THE IDEAS OF THE FALL
AND OF ORIGINAL SIN

THE IDEAS OF THE FALL
AND OF ORIGINAL SIN

A HISTORICAL AND CRITICAL STUDY

BEING EIGHT LECTURES DELIVERED BEFORE THE
UNIVERSITY OF OXFORD, IN THE YEAR 1924,
ON THE FOUNDATION OF THE REV. JOHN
BAMPTON, CANON OF SALISBURY

BY

NORMAN POWELL WILLIAMS, D.D.,

FELLOW AND CHAPLAIN OF EXETER COLLEGE, OXFORD

αἰτία ἑλομένου· θεὸς ἀναίτιος

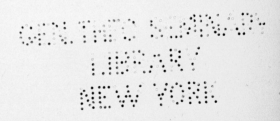

LONGMANS, GREEN AND CO. LTD.
39 PATERNOSTER ROW, LONDON, E.C.4
NEW YORK, TORONTO
CALCUTTA, BOMBAY AND MADRAS
1927

Made in Great Britain

EXTRACT

FROM THE LAST WILL AND TESTAMENT

OF THE LATE

REV. JOHN BAMPTON

CANON OF SALISBURY

'. . . I give and bequeath my Lands and Estates to
the Chancellor, Masters, and Scholars of the University of
Oxford for ever, to have and to hold all and singular the
said Lands or Estates upon trust, and to the intents and
purposes hereinafter mentioned ; that is to say, I will and
appoint that the Vice-Chancellor of the University of
Oxford for the time being shall take and receive all the
rents, issues, and profits thereof, and (after all taxes, repara-
tions, and necessary deductions made) that he pay all the
remainder to the endowment of eight Divinity Lecture
Sermons, to be established for ever in the said University,
and to be performed in the manner following :

' I direct and appoint that, upon the first Tuesday in
Easter Term, a Lecturer be yearly chosen by the Heads of
Colleges only, and by no others, in the room adjoining to
the Printing-House, between the hours of ten in the morning
and two in the afternoon, to preach eight Divinity Lecture
Sermons, the year following, at St. Mary's in Oxford,
between the commencement of the last month in Lent Term
and the end of the third week in Act Term.
' Also I direct and appoint, that the eight Divinity
Lecture Sermons shall be preached upon either of the
following Subjects—to confirm and establish the Christian

Faith, and to confute all heretics and schismatics—upon the divine authority of the holy Scriptures—upon the authority of the writings of the primitive Fathers, as to the faith and practice of the primitive Church—upon the Divinity of our Lord and Saviour Jesus Christ—upon the Divinity of the Holy Ghost—upon the Articles of the Christian Faith, as comprehended in the Apostles' and Nicene Creeds.

'Also I direct, that thirty copies of the eight Divinity Lecture Sermons shall be always printed, within two months after they are preached; and one copy shall be given to the Chancellor of the University, and one copy to the Head of every College, and one copy to the Mayor of the city of Oxford, and one copy to be put into the Bodleian Library; and the expense of printing them shall be paid out of the revenue of the Land or Estates given for establishing the Divinity Lecture Sermons; and the Preacher shall not be paid, nor be entitled to the revenue, before they are printed.

'Also I direct and appoint, that no person shall be qualified to preach the Divinity Lecture Sermons, unless he hath taken the degree of Master of Arts at least, in one of the two Universities of Oxford or Cambridge; and that the same person shall never preach the Divinity Lecture Sermons twice.'

PREFACE

PERHAPS the gravest of the intellectual difficulties which restrain men of thoughtfulness and goodwill from giving their allegiance to the Christian Faith is that which inheres—not in any one article or detail of our religion, not in its doctrines of the Triune being of God or of the two natures of Christ, not in Atonement, miracles, sacraments, or eschatology—but in its fundamental assertion that ' God is love.' It is not that such persons find an intrinsic improbability or logical incongruity in the ascription of those qualities which we know in man as righteousness, benevolence, compassion, and love to the mysterious Ultimate Source and Ground of things ; but rather that the assertion appears to them as irreconcileable with the facts of the world and of human life. ' Is it possible,' they ask, ' to believe that behind the cruel misfits, the senseless waste, the sordid ferocity with which organic nature, human and sub-human, is deeply marked, there really exists that dazzlingly perfect, that inconceivably glorious and blissful Being of whom Christian theology speaks ? Can we recognise in the infinite and eternal Energy, from which all things proceed, which seems with impersonal indifference to weave good and evil, love and hate, beauty and ugliness into the tissue of its phenomenal self-expression, the features of that loving heavenly Father whom Jesus claimed to reveal ? Is it not more honest to admit that we are confronted by a morally neutral universe ; and, if we keep the conception of " God " at all, to regard the God of religion as limited, as less than the Absolute, though greater than ourselves—our ally, perhaps, in the work of harnessing the blind forces of nature, without us and within, to ethically valuable ends, but like men ultimately dependent for His being on the inscrutable substrate of the world-process, which, for all we know, may in some unpredictable freak eventually crush both Him and us ? '

For Christians, the faith that God is infinite in power, love, and holiness alike is guaranteed by His revelation of Himself, imparted in the first instance through the Hebrew prophets, consummated in Jesus Christ, and authenticated by the witness of the Spirit within the believer's heart. Whatever use may be made of intellectual argument for establishing the probability of Christian theism, the conviction of its certainty must always rest upon experience of a supra-rational kind : and such experience is normally acquired and communicated through the spiritual contagion which clings about the organised fellowship of redeemed people, the visible Church of Christ upon earth. To those who doubt the friendliness and the love of the Power behind the universe, the ultimate appeal of Christians must be ' Come and see,' ' gustate et videte, quoniam suavis est Dominus.' Nevertheless, such an appeal, if it is to exert its full power, should be accompanied by some reasoned answer to the question ' How is the hypothesis of God's infinite goodness and compassion to be reconciled with the actual state of His world ? '

The answer given to this question by historical Christianity consists in the doctrine of the Fall and of its consequences. The world is what it is *despite* the goodness of its Maker, because it has apostatised from its Maker. But, owing partly to the verdict of Biblical criticism upon the ancient stories with which this doctrine has for many centuries been connected, partly to the revolution effected by modern science in our conception of the universe and of the place of man within it, the idea of the Fall may be said to have been for some time past under a cloud ; and such references as have been made to it by Christian thinkers, at least in areas of Christendom where heed is paid to science and Biblical criticism, have been hesitating and uncertain, except when they have involved its definite rejection. It seems, therefore, that there is room for a systematic study of the whole subject, such as is attempted in the following Lectures, a study which will not merely investigate the origins of the Fall-doctrine and trace the course of its development, but will seek to determine the extent of its acceptance by orthodox Christianity, and the degree of validity, if any, which it may claim before the bar of reason.

Such a study has indeed been made on an imposing scale by Dr. F. R. Tennant, in three works, of which the latest was published some fifteen years ago—namely, ' The Origin and Propagation of Sin ' (Hulsean Lectures, 1902), ' The Sources of the Doctrines of the Fall and Original Sin ' (1903), ' The Concept of Sin ' (1912). These books constitute the first, and so far the only, attempt in English to subject the Fall-doctrine to a severely scientific examination in respect both of its origin and of its truth, and my obligations to them will be obvious to the reader of these Lectures at every turn. Nevertheless, I have been impelled to essay the task again, partly because at various points I find myself in disagreement with Dr. Tennant's interpretation of the historical data, and partly because, since the publication of his last-mentioned work, the speculative situation has been largely modified by the development of what is known as the ' new psychology,' and also by the revival of a theory which at the time when Dr. Tennant wrote was not considered as a serious claimant to the attention of modern theologians, but which has been adopted as the basis of the constructive view set forth in the last of these Lectures— the theory, namely, of a transcendental, pre-human or pre-cosmic ' Fall.' This revival is mainly due to Canon Peter Green's book ' The Problem of Evil ' (1920) and Dr. C. W. Formby's ' The Unveiling of the Fall ' (1923) ; and I desire to acknowledge here the share which both of these books have had in moulding my own thought on the subject. Apart from these considerations, it has seemed worth while to endeavour to provide a treatment of the whole matter, both in its historical and in its dogmatic aspect, which should be included between the covers of one book : though it must be confessed that the discussion of so vast and intricate a question, raising as it does almost every other problem both in theology and philosophy, does not lend itself to compression within the limits of eight

Lectures; and, whilst rigidly confining myself, so far as
was possible, to the examination of the Fall-doctrine proper,
and abstaining from entering upon collateral fields of enquiry,
I have found myself compelled to make full use of the
privilege customarily conceded to a Bampton Lecturer,
that of printing considerably more than was actually
spoken in the pulpit of St. Mary's. The apparent dispro-
portion between the long and detailed study of pre-
Augustinian thought in Lecture IV and the cursory notice
of post-Reformation developments in Lecture VI is, I hope,
justified by the use made of the former in the constructive
part of the book.

I desire to express sincere gratitude to those who have
helped me in the preparation and revision of these Lectures
with information and advice : first and foremost to the
Rev. Canon Darwell Stone, D.D., who has found time
amidst his innumerable employments to read the whole of
the historical part of the book in typescript, and has freely
placed the immense resources of his patristic learning at
my disposal; then to the Rev. Canon Brightman, Fellow
of Magdalen College, Oxford, to whom I owe the substance
of Additional Note C ('Congregational Confessions of
Original Sin'); to Canon D. C. Simpson, D.D., Oriel
Professor of the Interpretation of Holy Scripture in the
University of Oxford; Professor Dr. Friedrich Loofs, of
Halle; Dr. Charles Singer; Dr. A. Büchler, Principal of the
Jews' College; Canon T. A. Lacey; and Mr. H. M. J. Loewe,
University Lecturer in Rabbinic Hebrew at Oxford. It is
doubtless unnecessary to add that these gentlemen are not
to be considered in any way responsible for any of the
opinions expressed in the book, or for any mistakes which
may appear in it. I must also thank the Ven. R. H. Charles,
D.D., F.B.A., Archdeacon of Westminster, and the Delegates
of the University Press for permission to make use of
quotations from the English translations of apocalyptic
documents contained in 'Apocrypha and Pseudepigrapha
of the Old Testament' (1913).

N. P. WILLIAMS.

OXFORD :
    January 1927.

SYNOPSIS OF CONTENTS

The Problem of Evil in general. No complete solution is possible ; but Religion ought to contain some indication of the direction in which the solution lies.

Three classical answers to the question have in the past been given by Religion in its higher forms : (1) the theory of 'unmoral monism,' characteristic of Hindu thought, according to which Good and Evil are alike appearances—presumably necessary appearances—of an Absolute which transcends them both ; (2) dualism, the view of later Mazdeism and Manicheism, which postulates co-eternal Powers of Good and Evil ; (3) the theory of a 'Fall' and of 'Original Sin,' inherited by Christianity from Judaism, and standing in sharp opposition to the two former views. The purpose of these lectures is a critical examination of this last theory, both as regards origin and validity.

General remarks as to the present position of the Fall-doctrine and of the conception of Redemption which is its inseparable corollary.

We are faced at the outset by the fact that much diversity has prevailed within historical Christianity as to the exact form and contents of the ideas of the Fall and of Original Sin. Before endeavouring to evaluate them, we must first of all determine what precisely they are. It is impossible to assume without enquiry that any existing confessional formulary adequately embodies the whole mind of traditional Christianity on these points : and there are no detailed definitions of oecumenical authority. We must therefore endeavour to arrive at the irreducible essence of Fall-doctrine to which Catholic Christianity is committed by a comprehensive survey of the history of the doctrine, employing the 'Vincentian canon' as a scientific—*not* as a authoritarian —criterion. The first six lectures will, accordingly, be historical in nature, intended to ascertain the origin and fix the essence of these ideas, and the last two, theological or philosophical, devoted to a discussion of their validity.

Our historical survey necessarily begins with the Old Testament. The Paradise-story of Gen. iii. contains no idea of 'Original Sin'; it is, therefore, not the historical source of the Fall-doctrine, which originated in the thought of post-exilic Judaism as the result of reflection on the empirical universality of Actual Sin. This observed fact suggested the presence of some inherent taint in human nature : the Jew's intense conviction of the Creator's goodness forbade the supposition that such a taint could have belonged to human nature as originally created : it thus seemed necessary to postulate a ' Fall,' or first sin. The necessity of a Fall having been thus arrived at by *a priori* reasoning, search was made in the Biblical narratives for some event which could be identified with the first sin ; this was found, at first, in the story of the lustful angels narrated in Gen. vi.

The theory that human wickedness is due to the unnatural mixture of divine and human essences involved in the union of the ' sons of God ' and mortal women is elaborated in the Book of Enoch, and other apocalyptic literature. It breaks down, owing to its failure to explain *post-diluvian* sin, and is gradually ousted from its position as the popular Fall-story by the Adam-narrative of Gen. iii. Traces of it are, however, to be found even in New Testament documents.

The fact that there has been this rivalry between the two Fall-stories, Gen. vi. and Gen. iii. (ending in the victory of the latter), confirms the conclusion that neither is the real basis of the doctrine : they are rather symbolic façades, clothing a conceptual structure which rests upon spiritual experience and introspection. And the suggestion of Gen. vi., that the origin of sin is due to lust, represents the first emergence of a *motif*, which runs through much of Christian Fall-speculation and seems to have reappeared in recent psychology of the Viennese school.

We now turn to the consideration of the story which finally became the official Fall-story of the Christian Church, that of Adam and Eve. It was pointed out in Lecture I that this story, in itself and for the mind of the Yahwistic writer, contained no doctrine of ' Original Sin ' and regarded ' the Fall ' merely as an exterior punishment, not as the acquisition of an interior taint or weakness. This statement must now be justified.

The story analysed. Though capable of conscious communion with God, the first men are not conceived as being very much higher than the beasts, in respect of physical and material conditions. There is no doctrine of ' Original Righteousness ' ; but Adam and Eve, in their unfallen condition, are not strictly ' non-moral,' for they know of at least two duties—work and abstinence from the forbidden fruit. For the Yahwistic writer, their sin lay in the illicit acquisition of scientific knowledge ; *cf.* the myth of Prometheus. J is a pessimist ; he thinks that civilisation is a mistake, and that the increase of knowledge brings sorrow in its train.

This naïve original significance, however, was obscured for the Jews of the Maccabean period by the canonical status and inspired character attributed to the Book of Genesis ; hence, the religiously higher idea—that the essence of the first sin consisted in the conscious transgression of a known law—could be and was read into it. The pre-Christian development of Fall-speculation, now firmly anchored to the Adam-story, summarised : we notice in particular the growth of (*a*) the idea that man's mortality is directly due to the first sin, and (*b*) the theory of ' Original Righteousness.' The theory of the *inquinamentum* (which reappears in the New Testament), according to which Eve was the sole source of human sin and misery, Adam being guiltless.

The two Fall-theories just discussed (that based upon Gen. vi., and its successful rival based on Gen. iii.) belong to *popular* religious thought. But, to gain a complete picture of the theological *milieu* into which Christianity came, and of the doctrinal background which the teaching of our Lord and His Apostles presupposes, we must consider the theory of the origin of evil held by official Rabbinical scholasticism—which is still held by the Jewish Church at the present day. This is the theory of the *yēçer ha-ra'*, or ' evil imagination.' Derivation of this conception from the words of Gen. vi. 5.

The ' evil imagination ' in pre-Christian literature, especially Ecclesiasticus. Further information about this idea may be derived from Talmudic sources. The conception of the *yēçer ha-ra'* in the Rabbis would seem to be almost identical with that of *libido* in Jung, if not in Freud. Difference between this idea and that of ' Original Sin.' The *yēçer* implanted by God in each individual soul.

This was the view of the official theology—as distinct from popular pietism. But the Adamic theory won such widespread support that the Rabbis had to take some account of it ; hence the idea of a forensic imputation of the first man's demerit to his descendants, *i.e.* the idea of ' Original Guilt,' as distinct from that of ' Original Sin.' This distinction, which will be of crucial importance for the understanding of Christian thought on the subject, explained.

Two attempts to combine the popular theory of Adam's Fall and ' Original Sin ' with the Rabbinical theory of the *yēçer ha-ra'*—the Syriac Apocalypse of Baruch, and the Ezra-Apocalypse. Philo's Platonism (really identical with what we described as the Hindu answer to the problem of the origin of Evil) forbids him to accept either the Fall or the ' evil imagination.'

Summary of the state of opinion within Judaism at the time when Christianity came into existence. The Fall-doctrine held *in* the Jewish Church, but not *by* the Jewish

Church as a whole. So far as the Elder Dispensation is concerned, it was never more than a ' pious opinion.' Any claim to the position of a ' revealed ' doctrine made on its behalf can only rest on the fact of its embodiment into the scheme of *Christian* doctrine.

The foregoing Lectures have described the source and contents of the main theories as to the origin of Evil—the angel-theory, the Adam-theory, and the idea of the *yēçer ha-ra'*—which prevailed within Judaism at the beginning of our era. We now have to face a crucial question : how was it that one of these theories (the Adam-theory) was taken over, to the exclusion of the others, by Christianity, and welded so firmly into the dogmatic structure of Christianity that succeeding ages have regarded it as a chief pillar of the Church's Faith ? The question is somewhat of an enigma in view of the fact that the direct authority of Christ cannot be claimed for this doctrine, or indeed for any other theory of the origin of evil, though His teaching assumes that mankind is in sore need of redemption from sin.

The only New Testament passages which definitely teach ' Original Sin ' and the Adamic theory of the Fall are contained in the writings of St. Paul (Jude and 2 Peter seem to assume the ' angel-theory '). It is noticeable that St. Paul is at no pains to *prove* the Adamic theory : he *takes it for granted*, in parentheses and *obiter dicta*, which he could hardly have done unless he had known it to be common ground between himself and his readers. But, how could he have assumed it, in this almost casual manner, as the common intellectual property of all Christians, if it had not direct Dominical authority behind it ? We must admit that the passage of the Fall-doctrine from Judaism into Christianity is involved in some obscurity ; but the following appears to be the most probable hypothesis :

(*a*) That the earliest adherents of our Lord, being rough Galileans, and destitute of Rabbinical culture, would know nothing about the *yēçer ha-ra'*, but would be well acquainted with the popular apocalyptic literature : and would therefore be likely, in the absence of direct Dominical instruction to the contrary, to take the pseudepigraphic theory of a Fall and Original Sin for granted, either in its ' angelic ' or its ' Adamic ' form.

(*b*) That our Lord, in accordance with His policy of assuming current Jewish theology wherever possible, tacitly acquiesced in this, and left His followers to decide for themselves between the Fall-stories of Gen. iii. and Gen. vi.

(*c*) That at first the Watcher-story enjoyed some popularity in Jewish-Christian circles : but that St. Paul's influence eventually dispossessed it in favour of the Adam-narrative, which thus became the official Fall-story of the whole Christian Church.   If this is so, St. Paul would seem to have done Christianity a considerable service, in view of the unedifying developments of which the angel-story from its nature is capable.

It is to be noted that although the Adamic theory as taught by St. Paul is mainly built upon the Biblical story, yet two passages in the Pauline *corpus* appear to presuppose the extra-Biblical legend of the *inquinamentum* (2 Cor. xi. 3 and 1 Tim. ii. 14) ; probably, however, this idea is merely used in the spirit of Philonic allegorism, to give point to practical exhortations.

We now turn to the task of reconstructing the Apostle's doctrine in detail.   The *loci classici* are to be found in Rom. v., vi., vii. ; 1 Cor. xv. ; Gal. v.   The relevant portions of these chapters imply that Adam's sin communicated to his posterity (*a*) physical mortality, and (*b*) a condition of ' suppressed sinfulness,' which is stimulated by knowledge of the Law to break out into sinful acts.   The remedy for this condition is Baptism : analogies to this conception in contemporaneous paganism.   St. Paul knows nothing of ' Original Righteousness ' or ' Original Guilt.'

The seat or *nidus* of the hereditary infection is the ' flesh,' the ' body of this death,' with its ' sinful passions.'   Is this conception based upon a Platonic or Oriental dualism ?   But we have seen that the Fall-theory is necessarily the sworn foe of dualism.   If a source other than St. Paul's own experience must be found for the idea of the φρόνημα τῆς σαρκός there is no need to go further than the yēçer ha-ra', with which the Apostle's Rabbinical training must have made him familiar.

A complete treatment of the problem of sin must endeavour to deal with the relation of evil in man to evil in Nature, or in the world outside men.   Many subsequent theologians have shirked this question ; but it is clear that the Apostle has faced it in his own private thoughts.   Not human nature alone is permeated by Evil : the malign infection extends downwards into the sub-human creation, which ' groans and travails together until now,' and upwards into the supernatural sphere, where it inspires the hateful energies of a ' spirit-world at war with God,' the malevolent ' world-rulers,' ' principalities,' and ' powers.'   For the content of these ideas St. Paul is indebted to the pre-Christian apocalyptists : but the form and the implications which he has imposed upon them are profoundly original.

Summary.   The doctrines which we are studying come to us on the authority of St. Paul and of the Church rather than on that of Christ : if, however, our final examination of them shows that they correspond to the facts of life, the circumstances of their entry into Christianity will constitute no argument against them, and we shall be at liberty to conclude that, whilst not strictly Dominical themselves, they are nevertheless implicit in the Dominical teaching as to the universal need of redemption. Though it gathers into a single system the ideas loosely scattered throughout the pre-Christian apocalyptists, the Apostle's doctrine is yet somewhat vague and elastic, and therefore much more reasonable than some of the more rigid products of later theology. Despite a few rhetorical turns of phrase, no trace is to be found in his Epistles of the impossible paradox that we are morally culpable for possessing instincts which we cannot help possessing. Apart from the synthetic work just mentioned, and the final expulsion of the Watcher-story, the most permanently significant of the Apostle's contributions to the growth of the Fall-doctrine are (a) the close connexion established, or pointed out, by him between Original Sin and Baptism, and (b) his great conception of the unitary nature of Evil as pervading the three planes of life, sub-human, human, and superhuman, with its corollary of a final redemption embracing the whole realm of animate and created being.

The Pauline teaching sketched in Lecture III was bound, when reflected upon, to raise certain great issues which have dominated the subsequent history of these doctrines. These issues are :

   (i) Is the Adam-story historic truth or allegory ?

  (ii) What was man's unfallen condition—non-moral innocence, or ' Original Righteousness ' ?

 (iii) What exactly is the undesirable thing, state, or quality alleged to have been communicated by the first man to his descendants ?

 (iv) What was the mode of this communication— physiological or merely social heredity, mystical or physical identity ?

  (v) What is the resulting state of human nature, with which Redemption now has to deal ?

It must therefore be expected that the task of fixing the outlines of the really ' Catholic ' or universal doctrine will become more complicated as our research moves down the centuries. In order to determine what precisely has been believed *ubique, semper, et ab omnibus*, we shall have to enquire, not merely whether the Fall-doctrine was or was not held by the Christian Church during a given period, but also (if we decide that it was) what answers were returned to these crucial questions during the epoch under discussion. As these ideas are ultimately based upon religious experience, we shall find that the opinions held with regard to these five issues tend to group and combine themselves into two well-defined versions of the Fall-theory, corresponding to the ' once-born ' and ' twice-born ' types of religious temperament.

The more or less straightforward path followed by the evolution of the Christian Fall-doctrine after the Apostolic age is sharply bisected by the figure of Augustine, which stands as it were on the watershed between classical antiquity and the Middle Ages. The remainder, therefore, of our historical survey falls naturally into three sections, concerned respectively with Christian opinion before Augustine, with the teaching of Augustine himself, and with the subsequent Western developments of Augustinianism. The first of these sections, to which this morning's lecture will be devoted, will be of peculiar importance for the task of settling what really has been believed ' everywhere, always, and by all,' inasmuch as in the primitive, pre-Augustinian Church we may reasonably expect to find nothing but the fundamental thought of historic Christianity on this subject, free from the ' personal equation ' introduced by Augustine's powerful individuality.

Only two, exceedingly faint and doubtful, traces of these ideas are to be found in the ' Apostolic Fathers ' ; the Apologists are more explicit, but their teaching is ambiguous and confused. The first appearance within Christianity of the conception of ' Original Righteousness,' and of the suggestion, destined to be elaborated by Duns Scotus, that the inherited infirmity consists in the lack of the supernatural endowments of the first man. It would seem that, whilst St. Paul's teaching was accepted, in a vague and general manner, by the Christian world, at least from the time of the canonisation of the Pauline *corpus* onwards, it was held very much in the background of the Church's mind during the first post-Apostolic century : and that the hypothesis of a multitude of personal demons attacking the soul from without possessed much more vivid reality for the earliest Christians, as the explanation of evil suggestions, than the more abstract idea of a hereditary bias influencing it from within.

The ideas of the Fall and of Original Sin emerged from this temporary eclipse as the result of the impact of Gnosticism upon the Church. Under the banners of this syncretistic movement, the two ancient foes of Jewish-Christian mono-theism—Hindu monism and Iranian dualism—once more advanced to the assault ; and, as in the Maccabean period, the Fall-theory was brought out of the Church's armoury as the tried shield against any theories which imply the eternity or necessity of evil. The first systematic consideration of the subject is found in Irenaeus ; the surprising modernity and reasonableness of his views on some of the five crucial issues.

With the two greatest anti-Gnostic champions of the following century—Origen in the East and Tertullian in the West—the two classical types of Fall-doctrine begin to distinguish themselves. Some care must therefore be devoted to the examination of these writers. Origen will naturally be considered first, as standing more directly in the succession of the earliest Greek-Christian thought.

Origen's two periods—the Alexandrine and the Caesarean. In the former, following the lead of Clement, he allegorises

Gen. iii., in accordance with the exegetical methods traditional at Alexandria, reading into it the theory, borrowed from Plato's Phaedrus, of a pre-natal fall of individual souls. ' Original Righteousness ' is thus affirmed, but referred to a transcendent and extra-temporal mode of existence, whilst ' Original Sin ' becomes a weakness rather than a disease, a *privatio* rather than a *depravatio*.

In the latter, he takes a more gloomy view of ' Original Sin ' as a positive, quasi-physical pollution, to which, in some inexplicable way, *guilt* attaches ; here the conception of ' Original Guilt ' creeps in by the side of ' Original Sin.' This change of view is probably due to the fact that at Caesarea he became acquainted for the first time with the practice of Infant Baptism, which seemed to necessitate some doctrine of inborn depravity or guilt. He also shows signs of reverting to a more literalistic exegesis of Gen. iii., and, for the time, abandons the theory of individual pre-natal falls for that of a collective Fall of humanity in Adam. But in both periods alike he remains convinced that ' Paradise ' belongs not to the material but to the supersensible world. This is an idea which may prove fruitful in suggestions when we approach the constructive part of our task.

The place of Tertullian in history as the father of Western and Latin theology, and the precursor of Augustine. The general texture and quality of his mind was unphilosophical, legalistic, materialistic. He is not prepared to predicate of unfallen human nature more than ' integrity ' (which does not amount to ' Original Righteousness ') ; but he adheres to a rigidly literal interpretation of Gen. iii. The fundamental element in his presentation of the Fall-doctrine is the belief in the corporeity of the soul : from this is derived the ' Traducianist ' view of the propagation of souls, on which a crude form of the theory of ' seminal identity ' is based. It is strongly asserted that ' Original Sin ' is a positive corruption and not a mere infirmity : but there is no idea of ' Original Guilt,' as Tertullian, unlike Origen, objects to the practice of Infant Baptism.

The two types of Fall-doctrine destined to be characteristic of Eastern and Western Christendom—that which starts from the conception of ' Original Sin ' as a *privatio* and that which regards it as a *depravatio*—thus emerge in the writings of these two great third-century teachers. Further developments in the East (Methodius, Athanasius, and the Cappadocians) and in the West (Cyprian, Ambrose, Ambrosiaster—the two latter approximating to the full Augustinian doctrine) briefly summarised.

Summary. From the evidence adduced it may be reasonably concluded that the Fall-doctrine was very generally assumed in the Church of the first four centuries, on the authority of the Old Testament as interpreted by St. Paul. But it was not the centre of much discussion or interest ; the demon-theory bulked more largely in the imagination of the ordinary Christian. Nor, in view of the fluidity of Christian thought at this epoch, can it be said to have been strictly *de fide*. It was not embodied in the baptismal Creeds, or regarded as part of the Gospel or the ' deposit of Faith ' ; it was viewed rather as part of the prolegomena to the Gospel, taken over from Judaism. The sense in which the Fall-doctrine may be said to have enjoyed this vague general acceptance does not go beyond the simple teaching of St. Paul and, perhaps, of Irenaeus ; this view, which regards the Fall as a *praevaricatio* rather than a *lapsus*, and ' Original Sin ' as a weakness rather than an offence or pollution, is not uncongenial to the ' once-born ' type of religious experience and the sunny genius of Christian Hellenism. But the more gloomy and fanatical temperament of Northern Africa was already in search of a severer theory, appropriate to the ' twice-born ' mode of feeling. The Augustinian version, which has dominated the West so completely that it is still thought by many to be the only Fall-doctrine, had not yet been constructed : but the materials for it were being accumulated.

Christian Doctrine, in its ' orthodox ' or ' historical ' presentation, is now conventionally divided into five great sections—the doctrine of the Trinity, of the Incarnation or the Person of Christ, of Grace or the Work of Christ, of the Church, and of the Sacraments. But in the primitive Church of the first four centuries, which claimed our attention in Lecture IV, Christian doctrine, so far as it had been formulated, consisted only of the first two of these sections—the doctrines of God and of Christ. Broadly speaking, the Church and the Sacraments were taken for granted as facts, and used rather than speculated about : and the problems which come under the head of the ' doctrine of Grace '—Sin, Atonement, Justification—received only cursory attention, nor were any specific opinions in regard to them treated as *de fide* or insisted on as terms of communion. The Fall-doctrine in particular, though enjoying a vague general acceptance, was not thought of as part of ' the Gospel,' and was largely obscured by the demonic theory. We have now to consider how ' the doctrine of Grace,' carrying a rigidly systematised and ' twice-born ' version of the Fall-theory embedded in it, came to be added to the doctrines of God and of Christ as a third great section of the Christian intellectual scheme, as that scheme was conceived in the Western Church. This enlargement of the area of authoritative dogma was mainly due to the teaching and influence of St. Augustine.

As the Fall-doctrine is based upon spiritual experience, it is desirable, at each crucial moment in its development, to examine the lives and temperaments of its greatest exponents, in order to lay bare the causes which have moulded their characteristic presentations of it. A brief review of Augustine's earlier life discloses three main factors which naturally disposed him towards the sterner and more rigorous type of Fall-theory: (1) his own passionate, introspective, and 'twice-born' genius, which had been deeply marked by the convulsions of sin, remorse, and instantaneous conversion ; (2) his contact with Persian dualism, the traditional foe of Jewish-Christian monotheism, in its Manichean form, which affected him first by attraction and then by repulsion ; (3) the tradition and temper of the North African Church, which made him heir to the more gloomy view of ' Original Sin ' first adumbrated by Tertullian.

Augustine's doctrine, which is the finished and classical expression of the ' twice-born ' view, took shape in his mind during the first ten years of his Christian and monastic life, as the result of his reaction from Manicheism, long before he had so much as heard of Pelagius. Its main points— ' seminal identity,' ' original guilt,' ' original sin ' viewed as a depravation and not as a mere privation, the intrinsically evil nature of ' concupiscence,' and the idea of fallen humanity as a *massa peccati*—appear in the treatise *ad Simplicianum*, as early as the year 397.

Meanwhile, by a remarkable chance—or providence—the ' once-born,' strongly ethical type of religious temperament found a powerful representative in another monk, the Irishman Pelagius, whose evangelistic methods presupposed an absolute indeterminism and an optimistic view of human nature, which was eventually worked out by himself and his friends, Caelestius and Julian of Eclanum, into an explicit doctrine of man and of sin now known as ' Pelagianism.' Down to the end of the fourth century the two monks, the Briton and the African, typifying and inculcating respectively the extremest forms of the ' once-born ' and ' twice-born ' views of sin and redemption, were unknown to each other ; but the stage was being set for the great conflict between these two theories, which has not even yet come to a final decision.

It will be convenient here to sketch the main principles of Pelagianism. It was not a ' formal ' heresy—nor, at the date of its first appearance, was it a ' material ' heresy, as no officially defined Fall-doctrine was yet in being. It was rather an attempt to provide a rationalised, non-mystical explanation of the Scriptural texts relating to Adam's transgression and the entrance of sin into the world. It started from the fundamental Christian idea of God as infinitely good, and from this deduced the immutable goodness of human nature. Hence Adam's sin only injured himself directly, though it may be said to have injured his posterity indirectly in so far as it provided a bad example for their imitation. There is no physical propagation of any undesirable state or quality, not even of a *privatio* or weakness ; every individual represents at his birth a fresh start in the moral history of the

race, and throughout the whole of his life retains absolute
free-will, entirely undetermined by habit or character. So far
as there is any transmission of evil from one generation to the
next, it is merely through ' social heredity,' bad examples,
customs, laws, and the like. Infant baptism confers positive
graces, but not ' remission of sins,' as infants have *ex hypothesi*
no sins or sinfulness to be remitted ; and the eschatological
aspect of the problem, which now for the first time emerges
in the question, ' What is the fate, after death, of those who die
unbaptised ? ' is dealt with, so far as infants are concerned, by
the hypothesis of *Limbo*.

The history of the Pelagian controversy summarised.
The North African bishops, headed by Augustine, succeeded
in forcing the stiff, ' twice-born ' doctrine upon the West ; but
their triumph was largely due to the secular arm of the Roman
Government, and did not extend to the East, where the
Pelagians found a natural ally in Theodore of Mopsuestia.
Eventually the remnants of Pelagianism were involved in the
downfall of Nestorianism ; but Canons 1 and 4 of Ephesus,
which represent the only approach to a conciliar definition of
oecumenical authority on this subject, noticeably abstain
from an affirmation of Augustinianism, and content themselves
with a cautious condemnation of Caelestius.

A critique of Pelagianism. Whatever we may think of the
methods employed to suppress Pelagianism, its disappearance
was, on the whole, a blessing for Christianity. Though some
of its positions are infinitely more reasonable and humane
than the corresponding Augustinian tenets, it must yet be
remembered that its vicious doctrine of unlimited indeterminism abolished the essence of true religion by abolishing
man's feeling of dependence on God, and, by exaggerating
every venial fault into a conscious mortal sin, turned
Christianity into a joyless and legalistic Puritanism.

This blessing was, however, dearly purchased by the
triumph of Augustinianism. We must now examine this
system in detail, as fully developed in St. Augustine's anti-
Pelagian writings. As in the case of the pre-Augustinian
Fathers, our method will be that of considering St. Augustine's
answers to the ' five crucial questions ' defined in Lecture IV
as naturally arising out of the Pauline doctrine.

(i) *The literal or allegorical interpretation of Gen. iii.*
After a momentary hesitation, Augustine decides for the
former.

(ii) *Man's unfallen state.* The Rabbinical idea of
' Original Righteousness ' is carried to the highest pitch,
in order to intensify the heinousness of the Fall ; Adam,
unfallen, is canonised as the ideal athlete, philosopher, and
saint.

(iii) *The exact nature of the disastrous legacy of the Fall.*
Augustine is the first to distinguish clearly between the
vitium and the *reatus* of ' Original Sin '—in other words,

between ' original sin ' as a psychological fact and ' original guilt ' as a forensic status.   Of these :

(a) The *vitium* consists in ' concupiscence,' which is transmitted in and through parentage, and is in itself evil.

(b) The *reatus* consists in legal responsibility for Adam's transgression, based on the theory of ' seminal identity.'

(iv) *The mode of transmission.*   As will be seen from (iii) (a) and (b), Augustine alternates between ' heredity ' and identity.   He never makes up his mind as between ' Creationism ' and ' Traducianism.'

(v) *The resulting state of human nature.*   Mankind is a *massa perditionis* ; but Augustine's Platonism, for which all being, in so far as it is true being, is good, arrests him just short of the Calvinistic doctrine of total depravity, and mercifully blunts the edge of the antithesis between ' nature ' and ' grace.'   Man was deprived of ' freedom ' by the Fall, but still possesses ' free-will '—an elusive and probably meaningless distinction.

To these we must add :

(vi) *The eschatological issue,* first brought out by the Pelagian controversy, ' What happens after death to those who die in original sin only, without having committed actual sin ? '   Augustine has no hesitation in consigning this whole class, including unbaptised infants, to everlasting flames.

A brief critique of the Augustinian doctrine.   Its key-conceptions are three—Original Righteousness, Original Sin, and Original Guilt.   As we have previously suggested, the first and third of these are intellectually indefensible, at any rate as Augustine phrased them and as they are embodied in the Western post-Augustinian systems : and his presentation of, the second seems strongly coloured by his early Manicheism.   If, then, it were true, as is often assumed, that ' the Catholic doctrine ' of the Fall and of Original Sin is identical with the Augustinian doctrine, Catholic Christianity would indeed be in evil plight.   But we have seen that Ephesus abstained from affirming Augustinianism ;   and no other Oecumenical Council has dealt with the matter.   Augustinianism cannot in any case claim to satisfy the test of *semper* ; but it will be well, for the sake of completeness, to enquire whether there was ever a time when it was accepted *ubique et ab omnibus.*

This last question must, it would seem, be answered in the negative.   The Christian East has never accepted the Augustinian version of the Fall-doctrine ; the Greek-speaking Church of the eighth century, as represented by St. John of Damascus, seems to leave the whole question shrouded in ' reverential vagueness.'   We therefore conclude that orthodox Christians as such are in no way committed to the Augustinian position ;   and that the Church of the future is likely to look to the Greek tradition, which expresses the ' once-born ' type of religious experience as its guide and

norm in this matter, though in any complete ' re-statement '
of the Fall-doctrine room must be found for an expression
of the permanent values disclosed by the rarer ' twice-born '
type.

It was shown in Lecture V that the Augustinian version
of the Fall-theory, never having been adopted by Eastern
Christendom, does not satisfy the criterion of acceptance
ubique, semper, et ab omnibus, and cannot therefore be described
as ' the ecclesiastical doctrine ' or ' the doctrine of the Christian
Church as a whole.' It might, however, be urged that the
non-acceptance of the Augustinian teaching by the East does
not necessarily invalidate its claim to be ' the Christian
doctrine,' inasmuch as the intellectual life of the Eastern
Church was (not exclusively through its own fault) comparatively stationary from the time of the Great Schism down to
the nineteenth century ; and that it is unfair to dismiss a
theory which has so deeply affected the religious life of Western
Europe, both in mediaeval and modern times, without having
considered the developments which it received at the hands of
some of the greatest Christian thinkers since the Patristic age,
both Schoolmen and Reformers. We do not wish to argue the
question of the true meaning of *omnes*, or to assume (for the
purpose of these Lectures) any particular view as to the extent
of ' the Church ' ; our desire is to arrive at conclusions which
will possess as much objectivity and breadth of appeal as
possible. We will therefore meet the hypothetical objector on
his own ground, and examine the post-Augustinian history of
Fall-speculation in Western Christendom, in order to decide
whether or not, within this restricted sphere, the classical
' twice-born ' theory can reasonably claim acceptance *ab
omnibus*, and in the hope that this part of our historical survey
may provide suggestions which may be of use in the constructive part of our task.

We need not consider the Semi-Pelagian controversy,
which was concerned rather with the operations of ' grace '
than with the nature of the Fall : it is to be noted, however,
that the second Council of Orange (A.D. 529), which brought
this controversy to an end, contents itself with affirming a
modified Augustinianism, which only predicates ' integrity '
of unfallen man, abstains from affirming ' Original Guilt,'
and asserts that whilst free-will was weakened by the Fall it
was not destroyed. Little of interest is to be gleaned from
the ' Dark Ages.' Augustine continues to dominate the West
down to the beginning of the scholastic epoch, though Anselm

revives the idea that 'original sin' consists mainly in the lack of 'original righteousness,' and Abaelard repudiates 'original guilt.'

The history of mediaeval thought on this subject is the history of the gradual decline of the Augustinian view. This decline manifested itself in two forms, associated respectively with the Dominican and the Franciscan theologies, which must be separately explained.

The Order of Friars Preachers was born in Provence, in the midst of the struggle between Catholicism and the Albigenses or Catharists, who represented a recrudescence of Manicheism. In accordance, it would seem, with a law already noticed, that the invasion of Christendom by Oriental dualism stimulates in the Church a revival of interest in, and a tendency to intensify, the Fall-doctrine, Dominican thought was naturally inclined towards the strict Augustinian teaching. But, all unconsciously, it was constrained to modify Augustinianism in order to preserve it. The teaching of St. Thomas Aquinas may be taken as representative, and briefly summarised : as before, we arrange it under the heads of the 'crucial issues' implicit in the Fall-doctrine.

The Thomist position.

(i) *Man's unfallen state.* The Augustinian antithesis between ' nature ' and ' grace ' reappears as a metaphysical distinction between the natural and the supernatural orders. Hence the distinction between the *donum super-naturale* of ' Original Righteousness ' and man's *pura naturalia* is emphasised and sharpened.

(ii) *The nature of ' Original Sin.'* The Fall was a fall from the supernatural to the merely natural plane. It follows that ' Original Sin ' consists in ' the lack of original righteousness,' and, logically, the *pura naturalia* should be regarded as remaining unimpaired. St. Thomas, however, feels obliged to retain the Augustinian idea of ' concupiscence ' as essentially evil, and hence he affirms that ' concupiscence ' constitutes the matter, and the ' defect of Original Righteousness ' the form, of Original Sin. Original Sin involves guilt. But baptism annuls the guilt of concupiscence, and leaves it as a morally neutral *fomes peccati*—an important modification of the Augustinian view.

(iii) *The mode of its transmission.* The conception of ' seminal identity ' is translated into terms of motion ; Adam becomes an ethical *primum mobile* who ' moves ' his descendants towards sin by begetting them.

(iv) *The resultant state of human nature.* The Augustinian position is, if anything, emphasised ; freewill is verbally affirmed and constructively denied.

(v) *The eschatological corollaries of Original Sin.* Augustine's condemnation of the unbaptised to eternal torments is tacitly dropped, and the more merciful conception of *Limbo* substituted ; this idea receives poetic consecration from Dante, *Inferno*, Cant. iv. Here we have a significant symptom of a tendency to revert to the earlier view of ' Original Sin ' as a *privatio* rather than a *depravatio*.

The Franciscan position embodies a more definite and decided revolt against Augustinianism, and shows a tendency to return to the ' once-born ' view : of this, Duns Scotus may be taken as the typical representative. His characteristic opinions may be summed up as follows :

(i) ' Original Righteousness ' was a provisional state, which would have been progressively confined by resistance to temptations ; this idea points in the direction of a return to the more primitive conception of the first man as un-developed. This involves a milder view of the Fall, of which the malice is expressly declared not to have been infinite.

(ii) Hence ' Original Sin ' is a mere *privatio* consisting solely in the lack of ' Original Righteousness,' and con-cupiscence is not sin at all in any sense. Scotus, however, cannot shake himself so far free from Augustinianism as to take the obvious next step of denying that this lack of ' Original Righteousness ' involves *guilt*.

(iii) Man, even as fallen, possesses full freedom of the will ; and a position as to the necessity of ' prevenient grace ' is taken up which approximates to Semi-Pelagianism.

(iv) *Limbo* is conceived as a state not merely of no pain but of positive pleasure.

Closely connected with this minimising version of the Fall-doctrine are (*a*) the Scotist view of the Incarnation, which holds that the Son of God would have in any case assumed flesh, even if man had never fallen, and (*b*) the belief in the exemption of Mary from Original Sin—a belief which becomes the easier of acceptance the less ' Original Sin ' is made to mean.

The allegiance of mediaeval thinkers was thus, broadly speaking, divided between the modified Augustinianism of St. Thomas and the almost anti-Augustinian view of Scotus. It will be convenient to complete the history of the subject so far as the Latin Church is concerned, before considering the views of the Reformers. The decisions of the Council of Trent represent a compromise between the modified Augus-tinianism, championed by the Dominicans, and the minimising view which the Jesuits had inherited from the Franciscans— a compromise which was strongly in favour of the latter. The subsequent condemnations of Baius and Jansen emphasised the anti-Augustinian direction of Roman thought on this subject, and the present Fall-doctrine of the Roman Church would appear to be largely Scotist, with the Augustinian idea of ' Original Guilt ' inconsistently adhering to it ; the triumph of Scotism was consummated by the definition of the Immaculate Conception in 1854.

The history of the Augustinian Fall-doctrine within Latin Christianity from Anselm to the present day might thus, on the whole, be graphically represented by a steadily descending curve. At the Reformation, however, and in the parts of

Christendom affected by it, the curve of Augustinian influence suddenly soared up into a peak. Luther and Calvin were responsible for an ultra-Augustinian doctrine of Man and Sin, which is still popularly supposed to be the orthodox Christian view, which was the basis of some of the more unlovely aspects of Puritanism, and against which the conscience of England and America has now largely revolted. Reasons for the embodiment in Protestant theology of a rigid ' twice-born ' anthropology : (1) the Reformation itself was a colossal recrudescence of the mystical, as opposed to the institutional, elements in St. Augustine's thought, and therefore demanded a theory of man and sin which would make salvation exclusively God's work and eliminate human effort and merit ; (2) Luther himself, like St. Paul and St. Augustine, possessed the ' twice-born ' temperament in a high degree.

The Reformation made the Fall-doctrine, almost for the first time, a matter of popular and not merely of theological interest : compare many Calvinistic liturgical confessions, which require the congregation to accuse itself of ' original ' as well as ' actual ' sin, with the Catholic *Confiteor*, which is a confession of actual sin only.

The differences between Lutheranism and Calvinism on this subject were inconsiderable, so that it is possible to deal with the Protestant Fall-doctrine as a single body of ideas. The foundation of the Reformers' position was the denial of the scholastic distinction between the *donum supernaturale* of ' Original Righteousness ' and the *pura naturalia*. Adam's supposed magnificent endowments were not conferred upon him by way of a superadded adornment, as the Schoolmen had taught, but belonged to him in right of his human nature. It follows that the Fall was a fall not from the supernatural to the natural plane (the scholastic teaching) but from the natural to a *sub*-natural plane. Hence the Fall was the most horrible catastrophe conceivable, and its result is to be found in the ' total depravity ' of human nature, which the Reformers depict in the blackest colours. All the actions of the heathen, even apparently virtuous actions, are really sins. The mere fact of the possession of ' concupiscence ' is a mortal sin, apart from and prior to its actual indulgence. ' Original Guilt ' is strongly affirmed, and, in the last analysis, ' Original Sin ' is the only real sin that exists, all actual sins being merely *epiphenomena* revealing its malignant presence. It would seem, in short, that it is criminal in the sight of heaven to be born or to be a human being at all.

It is hardly necessary to point out that this conception of human nature and sin rules out free-will : Luther is even more emphatic on this point than Calvin. But theism, rigid determinism, and the doctrine of ' total depravity ' taken together inevitably make God the direct author of evil ; and this conclusion was accepted in set terms by Melancthon and Calvin, who thus appear to land themselves in precisely that unmoral Hindu monism which the Fall-doctrine was designed to resist—a curious revolution of the wheel of thought.

The gloomy theory just described dominated Continental Protestantism for two centuries, but has now shared the fate of evangelical orthodoxy in general ; the now dominant system of Ritschlianism has no place for any kind of Fall-doctrine, Augustinian or other. The Anglican Articles were doubtless meant by their compilers to rivet a decided Augustinianism upon the English Church : but this interpretation was challenged by Jeremy Taylor in the seventeenth century and Bishop Porteous in the eighteenth : and it would seem that the relaxation of the terms of subscription in 1865 has set the English Church free to handle the matter afresh. If we set these facts side by side with the largely non-Augustinian character of the present Roman Catholic Fall-doctrine, it will be seen that the classical expression of the 'twice-born' view has now all but disappeared from Christian thought, and therefore fails to satisfy the Vincentian canon, even within the restricted area of Western Christendom.

As a result of the extended historical survey contained in the last six lectures, we are now in a position to attempt a definition of the 'Catholic' doctrine of the Fall and of Original Sin—understanding by the term 'the Catholic doctrine' (as previously explained) the irreducible minimum of Fall-doctrine which has been disclosed by our examination of the history of Christian doctrine. This may be expressed in the form of seven propositions, as follows :

(i) *God is infinitely good, and therefore the world as He made it must have been purely good, including no element of evil at all.*

(We note that the idea of Creation is here presupposed.)

(ii) *The origin of evil is therefore to be sought in the voluntary rebellion of some finite and created will or wills, such rebellion having taken place prior to the appearance of the human species on this planet.*

(The ultimate 'Fall' may, therefore, be conceived either in accordance with Origen's suggestion of a pre-natal fall of individual souls, or as a pre-cosmic 'fall of the angels,' such as was inferred by an uncritical exegesis from Rev. xii. 7 ff.—the passage about the war between Michael and the 'dragon.')

(iii) *Man, at his first entry into this world, was in moral and intellectual stature a babe, created frail, imperfect, ignorant, and non-moral, but endowed with self-consciousness and the power of self-determination, which constituted his starting-point for progress and upward evolution.*

(The 'irreducible residuum' does not contain the Rabbinical and non-Scriptural idea of 'Original Righteousness,' the abandonment of which abolishes the apparent conflict between the Fall-doctrine and the evolutionary view of human history.)

(iv) *The growth of man's moral ideas brought in its train some action whereby man aligned himself with the revolting power, partially identified himself with the forces of Evil, and entered upon a path largely divergent from that straight upward road which God had meant him to follow.*

(In other words, the first sin was not so much a 'Fall' as a failure to climb, or, more exactly, to climb as directly and perpendicularly as God desired. It will therefore be well to avoid using the term 'Fall' with reference to the first *human* sin, and to keep it for designating the ultimate pre-cosmic revolt, whatever that may have been. The term 'Fall,' again, is non-Biblical.)

(v) *Ever since this first transgression, human nature has displayed an inherent moral weakness or bias towards sin.*

(It is to be noted that this proposition abstains from asserting that the first transgression was the *cause* of the innate bias towards evil.)

(vi) *This innate bias or tendency towards evil is the effect and symptom of 'weakness of will,' or defective control of the lower emotional and instinctive nature by the higher self.*

(We have already seen, in Lectures V and VI, that Catholic or universal acceptance cannot be claimed for the specifically Augustinian or Western ideas of 'seminal identity,' 'Original Guilt,' and the intrinsic sinfulness of 'concupiscence'; all these ideas, consequently, go by the board. And the term 'Original Sin' itself is non-Biblical, and inextricably associated with the idea of 'Original Guilt'; we shall therefore avoid it for the future, and use instead the term 'inherited infirmity.')

(vii) *This quality of 'weakness of will' inheres in the human stock as a hereditary character transmitted from parent to offspring through biological and not merely through social heredity.*

Two corollaries which seem to follow from this general position should be mentioned : (*a*) the 'inherited infirmity,' being inherited and not wilful, cannot be thought of as deserving God's 'wrath'; (*b*) there is much to be said for the Pelagian and scholastic conception of *Limbo*—the Augustinian idea that unbaptised infants deserve hell is in any case intolerable.

Of these seven propositions, the first five deal with what is generally known as the 'Fall,' and the last two with 'Original Sin,' so called. But we have seen that the former idea was historically, and always must be, an inference from the latter. To-day, therefore, we will restrict ourselves to the task of deciding whether the 'inherited infirmity' is a psychological reality or not, leaving more metaphysical questions as to the origin of sin for our final lecture.

What is meant by the statement that the will is ' weak ' ? This assertion is meaningless if the will enjoys unlimited freedom, and equally meaningless if it is absolutely determined. ' Weakness ' must therefore imply the conception of ' partial determinism '—or ' partial indeterminism,' which comes to the same thing. This conception is intelligible enough ; the only question is whether it is true or not. To decide this, we must examine the structure and working of human personality in the light of recent knowledge. An apology should doubtless precede any fresh discussion of the world-old problem of ' free-will ' ; it may, however, be possible to speak, *nove, non nova.*

We proceed to sketch, in summary form, that picture of the soul which recent psychology has built up, making free use of symbol and metaphor.

(*a*) The three areas of the soul—generally spoken of as though they were three storeys in a building—the *conscious, preconscious,* and *unconscious.* The preconscious contains the ' sentiments ' or ' complexes,' conglomerates of ideas and images which are charged with psychic energy and toned with feeling. The unconscious is largely unexplored, but may contain ' complexes ' which have been ' repressed ' owing to their incompatibility with the dominant purposive organisation of the soul.

(*b*) The *instincts* : these are paths or channels conducting the energy of the soul from its obscure source in the unconscious, either directly into action or into the ' complexes ' where it is stored until evoked by the appropriate stimulus. Whatever the correct number and classification of the primary instincts may be, there are three of special importance and power—those connected with the maintenance and assertion of the self, with sex, and with the ' herd ' ; and the corresponding ' complexes ' constitute the chief springs of human action.

The main outlines of this structure are universally admitted to be fixed by heredity ; if, therefore, there is such a thing as the ' inherited infirmity ' assumed by traditional theology, it should be discoverable somewhere in this framework. But the alleged ' infirmity ' has to do with moral action ; we must therefore scrutinise the ' moral sentiment ' with some care. This is built upon the ' herd-complex ' ; but two cautions must be borne in mind during our further investigation : (i) we are not now concerned with the question of hereditary *criminality* : this is a ' varietal character,' and the ' infirmity ' postulated by theology is generic and universal ; (ii) the same individual may belong to many ' herds ' and so possess many herd-complexes : the only herd-complex which interests us is that which centres in the idea of ' human society.' Inspection shows us that this is normally far weaker than either the ego— or the sex-complex ; *we therefore identify the ' inherited infirmity ' of theology with ' inherited weakness of herd-complex.'* This is the *privatio,* revealed by the ' once-born ' type of religious experience, and exaggerated by the ' twice-born ' type

into a positive *depravatio*; it does not, strictly speaking,
amount to a tendency towards ' sin ' as such, but rather to a
tendency, experienced under *all* circumstances, towards action
which under given circumstances is sin. But this negative
conception of the ' inherited infirmity ' implies no extenuation
of the melancholy results to which it leads.

The existence of a hereditary condition which tends to the
indulgence of self-regarding and sensual impulses in despite of
' conscience ' or the ' moral sentiment ' would thus seem to
have been verified. But this line of thought, if followed out
consistently, proves too much for our purposes : for it lands
us, not in ' partial determinism,' but in a determinism just as
' absolute ' as that which results from the older mechanistic
view of the mind. In the preceding description of the
rationale of conation and action, hardly anything was said
about the conscious ego, which occupies—or rather is—the
uppermost storey of the house of personality ; and modern
psychology, especially of the medical type, is largely epi-
phenomenalistic, regarding the feeling of effort and struggle
as an illusion, and consciousness as the passive mirror of events
which it has had no share in causing. If we acquiesce in this
tendency to ignore the conscious ego as a real factor in the
causation of conduct, we shall have failed to vindicate what
our historical survey has taught us to regard as the basic
Christian doctrine of human nature ; Augustinianism, having
been driven from the field of theology by means of the
Vincentian canon, will have returned in triumph with the
assistance of Freud.

The situation in regard to the question as to whether a
true spontaneous causality, acting within limits fixed by
heredity and environment, can be ascribed to the ego or not,
has not essentially altered since Kant. Determinism is the
necessary methodological postulate of science ; but freedom
is the no less necessary assumption of moral education, and,
it may be added, of psycho-therapeutic practice as distinct
from theory. We do not pretend to be able to solve a problem
which is probably insoluble ; but we may point out that
determinism is only necessary to a psychology which studies
the mind objectively and *ab extra*, whilst the consciousness of
ability to exert or not to exert effort is, from the subjective
and introspective point of view, a datum of immediate experience. The doctrine of ' partial determinism,' which, whilst
admitting that conduct is the result of the interplay of stimulus,
complex, and instinct, nevertheless claims that consciousness
has, within limits, a real power of guiding the flow of psychic
energy into this complex rather than that, and of gradually
modifying the contents of the preconscious and unconscious by
voluntary ' sublimation,' would seem to be the only one which
does justice both to man's moral and to his intellectual
experience.

We have seen that the belief in a ' Fall ' is now, and—
despite the quasi-historical façade which has clung to it for
twenty centuries—always has been, an inference from the
fact of man's ' inherited infirmity,' when considered in the
light of the belief in the infinite goodness of his Creator : it
is not a premise given by history. The doctrine of the Fall
is logically dependent on the doctrine of ' Original Sin ' (so
called), and not *vice versa* ; it is a pinnacle, not a foundation,
of the Faith. It follows that Catholic Christianity as such is
committed to no more than the bare assertion that there *was*
a Fall—that is, a primal rebellion of a created will against
God ; any attempts to fix the exact nature of this event
belong to the realm of speculation. But, though this antecedently *contingent* catastrophe, which our monotheistic belief
and the fact of the ' inherited infirmity,' taken together,
compel us to postulate, lies far back beyond the beginnings of
recorded history, it may be possible to arrive at some dim
conception of its nature by a Method of Residues, ruling out
various hypotheses which appear to be inconsistent either
with scientifically ascertained facts or with our fundamental
axiom, which is the reality of the God revealed in the Bible
and through Christ.

When we have had occasion to mention the ' Fall ' hitherto,
we have spoken of it as though it were an event in time,
capable, if we only had the requisite knowledge, of being dated
in a given year B.C. But *a priori* reasoning, when applied to
the reconstruction of past events in time, lies under a not
undeserved suspicion. And as we have no evidence for a Fall
other than what can be derived from *a priori* reasoning, it is
natural to enquire in the first instance whether a temporal
conception of the Fall is rigorously necessitated by our two
premises, the goodness of God and the sinfulness of men.
May it not be easier to conceive the Fall as an extra-temporal
fact, the transcendental ' ground,' rather than the historical
' cause,' of the ' inherited infirmity ' and of all other forms of
concrete evil ? The simplest method of answering this question
will be to examine the two classical attempts which have been
made to lift the Fall out of the time-series—those associated
with the names of Kant and Hegel. If these philosophic
giants have failed to accomplish this feat, we may reasonably
conclude that it is in the nature of things impossible.

Kant's discussion of the idea of the Fall is contained in his
treatise, *Die Religion innerhalb der Grenzen der blossen Vernunft.*
The empirical universality of evil is admitted, though it is
regarded as an inseparable accident rather than as an essential
constituent of human nature. It arises out of the adoption by
man of ' law-contradicting maxims ' (*gesetzwidrige Maxime*)
as motives of action in place of the maxims dictated by the
moral law. These law-contradicting maxims are suggested by
the sensual nature, which, though not evil in itself, is the

source of evil in so far as it demands satisfaction regardless of moral restraints. The fact that the sensual maxims do secure universal acceptance is explained by the supposition of an 'inclination to evil' (*Hang zum Bösen*). This is inborn. But Kant, taking the Lutheran theology of his country for granted, assumes that moral and religious experience informs us that we are *blameworthy* for possessing this 'inclination to evil'; in other words, he assumes that religion as such is committed to the idea of 'Original Guilt.' The inbred propensity to evil must, accordingly, be somehow traceable to our own act.

But he sees the impossibility of basing the (supposed) blameworthy hereditary condition upon the theory of 'seminal identity' with Adam : in the case of each individual, therefore, it must be traceable to the individual's own act, and each man must be the Adam of his own soul. But we have possessed the inborn bias to evil from the moment of birth ; how or when, then, did we commit the act which produced it ? To solve this difficulty the dualism set up by Kant's general metaphysical position between the phenomenal and the noümenal selves is invoked. The 'phenomenal ego' is temporal and determined, and the 'noümenal ego' is timeless and free. It is, therefore, to the latter that the fundamental act of wrong choice must be assigned. The 'Fall' in the case of each individual is a 'timeless act' whereby his 'noümenal self' adopts the 'law-contradicting maxims' as principles of action. Instead of a single collective Fall in time, we have a multiplicity of individual and extra-temporal falls—an idea which bears some resemblance to Origen's earlier theory of a multiplicity of pre-natal falls.

This conception, when stripped of technical terminology, is open to grave objections. Strictly speaking, a 'timeless act' appears to mean nothing : for an 'act' must involve some change, if not in the world external to the agent, at least in the agent himself, and change implies succession and time. But if the word 'act' really means 'state,' we are left with the hypothesis of an eternal and presumably necessary evil principle existing in all noümenal selves, or all selves considered as noümenal. In other words, Kant's theory seems to be either meaningless or Manichean.

Hegel's reinterpretation of the Fall-doctrine is expounded in the *Philosophie der Religion*, 3. Theil (*Die absolute Religion*), § II (*Das Reich des Sohnes*). It finds the source of evil in the separateness of the individual soul from the rest of the universe—in other words, in individuality and self-consciousness. From this it follows that sin is a necessary phase of the soul's evolution, and, though undesirable in itself, is less evil than innocence. We have already met with this theory in the course of our historical review ; it is nothing other than a form of that Gnosticism which stimulated the revival and development of the Fall-theory by Irenaeus in the second century. It both involves and presupposes that conception of an unmoral and impersonal Absolute which lies at the root of the religious thought of India, but is totally irreconcileable with the conception of God characteristic of Semitic religion and of the Bible.

We conclude, then, that the instinct of the Maccabean Jews was right, and that it is impossible to lift the Fall out of the time-series without falling either into Manicheism or unmoral monism. Whether we like it or not, so much would appear to be certain (given our premises), namely, that ' the Fall,' whatever else it may have been, must have been an event in time. We now approach a second question raised by Kant, and by Origen before him, namely this : Is it necessary to suppose a single collective Fall, or will a multiplicity of individual falls suffice ? The latter would have to be conceived as pre-natal, inasmuch as (according to the conclusion just reached) they would have to be in time and yet outside our present phenomenal lives. This theory of pre-natal falls enjoys a certain popularity in connexion with Theosophy, and it will therefore be worth while to examine its classical presentation as embodied in Julius Müller's ' Christian Doctrine of Sin.' This examination, however, reveals two fatal objections : (1) Müller's theory makes heredity to be a mere illusion, produced by a mysterious pre-established harmony of the pre-existing psychic monads ; (2) it assumes an intolerably pessimistic (again, almost Manichean) view of this world and of human life as lived within it. We are, therefore, driven back upon the hypothesis of *a single, collective Fall in time* : Coleridge's suggestion of a Fall of the race-soul presents certain attractions.

This probably represents the furthest point in our regressive quest of the origin of evil that can be reached by *a priori* reasoning. We must, therefore, consider if the hypothesis formulated above can be given further substance and articulation by the consideration of *a posteriori* evidence provided by the history of the world and of our species as now known to us. Such evidence would seem to make it certain that the origin of evil cannot be found in ' the first human sin.' For :

(i) The continuity of man's upward evolution, both physical and psychic, from the brute, makes it very doubtful whether there ever was a single action which could be described in an absolute manner as ' the first sin ' ; instinct can only gradually have given birth to conscious self-determination, and non-moral reactions must have shaded by imperceptible degrees into moral behaviour.

(ii) Even if it were possible to fix upon some act of individual or group which could be labelled with certainty as the ' first known sin,' this could not be identified with ' the Fall ' ; for (a) it must have occurred far too long after the emergence of man as a distinct zoological species to have affected the whole stock ; (b) such an identification would presuppose the transmissibility of acquired characters, a hypothesis which is far too uncertain to be built on with safety. In any case, sin presupposes the moral sentiment, and this, as we have seen, is the outgrowth of ' herd-instinct ' ; it follows that the ' first known sin ' would be, not the cause, but the first known effect of that deficiency in ' herd-instinct ' with which we have identified the ' inherited infirmity ' of theology. The Rabbis were right when they said that Adam fell because he already had the ' evil inclination ' within him.

The cause of evil in man would thus seem to be historically prior to man. Can we assume that the defect of ' herd-instinct ' was simply inherited by man from his animal ancestors ? Apparently not : there is no reason for supposing that the ' sub-men ' were less loyal to their packs or hordes than wolves or hyenas now. The fact is that the defect of herd-instinct in man is relative to the enormous growth of self-consciousness which distinguishes him from the brutes ; the corporate instinct in him has not kept pace with the increasing demands of the complex societies which his expanding intellect has created. What is wrong with man is that he has just enough ' herd-instinct ' for an anthropoid, but not enough for a man ; he is suffering from *arrested development* of ' herd-instinct.' But what arrested the development ? At present we can only assume that some unknown and positively malignant factor intervened in the crisis of the birth of the race. (It must be expected that our conclusions will become less and less precise, the further we penetrate back into the tunnel of the past.)

Perhaps we may gain light upon the nature and source of this positive evil factor, which seems to have been revealed as lying behind the negative defect of ' weakness of herd-instinct,' if we consider man's context—that is, the rest of organic nature. Evil in sub-human nature (which mainly takes the form of ' cruelty ' or ' selfishness ') is positive and not merely negative, and objective in character, not subjective (*i.e.* to us, looking on as spectators, it appears as that which ought not to be, but to the beasts which work it in blind obedience to instinct it doubtless appears as natural). The cat has no qualms of conscience about playing with the mouse. Nevertheless we cannot but feel that we should not have created a universe containing the cobra and the bacillus of diphtheria, had we occupied the position of Demiurge ; why, then, should God have done so ? The answer can only be that He did not do so ; the evil which exists in organic nature, apparently coeval with it and worked into its very tissue, cannot be due to the all-loving Creator. We are thus led to the hypothesis of a pre-cosmic vitiation of the whole Life-Force, at the very beginning of cosmic evolution : this, it would seem, and not the failure of primitive man to escape from already existing evil, is the true and ultimate ' Fall.' Such a view of the Fall and its effects is much vaster and more awe-inspiring than that which makes it a purely human affair ; and it proportionately increases the amplitude and magnificence of Redemption.

To avoid both dualism and an infinite regress, we must suppose that the Life-Force corrupted itself—which means that we must conceive it as having been, at its creation, personal and free—a self-conscious *anima mundi*, like the ' only begotten universe-god ' of Plato's *Timaeus*. The Father of all things must have created this World-Soul good ; but at the beginning of time, in some transcendental and incomprehensible manner it turned away from Him and towards Self, thus staining its own essence and, perhaps, forfeiting self-consciousness, which it has only regained after aeons of myopic striving, in sporadic fragments, which are the separate minds of men. This interior perversion of its being—this orientation away from God, and in the direction of ruthless self-assertion—manifested itself in the struggle for existence, so soon as the *anima mundi* was able to express itself in organic forms at all ; it appears in the cruelty which ravages the animal world, in the unknown factor which hindered the due development of ' herd-instinct ' just when the anthropoids were becoming men, and in the mysterious outbreaks of fiendishness which we call ' criminality.'

The conception just outlined has some affinities with the thought of Plotinus, who makes the World-Soul the third member of his Trinity. But we diverge decisively from him in regard to two points, viz. : (i) the World-Soul for us is a *created* being, not an element in a part of, or a necessary emanation from, the Godhead ; (ii) whereas Plotinus finds (what corresponds to) the ' Fall ' in the detachment of the human soul from the World-Soul, we find the Fall in the voluntary deviation of the World-Soul from conformity with the will of the Creator. Yet, though we cannot identify the created *anima mundi* with the eternal Logos of God, Who is the ' express image of His substance,' we must recognise an intimate relation between the Life-Force of the universe and the Divine Person Who ' upholds all things by the word of His power.' This relation was meant to consist in the penetration, inspiration, and guidance of the created by the Uncreated power ; and the rebellion of the former has not banished the patiently working influences of the latter. Before man was, the Spirit of Christ was striving with the evil in nature : and since the emergence of man, the Word of God has worked in saint and sage to counteract the languor of the ' inherited infirmity,' finally assuming flesh as one of our own race to inaugurate the final act of salvation, whereby, in the perfected Kingdom of God, not only men, but superhuman and sub-human beings, and the basic World-Soul itself, will be redeemed from the bondage of corruption into the glorious liberty of the children of God.

ABBREVIATIONS

AV   Authorised Version.
CQR   Church Quarterly Review.
DB   Dictionary of the Bible (Hastings).
DCB   Dictionary of Christian Biography (Smith and Wace).
DTC   *Dictionnaire de théologie catholique* (Vacant-Mangénot).
EBi   Encyclopaedia Biblica.
ERE   Encyclopaedia of Religion and Ethics (Hastings).
ICC   International Critical Commentary.
JE   Jewish Encyclopaedia.
JQR   Jewish Quarterly Review.
JTS   Journal of Theological Studies.
PRE   *Real-Enzyklopädie für prot. Theologie u. Kirche*[3] (Herzog-Hauck,
          1896–1913).
PG   *Patrologia Graeca* (Migne).
PL   *Patrologia Latina* (Migne).
RV   Revised Version.
TR   *Textus Receptus* of the New Testament.
WH   Westcott and Hort's Text of the New Testament.

ERRATUM

Page 354 *n.* 3 : for *hist. ane.* read *hist. anc.*

I.

THE BEGINNINGS OF FALL-SPECULATION

Our life is a false nature—'tis not in
    The harmony of things,—this hard decree,
This uneradicable taint of sin,
    This boundless upas, this all-blasting tree,
    Whose root is earth, whose leaves and branches be
The skies which rain their plagues on men like dew—
    Disease, death, bondage, all the woes we see—
And worse, the woes we see not, which throb through
The immedicable soul, with heart-aches ever new.

BYRON, *Childe Harold's Pilgrimage*, iv. 126.

LECTURE I.
THE BEGINNINGS OF FALL-SPECULATION

Wisdom ix. 16.   Hardly do we divine the things that are on earth,
And the things that are close at hand we find with labour,
But the things that are in the heavens who ever yet traced out ?

THE problem of evil is at once the most momentous, most terrible, and most intractable question which has ever vexed the thoughts of man.   This vast and multiform enigma, written visibly upon the nature of things, has seemed in every age to cry aloud at least for such a measure of explanation as shall make its continued presence endurable, both in thought and life.   Whether it meets us in the sub-human world as *physical* evil, pain and suffering, the blind cruelty of Nature ' red in tooth and claw with ravin,' or in the works of man as *aesthetic* evil and ugliness, such as broods over the dreary streets of some squalid industrial town, or in the mind of man himself as *intellectual* evil, error or superstition, or in the central citadel of personality as *moral* evil, uncleanness, and sin, we instinctively feel ourselves in the presence of a single Protean power, which in all its manifold shapes is one in essence, springing from a single fount which lies beyond our ken.   It may still have been possible, exactly ten years ago,[1] at the beginning of the fateful year 1914, for men to dismiss the problem of its genesis with a light-hearted *solvitur ambulando*, and to console themselves for the impossibility of accounting for the origin of evil by the assurance of its necessary and speedy extinction, as the result of an irresistible upward trend of moral evolution

---

[1] The introduction to this first lecture is printed exactly as delivered.

assumed to be in automatic conformity with the ascending curve of material, mechanical, and scientific advance. But the events through which humanity has lived since then have for ever dispelled such a credulous optimism. The countless graves in which the most vigorous of the race now sleep, and the living legacy of mutilation, blindness, and madness which the great catastrophe has left behind it, have decisively refuted the dogma of a necessary moral progress implicit in mental evolution. Nor is it now possible to fall back upon the conception of an unlimited freedom of the will, and to regard evil as neither requiring nor being capable of any further explanation than the arbitrary and incalculable choice of conscious, self-determining agents, in the light of the melancholy, if less immediately disastrous, sequence of events which has unrolled itself since the peace. Humanity, as it feels itself slowly drawn, against its will, by the ever-quickening current of uncontrollable race-hatreds towards the Niagara of another disaster even more dreadful than that from which it has just emerged, has good occasion to utter from its heart the cry of the Apostle ' Who shall deliver me from the body of this death ? ' [1] If our race is to be saved from the inexplicable madness which from time to time impels it to destroy both itself and its achievements, it needs in the first instance light and knowledge—light upon the mysterious source and potency of Evil, and knowledge of its own wayward nature ; and whither should it look for light and knowledge but to Religion, its ancient kindly teacher, so long neglected during the days of prosperity, yet claiming still to be its heaven-descended guide ? No complete solution of the problem of Evil is attainable with our present faculties, still less a logically perfect Theodicy, or vindication of the ways of God to men : but Religion, if it is what it claims to be, must provide us at least with an indication, sufficient for the practical purposes of life, of the direction in which the solution lies.

If we study the history of Religion, we shall find in it three classical answers to the problem of Evil, which in their most typical forms are known to us as evolved by the

[1] Rom. vii. 24.

creative thought of three races, each corporately gifted in a
singular degree with that sensitiveness to the influences of
the Divine and that thirst for immediate contact with and
possession of Ultimate Reality which in the individual are
the hall-marks of spiritual genius. Perhaps the most
ancient of these reasoned answers is that which, ever since
the composition and canonisation of the Upaniṣads,[1] has
characterised the deepest philosophic and religious thought
of the Hindu branch of the Aryan race ; it consists in the
affirmation that Evil is appearance, the inevitable concomitant of individual, finite, and relative existence, and
that the Absolute, the eternal One which is the timeless and
changeless substrate of the fleeting phenomenal Many, lies
as infinitely far beyond the opposition of good and bad as
it transcends the distinction of personal and impersonal,
and even the final antithesis of Being and Non-Being, in
the incomprehensible depths of its all-embracing inanity.
This view of God, the World, and Evil may be compendi-
ously described as ' unmoral ' or ' praeter-moral ' monism. As
generally expounded in the Vedânta philosophy (that is,
the system of thought which is partly contained in, and
partly has been educed by commentators from, the
Upaniṣads) it does not deny an imperfect and subordinate
degree of reality to the phenomenal world,[2] but, as developed
to its extremest pitch in the teaching of Buddhism, it
involves as a necessary corollary the doctrine of Mâyâ or
illusion, that is, the belief in the complete non-reality and
non-entity of phenomena, including the individual self.
From this doctrine follows the profoundly pessimistic theory
of redemption offered to mankind by the pure and lofty
genius of Gautama—a theory which sees salvation only in
the dissipation of the illusion of self-hood, with its con-

---

[1] For the gradual revolution, marked by the growth of these books,
and covering the period from the eighth to the sixth century B.C., which
substituted the idea of the one supreme impersonal Being, called Brahman,
for the animistic pantheon of the Vedas, see J. N. Farquhar, *A Primer of
Hinduism* (1911), cc. IV, V (' The Philosophic Period ') ; *cf.* also Hastings,
ERE, art. ' Upaniṣads ' and P. Deussen, *Philosophy of the Upanishads*
(Edinburgh, 1906).

The most important Upaniṣads have been translated by F. Max Müller,
Sacred Books of the East, vols. i., xv.

[2] F. Max Müller, *The Vedânta Philosophy*, pp. 126–132.

comitant extinction of desire, and escape from the weary burden of Karma, achieved through successive cycles of reincarnation and death ; and bids men concentrate their hope upon the supreme moment when the soul attains Nirvana by stripping itself of the last shred of individual passion and self-consciousness, and slides like a drop into the ocean of the infinite Nothing, which is the All.

Second in order of time is the answer given by the other branch of the Eastern Aryan family, the Iranian Persians, in whose national religion, as elaborated by the Magi (though not as originally promulgated by Zarathushtra [1]), the mysterious power of Evil, vaguely felt as all-pervasive, is personified as a malevolent God, Angra Mainyu or Ahriman, locked in Titanic conflict with Ahura Mazdah, the God of wisdom, goodness, and light. This is the answer of dualism, which regards Good and Evil, light and darkness, as equally rooted in the structure of reality, not as mere appearances, but as coaeval hypostases or substantive beings, existing from eternity in their own right, and dividing the realm of phenomenal being between them. So far as this Magian dualism was able to evolve a theory of redemption at all, it did not progress beyond the crude conception of an unexplained future victory of the good God over the opposing power of evil, or of the ultimate collapse of the latter as

[1] I here follow the great authority of J. H. Moulton, according to whose *Early Zoroastrianism* (1913), p. 201 ff., Zarathushtra's own doctrine of evil, as expressed in the Gathas, ' amounted only to a strengthening of the Iranian doctrine of Truth as the highest virtue, with Falsehood as the sum of all evil. To that source of every wrong the Prophet attached a descriptive title, Angra Mainyu, which, however, he did not make into a real name. It seems a reasonable conjecture that the Magi commended their own dogma of a division of the world between good and evil powers— a mere relic of animism, which gave birth to a dreary ritual of apotropaic spells—by adapting the Gathic titles of Ahura Mazdah and Angra Mainyu ' (p. 202). A. V. Williams Jackson, on the other hand, thinks that Mazdean dualism is ultimately the product of Zarathushtra's own genius (' Die iranische Religion,' in *Grundriss der Iran. Philologie*, ii. (1900), pp. 627–631). In any case, however, the idea that there exists an evil Creator, independent of and hostile to the Good Spirit, is so thoroughly engrained into the later Avestan system as amply to justify the expression ' Persian ' or ' Mazdean ' dualism, which will frequently occur in the text ; see L. C. Casartelli, *Philosophy of the Mazdayasnian Religion under the Sassanids*, E. tr. (Bombay, 1889), pp. 50–54 ; and F. Cumont, *Oriental Religions in Roman Paganism*, E. tr. (Chicago, 1911), p. 151, ' Persia introduced dualism as a fundamental principle in religion.'

brought about by the malignant natural forces which are its own creations and instruments.[1] The means whereby man may assist Ahura Mazdah in his aeonian battle with Angra Mainyu, and prepare himself for eternal blessedness after death, consist in *manthras* or spells and purificatory rites of the most mechanical and materialistic description ; though the noblest form of the Iranian religion, Mithraism, deduced from the idea of the struggle between the good and the evil Gods, and of the obligation incumbent upon man to take an active part in the war on the side of good, an austere and exalted morality,[2] which, in the second and third centuries of our era made the religion of the ' unconquered Sun ' the most formidable rival of the religion of Christ, and all but secured for it the domination of Western Europe.[3]

Last of all, opposed in the sharpest possible manner to both of these theories, and destined to wage for twenty centuries unremitting warfare upon them, emerges the third classical answer which Religion has given to the enigma of Evil : the answer which was born of the spiritual experience of the Semitic race, flowering in the lofty ethical monotheism to which the people of Israel ultimately attained, the answer which, against all views, whether monistic or dualistic, involving the eternity or necessity of evil, proclaims its temporal character and contingency. This answer is what we are accustomed to call the doctrine of the Fall and of Original Sin. As developed by the Christian Church, which claims to be Israel's true representative and heir, it boldly asserts that Evil in all its forms—physical, aesthetic, intellectual, and moral—though to a certain limited degree and in certain spheres from a human point of view apparently inevitable, is yet from God's point of view *contingent* ; that

---

[1] Plutarch, *de Is. et Osir.* 47 : ἔπεισι δὲ χρόνος εἱμαρμένος, ἐν ᾧ τὸν Ἀρειμάνιον, λοιμὸν ἐπάγοντα καὶ λιμὸν, ὑπὸ τούτων ἀνάγκη φθαρῆναι παντάπασι καὶ ἀφανισθῆναι κ. τ. λ.

[2] Cumont, *Oriental Religions*, p. 157 f.

[3] In 307 A.D., six years before the liberation of Christianity by the Edict of Milan, the emperors Diocletian, Galerius, and Licinius met at Carnuntum on the Danube, and dedicated a sanctuary there to Mithra, ' the protector of their empire ' (fautori imperii sui) (*Corpus Inscr. Lat.* III. 4413 ; *cf.* Cumont, *Monuments et textes relatifs aux mystères de Mithra*, i. p. 281).

it might not, and need not, have been at all ; that its origin
is to be found in the self-determined rebellion, in some
' dark backward and abysm of time,' of a finite, created
will or wills against the all-holy will of the infinite Creator ;
and that this remote primaeval catastrophe has marred the
fair order of the universe and vitiated the stream of life in
brute and man and whatever there may be of discarnate
intelligence superior to man, in such a way that the tares of
pain and ugliness and sin are, in the world as we know it,
inextricably intermingled with the fair harvest which the
creative fecundity of the Divine Spirit has brought forth
in the wonders of nature and the triumphs of human
achievement. This is the traditional Christian solution,
or adumbration of a solution, of the problem of Evil. If
it is true, it would appear to embody precisely that information as to man's wayward nature and the relations in which
he stands towards the moral order of the universe which he
needs, and has never needed more than now, in order to
re-shape his course in accordance with reality in a world of
confusion and change. It may therefore be hoped that the
critical examination of these doctrines in respect of their
origin, content, and validity which the present lectures
purpose to undertake will be justified, not merely by the
theoretical interest which attaches to them in the mind of the
professed theologian, but by their profound and intimate
bearing, which affects theologian and layman alike, upon
the possibility of a moral re-orientation of mankind.

There is, however, a second reason, of no less weight for
the reflective Christian, which, as I venture to think, justifies
the choice of these mysterious doctrines as the subject of
our enquiry. Even if the question of the source of evil were
not suggested by the present condition of the world, it would
still be pressed upon our attention by the exigencies of
modern religious thought. There was a time when the
scheme of orthodox dogma appeared to all as an unshakeable
adamantine framework, reposing upon the two pillars of the
Fall and of Redemption. These two complementary conceptions—that of the great apostasy, which defaced the
image of God in man, and that of the great restoration through
the Incarnation and the Atonement, which renewed it—were

universally taken for granted as the twin focal points which determined the ellipse of traditional theology : and the imagination of Christians loved to play around the parallelism of Adam and Christ—' the first man, of the earth, earthy,' ' the second man ' who is ' of heaven '[1]—of the virgin Eve and the Virgin Mary,[2] of the death-bringing Tree of Knowledge and the life-giving Tree of the Cross.[3]   This idea of the double foundation of the Christian Faith is tersely summed up in Pascal's aphorism—' Toute la foi consiste en Jésus-Christ et en Adam : et toute la morale en la concupiscence et en la grace.'[4]   But the days when this conviction reigned unchallenged were days when most men believed that they dwelt in a comparatively small, geocentric universe, not more than five thousand years old, which had been constructed in six literal days, and still contained the terrestrial paradise with its flaming Cherubim and its wonderful trees, concealed by divine power in some inaccessible region of the earth.[5]   Since then, the world in which we live has expanded like a wizard's creation, at the touch of the magic wand of Science : the imagination is staggered by the illimitable leagues of interstellar space and the uncounted aeons of geologic time ; biology proclaims the unbroken continuity of man's descent from the brutes, and anthropology can find no room for the idea of his paradisal perfection.   It is not too much to say that, whilst for professed and genuine Christians the second great pillar of the faith, the doctrine of Redemption, remains unshaken, founded upon direct

---

[1] I Cor. xv. 47.

[2] For the beginnings of this idea in the Christian Fathers of the second century, see below, Lecture IV, p. 174.

[3] Cf. Iren. adv. haer. V, 19. 1, and also the second and third stanzas of the great Passiontide hymn Pange lingua (Venantius Fortunatus, 530–609 A.D.) :

> ' de parentis protoplasti fraude facta condolens
> quando pomi noxialis morte morsu conruit,
> *ipse lignum tunc notavit, damna ligni ut solveret.*
>
> hoc opus nostrae salutis ordo depoposcerat,
> multiformis perditoris arte ut artem falleret,
> *et medellam ferret inde, hostis unde laeserat.*'

with the parallels quoted by A. S. Walpole, Early Latin Hymns, p. 168.

[4] Pensées sur la Religion, Art. XVI, ii.

[5] Cf. S. Thomas Aq., Summa theol. iia iiae, q. clxiv. a. 2, ad 5.

experience of the redeeming love of God in Christ, even they have the uneasy feeling that the first pillar, the doctrine of the Fall, has been irretrievably undermined, and totters on its base, no longer capable of bearing its former share of the super-incumbent weight.   There are, indeed, those who urge that it is now a source of weakness rather than of strength to the fabric which it supported for so long, and should be razed to the ground.   Whether this be so or not, it will be admitted that there is urgent need for a re-investigation of the question, and, if not for an abandonment of the traditional doctrine, at least for a ' re-statement ' of it, in the strict and legitimate sense of that term.

Before, however, we can approach the task of evaluating the doctrines of the Fall and of Original Sin, with an eye to the possibility of such re-statement, another, much more difficult and delicate, operation must be performed, namely, that of defining what precisely they are.   It is noticeable that Dr. F. R. Tennant, in his monumental discussions of this subject, from time to time alludes to what he calls ' the ecclesiastical doctrine ' with regard to the Fall and Original Sin, without explicitly defining either the denotation or the connotation of this phrase.[1]   A careful examination of the contexts in which the phrase occurs seems to justify the inference that it is meant to denote either the doctrine contained in the Thirty-Nine Articles, or else the highest common factor of the doctrines contained in the Anglican Articles, the Decrees of the Council of Trent, and the Confessions of Augsburg and Westminster.[2]

[1] As, for instance, in *The Origin and Propagation of Sin*, 1902 (Hulsean Lectures), pp. 3, 4, 5 ; *Sources of the Doctrines of the Fall and Original Sin*, 1903, pp. 2, 104, 272, 274, 282, 299 (note 3), 343 ; art. ' Original Sin ' in *ERE* ix. pp. 558, col. b, 560, col. b, 564, col. a.

[2] It is, in fact, implied (*Origin and Propagation*, p. 5) that ' *the* doctrine of original sin ' (italics mine)—which presumably is the same thing as ' the ecclesiastical doctrine '—is for all practical purposes identical with the Augustinian teaching ; and Appendix A, *op. cit.*, p. 151, which is entitled ' The Doctrine of Original Sin in Christian Confessions,' confines itself to extracts from the Thirty-Nine Articles, the Decrees of Trent, and four Protestant Confessions.   It is remarkable that the teaching of the Eastern Orthodox Church is only alluded to in the vaguest possible manner (. . . ' it would appear that on several points the teaching of the Greek Church with regard to the Fall and original sin is in agreement with that of Rome ') ;   and yet the Holy Eastern Church by itself constitutes a fifth of Christendom.

If, however, we wish to consider the matter in a spirit of scientific impartiality, it will be impossible to assume, without previous enquiry, that any one of the types of teaching embodied in these Western and comparatively recent formularies, or even the highest common factor of them taken together, necessarily represents ' the ecclesiastical doctrine,' if this phrase be taken in its natural sense of ' the doctrine of the Christian Church as a whole.'   Though it is not necessary for our present purposes to lay down any detailed theory of ' the Church ' or to fix its exact limits, we shall hardly be challenged if we assume that the Universal Church of God is something far more vast and spacious than the Church of England, the Church of Rome, the Lutheran or the Calvinistic communions, and that no existing confessional document is likely to contain more than a partial and provincial expression of its fundamental mind.   But, when we enquire for an accurate index of that fundamental mind, a clear statement of the irreducible essence of Fall-doctrine to which historic Christianity as such is committed, we are faced by a remarkable absence of universally authoritative definition.   Neither the Nicene nor the Apostles' Creed contains any direct allusion to the subject, nor can any positive and detailed information be gathered from the decrees of the undisputed Oecumenical Councils.[1]   The only means, therefore, which will enable us to collect and fix the diffused essence of the Christian doctrines of Man and of Sin must be found in a comprehensive survey of the history of these ideas, combined with an application of the canon laid down some fifteen centuries ago, by St. Vincent of Lerinum, that that alone is to be accounted truly Catholic which has been believed ' everywhere, always, and by all.' [2]   Let me hasten to add that I propose in the first instance to employ this criterion, that of universal consent, as a means, not of establishing the objective truth of these doctrines, but merely

[1] For a discussion of the significance which may be attributed to the censure pronounced upon the adherents of Caelestius by the Council of Ephesus, see Lecture V, pp. 354, 387.

[2] *commonitorium*, ii. 6 : ' in ipsa item catholica ecclesia magnopere curandum est, ut id teneamus *quod ubique, quod semper, quod ab omnibus creditum est.   hoc est etenim vere proprieque catholicum*, quod ipsa vis nominis ratioque declarat, quae omnia fere universaliter comprehendit.'

of defining their exact content. When that content has
been finally determined—when we know what the doctrines
actually are—then, and not till then, can we address ourselves to the task of deciding whether they correspond to
the facts of nature and life or not. The first six lectures,
therefore, of this course will be historical in nature, intended
to ascertain the origin and fix the essence of these ideas,
and the last two, theological or philosophical, devoted to a
discussion of their validity and truth.

The Problem in the Old Testament

As the Christian Church claims to be continuously
identical with the ancient Israel, and as the Jewish Scriptures
are embodied in the Christian Bible, our historical survey will
naturally begin with the Old Testament ; by which term I
understand, for the purposes of this lecture, the total *corpus*
of Hebrew and Jewish literature contained in the longer or
Septuagintal Canon, a definition which includes the books
commonly called Apocrypha. The period of a thousand
years over which the dates of these documents range may
naturally be divided into three sub-periods, pre-Exilic,
Exilic, and post-Exilic ; and it will be convenient to arrange
our consideration of the growth of the Fall-doctrine in three
corresponding sections.

(*a*) It is not too much to say that the *first* of these periods,
that which ends with the Babylonian captivity, contains no
trace whatever of the existence of a belief in a ' Fall ' (as the
term is used in technical theology) or in ' Original Sin ' ; the
Paradise-story of Gen. iii, as we shall see in our next lecture,
forms no exception to the truth of this statement.[1] It is not
difficult to see why this must necessarily have been so.
These ideas—especially that of a hereditary bias towards
evil—even when held in the vaguest and most popular form,
and without any scholastic exactness of definition, are yet
of a somewhat artificial and abstract nature. They presuppose considerable powers of generalisation and induction
from the facts of history and also of introspective self-

[1] See Lecture II, p. 50 f.

analysis. Hence they are not likely to have arisen at a very early date in the history of the Chosen People. The idea of ' Original Sin,' even in the crudest form, can only come into being as the result of meditation on the fact of Actual Sin ; it can only be born in the mind of one who has felt within him the fierce wrestling of conscience and desire, swaying to and fro in the agonies of the moral struggle. Now the idea of Actual Sin itself, in its precise sense of the free and deliberate transgression of a known moral law, does not belong to the earliest strata of human thought as revealed by anthropological research. The most primitive peoples known to us conceive of evil, not so much in its ethical sense as a value, or negation of value, affirmed of actions, motives, or the will or character which prompts them, but rather in a quasi-physical sense, as a subtle contagion, an impalpable foetor, which exhales from uncanny persons and things, from material substances, such as shed blood, corpses, and objects placed under a religious ban, or from organic processes such as those of generation, birth, and death. At this early stage of thought, there can be no question of a ' Fall' or definite event giving rise to evil. For the distinction between bad and good *mana*, as inhering in uncanny things or persons, is not absolute, but relative to the circumstances of the percipient ; the emotions aroused by the uncanny are strictly ' ambivalent,' and may manifest themselves either as veneration or as horror.[1] As, therefore, there is no such thing for the savage as objectively or absolutely bad *mana*, the question of its origin does not and cannot arise.

It is only by slow and painful degrees that the strictly ethical idea of good and evil has been educed from the

---

[1] *Cf.* the double meaning of the Latin word *sacer* (' sacred ' and ' accursed '). For detailed exposition of the meaning of *mana*, in its generalised significance as a category employed by the science of Comparative Religion, see ' The Conception of Mana ' in *The Threshold of Religion*, R. R. Marett (1914) ; also the article ' Mana,' by the same author, in Hastings, *ERE* viii. p. 375. The idea of bad *mana*, owing to its vagueness, and (as explained in the text) owing to its relativity, cannot be claimed as identical with the later and more artificial *theologumenon* of ' Original Sin ' ; but lingering traces of it seem to have worked subconsciously in the minds of some Christian patristic writers on hamartiology, notably Origen and St. Augustine ; *v. infra*, Lect. IV, p. 226, and *cf.* V, p. 366.

ambiguous notion of beneficent-noxious *mana*. Amongst
the Greeks, the great tragedians allow us to see the process
actually at work ; the *Antigone* of Sophocles, for instance,
contains both conceptions, the ethical and the quasi-physical
side by side. The sin of Oedipus, which was *ex hypothesi*
unconscious and involuntary, is only a sin if evil is thought
to be a substantive miasma or pollution inhering in a person,
rather than a value which the mind attaches to his acts ;
whilst the heroism of Antigone is goodness in the modern or
ethical sense, being obedience to those eternal laws of which
she herself says :

For their life is not of yesterday or to-day, but from all
time, and no man knoweth when they first appeared.[1]

And, as with Greece, so it was with Israel. Like its
neighbours, Israel started on its career with what may be
called a merely zymotic theory of evil, which is clearly
visible in the story of Achan and the Babylonish garment,
and survives embalmed in much of the ceremonial of the
Priestly Law.[2] It was the work of the great prophets of
Israel's classical period to dislodge this barbarous conception from the national mind, to replace it by the spiritual
and ethical idea, and to proclaim that the Lord requires
nothing of man save ' to do justly, and to love mercy, and
to walk humbly with his God.'[3] But this was a task more
than sufficient to absorb the whole even of their volcanic
energies, and they would not have had time, even if they had

---

[1] Soph. *Ant.* 456, 457 :

οὐ γάρ τι νῦν γε κἀχθές, ἀλλ᾽ ἀεί ποτε
ζῇ ταῦτα, κοὐδεὶς οἶδεν ἐξ ὅτου ᾽φάνη.

[2] ' Exactly the same penalty is imposed for infringements of ritual
(Ex. xxx. 33, 38 ; Lev. xvii. 4, 9, 14 ; xix. 8) as for grave moral offences
(Lev. xviii. 29). Death is the penalty, alike for murder (Num. xxxv. 31)
and for Sabbath-breaking (Ex. xxxi. 15 ; xxxv. 2). Purification from
sin is prescribed after purely physical defilement, as through contact
with a corpse, and even for a house which has been affected by leprosy
(Lev. xiv. 49, 52 ; Num. xix. 12, 13, 19, 20 [the Heb. in these passages for
cleanse, purify is properly to ' free from sin ']). A sin-offering is also
sometimes enjoined for merely ceremonial uncleanness (*e.g.* Lev. v. 2, 6 ;
Num. vi. 9–11). . . . The principle of ceremonial cleanness and uncleanness, it may be noticed, was the point on which our Lord broke
most decisively with the Mosaic law' (S. R. Driver, art. ' Law (in Old
Testament) ' in *HDB* iii. p. 72.

[3] Micah vi. 8.

possessed the inclination, to raise the question of the origin
of moral evil ; whilst the hypothesis of an inbred tendency
to sin, with the element of qualified determinism which it
most always involve, would have been profoundly uncongenial to them as apparently offering an easy excuse for
continuance in evil-doing to the indolent and the hypo-
critical.[1] The insistence upon individual freedom and
responsibility which lies at the roots of the prophetic teaching rises to its highest point in the rigid ethical atomism
of Jeremiah and Ezekiel, as expressed in such sayings as :

In those days they shall say no more, The fathers have
eaten sour grapes, and the children's teeth are set on edge.
But every one shall die for his own iniquity : every man
that eateth the sour grapes, his teeth shall be set on edge [2] ;

and

The soul that sinneth it shall die. The son shall not bear
the iniquity of the father, neither shall the father bear the iniquity
of the son ; the righteousness of the righteous shall be upon
him, and the wickedness of the wicked shall be upon him [3] :

—utterances which, if pressed to their logical conclusion,
would seem to amount to a denial by anticipation of the
later doctrine of Original Sin, at any rate in its strictly
Augustinian form.

(b) In the course of our *second* period, that of the Exile,
a change begins to appear in Hebrew thought on the subject of sin. The great catastrophe had burnt the ethical
teaching of the prophets deeply into the mind of Israel,
had produced a poignant sense of sin, both national and
individual, and had fostered a mood of sombre introspective-
ness in which the soul seeks refuge within itself from the

---

[1] The passage Jer. xvii. 9 : ' The heart is deceitful above all things,
and it is desperately sick ; who can know it ? ' does not affirm a radical
evil in human nature ; it is merely a practical aphorism, warning the
prophet's hearers that ' No man ever knows fully his neighbour's thoughts
and motives, nor whether he will remain faithful to his engagements '
(L. E. Binns, *The Book of the Prophet Jeremiah*, 1919, p. 140).

[2] Jer. xxxi. 29 ; *cf.* Ezek. xviii. 2.

[3] Ezek. xviii. 20.   Although the whole of Ezekiel's prophetic ministry
falls chronologically within the period of the Exile (it may be dated 592–
570 B.C.) I have quoted this passage in my survey of the pre-Exilic
period, because of its logical connexion with the teaching of Jeremiah.

disappointments of the unfriendly world without, only to be confronted by the spectacle of weakness and disharmony within. It would seem, however, that the first essays of the Exilic period in the task of explaining evil were prompted by the desire to mitigate, by elucidating, the fact of suffering or pain, and therefore approached the problem primarily on its physical side. The facile optimism of Deuteronomy, which regarded happiness as the unfailing reward of virtue, and suffering as the invariable punishment of sin, indissolubly linked together within the bounds of this present life, had been refuted by history [1]; and, with the final adoption by Israel of a genuine monotheism, which regarded Yahweh, no longer as a local and limited tribal deity, but as the unique sovereign and creator of the universe, the problem of undeserved suffering called all the more insistently for a fresh solution. Abruptly challenging Mazdean dualism, which must have appeared as a simple and tempting solution to many of the exiled Jews, the audacious thought of Deutero-Isaiah attributes evil to the direct appointment of God. ' I am Yahweh, and there is none else. I form the light, and create darkness : I make peace, and create evil : I am Yahweh, that doeth all these things.' [2] Here there can be little doubt that both physical and moral evil are meant. But the genius of Hebrew religion, faithful to the lessons which it had learnt from the great pre-exilic prophets, could make no terms with a solution which by representing God as the author of evil sacrificed His righteousness in order to save His power. It was felt that somehow man, and not God, must be in the last resort responsible for evil, at any rate for the evil which appears in human history ; and the hypothesis of a direct causal relation between sin and suffering inevitably re-appeared,

[1] It is here assumed, in accordance with the generally accepted ' critical theory ' of the Pentateuch, that the composition of Deuteronomy was subsequent to the teaching of (the first) Isaiah, and cannot in any case be attributed to Moses ; see p. 19, n. 5.

[2] Isaiah xlv. 6, 7 ; *cf.* xxxi. 2, and Amos iii. 6. There are several earlier passages of the Old Testament in which Yahweh is represented as prompting men to particular evil actions (Ex. vii. 3 ; Judg. ix. 23 ; 1 Sam. ii. 25, xix. 9 ; 2 Sam. xxiv. 1) ; but Deutero-Isaiah would seem to be the first Hebrew writer to affirm the Divine authorship of evil as a universally valid proposition.

as in the discourses of Job's friends and comforters. The
author of Job rejects the naïve theory of a necessary
connexion between sin and suffering in this life ; but, in
the course of his meditations on this intractable problem,
he is led to admit the empirical universality of sin to such
an extent as to suggest something like an *a priori* necessity
for it, rooted in the nature of man. And here we come
upon the first dim traces of the ideas of which we are in
search. ' Can a mortal be just before God ? or can a
man be pure before his Maker ? ' [1] Or, again, ' Who can
bring a clean thing out of an unclean ? Not one.' [2] Or—
even more emphatically—' What is man that he should be
clean ? And he that is born of a woman, that he should be
righteous ? Behold, he putteth no trust in his holy ones ;
yea, the heavens are not clean in his sight.' [3] ' How then
can man be just with God ? Or how can he be clean that
is born of a woman ? ' [4]

This is not yet a doctrine of original sin, but it is well on
the way towards one. It would seem that the sinfulness
which the author of Job admits to inhere in man is regarded
by him as a necessary consequence of man's finitude and
creaturely character ; there is no thought of a ' Fall ' from
a supposed condition of original perfection. Moral frailty
is the inevitable corollary of physical weakness and limitation. It is to be noted that ultimately this solution of the
problem of evil is the same as the Second Isaiah's, because,
if sin is due merely to man's physical frailty, the ultimate
responsibility for it lies with the Creator who made him
frail ; and, indeed, the book of Job, for all its poetic sub-
limity, is a self-confessed failure considered as a theodicy.
It seemed as though Jewish thought was involved in an
endless circle, perpetually finding itself drawn back into the
position from which it most desired to escape, namely that
which makes God the ultimate author of evil. There was

---

[1] Job iv. 17 (tr. Driver and Gray, *ICC*).
[2] Job xiv. 4.   Driver and Gray translate : ' Oh that a clean thing could
come out of an unclean ! not one can.' Some critics regard this verse as
a marginal gloss which has crept into the text : see *op. cit., Philological
Notes*, p. 89.
[3] Job xv. 14, 15.
[4] Job xxv. 4.

only one way out of the difficulty. The conflict between the hypotheses of an inherent tendency to evil in man, and of the infinite goodness of God who created man, could only resolve itself by the assumption that human nature as it actually exists is not what God meant it to be, and that some historical catastrophe must be postulated in order to account for this otherwise inexplicable fact.

(c) This train of thought—in which the perception of the empirical universality of sin gives rise to a theory of inherited liability to sin, and this again when reflected on compels the assumption of a primal sin as its source—did not attain to complete definition and articulation until the *third* or autumnal period of Israel's history, the age known by the great name of the Maccabees. It is not on that account to be lightly set aside or disparaged. What Professor F. C. Burkitt has called ' the heroic age of Jewish history ' [1] had a providential function to discharge in fashioning and assembling much of the conceptual material which was to be built into the fabric of Christian theology, even before the birth of Christ, just as David before his death had accumulated timber and squared stones to be used in the construction of Solomon's temple. We need only instance the doctrines of the Logos, of the heavenly Son of Man, of the Church and the Communion of Saints, of the Resurrection and the Last Things, as ideas which our Lord and His Apostles did not create but took over as parts of an already existing theology. It was in the characteristic mind of this age, so strangely blent of touching piety and repulsive fanaticism, that the Jewish theories of the origin of evil assumed a relatively final shape.

We cannot here attempt to reconstruct the state of religious thought and feeling during the obscure beginnings of this epoch ; it must suffice to quote three testimonies to the deepening sense of sin, with its reflex tendency to stereotype and fix, by a kind of corporate auto-suggestion, the floating idea of hereditary sinfulness in the mind of the Jewish Church. These shall be taken from the hallowed and familiar words of three Psalms, dating from the Persian

---

[1] *Jewish and Christian Apocalypses*, p. 15 (1913).

and early Greek periods.[1] ' If thou, Lord, wilt be extreme
to mark what is done amiss, O Lord, who may abide it ? ' [2]
' Enter not into judgment with thy servant, for in thy sight
shall no man living be justified ' [3]—two utterances which
seem to show that the empirical universality of sin has
already been elevated to the rank of a dogma.   The next
step, that of ascribing this universality of actual sin to the
presence of a hereditary taint or weakness, is taken in the
most pathetic of all outpourings of repentant grief, the 51st
Psalm : ' Behold, I was shapen in wickedness, and in sin
hath my mother conceived me ' [4]—a saying which bears
the same unmistakeable significance, whether an individual
sinner or the personified community be regarded as the
speaker.   The time was ripe for the last step in the process,
that of tracing the hereditary taint back to a primal sin, the
uncaused cause or *primum mobile* of the whole disastrous
concentration.   As a matter of fact, though in all probability
the Psalmists knew it not, this step had already been taken.
Already during the fourth century before Christ an unknown
thinker had reasoned with himself to this effect—' Human
nature everywhere contains an innate bias towards evil.
This is clearly contrary to the intention of God, who must
have created man in a state of goodness ; therefore, there
must have been a primitive catastrophe, through which evil
invaded human life from without, from the unseen world of
spirits.'

This nameless philosopher, whose thoughts we have thus
speculatively reconstructed, was the person designated in
Hexateuchal criticism by the symbol R^{JP}—in other words,
the redactor who wove the Prophetic and Priestly strands
of the Hexateuch into the single history which we possess
to-day.[5]   Oppressed by the need for a final and specific

---

[1] This dating is taken from Briggs, *The Book of Psalms, ICC.* (1907) ;
he assigns Pss. li. and cxliii. to the Persian, cxxx. to the early Greek
period.   But the argument in the text will not be affected if all three are
assigned to the Greek period.

[2] Ps. cxxx. 3, RV., ' If thou, Lord, shouldest mark iniquities, O Lord,
who shall stand ? '

[3] Ps. cxliii. 2.   [4] *v.* 5.

[5] Though no reader who is in any degree conversant with the present
state of Biblical knowledge will require a detailed disproof of the Mosaic
authorship of the earlier books of the Old Testament as they stand, it may

event to explain the origin of evil, he searched through the ancient traditions which lay before him, and fixed upon the mysterious legend of the fallen angels narrated in Genesis vi. This story, it would seem, was the first Jewish Fall-story, not in the sense that it is more ancient in origin than the Paradise-story contained in Genesis iii., but in the sense that it was *the first to be fixed upon* as containing an explanation of the origin of evil in man. To it, therefore, some words of explanation and criticism must be devoted.

The Story of the Fallen Angels

The first eight verses of Genesis vi. are taken from the Yahwistic source, and have been placed in their present position to form an introduction to the Flood-story, which, as is well known, is composed of alternate sections of the Yahwistic and the Priestly narratives. In them we are told that certainly heavenly beings described as the *benē*

---

nevertheless be well to state explicitly that in this and the following Lecture I assume the outlines of the ' four-document ' critical theory of the Hexateuch, elaborated in its present form mainly by Kuenen and Wellhausen. This, very briefly summarised, regards the Hexateuch as a composite structure, built up in the main out of four primary elements, namely, (1) the ' *Yahwistic* ' *narrative*, so called from its use of the divine name YHWH, and usually designated by the symbol J : this may be roughly dated *c.* 850 B.C. ; (2) the ' *Elohistic* ' *narrative*, covering the same historical ground, but distinguished by its preference for the title, '*elōhīm* to denote God, and compiled, in all probability, about a century later than J ; this is referred to by the symbol E (the conflate history of the world and of Israel into which these two narratives were compounded towards the end of the eighth century B.C. is known as JE, or the ' Prophetic History ') ; (3) the *Book of Deuteronomy*, the central portion of which is regarded by most critics as the basis of Josiah's sweeping Reformation (2 Kings xxiii.), together with certain elements akin to Deuteronomy contained in other books, the whole being known as D ; (4) the great *Priestly Document*, which includes both an ecclesiastically coloured history and a collection of legal codes, and was reduced to its present form during and after the Exile (this is known as P). The final combination of JE, D, and P into the Hexateuch as we possess it may be assigned to the fourth century B.C. As both of the Genesis-passages which we shall have to examine are derived from J, it will not be necessary to go further into the refinements of Pentateuchal criticism, with regard to which much diversity of opinion still prevails amongst scholars (see *The People and the Book*, 1925, Essay VI).

ha-'elōhīm—the ' sons of the gods '[1]—(a trace of original polytheism which reveals the great antiquity of the narrative) saw the daughters of men that they were fair, and contracted marriages with them (*vv.* 1, 2). In *v.* 3, Yahweh, beholding this action from heaven, is said to have uttered words which, as represented in the English versions, appear somewhat cryptic : ' My spirit shall not strive with man for ever, for that he also is flesh ; yet shall his days be an hundred and twenty years.' [2] The fourth verse tells us of the *nephilīm*,[3] or giants, who existed upon the earth in those days, and also afterwards, whenever the ' sons of the gods ' united themselves with women. The presumption is that these giants were sprung from the union between divine and human partners. They are further identified with the *gibbōrīm* or ' mighty men ' of old, the traditional heroes of popular folk-lore. We are then told (*vv.* 5, 6) that Yahweh saw ' that the wickedness of man was great in the earth, and that every imagination of the thoughts of his heart was only evil continually ; and Yahweh repented that he had made man on the earth, and it grieved him at his heart.' He consequently resolves to destroy the human race by means of a flood. Noah, however, finds favour in the sight of the Lord.

As these verses stand, the only construction to be put upon them appears to be as follows : The ' sons of the gods ' are divine beings, of an order inferior to Yahweh—or, to employ a later and more familiar term, ' angels '[4]—who gave way to lust, and committed sin by deserting their heavenly abode and mingling the divine essence with the

[1] This translation seems to be necessitated by the presence of the definite article before אֱלֹהִים. ' Sons of God ' (AV., RV.) would presumably be בְּנֵי אֱלֹהִים, as in Job xxxviii. 7.

[2] See below, p. 23, n. 1.

[3] For an account of these mythical beings (containing a large element of conjecture) see T. K. Cheyne in *EBi* iii. *s.v.* Nephilim.

[4] *Cf.*, much later, the use of אֱלֹהִים in Ps. viii. 5 : ' Thou didst make him a little lower than the '*elōhīm*,' and Briggs' note *in loc.* (*ICC.*, Psalms, vol. i. p. 64) : ' We must think of the *Elohim* as comprehending God and angels, the latter being, in their historic origin, the ancient polytheistic gods, degraded to ministering servants of the one God Yahweh.'

seed of man. This unnatural action introduces the principle
of evil into humanity : a principle which finds its first and
most terrifying manifestation in the appearance of a monstrous brood of Titans, who disturb the moral order of the
earth by deeds of lawlessness. The chaos so created attains
to such dimensions as to provoke the Creator to visit the
earth with the Flood, so as to eliminate evil from the earth
by drowning both the giants and other members of the
human race who have been corrupted by their influence.
As the narrative stands, it appears to imply the existence of
a direct causal relation between the wickedness of the giants
and the lustfulness of their angelic sires ; this construction
of the story, however, is not actually stated in the text, and
careful examination seems to show that there is a perceptible
' suture ' or join between *vv.* 4 and 5. Verses 5–8, giving
the account of man's wickedness, lead directly into the
Yahwistic Flood-story ; but *vv.* 1–4, containing the legend
of the angels, seem to come from a cycle of tradition which
knows nothing of the Deluge ; for in Numbers xiii. 33
(a passage derived from JE) certain descendants of the
nephilīm, including the famous sons of Anak,[1] are said to
have been still surviving in Palestine at the time of the
invasion under Joshua, a statement which is obviously
inconsistent with the supposition that the giants were all
drowned in the Flood.   And the words attributed to Yahweh
in *v.* 3 seem inconsistent with the idea of a flood shortly
to follow ; for, if we follow the most probable hypothesis,
their meaning may be paraphrased as follows : ' My " spirit "
or essence ' (that is, the divine essence which the ' sons of the
gods ' have improperly introduced into the human stock by
their unnatural alliances) ' must not be allowed to remain
intermingled for ever with the essence of mortal man, who
is but flesh ' (*i.e.* not much more than an animal) ' and
therefore is not entitled to the permanent enjoyment of the
supernatural increase in knowledge and strength which
participation in the divine essence brings with it.   I will,

---

[1] But G. Buchanan Gray (*ICC.*, Numbers, p. 151) thinks that the
words בְּנֵי עֲנָק מִן-הַנְּפִלִים, ' the sons of ' Anāq are some of the *nephilīm,*'
are a gloss, as they are not represented in the LXX.

accordingly, reduce the average duration of human life to a period of a hundred and twenty years, in order to ensure that the divine essence is worked out of the human race within a comparatively brief period.' [1]   Again, it would seem that Yahweh's contemplation of so prolonged and cumbrous a method of eliminating from the human stock the divine element unlawfully introduced into it is quite inconsistent with the supposition that he was able, and intended, to destroy the whole human race *en bloc* by a sudden cataclysm within a few years. We therefore conclude that the Angel-story comes from sources entirely different from those of the Flood-story, and that it was prefixed to the Flood-story by R^{JP} in order to explain the universal wickedness which provoked the Deluge. In making it into a 'Fall-story' it is probable that R^{JP} has mutilated it, in order to abolish mythological features which offended his moral and religious sense.

THE ANGEL-STORY IN THE APOCALYPSES

The use of this earliest Fall-story is illustrated by its elaboration in the most interesting of all pseudepigraphic

---

[1] This very obscure and probably corrupt verse has been exhaustively discussed by J. Skinner (*Internat. Crit. Commentary*, Genesis, pp. 143 ff.). Its interpretation turns upon the meaning of the word רוּחִי (' my spirit ') and of the phrase לֹא־יָדוֹן, which the LXX represents by οὐ μὴ καταμείνῃ and the English versions by ' shall not strive.' The explanation adopted in the text is that given by Skinner, following Wellhausen (*Die Composition des Hexateuchs u. der historisch. Bücher des AT*, 2nd edn. 1889, p. 305 ff.). It is not an objection to this view that the shortening of the lives of individuals would not affect the characteristics acquired by the race through the divine-human unions ; for (assuming no further apostasies on the part of the *'elōhim*-beings) the amount of the divine essence latent in the human stock as the result of the original transgression would, presumably, be conceived as strictly fixed, and, with the increasing numbers of the race, would be regarded as subject in each generation to a process of continuous subdivision, so that eventually the quantity of it to be found in any given individual would be infinitesimal and so practically negligible. The reduction of the average life of the individual from nine centuries to a little more than one would be an obvious means of accelerating this process.

works—the *Ethiopic Book of Enoch*.[1] This book is a literary patchwork embodying the whole or fragments of at least six separate documents, belonging to dates ranging between the end of the third and the middle of the first century B.C. The most important of these documents are (1) the Book of Enoch proper, comprising Chapters 12–36 of our present text, which may be dated in the neighbourhood of 200 B.C. ; (2) the fragments of the Book of Noah, which is at least earlier than the persecution of Antiochus Epiphanes ; (3) the Visions of Enoch, written about 165 B.C., in the midst of the Maccabean struggle, and contemporaneously with the Book of Daniel ; and (4) the Similitudes, which appear to have been written between the years 94 and 64 B.C., during the reigns of Alexander Jannaeus and Alexandra. The most complete statement of the Fall-story as connected with the sin of the angels is contained in the fragments of the Book of Noah.[2] In this work the apostate angels are described by a term familiar to us from the Book of Daniel[3] as ' Watchers '—that is, spirits who are conceived in their heavenly home as ceaselessly *watching* the Almighty, so as to be in perpetual readiness to execute His commands. We are told that they were two hundred in number, and that, having bound themselves by a mutual oath to carry out the projected rape, they descended upon the summit of Mount Hermon.[4] The giants, who were their sons, are said

---

[1] For citations from the text of this book, as well as from other apocalyptic writings which it has been necessary to mention in this lecture, I have used the translations contained in the monumental *Apocrypha and Pseudepigrapha of the Old Testament*, Oxford, 1913, edited by Dr. R. H. Charles. In giving references, I have followed the common custom of designating the Ethiopic Enoch as 1 Enoch, and the ' Book of the Secrets of Enoch,' or Slavonic Enoch, as 2 Enoch.   [2] 1 Enoch vi–xi.

[3] iv. 13, 17, 23. The Aramaic word is עִיר, ' wakeful one,' which LXX and Theodotion transliterate as εἰρ; Aquila and Symmachus, however, render עִירִין by ἐγρήγοροι, which appears to have become a technical term denoting the order to which the peccant angels belonged, as it appears in the Slavonic Enoch under the curious form ' Grigori ' (2 Enoch xviii. A text ; the B text has ' Egoroi ' ; Charles, *Apocr. and Pseudep.* ii. p. 439).

[4] 1 Enoch, vi. 6. St. Hilary (*tract. in cxxxii. ps.* [*PL* X. 521]) quotes this detail with some hesitation from the Book of Enoch, which he describes as ' nescio cuius liber.' W. Robertson Smith (*Religion of the Semites*, 1914 edn., p. 446) suggests that the Watcher-story may have originally been a local legend connected with Mount Hermon.

to have been three thousand ells in height.   These Titanic
beings, we are told, ' consumed all the acquisitions of men.
And, when men could no longer sustain them, the giants
turned against them and devoured mankind. . . . And as
men perished, they cried, and their cry went up to heaven.' [1]
The engendering of giants, however, was not the only way in
which the fallen Watchers introduced wickedness into the
earth.   They corrupted the human race by imparting to it
knowledge which the Creator had not meant it to possess.[2]
Here we detect the emergence of a *motif* which reappears in
the second Fall-story, that of Adam and Eve, and is closely
paralleled by the Greek legend of Prometheus—the idea
being that God is jealous—τὸ θεῖον πᾶν φθονερόν, as the
Greeks put it [3]—that the Creator grudges His creatures the
possession of knowledge, and that all or many of their woes
are due to its unlawful acquisition.   Of the fallen angels,
Azâzêl taught men the art of working metals, and of making
knives, swords, and armour, and also instructed them in the
manufacture of jewellery and cosmetics, arts which naturally
led to the increase of homicide and impurity ;   whilst the
other angels reveal to men the sciences of magic, astrology,
and astronomy.[4]   Then, in Chapter 9, the Archangels
Michael, Uriel, Raphael and Gabriel look down from heaven,
and see the corruption and disorder which reign upon the
earth.   They complain to the Almighty, who charges them
to deal with the situation in different ways.   Uriel is commanded to warn Noah of the approaching Deluge ;   Raphael
is commissioned to bind Azâzêl, the leader of the rebel
angels, hand and foot, and to bury him in a hole in the
desert, piling upon him rough and jagged rocks, until the

[1] 1 Enoch vii. 4; viii. 4.   The arrogance of the giants is also mentioned
in 3 Macc. ii. 4 ;   Ecclus. xvi. 7 ;   Wisdom xiv. 6.

[2] ix. 6 :   *cf.* also lxiv. 2 (Similitudes).

[3] Herodotus i. 32, iii. 40 :   in these passages only material prosperity
is conceived as the object of the divine ' jealousy.'   Aristotle condemns
this opinion, especially in so far as it attributes to God a dislike of human
progress in knowledge :   εἰ δὴ λέγουσί τι οἱ ποιηταὶ καὶ πέφυκε φθονεῖν τὸ
θεῖον, ἐπὶ τούτου (*i.e.* in the matter of knowledge) συμβαίνειν μάλιστα εἰκὸς καὶ
δυστυχεῖς εἶναι πάντας τοὺς περιττούς.   ἀλλ᾽ οὔτε τὸ θεῖον φθονερὸν ἐνδέχεται
εἶναι, ἀλλὰ καὶ κατὰ τὴν παροιμίαν πολλὰ ψεύδονται ἀοιδοί κ.τ.λ. (*Met.* A.
ii. 10).

[4] 1 Enoch viii.

time is ripe for the last judgment, after which he is to be
cast into eternal fire.   The Lord's charge to Raphael continues—' Heal the earth which the angels have corrupted,
and proclaim the healing of the earth that they may heal
the plague, and that all the children of men may not perish
through all the secret things that the Watchers have disclosed and have taught their sons.   And the whole earth
has been corrupted through the works that were taught by
Azâzêl ; to him ascribe all sin.' [1]   The commissions of the
two other archangels seem to be derived from a different
cycle of tradition, inasmuch as Gabriel is commanded to
proclaim the destruction of the children of the Watchers
through internecine strife—a command that seems inconsistent with the hypothesis of a rapidly approaching Flood ;
whilst Michael is bidden to bind one Semjâzâ, who in this
version appears to be the leader of the apostates, in a ravine
of the earth, there to await the last great assize.   Such is the
haggadic amplification of the story contained in Genesis vi.
1–4 as it appears in the fragments of the Book of Noah
embodied in the Ethiopic Book of Enoch.   A supplemen-
tary detail is added in c. xv., belonging to the Book of Enoch
proper, in which the souls of the dead giants are said to have
become demons who afflict mankind.   It is very significant
that the author of this document is well acquainted with the
Paradise-story of Genesis iii.   On one of his tours through
the supramundane regions Enoch is shown the Garden of
Eden with the Tree of the Knowledge of Good and Evil
growing in the midst of it. [2]   His angelic guide explains that
this is the tree of which Adam and Eve ate, which opened
their eyes so that they knew that they were naked ; but it
is noticeable that this event is mentioned merely as an
interesting historical fact, and that no attempt is made to
trace the origin of human wickedness to it.   Evidently the
Watcher-legend of Genesis vi. is the only Fall-story of which
the Book of Enoch knows.

A symbolic version of the Watcher-legend occurs in the
third section of the Ethiopic Enoch, namely, the Visions,
which must have been written in the very midst of the
Maccabean struggle, almost contemporaneously with the

[1] 1 Enoch x. 7, 8.   [2] xxxii. 3, 4.

Book of Daniel. In the second ' Vision ' the history of the
world from the creation of man to the foundation of the
Messianic kingdom is told under the form of an elaborate
animal story.[1] The apostate Watchers are symbolised by
stars, the children of Seth, with whom they intermarry,
by oxen, and the evil brood of giants who sprang from these
unions by elephants, camels, and asses.[2] The Watcher-
legend is assumed once more in the Similitudes, which
Dr. Charles dates between 94 and 64 B.C. In cc. lxvi–lxix.
the emphasis is laid, not so much upon the lust of the angels
as upon their transgression of the divine ordinance, in
revealing to the human race secret knowledge which the
Creator had not designed for it. As before, sorcery, metallurgy, and the manufacture of weapons occupy a prominent
place among the forbidden arts in which the fallen spirits
instructed man [3] : the author of the Similitudes ingeniously
adds the art of writing with ink and paper as one of the chief
causes of human corruption for which the apostate Watchers
were responsible.[4]

Such was the earliest and crudest form in which the
doctrines of the Fall and of Original Sin obtained any wide
currency amongst the Jews—the naïve belief that the
universal sinfulness with which mankind appeared to be
infected flowed like a dark turbid river from a single fount,
namely, the unholy unions of angelic and human beings
narrated in Gen. vi. and the commixture of mortal and
immortal essences effected thereby. No less crude was the
theory of redemption dependent upon it. The world's
deliverance from sin was to be accomplished by purely
external and mechanical means—the imprisonment of the
Watchers, by God, or the Son of Man, in a lurid Gehenna,
and the burning out of the body of the human race of the
plague-spot which their lust had left behind, by the fires of
an eschatological cataclysm. Doubtless we must attribute
it to the distractions of the mortal conflict with the Seleucid
power in which the Jewish Church-State was for nearly

[1] i Enoch lxxxv.–xc. In c. lxxv., the creation of Adam and Eve, the
murder of Abel, and the birth of Seth are related in symbolic terms, but
there is no mention of the forbidden fruit or the expulsion from Paradise.
[2] lxxxvi.   [3] lxv. 6–8.   [4] lxix. 9, 10.

a generation involved, that an obvious internal difficulty exhibited by this artless theory was not at first perceived. The difficulty is this. Taking the story of Genesis vi., vii. literally, as the authors of Enoch took it (and ignoring the reference to the *nephilīm* in Num. xiii. 33), we learn that all living beings, except Noah and his family and the animals preserved in the Ark, were destroyed in the Flood. Presumably, therefore, the giants were drowned, and the whole seed of evil proceeding from the Watchers must have come to an end ; so that the Watcher-story in no way accounts for the fact of *post-diluvian* wickedness. The author of the Visions seems dimly to feel this difficulty, because, after stating that the elephants, camels, and asses, who symbolise the giants, perished in the Flood, he goes on to state that the three bulls, who symbolise the sons of Noah, procreated after the Deluge—for no assignable reason—a heterogeneous brood of lions, tigers, wolves, dogs, hyenas, wild boars, foxes, squirrels, swine, and other unclean creatures.[1] These, of course, are the Gentiles or wicked races of the earth ; but their appearance merely raises the problem of the origin of evil all over again, and leaves the apocalyptic thinker in the same condition of perplexity as before.

The interpolator of the *Book of Jubilees*, the main body of which may be dated about the end of the second century B.C., attempted to solve the problem by asserting that post-Noachian wickedness was due to the ghosts of the drowned giants, who continued to haunt the world as earth-bound spirits.[2] But the original author of Jubilees had already cut the Gordian knot by abandoning the Watcher-legend altogether, and fixing for his Fall-story on an entirely different passage of Scripture, namely, the Paradise-narrative of Genesis iii., which eventually, owing to the influence of St. Paul, became the official Fall-story of the Christian Church.[3] This writer cannot, indeed, claim to be the first inventor of this idea, inasmuch as the sin of Eve is asserted to be the beginning of wickedness and the cause of death by the Son of Sirach, writing some eighty years previously.[4]

---

[1] I Enoch lxxxix. 10.   [2] Jubilees, vii. 26–39; x. 1–15.   [3] iii. 17–35.
[4] Ecclus. xxv. 24 ; for an examination of this passage see below, Lecture II, p. 54.

But, from the Book of Jubilees onwards, during the course of the first century B.C., it is possible to trace the gradual suppression of the Watcher-legend by the Adam-story as the historical, or supposedly historical, explanation of the origin of human sin.

THE EMERGENCE OF GEN. III. AS THE POPULAR FALL-STORY

In the *Testaments of the Twelve Patriarchs* both stories seem to appear in this character. The Watcher-story appears in the Testament of Reuben, with a curious variant which makes the daughters of men take the initiative in seducing the angels,[1] and in the Testament of Napthali.[2] On the other hand, the Testament of Levi asserts that the redemption which the Messiah will bring will consist in the removal of the flaming sword which excludes man from Paradise, his restoration to the happy garden, and his being given to eat of the Tree of Life [3]—a prophecy which seems to presuppose the identification of the ultimate ' Fall ' with the sin of Adam and Eve. In the *Book of the Secrets of Enoch* (often called the ' Slavonic Enoch ') written, perhaps, contemporaneously with the life of our Lord, whilst both Fall-stories appear, all the emphasis is laid on the Paradise-story as narrating the origin of human wickedness in general, and the Watcher-legend is depressed to a comparatively subordinate role as the explanation merely of that particular episode in the history of human sin which was the occasion of the Flood. In the *Book of the Wisdom of Solomon*, which may be probably dated during the decade which followed the death of Christ,[4] there appears to be an incidental allusion to the Adam-story as the explanation of the cause

[1] Test. Reub. v. 5–7.
[2] Test. Napth. iii. 5.
[3] Test. Lev. xviii. 10, 11.
[4] A. T. S. Goodricke, *The Book of Wisdom*, 1913, Introd. § 2. But it must be confessed that much diversity of opinion has prevailed amongst scholars as to the period of this book's composition : Grimm dates it 150–145 B.C., Thackeray 130–100 B.C., Gregg 125–100 B.C., Gfrörer 100 B.C., Bousset under the Roman Empire, Farrar A.D. 40. For a full discussion of the question, see S. Holmes, *The Wisdom of Solomon*, introd. § 5 (in Charles, *Apocr. and Pseudep.* i. p. 520 f.).

of human mortality [1]; the Watcher-story is not mentioned. The *Ezra-Apocalypse*, commonly known as the Second or Fourth Book of Esdras, which dates from the last quarter of the first century A.D., seems to mark the complete disappearance of the Watcher-story, and the triumph of the Adam-narrative as the generally accepted Fall-story.[2] It need only be added, by way of epilogue to this earliest chapter in the history of the Fall-doctrine, that, when the angel-myth had finally ceased to be regarded as the inspired record of the origin of human sin, its somewhat carnal character gradually evoked, in the Israel of the Mishnic period, a strong repugnance to that literal, and, historically considered, correct interpretation of it which had hitherto held the field. The idea of sexual intercourse between celestial spirits and the daughters of men came to be abhorrent to the pious Jew; hence the *benē ha-'elōhīm* were rationalised into ' sons of the judges ' or ' of the mighty,' that is, purely human beings of princely rank,[3] and their sin was regarded merely as the first instance of seduction.[4] In the Middle Ages, the literal interpretation was revived by the authors of the Qabbālāh, and made the foundation of wild theosophical romances [5]; but the main body of Judaism, which had ceased to believe in angels as more than poetical personifications of the divine attributes, adhered to the rationalistic view until recent times. The comparative study of religions, whilst restoring the literal interpreta-

---

[1] ii. 23 ; *v. infra*, Lecture II, p. 55.

[2] *v. infra*, Lecture II, p. 79.

[3] See the references given in the *Jewish Encyclopaedia*, V. 333, art. ' Fall of Angels,' and R. H. Charles, *Book of Jubilees* (1902), pp. 33 ff., note. Symmachus embodies this interpretation in the text, rendering בְּנֵי הָאֱלֹהִים as υἱοὶ τῶν δυναστευόντων.

[4] Philo, however, characteristically allegorises the story, interpreting the lustful angels as being in reality ' the wicked, who slip into the name of angels, not knowing the daughters of right reason, the sciences and virtues, but captivated by the mortal offspring of mortal men, even pleasures, the bearers of no genuine beauty, which is seen by the understanding alone, but of a spurious gracefulness, through which the senses are deceived ' (*de gigant.* iv). But, as usual, the allegorical significance of the narrative does not exclude its literal truth (*ibid.* ii.). Josephus (*Ant.* i. 3. 1) reproduces the story without theological or other comment.

[5] Grünbaum, *Gesammelte Aufsätze zur Sprach- und Sagenkunde* (1901), pp. 70, 71.

tion of the phrase *bēne ha-'elōhīm*, has now dispelled any lingering traces of belief in the historical character of the story, within as without the modern Jewish Church.[1]

It is easy enough to dismiss this queer old legend, this superseded and forgotten Fall-story, as at the present day totally devoid of interest, except for the Orientalist and the student of folk-lore. But the time which we have spent upon its consideration will not have been wasted, if in the course of the discussion two points, which will play an important part in our final constructive synthesis, have been made to stand out with clearness; and this lecture may appropriately conclude with a summary re-formulation of them.

The first is this—that, considered historically and with regard to the circumstances of its origin, the theory of the Fall and of Original Sin does not rest upon the Paradise-story of Genesis iii. Its true foundations are psychological, based on bed-rock facts of ethical and spiritual experience —the consciousness of the moral struggle, and the feeling of a ceaseless strain and tension between duty and the clamorous appetites, which ever and anon burst victoriously forth into crude external expression, whilst reason looks on in helpless dismay and shame. *Video meliora proboque, Deteriora sequor* [2] : ' the evil which I would not, that I do ' [3] : the state of things described in these almost proverbial sayings may be taken for granted, as requiring no explanation, by the unspiritual and the thoughtless; but, when deeply pondered and brooded over by pure, reflective, and sensitive minds, it generates a mental atmosphere in which the predicate of evil tends to become detached from outer acts and transferred to the inner dispositions, even to the very essence, of the soul—an atmosphere in which the conception of penitence becomes invested with a new and deeper meaning. The ordinary man may feel ashamed of doing wrong : but the saint, endowed with a superior refinement of moral sensibility, and keener powers of introspection, is ashamed of being the kind of man who is liable to do wrong ;

---

[1] For the history of the Watcher-story, and of the Fall-story based upon it, within the Christian Church, see Lecture III, p. 113 f.

[2] Ovid, *Met*. vii. 21.   [3] Rom. vii. 19.

and, the more complete his mastery over the rebellious
impulses of his lower nature, the greater is the distress which
the mere existence of these impulses tends to cause him.
The ordinary man, if he repents at all, repents merely of
what he does, the saint repents of what he is : hence is
derived the standing paradox of sanctity, the fact that the
consciousness of sin actually deepens in and through the
process of liberation from its malignant power, and that it
is precisely the most spotless of men—with the arresting
exception of One Whom Christians believe to be more than
man—who have always proclaimed themselves to be the
' chief of sinners.'   This attitude of repentance of one's self,
translated into intellectual terms, becomes a belief in some
kind of ' radical evil' inherent in human nature.   But
human nature was created by God, and the passionate
ethical monotheism which is the heart of Judaism and
Christianity alike cannot endure the idea that God is the
author of evil ; hence it was concluded that evil in man must
be due to some spontaneous revolt against the Divine Law,
some voluntary aberration from the path marked out for
man by his Creator—in other words, to a ' Fall' of some
kind.   The necessity of a ' Fall' being thus established
nothing remained but to identify it with some ' fontal sin '
of man's infancy, and the unnatural marriages of Gen. vi.
seemed at first to be the catastrophe required.   Whatever
we may think of the validity of this regressive chain of
reasoning, from the facts of the moral struggle back to the
idea of an inherited taint and from that again to the conception of a primordial sin, it is clear that, inasmuch as the first
Fall-story was that of Gen. vi., the doctrines of the Fall and
of Original Sin cannot be regarded as standing or falling
with the historicity of Gen. iii.   The fact is that recent
research, which has disposed of the claims of these stories
to represent literal historic fact, has simultaneously disposed
of the idea that the Christian doctrines of Man and of Sin
are logically based upon them.   If the Fall-theory rested
upon moral and religious experience at the time of its first
appearance, and if, as we have seen, the Watcher-story and
the Adam-story were subsequently and successively applied
to it as what we may call decorative after-thoughts or

supposed historical verifications, it follows that, in principle, it must still claim to be based upon moral and religious experience—and for us, who know these ancient stories to be no more than folk-lore, upon moral and religious experience only.   Hence the assertion which has sometimes been made, to the effect that the idea of the Fall has been refuted by ' Biblical criticism,' would seem to be very wide of the mark.   A psychological and metaphysical theory can never be refuted by ' Biblical criticism '—it is vulnerable only by psychological and metaphysical criticism.   Whether the theory of an inherited taint or weakness actually corresponds to the facts of human nature or not—and whether, if it does so correspond, it is permissible to found upon it inferences as to the remote origin of human sin—are problems which must be reserved for discussion in the concluding lectures of this course ; but it will be sufficient for our present purposes if it has been made clear that the question of the truth of the doctrine is completely detachable from and independent of the question of the historicity of the stories.

To put the matter in the clearest light, I will venture to append a simile, drawn from the structure of those palaces of commerce or pleasure which line the streets of a modern metropolis.   From the pavement, the passer-by who casts his eye over one of these buildings sees a stately front, composed, it may be, of pillar, cornice, and architrave in strict accordance with the rules of Vitruvius or Palladio ; and the unskilled person may well imagine that the upper rooms and stories are supported by the seemingly massive columns which stand upon the roadway level.   But the trained glance of the professional architect discerns at once that the imposing front is merely a stone veneer, masking a constructional frame of steel girders which is a mechanically perfect and self-contained system, and that the sculptured columns seen from the streets are mere pilasters and decorative panels, which take none of the weight of the fabric. In like manner the Fall-story of Gen. vi. and that which eventually succeeded it, the story of Gen. iii., though long believed to be supports of the doctrines under discussion, have now been shown to be quasi-historical façades, successively attached to a conceptual structure which stands upon a psychological basis. The fact that the existing façade has now been discovered to consist of the gesso-work of poetry rather than the ashlar masonry of history does not in itself constitute any presumption against the soundness and stability of the interior framework.

The second point which claims attention arises from the nature of the Watcher-story itself. There can, of course, be no question of utilising this story as a source of historical information ; but the student of comparative mythology will not need to be reminded that stories which are valueless historically may have a profound significance for the psychology of races and peoples. Recent study of the mind and its workings has taught us that, in the individual, the dream may be the source of interesting and important information as to the contents of the dim, mysterious region of the Unconscious ; for, in the fantastic imagery of the dream, impulses, instincts, and wishes of which the conscious *ego* may be entirely ignorant find a symbolic expression, through the partial relaxation in sleep of the censorship exercised by the higher self. And myths are the dreams of the vast, slumbrous, diffused race-soul, embodying, in symbolic and generalised form, unmistakeable testimony to the mutual affinities and interpenetrations of the most fundamental emotions of human nature. Hence, it is deeply significant that, in the earliest Fall-story evolved by the ancient Church of God, the primal sin is one which, if the Decalogue could be supposed to have been in existence at the time of its alleged occurrence, would be described as a transgression of the Seventh Commandment. Though it is impossible now to develop the inferences suggested by this fact, it is worth while noting that, in the very beginnings of the idea of Original Sin, there emerges a tendency which has profoundly influenced the course of Christian speculation on the subject, more particularly in its Augustinian phase : and that is the tendency to regard the flaw or weakness inherent in the structure of human personality as caused by, or at least closely connected with, what is known in the language of technical theology as ' concupiscence.' We shall have to formulate a judgment as to the truth or value of this tendency, when we come to examine the bearing of modern psychology upon the problem of the origin of sin, and its detailed discussion must be deferred until then ; but, in our historical survey, we shall often have occasion to note resemblances, sometimes slight and superficial, sometimes astonishingly exact, between the idea of ' concupiscence,' as it appears in Jewish and Christian thought, and the Freudian conception of *libido*. Meanwhile, we may take our leave of this curious fragment of Semitic mythology, remembering that, despite the grotesque and even repulsive details with which it was bedizened by the riotous imagination of the apocalyptists, it has for a season served a providential purpose. It is one of the rough earthen vessels which for a time have enshrined a heavenly treasure, the treasure of the spirit of true peni- tence, which realises that man has good reason to feel sorrow, not merely for his actions but for his nature, and the treasure of faith in an All-Holy God, Who is ' of purer eyes than to behold evil,' and may not, therefore, without impiety be deemed to be its author or fount.

ADDITIONAL NOTE A

THE ORIGIN OF THE ARTS IN PSEUDO-ENOCH AND AESCHYLUS

It is instructive to compare 1 Enoch vii., viii., which tell how the apostate ' Watchers ' instructed mankind in the arts of civilisation, with the speech which Aeschylus puts into the mouth of the rebellious god Prometheus, who performs the same function in Greek mythology :

λέξω δέ, μέμψιν οὔτιν' ἀνθρώποις ἔχων,
ἀλλ' ὧν δέδωκ' εὔνοιαν ἐξηγούμενος·
οἳ πρῶτα μὲν βλέποντες ἔβλεπον μάτην,
κλύοντες οὐκ ἤκουον, ἀλλ' ὀνειράτων
ἀλίγκιοι μορφαῖσι τὸν μακρὸν βίον
ἔφυρον εἰκῇ πάντα, κοὔτε πλινθυφεῖς
δόμους προσείλους ᾖσαν, οὐ ξυλουργίαν·
κατώρυχες δ' ἔναιον ὥστ' ἀήσυροι
μύρμηκες ἄντρων ἐν μυχοῖς ἀνηλίοις.
ἦν δ' οὐδὲν αὐτοῖς οὔτε χείματος τέκμαρ
οὔτ' ἀνθεμώδους ἦρος οὔτε καρπίμου
θέρους βέβαιον, ἀλλ' ἄτερ γνώμης τὸ πᾶν
ἔπρασσον, ἔστε δή σφιν ἀντολὰς ἐγὼ
ἄστρων ἔδειξα τάς τε δυσκρίτους δύσεις.

καὶ μὴν ἀριθμόν, ἔξοχον σοφισμάτων,
ἐξηῦρον αὐτοῖς, γραμμάτων τε συνθέσεις,
μνήμην θ᾽ ἀπάντων, μουσομήτορ᾽ ἐργάνην.
κἄζευξα πρῶτος ἐν ζυγοῖσι κνώδαλα
ζεύγλαισι δουλεύοντα σάγμασίν θ᾽, ὅπως
θνητοῖς μεγίστων διάδοχοι μοχθημάτων
γένοινθ᾽, ὑφ᾽ ἅρμα τ᾽ ἤγαγον φιληνίους
ἵππους, ἄγαλμα τῆς ὑπερπλούτου χλιδῆς.
θαλασσόπλαγκτα δ᾽ οὔτις ἄλλος ἀντ᾽ ἐμοῦ
λινόπτερ᾽ ηὗρε ναυτίλων ὀχήματα. . .
τὰ λοιπά μου κλύουσα θαυμάσει πλέον,
οἵας τέχνας τε καὶ πόρους ἐμησάμην. . . . .

I will speak, not chiding mankind, but expounding the kindness that I showed them in my gifts. For, at the first, men seeing saw in vain, and hearing they heard not, but like unto dream-forms they mixed all things in wild confusion all their days. Naught they knew of brick-built houses, turned to face the sun, or of the joiner's craft ; they dwelt underground, like the tiny ants, in the sunless recesses of caverns. Nor was there any certain sign for them of winter, or bloomy spring, or fruitful summer, until I showed them the risings of the stars and their settings hard to be discerned. Number I found out for them, noblest of inventions, and groupings of letters, and memory of all things, creative mother of knowledge. I first yoked beasts of burden, and made them thralls to collar and pack-saddle, that they might relieve mortals of their heaviest toils ; and to the chariot I harnessed docile steeds, the splendid appanage of luxurious wealth. Nor did any other devise the mariners' canvas-winged wains that roam the sea. . . . Thou wilt wonder yet more, having heard the rest of my tale, what arts and contrivances I framed. . . .

He goes on to claim credit for having originated medicine, the art of divination, and (like Azâzêl) metallurgy :—

ἔνερθε δὲ χθονὸς
κεκρυμμέν᾽ ἀνθρώποισιν ὠφελήματα,
χαλκόν, σίδηρον, ἄργυρον, χρύσον τε τίς
φήσειεν ἂν πάροιθεν ἐξευρεῖν ἐμοῦ ;
οὐδείς, σάφ᾽ οἶδα, μὴ μάτην φλύσαι θέλων.
βραχεῖ δὲ μύθῳ πάντα συλλήβδην μάθε,
πᾶσαι τέχναι βροτοῖσιν ἐκ Προμηθέως.

And who before me could pretend to have discovered the treasures hid beneath the earth, brass, iron, silver, and gold ? no one, I wot, unless he willed to babble foolishly. In one short sentence learn the whole story : all the arts came to mortals from Prometheus. (*Prometheus Vinctus*, 447–468, 476–7, 500–6.)

In the Greek myth, knowledge is a blessing which the tyrant Zeus desires to withhold from men because he hates them ; in the Jewish story, it is, relatively to finite and imperfect beings, a curse from which the Lord would fain shield his children.

II.

THE ADAM-STORY AND THE
'EVIL IMAGINATION'

Love is the source both of virtue and of sin

' Nè creator nè creatura mai,'
    cominciò ei, ' figliuol, fu senza amore,
    o naturale o d'animo ; e tu il sai.
Lo natural è sempre senza errore,
    ma l'altro puote errar per malo obbietto,
    o per poco o per troppo di vigore.
Mentre ch'egli è ne'primi ben diretto,
    e ne'secondi sè stesso misura,
    esser non può cagion di mal diletto ;
ma, quando al mal si torce, o con più cura
    o con men che non dee corre nel bene,
    contra il fattore adopra sua fattura.
Quinci comprender puoi ch'esser conviene
    amor sementa in voi d'ogni virtute,
    e d'ogni operazion che merta pene.'

DANTE, *Purgatorio*, xvii. 91-105.

LECTURE II.

THE ADAM-STORY AND THE 'EVIL IMAGINATION'

Rom. v. 12 : ' Through one man sin entered into the world, and death
through sin.'

Gen. vi. 5 : ' And the Lord saw that the wickedness of man was great
in the earth, and that every imagination of the
thoughts of his heart was only evil continually.'

It was assumed in our last lecture that the Paradise-story
of Gen. iii., despite its traditional employment in later
Judaism and Christianity as a basis for the doctrines of the
Fall and of Original Sin, did not in the mind of the original
compiler of the Yahwistic source either explicitly or implicitly contain these doctrines, in any of their developed or
technical forms.[1] This assumption must now be justified
by a critical examination of that narrative which for many
centuries was venerated by Christians as the literal historic
record :

> Of man's first disobedience, and the fruit
> Of that forbidden Tree, whose mortal taste
> Brought Death into the world, and all our woe.[2]

The cadence of these stately lines should remind us of
a preliminary warning, which despite its frequent repetition
by commentators is not even yet superfluous, namely, that
which bids us resolutely banish Milton from our thoughts.
Probably most educated Englishmen who are not theological
specialists still tend unconsciously to read the highly
systematised doctrinal background of ' Paradise Lost ' into
the artless simplicity of the primitive Scripture. But the
student who is on his guard against the subtle influence
which half-remembered poetic echoes may exercise upon

---

[1] Lecture I, p. 12.   [2] Milton, *Paradise Lost*, i. 1.

the mind will see at a glance that the splendour of Milton's mighty epic bears much the same relation to the original story of Gen. iii. as Michael Angelo's basilica of St. Peter bears to its humble predecessor, the wattled oratory built by the earliest Christians upon the same site; and it is the original story alone which has any significance at this stage of our enquiry. To discover this significance, we must be prepared to examine the narrative without presuppositions, and with a certain necessary independence of its familiar and hallowed associations.[1]

The Paradise-story examined.

Approaching the story in this spirit, we naturally enquire first of all, What, in the mind of the Yahwistic author, was

---

[1] If the following exposition of the Paradise-story, insisting, as it does, upon the imperfect conception of the moral character of God which is involved in the idea of His grudging His creatures the possession of knowledge, appears to any readers difficult at first sight to reconcile with belief in the authority of the Old Testament as 'written for our learning, that we through patience and comfort of the scriptures might have hope' (Rom. xv. 4), I would ask the attention of such readers to the following words, which I am permitted to quote from a sermon preached by Dr. H. L. Goudge, Regius Professor of Divinity in the University of Oxford: ' There is a distinction which we must often remember as we read the Old Testament. It is the distinction between the original meaning of the words and the meaning which they now have for us. In early days the Jews were accustomed to treat their literature very freely. They combined old materials in a new way ; they corrected and added to what they found : and, as their interest in religion deepened, they put new and higher meanings upon old and familiar words. When the Christian Church took over the Old Testament from the Jews, it used a similar freedom. It did not, indeed, further alter the words which it found ; we read them to-day much as our Lord must have read them. But the fuller knowledge which the Church possessed enabled her teachers to find in the Old Testament a deeper meaning than even the Jews had found ; and it is with this deeper meaning that we are chiefly concerned to-day. What the words *originally meant* often matters little ; what they *mean as part of the Bible* matters a great deal' (italics mine). In accordance with the method explained in Lecture I, p. 12, the present portion of our enquiry is of a purely historical and scientific, not of a dogmatic or homiletic nature ; and it is therefore concerned solely with the question what the Paradise-story *originally meant*, in the ninth century B.C., for the Yahwist writer when he selected it from a mass of Babylonian traditions for embodiment in his history of God's dealings with man ; it does not touch upon the question, what this story *means now* as part of the Christian Bible, for instructed members of the Christian Church.

the condition of Adam and Eve [1] as first created? It is
clear that the physical and mental state of the first man is
not conceived as being very far exalted above that of the
beasts, because the sole object of the creation of animals,
according to the Yahwistic narrative of c. ii. 18–25, is to
provide Adam with a suitable companion, and the various
existing species of brutes represent so many unsuccessful
experiments made to this end by the Creator [2]; who,
indeed, only hits upon the idea of building up a rib drawn

[1] 'Adam' ('ādhām, אָדָם) is not really a proper name at all; it is the
ordinary Hebrew word for 'man,' homo. 'Eve' is a proper name, but
its Hebrew form is Ḥawwāh (חַוָּה, which in the LXX becomes Eὔa and
in the Latin 'Heva' or 'Eva,' whence the English 'Eve'). The Yahwist
connects Ḥawwāh with the verb ḥāyāh (חָיָה), to 'exist' or 'live,' and
explains that this name was conferred on the first woman by her husband
'because she was the mother of all living' (iii. 20, which comes in rather
oddly after the account of the first sin, and may be misplaced); but this
etymology may well be an ex post facto invention, and it is not improbable
that Ḥawwāh may be a 'depotentiated' Phoenician goddess of the
underworld, as the name חות (ḤWT) occurs on a Punic tablet described
by Lidzbarski, Ephemeris für semit. Epigraphik, i. pp. 26 ff.; see also
G. A. Cooke, North-Sem. Inscr., p. 135. To convey the full atmosphere of
this primitive folk-tale, we should, perhaps, designate the two human
actors in it as 'Man' (with a capital M) and 'Ḥawwāh' respectively;
but, as the use of 'Adam' and 'Eve' will be inevitable in those sections
of our enquiry which are concerned with the Christian development of
the Fall-doctrine, it seems best for the sake of verbal consistency to use
them here.

[2] In v. 18 Yahweh realises that solitude will be injurious to Adam,
and resolves to make him a suitable mate. He therefore (v. 19) forms
out of the ground 'every beast of the field and every fowl of the air,' and
brings them in succession to Adam 'to see what he would call them,' i.e.
to see whether he would manifest his acceptance of any one of them as a
life-companion by addressing it with some endearing epithet. The man
apparently greets them in turn with ejaculations of a disparaging nature,
each of which adheres to the particular animal which provoked it (for the
primitive Hebrew, words are semi-material things which may become
attached to living agents—compare the story of Jacob's theft of the
blessing designed for Esau) and becomes the animal's permanent generic
name ('whatsoever the man called every living creature, that was the
name thereof'). See Skinner, Genesis, ICC., p. 67 f.; the patristic
idealisation of the passage is discussed in Lecture V, p. 361 f. It is
hardly necessary to point out that this story, according to which man was
created before the brutes, and was, in fact, for some appreciable time the
only living organism in the world, is totally irreconcilable with the later
narrative of P (i. 20–27), according to which man was only created at
the close of the sixth day, after all the lower animals.

from Adam's own body into a separate person when he finds that none of his sub-human productions prove congenial to a being endowed with reason. Man is thus a frail creature, child-like in his ignorance and simplicity, qualities which are manifested and symbolised by his nakedness. His home is Yahweh's own private pleasaunce, set in the faery realm of 'Ēdhen towards the sun-rising, shaded by the solemn loveliness of the primaeval forest, and watered by the perennial fount which feeds the four great rivers of the ancient world, Pīshōn, Gīḥōn, Ḥiddeqel, and Euphrates [1]; in its midst stand up two trees endowed with magical properties, the Tree of Life and the Tree of the Knowledge of Good and Evil. His days are spent in the light and pleasant labour of dressing and keeping [2] the Garden. Apart from this duty, one law only is imposed upon him—the prohibition against eating of the Tree of Knowledge, the taste of which, he is told, is fraught with instant death.[3]

This detail raises a question of considerable importance for the true understanding of the story—the question of the moral condition of Adam and Eve before the first transgression. It is clear that the story contains no formal doctrine of ' Original Righteousness,' such as was later imagined in order to accentuate the malevolence of the first sin. But, on the other hand, the state of our first parents cannot be said to have been one merely of non-moral innocence : for they are conscious of at least two duties, those of doing a reasonable amount of work in the garden

[1] Ḥiddeqel is undoubtedly the Tigris ; it seems most probable that Pīshōn and Gīḥōn are the Ganges and the Nile respectively (the traditional identifications ; see Skinner, *ICC.*, p. 64 ff.). A prosaic critic might find a difficulty in the fact that the Euphrates, the Tigris, the Ganges, and the Nile have not and never have had, a common source ; but the topography of Fairyland need not be taken too seriously. For an attempt to extract definite spatial determinations from these poetic fantasies, see F. Delitzsch, *Wo lag das Paradies ?* (1881).

[2] That is ' guarding ' : against what sort of dangers, in an unfallen universe, is not clear.

[3] It may be observed that the convention of describing and depicting the fatal fruit as an ' apple ' (which goes back at least as far as Venantius Fortunatus in the seventh century A.D., who speaks of the ' pomum noxiale '—*v. supra*, p. 9, n. 3) is purely arbitrary. So far as the Yahwist visualised the magic trees at all, he must have thought of them as palms (like the sacred palms which appear in conventionalised form on many Babylonian sculptures) and of their fruit as dates.

and of abstaining from the forbidden fruit. It would seem truer to say that they are conceived as being in principle moral and responsible agents, but exempted by their ignorance and by the primitive simplicity of their paradisal state from most of the painful conflicts between conscience and appetite which more complicated conditions of life necessarily involve ; they are in possession of the forms or categories of ' Right ' and ' Wrong,' but their acquaintance with the content of these conceptions is imperfect and limited.

It is natural to enquire at this point ' If Adam and Eve are conceived in the story as possessed, even before their fatal act, of the knowledge of the distinction between right and wrong, what is meant by the description of the sinister Tree as " the Tree of the *Knowledge* of Good and Evil " ? ' The answer to this question seems to lie in the fact that the Hebrew words for ' good ' and ' evil ' (*ṭōbh* and *rā'*) do not necessarily or primarily signify *moral* good and evil : their fundamental meaning is rather that of ' good ' and ' evil ' relatively to the *physical* well-being of man, the expressions being transferred to virtue and vice only in so far as the consequences of these two states are advantageous or the reverse. In this phrase, therefore, *ṭōbh* and *rā'* may well be translated ' beneficial ' or ' useful,' and ' noxious ' or ' harmful,' respectively. The knowledge, therefore, of ' good ' and ' evil,' that is of ' beneficial ' and ' noxious ' things, which Yahweh forbids his creatures to acquire, would appear to be what we should call ' scientific ' knowledge rather than moral illumination. He does not wish them to know anything of the arts of civilisation, or of the sciences which make society and culture possible : he desires to keep them in happy, child-like ignorance, infinitely inferior to himself, but safeguarded from the sorrows which the increase of knowledge brings in its train. We shall see how this conception of the effects of the ill-omened tree lights up the whole story, as it appeared to the mind of the Yahwistic writer. Once more we are brought face to face with the Prometheus-*motif*, which we have already noted as running through ' Enoch's ' decoration of the Watcher-legend—the belief, that is, in a Divine jealousy which grudges man the possession of scientific knowledge, and exacts stern punishment for its illicit acquisition.[1] The main duty, therefore, of Adam and Eve, in their primal state, is to be ignorant : ' where ignorance is bliss, 'tis folly to be wise.'

Into this paradise of nescience there enters the sinister shape of the serpent, the most subtle of all the beasts of the field which Yahweh '*elōhīm* had made, the incarnation of the irrepressible spirit of intellectual curiosity. There can be no doubt that in the mind of J it is the literal serpent that is meant (at this early date, it is to be presumed that only one [2] specimen of the serpent race was in existence, the primitive progenitor of all subsequent members of the tribe). In the text as it stands, there is no suggestion whatever that he is Satan in visible form or that he is indwelt by Satan, or that he embodies any personal principle of evil external to or other than himself. With treacherous affability, he engages our unsuspecting ancestress in conversation. By adroitly exaggerating the extent of the divine prohibition (' Hath God said, Ye shall not eat of *any* tree of the garden ? '), he lures the too communicative woman into a discussion of the forbidden fruit and its properties : and points out (apparently with perfect truth, as we gather from the sequel) that the motives which have impelled her master to enact this prohibition are of anything but a disinterested nature, and that his warning as to the mortal effects of the tree is an empty threat. Yahweh is haunted by a jealous fear lest men, through the acquisition of scientific knowledge, should attain to a position of equality with himself, and he therefore endeavours to keep them in the dark by means of baseless menaces. Eve is deeply impressed by the uncanny creature's knowledge of these high mysteries, and her longing for wisdom is reinforced by the demands of natural appetite. She tastes the seductive fruit, and induces Adam to share her transgression. The immediate effects of the magic food are of a somewhat unexpected nature ; the man and the woman become

[1] See Lecture I, pp. 25 f.

[2] Or possibly two, if the Yahwist thought that sexual distinctions existed in the brute creation at this date ; in which case it may be presumed that the male serpent is here meant. But it is extremely improbable that our author had thought the matter out with this degree of minuteness.

suddenly conscious of the facts of sex, of which, it would seem, they had hitherto been ignorant, with the concomitant sense of physical shame : which impels them to enwreath their bodies, hitherto innocently naked, with extemporised aprons of fig-leaves.[1]   Then an ominous sound falls on their ears—they hear the approaching footsteps [2] of the Creator, who, with the most naïve anthropomorphism, is represented, like an earthly nobleman, as walking in his garden ' in the cool of the day.'   Instead of running to meet him, as on the occasions of his previous visits, with the artless affection of children, the conscience-stricken pair hasten to hide themselves in the undergrowth ; but are detected and summoned forth to give an account of this undutiful conduct.   The man incautiously alleges his nudity as an excuse, thus betraying the fatal fact of his sin, with which he is immediately taxed.   He confesses it, having no other resource, but, with unchivalrous cowardice, hastens to lay the blame on his wife, who in turn accuses the serpent ; the latter, unable to transfer the responsibility to any fourth party, maintains a guilty silence.   Then the judgment is pronounced.   The light and pleasant labour of tending the fertile garden is to be exchanged by Adam for the heartbreaking task of wringing a scanty sustenance from a thorny and stubborn earth.   The woman is punished for the unlawfully acquired knowledge of sex by subjection to the pangs of childbirth, which, despite its accompanying pain, the deepest instincts of her soul will drive her to desire ; whilst the serpent is deprived of the upright posture assumed to have been enjoyed by him hitherto, and is condemned to what our author evidently regards as a painful and ignominious method of locomotion, to food of dust, and to a condition of perpetual feud with the human race.   There follows the enigmatic sentence traditionally known as the *Protevangelium*, in which it is predicted that the seed of

---

[1] It seems unnecessary to attribute (as apparently do St. Augustine, *de civ. Dei*, xiv. 17, and Milton, *Par. Lost*, ix, 1011 ff.) strictly aphrodisiac effects to the forbidden fruit.   For the sex-*motif* in Fall-stories and Fall-speculation generally, see Lecture I, p. 34 ; II, pp. 58, 66.

[2] The word קוֹל, rendered by the English versions as ' voice ' (' the voice of the Lord God walking in the garden '), should be translated 'sound,' as RV. marg. ; see Skinner *in loc.*

the woman will crush the serpent's head, whilst the serpent will crush or bruise his heel. The mystical interpretation of this saying as a foreshadowing of Redemption is well known, and, within the sphere of devotion, doubtless legitimate ; the critical student, however, cannot feel confident that the original significance of the passage is more than aetiological, designed to explain the instinctive mutual antipathy which exists between men and snakes.

The primal curse having been thus pronounced, feelings of compassion seem, for a time, to come uppermost in the mind of the offended Deity ; for he condescends to manufacture, apparently with his own hands, garments of skins [1] to replace the drapery of fig-leaves with which the guilty pair had clothed themselves. We are not told who slew the animals from which these skins were procured ; it may be surmised that a paragraph narrating the beginnings of animal sacrifice, or of hostility between the animals (other than the serpent) and man, has here dropped out of the record. Then the feeling of jealous alarm for his own position once more revives in Yahweh's breast. He suddenly thinks of the possibility that man, having acquired potentialities of scientific knowledge equal to that of his Creator, may take the further step of seizing immortality by tasting of the Tree of Life—a step which would make Adam Yahweh's equal, and practically annul the judgment just pronounced against him. [2] To ensure effectually against this undesirable contingency, he expels the man and the woman from the garden, and places at its gateway the Cherubim and the whirling sword of flame, to bar for ever man's access to the Tree of Life.

This wonderful saga, both when read in the matchless English of the Authorised Version, and still more in the Homeric simplicity and directness of the Hebrew original, is instinct with a peculiar power and impressiveness, which is felt even by those for whom the story has no theological significance. And it may truly be claimed that, by removing

[1] For the allegorisation of these ' coats of skins ' by the Greek Fathers, v. infra, Lecture IV, pp. 229, 251, 275, 285.
[2] v. 22 : ' Behold, the man is become as one of us ' (i.e. of the 'elōhīm, Yahweh and his fellow gods) ' to know good and evil.'

the baroque magnificence with which the genius of Milton
had gilded it, and bringing to light the brilliant, yet grave,
archaic colouring of the authentic story, fresh from the
Semitic world of the ninth century before Christ, modern
criticism has rather enhanced than diminished the splendour
of its literary and artistic appeal.   It fulfils in a high degree
the function assigned by one of our great teachers to the
myths of Plato, that of evoking 'Transcendental Feeling'
in a singularly pure and poignant form [1]: it speaks like
solemn organ-music to the heart, awakening blended and
formless emotions of adoration, awe, and penitence.   From
this point of view alone, it is impossible not to perceive the
enormous superiority of the Adam-story of Gen. iii. to its
earlier rival, the Watcher-story of Gen. vi., a superiority
which is reflected by the measure in which the frieze of
gorgeous pictures conjured up by Milton out of the former
surpasses the weak and bombastic drama ('Heaven and
Earth') founded by Byron upon the latter.[2]   And, on any
showing, there can be no doubt that religion was the gainer
by the victory of Gen. iii.   It is not, indeed, necessary to
discuss the question of its historicity before an audience
such as this ; it has long since been recognised by educated
Christians that the sunlight of Eden, which falls upon the
magic trees, the talking serpent, and the man-like figure of
the Creator, walking in his garden in the cool of the day, is

> The light that never was on sea or land.[3]

A few words, however, devoted to the questions of its origin
and significance will involve no waste of time, for they will
confirm the judgment provisionally formulated in Lecture I,
as well with regard to the Paradise-story as to the tale of
the fallen Watchers, that these narratives are to be viewed
as façades successively attached to, rather than foundations

[1] See J. A. Stewart, *The Myths of Plato*, Introduction, 4 (p. 39).

[2] In this connexion, it is perhaps worth noting that the Fall-story
of Gen. vi. has widely been thought to have subconsciously inspired a
line of Coleridge's dream-poem, *Kubla Khan* :

> 'A savage place ! as holy and enchanted
> As e'er beneath a waning moon was haunted
> *By woman wailing for her demon-lover.*'

[3] Wordsworth, *Stanzas on Peele Castle.*

which carry the weight of, that theory of the origin of evil which is known as the doctrine of the Fall and of Original Sin.

It may be said at once that archaeology so far has failed to discover the ultimate source from which J obtained the story, though a few uncertain parallels to one or other of its characteristic details have been discovered in Babylonian and Zoroastrian literature.[1] Nor does its internal criticism afford us much help in ascertaining the date and place of its origin. A careful examination of it raises difficulties to which no obvious answer is forthcoming. If Adam was allowed to eat of all the trees of the Garden, except only of the Tree of Knowledge, why did he not eat of the Tree of Life, and so secure immortality, before the ' Fall ' ? Why does the threat of instant death to follow upon the taste of the Tree of Knowledge fail to secure fulfilment, with the result that the serpent's disparagement of the Creator's good faith is apparently vindicated ? And, lastly, what were the motives which actuated the animal tempter in his gratuitous interference with the happy condition of Adam and Eve ? As the story stands, the serpent appears to come very badly out of the affair. He loses various gratifying privileges, and gains nothing whatever—a result which his demonic subtlety might reasonably have been expected to foresee. These inconcinnities suggest that the Paradise-story contains two narratives imperfectly fused—whether by J himself, or by an earlier writer, cannot now be determined. Sir James Frazer has suggested [2] that one story may have embodied a theme widely disseminated in the folk-lore of the African peoples, the idea that God sends a message to man informing him how to attain immortality, and employing some animal as his messenger—and that man's present condition of mortality is due to the fact that the messenger spitefully falsified or suppressed the message.

---

[1] See Skinner, *ICC.*, pp. 90–93 ; and W. L. Wardle, *Israel and Babylon* (1925), c. vii., ' Paradise and the Fall,' which contains a criticism of the attempt made by S. Langdon to find a Babylonian version of the Fall-story in his *Sumerian Epic of Paradise, the Flood, and the Fall of Man* (1915). For a defence of Langdon's theories, Wardle refers to an article by Mercer, in the *Journal of the Society of Oriental Research*, iii. 86–88—a reference which I have not been able to verify.

[2] *Folk-lore in the Old Testament* (1919), i. 2 (pp. 45–77).

The other may have been based on another well-known legend, which accounts for the supposed immortality of the serpent by the fact that it periodically sheds its skin. It is conceivable that the original story may have combined these two ideas by telling how the serpent was commissioned by God to advise Adam to eat of the Tree of Life and so acquire immortality, and how through envy he perverted the divine message by persuading Adam to eat of the Tree of Death, and appropriated the gift of immortality by eating of the Tree of Life himself. This, however, remains no more than a brilliant conjecture.

The origin of the story is thus obscure : but the significance which it bore for the minds of those who embodied it in the great Prophetic history of God's dealings with man can be determined with much greater certainty. It has been already pointed out that the most important *prima facie* difficulties inhering in the story are cleared up if we assume that ' good ' and ' evil ' in the name of the fatal Tree mean physical, not moral, good and evil respectively, and that the sin of the first men consisted in snatching the treasure of scientific and cultural knowledge which the Creator had not destined for them. This conclusion is strikingly confirmed by the tenor of chapter iv., which narrates the first rude beginnings of culture, following immediately upon the expulsion from Paradise of the ancestors of the human race ; for it is precisely with this growth of civilisation that the two first instances of human cruelty and ferocity are connected. The development of agriculture and of cattle-keeping, with its corollary, the discovery [1] of the only kind of sacrifice acceptable to Yahweh, brings in its train the first murder, that of Abel.[2] The discovery of the art of working in metals by Tubal-Cain [3] leads to the fatal invention of the sword, and there follows the repulsive scene in which Lamech is apparently represented as brandishing the newly forged weapon, which he owes to the ingenuity of his son, before his wives Adah

---

[1] If it be thought probable, as suggested above, that a paragraph narrating the beginnings of animal sacrifice has dropped out between iii. 20 and 21, for the words ' discovery of ' should be substituted ' acquisition of the means of offering.'

[2] Gen. iv. 2–8.   [3] Gen. iv. 22.

E

and Zillah, and exulting in the bloody vengeance which he has taken for some trifling slight.[1] It would seem that, for J's sombre philosophy of history, civilisation and culture are, on the whole, a disastrous mistake. The undertones of pessimism and world-weariness which pervade the early sections of his narrative are easily discernible by an ear attuned to the finer vibrations of an unstudied literary style, and it can hardly be doubted that he would have given a whole-hearted assent to the Preacher's melancholy aphorism ' He that increaseth knowledge increaseth sorrow.' [2]

It will be seen that for this writer the first sin was indeed a ' Fall,' in virtue of its consequences, namely, the forfeiture of Paradise, the loss of the opportunity of obtaining immortality, and man's resulting servitude to hard work and death. But the causal link between the primal transgression and man's subsequent misfortunes is clearly of an *external* and, so to speak, mechanical nature : these misfortunes are represented as due, partly to the arbitrary decree of a jealous Creator, concerned to safeguard his unique prerogatives against a possible rival, and partly to the complicated conditions of social life inevitably engendered by the growth of ' scientific knowledge.' There is not a word in the narrative to suggest that the first sin produced a reflex psychological effect upon Adam and Eve, or infected them with an *interior* corruption or infirmity capable of being transmitted by physiological heredity to their descendants : that is to say, there is not a word which implies the theological doctrine of ' Original Sin ' in any of its historic forms. The mysterious phrase which has been sometimes interpreted as imputing to Cain an innate bias towards evil (' if thou doest not well, sin coucheth at the door '—at the door of what, is not explained) is textually so corrupt that its original meaning is irrecoverable, and nothing can legitimately be built upon it [3] ; even if it be

---

[1] Gen. iv. 23.
[2] Eccles. i. 18.
[3] Gen. iv. 7. It should, perhaps, be added that the reading of LXX (οὐκ ἐὰν ὀρθῶς προσενέγκῃς, ὀρθῶς δὲ μὴ διέλῃς, ἥμαρτες ; ἡσύχασον—' If thou didst offer rightly, but didst not rightly divide [the oblation], hast not sinned ? be silent ') gives a sense which is perfectly intelligible, and may well be original ; it represents Yahweh as insisting upon ceremonial

insisted that these words must at least be understood as attributing an evil nature to Cain, the verse is entirely silent as to any inheritance of this by Cain from his parents, and in no way excludes the supposition that it may have been formed by unrecorded acts of free, but wrongful, self-determination committed prior to the murder of Abel. We can, indeed, read the story in the light of ' Original Sin,' or read back the idea of ' Original Sin ' into the story—if we choose ; but we must recognise that this can only be done by the employment of a mystical or allegorical, not a scientific, method of interpretation. In the narrative of Gen. iii. and iv. as it stands, the only 'hereditary' influences which play any part are such as fall under the general description of ' social heredity,' which affects the individual from without, through the medium of laws, customs, institutions, traditions, conventions, and fashions, and which is to be sharply distinguished from ' biological heredity,' which determines the individual from within, through the invisible psychic characters borne by the fundamental germ-plasm from which he springs.

The Development of the Fall-theory in Connexion with the Paradise-story

We conclude, then, that in the intention of J, the writer to whom we owe its embodiment in our Scriptures, the Paradise-story was meant to narrate what may be called a ' Fall,' in an external or dramatic sense—that is, an act of ὕβρις or presumption which brought the Golden Age to an end : but that it does not contain the idea of a moral infirmity or corruption transmitted by biological heredity, an idea which is the necessary basis of the doctrine of ' Original Sin ' in all its forms. It must be remembered, however, that simple minds would find it difficult to distinguish clearly between ' social ' and ' biological ' heredity, in the sense defined above, and that the former conception

---

correctness in every stage of the sacrificial action, not merely in the first. But, so understood, the verse clearly contains even less suggestion of ' hereditary sinfulness ' than it does in the Hebrew version.

might well be expected to melt insensibly into the latter, a transformation which would accomplish itself with especial facility in an intellectual world still subconsciously saturated, despite the work of the prophets, by the old conception of evil as a quasi-material contagion. It will be appropriate to subjoin a few words with regard to the steps by which this metamorphosis was actually effected.

It was pointed out in Lecture I that the Fall-theory, in its earliest and vaguest form as a belief in a ' first sin ' of some kind which introduced an undefined poison into the stock of humanity, would seem to have been first connected with the Angel-story of Gen. vi., and that its attachment to the Adam-story was in the nature of an afterthought. It must be frankly admitted that any attempt to reconstruct the process whereby the Fall-theory became firmly anchored to the Adam-story must necessarily be conjectural as regards its earlier stages, owing to the paucity of literary data for the period between Nehemiah and the Maccabees. We can affirm with certainty that the process did in fact take place, and that the Adam-story did, almost though not quite completely,[1] extrude the Angel-story from its position as the popularly accepted Fall-narrative, during the last two centuries before Christ : references to the pseudepigraphic passages which mark the stages of this silent revolution were given in our last lecture,[2] and need not be repeated here. But it must be confessed that the pre-Maccabean beginnings of this process are at present veiled in obscurity. If, however, the provisional nature of all speculations as to the course taken by this development before the epoch at which it can be controlled through written evidence be borne in mind, it will be permissible to claim as much certainty as is possible under the circumstances for the following propositions :

(1) The ruling idea of the original narrative, that knowledge is intrinsically disastrous, presupposes a very primitive and naïve philosophy of life, and must have been obscured and forgotten by the time that speculation on the origin of evil began in earnest, after the Exile. It can hardly have survived the rise to power and influence of the

---

[1] See Lecture III, p. 113 f.   [2] Lecture I, pp. 28–30.

'wise men' (hakhāmīm) and the tendency to hypostatise and almost to deify Wisdom (ḥokhmāh). This idea once out of the way, the command to abstain from the fruit of a particular tree could be re-interpreted as a simple test of man's obedience to his Creator, and the first sin could be viewed as deriving its significance and guilt merely from the fact that it was a deliberate transgression of a known law. In this way, we may suppose, the story was brought into harmony with strictly ethical ideas of God and goodness, and fitted to become the basis of a reasoned and logical Fall-theory.

(2) It would seem that the first step in the construction of such a reasoned Fall-theory on the basis of the Paradise-narrative consisted in the affirmation of a causal connexion between Adam's sin and the fact of human liability to death, that is, in the reading into the story of the hypothesis that man at his creation was endowed with the gift of immortality, but that this was withdrawn from him as part of the punishment for his transgression.[1] In fact, the Scriptural text says nothing of the kind : it implies, on the contrary, that man was created mortal, formed of the dust and destined to return to it, though he might have made himself immortal by eating of the Tree of Life, even after his sin ; and that it was precisely in order to keep him mortal that Yahweh expelled him from the Garden and posted a cherubic guard to prevent his return. The point of Yahweh's warning in ii. 17 as to the fatal consequences which would follow a breach of his command is, not that man would become mortal after being immortal, but that man, mortal by nature and fated sooner or later to return to dust, would suffer death *forthwith* as a punishment for his sin ('*in the day* that thou eatest thereof thou shalt surely die') instead of living out his life to a ripe old age and being re-absorbed into his parent earth through a painless dissolution. It is the ruthless immediacy of the threatened death, not the mere fact of mortality (to which Adam was in any case subject by virtue of his creaturely nature), which constitutes the spear-head of the menace. It may be thought that the literal non-fulfilment

---

[1] This theory seems to underlie the words of our first text, Rom. v. 12 ; *v. infra*, Lecture III, p. 126 f.

of this warning, on which we have already commented, ought to have presented as patent a difficulty to the Jews of the post-exilic age as it does to us. But it must be remembered that thinkers who approached the story of Gen. ii. and iii. in a spirit of uncritical devotion would find it easy to surmount this difficulty by supposing that, whilst the taste of the Tree of Knowledge was intrinsically fraught with death, its fatal operation was suspended for some nine centuries by a special exercise of Divine mercy, and only allowed to take effect after Adam had lived for the best part of a millennium. Hence the son of Sirach, writing in the first quarter of the second century before Christ, is already able to affirm a direct causal relation between the first sin and the fact of human death, though his misogynist tendency leads him to saddle Eve with the sole responsibility for our woes :

From a woman was the beginning of sin, and because of her we all die.[1]

This aphorism cannot, indeed, be quoted as evidence for the existence in 180 B.C. of a doctrine of hereditary *sinfulness*, as distinct from hereditary mortality ; for the recovery of the Hebrew original of this part of Ecclesiasticus has shown that the phrase ' From a woman was the beginning of sin ' only means that Eve's sin was chronologically the first to be committed in human history, and does not imply that it was the cause of all subsequent sin.[2] It is probable, however, that the distinction between merely chronological and directly causal antecedence, even if consciously realised, would soon tend to become blurred in the non-speculative Jewish mind ; and the idea of inherited mortality would draw to itself, by a kind of capillary attraction, the floating idea of inherited sinfulness, so that both alike would come

---

[1] Ecclus. xxv. 24 :

ἀπὸ γυναικὸς ἀρχὴ ἁμαρτίας,
καὶ δι' αὐτὴν ἀποθνήσκομεν πάντες.

[2] The word ἀρχή stands for an original תְּחִלָּה, which means ' temporal beginning ' rather than ' efficient cause ' ; see Brown, Driver and Briggs, *Hebrew and English Lexicon of the O.T.*, s.v., p. 321. For the Hebrew text of Ecclus. xxv. 24, see *JQR*, xii. pp. 456 ff. (Schechter) ; *Facsimiles of the Fragments of the Book of Ecclesiasticus in Hebrew* (Oxford and Cambridge University Presses, 1901).

to be regarded as direct consequences of the primordial sin of the first man. It can safely be affirmed that this process had been consummated, at least in some Jewish circles, by the beginning of the Christian era. Even if the famous saying of the Wisdom of Solomon :

> God created man for incorruption
> And made him an image of his own proper being ;
> But by the envy of the devil death entered into the world,
> And they that are of his portion make trial thereof [1]

be interpreted as referring solely to physical death, the existence, at an epoch roughly coinciding with the life of Christ, of a fairly well-defined doctrine affirming that Adam's sin was the cause of spiritual death in his descendants— that is, of an embryonic doctrine of Original Sin—is proved by its explicit assertion in the Book of the Secrets of Enoch, in a passage describing a vision of the lowest hell which unrolled itself before the eyes of the terrified patriarch. In this abyss, he says, ' I saw all our forefathers from the beginning with Adam and Eve, and I sighed, and wept, and spake of the ruin *caused by* their wickedness ; Woe is me *for my infirmity and that of my forefathers.* And I meditated in my heart, and said : Blessed is the man who was not born, or having been born has never sinned before the face of the Lord, so that he should not come into this place, and bear the yoke of this place ! ' [2]

Before we leave the consideration of the Adamic Fall-doctrine as it appears in the Jewish Apocalypses—if ideas so hazy and fluctuating as were those of Adam's guilt and its melancholy inherited consequences in pre-Christian Judaism may legitimately be described as a ' doctrine '— certain developments and variations of it, which were not without influence in the formation of Christian thought on

---

[1] Wisdom ii. 23, 24 :
> ὅτι ὁ θεὸς ἔκτισεν τὸν ἄνθρωπον ἐπ᾽ ἀφθαρσίᾳ,
> καὶ εἰκόνα τῆς ἰδίας ἰδιότητος ἐποίησεν αὐτόν·
> φθόνῳ δὲ διαβόλου θάνατος εἰσῆλθεν εἰς τὸν κόσμον,
> πειράζουσι δὲ αὐτὸν οἱ τῆς ἐκείνου μερίδος ὄντες.

[2] 2 Enoch c. 40. It will be noticed that these words leave a loophole for the idea of human free-will. Like the Christian second Council of Orange and the Council of Trent, the Slavonic Enoch holds strongly that the taint inherited from Adam and Eve is not so powerful as to destroy the individual's responsibility for his own fate.

this subject, deserve to be briefly mentioned. The first and most important of these consists in the growth of an exalted theory of the state of unfallen man, which represents a striking departure from the picture of a frail and ignorant creature, not so very much higher than the beasts, contained in the text of Gen. ii. and iii. The belief that Adam before the ' Fall ' was, not merely in a position to acquire immortality, but actually immortal, naturally suggested the ascription to him of other physical, mental, and moral endowments of a supernatural kind, thus eventually giving rise to the idea of the original perfection of man, an idea known in its moral aspect to later Christian theology as that of ' Original Justice ' or ' Righteousness.' The growth of this conception was assisted by two factors : firstly, the tendency already mentioned, to heighten the bliss of Paradise and the supposed virtues of its inhabitants in order to bring into stronger relief the wilful malice of the first sin and the disastrous nature of its consequences ; secondly, the popular diffusion of versions of the Paradise-story, parallel to but more riotously imaginative and fantastic than the comparatively restrained presentation of it which secured admission to the Yahwistic document, and through this document to the text of canonical Scripture. It would seem that extra-Biblical traditions of this kind underlie the remarkable passage, Ezekiel xxviii. 11–19, in which the prophet compares the future fall of the king of Tyre to an expulsion (presumably the expulsion of Adam) from the Garden of Eden ; and (if it be admitted that a direct comparison of the Tyrian prince with Adam is here intended) by implication describes the first man unfallen, as an ' anointed cherub,' ' full of wisdom, and perfect in beauty,' perfect in his ways from the day he was created until unrighteousness was found in him, dwelling in Eden the garden of God and on the holy mountain of God, clothed in garments sewn thick with jewels, and so completely exempt from physical pain that he could walk up and down ' in the midst of the stones of fire.' [1] The doctrine of the

---

[1] On the ' fire-walk,' a religious practice, common to many nations, in which Adam is here said (by implication) to have been an expert, see J. G. Frazer, *Adonis, Attis, Osiris*, i. p. 114 f.

'original perfection' of man appears explicitly in the Book of the Secrets of Enoch, which describes the first man as 'a second angel, honourable, great, and glorious,' 'appointed as ruler to rule the earth, and to have God's wisdom,' and endowed with the beatific vision so that he could see 'the angels in heaven singing the song of victory and the gloomless light'[1]; for some reason, however, it is asserted that this condition of beatitude only lasted for five and a half hours.[2] It is a reasonable conclusion that by the time Christianity came into the world the idea of man's 'original perfection' had become more or less stereotyped as the logical *prius* or presupposition of the Adamic version of the Fall-theory, in those areas of the Jewish Church where this theory prevailed.[3]

From the extra-Biblical versions of the Paradise-story, which it thus appears necessary to postulate, would seem to be derived a repulsive variant of the Adamic doctrine of the origin of sin, which regards the 'Fall' as consisting in the seduction, in the restricted sense of that term, of Eve by the serpent, or by Satan appearing as the serpent; from which was later deduced a theory of the inherited taint as an *inquinamentum*, a gross physical pollution so communicated to her and through her to her posterity.[4] The Slavonic Enoch expresses this view of the Fall quite frankly:

On account of this (his expulsion from heaven) he (Satan) conceived designs against Adam; in such a manner he entered and deceived Eve. But he did not touch Adam.[5]

---

[1] 2 Enoch xxxi. (A text): *cf.* also the Book of Adam and Eve, i. 8.

[2] 2 Enoch, xxxii. (A text).

[3] It should be added that a fragment of the Book of Noah (1 Enoch lxix. 11) affirms the 'original perfection' of man, so far as righteousness and physical immortality were concerned, but attributes its loss to his intellectual development, stimulated by the instruction imparted by the fallen angels: 'For men were created exactly like the angels, to the intent that they should continue pure and righteous, and death which destroys everything could not have taken hold of them; but through this their knowledge they are perishing.'

[4] *v. infra*, Lecture III, p. 122; Lecture IV, p. 227.

[5] xxxi. 6. The words 'into Paradise' which Professor Sokolov's text adds after 'entered,' are a patent gloss, designed to remove the obvious (and to later minds unedifying) significance of the passage: Morfill and Charles, *The Book of the Secrets of Enoch* (1896), p. 45. See Tennant's full discussion, *Fall and Original Sin*, pp. 208, 209.

We observe once more the emergence of a *motif*, destined to exercise a powerful though largely hidden influence on the course of Jewish and Christian Fall-speculation, which we have already found strongly expressed in the Watcher-story, and less prominently in the Paradise-story (in connection with man's realisation of his nakedness)—namely, the idea that the first sin was a sexual one or in some way had reference to the instinct of sex.[1]   It is noteworthy that the theory of the Fall here expressed exempts Adam from all responsibility for it ; and it is impossible not to suspect that it may lie behind the cynical dictum of Ben Sirach, quoted above—' From a *woman* was the beginning of sin.' Strange though it may seem, we shall see in our next lecture that this hideous legend has shaped the form of two passages in the New Testament which allude to the first transgression.[2]   A less revolting, though hardly more reasonable, embodiment of the sexual interpretation of the Fall is contained in the Apocalypse of Abraham,[3] a pseudepigraph of uncertain date, in which it seems to be implied that the first sin consisted in the physical union of Adam and Eve, who had apparently been meant by the Creator to live in perpetual continence.   We may for the sake of completeness conclude this catalogue of apocalyptic variations upon and decorations of the Adamic Fall-theory by mentioning the idea, based upon the curse of Gen. iii. 17, 18, which doomed the earth to lose its primitive fertility and to bring forth thorns and thistles, that Adam's transgression had cosmic consequences of a far-reaching nature : the Book of Jubilees asserts that in consequence of this event the animals lost the power of speech which they had previously possessed, and the Syriac Apocalypse of Baruch attributes to it the beginnings of pain of every kind.

We have now briefly sketched the origins, and traced the pre-Christian development, of the Fall-doctrine proper —that is, of the theory (if the cloudy and confused trains of ideas running through the documents so far reviewed may

---

[1] See Lecture I, p. 34 ; II, p. 45.

[2] 2 Cor. xi. 2, 3 ; 1 Tim. ii. 14.   See Lecture III, p. 122.

[3] cc. xxiii, xxiv. (E. tr., G. H. Box, 1918, p. 69 ff. ; G. N. Bonwetsch, *Die Apok. Abrahams*, p. 33 f.).

be deemed to constitute a theory) which finds the origin of
evil in a first transgression, producing in its perpetrators
and their offspring a moral taint or infirmity which is conceived as transmissible by strictly physiological heredity.
The Fall-doctrine however (understood in this precise sense)
was by no means the only explanation of the origin of sin
which was held within the Jewish Church at the time of the
birth of Christ.   It will have been observed that nearly all
the evidence which we have adduced so far, of a date subsequent to the close of the canon of the Old Testament,
has been drawn from the Apocalypses ; and these books,
broadly speaking, represent the popular religious literature
of Hasmonaean Judaism, unofficial tracts and flysheets
designed to inflame patriotism, purify piety, and foster the
hope of the Messianic deliverance from Gentile tyrants,
which circulated amongst the unlearned masses of the people,
and especially, it would seem, amongst the semi-outcaste
population debarred by the necessities of its manual avocations from the full observance of the Law, and known by
the contemptuous name of the ʿam ha-ʾāreç, the ʿ people of
the earth.'   But, to obtain a complete picture of the intellectual influences which surrounded the cradle of Christian
doctrine, and, as we shall see, had no small share in determining the lines on which the Christian Fall-theory was destined
to develop, we must consider the characteristic ideas, not
merely of popular, unofficial, and unscientific pietism as
represented by the Apocalypses, but of the official and
technical theology as taught by the Rabbis.   The conception
of the psychological ground of sin which permeates this
latter stream of Jewish teaching is that of the yēçer ha-raʿ,
or ʿ evil imagination,' a phrase drawn from the Scriptural
passage (Gen. vi. 5) which I have used as the second of my
two texts.   This doctrine, whilst bearing some resemblance
to that of ʿ Original Sin,' has no place for the idea of a ʿ Fall,'
in the strict sense of the term, an idea which may consequently be said to be peculiar to the apocalyptic or popular
theology of sin.   The all but complete disappearance of the
apocalyptic scheme of ideas from the mind of Israel, due,
partly to the conversion to Christianity of those Jews who
held it, and partly to the apparent refutation of the glowing

millennial hopes which it embodied by the catastrophes of A.D. 70 (the destruction of Jerusalem by Titus) and of A.D. 135 (the overthrow of Bar Kokhba by Hadrian), has brought it about that the Fall-doctrine is now exclusively characteristic of the Christian, and the doctrine of the *yēçer ha-ra'* of the Jewish Church : and the theology of present-day Judaism is as devoid of any idea of a ' Fall ' as it is of the belief in personal angels and devils. To the consideration of this Rabbinical idea of the ' evil imagination,' and of the various attempts which were made, previously to and contemporaneously with the rise of Christianity, to blend it with the Fall-doctrine proper the remaining part of this lecture must be devoted.

THE DOCTRINE OF THE ' EVIL IMAGINATION '

Unlike the doctrine of the Fall, which, as we have seen, would appear to have been first constructed from data given by spiritual experience, and then successively read into two of the primitive stories embodied in Genesis, the doctrine of the *yēçer ha-ra'* arose directly from the exegesis of a Scriptural passage. ' God saw that the wickedness of man was great in the earth, and that every imagination (*yēçer*) of the thoughts of his heart was only evil continually ' (Gen. vi. 5). Here the evil ' form,' or ' fashion,' or ' imagination ' of man's thoughts is regarded as a factor which provokes the Almighty to wrath ; it is to be presumed, therefore, that man himself is responsible for its existence. A little later, however, in the same narrative we read (viii. 21) that, after the subsidence of the waters of the Flood, ' Yahweh smelled a sweet savour ' arising from Noah's sacrifice, and said in his heart ' I will not again curse the ground any more for man's sake, for that the *imagination* (*yēçer*) of man's heart is *evil* (*ra'*) from his youth.' Here the ' evil imagination ' is clearly regarded by Yahweh as constituting an *excuse* for human depravity, from which it would seem to follow that it is something which is given in the essential constitution of man's nature, an inherited infirmity of some kind which the individual cannot help possessing. It was inevitable that an idea based equally upon both of these texts should be somewhat ambiguous. In the light of the first, the *yēçer ha-raʿ* might be regarded as the sinful habit which man, by the repetition of wrongful acts, impresses upon his own soul ; in the light of the second as a ' form ' already imprinted upon him by the Creator.[1] But this very ambiguity may be said to have exercised a beneficent influence on the development of Jewish, and, later, of Christian dogma, inasmuch as it contained the potentiality of a doctrine of sin which would do equal justice to those elements of religious experience which assure man of the reality of his own free-will and to those which testify to the limitation of free-will by the sinister handicap of an innate moral weakness.

Owing to the vast extent of the documentary evidence contained in the Rabbinical literature, it is impossible to do more than indicate, in the briefest manner possible, the main outlines of this important and interesting conception. The recent discoveries of parts of the original Hebrew text of Ecclesiasticus have revealed these outlines as already existing, with tolerable clearness of definition, in the thought of Ben Sirach.   The most important passage is xv. 11–17,

---

[1] 'It is never doubted that God made the evil *yēçer*, yet man is responsible for controlling and subduing it.   The word itself suggested these two apparently contrary conceptions.   The verb יצר means to form, or fashion, and also, to form inwardly, to plan.   It was used as the technical word for the potter's work.   It was frequently used of God's forming of nature and of man, and also of his planning or purposing.   The יצר of man could therefore suggest either his form, as God made him, his nature (so Ps. ciii. 14) or his own formation of thought and purpose, " imagination " as the word is rendered in several Old Testament passages (Gen. vi. 5 ; viii. 21 ; Deut. xxxi. 21 ; Isaiah xxvi. 3 ; 1 Chron. xxviii. 9 ; xxix. 18).   In Deut. xxxi. 21, and probably Isaiah xxvi. 3, the word is used without the further definition "of the thoughts," "of the heart," which 1 Chron. retains.   The word had gained, therefore, in the Old Testament, a certain independence as meaning the nature or disposition of man, and this could be regarded as something which God made (Ps. ciii. 14) or as something which man works (Deut. xxxi. 21).   It is evident that the word was fitted by Old Testament usage for further development in discussions of the origin of sin and the responsibility of man ' (F. C. Porter, *The Yeçer Hara*, in the Yale Bicentenary Volume of *Biblical and Semitic Studies*, 1901, pp. 108, 109).   See also C. Taylor's note on יצר (*Sayings of the Jewish Fathers*, 1897 edn., p. 37, n. 36).

which, as literally translated from the Hebrew, runs as
follows :

11. Say not, My transgression was of God ;
    For that which he hateth he made not.
12. Lest thou say, He it was that made me stumble ;
    For there is no need of men of violence.
13. Wickedness and an abomination the Lord hateth ;
    And will not let it befal them that fear him.
14. For (?) God created man from the beginning,
    And put him into the hand of him that would spoil him,
    And gave him into the hand of his inclination (*yēçer*).
15. If thou choose, thou mayest keep the commandment ;
    And it is understanding to do his will.
    If thou trust in him, thou shalt even live.
16. Fire and water are poured out before thee :
    Upon whichsoever thou choosest stretch forth thy hands.
17. Death and life are before a man :
    That which he shall choose shall be given him.[1]

In this the author directly raises the eternal problem of
human wickedness in its relation to God's all-disposing
providence. He cannot allow man unlimited free-will, nor
can he admit that God directly moves the human soul
towards sin. His solution is to suppose that God has
created two mutually antagonistic powers, the evil *yēçer*
within the soul and the (Mosaic) Law without it, and that
man possesses just enough freedom of choice to be able to
surrender himself either to one or to the other. These alternative and mutually exclusive guides of life are symbolised
in *vv* 16, 17 as the fire and water, the death and life between
which the Israelite has to choose. This thought can be
paralleled exactly by one of the most important Rabbinical
sayings with regard to the *yēçer*, the latter part of which
seems to be a verbal quotation of 14*c* ; ' I created the evil
yēçer ; I created for it the Law as a remedy. If ye are
occupied with the Law, ye shall not be delivered into its
hand.' [2]

The second passage, in the Hebrew original of which the
word *yēçer* has been discovered to exist, is xxvii. 5, 6. The

---

[1] Schechter and Taylor, *The Wisdom of Ben-Sira* (1899), pp. xxxi, xxxii.
[2] *Qiddushin* 30[b].

verbal form of these verses is in one or two details not
absolutely certain ; but the following is, according to a high
authority, textually most probable, and gives an intelligible
and instructive sense :

5. A potter's vessel is for the furnace to bake ;
   And, like unto it, a man is according to his thought.
6. According to the husbandry of the tree will be its fruit ;
   So the thought is according to the *yēçer* of man.

If this text be accepted as authentic, it throws a considerable
light upon the providential function attributed by Sirach
to the *yēçer ha-ra*ᶜ. The paraphrase of its meaning given by
the same authority can hardly be bettered : ' A potter's
vessel is both tested and made by the fire ; so a man is
tested by his inner thought, it is this that both tries and
makes him (*cf.* Prov. xxiii. 7). . . . The husbandry of a
tree, *i.e.* the digging and pruning, both tests the life of the
tree and is the condition of its fruitfulness. So the thought-
life of man is tested and developed by the *yēçer*, which, like
the fire of the potter's furnace and like the labour of the
husbandman, is severe and may prove destructive, but is
essential to the making of a vessel and the growing of fruit.
A man is tested and made, not by appearances or deeds but
by his thought or reasoning, and his thought is tested and
made to be of worth by the evil inclinations within him,
that is, by moral struggle.' [1]

The third passage which may be quoted in this connexion
is one which has not yet been recovered in the Hebrew, but
in which the occurrence of the word *yēçer* is established by
the Syriac version. This is xxi. 11*a*, which is given in the
English Revised Version as :

He that keepeth the law becometh master of the intent thereof

—an apothegm of doubtful meaning—but in the Syriac
appears in a far more intelligible and significant form as :

He that keepeth the law getteth the mastery over his *yēçer*.

It can hardly be doubted that this is the original sense : and,
like the first of our quotations, it testifies to the existence,

---

[1] F. C. Porter, *op. cit.*, p. 142.

towards the beginning of the second century before Christ, of the belief, characteristic of later Rabbinical orthodoxy, in the ' evil impulse ' or ' imagination ' as a power rooted in the soul, prior to and independent of conscious choice, exerting from time to time an almost intolerable pressure in the direction of sin, yet capable of being tamed and subdued by the wholesome discipline of a rigorous observance of the Law.[1]

It is true that after its first occurrence in the Book of Ecclesiasticus the term *yēçer* disappears until the beginning of the Talmudic epoch. This, however, is due to the fact that most of the Jewish literature of the last two centuries before and the first century after the birth of Christ is only preserved in Latin, Greek, Ethiopic, or other non-Semitic languages ; and as, at the moment that Hebrew texts become available once more, the idea of the *yēçer* is found existing in full force, it is safe to assume that it existed during the period for which direct Hebrew or Aramaic evidence is lacking. And it is well known that the Mishnah and the Midrashim contain much material dating from times long anterior to those of their actual codification or composition in their present form. It will, therefore, be permissible to make a cautious use of Rabbinical and Talmudic data for the purpose of articulating and enriching the general picture of the doctrine of the *yēçer ha-ra‘* which we have constructed on the basis of the Sirach-passages, so as to be in possession of a roughly accurate idea of the degree of development which it had attained in Jewish thought at the beginning of the Christian era.

It will be convenient to summarise the additional information which may be obtained from these later sources under the three heads of the Seat, the Nature, and the ultimate Origin of the ' evil imagination.' (*a*) The Rabbis

---

[1] *Cf.* also xxxvii. 3, ' O evil imagination ' (ὦ πονηρὸν ἐνθύμημα, presumably = יֵצֶר רַע) ' whence camest thou rolling in To cover the dry land with deceitfulness ? ' : and xvii. 31, which W. Bousset (*Religion des Judentums im NTl. Zeitalter*, 1903, p. 384) restores as follows, after the Syriac version : ' What shines brighter than the sun ? yet it becometh darkened. So also is it with the man who subdueth not his *yēçer* ' (' seeing that he is flesh and blood ' Bousset thinks may be a gloss). On this latter verse, see also R. H. Charles, *Apocr. and Pseud.* i. p. 312.

are unanimous in placing the *seat* of the evil *yēçer* in the
'heart' (*lēbh*), that is, the inner self, the basal personality
of man.[1]   So intimately is the evil *yēçer* connected with the
'heart' that the latter term can be treated as almost
synonymous with the former : as when Ps. cix. 22, 'My
heart is wounded within me,' is interpreted to mean that
the Psalmist's 'evil impulse' has been wounded or slain,
from which the Rabbinical exegete deduces the consequence
that David is to be reckoned with Abraham, Isaac, and
Jacob, over whom the *yēçer ha-ra'* had no power.[2]   It has
recently been suggested that the 'heart,' in Hebrew psychology, denotes precisely that obscure and profound region of
the Self which underlies, yet continually influences, the surface play of thought and volition, and which modern writers
have named the 'Unconscious'—the dark and unexplored
home of instinct, emotion, and impulse, which, using an
inevitable spatial metaphor, we are accustomed to describe
as situated below the brilliantly lit area of the conscious
mind.[3]   Whether a simple equation of the 'heart' and the
'Unconscious' can be sustained—in view of the accepted
opinion, voiced by Driver and other critics, that the processes believed by the Old Testament writers to reside in the
heart were strictly *intellectual*, and that the emotions were
associated by the Hebrews with the 'reins,' or kidneys—
is a question which must be left to the decision of experts.
But the 'Unconscious' of modern psychology includes
thought as well as emotion, so that its connotation at least
overlaps to a large extent, even if it does not exactly coincide
with, that of *lēbh*.   We shall therefore not be far wrong if we
assume that in using the term 'heart' to describe the seat
of the evil impulse, the Jewish writers meant at least to
orientate their readers' attention in the direction of what
we now know as the 'Unconscious': and we shall see in a
moment that such an assumption has the effect of illumina-

[1] The question was raised, whether the 'evil imagination' resides in
beasts.   Rabbi Nachman ben Isaac is of opinion that it does, because they
bite and kick (*Berakhoth* 61ᵃ).   Angels, however, are exempt from it
(*Lev. rab.* 26 ; Bacher, *Amor.* ii. p. 419).
[2] *Baba bathra* 17ᵃ.   It would seem that the doctrine of the Immaculate
Conception is here anticipated, in reference to these four patriarchs.
[3] K. E. Kirk, *Some Principles of Moral Theology* (1920), p. 145.

F

ting and clearing up the second of our three questions, namely, that of the *nature* of the ' evil imagination.'

(*b*) This question naturally subdivides itself into two further problems, namely, (1) What is the predominant meaning of the substantive *yēçer*? and (2) What is meant by the adjective ' evil ' ?   The first of these has already been dealt with up to a point, in the comments on Gen. vi. 5 and viii. 21, prefixed by way of introduction to this section of our enquiry.   Etymologically, as we have seen, *yēçer* should mean a fixed habit or disposition, and it is sometimes used in this sense.   But, in by far the greater number of Rabbinical passages, it is clearly conceived, not so much as a static character but rather as a dynamic force, a strong current of emotional and conative energy which (if the use of a miscellany of metaphors may be allowed) can be resisted, fought, bridled, tamed, subdued, diverted into fresh channels, or harnessed to new purposes.   The ambiguity is, however, perfectly natural and intelligible.   When we think of a river, we may think either of its moving volume of waters, which, as instinct with dynamic energy, may operate turbines or demolish bridges : or else of the (relatively) fixed and permanent channel in which it flows, which may form the frontier separating parishes, counties, or empires. So what appears to be the element of innate sinfulness in human personality, which manifests itself with sudden and terrifying vividness in moments of temptation, may be viewed either as a dynamic uprush of psychic energy from the depths of the soul, or as the static channel, consisting of inherited psycho-physical dispositions, which directs this energy, harmless in itself, towards morally reprehensible ends.

This ambiguity in the use of the substantive, which the official Jewish theology never succeeded in resolving, explains an even more remarkable ambiguity in the use of the adjective.   The *yēçer* is evil, because it is perpetually pricking and prompting men to sin, and especially to sins against purity.   (We note once more the appearance of the King Charles' head which has obsessed so many speculators on the problem of evil in man.)   Anger and idolatry are also conspicuous manifestations of the *yēçer* ; and the pious Jew still entreats, in his morning prayers, to be guarded

from sin and temptation, and from the evil *yēçer*.[1] God
Himself, according to some authorities, repents of having
made the ' evil imagination ' ; ' It stands ill with the evil
yēçer, since even its creator calls it evil ' [2] ; ' Woe to the
dough, of which the baker himself testifies that it is bad ! ' [3]
Eventually the evil *yēçer* was, in some quarters at least,
identified with Satan ; ' Satan, the evil *yēçer*, and the angel
of death are one.' [4] Yet, paradoxically enough, there is a
certain amount of testimony to the essential *goodness* of the
evil *yēçer*. In expounding Gen. i. 31, ' And behold it was
very good,' R. Samuel ben Nachman says ' Is the evil *yēçer*
then very good ? Certainly, for without it man would not
build a house, nor marry, nor beget children, nor engage in
trade.' [5] Another Rabbi, Simon ben Eleazar, teaches as
follows :

' The evil *yēçer* is like iron. From iron one may make all
sorts of vessels if only he cast it into the fire. So one can
make the evil *yēçer* useful by the words of the Law.' This
is proved by Prov. xxv. 21 : ' If thou soothe thine enemy
(the *yēçer*) with bread and water (the Law), God will make it
thy friend.' [6] This apparent antinomy is easily resolved if
we understand the *yēçer* as a fountain of *conative energy*,
welling up from the ' heart,' that is, approximately, the subconscious self, intrinsically good, as having been created
by God, and remaining good, so long as it finds its outlet in
socially useful or legitimate activities, but becoming ' evil '
when allowed to overflow without restraint in the directions
of sexual indulgence or ruthless self-assertion in defiance of
the rights of God and one's neighbour.

The fact is that, in its quest for the source of evil in man,

[1] S. Singer, *Authorized Daily Prayer Book*, 4th edn., p. 7 (Morning
Service), ' O lead us not into the power of sin, or of transgression or iniquity,
or of temptation : *let not the evil inclination have sway over us.*' It is
impossible not to be struck by the similarity of these sentences to the
language of the Lord's Prayer as recorded by St. Matthew (vi. 9–13) ;
v. infra, Lect. III, p. 98, n. 2, and see also Taylor's discussion in *Sayings
of the Jewish Fathers* (1897), Excursus V (' The Lord's Prayer '), p. 128.

[2] *Qiddushin* 30b.

[3] *Num. rab.* 13 ; *Gen. rab.* 34.

[4] *Baba bathra* 16a ; Bacher, *Amor.* i. p. 354.

[5] *Gen. rab.* 9 ; *Eccles. rab.* 3, 11 ; Bacher, *Amor.* i. p. 487 f.

[6] Bacher, *Die Agada der Tannaiten*, ii. p. 436 ; the same saying is
also ascribed to R. Berachiah (Bacher, *Amor.* iii. p. 381 f.).

the official Jewish theology had stumbled upon, though it
never quite succeeded in disentangling from confusing associations, that central conception of modern psycho-analytic
theory which is generally designated by the term *libido*.
We may note in passing the remarkable fact that this
conception should twice in the history of thought have been
developed by men of Jewish blood, once in the Palestine
of the second century before the birth of Christ, and again
in the Vienna of the twentieth century after it.   It must be
added, for the sake of accuracy, that the idea of the *yēçer
ha-ra'* seems to be the equivalent of the idea of *libido* as
defined by Jung, rather than of the strictly Freudian conception ; for the *yēçer*, though largely, is not exclusively
sexual in nature.   A definition drawn from an authoritative
exposition of Jung's psychology will make this clear :
' (The *libido* is) a longing, a cosmic pressure or urge of the
life-force manifesting itself in the human individual, the
conation or striving which manifests itself not only in the
reproductive instinct but in such physiological and psychological phenomena as growth, development, hunger, and
other human activities and interests.' [1]   It is, consequently,
not surprising to find that, whilst the Rabbis occasionally
insist upon the necessity for ' repressing ' the ' evil impulse,'
the main tenor of their teaching finds the cure for it in what
is now called ' sublimation,' that is, the diversion of it into
good and lawful avenues of expression, the chief of which
are prayer and the exact observance of the *Tōrāh*.   (Ideally,
the observance of the Law is for the sincere and pious Jew,

---

[1] From the introduction (p. xvii), by Dr. Beatrice M. Hinkle, to Jung's
Psychology of the Unconscious (E. tr. 1922).   The whole passage, which I
have epitomised in the definition given in the text, runs as follows : ' Beginning with the conception of *libido* itself as a term used to connote sexual
hunger and craving, albeit the meaning of the word sexual was extended
by Freud to embrace a much wider significance than common usage has
assigned to it, Jung was unable to confine himself to this limitation.
He conceived this longing, this urge or push of life as something extending
beyond sexuality even in its wider sense.   He saw in the term *libido* a
concept of unknown nature, comparable to Bergson's *élan vital*, a hypothetical energy of life, which occupies itself not only in sexuality but in
various physiological and psychological manifestations such as growth,
development, hunger, and all the human activities and interests.   This
cosmic energy or urge manifested in the human being he calls *libido*, and
compares it with the energy of physics.'

not the enforced performance of a dull mechanical routine, but a joyful exercise, carried out with devotion and enthusiasm, which provides an ample outlet and satisfaction for great volumes of emotional energy.[1]) Yet the conclusion which might be expected to have been suggested by this remedial method, namely, that the *yēçer* in itself is neither good nor evil, but morally neutral and colourless, was never attained by Jewish thought. Even at the present day it seems to be generally assumed that the *yēçer* is essentially evil, though it may be endowed with a kind of artificial and adventitious goodness by being harnessed to good ends. In other words, Rabbinism never freed itself from what appears to us the self-evident fallacy of supposing that, because appetite under certain circumstances may lead to sin, it is therefore in itself sinful—a fallacy which, as we shall see in succeeding lectures, re-appears, with unfortunate results, in certain areas of Christian speculation with regard to the problem of sin.

(c) The question of *the ultimate Origin* of the 'evil imagination' can be dismissed in a few words. The origin of the evil *yēçer* is attributed by the Rabbis immediately to God : so immediately, in fact, that God is conceived, not as creating the *yēçer* in man at the beginning of human history, and leaving it to be propagated by heredity, but actually as implanting it *de novo* in the soul of every individual member of the race at the moment of his or her conception (or, according to some authorities, birth[2]). This is the cardinal point which distinguishes the official and scholastic doctrine of the *yēçer ha-ra'* from the popular and pseudepigraphic theory of the Fall—its denial that the 'evil impulse' in man is *hereditary*. According to the Rabbis, the individual sinner neither inherits the tendency

---

[1] We are here simply concerned with theoretical principles, and it would, therefore, be out of place to raise the historical question as to how far this ideal was in fact realised during the centuries immediately preceding and succeeding the Incarnation ; though it will be understood that a Christian author naturally assumes that there was ample justification for the attitude towards the Law and the halakhic tradition taken up by our Lord and by St. Paul.

[2] Rabbinical theology in general holds to the 'creationistic' hypothesis of the origin of the soul : see F. Weber, *System der alt-synagog. palästin. Theologie* (Leipzig, 1880), pp. 219, 220.

to sin from his parents nor transmits it to his children ; he receives it into his soul directly from God at the first moment of his existence, as his parents individually received it before him and his children will receive it after him.   It follows from this denial of the continuous transmission of the evil tendency that the existence of the *yēçer ha-ra'* is in no sense due to Adam's transgression ; on the contrary, Adam transgressed because the evil *yēçer* had already been planted in him by his Creator.   The disconcerting fact that, on this hypothesis, God is apparently made the author of evil, and the citadel of ethical monotheism in principle surrendered, never seems to have been adequately faced by the Jewish Church.

REACTIONS, REAL AND SUPPOSED, UPON EACH OTHER OF THE PSEUDEPIGRAPHIC AND THE RABBINICAL THEORIES

Such, then, were the two chief theories with regard to the origin of human sin which prevailed within the Jewish Church at the moment when Christianity came into the world—the popular and somewhat hazy theory of a primitive moral catastrophe and of some kind of hereditary corruption flowing from it, found in the Apocalypses, and the official, scholastic, and well-defined doctrine of an ' evil impulse ' planted by God in every human soul separately and individually which appears in the writings of the Rabbis. It would, however, be a mistake to exaggerate the division between the popular and the official theologies of Palestinian Judaism into an impassable gulf ; the spiritual aristocracy of Israel, the class of the scribes and of the rigid observers of the Law, must have shaded downwards by imperceptible degrees into the lower strata of Jewish society known as the ' people of the earth,' so that ideas could without great difficulty travel both up and down the scale ; and, in so small a country as Palestine, it is to be expected that the two worlds of thought, the apocalyptic and the Rabbinical, would overlap and interpenetrate one another at a thousand points.   Hence a full description of the immediately pre Christian state of Jewish opinion with regard to the origin and psychological ground of human sin must include some account of what appear to be half-conscious attempts to synthesise the two traditions, or at least to be instances of a tendency in one or other of these traditions to assimilate itself to its rival. A complete organic fusion of the Fall-theory and the *yēçer*-theory was never attained by Judaism ; that was a task which Providence reserved for Christian thought.

It is natural to classify the movements of thought just indicated under the two heads of (*a*) apparent approaches of Rabbinism towards the Fall-theory, and (*b*) leanings of the Fall-theory in the direction of Rabbinism, that is to say, in other words, developments of Rabbinical speculation with regard to Adam and his sin which seem to have been influenced by the apocalyptic vein of thought or at least by the extra-Scriptural traditions underlying it, and attempts made by the apocalyptic writers on their side to work the characteristic Rabbinical theology of sin into their presentation of the Adamic Fall-theory. Of these movements, the former class deserves prior consideration, inasmuch as some scholars of weight have believed that they could trace, running through it, the gradual fixation and crystallisation, as it were, of two of the most important ingredients in that version of the Christian Fall-doctrine which was taught by St. Augustine—the ideas, namely, of ' Original Righteousness ' or ' Perfection,' and of what we will take leave to call ' Original Guilt,' a term which will be presently explained.

With regard to the first of these ideas, that of the ' Original Perfection ' of man, it is perfectly true that Rabbinical theology developed it to an even more extravagant pitch than did the apocalyptic writings quoted above.[1] The ' image of God,' after which Adam was created, is made to include gigantic dimensions [2] (Adam is frequently said to have filled the whole world!), surpassing beauty of body, a degree of wisdom which almost suggests omniscience, an aureole of light eclipsing the radiance of the sun, powers of

---

[1] *v. supra*, p. 56.
[2] *Cf.* the following, from *Gesprächen der drei Heiligen* (*Denkschriften der Akad. zu Wien*, Bd. 24, S. 63) : ' quantum erat caput Adae ? responsio : tantum ut triginta homines in illud intrare possent.'

vision which enabled him to see the total extent of the earth at once, and the right to command the services of angels for the purpose of ministering to his physical comfort.[1] These marvellous endowments were forfeited as the result of Adam's sin, and the *Shekhīnāh* or divine glory withdrew itself from the earth. It would seem at first sight natural to conclude that Rabbinical thought must have regarded Adam's descendants in a certain sense as having been injured by their first father's transgression, inasmuch as they were born without the supernatural qualities which constituted 'Original Perfection'; and it is doubtless possible to see, implicitly contained in these fantastic speculations, the germ of the specifically Scotist doctrine of 'Original Sin' which defines it as consisting solely in the 'defect of Original Righteousness.'[2] But there is no proof that such conclusions were ever drawn by the Jewish theologians in a formal and explicit way; and the triviality which characterises most of the haggadic amplifications of the Biblical Paradise-story strongly suggests that this narrative was never taken in earnest by the Rabbis as the explanation of the ultimate origin of sin, and that the belief in Adam's 'original perfection' never decisively crossed the frontier which separates the realm of romantic imagination from that of serious theological thought.

A similar conclusion appears to be inevitable with regard to the supposed presence of the idea of 'Original Guilt' in the official theology of Judaism during the epoch which immediately preceded the birth of Christianity. Though we have not met with this conception hitherto, it is one which plays an important part in the history of the Christian doctrine of Man and Sin, and the present will therefore be an opportune moment for defining it. It is the idea that the sin of the first man is *legally imputed* to his descendants (either because they are supposed to have been physically included in him when he sinned, or because they are arbitrarily regarded by God as having been represented or typified by him) in such a way that every individual

---

[1] Quotations illustrating those beliefs have been collected by F. Weber, *System der altsynagog. Theologie*, pp. 214, 215.

[2] See Lecture VI, p. 410.

human being is born, not merely with the tendency to future
sins latent in him, but subject to the personal *guilt* of and
responsibility for the primal sin.   It will be seen that this
is a different idea from that of which we have hitherto been
tracing the history, the conception of a hereditary bias
towards evil, though it may be and in large areas of Christian
thought has been closely associated with it ; and it will be
convenient in our future discussion to keep the term
' Original Sin ' [1] for describing the innate tendency to sin,
which is a fact, or alleged fact, of the psychological order,
as contrasted with ' Original Guilt,' which is a juristic or
quasi-juristic conception.   It is this latter idea which
Ferdinand Weber asserts to be characteristic of Rabbinical
theology in all its periods, including, as we must suppose,
the immediately pre-Christian period.   His words are :
' There is a hereditary *guilt*, but no hereditary sinfulness
(*Es gibt eine Erbschuld, aber keine Erbsünde*) ; Adam's fall
has brought death upon the whole race, but not sinfulness in
the sense of a compulsion to sin ; sin is the result of each
individual's personal decision, which experience shows to
be in fact universal, but which, even after the Fall, is in no
sense theoretically necessary.' [2]   Here it is affirmed that
the Rabbis—including, presumably, the *Tannāīm* or
' Repeaters,' who were the dominant school of our Lord's
day [3]—whilst rejecting ' Original Sin,' nevertheless accepted

---

[1] Strictly speaking, of course, it is anachronistic to use the term
' Original Sin' in dealing with the ideas of any period prior to that of
St. Augustine (see Lect. V, p. 327), as it is to employ the word 'Fall' to
describe the first sin as conceived by writers earlier than Methodius of
Olympus (see Lect. IV, p. 252, n. 4) ; but, in the case of both terms, we
may plead that the anachronism is convenient and inevitable.

[2] *op. cit.* p. 217.   ' Es gibt eine Erbschuld, aber keine Erbsünde ;
der Fall Adams hat dem ganzen Geschlecht den Tod, nicht aber die
Sündigkeit im Sinne einer Nothwendigkeit zu sündigen verursacht ; die
Sünde ist das Ergebnis der Entscheidung jedes Einzelnen, erfahrungs-
gemäss allgemein, aber an sich auch nach dem Fall nicht schlechthin
nothwendig.'

[3] It may be of interest to set down here a list of the successive schools
of divines which held sway during the classical period of Rabbinism.
They were (1) The *Sōpherim*, or ' Scribes,' whose period lasted, roughly,
from Ezra to the age of the Maccabees ; (2) the *Zugōth*, or ' pairs,' so called
because it is alleged that there were only two of them in office at a time,
one being president, and the other vice-president, of the Sanhedrin—the
word is formed from the Greek ζυγόν, a yoke-pair ; their period lasted from

the idea of ' Original Guilt.'   If this conclusion could be
sustained, it would represent a fact of the highest importance
for the interpretation of the New Testament doctrine of the
Fall.   Dr. Tennant has, however, shown that this sweeping
assertion of Weber is, at the least, uncertain in the highest
degree, in so far as it refers to immediately pre-Christian
Rabbinism, in which alone we are interested for the purposes
of the present enquiry.[1]   It is, in fact, a precarious inference
from the supposition, itself unproved, that the *Tannāïm*
believed Adam's sin to have been the cause of mortality in
his descendants.   But, despite the fact that this latter
doctrine was held by Ben Sirach [2] and possibly by the author
of the Book of Wisdom,[3] there is no proof that it became
at all common in the Rabbinical schools before the third
century of our era.   It is, moreover, affirmed, in opposition
to Weber's contention, by two eminent authorities [4] on the
religion and theology of Judaism, that the generation of
Rabbis nearest the time of Christ held for the most part an
individualistic view of the connexion between sin and death,
maintaining that each man's death is due to his own sinful
acts (which, as we have seen, are deemed to arise from his
own culpable failure to control his *yēçer*) and not to any ancestral or racial sin.   The empirical universality of death would
thus be due merely to the empirical universality of actual
sin, and not to any *a priori* necessity or arbitrary Divine
decree.   It seems, therefore, safest to regard the attribution
of a belief in ' Original Guilt ' to the Rabbis of the first
centuries before and after the beginning of our era as an

---

the Maccabees till Herod the Great ;   (3) the *Tannāïm*, or ' repeaters '—who
flourished during the first and second centuries of our era ; (4) the '*Amōrāïm*
or ' interpreters,' from *c.* 200 to *c.* 500 A.D. ;   (5) the *Sabōrāïm*, or ' teachers,'
whose period coincides roughly with the sixth century A.D. ;   and (6) the
Geōnīm, or ' noble ones,' who taught from 609 to 750 A.D.   For further
information as to these schools, see Oesterley and Box, *Religion and
Worship of the Synagogue*, c. IV ii. ;   H. M. J. Loewe, art. ' Judaism,' in
ERE, vol. vii. ;   Oesterley and Box, *Short Sketch of the Literature of Rabbinical and Mediaeval Judaism* (1920), pp. 89–126.
    [1] *Sources of the Doctrines of the Fall and of Original Sin*, pp. 161–168.
    [2] Ecclus. xxv. 24.
    [3] Wisdom ii. 23, 24 ; see above, p. 55.
    [4] Ginzberg, *Monatsschrift für Geschicht eund Wissenschaft Judentums*,
Jahrg. 43, p. 153 f. ; Schechter, *Studies in Judaism*, pp. 260 ff.

anachronism ; and to assume that, within the sphere of the official theology, as it stood at this period, the hypothesis of a causal connexion between Adam's sin and the deaths of his posterity only existed (so far as it existed at all) in a vague and undefined form, as a haggadic and mythopoeic *motif* rather than as a reasoned intellectual theory.

It would seem, then, that the official theology of the Jewish Church in its immediately pre-Christian period only leaned towards the Adam-theory on its haggadic, that is, its imaginative, romantic, and mythological side, and that it exhibited no real approximation to what we are justified in calling the pseudepigraphic doctrine in the sphere of intellectual concepts. The case, however, is different when we turn to the latest Apocalypses which have any bearing on our enquiry, namely, the *Syriac Apocalypse of Baruch* and the *Second* or *Fourth Book of Esdras.*[1] These books are of peculiar interest for our present purpose, because both the composition of their several elements and their final redaction as literary wholes are generally admitted to fall within limits marked by the dates 50 and 120 A.D.— that is to say, within a period roughly contemporaneous with the development of Apostolic Christianity and the writing of the New Testament ; and they therefore may be taken as first-hand evidence for the background of Jewish thought on the origin and ground of sin which is presupposed by St. Paul's treatment of the subject. In them we shall find unmistakable evidence of the contacts and reactions between the scholastic and the popular opinions which must have been proceeding in the Jewish Church of our Lord's day—evidence which in the former book takes the shape of

[1] These documents have been edited, with English translation and full notes, by R. H. Charles and G. H. Box respectively, in *Apocrypha and Pseudepigrapha of the Old Testament*, vol. ii. (1913). Though the introduction to each contains a complete bibliography, it may be well to note here a few editions of importance : (1) (*Baruch*), R. H. Charles, *The Apocalypse of Baruch* (1896) ; Ryssel, in Kautzsch, *Apokr. u. Pseudepigr. des AT*, ii. 411 (1900) ; (2) (*Esdras*) R. L. Bensly and M. R. James, *The Fourth Book of Ezra* (the complete Latin version, including for the first time the missing fragment vii. 36–105, discovered by Prof. Bensly) ; *Texts and Studies*, iii. 2 (1895) ; Gunkel, in Kautzsch, *Apokr. u. Pseud.* ii. (1900) ; Bruno Violet, *Die Esra-Apocalypse* (*Die griech. christl. Schriftst. der ersten drei Jahrhund.* Bd. 18, 1910) ; G. H. Box, *The Ezra-Apocalypse* (1912).

an emphatic repudiation of the Fall-doctrine, and, in the latter, of a more or less successful attempt to fuse it with the *yēçer*-theory. Though it is certain that 2 Baruch and 4 Ezra (to employ the short titles under which scholars have agreed to designate these works) are closely related, in the sense that one was published as a conscious and deliberate reply to the other, there is at present no *consensus* of opinion on the question which came first ; and we shall therefore content ourselves with sketching the positions characteristic of these two books, without expressing any view as to which ought to be regarded as thesis and which as antithesis. As the Baruch-document represents what eventually became the permanent mind of post-Christian Judaism, it will be natural to examine this work in the first place, and to reserve 4 Ezra, which approximates more nearly than any other purely Jewish writing to the full Pauline doctrine of the Fall and Original Sin, for subsequent consideration.

It is noteworthy that all the passages in 2 Baruch which deal with the origins of sin occur either in that stratum of it which Dr. Charles denotes by the symbol A³ and assigns to the period prior to the destruction of Jerusalem, or in that designated by him as B², the composition of which he places in the epoch of despair which succeeded the catastrophe of A.D. 70.[1] But this difference of date between the two documents in question, even with the difference of world-outlook necessarily involved in it, does not affect their substantial identity of view with regard to the theology of sin,[2] and the relevant texts may therefore be considered together, without any attempt to group them chronologically. 2 Baruch admits, in accordance with the haggadic tendency noticed above, in our discussion of the Rabbinical interpretation of Gen. iii., that Adam's transgression was the starting-point of a long series of *external* or *material* disasters, in particular of physical death, or at least of its premature

---

[1] *Apocr. and Pseudepigr.* ii. pp. 474 ff.

[2] It should, however, be noted that in B² Adam's sin is the cause of *all* death, it being apparently assumed that, but for the Fall, man would have been immortal ; in A³, on the contrary, man was originally mortal, and Adam's transgression is the cause only of its premature occurrence.

occurrence [1] ;   this opinion finds expression in xxiii. 4 :
' Because when Adam sinned, and death was decreed against
those who should be born ' ; in xlviii. 42, 43 :

(42) O Adam, what hast thou done to all those who
          are born from thee,
 And what will be said to the first Eve who
        hearkened to the serpent ?
(43) For all this multitude are going to corruption,
 Nor is there any numbering of those whom the fire devours ;

and most conspicuously in lvi. 5, 6 :

(5) And as thou didst previously see on the summit of the cloud
 black waters which descended previously on the earth,[2] this
 is the transgression wherewith Adam the first man transgressed.

(6) For (since) when he transgressed
 Untimely death came into being,
 Grief was named,
 And anguish was prepared,
 And pain was created,
 And trouble consummated,
 And disease began to be established,
 And Sheol kept demanding that it should be renewed in
  blood,
 And the begetting of children was brought about,
 And the passion of parents produced,[3]
 And the greatness of humanity was humiliated,
 And goodness languished.

It will be noticed that *v.* 6 contains what looks like an
approximation to the later Augustinian doctrine of ' Original
Sin,' in the shape of a suggestion that the existence of sexual
passion is due to Adam's fall : this idea is further developed
in *vv.* 10 ff., where it is connected with the story of the
lustful angels :

For he became a danger to his own soul : even to the angels
became he a danger.   For, moreover, at that time when he was
created, they enjoyed liberty.   And some of them descended,

---

[1] See note 2, p. 76.
[2] The reference is to Baruch's vision, narrated in c. liii., in which the
history of mankind from Adam to the Messiah is symbolised under the form
of alternate showers of black and bright waters descending from a cloud.
[3] Italics ours.

and mingled with the women.   And then those who did so were
tormented in chains.

If these passages stood alone, we should be entitled to
describe 2 Baruch's views with regard to the significance of
Adam's sin as a compromise between the Rabbinical and
the popular traditions, the consequences of the Fall being
kept, in the main, on the purely external and mechanical
level in deference to the former, whilst a single interior and
psychological consequence—to wit, sexual emotion and
activity—is taken over, in isolation, from the latter.   It is
noticeable that no attempt is made to utilise the idea of the
yēçer ha-ra‛ in this connexion.   But we have to set against
the texts just quoted certain other passages in which the
robust ethical libertarianism, almost amounting to what
was known to later Christian theology as Pelagianism, of
the Rabbis is strongly affirmed, and the popular Adamic
Fall-theory is repudiated in explicit and energetic language.
Those which bear most directly on the subject of our enquiry
are xviii. 1, 2, where Moses is said to have lighted a lamp
for Israel (by promulgating the Law) but to have been
imitated by few, the majority of Jews having chosen to
‛ take from the darkness of Adam ’ (that is, to imitate his
sin) instead of rejoicing in the light of the lamp [1] ;   and
liv. 15 ff., which expressly states that Adam's sin introduced
premature death only, and in no way affected his descendants’
freedom of choice, in words characterised by such pointed
vehemence that they can only be interpreted as a direct
attack upon the Fall-theory :

(15) For though Adam first sinned
    And brought untimely death upon all,
    Yet of those who were born from him
    Each one of them has prepared for his own soul torment
        to come,
    And again each one of them has chosen for himself glories
        to come.

(19) *Adam is not therefore the cause, save only of his own soul,*
    But each one of us has been the Adam of his own soul.[2]

---

[1] *Cf.* John v. 35, in which a similar metaphor is applied to John the
Baptist : ἐκεῖνος ἦν ὁ λύχνος ὁ καιόμενος καὶ φαίνων· ὑμεῖς δὲ ἠθελήσατε
ἀγαλλιασθῆναι πρὸς ὥραν ἐν τῷ φωτὶ αὐτοῦ.

[2] Italics ours.

The patent inconsistency of this teaching with that of lvi. 5 ff., quoted above, is a striking reflection of the divided opinions with regard to this subject which prevailed within the Jewish Church, just at the time when St. Paul was laying down, in measured yet unhesitating words, the outlines of that Christian Fall-doctrine which ever since has formed the presupposition of the Catholic redemptive scheme.

With 4 Ezra we pass into a different atmosphere. This writer accepts the Rabbinical doctrine of the *yēçer ha-ra'*; but his experience of the actual sinfulness of Israel has led him entirely to reject its companion doctrine, that the Law is a sufficient remedy for the evil impulses connatural with the human soul, and that man can perfectly well obey the whole Law if he chooses so to do. Like St. Paul, though untouched by any spark of Christian faith or emotion, he has discovered that the Law produces only the ' knowledge of sin,' not the power to overcome it, and that in him, or in his flesh, there dwelleth no good thing.[1] He arrives at an explanation of this saddening fact by fusing the Rabbinical and the pseudepigraphic theories, admitting that the evil *yēçer* was planted (presumably by the Creator) in the heart of Adam at the moment of his creation, but supplementing this position by the implied assertions that its presence in him became fixed and habitual owing to the Fall, and that it is now hereditary in the human race, being communicated from Adam to the successive generations of his posterity by physical propagation. This, it will be seen, is for all practical purposes identical with the Pauline doctrine, save in so far as the Apostle abstains from affirming that the germ or potentiality of evil existed in Adam before the Fall ; and even this latter idea can be paralleled in the teaching of St. Augustine, who finds himself obliged to postulate a minute but appreciable amount of ' concupiscence ' in unfallen man, in order to explain the possibility of his being tempted at all.[2]

The relevant passages may here be given at length :

[1] Passages implying the empirical universality of actual sin are : iii. 35 f. ; vii. 46, 68 ; viii. 35.
[2] See Lecture V, p. 363, n. 3.

(*a*) For the first Adam, clothing himself with [1] the evil heart, transgressed and was overcome ; and likewise also all who were born of him. Thus the infirmity became inveterate ; the Law indeed was in the heart of the people, but (in conjunction with) the evil germ ; so what was good departed, and the evil remained (iii. 21–23).

(*b*) For a grain of evil seed was sown in the heart of Adam from the beginning, and how much fruit of ungodliness has it produced unto this time, and shall yet produce until the threshing-floor come ! (iv. 30).

(*c*) Then said he unto me : Even so, also, is Israel's portion ; for it was for their sakes I made the world ; but when Adam transgressed my statutes, then that which had been made was judged, and then the ways of this world became narrow and sorrowful and painful and full of perils coupled with great toils (vii. 11, 12).

(*d*) And I answered and said : This is my first and last word ; better had it been that the earth had not produced Adam, or else, having once produced him, (for thee) to have restrained him from sinning. For how does it profit us all that in the present we must live in grief and after death look for punishment ? O thou Adam, what hast thou done ! For though it was thou that sinned, the fall [2] was not thine alone, but ours also who are thy descendants ! (vii. 116–118).

In the first two of these passages the *yēçer ha-raʿ* is referred to as ' the evil heart,' ' the evil germ,' ' a grain of evil seed ' ; it may be added that in another passage (vii. 92, which I have not quoted because it does not directly bear upon the questions of the origin and transmission of evil) the *yēçer* is even more recognisably mentioned under the title of ' the innate evil thought ' (*cum eis plasmatum cogitamentum malum*). The third passage cannot, perhaps, be claimed as going beyond the haggadic tradition generally received by the Rabbis, namely, that Adam's Fall was the starting-point of material evil. But the transmission of the ' evil heart ' from Adam to his posterity would seem to be clearly implied in (*a*) and also in (*d*), the last sentence of

---

[1] So the Syriac and Ethiopic versions : the Latin has ' bearing ' or ' carrying ' (*i.e.* within him)—' cor enim malignum baiolans primus Adam transgressus et victus est.' See Bensly and James, *op. cit.*, p. 8. Box (*Ezra-Apocalypse*, p. 16, note *in loc.*) argues that the Latin *baiolans* represents a Greek φορέοας, which would be the equivalent of ' wearing ' or ' clothing ' himself with the ' evil heart,' as though it were a garment.

[2] For a note on this word, see Lecture IV, p. 252, n. 4.

which can hardly mean less than that Adam's descendants in some sense have shared in his sin owing to their physiological connexion and continuity with him.

It is impossible to read this Apocalypse, the last purely Jewish document to set forth the popular doctrine of an inherited interior weakness or disease, without feeling that a true organic synthesis of the two conceptions which the author of the main body of 4 Ezra somewhat mechanically juxtaposes lay all the time ready to his hand. From the standpoint of the dispassionate modern student, it must seem that it would not have been difficult to harmonise the official and the popular theories by taking advantage of the more reasonable form assumed by the scholastic doctrine in those passages of the Rabbinical writings which represent the *yēçer* as being in itself a morally neutral *libido* ; and, whilst admitting that the *yēçer* existed in Adam from the moment of his creation, to conceive the Fall as consisting in a mis-direction and fixation of this *libido* upon an improper object, a fixation which became stereotyped in him and was transmitted by him to his posterity. I am not concerned at this stage of our enquiry to maintain that such a view is possible for us, but merely that it would have been possible for 4 Ezra. But the opportunity was missed, and the synthesis which seems for a moment to have trembled upon the verge of consummation was never consciously achieved. The crowning disasters of Bar Kokhba's rebellion and its bloody suppression by Hadrian (A.D. 135) finally discredited the whole apocalyptic *genre* of literature and thought, which vanished into the limbo of forgotten things, taking with it (so far as Jewry was concerned) the half-developed ideas of the Fall and of Original Sin, and leaving the strict Rabbinical conception of the *yēçer ha-ra'*, as individually implanted by the Creator in each human soul and not hereditarily derived from any primaeval disaster, in sole possession of the field of Jewish orthodoxy.

PHILO'S IDEAS WITH REGARD TO THE 'FALL'

It should be added, before we close our survey of the Jewish antecedents of the Christian Fall-doctrine, that little

G

information of interest for our immediate purpose can be gleaned from the writings of Philo. His loyalty to the main tenor of the scholastic tradition leads him, in commenting on the early narratives of Genesis, to reproduce the current haggadic ideas regarding the supernatural endowments, physical, mental, and moral, enjoyed by the first man,[1] and the material or external disasters which were involved in his expulsion from the happy garden.[2] But the idea of an internal psychological malady, transmissible by physical heredity, and engendered by our first father's fall, is totally absent from his writings. It is probable that his deepest thought with regard to the story of Gen. iii. is that which finds expression in the treatise *de mundi opificio* : in which the Fall-narrative is said to be an allegory (though this does not imply that it is not also a record of literal fact) portraying in symbolic form the processes which normally precede the commission of actual sin, Adam typifying the rational and Eve the sensuous element in human nature, whilst the serpent signifies the sinister power of carnal lust and pleasure.[3]

It might have been expected that Philo, belonging as he did on his Jewish side to the world of official and Rabbinical theology rather than to the world of popular pietism in which the Apocalytic literature grew up, would have given an unfaltering allegiance to the idea of the

---

[1] *de mundi opif.* 50 (*Philonis Iudaei opera omnia*, ed. C. E. Richter, Lipsiae, 1828, i. p. 47 ; references to the volume and page of this edition are given in brackets after the references to the chapter or paragraph of Philo's text) : Adam ἐν ἀκράτῳ διέτριβεν εὐδαιμονίᾳ, and was in all things conformed to the will of his Creator ; *ibid.* 52 (i. p. 48) : the naming of the animals was a proof of Adam's supreme wisdom and sovereignty over the world (for the re-appearance of this idea in Christian thought, see Lect. V, p. 361) ; *quaest. in Gen.* i. 32 (vi. p. 266) : ' protoplastorum autem animae ut a malo mundae essent et intemeratae, acutae omnino erant ad perceptionem cuiuscumque vocis . . . illi vero quemadmodum corpus sortiti sunt nimis grande et proceritatem gigantis, necesse fuit ut prae se ferrent sensus etiam certiores, et quod his praestantius est, philosophicos intuitus auditusque. non enim frustra arbitrabantur nonnulli oculis illos praeditos esse, quibus potuerunt etiam eas quae in caelo sunt naturas essentiasque et operationes videre, quemadmodum et auribus cuiuscumque generis voces percipere.'

[2] *de mundi opif.* 60 (i. 54), an expansion of Gen. iii. 16–19 ; cf. *de nobilit.* 3, ad fin. (v. p. 262).

[3] *de mundi opif.* 56 (i. p. 51 f.).

yēçer ha-ra' as the ground or source of human sin. This idea does, indeed, seem to show itself, in a defaced and not easily recognisable form, as the totality of the 'passions' (πάθη) which are described as 'rooted in the flesh' [1] and as 'evils connatural with our race' [2]; and it is possible that we might be able to perceive its authentic lineaments in passages of the Philonian writings where its presence has not so far been suspected, had the Hellenistic Jews been able to agree upon one single Greek equivalent for the term *yēçer*.[3] But Philo was prevented from allowing this conception to attain its full Rabbinical development in his teaching by his great horror (which, as we have seen, the doctors of Palestinian and Babylonian Judaism do not seem to have shared [4]) of making God the author of evil. And, where his Rabbinism leaves him in the lurch, his Platonism emerges with redoubled power, and sets a masterful grip upon the reins of his speculation. He never attained to a single, internally harmonious explanation of the origin of sin; but there can be little doubt that the

---

[1] *quis rer. div. haer.* 54 (iii. p. 59) : νόθα γὰρ καὶ ξένα διανοίας τὰ σώματος ὡς ἀληθῶς πάθη, σαρκὸς ἐκπεφυκότα, ᾗ προσερρίζωνται.

[2] *ibid.* 55 (iii. p. 60) : τὰ σύμφυτα κακὰ τοῦ γένους ἡμῶν. Philo is deeply conscious of the universality or practical universality of innate sinfulness ; *cf. de vita Mosis*, iii. 17 (iv. p. 215) : παντὶ γεννητῷ καὶ ἂν σπουδαῖον ᾖ, παρ' ὅσον ἦλθεν εἰς γένεσιν, συμφυὲς τὸ ἁμαρτάνον ἐστίν ; *de confus. ling.* 17 (ii. p. 204) : <τὰ κακὰ> ἐφ' ἅπερ ἡ μοχθηρὰ φύσις δι' ἑαυτῆς βαδίζει ; *de mut. nom.* 6 (iii. p. 166 f.) : ἄπειρα μέν ἐστι τὰ καταρρυπαίνοντα τὴν ψυχήν, ἅπερ ἐκνίψασθαι καὶ ἀπολούσασθαι παντελῶς οὐκ ἔνεστιν. ἀπολείπονται γὰρ ἐξ ἀνάγκης παντὶ θνητῷ συγγενεῖς κῆρες, ἃς λωφῆσαι μὲν εἰκός, ἀναιρεθῆναι δ' εἰσάπαν ἀδύνατον : *de poenit.* 1 (v. p. 215) : τὸ μὲν γὰρ μηδὲν συνόλως ἁμαρτεῖν, ἴδιον θεοῦ, τάχα δὲ καὶ θείου ἀνδρός : *de sacr. Abel. et Caini* 33 (i. p. 259) : ἄγευστον γὰρ παθῶν ἢ κακιῶν ψυχὴν εὑρεῖν σπανιώτατον. Notice in this last passage the comparison of humanity to a φύραμα, or lump of dough, which re-appears in St. Paul (Rom. ix. 21, 1 Cor. v. 7), Tertullian (' conspersio'— *v. infra*, p. 328, n. 3), Ambrosiaster (' massa,' p. 310), and Augustine (p. 328).

[3] For יֵצֶר LXX has διάνοια (Gen. viii. 21), διαβούλιον (Ecclus. xv. 14), διαλογισμός (*ibid.* xxvii. 6), ἐνθύμημα (*ibid.* xxxvii. 3) ; etc.

[4] *de decem orac.* 33 (iv. p. 280) : θεὸς ἦν, εὐθὺς δὲ κύριος ἀγαθός, μόνων ἀγαθῶν αἴτιος, κακοῦ δὲ οὐδενός ; *quaest. in Gen.* i. 78 (vi. p. 290) : 'deus enim malorum nullo modo causa est' ; *ibid.* i. 89 (vi. p. 296) : 'minime pro causa < corruptionis > habentes divinitatem, quae immunis est malitia et malis : sola enim bona prius largiri est eius opus' ; *ibid.* i. 100 (vi. p. 304) : '< deus est > causa sane non omnium sed bonorum tantum eorumque qui secundum virtutem sunt ; sicut enim expers est malitiae, ita etiam nec causa' ; etc.

predominant factor in his thought on this subject is the
Platonic conviction (identical with what we have in Lecture I described as the ' Hindu ' or monistic solution of the
problem [1]) that evil is inseparably bound up with finite,
relative and phenomenal existence. With this conviction
naturally coheres another Platonic tenet, the belief in the
pre-existence of the human soul; and it is therefore not
surprising to find, in two passages at least,[2] inchoate
adumbrations of a theory (such as had been imaginatively
suggested by Plato himself in the *Phaedrus*, and as was
destined to be elaborated nearly two centuries later by
another great Platonist of Alexandria, Origen [3]) of a prenatal
fall of individual souls, drawn downwards from the transcendental plane, which is their true home, through a
sensual craving for earthly and bodily life, and contracting
the taint of evil from their voluntary self-imprisonment in
envelopes of material flesh. This idea, according to which
every human birth represents the voluntary fall of a pre-
existent spirit from the heavenly sphere, has played a
considerable part in non-Christian systems of religious
belief, will meet us more than once in the history of
Christian speculation on the origins of evil in man, and
will claim a measure of respectful consideration when we
approach our final task of determining what is the essential
Fall-doctrine of the Christian Church.[4] But it must suffice
at this point to emphasise the fact that the theory of
pre-natal falls was only hinted at, and never worked out in
detail, by Philo, and cannot, therefore, be reckoned amongst
the influences which contributed to the shaping of that
doctrine regarding the Fall and Original Sin which we shall
find in the pages of the New Testament.

---

[1] *v. supra*, Lecture I, p. 5.

[2] *de somn.* i. 22 (iii. p. 244) ; *de gigant.* 3 (ii. p. 53). But in *de confus.
ling.* 17 (ii. p. 265) the souls of the wise are said to have descended from
heaven to earth ' because of their love of contemplation and learning.'
The theory of pre-existence is generally believed to underlie Wisdom viii. 19 :

> ' Now I was a child of parts, and a good soul fell to my lot ;
> Nay rather, being good, I came into a body undefiled '

(though A. T. S. Goodricke, *The Book of Wisdom* [1913], pp. 212, 381 f.,
denies this). But Pseudo-Solomon does not suggest that the incarnation
of a pre-existent soul is to be regarded as a ' Fall.'

[3] *v.* Lecture IV, p. 212 ff.   [4] *v.* Lecture VIII, p. 507 ff.

SUMMARY AND CONCLUSION

In view of the vague and elusive nature of the ideas respecting the origin and ground of sin which prevailed within the Jewish Church, as it stood on the eve of the Incarnation, it would seem desirable, even at the cost of some repetition, to conclude our survey of the pre-Christian history of the Fall-doctrine with a brief summary of the results so far attained. We have seen that this doctrine is entirely absent from the Old Testament documents of a date prior to the Exile, and that its origin is to be found in the feeling of sin, understood now in a strictly ethical and not in a quasi-materialistic sense, which that great catastrophe inspired in devout and introspective souls. The dreary impotence which for the most part characterised the life of the restored community during the Persian and Greek periods impressed deeply upon the mind of the later Israel the idea of the empirical universality of sin. Reflection and self-analysis seemed to show, lying behind this fact, an innate sinfulness or tendency towards sin, deeply rooted in human nature. But this psychological phenomenon itself required an explanation. The piety of the common folk, which found expression in the apocalyptic literature, could not endure the supposition that human nature as it stands, with the evil impulse rooted in it, represents human nature as created by God; and was accordingly compelled to postulate a voluntary and deliberate declension of man from the moral ideal set before him by his Maker—in other words, a ' Fall.' The ancient traditions of Israel were ransacked in order to discover an event which could be identified with this hypothetical ' Fall '; and the first supposedly historical incident which was selected for this purpose was the unnatural intermarriage of divine and human beings narrated in Gen. vi. 1–4. But the difficulty of accounting, on this hypothesis, for the persistence of evil after the Flood forced the later apocalyptists back upon the Paradise-story of Gen. iii.; which seemed to provide an explanation of the origin of evil fitting the known facts of human nature and the supposed facts of human history much more closely than that based upon the Angel-legend, and, in course of time, pushed this earlier Fall-story into the background. Both of these Fall-theories, as elaborated in the apocalypses, are shot through and interwoven with frequent traces of two diverse, though not necessarily discrepant, ideas as to the nature and mode of propagation of sin—one which regards it as bound up with man's advance in knowledge, and one which finds it in intimate association with his sensual appetites, particularly with that appetite which subserves the continuation of the race.

Meanwhile, the official theology of the Jewish Church, as represented by the scribes, the authoritative custodians of its traditional deposit, was developing a solution of the problem of evil and its origin on largely different lines. Having (it is not unfair to suggest) a somewhat colder, more intellectualised and philosophical, conception of God than that which underlay the passionate piety of the pseudepigraphic writers, they felt less difficulty about attributing, or appearing to attribute, the ultimate responsibility for the existence of evil to Him ; and the robust ethical libertarianism [1] which they had inherited from the prophets made it impossible for them to allow the sinner a possible excuse for or palliation of his wrong-doing, such as he might have found in the theory of an involuntarily inherited propension towards sin. Hence Rabbinical theology rejects altogether the beliefs in a ' Fall,' and in a hereditary infirmity or taint, and substitutes the idea of the ' evil imagination,' individually implanted by the Creator in every man at his conception or birth—a mysterious tumultuous force perpetually welling up from the depths of the soul and appearing in consciousness as an imperious hunger for self-assertion, self-expression, and self-gratification, especially within the sphere of sex. (In the stress which they lay upon this matter, the scholastic and the popular theories join hands.) This impulse has been placed by the Creator in man, not

---

[1] This firm belief in free-will was held by the Rabbis side by side with an equally firm belief in the universality of the Divine prevision, as appears from the celebrated saying of R. 'Aqibah ' Everything is foreseen, and free-will is given ' (*Pirqe 'Abôth*, iii. 24 ; Taylor, *Sayings of the Jewish Fathers*, 1897 edn., p. 59). But Divine prevision, even if construed as predestination, does not in itself imply a radical evil in man.

indeed with the avowed object of causing him to sin, but rather to be the necessary pre-condition of moral virtue, which is only attained through its subjugation, by means of the Law, and its consequent direction towards good and noble ends. We have already suggested that this conception appears to be in essence identical with the *libido* of recent psychology, an idea which may prove useful when we approach the constructive part of our task. The Rabbis were, however, sufficiently far influenced by the movements of popular thought and by the vague body of extra-biblical legend floating around the figures of Adam and Eve to be willing to find a place, at least within the haggadic elements of their teaching, for the theory that the transgression of the first man, though not the source of human sinfulness, was nevertheless attended by many disastrous physical consequences affecting both himself and his descendants, and including the forfeiture of the supernatural perfections supposed to have been enjoyed by him in his paradisal state. The doctrine of ' Original Righteousness ' would thus seem to have been already present in the Jewish scholasticism which formed part of the intellectual *milieu* within which the Christian doctrines of Man and of Sin were first formulated ; and, though it would doubtless be anachronistic to attribute to the Rabbis an explicit belief in ' Original Guilt,' or the imputation of Adam's sin to his descendants, yet it can now be seen that the potentialities of such a belief lay dormant in the traditional mythology which treated the Fall as the origin of physical evil.

At the beginning, therefore, of our era three main theories as to the origin of human sin were current within that Jewish *Ecclesia* into which Christ and His Apostles were born, namely :

(1) The theory of the older apocalyptists, which finds the ground of moral evil in a hereditary taint introduced into the world by the unnatural angel-marriages of Gen. vi.

(2) The theory of the later apocalyptists, which traces the source of inherited sinfulness to the transgression of Adam and Eve narrated in Gen. iii. Under this head we must distinguish between (*a*) that form of the theory which, confining itself to the interpretation of the Biblical narrative, found the first sin in Adam's wilful transgression of a known divine command,

and (b) that based upon extra-biblical folk-lore, which regards the moral corruption of mankind as a consequence of the physical pollution of Eve by the serpent, or Satan.

(3) The theory of the Rabbinical, that is of the official and scholastic theology, that the psychological basis of sin consists in an ' evil impulse,' ' imagination,' or ' disposition,' which is not hereditary, but implanted by the Creator in each individual separately at the moment of conception or birth.

To these should perhaps be added (though, as already observed, it appears to have exercised no influence upon the earliest Christian thought) :

(4) The view of Philo, according to which evil is a necessary quality of finite and relative being, and is communicated to human souls through their individual falls to the material plane from the transcendental sphere in which they are conceived as having existed before their births in time—a view which appears to be substantially identical with what we have described as the ' Hindu theory ' in Lecture I.

These diverse and in many ways discrepant conceptions constituted the pile of raw material which lay ready to the hand of the earliest Christian theology, at the moment when first it bent itself to the task of building up a doctrine of Man and of Sin to serve as the logical presupposition and *prius* of its redemptive and soteriological scheme.

It may thus be claimed that a candid research into the origins and growth of the later or ' Adamic ' version of the Fall-theory has confirmed the conclusion which was provisionally formulated at the close of Lecture I, as the result of our investigation of the earlier or ' angelic ' version— namely, that the true basis of the pseudepigraphic doctrines of the Fall and of Original Sin (as of their scholastic rival, the doctrine of the *yēçer ha-ra‘*) is to be found in facts of inner spiritual experience, in particular the experience of moral struggle and failure and of penitence ; these beliefs are .rooted in psychology, not in history. The question may well be asked ' Does not this conclusion dispose of their claim to be based upon a Divine revelation ? ' : and the last words of this lecture shall be devoted to the presentation of a reply as definite as can be given at this stage of our argument without anticipating contentions which have yet to be developed.

The nature of this reply must necessarily be determined by the conception of ' Revelation ' which is in the mind of our imaginary interlocutor. If by ' Revelation ' he means a purely external, objective, and mechanical impartition to men's minds of Divine truth in a finished and unalterable form, the answer must be in the affirmative ; the facts which we have passed under review do indeed dispose of any claim which might be put forward on behalf of the Fall-doctrine that it rests upon such an outward, and, so to speak, tangible revelation. In all probability Man has lived upon this planet for not less than half a million years, and the Genesis-stories, in their present form, can hardly number thirty centuries of existence ; we cannot, therefore, regard them as based upon genuine reminiscences of the infancy of the human race. We have, moreover, seen that the Fall-doctrine came into existence as the result of human reflection upon the problem of human sin, and that it was not until after a century of experimentation with the Watcher-legend that the Paradise-story was finally chosen as the nail from which the inferred chain of the hereditary evil causality was to be suspended ; it is, therefore, equally impossible for us to accept that more refined form of the theory of an ' objective revelation ' underlying the Fall-doctrine which would see in the narrative of Gen. iii. an allegory directly dictated by the Holy Spirit in order to acquaint mankind with the forgotten first page of its own moral history.

But, when we deny that this doctrine originated in an exterior or objective revelation, conveyed through oracle, vision, or supernaturally dictated text, and affirm that its immediate historical source is to be found in human specu-lation, we do not thereby exclude the possibility that it may be ultimately attributable to a Divine *revelation of an interior or subjective kind.*   God fulfils Himself in many ways ; and the *praeparatio evangelica* which, as heirs of the ancient covenant, we Christians discern in the pages of the Old Testament, was unrolled before the eyes of the Jewish Fathers πολυμερῶς καὶ πολυτρόπως,[1] in many fragments and after many manners. Deep, searching, self-abhorring

[1] Heb. i. 1.

penitence, in which the whole theory is rooted and from which it draws its vitality, is in any case the gift of God ; and Christian believers should find no antecedent difficulty in the supposition that the same indwelling Spirit, who bestowed this poignant experience upon the noblest of the apocalyptic thinkers, may also, with delicate invisible touches, have so guided and shaped the course of their introspective meditations and reflections upon it as to educe from their tumultuous feelings a system of ideas—imperfectly defined and commingled for the time being with error and legend, yet containing a truer explanation of the origin of moral evil than any that the mind of man had hitherto evolved, and capable of purification during the following centuries in accordance with the mind of Christ and of ultimate incorporation into the majestic fabric of Christian belief. If this be a true account of the matter, and if the word ' Revelation ' may in this connexion be understood in the subjective sense indicated above, the doctrines of the Fall and of Original Sin may still claim to be founded in a Divine revelation, as surely as though they had been graven upon visible tables of stone or proclaimed in words of thunder from the smouldering steeps of Sinai.

Whether, indeed, such a hypothesis may legitimately be applied to the origin of these doctrines cannot be categorically decided until we have completed our final task of examining their permanent residuum, as it has emerged from the crucible of Christian thought, in regard to its psychological and metaphysical validity, and must depend upon the verdict at which we arrive in the course of our last two lectures. If we see reason to believe that these ideas embody the true explanation of the origin of evil, or an explanation as true as is attainable with our present faculties, we shall have no hesitation in assigning their ultimate source to the subtle, but none the less real, inspirations of the Divine ; if not, we shall conclude that they are mere human figments. Meanwhile, we may be content to observe that, as no consideration of *a priori* probability can be adduced which militates against the hypothesis of an interior and subjective revelation lying behind these doctrines, so also no *a posteriori* evidence fundamentally incompatible with such a hypothesis has been disclosed by a careful survey of their pre-Christian development. He who would unravel their obscure and confused beginnings must necessarily handle, as we have already seen, much that is fantastic and even repulsive. But it is to be expected that in imperfect and undeveloped phases of revelation good and evil, truth and error, should be found lying side by side ; and the searcher after Divine verity who is both qualified and prepared to discriminate between the gold of genuine spirituality and the mythological dross in which it is often to be found embedded, will not allow his judgment to be deflected by the repugnance which he will naturally feel towards the coarse or puerile details which occasionally disfigure the Fall-stories in some of their expanded haggadic versions. Whether or not he admits the validity of the logic which argues from actual sins to innate sinfulness, and from innate sinfulness to a primal fall, he will at least respect the experience which it endeavours to express, and will salute across the centuries the devotion and the penitence of the Maccabean saints, the holy and humble men of heart who waited for the consolation of Israel.

III.

THE FALL-DOCTRINE
IN THE NEW TESTAMENT

The expense of spirit in a waste of shame
Is lust in action; and till action, lust
Is perjured, murderous, bloody, full of blame,
Savage, extreme, rude, cruel, not to trust,
Enjoy'd no sooner but despised straight,
Past reason hunted, and no sooner had
Past reason hated, as a swallowed bait
On purpose laid to make the taker mad;
Mad in pursuit and in possession so;
Had, having, and in quest to have, extreme;
A bliss in proof, and, proved, a very woe;
Before, a joy proposed; behind, a dream,
 All this the world well knows: yet none knows well
 To shun the heaven that leads men to this hell.

       SHAKESPEARE, *Sonnet* CXXIX.

LECTURE III

THE FALL-DOCTRINE IN THE NEW TESTAMENT

I Cor. xv. 22 : 'For as in Adam all die, even so in Christ shall all be made alive.'

OUR last two lectures have been devoted to the task of investigating the origin and defining the content of the ideas which were prevalent within the Jewish Church with regard to the origin of evil, at the moment when Christianity appeared on the stage of human history. These, it will be remembered, were the popular beliefs in ' Original Sin ' and in a ' Fall,' identified at first with the sin of the fallen Watchers, but, in later Judaism, more often with the transgression of Adam—and the Rabbinical, scholastic, or official conceptions of the ' evil imagination ' and of the imputation of Adam's sin to his descendants. We now have to face a grave and momentous question—how did it come to pass that one only of these theories (the popular and pseudepigraphic Adam-theory) was taken over, to the exclusion of the others, by Christianity, and welded so firmly into the dogmatic structure of our religion, that succeeding ages have taken it for granted as one of the central pillars and supports of the Church's Faith ?

THE TEACHING OF JESUS CHRIST

It might naturally be supposed, by one who had never enquired very closely into the question, that the choice of this particular theory to constitute the official Christian explanation of the origin of evil and to provide a logical *prius* for Redemption was made by the supreme and final

authority of Christ.   But it must be said at once that an
examination of our Lord's sayings as recorded in the
Synoptic Gospels reveals no evidence for such a supposition.
It is, of course, true that He assumes the empirical universality of sin as a fact.   Even for those who fail to catch the
sombre undertones pervading all His teaching with regard
to the relations of God and man, this ought to be sufficiently
shown by the fact that His fundamental message, which He
proclaimed at the outset of His public ministry in Galilee,
and on which the rest of His exhortation was based, is to be
found summed up in the solemn cry, re-echoing the words
of the Baptist ' Repent ye, for the kingdom of heaven is at
hand.' [1]   Though this charge was addressed to the people
of Israel alone, yet if interpreted in its context of contemporary ideas it inevitably implies the strict universality of
the need for repentance ; for from the Jewish point of view
' Gentiles ' were *ex hypothesi* sinners. [2]   This universal need
of repentance and forgiveness is most clearly assumed in
the Parable of the Unmerciful Servant, [3] and the petition
for forgiveness included in the Lord's Prayer, and the
saying, preserved by St. Luke alone, with regard to the
Galileans ' whose blood Pilate had mingled with their
sacrifices,' and the eighteen upon whom the tower in Siloam
fell—' Except ye repent, ye shall all likewise perish.' [4]
(The reference to the ' ninety and nine just persons who need
no repentance ' [5] can hardly be other than ironical.)   Three
sayings can indeed be cited (two of which at least are
respectively derived from two of the earliest sources of the
Synoptic Gospels, St. Mark and Q) which appear to take
the further step of assuming, behind the empirical universality of actual sin, some kind of sinful disposition naturally
inherent in the human soul ; these are (*a*) St. Mark vii.

[1] Matt. iv. 17 ; Mark i. 15.
[2] Even St. Paul, twenty years later, can allow himself to use the phrase
' We who are Jews by birth, and not sinners of the Gentiles ' (Gal. ii. 15).
For a lurid description of the hatred and contempt felt by strict Jews
towards all Gentiles as such, see Edersheim, *Life and Times of Jesus the
Messiah* (1901 edn.), i. 90–92.
[3] Matt. xviii. 23–35.   [4] Luke xiii. 2–5.
[5] Luke xv. 7 ; *cf.* Matt. xviii. 12, 13.   This interpretation clearly
applies also to a similar saying, Matt. ix. 13 : ' I came not to call the
righteous, but sinners.'

21, 22 (= St. Matthew xv. 19) : ' For from within, out of
the *heart* of men, evil thoughts proceed, fornications,
thefts, murders . . . all these evil things proceed from
within, and defile the man ' ; (*b*) Matt. vii. 11 (= Luke xi. 13) :
' If ye then, *being evil*, know how to give good gifts unto
your children, how much more shall your Father which is
in heaven give good things to them that ask him ? ' [1] and
(*c*) Matt. xii. 33, 34 : ' Either make the tree good and its
fruit good ; or else make the tree corrupt and its fruit
corrupt : for the tree is known by its fruit. Ye offspring
of vipers, how can ye, *being evil*, speak good things ? for
out of the abundance of *the heart* the mouth speaketh.' [2]
But the affirmations that this evil tendency or quality is
transmitted by physiological heredity, and is ultimately
derived from a primordial transgression—affirmations which
we have seen to be necessary constituents of a ' Fall-
doctrine '—are conspicuous by their absence. If, indeed,
it is possible to connect the ideas underlying these sayings
with current Jewish thought at all, the particular theory
of which they are reminiscent would seem to be that of the
yēçer ha-ra' : for, as we have already seen, the ' heart,'
which in (*a*) and (*c*) is implicitly asserted to be the home of
sinfulness, is again and again described by the Rabbis as
the source of the ' evil imagination ' : and it is possible
that the phrase ' bad ' (or ' evil ') thoughts (διαλογισμοὶ
κακοί Mark ; πονηροί Matt.) in the first of these sayings
may be a direct translation of an original *yēçer ra'*.[3] But
this coincidence of thought and language cannot legitimately
be pressed so far as to yield the further conclusion that our
Lord held the distinctive position of the Rabbinical doctrine,
namely that the ' evil imagination ' is, not inherited, but
separately implanted by the Creator in the heart of each
individual : and such a position would seem to be in sharp

[1] This saying is assigned to Q by such representative authorities as
Harnack, Sir John Hawkins, and Canon Streeter. St. Luke has ' holy
spirit' (πνεῦμα ἅγιον, without the article) for ' good things' in the apodosis
of the sentence.

[2] The Lukan parallel is vi. 43–45, which, however, omits the question
' How can ye, being evil, speak good things ? ' A ' doublet ' of the first
part of this saying (the tree known by its fruits) is found in Matt. vii.
16–19.

[3] In Ecclus. xxvii. 6 LXX διαλογισμός is used to render יֵצֶר.

H

contradiction to the whole tenor of His teaching about God. So far, therefore, as the Synoptic evidence goes, it appears that our Lord never raised the question of the ultimate origin of human sin at all, and never gave any authoritative decision as between the three current theories of ' original sin ' flowing from the fall of the Watchers, of ' original sin ' flowing from the fall of Adam,[1] and of an ' evil imagination ' implanted separately in each individual at birth.[2]

If we turn to the Fourth Gospel, we shall find only two texts which have any relevance to the subject of our enquiry. The less important of these is the passage ix. 2, 3, in which the intention of the Evangelist may be to represent our Lord as condemning the Philonian or Platonic theory of a pre-natal fall of individual souls, with reference to the problem of the man born blind [3] ; it does not, however, contain any positive information as to the real source of evil, physical or moral. The more important passage is iii. 1-21, which gives us the wonderful scene in which our Lord instructs Nicodemus by night—a passage destined, as we shall see, to play an important part in the Pelagian controversy.[4] Here the Saviour is recorded to have taught a ' ruler of the Jews ' that man needs to be ' born anew '— in order to see the kingdom of God, a saying which would certainly seem to imply that his present state, derived from his first or natural birth, is in some way sinful or pre-disposed

[1] It is a significant fact that the only allusion to Adam and Eve (other than the bare mention of Adam in St. Luke's genealogy of Christ) contained in the whole of the Gospels has reference to their original creation as male and female (Mark x. 6 = Matt. xix. 4), not to the ' Fall.'

[2] Some eminent authorities (C. Taylor, *Sayings of the Jewish Fathers*, 1897, p. 128 ; W. C. Allen, *ICC. St. Matthew, in loc.* ; C. G. Montefiore, *The Synoptic Gospels*, ii. 535) discern an allusion to the *yēçer ha-ra'* in the petition ' Deliver us from evil ' which stands in the Matthaean version of the Lord's Prayer, and draw attention to the similar request contained in the Jewish Liturgy ' O lead us not into the power of sin, or of transgression or iniquity, or of temptation : let not the evil inclination have sway over us ' (quoted above, Lecture II, p. 67, n. 1). This suggestion, however, though attractive, seems incapable of positive proof.

[3] It is possible, however, that what is condemned in this passage is the curious Rabbinical belief in the possibility of *foetal* sin, *i.e.* sin committed by the embryo between conception and birth : see J. Lightfoot, *Horae Hebraicae et Talmudicae in Quatuor Evangelistas* (Lipsiae, 1675), p. 1050, for Midrashic and Talmudic instances of this idea.

[4] See Lecture V, p. 378.

to sin ; and the new birth, which is to be mediated through
' water and the Spirit ' would certainly have been understood by the Evangelist's readers, towards the end of the
first century A.D., to be Christian Baptism. If we could
rely upon this passage as reproducing the *ipsissima verba* of
Christ with the accuracy of a modern stenographic report,
we should doubtless be entitled to combine this saying with
the two Synoptic passages mentioned above as implying
a radical evil inherent in the heart of man, and to infer, or
at least to presume, that the linked conceptions of ' original
sin ' and of Baptism as the remedy for it, which we shall
soon encounter in the writings of St. Paul, were already
present, undefined yet unmistakeable, in our Lord's own
teaching as given during His earthly life. But those who
are acquainted with the present stage of scholarly opinion
with regard to the origins and character of the Fourth
Gospel will be aware that the matter is not quite so simple
as it may appear at first sight. It is impossible here to
enter upon an exhaustive discussion of the Johannine
problem ; but the position upon which the greater number
of moderate and reasonable students, both of the ' con-
servative ' and ' liberal ' schools, appears (so far as I can
judge) to be converging may be summarised, and its bearing
upon the point now under discussion briefly indicated.

The Fourth Gospel and the three Johannine Epistles,
it is now coming to be agreed, were written by a great primitive teacher, John of Ephesus, commonly known as the
' Presbyter ' or ' Elder ' whose presence in Asia towards the
end of the first century of our era is attested by Papias
and other writers of the second century.[1] There are still
scholars [2] who are prepared to identify this venerated

---

[1] The necessities of compression will doubtless be accepted as a valid
excuse for what may seem to be the somewhat curt and dogmatic manner
in which the vast and intricate Johannine problem is treated in the text.
The same consideration must also justify the omission of any account
of the enormous mass of literature dealing with the subject ; for this,
the student must be referred to Moffatt, *Introduction to the Literature of
the New Testament* (1911), pp. 515 ff. To the bibliography there given
must now be added Streeter, *The Four Gospels*, Part III, ' The Fourth
Gospel.'

[2] *e.g.* Dom John Chapman, O.S.B., *John the Presbyter* (1911) ; Bishop
Gore, *Belief in Christ* (1922), c. iv.

personage with the Apostle John, brother of James and son
of Zebedee, and with the ' beloved disciple ' mentioned in
the Fourth Gospel itself, and it would be rash to predict
that there will never be a reaction in favour of this view ;
it would seem, however, that those who hold it are at present
in the minority, and that the main body of learned opinion,
whilst rejecting the counsel of despair which assigns this
Gospel to a ' Great Unknown ' of the second century, is
divided between (a) the theory of Delff,[1] which identifies
the Asian John with the ' beloved disciple,' believed to be a
Jerusalemite and a youthful member of the sacerdotal caste,
who, on the occasions of our Lord's visits to the Holy City,
spent as much of his time as he could in the Master's company, but was not one of the Twelve who were permanently
and continuously attached to Him—and (b) that associated
with the name of Weizsäcker, according to which the Asian
John was—not the ' beloved disciple,' but—the pupil or
epigonus of the ' beloved disciple ' (that is, on this hypothesis,
of John the Apostle), from whom he derived the information
which he has worked up in the Gospel.[2]   In any case, however,—whether the Fourth Evangelist was the son of Zebedee,
or the young priestly aristocrat of Delff's theory, or the
disciple of the son of Zebedee—we are justified in claiming
a fairly general consensus of unprejudiced opinion for the
disjunctive proposition that he was *either* an eye-witness
or the direct hearer of an eye-witness.   This proposition, if
accepted, establishes a *prima facie* presumption in favour
of the trustworthiness, broadly understood, of the strictly
narrative elements in the Gospel—a presumption which is
confirmed by their many vivid, human and realistic touches,
and by the fact that in regard to certain questions of detail,
such as that of the date of the Crucifixion, they appear to
be in the right as against the Synoptists.   It must further
be remembered that the Evangelist's fundamental conviction that the Word was in very truth made flesh, and that
the Divine glory was indeed manifested in true humanity

---

[1] *Geschichte des Rabbi Jesus von Nazareth* (1899) : the substance of
this theory has been adopted by Dr. C. F. Burney, *The Aramaic Origin of
the Fourth Gospel* (1922) c. ix.

[2] See Stanton, *The Gospels as Historical Documents* (1920), Part III ;
Streeter, *op. cit.* Part III.

within the bounds of space and time, would inevitably debar him from the conscious invention of fictitious narrative. Unreal incidents would be the poorest of weapons to employ against the Docetic Gnostics who affirmed the unreality of Christ's whole human life.[1] If, therefore, we leave out of account those incidents which, owing to their miraculous character, still tend to divide critical opinion, we may claim to be justified (quite apart from any dogmatic prepossessions, and solely upon the basis of an increasing consensus amongst scholars) in regarding the main historical framework of the Fourth Gospel as embodying good and reliable tradition ; and we need not doubt that the interview with Nicodemus, which is the point of immediate interest for our present enquiry, is not a mere dramatic invention, but a fact of objective history.

This conclusion, however, does not necessarily settle the question, what precisely was *said* on that occasion. Given the ancient conception of history as a branch of letters rather than of science, it follows that the considerable measure of factual solidity which may be attributed to St. John's [2] narrative framework does not of itself guarantee the literal accuracy of the reports of the Lord's sayings contained within that framework : the speeches in Thucydides are well-known instances of the classical custom of placing in the mouths of historic characters, not the exact words which they employed on given occasions, but what they might have been expected to say,[3] or what appeared to the

---

[1] *Cf.* Streeter, *The Four Gospels* (1924), p. 389 : ' The familiar observation, that in John the miracles are " acted parables " is absolutely correct ; only it does not go far enough. To John the whole of the appearance in history of the Word-made-Flesh is an acted parable—including the Death and Resurrection. That being so, it is essential surely to his whole theological position, whether against the Docetic Gnostics, who denied the reality of Christ's human body, or against the passionless Christ of Cerinthus, to affirm that the parable *really was acted out* in the plane of material existence in this world of fact.'

[2] By ' St. John ' I mean here and in the following pages simply ' the Fourth Evangelist,' whoever he may have been.

[3] *Cf.* Thuc. i. 22 : ὅσα μὲν λόγῳ εἶπον ἕκαστοι ἢ μέλλοντες πολεμήσειν ἢ ἐν αὐτῷ ἤδη ὄντες, χαλεπὸν τὴν ἀκρίβειαν αὐτὴν τῶν λεχθέντων διαμνημονεῦσαι ἦν ἐμοί τε ὧν αὐτὸς ἤκουσα καὶ τοῖς ἄλλοθέν ποθεν ἐμοὶ ἀπαγγέλλουσιν· ὣς δ' ἂν ἐδόκουν ἐμοὶ περὶ τῶν αἰεὶ παρόντων τὰ δέοντα μάλιστ' εἰπεῖν, ἐχομένῳ ὅτι ἐγγύτατα τῆς ξυμπάσης γνώμης τῶν ἀληθῶς λεχθέντων, οὕτως εἴρηται. ' As for

historian to embody the general spirit of their ideas and to represent legitimate inferences from and developments of those ideas. Now it is a striking fact that the style of Christ's speeches in the Fourth Gospel is thoroughly homogeneous with the style of the narrative portions of the Gospel, and with that of the First Epistle ; so much at least is therefore clear, that the Evangelist has clothed the ideas of his Master in his own characteristic language. And, when this has been admitted, the further suggestion is inevitably raised, that St. John may have, consciously or unconsciously, blended with the teaching of Christ as he remembered it, or as he received it from his instructor, his own meditations on that teaching. There is, indeed, no reason why he should not have done so consciously ; though a Jew in race and mind, the Fourth Evangelist, as writing for Gentiles and in a Gentile environment, might well have felt himself at liberty to follow the Graeco-Roman custom of reproducing the general spirit and essence of a great philosopher's teaching by means of imaginative discourses freely composed and attributed to him, and to discard the Jewish tradition which must have governed the compilation of Q, that namely which prescribed the preservation of a Rabbi's apothegms as nearly as possible in their original verbal form.

If the words and speeches of Christ contained in the Fourth Gospel be interpreted in accordance with the view just indicated, as a blend of authentic *logia* and Johannine commentary, many difficulties melt away which have long defied solution. I do not know of any other hypothesis

---

the actual words used by individuals at the outset of the war or during its course, it has been difficult to record their exact text, both for me in regard to speeches which I heard myself and for my informants in regard to other speeches ; I have therefore set down *what it seemed to me likely that the individual speakers would have said* in dealing with given emergencies, keeping as closely as possible to the general sense of what was actually said. An even more striking and suggestive instance of the liberty allowed themselves in this regard by ancient writers is to be found in the Dialogues of Plato, who may be said to have been a ' beloved disciple ' of Socrates, and, perhaps for that reason, has not hesitated to place his own developed philosophy in the mouth of his master, without feeling himself fettered by what a modern author would consider the claims of historical veracity.

which adequately explains the fact that—whilst the Synoptists represent the intuition of our Lord's Messiahship and Divine Sonship as dawning very slowly and gradually in the minds of the Twelve, and as not vouchsafed at all to the generality of His hearers (the demoniacs who blurt out the secret of His being are sternly silenced)—the Fourth Gospel ignores this whole perspective and development of the Messianic revelation, and portrays the Incarnate Logos as both publicly claiming, and as being confessed by others, to be Son of God, from the first moment of His ministry. Sometimes, indeed, the two strands which compose the didactic element in the Gospel (the words of Christ, and the Evangelist's commentary on them) are easily distinguishable ; in this very passage, for instance, it seems clear that verses 10–15 are meant to be the Lord's own words, whilst verses 16–21 are a devotional commentary on them, the fruits of a lifetime of devout meditation and ripe spiritual experience. It is evidently in St. John's manner to glide half unconsciously from a report of Christ's sayings into a train of exalted and mystical thoughts suggested by them : and it is, therefore, all the more difficult not to suppose that, in many or all of the speeches, the text of what the Lord actually said, and the commentary supplied by His servant's spiritual experience, have become fused into one indissoluble and indistinguishable mass. It may be added that the proportion borne by the strictly Dominical element in the Johannine discourses to that which must be attributed to the Holy Spirit informing and penetrating St. John's own meditations is not by any means constant ; it seems to vary from point to point of the text, a few passages being almost demonstrably verbal transcripts of *logia* which were actually spoken by the Saviour in the days of His flesh,[1] whilst, at the other end of the scale, great tracts of discourse-matter approximate to the purely ideal utterances ascribed to the Voice of the Master by the author of the *Imitatio Christi*. We have, in short, to

---

[1] John iv. 44 (' a prophet hath no honour in his own country ') ; xii. 25 (' he that loveth his life loseth it ') ; xiii. 20 (' he that receiveth me receiveth him that sent me ') ; xiii. 16 = xv. 20 (' a servant is not greater than his lord ').

recognise that this wonderful book eludes all attempts
to force it into either of the hard categories of ' purely
historical ' or ' purely devotional ' literature, and that no
better description of it has yet been found than the
Alexandrine Clement's phrase ' a spiritual gospel ' (πνευματικὸν
εὐαγγέλιον [1]) ; we must think of it as an embodiment of
the idea which it enshrines in a sentence ascribed to the
Master Himself ' It is the spirit that quickeneth, the flesh
profiteth nothing ; the words that I have spoken unto you
are spirit, and are life.' [2]

In the light of all these considerations, whilst we may
feel reasonably confident that the interview with Nicodemus
actually happened, and that the Redeemer did actually
impress upon His disciple the need for a change of heart so
deep and complete as to deserve the name of a ' new birth,'
we shall not be equally sure that this exhortation was
accompanied by a prediction of the future effects of the
Sacrament of Christian Baptism. We must leave open the
possibility that, in the Evangelist's mind, the developed
sacramental theology of the Christian Church, as it stood
at the end of the first century, may have been as it were
projected backwards, and that the liturgical point of the
saying, which resides in the phrase ' by *water*,' may represent
not so much what the Lord actually said as what the
Evangelist after a lifetime of missionary experience was
convinced that He meant.[3] If this be the true account of
the genesis of this particular passage in its present verbal
form, it would not by any means follow that the Evangelist
was wrong in the interpretation which he has given of the
Saviour's mind. But it would follow that we could not
regard ourselves as entitled in default of further evidence
to use the passage as a proof that our Lord explicitly taught
the correlation of ' Original Sin ' and Baptism, as disease

---

[1] Clem. Al. *ap*. Eus. *H.E.* vi. 14.

[2] vi. 63.

[3] Similarly many scholars would now hold that the other great sacramental passage in the Fourth Gospel, the Discourse on the Bread of Life,
as it now stands in vi. 32–59, represents in the main the Eucharistic experience of the Apostolic Church, though it may well have been built upon
a recollection of historical sayings of the Lord referring to the Messianic
Banquet.

and remedy, during His earthly, not-yet-Risen, and not-yet-Ascended life. It is not, indeed, proved, nor can it, so far as we can see, ever be proved, that our Lord did *not* use the crucial words ' by water ' on this occasion.[1] But so long as the doubt exists whether He did so or not, we cannot legitimately build any conclusion upon them.

It must further be added that, even if we could rely upon the verbal form of this saying with as much confidence as though it were a *logion* preserved by Mark or Q, it would yet be uncertain whether the implied undesirable state of human nature, which is to be done away through baptismal regeneration, is meant to be conceived in terms of the Fall-theory or of the doctrine of the *yēçer ha-ra'*. There is no allusion in the context to the Fall of Adam, and no reference to the question, how man came by the disordered or sinful nature of which he must needs rid himself in order to see the Kingdom of God.[2]

Neither the Fourth Gospel, therefore, nor the Synoptists provide us with any certain proof that the teaching given by our Lord during His earthly life contained the doctrine of the Fall, either in its ' Adamic ' or in any other version. The most that can safely be asserted on the basis of the available evidence is that on two or three occasions He used language which is doubtless compatible with it, but is also equally compatible with the doctrine of the evil *yēçer*. It seems clear that our Lord did not regard it as part of His immediate mission, during the period of His

---

[1] According to Kirsopp Lake, *ERE* ii. p. 384, art. ' Baptism (Early Christian) ' the words ' seem to have been unknown to Justin Martyr ' ; this is presumably based on the fact that they do not occur in his loose quotation of John iii. 3, or 5, in 1 *Apol.* 61, 4. But this contention would prove too much ; for Justin also omits ' by the Spirit,' words which cannot be excised from John iii. 5 without making nonsense of the verse.

[2] It may not be irrelevant to add that no explanation of the *origin* of evil is to be found in any of the documents which form the Johannine *corpus*. It has been suggested that the sharp contrast between τὰ ἄνω and τὰ κάτω, between ' light ' and ' darkness,' which pervades St. John's writings, is the reflection of Philonian dualism ; and that the statement that the devil ' was a murderer from the beginning ' implies the eternity of a personified evil principle. I do not wish to be understood as supporting these contentions ; but the fact they have been brought forward emphasises the absence of a definite Fall-theory from the existing Johannine literature.

public ministry, to decide between the various theories of the origin of evil then current in the Jewish Church.

This, indeed, is not to be wondered at in the light of a true conception of the purpose and method which governed His teaching activity during the two [1] crowded last years of His life on earth. His purpose was to prepare the way for the coming of the Kingdom of God, *firstly* by bringing the members of the ancient Ecclesia, out of which that Kingdom was to be developed, or upon which it was to be divinely superimposed—the two conceptions are complementary and not contradictory—to repentance and moral transformation ; and *secondly*, by the intensive training, in closest contact and association with Himself, of a band of twelve men, reproducing the mystical number of the twelve sons of Jacob who were the eponymous ancestors of the traditional divisions of the Jewish race, to be the princes or satraps of the Kingdom, sitting ' upon twelve thrones, judging the twelve tribes of Israel.' [2] The method of His instruction was therefore two-fold. To the multitudes, on the plain or by the lake-shore, He taught in homely simile or arresting parable, the moral ideals and values which were the completion of the Old Law and the necessary basis of the reign of God in men's hearts. But to the inner circle of the Twelve, the mysteries of the Kingdom—the Messiahship and Divine sonship, the life given as a ransom for many—were more fully unveiled, yet by hint and implication and apparently casual saying, rather than by anything that could be described as systematic theological instruction ; even for the future leaders of the Christian movement, ethical and spiritual discipline was more important, and claimed much more of the scanty time available for their training, than purely intellectual illumination. Of this latter, it is clear that our Lord during His earthly lifetime

---

[1] I have written ' two,' in accordance with the views expressed above as to the general reliability of the historical framework of St. John's Gospel. But the argument which follows is not weakened—it is, rather, strengthened—if we take the Synoptists as our sole authorities, and assume that the public ministry lasted for little more than one year.

[2] Matt. xix. 28 = Luke xxii. 30, beyond doubt a Dominical phrase. For remarks on the literary relationship of these two passages, see Streeter, *Four Gospels*, p. 288.

imparted to His Apostles no more than was absolutely necessary to give a right initial orientation to their thoughts and feelings with regard to His own Person and Work ; with regard to other matters concerning God and the Kingdom (the being of the Holy Spirit, angels, the Law, the Ecclesia, merit and good works, eschatology) He was content to assume or to tolerate the current Pharisaic theology, only occasionally correcting its more materialistic or unintelligent conceptions (as when He repudiated the authority claimed for the Rabbinical *halākhōth*—the ' traditions of the elders ' [1] —or condemned a grossly carnal idea of the resurrection [2]). The fuller elucidation and definition of the significance of His Life and Death, and the complete sifting out of the permanently valuable elements in the Jewish doctrine of His day from the worthless or untrue, were tasks which, it would seem, He deliberately left to be carried out by the Christian Church, when His visible presence should have been removed from the earth. Whether it is to be regarded as paraphrasing a historical *logion* or not, the saying ascribed to Christ by the Fourth Evangelist has admirably caught and expressed the true inwardness of His educative method : ' I have yet many things to say unto you, but ye cannot bear them now : howbeit when he, the Spirit of truth, is come, he shall guide you into all the truth . . . for he shall take of mine, and shall declare it unto you.' [3]

This general conception of the scope and method of our Lord's teaching would seem to justify us in concluding that the silence of the Gospels with regard to the Fall of Adam, and, indeed, with regard to the whole question of the origin of evil, is not merely accidental. If we may without irreverence or presumption endeavour to penetrate the mind of the Master as revealed to us in His recorded words and deeds, we may surmise that the predominantly practical purpose of His instruction, and the shortness of the time during which His teaching activities lasted, would naturally exclude from the subject-matter of His discourses, both public and private, all questions which might appear to be

[1] Matt. xv. 3 ff. = Mark vii. 8 f.
[2] Matt. xxii. 29 ff. = Mark xii. 24 ff. = Luke xx. 34 ff.
[3] John xvi. 12–14.

in the main of merely theoretical and speculative interest, such as the question of the precise way in which sin came into the world.[1] It was enough for Him that sin existed, and was in some sense rooted in the ' heart ' of man ; the abolition of its malevolent power self-evidently was, and still is, a vastly more important task than the philosophic explanation of its origin. He came to call sinners to repentance, and, by insisting that the guilt of the wilfully indulged thought is no less in the sight of God than that of the consummated act, to intensify and deepen the basic spiritual experience out of which, as we have seen, the Fall doctrine had arisen ; but it would seem that He left it to His future Church to decide whether the doctrine was the truest explanation of the experience, or no.

This conclusion is supported by a consideration which can hardly be omitted from a discussion of our Lord's teaching with regard to the source or ground of sin. It is a fact of some interest that—whereas we have only discovered in His recorded sayings some three or four which appear to contain the idea of an evil quality innate in man (and none which imply the Fall-theory proper, as distinct from the doctrine of the *yēçer ha-ra'*)—His discourses, as reported in the four Gospels, embody more than twice that number of expressions of a belief which might well appear *prima facie* to be, and during the sub-apostolic age in point of fact was,[2] an alternative and perhaps even a rival explanation of human sinfulness. This belief, which we have not before had occasion to mention at any length, but which permeated Rabbinical and Apocalyptic Judaism alike, thus forming an integral part of that background of Jewish religious thought presupposed by the words of Christ, is the belief in a host of personal devils attacking the human race with evil solicitations *from without* and obsessing the souls and bodies of individual men.[3] To their malign activities were

---

[1] Another such question, which, so far as we can judge, was entirely ignored by our Lord, is that of the conditions of the intermediate state between death and the Last Judgment—the question to which the Western doctrine of purgatory attempts to give an answer.

[2] See below, Lecture IV, pp. 175, 177.

[3] This aspect of Jewish (and indeed of Christian) demonology, as objectifying, externalising, and (in current psychological terminology)

attributed, not merely the phenomena of demoniacal possession in the restricted sense of the term, but sin and temptation of every kind and even physical diseases, such as deafness, dumbness, and paralysis. From this point of view, the sinful disposition which is antecedent to actual sin is conceived not in medical terms as a disease, but rather in what may be called political terms, as servitude to a tyrant or robber chief; and redemption becomes not so much the restoration of spiritual health as deliverance from an external yoke or bondage.[1]

We are very far from asserting that the beliefs in an interior innate corruption, and in an exterior personified power of evil, are logically irreconcilable or incapable of being simultaneously held by the same person; they were actually held together by the Jews of our Lord's day, with little attempt at harmonisation (though some Rabbinical authorities [2] affirm, in some sense, the identity of Satan and the *yēçer ha-ra'*), and they are still held together by the great mass of orthodox Christians. But it is clear that either belief, if insisted upon as an *exhaustive* account of the genesis of sin, makes the other otiose. Nor is this statement of the logical relations of the two theories, considered in the abstract and merely as theories, affected by the historical fact that the Jewish Fall-doctrine in both of its classical versions presupposes a supernatural tempter or tempters—Satan dwelling in the serpent, or the lustful sons of the *'elōhīm*—as the efficient cause of the assumed primitive catastrophe.

' projecting ' the evil power which makes itself felt in the experience of temptation, is strongly emphasised by the Bishop of Gloucester (*Life and Teaching of Jesus Christ*, 1923, p. 126). ' The belief in a personal evil spirit and a kingdom of evil implies that sin is no part of man's nature. His flesh may be weak, his heart may become full of evil imaginings; but the source of these is outside him. He listens to temptation, but it comes to him. No part of him is necessarily evil, no part need be cast away.' It may be assumed, however, that these words are not meant to imply the incompatibility of a belief in the devil with a belief in original sin : see below, p. 110.

[1] For the distinction between the ' medical ' and the ' forensic ' metaphors as applied to sin, see Lecture II, p. 73 ; and for later and perverse developments of the ' political ' conception of servitude to the devil, see below, p. 292 ff.

[2] See above, Lecture II, p. 67, n. 4.

For in both versions the only necessary function of the evil spirit or spirits is to effect the introduction of the hereditary poison into the human stock ; once introduced, the poison may well be deemed a sufficient explanation of all subsequent actual sins, and no further intervention by the demons appears in principle to be required. It would not in fact be difficult to work out a Fall-theory (assuming liberty to neglect the details of the Genesis-stories) which would dispense altogether with the figure of an external tempter, and find the primal source of sin solely in the free, self-determining will of the first man. We are therefore entitled to describe the hypotheses of ' original sin ' and of a personal devil or devils—in modern terminology, of ' auto-suggestion ' and of diabolical ' hetero-suggestion '—as *alternative*, though not necessarily incompatible or mutually exclusive, explanations of the immediate source of temptation and sin.

It is probably not unfair to suggest that, in the sermons and devotional literature of the present day, the question whether, in a given passage, the sudden thrill of an impulse condemned by conscience is to be accounted for by the hypothesis of an evil thought arising *from within*, spontaneously engendered by man's ' fallen ' nature, or by the hypothesis of an evil suggestion communicated by Satan *from without*, is usually determined by the rhetorical exigencies of the context rather than by any strictly scientific criterion. At any rate, whether for this reason or not, it is the case that in such literature the two explanations occur in fairly equal proportions. In the light of this fact, the apparent preference shown by our Lord for that explanation of the *provenance* of sinful thoughts and impulses which attributes them to the activity of Satan is not without significance. The four Gospels, taken together, give us no fewer than twelve separate sayings of this type,[1] as against

---

[1] The Dominical sayings in question (we are not concerned with *obiter dicta* of the Evangelists themselves, such as those in which St. Luke and St. John ascribe the treachery of Judas to the inspiration of Satan) are the following :

(1) Matt. v. 38 : ' Whatsoever is more than these ' (' Yea' and ' Nay ') is of the Evil One.'

(2) Matt. vi. 13 : ' Deliver us from the Evil One ' in the Lord's Prayer (but see p. 98, n. 2).

the three or four which imply that the seat of evil is within the heart of man. If we read such characteristic *logia* as the following :

> Straightway cometh Satan, and taketh away the word which hath been sown in them.
> The enemy that sowed them [the tares] is the devil.
> Then goeth <the unclean spirit>, and taketh with himself seven other spirits more evil than himself, and they enter in and dwell there, and the last state of that man becometh worse than the first.
> Satan asked to have you, that he might sift you as wheat.
> Ye are of your father the devil, and the lusts of your father it is your will to do.

—simultaneously bearing in mind the total absence from our Lord's discourses of any allusion to the Fall of Adam— and if we assume that, on the whole, the sayings preserved in the Gospels fairly represent not merely the content but

---

(3) Matt. xii. 43–45 = Luke xi. 24–36 : ' When <the unclean spirit> is gone out of the man ' . . . etc.

(4) Mark iv. 15 = Matt. xiii. 19 = Luke viii. 12 : ' Straightway cometh Satan, and taketh away the word which hath been sown in them.'

(5) Matt. xiii. 38–39 ' The enemy that sowed them ' (the tares) ' is the devil.'

(6) Mark viii. 33 = Matt. xvi. 23 (Peter addressed as ' Satan,' a passage which presumably implies the diabolical origin of mean or unworthy thoughts).

(7) Luke xxii. 31 : ' Satan asked to have you, that he might sift you as wheat.'

(8) John viii. 44 : ' Ye are of your father the devil . . .'

(9) John xii. 31,

(10) John xiv. 30, and

(11) John xvi. 11 (Satan described as ' the prince of this world ').

(12) John xvii. 15 : ' I pray not that thou shouldest take them from the world, but that thou shouldest keep them from the Evil One ' (for this translation of ἐκ τοῦ πονηροῦ, see Westcott's note *in loc.*). The five Johannine passages are, of course, quoted not as verbally exact transcripts of individual Dominical *logia* but as generally reliable evidence for the trend of our Lord's teaching in regard to this matter ; see the statement of the position assumed in this section with regard to the Fourth Gospel, *supra*, p. 101 f. The list includes only sayings which trace the origin of *moral* evil to Satan ; if physical evil, such as disease, were also in question, the list could be considerably lengthened. The most impressive testimony to our Lord's use of the Satanic hypothesis as the explanation of evil solicitations does not reach us in the form of a ' saying ' at all ; it is the whole narrative of His own Temptation, which must be derived ultimately from Him.

the balance and proportion of His teaching—it is not unreasonable to suggest that we shall find ourselves confirmed in the conclusion that the Fall-doctrine never received any explicit sanction from the lips of Christ Himself, such as that which He undoubtedly gave to the belief in the existence and activity of demons.

It does not follow in the least that He condemned or rejected the Fall-theory : we are justified in presuming that, if He had disapproved of the possible holding of this doctrine by His followers, He would have denounced it in terms so direct and trenchant that they would inevitably have found a place in the primitive collections of His sayings which underlie our present Gospels.[1] The argument from the silence of the Gospels is double-edged : it can be used as well to show that Christ did not explicitly condemn the doctrines of the Fall and of Original Sin as to show that He did not explicitly approve or promulgate them. But further than this we have no warrant for going. We must for the moment content ourselves with the only conclusion which can safely be based upon the evidence, namely that (to the best of our knowledge) our Lord said nothing either for or against any one of the theories respecting the origin of human sin which in His day prevailed amongst the Jews —save only in so far as a considerable number of His sayings may be taken to sanction the current belief in the existence of personal evil spirits.

THE ' WATCHER ' AND ' ADAM ' STORIES IN THE APOSTOLIC WRITINGS

It would seem, therefore, that the Gospels yield us no information with regard to this interesting question—how

---

[1] Those who do not admit the assumption made here and also towards the end of the last paragraph must in logic renounce any attempt to grasp or to formulate the teaching of the historical Jesus as a coherent whole. But the validity of this assumption is guaranteed for the vast majority of students of the Life of Christ by the overwhelming impression which His recorded teaching produces of an internal harmony and unity so all-pervasive and satisfying that it cannot be attributed to chance or to subsequent redaction.

was it that Christianity became committed to the Adamic version of the Fall-doctrine rather than to any other of the theories then current ? We must, accordingly, turn for light to the Epistles. The facts disclosed by an examination of these documents may be very simply summarised. The sole authority within the New Testament for the Adam-theory is to be found in the writings of St. Paul. The only passages which can be adduced as embodying this doctrine in one or other of its aspects are certain portions of the 5th, 6th, and 7th chapters of the Epistle to the Romans : the exposition of the parallelism between the two Adams, contained in 1 Cor. xv. ; and the brief description of the inbred hostility between ' flesh ' and ' spirit ' in Gal. v.[1] It will be noticed that these Epistles all belong to the group recognised by Baur and the radical critics of Tübingen as ' pillar-Epistles,' so that we may reasonably consider our-selves dispensed from the preliminary task of vindicating their authenticity : and also that they belong to the same period of the Apostle's life, the period of the missionary journeys and the Judaistic controversy, so that we need not expect to find any pronounced development or change of opinion within them, and may assume that they express a single, internally harmonious view. The scope of our immediate enquiry is thus fortunately circumscribed and simplified. But it remains true to say that if we confine our attention to the New Testament, St. Paul, rather than Christ, is the teacher on whose authority these Jewish doctrines have descended to the modern world.

A complete statement, however, of the data on which our judgment must ultimately be based should include the very striking and remarkable fact that, whilst the only

---

[1] The sentence which has often been quoted from Eph. ii. 3 as a ' proof-text ' establishing the doctrine of original sin—' we . . . were by nature children of wrath ' (ἤμεθα τέκνα φύσει ὀργῆς)—is now generally admitted to have no relevance to the matter, and is therefore not mentioned in the text. ' By nature ' (φύσει) means no more than ' in ourselves,' and ' children of wrath ' is a Hebraism meaning ' objects of the Divine wrath.' All, therefore, that the text means is that Jews and Gentiles alike, prior to their acceptance of Christianity, were de facto actual sinners and as such deserving of God's wrath : there is no suggestion of a here-ditarily acquired sinfulness antecedent to actual sin. See J. Armitage Robinson, St. Paul's Epistle to the Ephesians, 1909, pp. 50 and 156.

I

Fall-theory known to the Pauline *corpus* is that based upon the story of Gen. iii., the Catholic Epistles present two clear traces of the influence of the Watcher-legend. The Epistle of St. Jude alludes to the ' angels which kept not their own principality but left their proper habitation ' ; these are described by implication as ' giving themselves over to fornication and going after strange flesh,' for which reason they are declared in the true Enochian vein to be ' kept in everlasting bonds under darkness unto the judgment of the great day.' [1]   And the so-called Second Epistle of Peter, which is generally assigned to the second Christian century, speaks of ' the corruption that is in the world through lust ' [2] —that is, the lust of the fallen angels, who are affirmed, as in the Epistle of Jude, to be ' cast down to hell and committed to pits of darkness to be reserved unto judgment.' [3] It is a striking testimony to the vitality of the older Fall-theory that a recrudescence of it should be found in a document written more than a century after the beginnings of Christian history. To these traces of the Watcher-story in the non-Pauline Epistles we must add the fact that it appears to have inspired St. Paul's celebrated injunction that women are to be covered in the church ' because of the angels,' [4] though his loyalty to the Adam-tradition prevents him from making any use of this earlier theory as the explanation of the ultimate origin of sin.

The situation, therefore, which the Epistles reveal to us as existing within Christianity towards the end of the first generation is this. It is probable that the Watcher-theory, inherited from the Judaism of the second century B.C. through the Book of Enoch and similar works, still lingered in some Jewish-Christian circles. But the Adam-theory, derived from the tradition which expresses itself in Jubilees, 2 Enoch, and Wisdom, must have predominated within Jewish Christianity as within non-Christian Judaism. And it would seem to have been the only Fall-theory known within the borders of Gentile Christendom. This latter conclusion, paradoxically enough, can be shown from the small amount of space which is devoted to the subject— a point which needs a word of elucidation.

[1] *vv.* 6, 7.   [2] 2 Peter i. 4.   [3] 2 Peter ii. 4.   [4] 1 Cor. xi. 10.

Nearly seventy years ago Dr. Jowett, in his Commentary on the Epistle to the Romans, suggested that the small amount of space occupied in the New Testament by the texts implying the doctrine of a hereditary sinfulness flowing from Adam constituted a clear proof of the uncertainty and unimportance of this doctrine.[1] It would seem that in formulating this argument Dr. Jowett was still unconsciously dominated by the old artificial conception of Scripture as a systematic handbook of theology, a magazine of proof-texts, in which the importance of a particular subject can be measured by the amount of space devoted to its consideration. To-day, however, the interpretation of St. Paul's writings is largely governed by an entirely contrary principle, which is based upon the psychology of letter-writing, and cannot be better stated than in the words of Professor Kirsopp Lake :

Treat the Epistles as letters ; and recognise that in letters the subjects discussed are not those on which all parties are agreed but those on which there is a difference of opinion ; so that the really central points [of the Christian Faith, that is] are not those which are supported by arguments but those which are assumed as generally believed.[2]

Apply this principle to the two Epistles in which the Adamic theory is expressly mentioned, Romans and 1 Corinthians, and a clear result emerges. The problems upon which the Apostle lavishes a wealth of laborious dialectic, of glowing eloquence, or of mordant irony—such questions as the value of faith as compared with works, the function and nature of the Mosaic Law, the constitution of the resurrection body —are precisely those upon which Christian thought is not agreed, and in regard to which St. Paul has to wage a

---

[1] *op. cit.* (1855 edn.), p. 162. ' How slender is the foundation in the New Testament for the doctrine of Adam's sin being imputed to his posterity ! ' (but it seems clear that Dr. Jowett is thinking not merely of ' Original Guilt ' but also of ' Original Sin ') ' two passages in St. Paul at most, and these of uncertain interpretation. The little cloud, no bigger than a man's hand, has covered the heavens. To reduce such subjects to their proper proportions we should consider : First, *what space they occupy in Scripture* ' . . . (italics ours), etc.

[2] *Earlier Epistles of St. Paul*, p. 424.

stubborn fight for the triumph of his own view. But behind this array of hotly disputed questions it is easy to discern a solid nucleus of generally accepted ideas, or what St. Paul assumes to be such, which only come to the surface of his thought as it were accidentally, in unpremeditated interjections or passing allusions ; or, if designedly mentioned, are adduced, not as subjects of discussion, but as universally admitted premises to be used for the establishment of further truth. And to this residuum of beliefs which the Apostle assumes to be common ground to himself and his readers, it would appear that the Fall-doctrine belongs, precisely because of the cursory and casual nature of the allusions which are made to it. In neither of these Epistles does St. Paul make any attempt to prove the Adamic theory : on the contrary, he takes it for granted, in parentheses and *obiter dicta*, as though it were a matter about which there was admittedly no dispute, and uses it to support or illustrate some further position—the universality of grace or the logical necessity for a resurrection. Nor is there any reason for supposing that Rome and Corinth were peculiar in this regard amongst the churches of the Gentile-Christian world. In the Roman letter, indeed, the Apostle's quiet assumption of these ideas as indisputable truths is specially impressive in view of the fact that the Roman Christians were not his own converts and (at the time when he wrote to them) had never seen him in the flesh. If, therefore, the exegetical canon formulated by Professor Kirsopp Lake be valid, we are entitled to conclude that the Adamic Fall-doctrine was generally accepted throughout the churches of the Uncircumcision.

It would save us some time and trouble at a later stage in the enquiry [1] if we could accept the principle that what St. Paul takes for granted and does not labour to prove must have been explicitly accepted by the totality of his readers, *au pied de la lettre*. But I must needs think that Professor Lake has, in the passage quoted, phrased the principle rather too absolutely, and that, in an unqualified form, it is as unreliable an instrument of interpretation as the opposite

---

[1] See Lecture IV, p. 177 ff.

maxim which it has superseded, and of which we cited a characteristic expression from Dr. Jowett. As it stands, it ignores the fact that a man of masterful character and intense conviction, such as was St. Paul, is often prone to assume that his hearers, or readers, consciously agree with him, when in point of fact they are merely not prepared to contradict him. It appears to me that Professor Lake's principle must be somewhat modified in the light of this psychological law, and that the utmost which can be safely inferred from St. Paul's confident assumption of the Adam-doctrine is that *no other theory of the origin of evil was in possession of the Gentile-Christian field* at the time when he wrote. It is possible that some Corinthian and Roman Christians, who were by birth Hellenistic Jews or had been ' God-fearers,' may have already been in possession of a belief in the Adamic theory, as the result of a study of Ben-Sirach, or the Book of Wisdom, but that we cannot tell ; it is also possible that many of those who had been converted directly from paganism to Christianity had never given a thought to the question of the ultimate origin of evil at all. The facility with which St. Paul assumes the Adam-theory merely proves that it was self-evident *for him* ; so far as the Gentile-Christian world is concerned, we cannot infer more from his language than that no other theory was a serious rival to it.

It would seem, then, that when St. Paul wrote 1 Cor. and Rom., rather less than thirty years after the death of Christ, the Adamic Fall-doctrine existed *within* the Christian Church. But it can hardly be said as yet to have been universally and consciously accepted *by* the Christian Church as such ; there is some evidence which suggests that its older rival, the Watcher-theory, still lingered in Jewish-Christian circles, and it is possible that many Gentile Christians may, at this early date, never have heard of it. The question as to the effects produced on Christian thought by St. Paul's unhesitating adoption of this doctrine in the two Epistles just mentioned must be reserved for discussion in our next Lecture.[1] There is no trace in the New Testament of the Rabbinical view that the bias towards evil

[1] p. 180 f.

is not inherited, but freshly implanted by God in every individual at birth.[1]

A Suggested Theory regarding the Passage of the Fall-doctrine from Judaism into Christianity

It must be observed, however, that this general and preliminary review of the Epistles has by no means solved, but rather accentuated, the problem of the precise way in which the Fall-doctrine passed over from Judaism into Christianity. In view of the solemnity with which St. Paul assures his Corinthian converts ' I received of the Lord that which I also handed on to you,'[2] the question becomes more insistent than ever, How could the Apostle have taken these doctrines for granted, especially in writing to Christians whom he had never seen, if they had not direct Dominical authority behind them ? It would be a counsel of despair to suggest that Christ must have given instruction, of which no record has survived, on these mysterious subjects during the ' Great Forty Days ' which intervened between His Resurrection and Ascension. We must frankly admit that the process by which the Fall-doctrine, or rather one parti-cular version of it, was inherited by the Christian Church from its Jewish mother is involved in some obscurity, and that we are moving in the realms of speculation ; but, if we bear in mind the fact that Christianity was conceived by its earliest adherents, not as a new religion intended to compete with Judaism, but rather as an *improved form* of Judaism—improved, that is, by the knowledge of the identity of the Messiah and the consciousness of the possession of the Spirit—it will not be difficult to frame a hypothesis which will amply account both for the silence of our Lord and for the confidence of St. Paul in regard to the Adamic doctrine of the origin of human sin.

[1] James i. 13, 14 (' God cannot be tempted with evil, and he himself tempteth no man ; but each man is tempted, when he is drawn away by his own lust [ἐπιθυμία] and enticed ') may represent a Jewish-Christian attempt to retain the general idea of the *yēçer ha-ra'* whilst repudiating the belief that its evil nature is due to God.

[2] 1 Cor. xi. 23 ; *cf.* also 1 Cor. xv. 3.

Such a hypothesis, it seems to me, may reasonably be founded upon the fact that the original birthplace of Christianity, the scene of our Lord's childhood, youth, and early manhood, the principal theatre of His public labours and the home of eleven of His apostles,[1] was Galilee. The remoteness of Galilee from the official centre of Judaism at Jerusalem, and perhaps the genial and smiling aspect of external nature, tended to develop amongst its sturdy peasantry a freer and more imaginative type of piety than that which prevailed in the neighbourhood of the capital, under the shadow of the Temple and the Rabbinical schools, upon the bare, rugged hills of Judaea ; and it is known that the religiously outcast stratum of Jewry, contemptuously described as the *'ām ha-'āreç,* the ' people of the earth,' whose manual avocations debarred them from the full observance of the Law, lay thick amongst the population of this northern province.[2] The assertion sometimes made, that the pseudepigrapha, and the apocalyptic *genre* of thought which they illustrate, were especially popular in Galilee cannot, indeed, be proved, but, in view of the circumstances just mentioned, it would seem to be highly probable ; and Christianity itself must have at first appeared to be, even if in fact it was not, a movement for hastening the eschatological cataclysm which this literature had, with such a wealth of lurid imagery, described. Nothing, therefore, could be more natural than that the rough fishermen and artisans who were the first to follow our Lord should have known and cared little about the learned speculations of the great scholars and divines of Jerusalem with regard to the *yēçer ha-ra'* ; nor is it less natural that, with minds steeped in the apocalyptic literature, they should have carried on into the new movement the ideas about a

[1] Kerioth, the birthplace of Judas, was in the Negeb of Judaea. See Hastings *DB. s.v.* Kerioth.

[2] For a description of the religious state of Galilee in the days of Christ, bringing out the theological and other differences between Galilean and Judaean piety, see A. Edersheim, *Life and Times of Jesus the Messiah* (1901 edn.), i. 223 ff. *Cf.* also E. Schürer, *History of the Jewish People* (E. tr. 1893), ii, 1, pp. 3–5 ; A. C. Headlam, *Life and Teaching of Jesus Christ* (1923), pp. 110 ff., and the works there referred to ; A. Neubauer, *Géographie du Talmud* (1868), pp. 177–233, and Merrill, *Galilee in the Time of Christ* (1885).

primitive catastrophe and a consequent inherited corruption which they had imbibed from Enoch, the Book of Jubilees, or the Testaments of the Twelve Patriarchs. Indeed, it is difficult to see any reason why they should have exchanged these ideas for others, in default of explicit instruction on the subject by the Master Himself. The only assumption, therefore, that need be made in order to obtain a satisfactory explanation of the passage of the Fall-doctrine from Judaism into Christianity is the very simple assumption which, as we have seen, is amply consistent with, if not necessitated by, the evidence of the Gospels— namely, that our Lord abstained from taking any steps to eradicate this belief from the minds of His disciples ; in other words, that He tacitly acquiesced in the continued existence within His movement of the ideas of a ' Fall ' of some kind and of a hereditary corruption derived from it. If this hypothesis be correct—and I do not know of any other which covers all the facts—it would follow that these doctrines are not altogether devoid of Dominical sanction ; they must be deemed to enjoy at least such a measure of approbation as is involved in the fact of deliberate toleration. At any rate we may assume that the Twelve and the Galilean nucleus of the primitive community would continue to take the Fall-conception for granted, because they had no reason for not doing so.

The newly converted Saul would thus find himself introduced into a community of which the leaders were Galileans, and therefore presumably believers in the Fall-theory. What his pre-Christian ideas on the subject of the origin of sin had been it is impossible to tell; he was doubtless familiar with the Rabbinical stories about the disastrous physical consequences of Adam's sin, and he may well have learnt ' at the feet of Gamaliel ' the doctrine of the evil *yēçer*, an idea which, as we shall later see, the Apostle Paul did not altogether discard. But it is reasonable to assume that after his conversion he received some instruction in the essential ideas underlying the Christian movement, whether from Ananias and the Christians of Damascus, or at a later stage from the original Twelve. If, then, he found that the Fall-doctrine was very generally assumed in the society which he had entered, that it was held by those who had known the Lord in the flesh, and that, if not strictly part of the Gospel, it was tacitly assumed as part of the setting of the Gospel, by many or most of those who ' seemed to be pillars,' it would be the most natural thing in the world that he should himself adopt it without question, and use it in at least two of his letters as though it were an axiomatic truth undisputed by any Christian.

The passage of the Fall-doctrine into Christianity may thus be considered to have been provisionally accounted for. But we have still to explain the immensely greater popularity, which ultimately became an exclusive dominance, within the Church of the Adamic theory of the Fall as contrasted with the Angel-theory. It is clear that, as we have said, our Lord gave His followers no guidance whatever on this subject ; even if we suppose, as suggested above, that He consciously permitted a germinal theory of ' original sin ' to pass on into Christianity, it would seem that He left His Church to choose for itself between the two traditional Fall-stories. If we assume that the Epistle of St. Jude really comes from the pen of one of the Lord's ' brethren,' this supposition receives an almost startling confirmation : for the passage which we have already cited (v. 6) (cf. v. 14) would then prove that the inspiration of the Book of Enoch —and strongly suggest that the ' angelic ' theory of the Fall—was accepted within Christ's own family circle, presumably without any protest on His part. But we have seen in Lecture I, that by the beginning of the Christian era the Adam-story had already attained to a position of predominance over its earlier rival, even within the Jewish Church ; and, if any further reason be required at this stage for its later triumph within Christianity, it may plausibly be suggested that the deciding factor was the personal influence of St. Paul himself. We may well believe that the great Apostle's keen spiritual and ethical perceptions were revolted by the unedifying emphasis laid on sexual sin by the Watcher-story, especially as expanded in the Book of Enoch, and that its eventual dispossession in favour of the more austere and elevated Adam-story was not the least of the services which his genius rendered to the Christian Church.

We need not be deterred from attributing the final expulsion of the Watcher-theory from Christianity to the influence of St. Paul by the fact that he makes one, or, if the Pastoral Epistles be reckoned as completely Pauline, two allusions to a theory which is even more liable than the Watcher-story to the objection just mentioned, that is, the theory which exempts Adam from all responsibility for the Fall and finds the source of evil in a physical pollution or *inquinamentum* communicated to Eve by the tempter.   The first and most certainly Pauline of these allusions is that contained in 2 Cor. xi. 2, 3 : ' I am jealous over you with a godly jealousy : for I espoused you to one husband, that I might present you as a pure virgin to Christ.   But I fear lest by any means, as the serpent beguiled Eve in his crafti-ness, your minds should be corrupted from the simplicity and the purity that is toward Christ.'   If these two verses be considered together, the underlying thought is not difficult to discern.   The second is that contained in 1 Tim. ii. 14, in which the author gives as the reason for his objec-tion to women preachers the statement that ' Adam was first formed, then Eve ; and Adam was not beguiled, but the woman being beguiled hath fallen into transgression.' [1] It is noticeable that the word translated ' beguile ' ($\dot{\epsilon}\xi a\pi a\tau \hat{a}\nu$) is the same in both passages, being doubtless used with a certain implied *nuance*, very much like the English word ' seduce.' [2]   Even if, however, we assume that both these passages alike come from the lips of St. Paul, there can be no doubt that nothing is further from his mind than the idea of seriously employing this unpleasant piece of haggadic mythology as the basis of his doctrine of sin : these two allusions to it are of the most cursory nature, conceived in the spirit of Philonic allegorism, and are merely intended to sharpen the literary form of his moral and practical exhortations.

[1] For a full discussion of these passages, see H. St. John Thackeray, *The Relation of St. Paul to Contemporary Jewish Thought*, cc. ii. iii. (pp. 50–57).

[2] The use of this verb was, no doubt, suggested primarily by Gen. iii. 13, LXX—$\dot{o}$ $\ddot{o}\phi\iota\varsigma$ $\dot{\eta}\pi\dot{a}\tau\eta\sigma\dot{\epsilon}\nu$ $\mu\epsilon$, $\kappa a\dot{\iota}$ $\ddot{\epsilon}\phi a\gamma o\nu$. But it is significant that $\dot{a}\pi a\tau \hat{a}\nu$ is twice at least used by LXX as = ' seduce,' in the narrower sense of the term (Exod. xxii. 16 ; Judith xii. 16).

THE PAULINE DOCTRINE. (*a*) THE FALL

The foregoing observations have, it may be hoped, explained—so far as it is possible to explain—the transit of the Fall-doctrine, and particularly of its Adamic form, from the Jewish into the Christian Church. We now approach a second and no less important task, that of examining the classical Pauline passages, with the object of reconstructing in detail what may be called the most primitive systematic presentation of the doctrine within Christianity ; it is doubtless unnecessary to prove at length that the results of this enquiry must, in the nature of the case, have the most vital bearing upon our ultimate definition, of ' that which has been believed everywhere, always, and by all.'

The earliest passage in the Pauline writings which refers to Adam's Fall is 1 Cor. xv. 21, 22 :

21. For since by man came death, by man came also the resurrection of the dead.
22. For as in Adam all die, so also in Christ shall all be made alive.

(The second allusion to Adam which occurs in the same celebrated chapter, *vv.* 45–49, does not refer to his transgression, but only to his ' psychic ' (ψυχικός, which may be roughly translated ' animal ') or ' earthy ' (χοϊκός) nature or constitution—a nature which, it is implied, was given him at his creation,[1] and cannot therefore be regarded as a consequence of the Fall. These latter verses, accordingly, are irrelevant to the subject of our enquiry, and need not be further discussed.)

The two verses 21, 22 quoted above do not raise the question of hereditary sinfulness, and deal solely with the origin of physical death. This is asserted to be a direct consequence of Adam's sin. The phrase ' since by man *came*

---

[1] Verse 45 : ' So also, it is written, The first man Adam became a living soul ' (ἐγένετο . . . εἰς ψυχὴν ζῶσαν, quoted from Gen. ii. 7, LXX). It is worth noting that the almost contemptuous terms in which the Apostle speaks of the first Adam's constitution, as ' earthy ' and merely ' psychic ' or animal, suggest that he cannot have held any exalted doctrine of ' Original Perfection ' or ' Righteousness.'

death ' (v. 21) must refer to some one specific event marking the entry of death into the world, and this event can hardly be anything other than the primal transgression.   And the words ' in Adam ' (v. 22), modelled as they are on the pattern of the great phrase ' in Christ,' [1] which pervades the Pauline writings from the earliest to the latest, cannot mean less than ' by virtue of their organic union or continuity with Adam,' that is, in other words, ' by virtue of their descent from him.'   This passage, therefore, asserts that physical mortality is a universal hereditary consequence of Adam's Fall.   It will, however, be seen at once that this position does not go beyond that of the Wisdom of Solomon (' by the envy of the devil death entered into the world,' ii. 24), a book with which St. Paul may well have been familiar [2] ; it appears to be assumed by the Apostle as by Pseudo-Solomon, that Adam was created, and but for his Fall would have remained, in a condition of immortality.   To ascertain St. Paul's beliefs with regard to the ethical and psychological results of the Fall, we must turn to the Epistle to the Romans, which contains the palmary texts or *loci classici* upon which the whole subsequent development of the Fall-doctrine within Christianity has been founded.

The first and most crucial of these texts is the celebrated passage Rom. v. 12–21, round the interpretation of which controversy has raged continuously, at least from the days of Origen onwards.   In studying these obscure and tangled sentences we must bear in mind the fact that St. Paul is dictating his letter to the Roman Church ; that dictation to a stenographer, although an easy and rapid method of composition, involves the inconvenience of inability to see at a glance what has just been dictated ; and that consequently, in dictated prose, sentences are liable to remain incomplete, subordinate clauses are left hanging in the air with no principal sentence on which to depend, and essential

---

[1] On this phrase see Deissmann, *Die neutestamentliche Formel in Christo Jesu*, Marburg, 1892, and the note in Sanday and Headlam, *ICC.*, *Epistle to the Romans*, on Rom. vi. 11.

[2] *Cf.* the note in Sanday and Headlam, *Romans* (1905 edn.), pp. 267 ff. : ' The relation of St. Paul's argument in chap. ix. to the Book of Wisdom ' ; and above, Lecture I, p. 29, n. 4, for the various dates which have been suggested for the composition of Wisdom.

links of thought are apt to remain in the author's mind and
never to appear on paper at all.   Ordinarily such blemishes
are remedied by a careful revision of the stenographer's
copy ; but the frequent anacolutha and inconcinnities which
abound in St. Paul's letters make it clear that he had no
time for the processes of grammatical, stylistic or logical
polishing, and that he usually contented himself with scrawl-
ing a final personal message, in the large letters which may
have been necessitated by defective eyesight,[1] at the end
of Tertius' manuscript, which was forthwith despatched,
unrevised, to its destination.   In order, therefore, to reconstruct in its fullness the series of ideas lying behind a difficult
passage such as this, our exegesis must be prepared to supply
a certain number of missing members by the judicious use
of conjectural restoration.

It will be convenient to consider the passage in two
divisions (a) vv. 12–14 and (b) vv. 15–21 ; the first of these
may now be given at length.

12. Therefore, as through one man sin entered into the
world, and death through sin ; and so death passed unto all
men, for that all sinned :

13. For until the law sin was in the world : but sin is not
imputed where there is no law.

14. Nevertheless death reigned from Adam unto Moses, even
over them that had not [2] sinned after the likeness of Adam's
transgression, who is a figure of him that was to come.

It is clear from the context that St. Paul, when he began
this section, had no idea of writing a formal dissertation on

---

[1] Cf. Gal. vi. 11 : ἴδετε πηλίκοις ὑμῖν γράμμασιν ἔγραψα τῇ ἐμῇ χειρί.

[2] The argument developed in the text depends upon the retention
of this ' not ' (μή) ; which has the all but unanimous testimony of the
Greek MSS. behind it, and appears in TR., Vulg., WH., and RV.   But
there is some authority for its omission : Prof. Souter's note (in his critical
edition of the Revisers' Greek Testament) runs as follows : μή om. 424* *
al. pauc. 𝕷 (vt.d *) Orig. (Tert. Cypr. Victorin.) codd. uetusti ap. Ambst.,
quos sequitur ipse, codd. plur. ap. Aug., qui omnes uel fere omnes om. etiam
καί.'   It will be noted that, with the exception of Origen, the corrector
of 424, and the text of three other cursives, these authorities are all Latin.
We may appeal with confidence to the maxim difficilior lectio potior in
support of μή, as its omission (by making all who died between Adam and
Moses guilty of actual sin) might easily have been thought by an unintelligent scribe or translator to simplify the passage ; whereas its insertion
into a text which did not contain it would be psychologically inexplicable.

the Fall ; he may indeed have had no definite intention even of touching upon it.   The first eleven verses of c. v. are of a purely practical and hortatory character, designed to impress upon his Roman readers the duty of cultivating in themselves dispositions of hope, interior peace, and confidence in God, and appealing to the immediate consciousness (which he assumes to be possessed by all Christians) of redemption through the atoning Blood of Christ and sanctification by the indwelling Spirit, as the all-sufficient logical ground of these virtues.   It then occurs to him that the parallel between the first and the second Adams, the natural and the spiritual heads of the race, which (as we have just seen) he has already employed in 1 Cor. xv. to establish the congruity of an eschatological resurrection, may at this point be effectively re-used, in order to enhance the glories of Christ's saving work by momentarily opposing to them the sombre consequences of Adam's Fall, and so to deepen in the minds of his readers the sense of Redemption as a solid and reasonable basis for Christian confidence and peace.   He accordingly begins his next sentence (v. 12) ' Therefore, as through one man sin entered into the world, and death through sin,' intending doubtless to supply the words ' so also through one man righteousness came into the world, and through righteousness life,' or some similar phrase, to serve as its principal clause.   Unfortunately, however, for the structure and symmetry of his sentence— though fortunately for our comprehension of his theology of sin—having once raised the question of the connexion between death and sin, he cannot resist the temptation to insert a parenthetic explanation of it into the ' as ' clause ; one idea brings up another by the chain of inevitable association, and the parenthesis expands to such a length that it overpowers the ' as ' clause, and drives the principal sentence for the time being entirely out of his mind.   What had, therefore, been intended merely as a passing allusion to the contrast between the typical acts of Adam and Christ and their respective consequences becomes in effect a short excursus on the subject of the Fall.   For the immediate purpose of our enquiry we may neglect the disordered syntactical structure of these three verses, and treat their contents as a series of detached propositions which, taken together, will reveal to us in its main aspects the doctrinal idea which is in the Apostle's mind.

Examined in this way, the first two affirmations contained in *v.* 12 do not seem to present any difficulty. Sin entered into the world (presumably from some external source, which may be identified with Satan or the serpent of Gen. iii.) through the transgression of Adam. Simultaneously physical death entered into the world as an inseparable concomitant of sin. So far all is plain sailing.

With the third affirmation we begin to get into difficulties. The Apostle continues ' And thus ' (that is, in consequence of the Fall) ' death passed abroad unto all men,' in other words, was distributed or disseminated like a plague amongst all men, ' *because all* sinned ' (ἐφ' ᾧ πάντες ἥμαρτον).[1] These words bring us to the central crux of this difficult passage. In what sense does he mean that all men ' sinned ' ? Does he mean that, when Adam sinned, all men constructively or potentially sinned *in* him, because they were all contained in his loins at the moment when he sinned ? or, that in subsequent centuries all men actually did commit wrongful acts, thereby imitating the first man, although they were in no way obliged or hereditarily inclined to sin ? or is his fundamental thought merely this, that all men were in some vague sense ' sinful,' in virtue of having a tendency to sin within them ? The next verse (13) will throw light on this problem.

The Apostle has just stated, with bald simplicity, that all Adam's descendants ' sinned.' He has no sooner dictated these words than a difficulty occurs to his mind, arising out of one of his own leading ideas, namely, the correlative connexion of ' sin ' and ' law.' He naturally assumes that the essence of ' sin ' lies in the conscious transgression of God's law[2] ; and when (as here) the influences

---

[1] It is sufficient to refer to Sanday and Headlam, *ICC.*, note *in loc.*, for proofs that the phrase ἐφ' ᾧ simply means ' because.' For remarks on Ambrosiaster's misunderstanding of the inaccurate Latin rendering *in quo*, see Lecture IV, p. 308.

[2] *Cf.* Rom. ii. 23, 25 ff. ; vii. 16, 22 ff. ; 1 Tim. i. 8 ff. This assumption is formulated in so many words by the author of the First Johannine Epistle : ἡ ἁμαρτία ἐστὶν ἡ ἀνομία (iii. 4).

of his Jewish ancestry and education are uppermost in his mind, ' God's law ' for him becomes identified with the concrete historical Law promulgated by Moses. The question is therefore inevitably raised ' What about the people who lived *between Adam and Moses* ? '—that is, between the ' Fall ' and the giving of the *Tōrāh*, or—as we might express it in rough figures based upon the Old Testament chronology, which St. Paul, of course, took for granted —between 5000 and 1200 B.C. ' They all died,' he reflects, ' therefore, they must have sinned in *some* sense ' (death and sin being inseparably connected) : ' and yet they cannot have sinned in the *strict* sense of the term—they cannot have sinned in the precise way in which Adam sinned ' (' after the likeness of Adam's transgression ') ' by wilfully breaking a known commandment, because, prior to the publication of the Decalogue, there was *ex hypothesi* no commandment for them to break. No law, no sin. In what sense, therefore, can the post-Adamic but pre-Mosaic generations be said to have " sinned " ? '

To us at the present day the difficulty will doubtless appear entirely unreal, because we do not accept its root-assumption that a person who has never heard of Exodus xx. can have no idea of the moral law [1] : but it is real enough for St. Paul. He is not, however, at a loss for a solution. If we may judge by the general tenor of the verses which follow (15–21), the answer to the problem which shapes itself in the Apostle's mind is, that during the pre-Mosaic period the human race, though incapable of committing ' sin ' in the strict sense of the term, was nevertheless *penetrated and infected by the miasma of a vague and undefined abstract ' sinfulness.'* It would seem, in other words, that he invokes in his own thoughts the conception of ' original sin,' in what the sequel will show to have been a somewhat nebulous form, in order to explain the universal domination of death at an epoch when, according to the Jewish view of the Decalogue as the sole embodiment of the moral law,

---

[1] A similar puzzle with regard to the good deeds of virtuous Gentiles, based upon the assumption that Gentiles as ἄνομοι, *i.e.* ignorant of the *Tōrāh*, must be *ipso facto* non-moral and incapable of meritorious action, is discussed in c. ii. 12–15.

' actual sin ' did not and could not exist. ' Until the Law
sin (= " original sin ") was in the world ' ; that is, the soul
of man is conceived, as having suffered, before the giving
of the *Tôrāh*, from a kind of ' suppressed sinfulness,' much
as his body may suffer from a latent fever or imposthume.
This conception, however, remains for the time being in
the Apostle's mind, and only reveals itself by degrees in the
following section (*vv.* 15–21). At the moment, it occurs to
him that he is in danger of being drawn into the quagmire
of an interminable discussion as to whether ' sin ' which is
merely an unconscious state really is sin or not ; and he
consequently extricates himself from this perilous ground
as rapidly as possible. He hastily drops the whole problem
of the moral condition of pre-Mosaic mankind, leaving the
complicated string of clauses which he has begun in *v.* 12 as
a hopeless anacoluthon, and reverts to the main thought
from which he has been drawn aside by these subtle speculations, so that (in the course of *vv.* 15–19) the ' as ' clause
which begins *v.* 12 receives in substance, though not in form,
the principal sentence with which he has forgotten to provide
it. The abruptness of the transition, and the mutilated
shape of the argument contained in *vv.* 12–14, leading up
as it does to a conclusion which is not spoken, but only
formulated in thought, will be graphically represented if we
employ the modern typographical device of inserting a row
of dots between the end of *v.* 14 and the beginning of *v.* 15.
' Death reigned from Adam unto Moses, even over them that
had not sinned after the likeness of Adam's transgression,
who is a figure of him that was to come. . . . But not as
the trespass,' etc. If we assume that in the parenthesis
which begins with *v.* 13 St. Paul is not really arguing with
anyone in particular, but only thinking aloud, it will be
easy to see that the dots stand for an unspoken thought,
which may be formulated as follows :

' The solution, of course, lies in the fact that though the
pre-Mosaic generations could not commit sinful *acts*, they
were hereditarily constituted in a sinful *state*. But the
question how a mere " state," acquired by birth and not
by the individual's personal act, can be " sinful," is too
abstruse to be discussed now : I will therefore return to the

K

point from which I started, the parallelism between the first Adam and the last.'

This parallelism is now expounded in a series of comparisons and contrasts, the verbal expression of which, however, is compressed by the seething uprush of the Apostle's thought into a highly elliptical form which does not conduce to lucidity. It will be, once more, well to give the passage at length : I will, however, at this point desert the English Revised Version, and print a somewhat paraphrastic version of my own, in order to minimise its obscurity and render detailed commentary as far as possible unnecessary :

15. But the bounty procured by Christ's atonement is not in all points analogous to the sorrowful legacy of Adam's transgression. By the transgression of the one Adam mankind in its myriads died ; but the kindness [1] of God, and the gift won by the kindness of the one Man, Jesus Messiah, have redounded to the welfare of mankind in its myriads [2] in infinitely greater measure.

16. And the boon of salvation is not exactly parallel to the disastrous achievement of the one individual who sinned ; for God's Judgment began from the one (Adam) and ended in (universal) condemnation, whilst His free gift began with the myriad offences which called it forth, and has ended in (potentially universal) acquittal.

17. It is true that by the transgression of the one individual death became king of mankind, through the instrumentality of that one individual ; but much more shall they who are receiving the abundance of God's kindness and of His gift of righteousness reign as kings in life eternal through the one Man Jesus Messiah.

18. So then, as the first process, that of the propagation of sin, began from one transgression, infected all men, and involved them in universal condemnation, in like manner the second process, that of salvation, began from one verdict of acquittal, is designed to diffuse its beneficent operations amongst all men, and leads to God's acquittal, which brings life.

---

[1] Gr. χάρις : on this word, usually translated ' grace,' see below, p. 138, n. 1.

[2] Gr. οἱ πολλοί, ' the many,' that is, the human race considered in its multiplicity. The AV. rendering ' many ' (without ' the ') is a mistranslation, which has been abused to support the Calvinistic doctrine of ' particular redemption.'

19. For as through the disobedience of the one man the myriads of mankind were constituted (κατεστάθησαν) sinners, so also through the obedience of that other One Man the myriads of mankind shall be constituted righteous.

20. And Law came into the process of human history as an afterthought, in order that the transgression might be multiplied ; but where sin was multiplied, God's kindness superabounded,

21. In order that, as sin reigned in a world penetrated by death, so also the Divine favour might reign by means of righteousness, leading men on to life eternal, through Jesus Messiah our Lord.

We need not follow this complicated passage through all the changes which it rings upon the phrases ' the one ' and ' the many,' now comparing and now contrasting ' the one man,' Adam, and ' the many ' who were injured by his fault, ' the one man ' Jesus Messiah, and ' the many ' who reap the benefits of His Atonement. A broad general view of it is enough to show that here, at last, we have in fully developed shape, albeit stated without any scholastic preciseness of definition, that momentous doctrine of the Fall and the Redemption as correlative conceptions, as twin pillars bearing up the fabric of Christian soteriology, which we saw in Lecture I to be distinctive of the orthodox or traditional presentation of our religion. It is clear that the transgression of Adam is conceived as standing in a *causal* relation to the subsequent death, sin, and condemnation of his descendants—nothing less than this can be meant by the word κατεστάθησαν (' were constituted ') in *v.* 19— though the exact nature of the link between this primal cause and its multitudinous effects is not expressly indicated. But we have already gathered from our consideration of 1 Cor. xv. 22, which may be regarded as a preliminary sketch or *Vorstudie* for this extended exposition of the idea of the two Adams, that St. Paul believed physical mortality to be a hereditary consequence of the first Adam's fault ; if, then, death and sin are inseparable associates (as is implied all through *vv.* 12–14), the Apostle must have held that sin also—in the vague sense of inherent sinfulness or propensity towards evil—is hereditarily transmitted.

This conclusion is confirmed by the fact that the last

two verses of this chapter (20, 21) are most easily explicable in accordance with the hypothesis adumbrated above, in connexion with *vv.* 12–14—namely, that the conception which is struggling for expression in St. Paul's mind is that of a hereditary disease, somehow introduced into the human stock by Adam's sin, existing in a suppressed form in the pre-Mosiac generations, but since the promulgation of the Decalogue manifesting itself in a perpetual irritation and stimulus towards wrong-doing. For, we are told in a brilliant and audacious paradox, the Law came in as an 'episode,' an afterthought, a temporary expedient which would not have been needed had there been no Fall, in order that the transgression might abound (*v.* 20) ; in other words, the Ten Commandments were given precisely in order that they might be broken as much and as often as possible. And this multiplication of actual sins was divinely ordained in order that God's kindness might abound, that is to say, in order that God might be moved to bestow upon mankind the gift of redemption and the reign of divine kindness through Jesus Messiah our Lord.

Whatever may be thought of this attempt to describe in human language the providential processes of the Mind of God, the doctrine of Man and of sin which underlies the whole passage *vv.* 12–21 should now be sufficiently clear. Man derived from Adam—we have been constrained to conclude, by physical heredity—the poison of suppressed sinfulness, which during four millenniums or thereabouts was unable to find its natural outlet in law-breaking, because there was no law to break. The Mosaic Law was then applied to mankind, as a sort of sharp, stinging fomentation, designed to bring this innate but suppressed poison up to the surface of the individual consciousness, so that it might discharge itself in the shape of actual sins. Sin, having been thus externalised and concretised, could then be dealt with by God on forensic lines, by means of a judicial atonement and acquittal. It would seem that at this point St. Paul assumes that ' innate sinfulness ' is a thing too vague, subtle, and elusive for God to treat directly : He needs a tangible subject-matter, in the shape of Actual Sin, before He can set His restorative processes in motion.

This curious assumption is, however, clearly bound up with the common Jewish idea that the moral law was uniquely and exclusively embodied in the Decalogue ; we need not, therefore, devote further consideration to it now. It will be sufficient for the purposes of our historical enquiry if it has been shown that the language of this crucial passage explicitly asserts the existence of a causal relation between Adam's sin and subsequent sin and death, and that the Apostle's language is most easily explicable on the supposition that there underlies it a half-thought-out idea of a hereditary spiritual disease, of an unconscious suppressed sinfulness, which when stimulated by the external impact of the Law, with its blunt, uncompromising series of commands and prohibitions, naturally wells up into the field of conscious volition.

It should be added that there is nothing in this passage which implies that ' suppressed sinfulness ' actually involves *guilt* in the sight of God, previously to and independently of the commission of actual sin ; and, indeed, the phrase in *v.* 13, ' sin is not imputed where there is no law ' [1] (ἁμαρτία δὲ οὐκ ἐλλογεῖται μὴ ὄντος νόμου), would seem to deny by anticipation the later Augustinian conception of ' original guilt,' at any rate in the case of the pre-Mosaic men. If we may judge by his general *usus loquendi*, St. Paul shares the opinions of the ' plain man ' on this point. The word ' guilt,' with the whole apparatus of forensic terminology to which it belongs, ' judgment ' (κρίμα), ' condemnation ' (κατάκριμα), ' acquittal ' (δικαίωσις), and the like, is only applicable to voluntary and responsible actions, that is, to actual sins : the ' inherited tendency to sin,' or ' original sin,' so called—if a fact—must be conceived as a disease, and medical terminology alone is appropriate in speaking of it. Neither here nor elsewhere does the Apostle make any attempt to explain how it is that a state for which we are not responsible manifests itself in acts for which we are, or why a guiltless malady should issue in symptoms to which guilt attaches—problems

---

[1] These words might be paraphrased thus : ' " Original " sin by itself, which has not expressed itself in the breach of a known commandment, is not considered by God to be sin in the true sense of the term.'

which have baffled the philosophers, theologians, alienists, and penologists of all ages.

THE PAULINE DOCTRINE.

(b) 'INHERITED SINFULNESS' AND BAPTISM

The process of unravelling St. Paul's profoundest thought is necessarily difficult, and may, I fear, have been in the present instance somewhat tedious, to follow in detail. It will, therefore, be appropriate, before we turn to the consideration of a second and hardly less important division of the Apostle's 'anthropology,'[1] namely, his teaching with regard to the nature and seat of 'inherited sinfulness,' to conform to the actual order of the Epistle to the Romans, and devote a few words to a more practical and more easily comprehensible aspect, or corollary, of the Pauline doctrine of Man and of Sin—that is, its conception of baptism.

In the light of certain ideas which are familiar to us from the teaching of the Prayer Book offices and the Catechism, it is at least interesting to find that the discussion of the universal and hereditary 'sinfulness' of mankind (v. 12–21) is immediately followed by a deeply mystical passage (vi. 1–11) in which the dominant thought is that of the saving effects of Baptism. We are at once reminded of the Nicodemus-scene in the Fourth Gospel (iii. 1–15) in which the words of Christ, as recorded by St. John, seem to speak of Baptism as the remedy for some implied and undefined defect inherent in human nature.[2] As we have already seen, the modern critical study of St. John's literary methods makes it difficult to be sure that our Lord Himself did actually point the sacramental moral of His exhortation as explicitly as the narrative represents ; but in the passage about to be discussed we have the *ipsissima verba* of the Apostle of the Gentiles, fixed and preserved for all time by Tertius' shorthand as they fell from his very lips. I cannot

---

[1] It need hardly be said that this term is here used in its theological, not in its modern scientific sense.

[2] See above, p. 98 ff.

doubt that the key to the interpretation of vi. 1–11 is given us in the words of Professor Kirsopp Lake :

> Baptism is for St. Paul and his readers universally and un-questioningly accepted as a mystery or sacrament which works *ex opere operato* ; and from the unhesitating manner in which St. Paul uses this fact as a basis for argument, as if it were a point on which Christian teaching did not vary, it would seem as though this sacramental teaching is central in the primitive Christianity to which the Roman Empire began to be converted.[1]

Given this hypothesis, which illuminates the relevant passages [2] of the Pauline writings as no other does or can do, and which can only be refuted on the basis of *a priori* assumptions as to what the Apostle ought to have believed —the articulation and sequence of St. Paul's ideas about Sin and its remedy stand out with photographic clearness. Mankind inherited physical mortality and ' suppressed sin-fulness ' from Adam, who himself acquired them by his Fall. The promulgation of a Law which man had not the strength to obey stimulated this subconscious sinfulness to pullulate in a multitude of actual sins. In due season, whilst we were yet (actual) sinners, Christ died on behalf of the ungodly. Thenceforward, ' Faith,' that is, unreserved mental, moral, and emotional self-surrender to Jesus as risen, Messiah, and Lord, procures for the believing soul ' justification,' or judicial acquittal from the burden of actual offences : and Baptism, which is the indispensable external expression and crowning moment of the act of Faith, mystically unites the neophyte to the Saviour, in whose death and resurrection, viewed *sub specie aeternitatis* as timeless facts, he sacramentally participates, and through the infusion of whose divine life he wins, as it would seem, the complete and final cure of the inherited disease of ' suppressed sinfulness.' [3] Faith, in short, brings ' release

---

[1] *Earlier Epistles of St. Paul*, 1911, p. 385. Professor H. A. A. Kennedy's attempt to disprove this hypothesis (*St. Paul and the Mystery Religions*, 1913, pp. 232 ff.) seems to me quite unconvincing ; I may, perhaps, be permitted to refer to my observations on ' The Origins of the Sacraments,' in *Essays Catholic and Critical* (1926), p. 389, n. 7.

[2] Gal. iii. 27 ; 1 Cor. vi. 11 ; x. 1, 2 ; xii. 13 ; Col. ii. 12 ; Eph. iv. 5.

[3] This idea—natural enough in the Church's enthusiastic infancy— that the regenerated Christian is from the moment of his baptism onwards strictly *incapable* of sinning—reappears in 1 John iii. 9 : ' whosoever is

from sin' in the 'forensic,' and Baptism in the 'medical,' sense, of these words.

Know ye not that all we who were baptised into Messiah Jesus were baptised into His death ? So then we were buried together with Him through our baptism so as to share in His death. . . . For if we became incorporate with the likeness of His death, surely also we shall be incorporate with the likeness of His resurrection ; knowing this, that our old man was cruci-fied together with Him in order that the body of sin [*i.e.* the physical nature of man in which, as we shall see, this hereditary disease of sin inheres] might be annulled or abolished, so that we should no longer be the slaves of sin.[1]

There can, I venture to think, be no reasonable doubt as to the meaning of these words. Baptism is assumed by St. Paul to be a cathartic and therapeutic rite, the logical parallelism of which with some observances of the Greek and Oriental mysteries he would not have repudiated,[2] which unites the sick soul to the strong and stainless Redeemer-God, conferring upon it, through a mystical death and resurrection, the heavenly gifts of healing, purity, and inward peace.

It is one of the inevitable inconsistencies to which pioneers in any sphere of thought are liable, that this description of baptism as the infallible medicine which heals the disease of sinfulness and 'annuls' the 'body of sin' should occur in a context which is devoted to imploring the Roman Christians to abstain from sin. It might well have

---

begotten of God doeth no sin, because His seed abideth in him ; and he *cannot* sin (οὐ δύναται ἁμαρτάνειν), because he is begotten of God ' ; *cf.* also *v.* 18.

[1] Extracts from vi. 2–6, freely translated. The original Greek is appended : ἢ ἀγνοεῖτε ὅτι ὅσοι ἐβαπτίσθημεν εἰς χριστὸν Ἰησοῦν, εἰς τὸν θάνατον αὐτοῦ ἐβαπτίσθημεν ; συνετάφημεν οὖν αὐτῷ διὰ τοῦ βαπτίσματος εἰς τὸν θάνατον . . . εἰ γὰρ σύμφυτοι γεγόναμεν τῷ ὁμοιώματι τοῦ θανάτου αὐτοῦ, ἀλλὰ καὶ τῆς ἀναστάσεως ἐσόμεθα· τοῦτο γινώσκοντες, ὅτι ὁ παλαιὸς ἡμῶν ἄνθρωπος συνεσταυρώθη, ἵνα καταργηθῇ τὸ σῶμα τῆς ἁμαρτίας, τοῦ μηκέτι δουλεύειν ἡμᾶς τῇ ἁμαρτίᾳ. The depth of St. Paul's belief in the absolute efficacy of baptism is shown by the fact that Col. ii. 11 re-echoes the thought of this passage, affirming the 'putting off of the body of the flesh' to be a result of Christian initiation, which is again described as being ' buried with him in baptism.'

[2] I do not, of course, mean to imply that St. Paul's ideas with regard to the Sacraments were *derived from* the Mysteries ; see above, p. 135, n. 1.

been asked by an external critic of the first century A.D.
' If the rite of Baptism has this immediate and all-sufficient
effect in annihilating the power of innate sinfulness, why
should it be necessary to urge baptised Christians to maintain a high standard of moral life ? How is it possible to
reconcile the liability to backsliding which these exhortations presuppose with the permanent and irrevocable effect
which Baptism is assumed to produce ? ' The answer, of
course, is that it is not really possible, and that St. Paul at
this early date had not fully thought out the implications
of the fact of post-baptismal sin, which he is curiously loth
to face. The logical difficulty in which he finds himself
involved in exhorting people to refrain from sin who, on his
own hypothesis, were incapable of committing it, was in
a later age solved in theory by admitting that baptism did
not destroy ' concupiscence ' [1] ; and the practical difficulties
which arose in connexion with the treatment of Christians
who had sinned after baptism gave birth to the sacrament
of penance, at first available only once in a lifetime for the
post-baptismal offender, and then only to deal with one
or more of the three capital sins, homicide, impurity, and
apostasy, later expanding and ramifying so as to cover
every type of sin and to be available as often as required.[2]
When the Apostle wrote, however, these developments still
lay in the future (the occasions on which he administered
penitential discipline at Ephesus [3] and Corinth [4] would
appear to him as purely exceptional events, which were not
likely to recur before the Parousia) : and he has therefore
to content himself with the position ' You cannot, and
therefore you ought not to, commit sin '—a reversed and

---

[1] *Cf.* Article IX, ' this infection of nature doth remain, yea in them
that are regenerated,' etc. ; *conc. Trident.* Sess. V. 5 : ' manere autem
in baptizatis concupiscentiam vel fomitem, haec sancta synodus fatetur
et sentit,' etc. (the whole passage is quoted below, Additional Note F,
' Formularies,' p. 539).

[2] For the details of this development, see O. D. Watkins, *History of
Penance* (1920). A convenient summary of the development of Penance
up to A.D. 400 may be found in Haslehurst, *Penitential Discipline in the
Early Church* (1921).

[3] Acts xix. 18 : πολλοί τε τῶν πεπιστευκότων (*i.e.* of the baptised
Christians) ἤρχοντο ἐξομολογούμενοι καὶ ἀναγγέλλοντες τὰς πράξεις αὐτῶν (presumably with a view to receiving some sort of absolution).

[4] I Cor. v. 3, 5 ; 2 Cor. ii. 6 ff.

negative form of the Kantian dictum ' I ought, therefore
I can,' which the most superficial analysis will show to be
a patent self-contradiction. The fact is, that he is on the
verge of raising, though he does not actually raise, a philosophic problem which is implicit in the idea of Original
Sin and of sacramental grace as the remedy for it, namely
this : ' Is it possible for there to be a presentation of the
Fall-doctrine which will be sufficiently *deterministic*—which
will lay sufficient emphasis on man's hereditary weakness—
to establish the need for " grace," in the technical theological
sense,[1] and for sacraments ; but will also be sufficiently
libertarian to preserve the idea of man's freedom and moral
responsibility ? ' But, interesting and important as this
question is in its bearings upon modern religious life and
thought, considerations of time compel us to defer its
examination to the constructive part of this course, and to
resume the thread of our main task, that of studying the
Apostle's conception of the state of human nature which
in his view made baptism and all other elements in the
redemptive process necessary.

The Pauline Doctrine.

(c) ' Inherited Sinfulness,' its Nature and Seat

We have seen that St. Paul assumes the existence of a
vague hereditary sinfulness, transmitted by Adam to his
posterity, as the presupposition of Actual Sin and consequently of Redemption ; and we have now to examine
more narrowly his conception of this inherited infirmity or
taint. It is probable that we shall gain most light on this
point if we begin by investigating the question of the *seat*

---

[1] That is, *gratia sanctificans*, which in the common usage of Western
theology denotes positive Divine assistance given *ab extra* to the struggling
soul ; this is a different idea from that conveyed by the term χάρις as
used by St. Paul, which means the sentiment of ' favour ' or ' loving-
kindness '—' graciousness ' rather than ' grace '—with which God regards
His creatures. No doubt the practical consequence of God's attitude of
χάρις is His bestowal of *gratia sanctificans* ; but much confusion has been
caused by the failure to realise that what St. Paul means by χάρις is not
precisely the same as what St. Augustine means by *gratia*.

of the congenital malady, that is, of the precise ' part ' ¹ of human nature in which it resides and through which it is transmitted. A careful study of cc. vi. and vii. of the Epistle to the Romans will leave us in no doubt as to St. Paul's view of the matter. The seat of hereditary sinfulness is ' the flesh,' that is, the strictly physical or animal nature of man. It is well known that the Apostle's theory of human nature is trichotomous, dividing the domain of personality into three clearly cut areas, namely (a) the ' flesh ' or the ' body,' (b) the ' soul ' (ψυχή), the principle of organic life which we share with the animals, a concept which is the practical equivalent of Aristotle's ' vegetative soul,' ² and (c) the ' spirit ' (πνεῦμα) which includes the highest intellectual, moral, and religious faculties.³ And what distinguishes St. Paul's ideas with regard to the subject of innate sinfulness from those of the other thinkers whom we have noticed up to this point, is the fact that he confines the seat of the inbred evil rigidly to the ' flesh,' apparently exempting the ' soul ' and the ' spirit ' from any sort of inherent taint, and only conceding that they may be polluted as it were *per accidens*, by the maleficent influences arising out of their physical substratum.⁴ So we find that the effect of union with Christ in baptism is to ' annul,' to ' bring to nought,' the ' sinful body ' ⁵ (vi. 6)—in plainer language, to paralyse, or rather to annihilate, sinful impulses assumed to be rooted in the body. More explicitly, the hidden sources of sin are described as ' the sinful passions which come through the Law ' ⁶ (vii. 5)—in other words, the evil impulses stimulated into life, in a way which will

¹ An apology is doubtless due for the use of this word ; but it will be remembered that we are investigating ancient, not modern, psychology.

² Cf. *Eth. Nic.* I. vii, 12 : *de anima* 413 b 7.

³ See arts. ' Soul,' ' Spirit,' by J. Laidlaw, *HDB* ; and *cf.* R. H. Charles, *Eschatology, Hebrew, Jewish, and Christian* (1899), pp. 409–15, for an elaborate, if occasionally arbitrary, analysis of St. Paul's trichotomous psychology.

⁴ The perversion of the intellect by sensuality is the last stage of moral degradation ; the final punishment of the vicious Gentiles is to be abandoned by God εἰς ἀδόκιμον νοῦν (Rom. i. 28), and, conversely, the ' renewal of the intellect ' (ἀνακαίνωσις τοῦ νόος) is the final stage of post-baptismal sanctification (Rom. xii. 2).

⁵ τὸ σῶμα τῆς ἁμαρτίας.

⁶ τὰ παθήματα τῶν ἁμαρτιῶν τὰ διὰ τοῦ νόμου.

be presently explained, by the prohibitions and threatenings of the Law ; and these are said, with reference to the unregenerate state in which both the Apostle and his readers once lived, to have been ' active in our members.' [1] As inherent sinfulness is thus connected with passion and impulse, it would seem that he would have spoken more accurately if he had affirmed the innate source of sin to lie in the ψυχή or ' vegetal soul ' ; we must, however, take his language as we find it ; and his apparent determination to saddle ' the body,' or ' the flesh,' with the sole responsibility for being the home of sin, by its *prima facie* inconsistency with his own trichotomous theory of human nature,[2] may well suggest that it is prompted by some unconscious psychological cause, lying deep in his personal idiosyncrasy, rather than by considerations of the strictly logical order.

The Pauline theory, if such it may be called, regarding the nature and seat of ' innate sinfulness,' and regarding the psychological *rationale* of its externalisation in the shape of actual sins, under the stimulus of acquaintance with the Law, may be studied at length in vii. 7–25 ; in what appears from the directness and poignancy of its language (it is difficult to believe that its use of the first person singular is a mere literary device) to be a sketch of the Apostle's own moral autobiography, a miniature analogue of the *Confessions* of St. Augustine. The passage deserves

---

[1] ἐνηργεῖτο ἐν τοῖς μέλεσιν ἡμῶν.

[2] The sharp contrast between ' flesh ' and ' spirit ' discussed later in the text seems to insist on a dichotomy rather than a trichotomy. According to W. Bousset (*Religion des Judentums im NTlichen Zeitalter*, 1903, p. 381) the Jewish psychology of St. Paul's day treated the terms ' spirit ' and ' soul ' as identical in meaning, thereby diverging from Old Testament usage, which had recognised a subtle difference of connotation between them, the former emphasising the element of Divine force which permeates and sustains all organic being, the latter laying stress on the separate psychic life of the individual organism (H. Schultz, *ATliche Theologie*[5], 1896, p. 492 ff.). St. Paul's normal use of the terms seems to accord with the practice of the Old Testament writers ; he distinguishes sharply between τὸ πνεῦμα and ἡ ψυχή in 1 Thess. v. 23. But in writing the passages discussed above he may well have felt the dichotomous *usus loquendi* of his Rabbinical instructors to have been better adapted to the clear exposition of the point at issue than the trichotomous category which is more characteristic of his own thought. See, however, R. H. Charles, *op. cit.*, pp. 412–13.

to be quoted at length, both because of its intense human interest and because of the light shed by it upon the difficult conceptions with which we are dealing.

What shall we say then ? Is the Law sin ? God forbid. Howbeit, I had not known sin except through the Law. For I had not known desire, except the Law had said 'Thou shalt not desire[1] (wrongfully).' But Sin, finding an occasion (or, starting-point), wrought in me through the Commandment all manner of (wrongful) desire ; for apart from the Law Sin is dead. Now I was alive apart from the Law once : but, when the Commandment came, Sin revived, and I died. And the Commandment, which was unto life (*i.e.* meant by God to promote my true life), this I found to be unto death : For Sin, finding its occasion (or starting-point) through the Commandment, beguiled me, and through it slew me. So that the Law is holy, and the Commandment holy, and righteous, and good. Did then that which is good become death unto me ? God forbid. On the contrary, Sin, that it might be shewn to *be* Sin, by working death to me through that which is good . . . that through the Commandment Sin might prove to be superlatively sinful . . . (an unfinished sentence). For we know that the Law is spiritual : but I am a *being of flesh* [2] sold under the power of Sin. But that which I do I know not : for, not what I would, that do I practise ; but what I hate, that I do. But if what I would not, that I do, I consent unto the Law that it is good. So now it is no more I that do it, but Sin which dwelleth in me. For I know that in me—*that is, in my flesh*—dwelleth no good thing : for to will is present with me, but to do that which is good is not. For the good which I would I do not : but the evil which I would not, that I practise. But if, what I would not, that I do—it is no more I that do it, but Sin which dwelleth in me. I find then the law,[3] that to me, who would do good, evil is present. For I delight in the Law of God after the inward man (or, so far as my inner self is concerned) : But I see a different Law *in my members*, warring against the Law recognised by my intellect, and bringing me into captivity under the Law of Sin which is *in my members*. O wretched man that I am ! who shall deliver me out of *the body* of this death ? . . . I thank God through

---

[1] οὐκ ἐπιθυμήσεις—the first words of the Tenth Commandment as given in Exodus xx. 17 (LXX).

[2] σάρκινος : this word merely means 'made of flesh,' and should be carefully distinguished from σαρκικός, 'carnal' in the bad sense, a distinction which RV. fails to recognise. See Grimm-Thayer, *Greek-English Lexicon of the N.T.*, s. vv.

[3] τὸν νόμον must here, I think, mean 'the general rule,' or 'constraining principle' ; see Sanday and Headlam's note.

Jesus Christ our Lord.—So then I myself with the intellect serve the Law of God ; but with *the flesh* the Law of Sin.[1]

The connexion of these verses with what precedes them is easily intelligible. The two passages on which we have just commented (v. 12–21 and vi. 1–11) are, as we have seen, pervaded by the theory that mankind inherited a suppressed or latent sinfulness in virtue of its descent from the first sinner Adam, but that this hereditary taint did not manifest itself in actual wrongdoing until stimulated by knowledge of the Law. A somewhat obtuse imaginary critic is represented as objecting that, if the effect of acquaintance with the Law is the commission of actual sin, the Law itself must be supposed to be in some way an evil power or agency (*v. 7*). The Apostle repudiates this suggestion with a stern ' God forbid,' but feels it necessary to provide against future misconceptions of the kind by clearing up, once and for all, the relations of ' suppressed sinfulness,' the Law, and actual sin. He therefore proceeds to elucidate the nature of ' suppressed sinfulness ' (designated in these verses simply as ' Sin ') by examining its operation on a small scale, within the compass of a single soul (in point of fact, as we have suggested, his own)—thereby reversing the procedure of Plato's *Republic*, which endeavours to elucidate the nature of Justice in the individual soul by examining its workings on a large scale in the State. The parallel centres on the idea of the Law, the learning of which during childhood, from the lips of parent or *ḥazzān*,[2] constitutes a moral Rubicon in the life of the individual, like that which its proclamation from Sinai constituted, as the Apostle believes, in the collective life of the race. If he had been acquainted with modern biological science, he might well have adapted one of its maxims to his purpose, and written ' (ethical and spiritual) ontogeny is the recapitulation of (ethical and spiritual) phylogeny,' as the premise from which his exposition is derived.

---

[1] RV., somewhat modified and expanded. I have italicised the references to ' the flesh,' ' the body,' and ' the members,' in order to make the underlying theory of the seat of sin stand out with clearness.

[2] The synagogue attendant, or professional reader, who often acted as schoolmaster.

In three or four vivid words (*v.* 9) he sketches the golden age of earliest childhood, during which he was alive,[1] ' in the purely physical sense,' without the Law ; that is, during which he was a non-moral organism, swayed solely by instinct, ignorant of the Decalogue, and therefore incapable of actual sin. This state of innocence was brought to an end by the coming of the Commandment, through instruction in the Law, which for the son of pious Jewish parents followed immediately upon the dawn of reason and moral responsibility. The effect of acquaintance with the Law was to rouse into venomous life the latent power of ' Sin ' (that is, ' original sin,' or the sinful tendency) which during infancy had been slumbering within him, inert, like a frozen snake. Through some strange psychic chemistry, the stern warning ' Thou shalt not desire . . .' provoked in his soul a passion of guilty desire to which he has hitherto been a stranger (*v.* 8) ; and, before he has had time to understand or adjust himself to the surging impulses which have broken out within him, he finds that he has committed some act which is condemned by the Law. It is difficult to avoid the impression that we have in *vv.* 8, 9 a generalised description of the psychic disturbances incidental to puberty and adolescence : though the language which describes an almost personified Sin as using the Commandment for a fulcrum whereby to push the tempted soul into spiritual death is equally applicable to the moral struggles of adult life.

The idea which St. Paul endeavours to express by this picture of an awakened ' endopsychic ' demon of Sin utilising the Law as a ποῦ στῶ for accomplishing its fell designs, is that summed up in the proverbial phrases ' *nitimur in vetitum semper*,' ' Stolen fruits are sweetest.' It is an idea which is, perhaps, rather less perplexing to us than it was to him : for we now know that the singular attraction exercised by the thought of forbidden conduct, merely because it is forbidden, over child-like and undisciplined minds, and it may be over others, arises from certain fundamental facts of human nature. A modern neurologist

---

[1] ἔζων : ζῆν means to ' be alive ' in a merely animal sense, βιώσκειν to ' live ' a fully developed human, rational, and civilised life ; *cf.* the English words zoology, biography.

might describe these facts in physiological terms, pointing out that it is impossible for the thought of a given action to be suggested to consciousness without a concomitant stimulation, in however minute a degree, of the kinaesthetic area of the cerebral cortex : and that such stimulation inevitably causes a discharge of energy, however infinitesimal in quantity, into the efferent nerves connected with the appropriate muscles, thereby producing a faint impulse towards the externalisation in act of the suggested thought. A psychologist, on the other hand, might prefer to speak of the ' phantasy ' of a particular action as exciting the cognate ' complex,' and of this latter as thereupon tending to release its accumulated *libido* into the conational channels leading to the realisation of the ' phantasy.' But, in whichever way we choose to envisage the mechanism of conduct, whether psychologically or psycho-physiologically, it remains true to say that the idea of an action, once suggested to the mind, has a slight but distinct tendency to realise itself. The whole curative method associated with the names of M. Coué and M. Baudouin is built upon this principle. Now the Law, by the very fact of prohibiting a certain mode of conduct, necessarily suggests to the mind the idea of such conduct, and therefore cannot help arousing some degree of propension towards that which it is designed to forbid. And when the prohibited conduct happens to be the normal expression of one of the cardinal instincts of human nature, the clumsy threatenings of the Law may well evoke, from the mysterious depths of the unconscious self, mighty forces which are seemingly beyond the power of the conscious ego to bridle or repress. A merely ' ideomotor ' impulse is doubtless too feeble and evanescent even to make itself felt in consciousness : but an ideomotor impulse reinforced by a flood-wave of animal appetite or elemental emotion inevitably passes over into action, unless dammed in by the barrier of habit or of intense volitional effort. Such spates of psychic energy, released in the way just described, are what the Apostle means by ' the sinful passions roused by the Law '; they constitute the ' second Law ' (ἕτερος νόμος) which hales us along as captives of the law of sin which is in our members.

But the question still presses for an answer, With what precisely, in the Apostle's thought, is ' Sin ' in the sense of these verses (that is, ' original sin ') to be identified ? Is it simply another name for the natural appetites of the body ? or is it the exaggeration of appetite ? Is it the psychic energy alluded to above, or the weakness of will which fails to tame its undisciplined uprushes ? We will, nevertheless, postpone these questions for a moment, in order to complete our review of the passage. Verse 13 attempts to account *ex parte Dei* for the paradoxical fact that the revelation of the Law is found in experience to stimulate law-breaking, by suggesting that this has been providentially allowed in order that man may realise the full horror of Sin by seeing that it is capable of utilising the sanctities of the Law as the instrument of its detestable purposes. With *v.* 14, we pass into a tragic description of the conflict between reason and appetite which once racked the writer's unconverted soul, a conflict in which appetite was continually victorious ; and the Apostle piles up rugged antithetical phrases (' it is not what I would that I practise : but what I hate, that I do,' and the like) to emphasise the complete dissociation which seemed to have taken place between his conscious *ego* and the control of his body. ' Sin,' like some malignant secondary personality, has got possession of his limbs, and uses them as it thinks fit, quite regardless of the commands of his real self. This real self, the ' inner man,' or the intellect (νοῦς), is strongly asserted to be morally sound, perfectly cognisant of the commands of the Law and perfectly loyal to them ; the whole blame for the aberrations of his actual conduct is laid upon ' the flesh,' or ' the flesh ' as controlled by ' Sin.' The state of interior schism thus depicted would seem to be exactly identical with what Aristotle terms ἀκρασία or ' incontinence,' the condition of the man who recognises the obligation of the moral law, but is too weak to conform to it, as distinct from the condition of the σπουδαῖος or ' good ' man, who both recognises and obeys the law, on the one hand, and that of the ἀκόλαστος or ' profligate ' man, who both rejects the law interiorly and disobeys it exteriorly, on the other.[1]

[1] *Eth. Nic.* vii. 1–10 (1145 a 15–1152 a).

L

But it is described by the fiery Apostle in words of burning
shame and remorse such as would have been quite unintel-
ligible to the phlegmatic Stagirite. And the philosopher,
unlike the Apostle, can only analyse the moral struggle,
and cannot suggest any means of bringing it to a satisfactory
end. The whole difference between the spirit of pagan
Hellenism and the spirit of Christianity is summed up in the
contrast between the cold aphorism with which Aristotle
concludes his dissertation on the character of the ' incontinent man ' (' Those who are incontinent through habit
are more easily curable than those who are such by nature ;
for it is easier to alter a habit than to alter one's nature ' [1])
and the exultant cry of the redeemed and converted Paul
' I thank God through Jesus Messiah our Lord.'

It is not necessary to dwell for more than a moment
upon two other well-known texts which should be noticed
in any attempt to elucidate St. Paul's conception of ' the
flesh '—those, namely, which expound the characteristically
Pauline antithesis of ' flesh ' and ' spirit,' Rom. viii. 3–13,
and what may be described as a rough preliminary study for
this passage, Gal. v. 16–24. We observe that in the former
of these texts it is not always certain whether the ' spirit '
which constitutes the second member of the contrasted
pair is meant to be man's own spirit, or the Spirit of God [2];
but, whichever it is, the ' flesh ' with its physical appetites
and cravings is conceived as standing in sharp opposition
and hostility to it. The $\phi\rho\delta\nu\eta\mu a$, the ' mind ' or ' disposition ' of the flesh—that is, the subconscious mental
qualities revealed in its instinctive desires—is said to be
death ; it is hostility towards God : it is not subject to the
Law of God, nor indeed can be.[3] ' The flesh desires con-

---

[1] Ar. *Eth. Nic.* vii. 10, 4. (1152 a 29) : [εὐιατότεροι] οἱ δι' ἐθισμοῦ ἀκρατεῖς
τῶν φυσικῶν· ῥᾷον γὰρ ἔθος μετακινῆσαι φύσεως.

[2] As the autographs of St. Paul's Epistles must have been written
in uncials, our modern typographic device of denoting the Spirit of God
by means of a capital initial letter was not available for his amanuensis :
so that we can only judge in a given passage, whether τὸ πνεῦμα, used
absolutely, means the Spirit of God or the spirit of man, from the general
sense of the context.   RV. is, I think, right in translating τὸ πνεῦμα in
Rom. viii. 4–9 as ' the spirit' (= the human spirit) and in Gal. v. 16–25
as ' the Spirit' (= the Spirit of God).

[3] Rom. viii. 7.

trariwise to the Spirit, and the Spirit contrariwise to the flesh ; for these two powers are directly opposed to each other, so that you do not actually do what you wish to do (*cf.* Rom. vii. 15, " not what I would, that do I practise " etc.). . . . Now the works of the flesh are manifest, which are these, fornication, uncleanness, lasciviousness, idolatry, sorcery, enmities, strife, jealousies, wraths, factions, divisions, sects, envyings, drunkenness, revellings, and such like.' [1] The ' flesh,' in short, is the seat or *nidus*, not merely of the bodily appetites which may be summed up under the head of sensuality, but also of the self-assertive instincts which fall more naturally under the head of pride. All these hateful impulses, however, are believed, in accordance with the absolute view of the efficacy of baptism noted above, to have been destroyed once and for all, in Christians, by the mystic death through which they were united to the Saviour and initiated into the fellowship of the Church. ' *Ye* are not in the flesh, but in the spirit, if—as you know to be the case [2]—the Spirit of God dwelleth in you.' [3] ' They that belong to Messiah Jesus have crucified the flesh with its passions and its appetites.' [4]

Our survey of the relevant passages of the Pauline writings has now placed us in a position to essay a solution of this most subtle and difficult of exegetical problems, the exact nature of ' inbred sinfulness ' and of its relation to ' the flesh,' as conceived in the Apostle's thought. It will clear the ground if we deal briefly, first of all, with a popular theory, not devoid of a superficial simplicity and attractiveness, which sees in the famous antithesis of ' flesh ' and ' spirit ' a reproduction of the Platonic dualism of matter and mind,[5] in which the former, when organised as a ' body,'

---

[1] Gal. v. 19.　　　[2] $\epsilon\check{\iota}\pi\epsilon\rho$, *siquidem*, appeals to an admitted fact.
[3] Rom. viii. 9.　　　[4] Gal. v. 24.
[5] The most noteworthy exposition of this theory is that given by O. Pfleiderer, *Paulinism* (E. tr. 1877), i. 47–68. W. Bousset (*Rel. des Juden-tums*, p. 386, 1903) is in general agreement with Pfleiderer : ' Wenn Paulus πνεῦμα und σάρξ als zwei den menschlichen Willen unbedingt beherr-schende und diesen niederzwingende Mächte anschaut, und wenn er die Wurzel der σάρξ doch wesentlich in dem leiblich-sinnlichen Wesen des Menschen sucht, so geht er damit seine Wege abseits von rabbinischer Theologie und bringt eine specifisch hellenische Auffassung an das Christ-entum heran.'

is regarded as the impure clog or fetter which weighs down the heavenward strivings of the latter.[1] It would not be difficult, did time allow, to rebut this contention by an extended demonstration of the intensely Hebraic character of St. Paul's thought in general which certainly betrays no other trace of Platonic influence ; and it would be even easier to set against it the passages in which the body is clearly conceived as a holy thing, created ' not for fornication, but for the Lord,'[2] the temple of the Holy Spirit,[3] destined at the Last Day to be transubstantiated, by some celestial alchemy, into a ' body of glory,'[4] an ethereal envelope which will be the perfect instrument and vehicle of the immortal soul. But the simplest and, I venture to think, the most convincing reply to this suggestion is one which bases itself directly on the logical structure and interrelation of the ideas which form the subject-matter of our enquiry. It may be phrased as follows : We may admit that the passages just cited, which find the seat of sin in the body and its appetites, if considered by themselves and in isolation from the rest of the Apostle's teaching, might appear to pre-suppose some kind of Platonic or Oriental dualism, were it not for the fact that the Apostle, in two classical texts (Rom. v. 12–19 and 1 Cor. xv. 21, 22), has left on record his conviction that the origin of evil, physical and moral, is to be traced, not to the essential constitution of human nature or of the material universe, but to the voluntary transgression of the first man—in other words, to the ' Fall.' It is the idea of the Fall, with its necessary implication of the contingency and temporality, as opposed to the eternity and necessity, of evil, which makes all the difference ; without the belief in the Fall, the doctrine of ' Original Sin ' *is* Manicheism. It is doubtless unnecessary to repeat the warning that we are not at the moment discussing the question of the Fall on its merits ;

[1] This point of view actually appears in Wisdom, a book which is permeated by Alexandrine-Jewish Platonism : ' For a corruptible body weigheth down the soul, And the earthy frame lieth heavy on a mind that is full of cares ' (ix. 15).

[2] 1 Cor. vi. 13.
[3] *ibid.* 19.
[4] 1 Cor. xv. 35 ff.

that question belongs to the second or constructive part of our enquiry, in which we shall see that, from the purely intellectual point of view, there is much to be said for Manicheism ; we are only concerned now to emphasise the consideration, explained at length in Lecture I, that the Fall-theory and dualism are in principle, and always have been in history, mutually exclusive hypotheses. It follows that St. Paul's emphatically asserted allegiance to the first is the surest proof that he cannot have held the second. There are those who would reply that strict logic was not the Apostle's strongest point ; that he may well never have had time to think the matter out with so much thoroughness as to become clearly conscious of the contradiction ; and that the occurrence of a ' Fall-theory ' in Rom. v. 12 ff., and of a ' flesh-theory ' immediately afterwards, in cc. vi. and vii., merely constitutes one more instance of that power of simultaneously holding incompatible theories, and of using each in turn as his dialectical exigencies require, which is most conspicuously displayed by his successive assumption of the predestinarian and of the libertarian standpoints, in the great Theodicy of Rom. ix.–xi. But the argument just advanced, that if St. Paul believed in a Fall he cannot have held any sort of dualistic theory, is based upon foundations which go far deeper than the canons of formal logic. Dualism, with its assertion of a realm of being (namely, matter) from which the will and power of the Most High are partially or entirely excluded, assumes a conception of God differing *toto caelo* from that ethical monotheism which was the supreme achievement of the Jewish Church, and a conscious relation to God fundamentally other than that possessed by the illustrious line of its prophets and saints. Dualism is treason to everything that is summed up in the *Shema'*, the Apostles' Creed of Judaism—' Hear, O Israel, Yahweh thy God, Yahweh is One.' To suppose that St. Paul was capable of such treason is to suppose not merely a psychological but an ethical and spiritual impossibility.

The 'Mind of the Flesh' and the 'Evil Imagination'

In point of fact, the student who remembers that St. Paul was before all things a 'Hebrew sprung from Hebrews,'[1] an 'Israelite,'[2] 'brought up at the feet of Gamaliel,'[3] has not very far to look for the true answer to the question, What precisely was it that St. Paul believed to have been introduced into the human stock by Adam's sin, to reside in 'the flesh,' and to constitute the psychological ground of actual transgression? The various phrases which we have passed in review during our exposition of the chief relevant texts—'Sin,' 'the old man,' 'the sinful body,' 'the body of this death,' 'the sinful passions aroused by the Law,' 'the mind of the flesh'—are all, I would submit, so many picturesque and paraphrastic names for the *yēçer ha-ra'*. Indeed, it may be tentatively suggested that the last of these terms—the φρόνημα τῆς σαρκός—almost amounts to a literal translation of the Hebrew phrase: we have seen that Hellenistic Judaism never fixed upon any one Greek word as the standing equivalent of *yēçer*, and the φρόνημα of Rom. viii. 6 would seem to come as near to its meaning as the word employed by the grandson of Ben Sirach, διαβούλιον (Ecclus. xv. 14). If the genitive 'of the flesh' may be taken as a Hebraism (= 'fleshly'), the words τὸ φρόνημα τῆς σαρκός then represent 'the fleshly *yēçer*,' and the corresponding phrase, τὸ φρόνημα τοῦ πνεύματος ('the mind of the spirit'), might be translated 'the spiritual *yēçer*'; so that the passage Rom. viii. 6, 7 would embody the first occurrence in Christian literature of the doctrine of the Two *Yeçārim*, bad and good, which strive for the mastery within the soul of man.[4] But,

---

[1] Phil. iii. 5. [2] Rom. xi. 1. [3] Acts xxii. 3.

[4] This development of the *yēçer*-conception appears first in *Test. xii. Patr.*, *Test. Asser*, I–IV. 6: 'Two ways hath God given to the sons of men, and *two inclinations* (δύο διαβούλια)' . . ., etc.; see the whole passage. The idea of the 'Two Ways,' which is built upon that of the Two *Yeçārim*, is found in the *Didache*, 1–6, and in the Epistle of Barnabas, 18–20. The Two *Yeçārim* themselves reappear in Hermas, *Mand.* xii. (*cf.* Lecture IV, p. 172).

whether this be so or not, it remains true to say that there
are a thousand chances to one in favour of any explanation
of a given Pauline concept which traces its genesis to Jewish,
rather than Greek, Persian, or other Gentile sources ; and
that, in this particular instance, the idea of the ' evil
imagination,' as we have met with it in Rabbinical thought
—of the turbulent stream of psychic energy perpetually
boiling up from the depths of the soul and appearing in
consciousness as sensual and self-assertive impulses—provides us with precisely the category which we need in order
to subsume into a unity the various aspects of inbred evil
in man which are reflected in the Apostle's passionate words.

When, however, we suggest that the key to the Pauline
doctrine of ' Original Sin ' lies in the hypothesis that he has
brought over with him into Christianity, from his Rabbinical
training, the idea of the *yēçer ha-ra'*, we must add that, in
embodying it into his own system, he has stamped it with
a threefold difference.

(1) In the first place, he has permanently welded into
it the idea of the Fall of Adam as its source, thereby creating
that synthesis of the apocalyptic and the scholastic theories
of the origin of evil, which (as we have seen) the author of
4 Ezra, writing in complete independence of Pauline and
Christian influence, seems to have achieved a generation later.[1]
We may surmise that he had learnt of the *yēçer*-theory from
Gamaliel, and already held it prior to his conversion to
Christianity, but that he only came to hold the Adamic
Fall-theory as the result of intercourse with the original
Apostles and other Galilean followers of our Lord. It is
doubtless true that his combination of the two theories is
more in the nature of a mechanical conjunction than of a
complete organic fusion ; for, whilst implicitly affirming the
yēçer to be the *effect*—and not, as the Rabbinical theology
asserted, the *cause*—of Adam's transgression, he nowhere
explains why a single act of wrongdoing should have had
such a mighty reflex consequence as the birth of an interior
power of evil, universally propagated by physiological
heredity, and unconquerable save by supernatural assistance ; the classical Fall-text, Rom. v. 12 ff., passes over this

[1] See above, Lecture II, p. 79.

question in silence ; nor, as we shall see, has this patent gap in his exposition ever been satisfactorily filled by any of his commentators or successors. But the Pauline blend of the two Jewish traditions, the popular and the official, possesses a strength which cannot be attributed to either of them separately : it supplies intellectual reinforcement to the Fall-idea by giving it a more or less defined psychological content, and it heightens the spiritual value of the *yēçer*-conception by denying that God is the author of the ' evil impulse,' and so bringing the idea into full accord with ethical monotheism. Abstracting from the question of its objective truth—a question with which, as has often been said, we are not in this the first and historical stage of our enquiry concerned—we may attribute its survival in great measure to its association of ethical and religious value with a tolerable, though by no means excessive, degree of conceptual precision.

(2) The second difference which St. Paul has impressed upon the *yēçer*-idea consists in the striking fact, already noticed, that—breaking away from the *usus loquendi* common to the prophets and the Rabbinical theologians, and endorsed by our Lord Himself, according to which the seat of the evil power in man is the ' heart ' [1]—he insists again and again that the inbred disease resides in the ' flesh,' the ' body,' or the ' members.' This is by no means a mere variant in terminology. In the rough and ready psychology of the Old Testament which lies behind all the Apostle's thought and language with regard to these subjects, the ' heart ' (*lēbh*), paradoxically enough, is not a part of the ' flesh ' (*bāsār*) : it is the whole personality, or perhaps rather that deep hidden part of the personality which we now call the Unconscious. The ' flesh,' on the other hand, means the literal flesh, the organic tissue of which the body is composed : and as such it is for the Old Testament writers morally neutral. When, therefore, St. Paul transfers the seat of innate evil from the ' heart ' to the ' flesh,' he is to be understood—so far as his words go—as exempting the mental and psychic life of man, even in its subconscious processes, from the infection of sin, and concentrating this

[1] See above, Lecture II, p. 65 ; Lecture III, p. 97.

almost exclusively in the physical body.   Actually, he fails
to maintain a sharp line of demarcation between body and
mind or to keep inherited sinfulness strictly on the physical
side of the line.   But it is difficult to escape from the
impression that his language in this connexion is dictated
by the fact that (like many of his predecessors and also of
his successors in the path of hamartiological speculation)
he is in the main, perhaps unconsciously, thinking of ' sins
of the flesh ' in the most restricted sense of the term ;
though, in the passage before noticed, Gal. v. 19, 20, he
endeavours to correct the balance of his thought by expressly
including amongst the ' works of the flesh ' those sins which
arise from cruelty and pride.

(3) It must be noticed, in the last place, that for St.
Paul the innate ' impulse towards sin ' is unreservedly evil,
and that he shows no traces of sympathy with that more
humane view held by some of the Rabbis, who (as we saw
in Lecture II) taught that the yēçer is, considered in itself,
a morally neutral *libido* : which, in the uninstructed man,
may and generally does discharge itself in unlawful acts,
but which is also the driving force behind all creative
achievement, whether in the economic, the political, or the
intellectual spheres, and which by the study of the Law can
be completely ' sublimated ' and diverted into socially
useful channels.   The Apostle will have none of this : for
him sin, even as innate and potential, is ' quite superlatively sinful ' [1] (καθ' ὑπερβολὴν ἁμαρτωλός), and the
Law, however long or intently it may be studied, quite
impotent to subdue it (on the contrary, as we have
seen, the Law merely stimulates the sinful impulse to fresh
vigour) ; nothing less than the living power which flows
forth from the Incarnation and the Atonement can quench
the flames of temptation.   ' That which the Law could not
do—that in which its impotence was exhibited through
(the power of Sin dwelling in) the flesh—God (actually did,
namely this)—having sent His own Son in the likeness of
sinful flesh and as a sin-offering, He condemned sin within
(that very sphere of) the flesh (in which it had hitherto
reigned without a rival).' [2]   So deep is St. Paul's conviction

[1] Rom. vii. 13.   [2] Rom. viii. 3 (freely translated).

of the sinfulness of the sinful impulse, and of its intimate and subtle diffusion throughout man's physical nature, that he is prompted to describe the stainless humanity of the Incarnate Son in a phrase which trembles on the verge of Docetism—' the *likeness* of sinful flesh.' [1]   Though, as will be argued later, the Augustinian doctrine of ' Original Sin ' represents a one-sided distortion of the fundamental Pauline ideas, it cannot be denied that the Apostle's language affords some excuse for those later Christian thinkers who saw in it an affirmation of the essentially sinful nature of ' concupiscence,' both in its general and in its specifically sexual significance.

THE INFLUENCE OF ST. PAUL'S TEMPERAMENT UPON HIS DOCTRINE

In the light of the facts reviewed in our previous Lectures, it will be clear that the special characteristics of the Pauline doctrine summed up under the last two heads (2) and (3)— that is, the affirmations of the intensely evil nature of the innate disease and of its close connexion with the physical organism—are *idiosyncratic* :   they represent the stamp which the Apostle's vivid and passionate temperament has impressed upon the materials combined by his genius. Not merely has he driven out the Watcher-theory, and exalted the Adam-story to the position of the one and only Christian Fall-narrative ;   not merely has he remedied the fatal weakness of the apocalyptic Fall-theories, which lay in the extreme vagueness with which the disastrous consequences of the primal sin were conceived, by formulating those consequences in terms of the scholastic *yēçer*-theory; he has embodied part of himself, of his living experience, in the great *theologumenon* which he has bequeathed to posterity.   The finished, or relatively finished, product has been deeply coloured by the crucible in which it has been compounded.   It will be appropriate to conclude our survey of the Pauline doctrine of Man and of Sin with a few words drawing out the significance of this fact.

[1] Rom. viii. 3.

We have seen that all the theories with which we are immediately concerned take their rise from introspective reflection upon the experience of repentance. In the case of most religious men, repentance, and its corollary ' conversion '—that is, the complete detachment of all impulses and desires, conscious or unconscious, from unworthy objects, and their complete concentration on the supreme good, however that may be conceived—are gradual ever-deepening processes, spread out over the whole life, and never, perhaps, consummated on this side of the grave. But in souls of a rarer mould, endowed with that highly sensuous temperament which is common to the voluptuary and to certain types of saint, the whole current of emotional and conative energy which ceaselessly wells up from the depths of the Unconscious may—through some minute and apparently accidental shock, physical or psychical—be in a moment diverted from one mental channel to another, and its manifestation in consciousness may be transformed from fleshly desire into the mystic thirst for God and goodness, in the experience known as ' instantaneous conversion.' It is no mere accident that the three great dominating figures in the history of the Christian Fall-doctrine—Paul, Augustine, Luther—belonged to this type, and passed through this experience. We shall have occasion again to examine the subtle influence exercised upon the more developed versions of the Fall-doctrine by the temperaments of their chief expounders ; it must suffice here to point out that the ' twice-born ' man (as William James has taught us to call him[1]) is usually an extremist, both as a sinner and as a saint ; that the same emotional energy which before his conversion expressed itself in sensuality or sensual temptations usually appears after conversion as a fanatical horror and hatred of sensuality ; and that this horror of sensuality is apt to cover everything even remotely connected with the senses, so that the suddenly converted man is less capable of viewing the fact of bodily appetite calmly, and of distinguishing between natural impulse and its excessive or anti-social indulgence, than his ' once-born ' fellows. Such a one is prone to an ultra-ascetic and puritanical

---

[1] *Varieties of Religious Experience* (1902), Lecture VIII.

condemnation of physical appetite as such, and specially of the sexual appetite ; it is noticeable, in this connexion, that St. Paul, in what may perhaps be described as a moment of unguarded soliloquy, expresses the wish that all men were celibates.[1] It is to the Apostle's ' twice-born ' temperament, and to intensity of feeling rather than to reasoned theory, that we must ascribe the causes which prompt him to an occasional, and possibly incautious, use of words which appear to identify the hereditary tendency to sin with the natural appetites of the body ; though, as we have already pointed out, it is not difficult to correct the *prima facie* impression which these words might produce by counterbalancing them with other passages in which the body and its divinely implanted instincts receive their proper honour, and ' the flesh ' is given the neutral meaning which it bears in the Old Testament Scriptures.

If we eliminate this accidental and temperamental colouring which clings to St. Paul's language about ' the flesh,' and endeavour to state the permanent essence of his conception of ' Original Sin ' in the terms which we may suppose that he *would* have used if he had been on his guard against the unconscious bias mentioned above, we shall be justified in describing the inherited moral disease as the hypertrophy, even the elephantiasis, of those non-rational and non-volitional elements in human nature which are summed up under the names of ' emotion,' ' feeling,' ' instinct,' ' appetite.' But the Apostle's letters contain no word which definitely asserts that *guilt* is attached to the state of subjection to this disease. Even though, in a highly rhetorical passage, inbred Sin is said to ' prove itself superlatively sinful,' this *dictum* must be understood in an abstract and proleptic sense, in other words, as implying no more than (*a*) that the inherited infirmity is, so to speak, *aesthetically* objectionable seen from God's point of view, and (*b*) that it may be described as ' sin ' in a metaphorical and improper sense, in virtue of its tendency to produce actual transgressions ; for only so can it be harmonised with the deeper, more deliberate, and more authoritative sentence, that where there is no consciousness of Law (as

[1] 1 Cor. vii. 7.

in the race between Adam and Moses, and in the individual before the dawn of reason) sin is not accounted to be sin (that is, does not involve guilt). St. Paul knows nothing of a mystical or pre-natal participation of Adam's posterity in the sin of their first father, nor of the idea that inherited, and therefore involuntary, infection with ' concupiscence ' is in itself deserving of punishment, even prior to and apart from actual offences ; in other words, he knows nothing of the conception of Original Guilt.

The Context of Evil in Man

(a) Evil in the sub-human World

It might well be supposed that the foregoing exposition, lengthy as it has inevitably been, would have exhausted the hamartiological doctrine even of so profound and original a thinker as the Apostle of the Gentiles. But the problem of evil in man presents yet a further aspect, with which we should expect a great Christian teacher to deal ; and that is the problem of its relation to evil *outside* man, to evil as it exists, or may be thought to exist, in the planes of being which lie above and below him, in the world of sub-human nature, animate and inanimate, and in the world of super-human spirits. And we shall find that, unlike many lesser thinkers who have been content to ignore this question and to treat evil as though it were a purely human phenomenon, St. Paul has faced it in his private communings with God and his own soul. His explanation of the evil which prevails in Nature is enshrined in words of almost lyrical beauty and power, to paraphrase which would be a profanation :

For I reckon that the sufferings of this present time are not worthy to be compared with the glory which shall be revealed towards us. For the earnest expectation of the creation waiteth for the revealing of the sons of God. For the creation was subjected to vanity, not of its own will, but by reason of him who subjected it, in hope that the creation itself also shall be delivered from the bondage of corruption into the liberty of the glory of the children of God. For we know that the whole creation groaneth and travaileth in pain together until now.[1]

[1] Rom. viii. 18–22.

Commentators are not agreed whether the mysterious reference to ' him¦ who subjected the creation to vanity ' is meant to indicate Adam or the Creator ; in any case, however, the meaning is that the woes of the animal creation are directly due to the Fall.   The roots of this idea, as of the other elements which make up the Adamic theory, lie deep in the thought of the pre-Christian apocalyptists.   The belief that Nature was corrupted by the Fall of Adam is derived ultimately from the primal curse pronounced, according to the Genesis-story, upon the earth—' Thorns also and thistles shall it bring forth unto thee '[1] ; and this was expanded by the pseudepigraphic writers so as to include among the consequences of the Fall inclement seasons, earthquakes and all destructive or terrifying natural phenomena, the ferocity of the animal tribes.

The Apostle reproduces this belief, but with an impressive difference.   The apocalyptists had thought of the discords in Nature as evil merely from the point of view of man, as prejudicial to man's comfort or physical well-being, as entailing fear, or pain, or death upon man.   With amazing modernity of feeling, St. Paul merges himself in Nature, and looks at the terror of existence, if we may so say, from Nature's point of view and through Nature's own multitudinous eyes.   The vanity and futility which mark the sub-human universe, the prodigal waste of life which the teeming generative forces of the world inevitably involve, procreating a million seeds to perish and decay for one that attains to full development, the ceaseless, silent, ruthless struggle for existence that underlies the smiling beauty of a summer landscape—these things appear to him as evil and God-defying in themselves, and not merely as perceived by, or in their relations to, man.   ' He is one of those, like St. Francis of Assisi, to whom it is given to read the unconscious thoughts of plants and animals.   He seems to lay his ear to the earth, and the confused murmur which he hears has a meaning for him.   It is creation's yearning for that happier state intended for it and of which it has been defrauded.'[2]   We cannot, indeed, in the light of modern knowledge, accept his naïve theory that waste, and vanity,

---

[1] Gen. iii. 18.   [2] Sanday and Headlam, *op. cit.*, p. 212.

and internecine hostility have been inflicted upon sub-
human life as a sort of vicarious punishment for the sin of
man ; for we know that pain and death existed upon this
planet millions of years before man was born. But we may
see beneath the Apostle's words an intuition of the profound
truths that man is organic to nature, inseparable from his
context in the sub-human creation, and that evil in man
is homogeneous with, and not explicable apart from, evil
in the world at large. These vast problems cannot be
adequately dealt with now ; but we may confidently claim
St. Paul's authority in support of our modern faith

> That nothing walks with aimless feet,
>   That not one life shall be destroyed,
>   Or cast as rubbish to the void,
> When God hath made the pile complete,[1]

and that, whether individual immortality be the destiny of
the lower animals or no, the sub-human universe of sentient
life can claim the ultimate fulfilment and perfection of its
being from the justice and love of its Creator, with no less
assurance, though with infinitely less of comprehension,
than the favoured race of man.[2]

THE CONTEXT OF EVIL IN MAN

(b) EVIL IN THE WORLD OF SPIRITS

Evil in man thus appears as set in a context or frame,
of which one side is the unconscious evil with which the
sub-human world is infected. The other side of this frame
is constituted by the evil which St. Paul believes to exist
on the superhuman plane, the ' spiritual powers of wickedness in the heavenly places.' [3] The Pauline demonology is
in complete continuity and identity with that which we
have already noted in the Synoptic Gospels, and like it

---

[1] Tennyson, *In Memoriam*, liv.

[2] *Cf.* the great description of the Messianic millennium in Isaiah xi.
–9. G. A. Smith draws attention to the fact that ' Isaiah and Paul,
chief apostles of the two covenants, both interrupt their magnificent odes
upon the outpouring of the Spirit, to remind us that the benefits of this
will be shared by the brute and unintelligent creation ' (*The Book of Isaiah*,
1889, vol. i. chap. x. III).

[3] For a detailed treatment of this subject see O. Everling, *Die paulin-
sche Angelologie u. Dämonologie* (1888).

reproduces the main characteristics of current Jewish
opinion with regard to Satan and his aery host. The
demons have the power of plaguing men with physical
evils,[1] such as the infirmity to which the Apostle alludes
under the name of a ' stake in the flesh,' and which he
regards as a ' messenger of Satan to buffet him '[2] ; they
foment dissension in the Church,[3] and contrive hindrances
to St. Paul's missionary plans[4] ; they torment the faithful
with sinful solicitations and temptations.[5]   (It is to be
observed that St. Paul's extant letters do not contain any
attempt to synthesise the theory which finds the origin of
temptation in diabolic suggestions from without and that
which regards it as rooted in sinful impulses, connatural
with the flesh, welling up from within ; doubtless it had
not occurred to him that these views required harmonisation.)   But the chief theatre of their power is the pagan
Graeco-Roman world lying outside the spheres both of
Law and of Grace.   They give reality and personality to
the imaginary gods of heathendom, communicating their
impure essence to their benighted votaries through the
pagan Mysteries, even as Christ bestows the participation
in His Body and Blood upon His worshippers through the
Christian Eucharist[6] ;   their power over this outlying
domain of darkness and sin is so great that they are
described as ' the princes of this age '[7] who (through the
agency of Pilate, the representative of the heathen empire)
crucified the Lord of glory, and their chief is even styled
' the god of this age.'[8]   In the Epistle to the Ephesians,
which, if not Pauline in authorship, is at least thoroughly
Pauline in sentiment and thought, some of them are
apparently identified with the ' world-rulers,'[9] the malignant

---

[1] The Church can in a sense utilise this diabolical power for disciplinary purposes, by handing the excommunicate person over to Satan
' for the destruction of the flesh, that the spirit may be saved in the day
of the Lord Jesus ' (1 Cor. v. 5) ; cf. also 1 Tim. i. 20.

[2] 2 Cor. xii. 7.   [3] 2 Cor. ii. 11.   [4] 1 Thess. ii. 18.

[5] 1 Cor. vii. 5 ; this conception would also seem to be implied in Rom.
xvi. 20.

[6] 1 Cor. x. 20, 21.   [7] 1 Cor. ii. 8.   [8] 2 Cor. iv. 4.

[9] Eph. vi. 12 ; cf. also the reference to the στοιχεῖα or elemental
spirits, in Gal. iv. 9.   For information about the κοσμοκράτορες in Gnosticism, see Edwyn Bevan, *Hellenism and Christianity* (1921), pp. 77 ff.

planetary spirits who, according to the lore of the Gnostics, drawn from the astral cults of Babylonia, shed disastrous influence upon the destinies of men : others, of humbler rank, find their home in the lowest or sublunary firmament, through which they ride the midnight gales, under the leadership of the ' prince of the power of the air.' [1]

It is natural at this point to raise the question, How, in St. Paul's view, had the evil spirits *become* evil ? (We must assume that the ethical monotheism, in which, as a devout Israelite, he believed, would have prevented him from holding that they had been created evil by God, or that they were co-eternal with God.) Various answers were given by the Apostle's Jewish contemporaries to this question. Josephus holds that the demons are the souls of wicked men departed.[2] The apocalyptic writers who were influenced by the older Fall-tradition identified them with the fallen Watchers and the spirits of the dead giants their sons [3] ; those who adhered to the newer Adamic theory doubtless believed in some sort of ultimate pre-mundane ' fall of the angels,' such as is described by the Slavonic Enoch in the following passage :

And one from out the order of angels, having turned away with the order that was under him, conceived an impossible thought, to place his throne higher than the clouds above the earth, that he might become equal in rank to my [that is, God's] power. And I threw him out from the height with his angels, and he was flying in the air continuously above the bottomless (abyss).[4]

It might be presumed *a priori* that St. Paul, as a believer in the Adam-tradition, would have given his allegiance to

---

[1] Eph. ii. 2. For the idea that the earth's atmosphere is the special haunt of evil spirits, *cf.* the passage 2 Enoch xxix. 4, quoted above, and the parallels adduced by Morfill and Charles, *Book of the Secrets of Enoch* (1896), note *in loc.*

[2] *B.J.* vii. 6, 3.

[3] So 1 Enoch vi.–xi., cvi. (fragments of the ' Book of Noah ') ; xv., xvi. (from the original ' Book of Enoch '). But it should be noted that the ' Similitudes ' distinguish sharply between the ' Watchers ' who fell in the days of Jared, and the ' Satans ' who are said to have corrupted them, and who must therefore be presumed to have become wicked themselves at some earlier period (lxix. 4, 5).

[4] 2 Enoch xxix. 4.

M

this last view; and in point of fact the language which he uses in 2 Cor. xi. 3 (the passage already quoted regarding the seduction of Eve by the serpent) and Rom. v. 12 (' through one man sin *entered* into the world '—presumably from some already existing external source) presupposes a tempter who is already corrupt himself before he corrupts our first parents. It is therefore reasonable to conclude that in the Apostle's thought there lies, dimly descried behind the historical, or supposedly historical, Fall of Adam, a much more ancient, remote, and mysterious ' Fall ' of conscious and intelligent beings, an ultimate and transcendental ' Fall ' from which the malign infection of evil has percolated downwards through the transgression of Adam into the human stock, and through the Divine sentence consequent upon that transgression into the sub-human creation. Immense vistas of speculation are opened up by these audacious conceptions: but the attempt to penetrate them must be reserved for the constructive and concluding part of our enquiry.

CONCLUSION

We have thus seen that the doctrines of the Fall and Original Sin come to us on the authority of St. Paul and of the Church, rather than on that of Christ, though it is not unreasonable to claim for them at least as much Dominical sanction as is implicit in the fact of non-prohibition. It is possible that in the final lectures of this course we may be able to go further; if our examination of these beliefs on their intrinsic merits shows that they correspond to the facts of human life, we shall be entitled to conclude that they represent the working out, into clear-cut and explicit form, of what is tacitly implied in our Lord's undoubted teaching as to man's universal need of salvation. Meanwhile, it is impossible not to be impressed by the extreme humanity and reasonableness of the Apostle's teaching, as compared with some of the more rigid products of later theology. Though he seems to assume the natural immortality of unfallen man,[1] he teaches no doctrine of ' Original

---

[1] See above, p. 124.

Righteousness' or perfection; the Rabbinical fictions which represent Adam as surpassing the angels in glory, intellectual power, and conscious holiness are totally absent from his pages. Nor can his words be cited in defence of the idea of 'Original Guilt'; despite a few rhetorical turns of phrase, no trace is to be found in his Epistles of the irrational paradox, that we are morally culpable for possessing instincts which we cannot help possessing. And blended with this Pauline thought, which is so reasonable precisely because so little defined, is the great conception which we may well be disposed to borrow, at a later stage, as the foundation-stone of a modern and constructive interpretation of the doctrines of the Fall and of Original Sin: the conception of the unitary nature of Evil as pervading the three planes of life, sub-human, human, and superhuman. It was St. Paul's prophetic intuition which first saw clearly that moral evil in man is no unique and isolated phenomenon, standing out with stark inexplicability in the midst of an otherwise moral and orderly cosmos; that it has upward connexions, joining it with the 'spiritual things of wickedness in the heavenly places,' and downward ramifications, running into the ferocious egotism and the diabolical cruelty which mar and ravage the infra-human world. The moral struggle in man is not a single combat waged within the narrow lists of the individual soul: it is part of a vast battle-front formed by the interlocked forces of Good and Evil, swaying to and fro in a conflict which is not indeed eternal (for to admit that would be a surrender to the ancient foe of dualism) but which is as old as Time and as wide as space, and which moves to the predestined climax of a Redemption in which not man alone, but the whole extra-human universe, in all its ordered hierarchical gradations from the highest discarnate intelligence [1] to the lowliest speck of animated tissue may be delivered, through the all-prevailing Blood of Jesus Christ, from the servitude of corruption into the liberty of the glory of the Children of God.

[1] Col. i. 19, 20 asserts that the benefits of the Atonement extend even to the hostile spirit-world : ' For it was the good pleasure of the Father . . . through him to reconcile all things unto himself, having made peace through the blood of his cross ; through him, I say, whether things upon earth or *things in the heavens.*'

IV.

THE FALL-DOCTRINE IN THE CHURCH OF THE FIRST FOUR CENTURIES

ἔστιν ἀνάγκης ῥῆμα, θεῶν ψήφισμα παλαιόν,
ἀΐδιον, πλατέεσσι κατεσφρηγισμένον ὅρκοις,
εὖτέ τις ἀμπλακίῃσι φόνῳ φίλα γυῖα μιήνῃ
‹νείκεΐ θ᾽› ὅς κ᾽ ἐπίορκον ἁμαρτήσας ἐπομόσσῃ,
δαίμονες οἵτε μακραίωνος λελάχασι βίοιο,
τρίς μιν μυρίας ὥρας ἀπὸ μακάρων ἀλάλησθαι,
φυομένους παντοῖα διὰ χρόνου εἴδεα θνητῶν,
ἀργαλέας βιότοιο μεταλλάσσοντα κελεύθους,
αἰθέριον μὲν γάρ σφε μένος πόντονδε διώκει
πόντος δ᾽ ἐς χθονὸς οὖδας ἀπέπτυσε, γαῖα δ᾽ ἐς αὐγὰς
ἠελίου φαέθοντος, ὁ δ᾽ αἰθέρος ἔμβαλε δίναις,
ἄλλος δ᾽ ἐξ ἄλλου δέχεται, στυγέουσι δὲ πάντες.
τῶν καὶ ἐγὼ νῦν εἰμί, φυγὰς θεόθεν καὶ ἀλήτης,
νείκεΐ μαινομένῳ πίσυνος.

EMPEDOCLES.

Zwei Seelen wohnen, ach ! in meiner Brust,
Die eine will sich von der andern trennen ;
Die eine hält in derber Liebeslust
Sich an die Welt mit klammernden Organen ;
Die andre hebt gewaltsam sich vom Duft
Zu den Gefilden hoher Ahnen.

GOETHE : *Faust*, Teil i.

LECTURE IV.

THE FALL-DOCTRINE IN THE CHURCH OF THE FIRST FOUR CENTURIES

Rom. v. 19 : ' As through the one man's disobedience the many were
made sinners, even so through the obedience of the
one shall the many be made righteous.'

HITHERTO our research into the origin and growth of the
doctrines of the Fall and of Original Sin has moved in an
exclusively Semitic and Jewish environment. With the
missionary labours of St. Paul, Christianity crosses from
Asia into Europe, and the point upon which our historical
research is focussed crosses with it. The transplantation
of our religion from its Syrian birthplace into the Western
and Aryan world, the world of Graeco-Roman culture, of
science and philosophy, inevitably involved the subjection
of its main constitutive ideas to a process of intellectual
scrutiny, analysis, and discussion, out of which grew up the
great fabric of Catholic theology, broad-based upon the
foundations laid by St. Paul and St. John : and the ideas
of the Fall and of the hereditary taint or weakness, vague
and ill-defined as they had been in Jewish and primitive
Christian thought, were now destined to share in this
process, to shed the pictorial and mythological guise which
they had hitherto worn, and, within the realm of Western
Christian theology, to assume an armour of clear-cut
conceptual forms, moulded in the furnace of acrimonious
controversy. It is clear that the somewhat general and
elastic doctrine of St. Paul described in our last Lecture
was bound, when subjected to rigorous examination, to
raise certain great issues which have dominated the subsequent history of these ideas, and it will facilitate the
further course of our study if we define these issues at once.

They may be formulated in the shape of five questions, as follows :

Firstly.   Is the Paradise-story of Gen. iii. to be regarded as literal history or merely as an allegory symbolising ethical and spiritual truths ?

Secondly.   What was the condition of man before the Fall ?   Is this to be described as one of ' non-moral innocence,' analogous to the state which we attribute to the animals ?   or is it possible and necessary to assume that he enjoyed that exalted state of moral and spiritual perfection which is described, by those theologians who accept this hypothesis, as ' Original Righteousness ' ?

Thirdly.   What is the precise nature of the *damnosa haereditas* alleged to have been bequeathed, as the result of the Fall, by the first man to his descendants ?   Is it a positive infection or corruption, or merely a negative weakness ?   Is it the fact of physical desire, or inability to control it ?   Is it merely a psychological state, involving liability to sin in the future, or does it also include a juridical status of responsibility for the sin committed by our first ancestor thousands of years before we were born ? In other words, what is ' Original Sin ' ?   and does it include ' Original Guilt ' ?

Fourthly.   Assuming that Adam communicated ' Original Sin ' to his descendants, in what way is the *mode* of this communication to be conceived ?   Is it to be regarded as consisting in the entail of physiological heredity, or merely in the concatenation of example and imitation, such as is called ' social heredity ' ?   Or are we to assume that Adam, when he fell, actually *was* the whole of humanity, mystically or literally, in such a way that, as we were in him, his sin is our sin ?

Fifthly.   What, in the light of any conclusions which may be reached with regard to the foregoing issues, is the present state of human nature, with which Redemption now has to deal ?   Is it totally depraved and corrupted in all its faculties, or is the hereditary wound to be regarded as a comparatively unimportant scratch ?   or, if the truth lies somewhere between these two extremes, at what precise point is it to be fixed ?

These are questions which are both momentous and subtle, and it must therefore be expected that the task of determining the outlines of the really ' Catholic ' or universal doctrine will become more complicated as our research moves down the centuries. In order to decide what precisely has been believed *ubique, semper, et ab omnibus*, it will be necessary to enquire, not merely whether the Fall-doctrine can be said to have been held by the Christian Church as a whole during a given period, but also (if we conclude that it was) what answers were returned to these crucial questions during the epoch under discussion. It need not, however, be feared that the subject-matter of our research will swell to unmanageable dimensions. As the ideas of the Fall and of Original Sin, despite their apparent logical dependence upon the story of Adam and Eve, are really rooted in, and derive their long-continued vitality from, the facts of spiritual and ethical experience, in particular from the experience known as repentance, we shall find that the opinions held by Christian thinkers with regard to these five cardinal issues tend to group and combine themselves into two well-defined versions of the Fall-doctrine, corresponding to those two contrasted types of religious temperament which William James has conveniently labelled as the ' once-born ' and the ' twice-born ' respectively.[1] The ' once-born ' or ' healthy-minded ' man, whose religious life has unfolded itself in equable and passionless development, exempt from crises or storms, thinks of sin in the light of human freedom and responsibility, and tends to minimize, ignore, or deny the suggested element of inherited obliquity within his soul. So far as he concedes its existence at all, it is for him a weakness, a lack or deficiency, not a corruption or an offence, and deserves the compassion rather than the wrath of an all-just Creator. But the ' twice-born ' man, the ' sick soul,' the Augustine or the Bunyan blessed or cursed from birth with the mysterious heritage of neural and emotional instability, whose passions have been transformed, whose communion with God and peace of mind have been won through the paroxysm of an

---

[1] This distinction has been already mentioned in connexion with St. Paul's doctrine of sin : see above, Lecture III, p. 155 f.

instantaneous conversion, thinks of himself as a ' brand plucked from the burning,' by no effort or volition of his own, and of his unconverted nature as saturated with moral evil and intrinsically hateful to God even before and apart from any particular or concrete transgressions of His law. That portion, therefore, of our historical survey which deals with the evolution of the ideas of the Fall and of Original Sin within Christianity after the Apostolic age will be largely devoted to the task of tracing the parallel growth and studying the mutual interactions of the two classical versions of the Fall-doctrine, to which these two types of spiritual experience have necessarily given birth.

This post-Apostolic history falls naturally into three sections, concerned respectively with Christian opinion between St. Paul and St. Augustine, with the teaching of St. Augustine himself, and with the subsequent developments of Augustinianism. The figure of Augustine, probably the greatest man, next to St. Paul, whom the Christian Church has ever known, stands like a Colossus upon a mountain crest, marking the watershed between the ancient and the modern worlds, and casting its shadow far along the road by which the Fall-doctrine was destined to travel. But the overwhelming influence which the Doctor of Hippo exercised both upon the form and upon the content of these ideas, as upon the rest of Christian theology, at any rate in Western Europe, renders it all the more important, for our purpose of arriving at an accurate formulation of the deep under-lying mind of historic Christianity in regard to this subject, that we should give special attention to the thought of the primitive, pre-Augustinian Church, the Catholic Church of the first four Christian centuries. If, without inelegant abruptness, a second and entirely different metaphor may be employed to illustrate this great man's place in the history of Christian thought, we will venture to suggest that a giant personality such as his might be expected to have the effect of warping and drawing out of proportion the thought of his age, much as the passage of a comet near the solar system has the effect of perturbing and distorting the orbits of the planets. But, in the writers of the epoch which preceded the transit of Augustine across the theological

firmament, we may be confident that we shall find nothing
but the unruffled, uncorrupted thought of historic Christianity, free from the tremors and oscillations which the
gravitational influence of this majestic luminary might
a priori be deemed likely to produce.

The Fall-Doctrine during the Sub-Apostolic Age

Without further preface, then, we resume the thread of
our historical investigation, which now leads us into the
obscure and dimly lighted region of the sub-Apostolic age ;
by which term I mean for the purposes of the enquiry to
denote the hundred and twenty years, more or less, which
elapsed between the deaths of the chief Apostles, St. Peter
and St. Paul (which probably took place in the year A.D. 64),
and the birth of systematic theology in the writings of
Irenaeus (*c.* A.D. 180). Our evidence for this period consists
in the remains of the so-called ' Apostolic Fathers,' and of
the early Apologists (Aristides, Justin Martyr, Tatian,
Theophilus). It is a striking fact, the significance of which
will presently be discussed, that amongst the documents
which have survived from the first ninety years after the
deaths of the chief Apostles, that is which are of a date
anterior to the works of Justin Martyr (who wrote *c.* A.D.
150–155), only one can be found containing an apparent
allusion to the Adamic Fall-theory. This is the anonymous
treatise known as the *Epistle of Barnabas*, dated by
Lightfoot as early as A.D. 70–79, but by the majority of
scholars about A.D. 130,[1] in which it is asserted that there
is a parallelism between the serpents which attacked the
Israelites in the wilderness [2] and the serpent through which
' *the* transgression ' (ἡ παράβασις, the technical term employed by later Greek theology for the ' Fall ' [3]) was wrought
in Eve.

[1] See Harnack, *Chronol. der altchristl. Litteratur* (1897), i. 410–428.
Bardenhewer, *Patrology* (E. tr.), p. 24, following Hilgenfeld, dates it during
the reign of Nerva, A.D. 96–98.

[2] Numbers xxi. 6–9.

[3] See below, p. 252 n. 4.

' For the Lord caused all manner of serpents to bite
them, and they died (forasmuch as the transgression was
wrought in Eve through the serpent) that He might convince
them that by reason of their transgression they should be
delivered over to the affliction of death.' [1]

But this passage stands by itself. Not a word can
be quoted from Clement of Rome, the *Teaching of the
Apostles*, the Epistles of Ignatius and Polycarp, or the
earliest surviving Apology, that of Aristides, as evidence
for the existence of a belief in the Fall of Adam as the fount
of human sin. In short, it would seem true to say that
(with the exception of the doubtful allusion just mentioned)
no trace is found of the Adamic Fall-theory in what survives
of the Christian literature written between the Epistle to
the Romans and the works of Justin Martyr. It is further
to be noted that this solitary allusion (if such it is to be
deemed) to the Fall-theory based upon Gen. iii. is balanced
by allusions to the two other Jewish theories regarding the
origin of evil, one to each, occurring in the documents of
this period. The canonical ' Second Epistle of Peter '
(which is now admitted on all hands to be a polemical
treatise, cast, in accordance with a literary convention
common in the ancient world, into the form of a letter
supposed to have been written by the martyred Prince-
Apostle, and dating from *c.* A.D. 150) refers twice to
the Watcher-theory [2] ; whilst the *Shepherd* of Hermas
(written not earlier than A.D. 90 or later than A.D. 140)
appears in one passage [3] to assume the doctrine of the *yēçer
ha-ra'* (ἐπιθυμία πονηρά), which it asserts to be a ' daughter
of the devil.' We will content ourselves for the moment with
noting the fact that each of the three Jewish theories of the
origin of sin can claim one reference in the scanty literary
detritus which has come down to us from the dark period

---

[1] xii. 5. ἐποίησεν γὰρ Κύριος πάντα ὄφιν δάκνειν αὐτούς, καὶ ἀπέθνησκον,
ἐπειδὴ ἡ παράβασις διὰ τοῦ ὄφεως ἐν Εὔᾳ ἐγένετο, ἵνα ἐλέγξῃ αὐτοὺς ὅτι διὰ
τὴν παράβασιν αὐτῶν εἰς θλῖψιν θανάτου παραδοθήσονται.

[2] i. 4 ; ii. 4 ; see Lecture III, p. 114.

[3] *Mand.* xii. ; this passage, in fact, contains a statement of the doctrine
of the Two *Yeçārīm* (ἐπιθυμία πονηρά and ἐπιθυμία ἀγαθή)—an interesting
instance of the way in which Rabbinical influences continued to penetrate
the Christian Church long after its formal separation from Judaism.

between the deaths of the Apostles and the point at which the nascent Catholic Church begins to stand out in the light of comparatively full documentary evidence. When we pass this point, a change comes over the scene. The last thirty years of the ' sub-Apostolic age ' (c. A.D. 150–180) are marked by a constellation of three Apologists, *Justin, Tatian, Theophilus* ; each of whom contains testimony to the existence of the Adamic doctrine, testimony which is perhaps vague enough when contrasted with the rigid confessional statements familiar to us, but which (at any rate in the case of the two last-named writers) wears an appearance of almost startling definiteness to one who approaches it fresh from the apparent blankness and inconclusiveness of the records of the first ninety years. To these authors, therefore, our attention must now be turned.

(1) *Justin Martyr*. This philosophic convert to Christianity must be pronounced even by the most indulgent critic to be a singularly hazy and confused thinker. We need adduce no further proof of this than his interpolation of the ' host of good angels ' between the Son of God and the Holy Spirit in his enumeration of the objects of Christian worship.[1] We shall therefore be prepared to find that such passing allusions to the subject as are contained in his writings are marked by confusion of thought and lack of mental grip. There is no systematic treatment of the subject, but there are scattered and incidental observations which, when collected, would seem to imply the presence in his thought of something like the Pauline doctrine. The empirical universality of sin is affirmed in the *Dialogue with Trypho the Jew* (c. 95) in which it is asserted that the whole race of man lies under a curse.[2] Though the immediate grounds of the curse are subsequently defined as actual sins, it is natural to suppose that there is a connexion between the idea of the empirical universality of sin and the ideas expressed in the preceding chapter (94) in which Justin borrows the curious conceit of ' Barnabas ' with regard to the parallelism between the serpent which tempted our first parents and the serpents which attacked the Israelites in the

---

[1] 1 *Apol.* 6.

[2] καὶ γὰρ πᾶν γένος ἀνθρώπων εὑρεθήσεται ὑπὸ κατάραν ὄν.

wilderness, and affirms that the purpose of the Incarnation
was to destroy the power of the old serpent, and to bring
man salvation from his bites, which are evil deeds, idolatries,
and other acts of unrighteousness. It would seem that the
underlying thought implies some sort of causal connexion
between the act of the serpent narrated in Gen. iii. and the
present sinful condition of mankind, though this connexion
is not of so stringent a character as to impair the reality of
human free will. In c. 88 of the *Dialogue*, the influence of
the first man's sin and the personal guilt of each of his
descendants are set side by side, without any attempt at
synthesis, in an allusion to—

. . . the race of men, who from Adam had fallen under
death and the deceit of the serpent, not to mention the individual
responsibility of each member of the race who sinned on his own
account.[1]

But the Fall finds its predestined counterpart in the
Redemption wrought by Christ ; and in c. 100 of the same
treatise we meet for the first time the famous parallel of
Eve and Mary, which was seized upon by Christian imagi-
nation as a natural pendant to the Pauline comparison of
Adam and Christ :

He was made man of the Virgin, that by the same way in
which the disobedience which proceeded from the serpent took
its rise, it might also receive its destruction. For Eve when a
virgin and undefiled conceived the word of the serpent, and
brought forth disobedience and death. But Mary the Virgin,
receiving faith and joy, when the angel Gabriel told her the good
news that the Spirit of the Lord should come upon her . . .
answered, Be it unto me according to thy word.[2]

Little or nothing is explicitly said as to the exact nature
of the causal link between the first man's sin and the sins of

---

[1] οὐδὲ τὸ γεννηθῆναι αὐτὸν καὶ σταυρωθῆναι, ὡς ἐνδεὴς τούτων, ὑπέμεινεν,
ἀλλ' ὑπὲρ τοῦ γένους τοῦ τῶν ἀνθρώπων, ὃ ἀπὸ τοῦ Ἀδὰμ ὑπὸ θάνατον καὶ πλάνην
τὴν τοῦ ὄφεως ἐπεπτώκει, παρὰ τὴν ἰδίαν αἰτίαν ἑκάστου αὐτῶν πονηρευσαμένου.

[2] καὶ διὰ τῆς παρθένου ἄνθρωπον γεγονέναι, ἵνα καὶ δι' ἧς ὁδοῦ ἡ ἀπὸ τοῦ
ὄφεως παρακοὴ τὴν ἀρχὴν ἔλαβε, καὶ διὰ ταύτης τῆς ὁδοῦ καὶ κατάλυσιν λάβῃ.
παρθένος γὰρ οὖσα Εὔα καὶ ἄφθορος τὸν λόγον τὸν ἀπὸ τοῦ ὄφεως συλλαβοῦσα
παρακοὴν καὶ θάνατον ἔτεκε· πίστιν δὲ καὶ χαρὰν λαβοῦσα Μαρία ἡ παρθένος
εὐαγγελιζομένου αὐτῇ Γαβριὴλ ἀγγέλου ὅτι πνεῦμα κυρίου ἐπ' αὐτὴν ἐπελεύσεται . . .
ἀπεκρίνατο· γένοιτό μοι κατὰ τὸ ῥῆμά σου.

his posterity. A phrase, indeed, which occurs in the first Apology (c. 10)—' the universally evil and manifold appetite which exists in each man ' [1]—is reminiscent of the idea of the ' evil imagination.' But it is possible that a vague and fugitive allusion to some kind of hereditary taint or flaw may be discovered in his exposition of the regenerating effects of baptism, in which we are told that man by birth is ' a child of necessity and ignorance,' but that by baptism he becomes ' a child of choice and knowledge.' [2] It is evident that Justin regarded the sin of Adam as having had some kind of evil influence upon the race, but it is not clear whether he regarded this evil influence as having been propagated by way of physical or merely of social heredity. In other words, his ideas on the subject would seem to be considerably vaguer than those of St. Paul ; and it is certain that the explanation of evil which interests him most, and occupies the forefront of his thinking on the subject, is to be found in his conception of the ' evil demons,' who according to primitive Christian thought swarmed everywhere, speaking through the pagan oracles, working lying wonders, and obsessing the bodies and souls of men.

Much more explicit and exhaustive treatments of the subject are to be found in the Apology of *Tatian*, the Syrian ascetic and student of the Gospels, and in the treatise *To Autolycus* of *Theophilus*, reckoned by tradition as the sixth Bishop of Antioch after St. Peter ; both of which documents may be dated somewhere between A.D. 170 and 180.

(2) *Tatian* tells us that man was created free and non-moral.[3] He was not created good, for God alone is good by nature, but was created with a capacity for goodness ; and the assistance of the Spirit or the Logos (Christian theology

---

[1] τὴν ἐν ἑκάστῳ κακὴν πρὸς πάντα καὶ ποικίλην φύσει ἐπιθυμίαν. It is noteworthy that the ' evil demons ' are in this passage said to take the κακὴ ἐπιθυμία as an ally (σύμμαχος)—an anticipation of the familiar homiletic method of combining the theories which respectively attribute temptation to the suggestion of Satan and to the inbred fault of human nature.

[2] 1 *Apol.* 61. ὅπως μὴ ἀνάγκης τέκνα μηδὲ ἀγνοίας μένωμεν ἀλλὰ προαιρέσεως καὶ ἐπιστήμης. But see the whole passage, which appears in a vague and elusive way to bracket together ' physical ' and ' social ' heredity as grounds of the evil tendency in man.

[3] *oratio contra Graecos*, 7.

is still not very clear as to the distinction between the two)
was given him in order to help him to realise this capacity.
As a result of his sin[1] the guidance of the Spirit was withdrawn ; man became mortal, and was shut out from intercourse with God.   Hence the human soul is afflicted by an
inherent weakness which renders it susceptible to the
assaults of the demons.   This weakness, however, is not so
grave as to destroy the power of self-determination and
consequent responsibility, on which Tatian strongly insists.
If we allow for the difference of times and the absence of
technical terminology, this is almost exactly the doctrine
of Duns Scotus, which finds the essence of ' Original Sin '
in the lack of the supernatural gifts of grace enjoyed by
the first man in his paradisal condition.[2]   (3) A similar presentation of the subject is found in the Apology addressed
by *Theophilus* to Autolycus.[3]   Man was created neither
mortal nor immortal, but capable of either state.   God gave
him ' a starting-point for progress ' ($\dot{a}\phi o\rho\mu\dot{\eta}$ $\pi\rho o\kappa o\pi\hat{\eta}s$), and if
he had made good use of this he would have developed
rapidly in the way of sanctification and intellectual perfection, finally becoming refined into pure spirit and
assimilated to the divine nature.   His unfallen state is said
to have been infantile and undeveloped,[4] and it is on this
basis that Theophilus explains the divine prohibition
against man's acquisition of knowledge.   Knowledge in
itself is good, but some kinds of knowledge are undesirable
for children.   If man had followed the upward path of
development, as his Creator had intended, the ban upon the
acquisition of knowledge might possibly have been removed
at a later date.   All the physical woes of human life are to
be reckoned as the consequences of man's expulsion from
Paradise ; but there is no mention of a train of interior and
psychological effects flowing from the sin which merited this
expulsion.   Again, however, as in the case of Justin, though
both Tatian and Theophilus seem to accept the general

---

[1] This is vaguely described as ' following that one of the angels who
was wiser than the rest, because he was the first-created ' and ' regarding
him as God.'

[2] See Lecture VI, p. 410.   [3] *ad Autol.* ii. 24, 25.

[4] *ibid.* 25 : ὁ Ἀδὰμ ἔτι νήπιος ὤν : *cf.* also ἅμα δὲ καὶ ἐπὶ πλείονα
χρόνον ἐβούλετο ἁπλοῦν καὶ ἀκέραιον διαμεῖναι τὸν ἄνθρωπον νηπιάζοντα.

teaching of St. Paul as to the entrance of sin into the world through Adam, it is nevertheless clear that the theory which really dominates their minds, and is instinct with the poignancy born of direct experience (real or supposed), is that of an airy multitude of demons which haunt the earth and the lower atmosphere, sometimes appearing visibly in the character of the pagan gods and perpetrating monstrous crimes, and always assailing the individual Christian with the invisible weapons of evil imaginations and thoughts. As we have before pointed out,[1] the hypotheses of diabolical suggestion *ab extra* and of evil auto-suggestion *ab intra*, arising from an inherited inclination or predisposition of the soul towards sin, are by no means to be considered as mutually irreconcileable explanations of the fact of wrongful impulse ; but they are distinct, and at least potentially alternative, explanations ; and it would seem that in the minds of these three Apologists, typical, we need not doubt, of the Roman[2] and Syrian Churches of their day, whilst the second is formally believed, it is the first which is most intensely felt and which has the greatest share in determining Christian practice. All the writers of this epoch insist strongly upon the reality of man's free-will.[3]

The Relation of St. Paul's Teaching to the Thought of the Sub-Apostolic Age

At the close of the sub-Apostolic age it is natural to pause for a moment, in order, if possible, to discover an

[1] Lecture III, p. 109.

[2] After his baptism, Justin appears to have resided at Rome (Eus. *H.E.* iv. 11) and to have been martyred there (*ibid.* iv. 16).

[3] It may be added, for the sake of completeness, that the literature of this period contains three allusions, other than those discussed in the text, to the Paradise-story of Gen. iii. : namely, *Epistle to Diognetus*, 12 (a rhetorical allegorisation of Paradise) ; a saying of an unnamed ' Presbyter ' (that is, one who had been taught by Apostles) preserved by Irenaeus, *adv. haer*. III. xxxiii. 2 (Harvey); and another saying of unnamed ' Presbyters,' *ibid.*, V. v. 1. None of these allusions, when examined, yields any testimony to the existence of a Fall-*doctrine*. Athenagoras, *libellus pro Christianis*, 24, 25 (ed. E. Schwartz, in *Texte u. Untersuch*. iv. 2) alludes to the Watcher-story of Gen. vi., but uses it merely as an explanation of the origin of the demons, whom he (doubtless following 1 Enoch) identifies with the lustful angels and the spirits of the giants their sons.

explanation of certain remarkable phenomena disclosed by
our survey of its literary remains.   These are, *firstly*, the
fact that—whereas St. Paul, writing to the Corinthian and
Roman churches, in A.D. 52 and 56 respectively, seems to
assume the Adamic Fall-doctrine with the greatest confidence, as an idea entirely familiar to his readers, and therefore presumably to all Christians—no other trace of this
doctrine (with the exception of the doubtful passage in
' Barnabas ' mentioned above) is found in Christian literature
until we come to Justin Martyr, nearly a hundred years later
than the dates of I Corinthians and Romans ; and, *secondly*,
the fact that when we have once passed the mysterious
date *c.* A.D. 150, unmistakeable allusions to the Fall-doctrine
begin to occur, and, as we shall see, are found in ecclesiastical
writers with increasing frequency the further we descend the
stream of the centuries.   It is tempting to explain the (all
but complete) silence of the first ninety years by the suggestion that this is merely apparent, due to the scantiness of the
literary evidence ; and that, for all we know, the Expositions
of Papias, the Apology of Quadratus, the Dialogue of Aristo
of Pella, and other writings of this remote epoch which have
perished through the lapse of time or the rage of persecutors,
may have abounded in references to the sin of Adam and
its disastrous results.   But the historical causes—accident,
persecutions, and the like—which have destroyed so many
of the documents produced during this period, must clearly
be deemed, precisely because from our point of view they
were blind and fortuitous, to have operated with complete
impartiality as between the ideas which may have been
expressed in those documents.   The doctrine of chances,
therefore, compels us to assume that, on the whole, the
proportion which the various ideas of the Faith bear to each
other in such sub-Apostolic literature as actually survives
does roughly represent the balance of the collective mind of
Christendom as it existed during this epoch.   If this be so,
we are driven to the conclusions that the Church of the first
three generations after the Apostles, whilst holding, in
undefined and rudimentary form, the great beliefs in the
Godhead of Father, Son, and Holy Spirit, in Christ's death
for man, and in the Divine power of the sacraments, had

made little effort to grapple with the question of the ultimate origin of evil; that, so far as this question had been raised at all, Christians were still divided between the three views which had prevailed in the Jewish Church (namely, the Adam-theory, the Watcher-theory, and the doctrine of the *yēçer ha-ra'*); and that St. Paul's teaching, as contained in 1 Corinthians and Romans, had had comparatively little effect on Christian thought. The question becomes all the more insistent—If the Pauline doctrine was in practice ignored down to the middle of the second century, what was the unknown factor which at that time suddenly came into play, disseminating and popularising this doctrine in such a manner that within another two generations it had become the sole official and ecclesiastical theory of the origin and ground of sin?

In order to answer this question satisfactorily, it is necessary to find a hypothesis which will at once explain St. Paul's confident assumption of the Fall-theory, its apparent eclipse for nearly a hundred years after the date of Romans, and its re-appearance in the writings of Justin Martyr and the later Apologists. To do this, we are constrained to re-traverse some of the ground which was covered in our last lecture. It was there suggested that St. Paul derived this belief, along with the essential Christian message, from the elder Apostles and other Galilean followers of our Lord, who themselves may be supposed to have imbibed it, not so much from any direct teaching of the Master, as from the apocalyptic literature with which they had been familiar long before they met Him. If the Fall-doctrine came to St. Paul as part of the setting of the Gospel, on authority so impressive as that of the original friends and Apostles of Jesus, it is natural that he should have taken it for granted as an indisputable truth; and, as we have seen, his own ethical and spiritual sense is a sufficient explanation of his emphatic preference for the ' Adamic ' as against the ' angelic ' version of the theory. But it was pointed out at the same time that the fact of St. Paul's taking this idea for granted in writing to Corinth and Rome does not necessarily prove that it was already accepted, consciously and explicitly, by all of his readers: it merely proves that no other theory held an exclusive dominance of the field.[1] It is characteristic of men of sanguine and enthusiastic temperament, such as was the Apostle of the Gentiles, to assume that those consciously agree with them who are merely not prepared to contradict them. The most, therefore, of which we can be certain with regard to the state of opinion in Gentile Christendom when St. Paul wrote his Epistles amounts to this—that the ' Adam-theory ' was known to some Gentile Christians, and not denied by any.

It may, however, be asked ' Even if this were the case at the moment when St. Paul wrote, should we not expect that the unhesitating assumption of the Adamic Fall-doctrine by so mighty a teacher as the Apostle of the uncircumcision, the Primate and Father of the Gentile Churches, would have had the effect of causing all his readers to give their allegiance to this doctrine at once, in submission to his inspired authority ? ' In reply to this question, it must be pointed out that St. Paul, when he wrote his letters, had no idea that he was writing ' Scripture,' nor were those letters regarded as ' Scripture,' though they were doubtless treated with the greatest respect and veneration, by their immediate recipients. For the first century of its existence, the Christian Church possessed no ' Scriptures,' recognised as such, other than the Scriptures of the Jewish Church ; the only ' Bible ' known to St. Paul's converts, to the Apostolic Fathers, and to the earliest Apologists was roughly identical with what we should call the Septuagint Old Testament [2] ; and even with reference to a date as late as A.D. 120, it would be true to say that the whole conception of a ' New Testament,' composed of authoritative Christian writings, and claiming a canonicity and inspiration equal to that of the Law and the Prophets of the elder dispensation, still lay in the womb of the future. Hence it is not to be expected that a couple of *obiter dicta*, one of them couched in somewhat obscure language, would immediately leaven the whole of Christian

---

[1] See above, Lecture III, p. 117.

[2] See three articles by Sir Henry Howorth on ' The influence of St. Jerome on the (Biblical) Canon of the Western Church,' *JTS*, July 1909, April 1910, Oct. 1911.

thought, or meet with instant comprehension and acceptance by the totality of Gentile believers. If it be remembered that the minds of St. Paul's readers must have been super-saturated with the belief in demons as the immediate authors of all evil—a belief which would be reinforced, not merely by the influences of their pagan environment, but by many recorded sayings of the Lord Himself—it is easy to see that the Pauline teaching about Adam and the consequences of his sin would be likely, so far as it was noticed or com-prehended at all, to remain for some considerable time in the dim background or penumbra of the Church's thought ; and that its gradual penetration into the central areas of that thought would naturally proceed at a very slow rate, until accelerated, towards the middle of the second century, by the canonisation of the documents in which it was embodied as part of the Pauline *corpus*, the second main constituent, after the Gospels, of the ' New Testament.'

It is, I would suggest, with this event—the formation of the Canon of the New Testament—that the sudden revival of the Fall-doctrine, after a period of apparent abeyance, is in the first instance to be connected. It will have become clear from the foregoing exposition that some occurrence of ecclesiastical or theological importance, the beginnings of which may be dated *c.* A.D. 140–150, is needed in order to explain the silence of Christian writers prior to that date, and the ever-increasing crop of allusions which springs up immediately after it ; and the canonisation of the New Testament is precisely what we require. The exaltation of the First Epistle to the Corinthians and the Epistle to the Romans from the rank of venerable monuments of primitive devotion to that of divinely inspired oracles, co-ordinate with the Law and the Prophets, would implicitly carry with it the promotion of the Adamic Fall-doctrine from the status of a ' pious opinion ' to something like that of a revealed dogma : and it may well seem that, within the sphere of external or superficial causes, no further explanation need be sought.

But no serious student of human ideas will need to be reminded that the procession of visible external happenings, controversies, definitions, and the like, which makes up what is called the 'history of dogma' (*Dogmengeschichte*) in the text-book sense of the term, is but the *epiphenomenon*, the surface ebullition and agitation which both veils and symbolises the play of mightier and more primary causes beneath, operating in the dim region of instinct and sub-conscious thought which must be assumed to lie at the base as well of a 'group-mind' like that of the Christian Church, considered in respect of its corporate organic life, as of an individual human mind.   It is not difficult, in the present instance, to descend from the outer to the inner, and to lay bare the deeper causes to which, in the last resort, the seemingly sudden popularisation of the Fall-doctrine which took place towards the end of the second century must be attributed.   The formation of the Canon of the New Testa-ment, like the elaboration of baptismal creeds, and the universal adoption of monarchical, in the place of collegiate, episcopacy, was part of the half-conscious process whereby the still young and tender Church developed, as it were automatically, a hard protective shell or armour, doctrinal and institutional, to safeguard the principle of its life against the vast, creeping, impalpable menace of Gnosticism. This extraordinary movement—the forms which it assumed were too bewilderingly manifold, and its intimate essence was too chameleon-like and elusive, to justify us in describing it as a doctrine or a system—arose prior to the birth of Christianity and in purely heathen environments.   But, immediately upon coming into contact with our religion, Gnosticism discovered a peculiar and, so to speak, parasitic affinity with it, adhering like a fungoid growth to the body of the 'Great Church' and striving to penetrate it at every pore, deftly disguising itself in Christian forms, borrowing the names of Christ and the Holy Spirit, claiming, finally, to be the true and authentic version of Christianity, handed down by a secret tradition known only to an inner circle of adepts, and standing in sharp opposition to what it alleged to be the vulgar, 'psychic,' or carnal version transmitted by the public tradition of the Apostolic Churches.   The beginnings of these syncretistic infiltrations are already a source of anxiety to some of the New Testament writers : witness the Apostolic denunciation of philosophy, exaggerated asceticism, and angel-worship directed to the Colossians,[1] and the Pauline, or deutero-Pauline, condemnation of ' Gnosis falsely so called.' [2]

It is impossible here to analyse the genesis of this primitive theosophy, or to disentangle the diverse elements, Mazdean, Babylonian, Hindu, Egyptian, which entered into its composition ; nor indeed are those scholars who have devoted long years of research to the subject of Gnosticism as yet agreed upon a single theory of its origin.[3] The two facts which emerge with unmistakeable clearness from the welter of conflicting systems are these—(a) that the root-idea of Gnosticism, underlying equally all its multitudinous shapes, was cosmic *pessimism*, the conviction that evil is eternally and necessarily bound up with the existence of the universe of finite, relative, and material being, and (b) that its redemptive method was conceived as purely intellectual, mediated through the acquisition of esoteric knowledge. The basal pessimism of the movement expressed itself sometimes in a *monistic* world-theory, such as that of Valentinus, with its hierarchy of aeons or emanations bridging over the gulf between the Absolute and matter, sometimes in an explicit *dualism*, which maintained a Demiurge or evil Creator, co-eternal with the good God ; of this latter tendency, Marcion, who identified the Demiurge with Jehovah, the God of the Jews and of the Old Testament, is perhaps the most typical representative. But, whichever type of Gnosticism—monistic or dualistic—at any given moment confronted her, the instinctive reaction of the ' Great Church ' towards it was always the same : she recognised intuitively that she was in the presence of the ancient and most deadly foe of that ethical monotheism which she had inherited from Judaism as the foundation and presupposition of the Gospel message. The lists were set for the next battle in the agelong struggle of the Asiatic

---

[1] Col. ii. 16 ff. See Bishop Lightfoot's commentary *in loc.*, and his Introduction, § II, ' The Colossian Heresy.'

[2] 1 Tim. vi. 20.

[3] The most recent survey of the data now available with reference to this vast problem seems to be the latest edition (1911) of W. Bousset's *Hauptprobleme der Gnosis* ; see also the articles in *PRE*, vi. p. 728 (' Gnosis, Gnosticismus,' G. Krüger) and *ERE*, vi. p. 231 (' Gnosticism,' E. F. Scott).

philosophies which affirm the eternity and necessity of evil
with the Judaeo-Christian belief in the supremacy of good
and the consequent contingency of sin ; and the inevitable
effect of the pressure of Gnosticism upon the Church was
to compel Christian thinkers to face the question of the
ultimate origin of evil, and, we may reasonably surmise,
to force them back upon a neglected element in St. Paul's
teaching, namely, the doctrine of the Fall. As in the
Maccabean period of the elder dispensation, so also at the
close of the sub-Apostolic age, the doctrine that evil is not
eternal or necessary, but traceable to a primitive self-
perversion of finite wills—a self-perversion which *ex hypothesi*
need not have happened—was brought out of the Church's
armoury, where it had rested unused and almost unnoticed
for a hundred years, to serve as the sure shield for safeguarding the Biblical conception of God. We shall have
occasion again in the course of our historical survey to note
the significant fact that the invasion of Christendom by a
wave of Oriental pessimism or dualism is usually followed
by a striking development of Fall-speculation within the
Church. Meanwhile, we may be content, so far as this
stage of our enquiry is concerned, with the conclusion—
paradoxical enough at first sight, yet fitting the known facts
so accurately as to admit of little doubt, in the present state
of our knowledge—that it was Gnosticism which indirectly
saved St. Paul's teaching with regard to the Fall and
' Original Sin ' : partly by its claim to be authentic Christianity, which brought about the canonisation of the first
Epistle to the Corinthians and the Epistle to the Romans,
but mainly by its fundamental affirmation of the *necessity*
of evil, which stimulated in the Catholic Church a revival of
the only authoritative doctrine in which the idea of the
contingency of evil was enshrined.

THE VINCENTIAN CANON AND THE SUB-APOSTOLIC AGE

If the preceding argument is well founded, our map of
the route by which the Fall-doctrine found its way into
accepted Christian teaching is now complete. The line of

that route, starting in the immediately pre-Christian pseudepigrapha, runs first through Galilee and the beliefs of our Lord's earliest disciples and followers, then through the mind of St. Paul, as instructed by St. Peter and the original Apostles, then, from the letters of St. Paul, after they had been canonised and placed on a level with the Jewish Bible, into the speculations of the later second-century Apologists, and so into the developing fabric of orthodox Christian theology. We have already drawn attention to the fact that the line does not, so far as we have been able to gather, run directly through the primary source of specifically Christian doctrine, namely the teaching of our Lord Himself, but rather, if we may say so, leaves it somewhat to one side. But it was at the same time pointed out that this fact would not in itself militate against the right of the Fall-doctrine to be considered as a member of the system of Christian truth, if the constructive part of our enquiry were to justify its claim to be a necessary outcome of the experience of penitence and an inevitable inference from the Christian conception of God and of His relation to the world. Our review of the sub-Apostolic age has, however, raised another question, of a formal rather than of a material nature, which must be disposed of before our research can proceed upon its way. 'If,' it may be asked, ' the object of your historical survey is to discover the precise maximum of Fall-doctrine which may be said to have been accepted by the Christian Church as a whole —and if the criterion of acceptance by the Church is that defined by the Vincentian Canon, namely, acceptance *ubique, semper, et ab omnibus*—is not a serious obstacle to further enquiry created by the conclusions which you have just formulated with regard to the sub-Apostolic age ? For, according to those conclusions, the Church of the period between St. Paul and Justin Martyr had not yet decisively made up its mind between the three Jewish theories of the ultimate origin of evil, and was not in possession of any one universally accepted Fall-doctrine. The Adamic-theory, therefore, fails to fulfil the test embodied in the word *semper* ; and it would seem useless to proceed any further down the stream of history. If the Fall-doctrine as a whole

is ruled out of the sphere of ideas which have been accepted
semper—that is, on your own hypothesis, out of the sphere
of ideas to which the Christian Church as such may be said
to be traditionally committed—by this disconcerting gap
of a hundred years at the beginning of its Christian
history, it will be waste of time to discuss its later
developments.'

It is undoubtedly true that—despite its *prima facie*
lucidity and convenience as a working ' rule of thumb '—
the Vincentian Canon can easily be made to generate a host
of logical puzzles, if severely analysed. And it may be
admitted at once that if the terms ' everywhere,' ' always '
and ' by all ' are to be tightly shackled together, so as to
constitute one single criterion, instead of three loosely
connected and potentially alternative criteria—and if the
single criterion so obtained is to be rigorously pressed, in
the strict and literal sense of each of its three component
terms—the consequence suggested by the objector necessarily
follows. But this mechanical method of construing the
Vincentian test speedily reduces itself *ad absurdum* ; for it
would also rule out the canonicity of the New Testament
itself, and compel us to assert that ' Catholic ' belief can
only be said to recognise the Bible of the Jews, that is the
Old Testament, as inspired, inasmuch as during the greater
part of the sub-Apostolic age the idea of a ' New Testament '
parallel to and of equal authority with the Hebrew Scriptures
was unknown. And yet no reasonable person would deny
that, if there are any principles to which the whole Church
may be said to be committed (however ' the whole Church '
may be defined), the authority of the New Testament is one
of those principles. It may be added that such a rigorous
interpretation of the Vincentian Canon would render it
useless for the purposes of the modern critical student of
Christian doctrine ; for he could not employ it in this form
without accepting the assumption, which it would then imply, that the essential ideas of historical Christianity must
constitute a static, crystalline, lifeless system, incapable
of growth or development in respect either of verbal expression or of logical articulation—an assumption which
is contradicted by the most patent facts of history,

and indeed was repudiated by St. Vincent of Lerins himself.[1]

It will be clear that the sense in which we adopted, and propose to employ, the Vincentian Canon as a working standard is considerably more elastic than that presupposed by our hypothetical critic. We have already been at pains to point out that our use of this principle is meant, not to guarantee the objective truth of the ' Catholic ' doctrines of the Fall and of Original Sin—for that is precisely the question which we have reserved for discussion in our last two lectures—but merely to enable us to define their exact content. In any case, however, it follows from the fact of doctrinal evolution that the Vincentian test must always be employed with a certain spirit of accommodation, as a μολύβδινος κανών or flexible rule,[2] continuously adapting itself to the differing stages of development which Christian thought and belief had reached at successive epochs of their history. The reasonable enquirer, who recognises that historic Christianity is a living growth, to be interpreted by means of biological rather than mechanical categories, will not expect to find all the lineaments characteristic of adult maturity present with equally sharp definition in the plastic vagueness of infancy ; nor will he be surprised if the Christian ideas regarding human nature and the sinful tendency prove at their beginnings to have passed through an ambiguous or neutral phase, analogous to that disclosed by science in the foetal life of animals, a phase during which it would have appeared uncertain to an external observer which of two alternative characters the fully grown organism was destined to bear. Supposing, in short, that the Fall-doctrine is eventually shown to fulfil the tests of acceptance *ubique* and *ab omnibus* for the immensely greater part of the Church's history, such an one will consider that the test of *semper* has been sufficiently satisfied if the idea in question was accepted at least by some members of the Church during

---

[1] *commonitorium*, c. xxiii. ' sed forsitan dicit aliquis : nullusne ergo in ecclesia Christi profectus habebitur religionis ? habeatur plane, et maximus.' See the whole of this chapter, which treats of dogmatic development.

[2] Ar. *Eth. Nic.* v. X, 78 (1137 b. 30).

its infantile and formative age. Our description of Christ's methods of instruction[1] will have prepared him for the fact that the history of Christian doctrine begins with a period of intellectual immaturity and (relative) indetermination, during which the general diffused mind of the Church was slowly clearing itself in regard to the question, which parts of the apocalyptic theology current in our Lord's lifetime were so intimately presupposed by His explicit teaching that they must needs be regarded as *implicitly* belonging to the essence of Christianity, and which parts deserved to be discarded as useless lumber or pernicious superstition.[2] And, in the light of this fact, he will not quarrel with a slight glossatory expansion of the Vincentian formula which would make it read ' quod *semper* quidem ab aliquibus, iam pridem vero *ubique et ab omnibus* creditum est.'

That the Fall-doctrine must have been believed *by some* during the sub-Apostolic age is guaranteed by its occurrence in two of St. Paul's chief epistles, which, though not yet formally canonised, can be shown from the fragments surviving from the literature of this age to have enjoyed great veneration and authority.[3] We shall, accordingly, deem that its claim to have been believed *semper* is not prejudiced by the fact that the Pauline teaching took a hundred years to sink into the general mind of the Christian society, and (humanly speaking) was only stereotyped as a fixed idea in that mind by the assaults of the rival doctrines (' unmoral monism ' and ' dualism ') which inspired the Gnostic movement. How, and when, it came to be accepted *ab omnibus*, we must now proceed to enquire.

---

[1] Lecture III, p. 106 f.

[2] The belief in a millennial reign of the Messiah and His saints upon this earth is an instance of a Jewish apocalyptic idea which, though widely held by primitive Christians, including Irenaeus, Lactantius, Methodius of Olympus, and, for a time, Augustine himself (*de civ. Dei*, xx. 7), was eventually discarded by the collective mind of the Church as not contained or implied in our Lord's teaching : it will be argued in the following pages that the belief in a ' Fall ' of some kind is an instance of an idea of similar *provenance* which, on the contrary, has been recognised and accepted by the Church as tacitly presupposed by the Gospel message.

[3] See *The New Testament in the Apostolic Fathers* (Oxford, 1905).

THE DOCTRINE OF THE FALL IN IRENAEUS

The Christian literature of the ' sub-Apostolic ' age, so far as we can judge from its surviving fragments and from notices of now lost works in Eusebius and other later writers, consisted in the main of occasional and unsystematic[1] compositions, written to deal with particular emergencies or to fulfil special purposes, homiletic, apologetic, or polemical. No synoptic treatment of the whole body of Christian ideas is therefore to be found in what remains of it ; the scope of the Apologies designed to vindicate the Faith in the judgment of the Roman Government and of the educated non-Christian public was limited by the natural unwillingness of the Church to disclose more than could be helped of her mysteries to profane eyes ; and it may, indeed, be doubted whether the great constitutive conceptions of our religion had as yet attained to a degree of fixity and definiteness sufficient to allow of their being formulated in any shape approximating to that of a text-book or *Summa* of dogmatic theology. But the increasing pressure of the Gnostic movement, which found its spear-head in the organisation of the first Christian schism, the powerful Marcionite Church, compelled the ' Great ' or ' Catholic ' *Ecclesia* to follow up the measures of instinctive self-defence which we have already noted (the development of the Canon of the New Testament, of the baptismal Creeds, and of the universal Episcopate) by the production of more or less systematic expositions of orthodox Christianity, endeavouring to embody the whole contents of the Apostolic tradition and to exhibit them as a coherent *corpus* of truth. The first ecclesiastical writer to undertake the task of framing such an exposition was *Irenaeus* (c. A.D. 130–c. 202), native of Asia Minor, pupil of Polycarp and other unnamed ' Elders,' and Bishop of Lyons in Gaul, whose great treatise

[1] The lost *Syntagma* of Justin, as its name suggests, may have been ' systematic ' in the sense of possessing a logical order or arrangement ; but it is not likely to have been a work of ' systematic theology ' as the term is now used, inasmuch as its purpose would seem to have been rather that of refuting heresies than of formulating orthodoxy (Justin, 1 *Apol.* xxvi. 8).

against Heresies may with probability be assigned to the period A.D. 175-185.

Substantially the same doctrine as to the Fall and Original Sin is found in the work just mentioned and in the lately discovered *Demonstration of the Apostolic Preaching*,[1] though we may note that the latter embodies the Watcher-story [2] in a form which is clearly based upon 1 Enoch vii. 1 ; here, however, the sin of the angels is not regarded as being itself the ' Fall,' but is merely narrated as a consequence of the Fall, which, in conformity with the now all-powerful teaching of St. Paul, is identified with the transgression of Adam. The doctrine of Irenaeus in the main continues and develops that which we found hazily presupposed in Justin and more clearly stated in Tatian and Theophilus. The main points of the fundamental Pauline scheme, namely, that sin came into the world mediately or immediately through the first man's transgression, that there is a causal connexion of some kind between Adam's sin and the sinfulness of his posterity, and that the infirmity or taint so attaching to human nature is cancelled and done away by baptism, are such commonplaces of his teaching that it is unnecessary to refer to individual passages. We may content ourselves with noting the interesting fact that he repeats the famous parallel first drawn by Justin Martyr between the virgin Eve and the Virgin Mary,[3] adding to it

---

[1] εἰς ἐπίδειξιν τοῦ ἀποστολικοῦ κηρύγματος. An Armenian translation of this long-lost work of Irenaeus was discovered at Eriwan in Armenia, by Dr. Karapet Ter-Mekerttshian, in 1904 ; the text with a German translation was published by him in collaboration with Dr. Erwand Ter-Minassiantz, in *Texte u. Untersuch.* xxxi. 1. An English translation, with introduction and notes, was published by Dr. J. Armitage Robinson in 1920 (S.P.C.K. ' Translations of Christian Literature ') : I have used it for the quotations which occur in the text. The passages in this work which deal with the Fall are cc. 12-18, 31-33.

[2] c. 18.

[3] Justin, *Dial.* 100 (see above, p. 174) ; Irenaeus, *adv. haer.* III. xxxii. 1, ' eam quae est a Maria in Evam recirculationem significans ' ; V. xix. 1, ' et si ea inobediret Deo, sed et haec suasa est obedire Deo, uti virginis Evae virgo Maria fieret advocata ' (see the whole context of both these citations). All references to the *adv. haer.* in the following pages are given in accordance with Harvey's edition of Irenaeus. *Demonstration*, 33, ' For it was necessary that Adam should be summed up in Christ, that mortality might be summed up and overwhelmed by immortality ; and Eve summed up in Mary, that a virgin should be a virgin's intercessor,

the second, equally celebrated parallel between the Tree of the Knowledge of Good and Evil and the Tree of Calvary [1] ; and with summarising certain striking and original views which he holds with reference to three of the five cardinal issues formulated at the beginning of this lecture. It will be noticed that Irenaeus is the first author whose Fall-doctrine possesses a content rich and stable enough to necessitate the employment of these logical subdivisions of the subject, which can hardly be applied to the vague and unsystematised ideas of the writers reviewed so far.

(i) The first of the cardinal issues is that of the literal historicity of the Adam-story. There can be no doubt that Irenaeus, like St. Paul and most of the Fathers, believed in the reality of a first man (he seems to recognise that ' Adam ' is not a proper name [2]) and of a first woman, called Eve. But, if the long fragment of a lost treatise of his preserved by Anastasius Sinaita,[3] a seventh-century writer, be genuine (as there seems no reason to doubt), he took a remarkably modern view of the story of the serpent and the forbidden fruit. The quotation of a few sentences will make this clear.

How is it possible that the serpent which was created by God naturally devoid of speech and reason should utter reasonable and articulate language ? If it spontaneously acquired for itself reason and discernment and understanding and the power to answer what was said by the woman, then there is no reason why any serpent should not do the same. But if they [presumably the Ophites, against whom these words were written] assert that it was enabled to address Eve with a human voice by a Divine plan and dispensation, then they set up God as the author of sin. Nor, moreover, was it possible for the wicked

---

and by a virgin's obedience undo and put away the disobedience of a virgin.' Cf. Tertullian, de carne Christi, 17, ' crediderat Eva serpenti : credidit Maria Gabrieli. quod illa credendo deliquit, haec credendo delevit.'

[1] adv. haer. V. xvi. 2 ; xvii. 4 ; Demonstr. 34.

[2] adv. haer. III. xxxiii. 1.

[3] In considerationes anagogicae in Hexaemeron, X (PG LXXXIX, 1013B–1014C). Anastasius says that the passage was written by Irenaeus against the Ophites, the Gnostic sect which worshipped the serpent of Gen. iii. Harvey, who numbers the fragment XIV (vol. ii. of his edition, pp. 483–6), doubts its genuineness, but merely on the subjective ground that it deals too brusquely with Holy Scripture.

demon to bestow reason upon a nature devoid of reason, and so to summon an endowment out of non-existence into existence ; for < if this had been possible > he would never have ceased to converse with men, with a view to deceiving them, by means of serpents and beasts and birds, and so to lead them astray.

He proceeds to apply a similar rationalising criticism to other details of the Fall-story, such as the serpent's knowledge of the Divine command, his accosting Eve in the first place instead of Adam, the weakness which Adam displayed in falling without a struggle. If we set this fragment side by side with the passages in the *adversus haereses* and the *Demonstration* in which the Fall is alluded to—noting that in most of these passages, whilst insisting upon the reality of our first parents' transgression, he seems carefully to refrain from specifying its exact nature—we shall conclude that he must have taken the episode of the serpent and the fruit in a purely allegorical sense, as veiling some sin of which the character is unknown to us.

It does not follow that he interpreted the rest of the Biblical history of Adam and Eve in the same way ; from his treatment of Eve's creation, the expulsion from Paradise and Cain's fratricide, we should naturally infer that his view of these incidents was strictly realistic. Modern readers may, indeed, find it difficult to believe that Irenaeus does not mean to allegorise the whole story from beginning to end, when they come across expressions of ideas which he shared with and doubtless inherited from the Slavonic Enoch and St. Paul : namely that the ' Paradise ' from which our first parents were ejected is situated *outside* the world which we know, on some transcendental super-terrestrial plane (described in terms of Rabbinical cosmology as the ' third heaven ' [1]) ; that it is identical with the Paradise in which repose the spirits of just men made perfect, and that even in this life the favoured saint may be for a brief space caught up thither in mystic rapture, as was the Apostle of the Gentiles in the ecstasy which he has himself described.[2]

---

[1] See 2 Enoch, viii (Charles, *Apocr. and Pseudepigr.* ii. p. 433 f.) ; 2 Cor. xii. 2–4.

[2] *adv. haer.* V. v. 1 : ποῦ οὖν ἐτέθη ὁ πρῶτος ἄνθρωπος ; ἐν τῷ παραδείσῳ δηλονότι, καθὼς γέγραπται . . . καὶ ἐκεῖθεν ἐξεβλήθη εἰς τόνδε τὸν κόσμον παρακούσας. διὸ καὶ λέγουσιν οἱ πρεσβύτεροι, τῶν ἀποστόλων μαθηταί, τοὺς

But it must be remembered that Irenaeus lived long before the days of Copernican astronomy, and that, at a time when the firmament was believed by all to be a solid vault arching over the earth, the affirmation of a geographical Paradise situated in ' the third heaven '—that is, somewhere above this vault—would not have appeared to his readers as meant to be other than a statement of objective fact. Hence the assertion that Adam, ' having disobeyed God, was cast out from thence into *this* world,' [1] is to be taken quite literally. No doubt the conception of Paradise as placed at a vast distance above the terrestrial globe, which is not uncommon in the Greek Fathers, easily lent itself to a process of refinement and sublimation, which tended to transform the idea of a material and spatial garden into that of a metaphysical and transcendental state. We shall find this metamorphosis complete in Origen ; but it would be an anachronism to read it into the thought of Irenaeus.

(ii) The second of the great issues, in regard to which this pioneer of systematic theology has expressed a definite view, is the question of the condition of Man *before* the Fall. We have seen that St. Paul asserts nothing about Adam's paradisal state, save in so far as he implies that it included the possession of free-will and physical immortality.[2] Irenaeus strongly re-affirms the position of Tatian and Theophilus, that unfallen man was an imperfect, undeveloped, and infantile creature,[3] thereby denying by anticipation

---

μετατεθέντας ἐκεῖσε μετατεθῆναι· δικαίοις γὰρ ἀνθρώποις καὶ πνευματοφόροις ἡτοιμάσθη ὁ παράδεισος, ἐν ᾧ καὶ Παῦλος ἀπόστολος εἰσκομισθεὶς ἤκουσεν ἄρρητα ῥήματα, ὡς πρὸς ἡμᾶς ἐν τῷ παρόντι, κἀκεῖ μένειν τοὺς μετατεθέντας ἕως συντελείας, προοιμαζομένους τὴν ἀφθαρσίαν. Cf. also *Demonstr.* 12 : ' And, that man might have his nourishment and growth with festive and dainty meats, He prepared him a place *better than this world* . . . and its name is Paradise ' ; 17 : ' when they were put out of Paradise, Adam and his wife Eve fell into many troubles of anxious grief, going about with sorrow and toil and lamentation *in this world.*'

[1] *adv. haer.* V. v. 1, quoted above.　　　　[2] Lecture III, p. 124.

[3] *adv. haer.* IV. lxii. This original imperfection of man is asserted to be a necessary consequence of his creaturely status : τὰ δὲ γεγονότα (as opposed to the eternally self-subsistent Creator) καθὸ μετέπειτα γενέσεως ἀρχὴν ἰδίαν ἔσχε, κατὰ τοῦτο καὶ ὑστερεῖσθαι δεῖ αὐτὰ τοῦ πεποιηκότος· οὐ γὰρ ἠδύναντο ἀγέννητα εἶναι τὰ νεωστὶ γεγεννημένα· καθὸ δὲ μή ἐστιν ἀγέννητα, κατὰ τοῦτο καὶ ὑστεροῦνται τοῦ τελείου. καθὸ δὲ νεώτερα, κατὰ τοῦτο καὶ νήπια, κατὰ τοῦτο καὶ ἀσυνήθη, καὶ ἀγύμναστα πρὸς τὴν τελείαν ἀγωγήν. ὡς οὖν ἡ μήτηρ

the doctrine of 'Original Righteousness.' According to this great primitive writer, perfection, moral, spiritual, and intellectual, was not the original endowment of mankind, but the goal which it was intended to attain, presumably after long centuries of evolution.[1] Human nature was indeed capable of immortality and incorruptibility; but at the beginning it was not actually possessed of these gifts. It is true that man was created in the 'image and likeness' of God: but whilst the divine 'image' (εἰκών) is expressed in man's flesh,[2] the divine 'likeness' (ὁμοίωσις) is developed in his soul gradually and slowly, through the possession of the Spirit and fellowship with God[3]; it therefore can have existed in the first man only as a germ. His ethical condition was one of innocence, not of virtue, inasmuch as he was unable to distinguish between good and evil.[4] If it is permissible, with Harnack,[5] to refer the rhetorical question 'quemadmodum igitur erit homo Deus, qui nondum factus est homo? quomodo autem perfectus, nuper effectus?'[6] to man's unfallen condition, it will be hardly an exaggeration to suggest that the Adam of

---

δύναται τέλειον παρασχεῖν τῷ βρέφει τὸ ἔμβρωμα, τὸ δὲ ἔτι ἀδυνατεῖ τὴν αὐτοῦ πρεσβυτέραν δέξασθαι τροφήν· οὕτως καὶ ὁ θεὸς αὐτὸς μὲν οἷός τε ἦν παρασχεῖν ἀπ' ἀρχῆς τῷ ἀνθρώπῳ τὸ τέλειον, ὁ δὲ ἄνθρωπος ἀδύνατος λαβεῖν αὐτό· νήπιος γὰρ ἦν. This position is emphatically repeated in lxiii. 1. Cf. also Demonstration, 12: 'The lord (of the earth), that is, man, was but small; for he was a child; and it was necessary that he should grow, and so come to his perfection'; 'Man was a child, not yet having his understanding perfected; wherefore also he was easily led astray by the deceiver.'

[1] adv. haer. IV. lxiii. 2: τοῦ δὲ ἀνθρώπου ἠρέμα προκόπτοντος (cf. the ἀφορμὴ προκοπῆς of Theophilus) καὶ πρὸς τέλειον ἀνερχομένου . . . ἔδει δὲ τὸν ἄνθρωπον πρῶτον γενέσθαι, καὶ γενόμενον αὐξῆσαι, καὶ αὐξήσαντα ἀνδρωθῆναι, καὶ ἀνδρωθέντα πληθυνθῆναι, καὶ πληθυνθέντα ἐνισχῦσαι, καὶ ἐνισχύσαντα δοξασθῆναι, καὶ δοξασθέντα ἰδεῖν τὸν ἑαυτοῦ δεσπότην (that is, God). The vision of God is that which ultimately produces ἀφθαρσία or incorruptibility. In the Demonstration, however, man is said to have been physically immortal before the Fall (c. 15). Too great consistency must not be expected from the first systematic theologian.

[2] adv. haer. V. vi. 1: 'perfectus autem homo commixtio et adunitio est animae assumentis Spiritum Patris, et admixta (? legendum admixtae) ei carni, quae est plasmata secundum imaginem Dei.'

[3] ibid. 'cum autem spiritus hic commixtus animae unitur plasmati, propter effusionem Spiritus spiritalis et perfectus homo factus est; et hic est qui secundum imaginem et similitudinem factus est Dei.'

[4] adv. haer. IV. lxiv. 1.

[5] History of Dogma (E. tr.), ii. 270, n. 2.   [6] adv. haer. IV. lxix. 2.

Irenaeus belongs, in respect of his moral status, to the category of *hominidae* or ' sub-men ' rather than to that of *homo sapiens* ; but for the fact that his early home was in an extra-mundane ' third heaven,' he might pass for the immediate progenitor of the semi-human race of Neanderthal. If this primitive Hellenic-Christian conception of man's primaeval state had never been overlaid by the Rabbinical imaginations as to Adam's supernatural perfection and splendour, later Christianity might have been spared even the appearance of a conflict with Darwinism.

In the light of this conception, it will not appear surprising that Irenaeus does not attach a very high degree of guilt or culpability to the 'Fall.' God Himself pities, rather than condemns, His frail, imperfect, inexperienced creature for succumbing to the wiles of a cunning and powerful foe.[1] Man's first sin was one of thoughtlessness rather than of malice ; the devil acquired power over him unfairly, by a trick.[2] Closely connected with these ideas is the even more startling speculation that the Fall was in some ways positively beneficial to mankind. Viewed objectively, and in regard to its historical effects, it almost becomes what has been called a ' Fall upwards,' inasmuch as it conduced to man's fuller and richer ethical evolution ; just as the individual learns the meaning of a ' bitter ' taste by actual sensation, so man learnt by painful experience that sin brings separation from God and spiritual death.[3] This,

[1] *adv. haer.* III. xxv. 2 : ' eum enim odivit Deus, qui seduxit hominem ; ei vero qui seductus est, sensim paulatimque misertus est ' ; IV. lxvi. 2 : ' eum autem, qui negligenter quidem sed male accepit inobedientiam, hominem miseratus est.'

[2] That is, by promising him equality with God, a gift which it was not in the devil's power to bestow. *adv. haer.* III. xxxii. 2 : ' primum enim possessionis eius vas Adam factus est, quem et tenebat sub sua potestate, hoc est, praevaricationem inique inferens ei, et per occasionem immortalitatis mortificationem faciens in eum ' ; *cf.* V. i. 1 : ' quoniam iniuste dominabatur nobis apostasia.'

[3] *adv. haer.* IV. lxiv. 1 : ' quemadmodum enim lingua per gustum accipit experimentum dulcis et amari, et oculus per visionem discernit quod est nigrum ab albo, et auris per auditum differentias sonorum scit, sic et mens per utrorumque experimentum disciplinam boni accipens, firmior ad conservationem eius efficitur, obediens Deo : inobedientiam quidem primum respuens per poenitentiam, quoniam amarum et malum est ; deinde ex comprehensione discens, quale sit quod contrarium est bono et dulcedini, ne tentet quidem unquam inobedientiam gustare Dei.'

however, does not mean that God directly decreed the Fall, but merely that He foresaw and tolerated it (not willing to interfere with man's free-will) and overruled its consequences for good ends.[1]

(iii) The third crucial issue which emerges in the writings of Irenaeus is the question of the exact nature of the causal link between Adam's sin and the sinfulness of his posterity. The task of bringing to light the unexpressed assumptions underlying the vague language of a primitive writer is necessarily delicate and precarious; but it must, nevertheless, be attempted. So much, at least, would be generally admitted, that in Irenaeus we find (for the first time, if our analysis of St. Paul's doctrine has been sound) that conception of the causal link which may be described as the 'mystical identity' of Adam and his descendants—the idea being that Adam was in some undefined sense the representative of mankind and that, therefore, the race was somehow committed by his transgression to an attitude of defiance towards God, in much the same way in which a nation may be committed to a war with its neighbours by a speech or an act of its Prime Minister. This theory is nowhere formulated in express words; but it appears in many turns of phrase and diction, as when he asserts that 'men' in general, or 'we,' transgressed God's law and forfeited Paradise.[2] Such a conception clearly contains the potentiality of a theory of 'Original Guilt,' though this is not explicitly developed.

It must, however, be pointed out that the theory—if such it can be called—of a merely 'mystical' identity can only maintain itself in a mind which has not the time or is unwilling to probe very deeply into the problem. If it is

---

[1] *adv. haer.* III. xxi. 1, 2. (God allowed Jonah to be swallowed by the great fish, not that he might perish, but that he might be delivered and glorify God the more: so also He permitted man to be swallowed by the author of the Fall, *i.e.* the devil, that man might learn not to consider himself like unto God.) *Cf.* also IV. lxi. 2 : ' Deo quidem magnanimitatem praestante in apostasia hominis; homine autem erudito per eam, quemadmodum propheta ait : *emendabit te abscessio tua* ; praefiniente Deo omnia ad hominis perfectionem, et ad aedificationem, et manifestationem dispositionum.'

[2] *e.g.* in III. xix. 6 ; xxi. 2 ; xxxiii. ; V. xvi. 2 ; xvii. 1 ' ⟨Deus⟩ in quem peccaveramus in initio ' ; and many other passages.

seriously reflected upon, it must either relapse into meaning-
lessness or transform itself into the theory of 'Seminal
Identity,' according to which Adam represented humanity
precisely because, at the time of his Fall, he *was* humanity,
the whole of his posterity existing seminally in his loins,
and consequently sharing in his sin ; just as (according to
the writer of the Epistle to the Hebrews) Levi existed
seminally in Abraham when he met Melchisedek, and
consequently participated in Abraham's payment of tithes
to the mysterious priest-king.[1] The indefinite character of
Irenaeus' language debars us from attributing this theory to
him in anything like that precise and fully articulated shape
which it wears in the thought of Ambrosiaster and Augustine, some two centuries later. But I must needs think that
a rude and inchoate form of it is implicit in his frequent use
of the phrase ' in Adam ' to describe the *rationale* of man's
subjection to sin and death.[2] I find it very difficult to affix
any other significance to passages such as the following :

(Christ was incarnate) that, *what we had lost in Adam*, that is,
being after the image and likeness of God, we might recover in
Christ Jesus.[3]

In the first Adam indeed we offended (God), not performing
His command ; but in the second Adam we have been reconciled to him, having been made obedient unto death.[4]

But ' the grief of their wound ' is the grief of that wound
by which *at the beginning man was smitten in Adam*, namely,
death. . . .[5]

This conception underlies, and forms the logical *prius* of
that view of redemption which is characteristic of Irenaeus,
and is denoted by the term ' Recapitulation ' (ἀνακεφαλαίωσις).
The passages in which this word and its cognates occur are
somewhat obscure, and its usage is not absolutely invariable ;
though that which the Redeemer ' recapitulates ' or ' sums

---

[1] Heb. vii. 9, 10.

[2] I here diverge from Dr. Tennant, *Sources*, p. 289 f.

[3] *adv. haer.* III. xix. 1.   This passage contains a classical statement
of the idea of ' Recapitulation,' on which see the text above.

[4] V. xvi. 2 : ἐν μὲν γὰρ τῷ πρώτῳ Ἀδὰμ προσεκόψαμεν, μὴ ποιήσαντες
αὐτοῦ τὴν ἐντολήν· ἐν δὲ τῷ δευτέρῳ Ἀδὰμ ἀποκατηλλάγημεν, ὑπήκοοι μέχρι
θανάτου γενόμενοι.

[5] V. xxxiv. 2 : ' *dolor* autem *plagae* est, per quam percussus est homo
initio in Adam inobediens, hoc est, mors. . . .'

up' is ordinarily 'man' or 'Adam' or 'human life,' yet
Christ is said in one place to have 'recapitulated' Adam's
disobedience,[1] and in another the primal enmity of man
towards the serpent.[2] If, however, we neglect these two
passages as employing the word in a somewhat abnormal
sense, it is possible to draw out the sequence of thought
which the great Gallican bishop has constructed by combining St. Paul's parallelism between the first and the
second Adams, drawn in two of his earlier Epistles,[3] with
the hints contained in Eph. i. and ii. as to a 'summing up'
(ἀνακεφαλαίωσις) of all things and a union of Jew and
Gentile into 'one new Man,' in the Mystical Body of the
exalted Christ [4] somewhat as follows.

Adam, being in his paradisal state co-extensive with
humanity, possessed the 'image and likeness' of God, and
then lost it by the Fall : the subsequent multiplication of
the human race is nothing other than the proliferation and
subdivision [5] of this original Adam into myriads of individual men, each, in consequence of the Fall, destitute of
the divine image. Christ then came as the Logos, who is
the perfect divine image, and as the second Adam, the
Ideal Man or Son of Man, who sums up in Himself all the
splendours which man's unfallen state had potentially [6]

---

[1] adv. haer. V. xix. 1.   [2] ibid. V. xxi. 2.
[3] 1 Cor. xv. ; Rom. v.   [4] Eph. i. 10, 23 ; ii. 13 ff.

[5] Nevertheless, although Adam as the universal of humanity splits up
into a multiplicity of descendants, considered as a particular man he retains
his own identity ; for Irenaeus is at pains to assert, as against Tatian, that
(the individual) Adam has been saved (adv. haer. I. xxvi. 1 ; III. xxxvii.).

[6] I here assume that the passages quoted above (p. 193, n. 3) which
portray unfallen man as a 'babe,' that is, a frail and undeveloped
creature, represent Irenaeus' real belief with regard to the state of man
before the Fall—an assumption which involves the consequence that this
Father cannot have attributed to our first parents more than a rudimentary
form of the 'image and likeness' of God, or more than a potential possession
of perfection. Harnack, however, maintains (History of Dogma, E. tr.,
ii. 273) that the idea of 'Recapitulation' presupposes the doctrine of
'Original Righteousness' or 'Perfection,' on the ground that what is
summed up and restored in the Second Adam must be supposed to have
had an actual and not only a potential existence in the First. I cannot
follow him in deducing this momentous consequence from the mere word
'Recapitulation'; and, though adv. haer. III. xxxv. 1 explicitly attributes a 'robe of sanctity' to unfallen Adam ('eam quam habui a Spiritu
sanctitatis stolam'), this is no more than a verbal inconsistency with
Irenaeus' general ascription of νηπιότης to the first man, an instance of

possessed, and purposes to gather into Himself, by sacramental incorporation into His Mystical Body, the countless individuals into which the ancient protoplast has split up, thereby re-uniting humanity into one single organism, endowed with the image and likeness of God, as at the beginning.

It is worth noting that Irenaeus make no effort to develop St. Paul's teaching with regard to the flesh as the seat of the hereditary infirmity and the connexion of sin with physical appetite. This element in the Pauline anthropology is almost entirely [1] absent from his writings— a circumstance doubtless to be accounted for by the fear of Gnosticism, all forms of which (as we have seen) agreed in regarding the material world, and therefore the body, as essentially evil.

The Bifurcation of the 'Once-born' and 'Twice-born' Versions of the Fall-Doctrine during the Third Century

Our study of these primitive Greek-Christian writers has thus revealed, gradually taking shape within the Catholic Church of the late second century, an interpretation of the Fall-doctrine which, whilst preserving the essential outlines of the Pauline teaching, wears a humane, reasonable, and curiously modern complexion. It does not, indeed, betray any suspicion that Adam and Eve may not

---

which, indeed, occurs in the same section (' indolem et puerilem amiserat sensum,' *ibid.*).

It may be added that Eusebius (*H.E.* v. 27) bears witness to the interest aroused by the question of the origin of evil at the end of the second century, and mentions a treatise written on this subject against the heretics (presumably the Gnostics) by one Maximus. Nothing of this book now remains : the passage quoted by Eusebius elsewhere (*Praep. Evang.* vii. 22), which purports to be an extract from it, but is verbally identical with a section of the Dialogue of Methodius of Olympus on Free Will (Bonwetsch, *Methodius*, Schriften i. 15–38), has been shown by Dr. J. A. Robinson (*Origenis Philocalia*, p. xl ff.) to be the work of the latter author.

[1] A suggestion of it is found in *adv. haer.* III. xxv. 1, which, describing the immediate consequences of the Fall, tells us that Adam clothed himself with fig-leaves ' retundens petulantem carnis impetum.'

have been historical personages. But it gives us a picture of primitive man as frail, imperfect, and child-like—a picture which is on the whole unaffected by the Rabbinical figment of Adam's ' Original Righteousness,' and is by no means incapable of harmonisation with the facts revealed by the science of to-day. It exaggerates neither the height from which, nor the depth to which, the first men are alleged to have fallen. It finds in the inherited disorder of our nature rather a weakness to be pitied than an offence to be condemned ; and, in so far as man is conceived as being under a curse or enslaved by the power of evil, a large part of the blame for this is divided between his own folly and the malice of a personal Satan. As held by the Apologists, it would seem to have contained no hint of the conception of ' Original Guilt '—a conception which presents equal difficulties to a reasoned faith in the Divine justice, whether the supposed ' guilt ' be regarded as accountability for the sin of a remote ancestor or accountability for the possession of instincts which we cannot help possessing. We must admit that (if our exposition of the theory of ' Recapitulation ' is correct) Irenaeus seems, in some passages, to have given what must be regarded as a wrong direction to the progress of Fall-speculation by interpreting the vague Pauline phrase ' in Adam ' in a sense which would assimilate it to the ' in Abraham ' of Heb. vii. 9, and would harden the undefined idea of our hereditary connexion with Adam into a stiffly realistic idea of our pre-natal existence in his loins. But this implied theory as to the link between Adam and his posterity is only used to account for our *de facto* lack of the Divine image, and the idea of our present personal responsibility for our first father's primaeval sin appears hardly, if at all.

This earliest patristic version of the Fall-doctrine, which we have reconstructed from the passing allusions of Justin, Theophilus, Tatian, and Irenaeus, is the natural product of the ' once-born ' type of religious experience, which alone would seem to be characteristic of the sunny genius of Hellenic Christendom, at that time the sole laboratory of Christian theology ; and in some ways it might have been well if this version had continued to prevail without a rival.

But a universal Church must embrace all nations and all types of religious temperament ; and the sterner and more terrifying elements of our religion had yet to receive their due recognition within the sphere of Christian anthropology. If the ' once-born ' temperament constitutes the ballast of the Church, the ' twice-born ' is, under God, its motive power ; and both modes of religious feeling should be represented, through their appropriate intellectual expressions, in the final and balanced estimate of human nature which a fully reasoned theory of Redemption requires as its presupposition. The point at which the single rivulet of primitive Christian Fall-tradition bifurcated into two distinct, and in some important respects divergent, streams of doctrine—the one preserving the relative indefiniteness of the Pauline conceptions and the emphasis on human freedom characteristic of Hellenic optimism and sanity, the other flowing in specifically Western and Latin channels, and deeply coloured by the pessimism of the ' twice-born ' religious temperament—lies in the early decades of the third century ; a review of which, in regard to its influence upon the developing doctrines of Man and of Sin, must form the next section of our narrative. The elemental force which stimulates the further growth of Fall-doctrine during this period is still the unquenchable determination of the Christian society to safeguard the ethical monotheism, inherited from the ancient Israel, which was the heart of its message and the mainspring of its life, against the slackening, but yet formidable, assaults of Gnosticism.

The writers whose opinions now demand our study are the illustrious Platonists of Alexandria, Clement and Origen, leaders of Christian thought in the East, and the fierce Tertullian, father of the characteristic theology of the West. It is in the Alexandrine and the African schools respectively that the two classical versions of the Fall-doctrine begin to appear differentiated from each other ; and their teaching must therefore be examined in some detail. The Eastern school has a prior claim to consideration, as standing in more direct continuity with the early Greek-Christian thinkers discussed above, and as having produced, in the speculations of Origen, some remarkable and brilliant developments of the Fall-doctrine, which will require attention in due course. A few words must be devoted in the first place to certain traces of the Fall-theory which, as I believe, may be discerned in the writings of Clement of Alexandria, side by side with much which appears to deny or ignore it.

CLEMENT OF ALEXANDRIA ON THE SIN OF ADAM

These traces appear in two passages, which shall be reproduced at length. The first of them runs as follows :

But contemplate for a moment, if you will, the Divine benefits bestowed upon us, looking back to their very beginning. There was indeed a time when the First Man sported in Paradise, free from all constraint, seeing that he was a child of God ; but there came a time when he fell under the power of pleasure (for by the serpent pleasure creeping on its belly is in a figure signified, and earthborn wickedness, which is nourished up as fuel for the flames). So then the child was led astray by lusts, and grew to manhood in disobedience, and having disobeyed his father he dishonoured his God. What was the might of pleasure ! man, who by reason of his simplicity had been free from constraint, was found bound with sins. This same man ($\tau o\hat{\upsilon}\tau o\nu$) the Lord then willed to loose from his bonds ; and being Himself bound in flesh (a divine mystery), by this mystery worsted the serpent and enslaved the tyrant, even Death. And—the most astounding thing of all—that same man who had been led astray through pleasure, that same who had been bound by corruption, him the Lord shewed set free with hands unfettered. O mystical wonder ! the Lord is bowed down, and man raised up ! and he who fell from Paradise receives as the prize of obedience something greater than Paradise, namely, heaven itself.[1]

[1] *protrepticus*, xi. 111 (ed. Dindorf, 1859) : μικρὸν δὲ, εἰ βούλει, ἄνωθεν ἄθρει τὴν θείαν εὐεργεσίαν. ὁ πρῶτος ὁτὲ μὲν ἐν παραδείσῳ ἔπαιζε λελυμένος, ἐπεὶ παιδίον ἦν τοῦ θεοῦ, ὁτὲ δὲ ὑπέπιπτεν ἡδονῇ—ὄφις ἀλληγορεῖται ἡδονὴ ἐπὶ γαστέρα ἕρπουσα, κακία γηΐνη, εἰς ὕλας τρεφομένη—παρήγετο ἐπιθυμίαις ὁ παῖς ἀνδριζόμενος ἀπειθείᾳ καὶ παρακούσας τοῦ πατρὸς ᾐσχύνετο τὸν θεόν· οἷον ἴσχυσεν ἡδονή ; ὁ δι᾽ ἁπλότητα λελυμένος ἄνθρωπος ἁμαρτίαις ηὑρέθη δεδεμένος. τῶν δεσμῶν λῦσαι τοῦτον ὁ κύριος αὖθις ἠθέλησεν, καὶ σαρκὶ ἐνδεθείς, μυστήριον θεῖον, τούτῳ τὸν ὄφιν ἐχειρώσατο καὶ τὸν τύραννον ἐδουλώσατο, τὸν θάνατον. καὶ τὸ παραδοξότατον, ἐκεῖνον τὸν ἄνθρωπον τὸν ἡδονῇ πεπλανημένον, τὸν τῇ φθορᾷ δεδεμένον, χερσὶν ἡπλωμέναις ἔδειξε λελυμένον. ὦ θαύματος μυστικοῦ· κέκλιται μὲν ὁ κύριος, ἀνέστη δὲ ἄνθρωπος, καὶ ὁ ἐκ τοῦ παραδείσου πεσὼν μεῖζον ὑπακοῆς ἆθλον οὐρανοὺς ἀπολαμβάνει.

In this passage we notice, first of all, the naturalisation within Christian thought of the allegorical method of exegesis borrowed from Philo, which we shall find used with such striking results by Clement's great pupil and successor, Origen. Secondly, we remark that—continuing what has been the uniform teaching hitherto of those Christian teachers who have alluded to the subject at all—Clement affirms the condition of the first man to have been that of a child, characterised by imperfection and innocence ; in other words, he knows nothing of the doctrine of ' Original Righteousness.'[1] Thirdly—and this is the point of greatest interest for our present enquiry—it is to be observed that the ' man ' who was freed by Christ from the chains of sin and from bondage to corruption is emphatically, even though implicitly, asserted to have been identical with the ' man ' who had been seduced by pleasure ; that is to say, ' Adam ' and the human race are identified as one entity. I venture to suggest that sufficient weight has not been allowed by previous students of the passage to the equation which it clearly presupposes between the universal ' man ' and the individual ' first man.' Such an allegorisation of the figure of Adam is by no means unnatural, because, as Origen later points out,[2] the Hebrew word Adam ('ādhām, אָדָם) is not a proper name at all—it is the ordinary word for ' man,' homo.[3] The paragraph is, of course, highly poetical in character ; but none the less it would seem clear that the underlying thought is that which we have already found in Irenaeus, the vague idea of a certain solidarity of mankind with Adam, which is capable of being expressed in terms of either ' mystical ' or ' physical ' identity, a solidarity which necessarily involves mankind in the bondage to ' pleasure,' that is, to the sensual appetites, first incurred by its common father. This is at least a minimal doctrine of ' Original Sin,' even though, as Dr. Bigg justly points out, it contains no suggestion of the idea of ' Original Guilt.'[4]

[1] *Cf. strom.* iv. 23, 150 (Adam was only ' perfect ' in the sense that no specifically human characteristics were lacking to him) : *ibid.* vi. 12, 96 (Adam was created, not morally perfect, but capable of acquiring virtue).

[2] See below, p. 229.   [3] See Lecture II, p. 41, n. 1.

[4] *Christian Platonists of Alexandria* (1913 edn., with some additions and modifications by F. E. Brightman), p. 112, n. 1.

The second passage contains an interesting speculation as to the exact nature of the first sin : it occurs in a context which is devoted to a defence of marriage against the attacks of the Gnostic Julius Cassianus, who had cited 2 Cor. xi. 3— ' I fear lest, by any means, as the serpent beguiled Eve in his craftiness, your minds should be corrupted,' etc.—to show that St. Paul disapproved of marital intercourse.

For (human) generation is a created thing and a creation of the Almighty, who assuredly would never depress the soul from a better to a worse state. Nay, rather was it the case that the Saviour came unto us who had gone astray as to our *minds*, which had been *corrupted* as the result of the disobedience committed by us, pleasure-loving as we were, against the commandments ; the first-formed man, perchance, having anticipated our season [that is, presumably, the season at which God willed that we, Adam's posterity, should be begotten] and before the time of the grace of matrimony having experienced desire and committed sin (for ' every one that looketh on a woman to lust after her hath committed adultery with her already,' not awaiting the season of the Divine Will).[1]

Here it is suggested that the ' Fall ' may have consisted in the first stirrings of lustful appetite, which may have led to the *premature* union of Adam and Eve, before the time appointed by God for their marriage. (We notice once more the tendency to which attention has already been drawn, to assign a sexual character to the first sin.[2]) The passage is elusive in style : but there is clearly meant to be implied *some* connexion between the sensuality attributed to Adam in the last clause and the ' love of pleasure ' which is, immediately before, said to be the source of our disobedience or actual sin. Is this connexion that of cause and effect, or merely that of type and antitype ? If the latter, it would seem that the whole sentence about Adam becomes an irrelevant rhetorical flourish. But if a *causal* connexion

---

[1] *strom.* iii. 15, 94 : κτιστὴ γὰρ ἡ γένεσις καὶ κτίσις τοῦ παντοκράτορος, ὃς οὐκ ἄν ποτε ἐξ ἀμεινόνων εἰς τὰ χείρω κατάγοι ψυχήν, ἀλλ' εἰς τοὺς πεπλανημένους τὰ νοήματα εἰς ἡμᾶς ὁ σωτὴρ ἀφίκετο, ἃ δὴ ἐκ τῆς κατὰ τὰς ἐντολὰς παρακοῆς ἐφθάρη φιληδονούντων ἡμῶν, τάχα που προλαβόντος ἡμῶν τὸν καιρὸν τοῦ πρωτοπλάστου καὶ πρὸ ὥρας τῆς τοῦ γάμου χάριτος ὀρεχθέντος καὶ διαμαρτόντος, ὅτι πᾶς ὁ βλέπων γυναῖκα πρὸς τὸ ἐπιθυμῆσαι ἤδη ἐμοίχευσεν αὐτήν, οὐκ ἀναμείνας τὸν καιρὸν τοῦ θελήματος.

[2] Perhaps Clement may have borrowed the idea set forth in the passage under discussion from the *Apocalypse of Abraham* ; see Lecture II, p. 58.

may be assumed, the whole argument at once falls into place, and aligns itself with the thought of the passage quoted above from the *protrepticus*. It may then be paraphrased as follows : ' St. Paul's saying about the deception of Eve by the serpent cannot be quoted as a disparagement of conjugal union. This was ordained by God, and cannot therefore in itself be an evil thing. It is true that the serpent signifies bodily pleasure, and that the inordinate love of pleasure which lies at the root of our concrete sins flows from a primitive act of surrender to bodily pleasure committed by our first parents. But the wickedness of this act consisted not in its sexual nature, but in its *prematureness* ; and this judgment is based upon a permanently valid ethical principle, which is embodied in our Lord's words recorded in Matt. v. 28. What He condemns is, not the appetite, but the unwillingness to wait for the time when the satisfaction of the appetite will have become legitimate.'

There is a third passage relative to the sin of Adam which deserves mention in this connexion, though its purport appears to be designed rather to refine away ' Original Sin,' on what would later have been called ' Pelagian ' lines, than to affirm it in the sense which we have found in the two places just discussed. This is a sentence occurring in the *adumbrationes*, or ' Outline Notes,' on the Catholic Epistles,[1] which are recognised by most scholars as coming in substance from the hand of Clement. Commenting on

---

[1] Printed in vol. iii. of Dindorf's edition, pp. 479–489. These *adumbrationes* are generally believed to be a dogmatically expurgated Latin version, made by Cassiodorus, of the commentaries on 1 Peter, Jude, 1 and 2 John, contained in Clement's now lost *hypotyposes* (ὑποτυπώσεις, = ' outlines '). For discussions of them, see Zahn, *Forschungen zur Gesch. des neutestamentl. Kanons*, iii. (1884), pp. 79–103 ; Preuschen, in Harnack's *Gesch. der altchristl. Literatur*, i. p. 306 f. Westcott, however, (art. ' Clement of Alexandria,' *DCB*, vol. i. p. 564,) doubts whether the *adumbrationes* as they stand are the work either of Clement or of Cassiodorus, though he thinks that they may include important fragments of Clement's Commentary ; and Bigg (*Christian Platonists*, p. 112, n. 1), though not, apparently, raising any question about the authenticity of the *adumbrationes* as a whole, doubts the context in which the sentence ' sic etiam peccato Adae ' stands, on the ground that it goes on to lay down ' the doctrine of reprobation.' I do not myself think that it does : but space forbids a discussion of the matter here. I have felt justified in quoting the sentence as Clement's in view of the agreement of the majority of scholars.

Jude 11—' Woe unto them ! for they went in the way of Cain '—he observes, according to the Latin translator, ' Sic etiam peccato Adae subiacemus secundum peccati similitudinem.' The fact that the Adumbrationes are no more than summaries of the Greek original makes it difficult to be certain of the precise sense intended by the author : but it seems clear that the phrase ' secundum peccati similitudinem ' is reproduced from Rom. v. 14 (' after the likeness of Adam's transgression ').[1] In view of its context, the only meaning which I can assign to the sentence is as follows : ' (The sinners denounced by Jude are said to have gone in the way of Cain, that is, to have imitated the sin of Cain) ; and in the same way we all are subject to the sin of Adam, *by imitating his sin.*' So interpreted, this aphorism would not directly deny the hypothesis of the solidarity of the race with its sinful parents ; but it must be admitted that it looks very like an attempt to supersede the conception of ' mystical identity ' by that of ' social heredity,' which regards Adam's transgression as influencing his posterity towards evil only in so far as it provided a bad example for this imitation.[2]

We have thus two passages in which the Adamic Fall-doctrine appears to be affirmed or implied, and probably one in which it is recognised, but recognised only in order to be rationalised away. But these passages, taken together, bear an exceedingly small proportion to the total contents of Clement's surviving works ; and against them we must set the whole trend and predominant tendency of his general treatment of the moral life, which, in strict accord with Hellenic-Christian tradition, insists strongly upon the autonomy of the will,[3] and makes little allowance for the fact of the moral struggle. It would not be justifiable to

---

[1] It is a probable inference from this sentence that Clement's text of Rom. v. 14, like Origen's, did not contain the word μή before ἁμαρτήσαντας : see Lecture III, p. 125, n. 2.

[2] The following curious passage should perhaps be mentioned in this connexion : *Protrept.* ii. 12 : Διόνυσον μαινόλην ὀργιάζουσι Βάκχοι ὠμοφαγίᾳ τὴν ἱερομηνίαν ἄγοντες καὶ τελίσκουσι τὰς κρεανομίας τῶν φόνων, ἀνεστεμμένοι τοῖς ὄφεσιν, ἐπολολύζοντες Εὐάν· Εὔαν ἐκείνην, δι' ἣν ἡ πλάνη παρηκολούθησεν. καὶ σημεῖον ὀργίων βακχικῶν ὄφις ἐστὶ τετελεσμένος. αὐτίκα γοῦν κατὰ τὴν ἀκριβῆ τῶν Ἑβραίων φωνὴν τὸ ὄνομα τὸ Εὔϊα δασυνόμενον ἑρμηνεύεται ὄφις ἡ θήλεια.

[3] *Cf. strom.* ii. 14, 60 ; 15, 66 ; and frequently.

assume that a belief in free-will is logically incompatible with the belief in any kind of inherited handicap ; and we have seen that both convictions were simultaneously held by the second-century writers reviewed above. But it cannot be denied that Clement's expression of the former is emphatic and enthusiastic, whilst his admission of the latter is scanty and grudging. In the Fall-passages which we have noticed, he conveys the impression of one who is rendering lip-homage to an idea which has too much traditional and Scriptural authority to be totally discarded, but which is really alien to the general direction of his own thinking. The truth is that Clement's own temperament is as definitely and typically ' once-born ' or ' healthy-minded ' as Augustine's or Luther's was to be ' twice-born ' [1] ; and it may be doubted whether his feeling of the sinfulness of sin was not somewhat less intense even than that of the normal ' once-born ' religious man. Such a conclusion is at least suggested by a sentence which defines the causes of moral evil as consisting in the ' weakness of matter,' that is of man's material body, and the ' involuntary impulses of ignorance.' [2] Hence, it is not surprising to find that in one place the conception of ' Original Guilt ' is rejected in scornfully explicit terms,[3] and that elsewhere words are used which, if taken at their face value, would deny even the mildest interpretation of ' Original Sin.' [4]

[1] Compare Bigg's phrase, ' the blithe geniality of Clement, whose cloistered life seems never to have felt a storm' (*Christian Platonists*, p. 168).

[2] *strom.* vii. 3, 16 : κακῶν δὲ αἰτίαν καὶ ὕλης ἄν τις ἀσθένειαν ὑπολάβοι καὶ τὰς ἀβουλήτους τῆς ἀγνοίας ὁρμάς.

[3] *ibid.* iii. 17, 100 : λεγέτωσαν ἡμῖν ποῦ ἐπόρνευσεν τὸ γεννηθὲν παιδίον, ἢ πῶς ὑπὸ τὴν τοῦ Ἀδὰμ ὑποπέπτωκεν ἀρὰν τὸ μηδὲν ἐνεργῆσαν . . . . καὶ ὅταν ὁ Δαβὶδ εἴπῃ, Ἐν ἁμαρτίαις συνελήφθην καὶ ἐν ἀνομίαις ἐκίσσησέν με ἡ μήτηρ μου, λέγει μὲν προφητικῶς μητέρα τὴν Εὔαν · ἀλλὰ ζώντων Εὔα μήτηρ ἐγένετο, καὶ εἰ ἐν ἁμαρτίᾳ συνελήφθη, ἀλλ' οὐκ αὐτὸς ἐν ἁμαρτίᾳ οὐδὲ μὴν ἁμαρτία αὐτός. ' Let them tell us, where the newly born child committed fornication, or how a thing that has performed no action at all has fallen under the curse of Adam ? . . . And when David says " I was conceived in sins and in iniquities did my mother bear me," he is alluding in prophetic wise to Eve as his mother ; but Eve became the mother of all living, and even if David was " conceived in sin," yet he is not thereby involved in sin, nor indeed is he himself sin.'

[4] *strom.* iii. 9, 64. Here the crucial passage Rom. v. 12 is quoted ; but Clement's only comment on it consists in the assertion that death is produced by natural necessity, flowing from the Divine governance of the

The exaggerated optimism with which Clement regards human nature reflects itself in his failure to appreciate the saddening and perplexing facts of evil in the extra-human universe.[1] The apparently purposeless cruelty which ravages the animal world, which, as we have seen, so deeply affected the imagination of St. Paul,[2] and which has led many thinkers, both ancient and modern, to take refuge in dualism as the easiest explanation of the present state of sub-human Nature, seems to have made no impression upon him. And as he never realised the genuine weight and force of Marcion's case against the monotheistic belief of the Great Church, he lacked the incentive to study and develop the one existing theory of the origin of evil which was capable of shielding that belief.   Hence the great architectonic idea of the parallelism between and the mutual implication of the Apostasy and the Redemption, which had been sketched out by St. Paul and elaborated by Irenaeus, is all but absent from the pages of Clement ; and the doctrine of the Fall is little more than a useless excrescence on his theology, only of significance in so far as the fact that he does not feel able to ignore it altogether may be regarded as testifying to the measure of acceptance which it had already won in contemporary Christian thought.

ORIGEN AND THE ' TRANSCENDENTAL ' FALL-THEORY

Far different is the place held by the Fall-doctrine in the writings of Clement's famous pupil Origen, perhaps the mightiest doctor of pre-Augustinian Christendom, the austere and fiery spirit of whom it has been said by one of my most eminent predecessors in this Lectureship ' There has been no truly great man in the Church who did not love him a little.' [3]

---

universe. He proceeds (in 65) to say that Eve was called ' Life,' because she was the mother of all, both of just and of unjust, ' each one of us justifying himself or again making himself disobedient' (ἑκάστου ἡμῶν ἑαυτὸν δικαιοῦντος ἢ ἔμπαλιν ἀπειθῆ κατασκευάζοντος).

[1] Cf. R. B. Tollinton, *Clement of Alexandria* (1914), ii. p. 254 ; Bigg, *Christian Platonists*, p. 109.

[2] Rom. viii. 18–25 ; see Lecture III, pp. 157 ff.

[3] Bigg, *Christian Platonists*, p. 329.

In order to elucidate the successive phases through which his peculiarly daring and imaginative Fall-speculations passed, it is necessary to refer briefly to the circumstances of his life. Origenes Adamantius was born A.D. 185-6, under the Emperor Commodus, and died in his sixty-ninth year, in the reign of Gallus (A.D. 251-254).[1] According to the generally accepted statement of Epiphanius,[2] he was a Copt, sprung from the native population of Egypt ; his father was the martyr Leonides, and shortly after his eighteenth year he was appointed by the Bishop Demetrius to succeed Clement in the headship of the great Christian institution known as the Catechetical School of Alexandria. Until A.D. 231 his days were devoted to the vast encyclopaedic labours, critical, philosophical, and theological, which made him the dominant intellectual force in the Eastern Christendom of his day, and to the public exposition of the Scriptures in the lecture-room and in the church. The stern asceticism of his private life, which aspired to an unreserved conformity with the precepts of the Gospel, even to the extent of a literal acting upon the commendation of those who have 'made themselves eunuchs for the kingdom of heaven's sake,' marks him as a typically 'twice-born' Christian, standing in this respect at the opposite pole to his master Clement ; but this temperamental bias was to a certain extent corrected by the Hellenic sanity, balance, and sense of proportion with which he was imbued by his studies at the Museum, or University of Alexandria [3] ; and we shall see that the character of his Fall-doctrine has been largely determined by the interplay of his passionate African idiosyncrasy and the calming influences of the philosophic culture, with its 'once-born' associations and tone, which he inherited from the Macedonian conquerors of his country.

[1] Westcott, art. ' Origenes ' in *DCB*, iv. p. 98, calculates these dates from the statements of Eusebius, *H.E.* vi. 2, vii. 1 ; for slightly different estimates by other scholars (not, however, varying by more than a year or two) see Weingarten, *Zeittafeln u. Überblicke zur Kirchengesch.* (1905), p. 17.

[2] *haer.* lxiv. 1 : Αἰγύπτιος τῷ γένει : a statement which is confirmed by the etymology of his name Origen ('Ωριγένης, ' sprung from the god Horus ').

[3] According to Porphyry (*ap.* Eus. *H.E.* vi. 19), under Ammonius Saccas ; Bigg, however, disputes this (*op. cit.*, p. 156, n. 3).

In the year last mentioned, he fell foul of Demetrius, the bishop to whom he owed his appointment as head of the Catechetical School, owing to his uncanonical acceptance of ordination to the priesthood, whilst on a visit to Caesarea, at the hands of certain Palestinian bishops. Being condemned and, perhaps, deposed from the priesthood [1] by Demetrius and an Egyptian synod, he quitted Alexandria ; and, as the churches of Palestine refused to recognise the censures of Demetrius, took up his abode at Caesarea, which, for the remaining twenty years of his life, was the scene of his multifarious literary activities. His writings consequently divide themselves into two well-defined groups, belonging respectively to the Alexandrine and the Caesarean periods of his life ; and, as we shall see, this chronological division corresponds to a significant difference of orientation in their treatment of the Fall-doctrine.

(i) THE ALEXANDRINE PERIOD—THE ' PRE-NATAL FALL '

The most notable work of Origen's first period is the great treatise ' On First Principles ' (περὶ ἀρχῶν, de principiis), which contains what at first sight appears to be a unique and original version of, or at least substitute for, the Fall-theory. As this work marks the first appearance within Christianity of a line of thought which has in more modern times led to some striking speculative developments, and which may well exert an important influence upon the final formulation of our constructive conclusions, it will be well to state the view of the origin of evil therein put forward with some degree of fullness.[2]

---

[1] So Photius (bibliotheca, 118, [PG CIII. 398, 93a]), following the Apology of Pamphilus and Eusebius.

[2] For the text of the de principiis I have used the critical edition of P. Koetschau (1913) in Die griech. christl. Schriftsteller der ersten 3 Jahrhunderte, herausg. von der Kirchenväter-commission der kgl. Preuss. Akademie der Wissenschaften. Reference to this will show that I have relied upon Koetschau's restoration of the Greek original, in places where Rufinus has apparently altered or suppressed what appeared to him doctrinally objectionable passages, from such sources as the anathemas of the Constantinopolitan synod of 543, and the Letter of Justinian to Mennas. I have also used the ' Berlin ' text of the commentary on St. John's Gospel

Unlike Clement, Origen is deeply sensitive to the inequalities, injustices, and miseries which are plainly manifest in human life, and may be dimly discerned in the superhuman and sub-human worlds. (We note the Pauline sweep and comprehensiveness of his envisagement of reality.) The Apostle tells us that one star differeth from another star in glory,[1] and for Greek thinkers of the third century (as still for Aquinas in the thirteenth [2]) the stars were, or were moved by, conscious minds; why should there be an apparently arbitrary inequality amongst these glorious beings? The diversities of human fortune present an even more perplexing problem. ' Some are barbarians, some Greeks; and of barbarians some are more cruel and fierce, some more gentle. Some men live under admirable laws, some under laws which are contemptible or harsh, some are governed by inhuman and bestial customs rather than by laws. Some men from the moment of their birth are placed in a state of humiliation and subjection and are brought up in servile fashion, under the rule of masters, princes, or tyrants; others are reared in a more liberal and reasonable condition. Some are born with healthy bodies, some with congenital disease or defect. . . . Why should I enumerate the whole catalogue of human calamities and miseries, from which some are exempt, and in which others are involved . . . ? '[3] The question of animal suffering is too embarrassing to be faced directly, and is dismissed with the curious observation that ' these things are secondary results, not primary causes.'[4]

To the question, Why is the world vexed by so many inexplicable inequalities and apparently undeserved sufferings? dualistic Gnosticism had an easy reply: these things

---

(E. Preuschen, 1903) and of the first four books of the *contra Celsum* (P. Koetschau, 1899). All quotations from other works of Origen are taken from Lommatzsch's edition (Berlin, 1831).

[1] 1 Cor. xv. 41.

[2] See the quotations given by P. H. Wicksteed, *Reactions between Dogma and Philosophy* (1920), pp. 73–76.

[3] *de princ.* ii. 9 (Koetschau, p. 166 f.).

[4] So at least I understand Rufinus' rendering ' cum haec non principalia sed consequentia accipi debere certum sit ' (*ibid.*, Koetschau, p. 167), which presumably represents an original ἐπεὶ ταῦτα οὐκ ἀρχὰς ἀλλὰ ἀκόλουθα χρῆ νομίζειν, or some similar phrase.

are the work of the evil Power co-ordinate and co-eternal with God. But Origen's Christian monotheism decisively rules out such a solution. God is the creator of all that is, and His goodness forbids the supposition that He has inflicted unmerited pain on any of His creatures. The inequalities of fortune and opportunity, and the sufferings which are actually endured by men, must therefore be *deserved* ; and as *ex hypothesi* these evils are congenital, and cannot have been deserved in this life, it follows that they must have been incurred by some transgression committed in a previous life. This is the logical basis of the theory of a pre-natal or extra-temporal ' Fall ' of individual souls, which represents the first conscious attempt of Christian theology to remove the origin of evil out of the phenomenal into the intelligible or supersensible sphere, and which may therefore be described as the earliest form of the ' transcendental,' as distinct from the ' historical,' Fall-doctrine.

Origen's exposition of this audacious speculation starts from the assertion that in the beginning God, of His pure goodness, created a fixed number of intellectual essences (νοεραὶ οὐσίαι) or rational beings, as many as He could keep under the control of His Providence. (The God of Origen is not unlimited ; for if He were, He would be incomprehensible even to Himself.[1])

All these immaterial and bodiless essences were created equal in goodness and like in status ; for the Creator, being himself exempt from variety or changeableness, could have had no motive for producing a variety of creatures [2] ; and, in virtue of their identity of nature and operation, they constituted a Henad (ἑνάς) or Unity, a collegiate organism intimately inspired and illuminated by the Divine Logos.[3] But, being created, they were necessarily capable of change ; and, being rational, they were gifted with freedom and the faculty of choice. This momentous endowment was used

[1] *de princ.* ii. 9, 1 (Koetschau, p. 164, where a fragment of the Greek original, from which these statements are taken, is restored from Justinian, *ad Mennam*).

[2] ii. 9, 6.

[3] ii. 8, 3 (Koetschau, p. 159). The affinities of this idea to the Gnostic conceptions of the Pleroma, the Ogdoad, Dodecad, etc., will be obvious.

by different groups of them in different ways. Some persevered in virtue and retained the status in which they were created ; others gave way to ' idleness, and weariness of the labour of preserving goodness ' (' desidia et laboris taedium in servando bono ' [1]) or to ' satiety of the divine love and contemplation ' (κόρος τῆς θείας ἀγάπης καὶ θεωρίας),[2] and fell from the supersensible world to various depths, so becoming enmeshed in matter to a greater or lesser extent and enclosed in corporeal envelopes of varying degrees of fineness and subtlety. The most rebellious sank to the deepest abyss, and became demons, clothed upon with ' cold and dusky ' bodies ; the less corrupted, whose love of God was cooled but not extinct, fell only as far as the earth-plane and became (human) ' souls ' (ψυχαί, fancifully derived from ψυχρός, cold [3]) ; those whose error was slightest descended only a little way from the Henad and became angels, Cherubim, principalities and powers in their various ranks, and the spirits animating the sun, moon, and stars. On earth, the fallen ' souls,' who are ourselves, immured in human bodies, are meant to

dree their penance step by step

and to win restoration through chastisement and discipline. To such a pre-natal transgression, committed in the transcendental sphere, the Psalmist makes mystical allusion in the verse ' Before I was humbled, I went wrong : but now have I kept thy word ' [4]—meaning by the phrase ' before I was humbled ' ' in my pre-natal life, before I was banished from the heavenly place, and confined in this humbling prison-house of flesh.' [5]

---

[1] ii. 9, 2 (Koetschau, 165).

[2] ii. 8, 3 (Koetschau, p. 159).

[3] ii. 8 (Koetschau, p. 158). The derivation of ψυχή from ψύξις, cooling, is also found in Philo, de somn. i. 6.

[4] Ps. cxviii. (cxix.) 67, LXX.

[5] de princ. ii. 8 (Koetschau, p. 158). τὸ γὰρ εἰπεῖν τὸν προφήτην, πρὶν ἢ ταπεινωθῆναί με, ἐγὼ ἐπλημμέλησα, ἐξ αὐτῆς φησι τῆς ψυχῆς ὁ λόγος, ὡς ἄνω ἐν οὐρανῷ ἐπλημμέλησε, πρὶν ἢ ἐν τῷ σώματι τεταπεινῶσθαι. The counter-argument from Scripture, based on St. Paul's words about Jacob and Esau (' the children being not yet born, neither having done anything good or bad,' Rom. ix. 11), is parried by the arbitrary glossing of the phrase ' cum . . . neque aliquid egissent boni neque mali ' with the words, ' in hac scilicet vita ' (ii. 9, 7).

This, of course, is the exact theory of the origin of evil—at least of physical evil—which was hinted at by Philo,[1] and is apparently condemned by the Christ of the Fourth Gospel.[2] Whilst in a general sense its source may be said to lie in Origen's Platonism, it is impossible to fix with precision the particular writings which may have moulded his presentation of it. Perhaps the idea first came to him from Philo, and was impressed upon his mind by the great myth contained in Plato's *Phaedrus*.[3] In this, the pre-existent soul is portrayed as a winged charioteer, guiding a pair of unequally yoked steeds, the white steed of Reason, and his dark unruly mate of Desire. Ever and anon one of these charioteers, as he follows in the train of Zeus, soaring upward to the heaven beyond the heavens, fails to curb the rebellious curvettings and prancings of the dark steed ; and is flung, like Phaethon, from the roof of the firmament down to this gross world of matter, shedding his wings as he falls, and becoming incarnate in the person of an individual man. Or we may find the immediate fount of Origen's Fall-theory in the Myth of Er,[4] embodied in the Tenth Book of the *Republic*, in which the souls who are about to be born into this world freely choose their future lots, drawn from the lap of Lachesis. This splendid fantasy clearly displays the fundamental *motif* of Origen's thought on this subject—namely, the determination to save God from the reproach of causing evil which lies behind all Fall-theories and all other theodicies—in the heavenly prophet's mystic cry, αἰτία ἑλομένου· θεὸς ἀναίτιος (' He who hath chosen shall answer for it : God is not answerable '). If the question of the more remote affinities of Origen's theory be raised, we may point out that the idea of the fall of the soul from a super-celestial state, acquiring various elements of impurity from the planetary spheres through which it passes

---

[1] See Lecture II, p. 84.

[2] John ix. 2, 3 ; see Lecture III, p. 98. As the relevant portion of Origen's Commentary on St. John's Gospel is no longer extant, we cannot tell how he evaded the difficulty which this passage must have raised for his theory.

[3] *Phaedrus*, 246 A–257 A.

[4] *Republic*, 613 E–621 D. On both of these myths see J. A. Stewart, *The Myths of Plato*.

on its downward way to be born in this world, was in the third century widely diffused, both within and without Gnosticism [1] : and Origen, like many other theologians since, may well have been unconsciously influenced by the very beliefs which he set out to refute. Living, too, in Alexandria, the great emporium and meeting-place of East and West, he may have been subtly affected by the Hindu belief in re-incarnation and *karma*, though he steadfastly refuses to admit more lives than three—pre-natal, present, and future.[2]

But, whatever the exact sources from which this theory arose, one thing is clear. Origen has grasped, as no other before him and very few since, the all-important principle laid down in Lectures I and II, that the Fall-doctrine really rests upon an inference from the phenomena of evil considered in the light of ethical monotheism, and not upon the Paradise-narrative of Gen. iii. He has realised that faith in the God of Christianity and ratiocination from observed facts form the only foundation on which a satisfactory theory of the origin of evil can be built, and that the story of Adam and Eve is not and cannot be more than a pictorial façade. Hence the exposition contained in the *de principiis* makes no attempt to base itself upon the Adam-story ; which, in another connexion,[3] is emphatically declared to

---

[1] See W. Bousset, *Hauptprobleme der Gnosis*, pp. 361–369, Exkurs IV, ' Der anthropologische Dualismus ' ; he gives copious references to ancient authorities, including Servius on Verg. *Aen.* vi. 714, xi. 51, Varro, Macrobius, Porphyry, Proclus, the *Corpus Hermeticum*, and *Pistis Sophia*. *Cf.* also Lobeck, *Aglaophamus*, ii. p. 932 f.

[2] Passages from Origen's works expressly repudiating metempsychosis have been collected by Bigg, *op. cit.*, p. 241, n. 1 ; see also P. D. Huet, *Origeniana*, ii. q. 6, §§ 18, 19.

[3] *de princ.* iv. 3, 1 (Koetschau, p. 323) : τίς γοῦν νοῦν ἔχων οἰήσεται πρώτην καὶ δευτέραν καὶ τρίτην ἡμέραν ἑσπέραν τε καὶ πρωΐαν χωρὶς ἡλίου γεγονέναι καὶ σελήνης καὶ ἀστέρων ; τὴν δὲ οἱονεὶ πρώτην καὶ χωρὶς οὐρανοῦ ; τίς δ' οὕτως ἠλίθιος ὡς οἰηθῆναι τρόπον ἀνθρώπου γεωργοῦ τὸν θεὸν πεφυτευκέναι παράδεισον ἐν Ἐδὲμ κατὰ ἀνατολάς, καὶ ξύλον ζωῆς ἐν αὐτῷ πεποιηκέναι ὁρατὸν καὶ αἰσθητόν, ὥστε διὰ τῶν σωματικῶν ὀδόντων γευσάμενον τοῦ καρποῦ τὸ ζῆν ἀναλαμβάνειν· καὶ πάλιν καλοῦ καὶ πονηροῦ μετέχειν τινὰ παρὰ τὸ μεμασῆσθαι τὸ ἀπὸ τοῦδε τοῦ ξύλου λαμβανόμενον ; ἐὰν δὲ καὶ θεὸς τὸ δειλινὸν ἐν τῷ παραδείσῳ περιπατεῖν λέγηται καὶ ὁ Ἀδὰμ ὑπὸ τὸ ξύλον κρύπτεσθαι, οὐκ οἶμαι διστάξειν τινὰ περὶ τοῦ αὐτὰ τροπικῶς διὰ δοκούσης ἱστορίας, καὶ οὐ σωματικῶς γεγεννημένης, μηνύειν τινὰ μυστήρια. ' What man of sense will suppose that there was a " first," " second," and " third day," both

be a ' seeming history,' revealing ' certain mysteries,' of which the nature is not explicitly defined. If by these ' mysteries ' he means, as would seem probable, his theory of the origin of evil, this declaration is an extreme instance of the power of that exegetical alchemy known as ' allegorism ' to make anything mean anything ; for this interpretation of the story generalises ' Adam ' out of all recognition, and dissolves even the extra-mundane, but still concrete, Paradise of Irenaeus into a rarefied metaphysical abstraction.

It must be observed, further, that he tacitly abandons (during this period), not merely the literal acceptation of the Adam-narrative, but what is the core of the Adamic theory, namely, the conception of a single collective Fall of humanity involved in or caused by its first parents' fault. For this he substitutes a multiplicity of individual falls ; the souls which were to become men ' fell ' independently and one by one. It follows from this that the unity of mankind, *qua* mankind, though real enough, is a consequence, and not an antecedent condition, of the ' Fall,' or the ' falls ' ; it is the unity of those who have suffered the same misfortune before birth, and now find themselves clothed in the same ' muddy vesture of decay.' [1] Nevertheless, there is one exception to the rule that birth into this world is a proof of pre-natal transgression—the human soul of Jesus, which like all other human souls pre-existed in the transcendental sphere, preserved its purity intact, and descended voluntarily in order to form part of the human nature which the Logos

---

evening and morning, without sun, moon, and stars ? and the alleged "first day" without even a heaven ? And who is so silly as to suppose that God literally " planted a garden," like a human farmer, in Eden towards the sun-rising, and that He made in it a visible and perceptible Tree of Life, so that one tasting of its fruit by means of his bodily teeth would receive (eternal) life ? or again, that a man could receive (the knowledge) of " good and evil " from having chewed the fruit of the Tree so called ?   And if God is said to walk in the garden in the evening, and Adam to hide under the tree, no one, I imagine, will doubt that such words are meant to reveal certain mysteries metaphorically, through a seeming history, not one which happened in concrete fact.'

[1] The only original and essential unity in which, according to Origen, all men participate is the unity of all intellectual natures, the ' Henad ' alluded to above (p. 212).

assumed at His incarnation [1] ; and the souls of a few of the greatest saints may also be assumed to have left the super-sensible world, not as the result of sin, but obeying a specific Divine command to co-operate in the regeneration of mankind.[2]

Such is Origen's earliest reconstruction of the idea of the Fall. The question still remains to be answered, What, in his view, were the results of the pre-natal transgression, other than the banishment of the peccant soul to this world ? It will be seen at once that the substitution of a series of individual and transcendental ' falls ' for a single ' Fall ' in time of a common ancestor entirely does away with any idea of an inherited bias towards evil (' Original Sin ') or of an inherited status of guilt (' Original Guilt '). Given this hypothesis, it is impossible to speak of any sort of sinfulness as inherited : whatever moral infirmity or consciousness of guilt may inhere in the individual has been *acquired* by him, as the result of his own act, pre-natal or post-natal. As we have seen, the unity of the human race *as such* is, for Origen's individualistic and atomistic anthropology, acci-dental, not essential [3] ; it is the result of sin, not the basis of sinfulness. It is impossible, therefore, to regard him as having held the doctrines of ' Original ' or racial sin or guilt, during the Alexandrine period of his career.

It might have been supposed that—given the stability which the theory of Adam's Fall as in some sense the cause of subsequent transgressions had by this time, in virtue of the Pauline teaching, attained within the Church—Origen would at least have felt obliged to provide a substitute for the idea of ' Original Sin ' in the shape of a conception of a *pre-natally acquired* bias towards sin. But no very clear expression of any such conception can be found in the

---

[1] *de princ.* ii. 6, 3 (Koetschau, p. 142 : see the references and parallels given in the foot-notes) ; iv. 4, 4 (Koetschau, p. 353).

[2] Such were Isaiah, Jeremiah, Ezekiel, John the Baptist (*in Ioann.* ii. 30 [Preuschen, p. 86 f.] ; this part of the Commentary was written before A.D. 231, according to Eus. *H.E.* vi. 24). We may perhaps compare the Lamaist idea of the successive incarnations of a series of Buddhas, for the purpose of teaching mankind the way of virtue. For a similar idea in Philo, see Lecture II, p. 84, n. 2.

[3] See note on p. 216, above.

de principiis.[1] (The idea, that the soul begins its life
here in a ' cooler ' condition, relatively as to its love of God,
than that which it enjoyed in the super-sensible sphere, is
hardly definite or positive enough to be construed in this
sense.)   The traditional Hellenic and Stoic[2] belief in the
absolute autonomy of the will, so strongly characteristic of
the primitive Greek-Christian writers—a belief which is all
but irreconcileable with the hypothesis of an *a priori* inclination to wickedness—has really overpowered in his mind the
authority of St. Paul, though he is, of course, quite unaware
of the fact.   So unqualified and inalienable is the power of
self-determination in all conscious beings—angels, men, and
fiends—that the fiends may, if they choose, exalt themselves
in the long run to human or angelic status, the angels may
correspondingly degrade themselves, and men may either
rise to the highest or sink to the lowest point in the scale of
created being.[3]   Origen quotes, indeed, the Apostle's words
—' The flesh lusteth against the spirit,'[4] but explains them
away as meaning merely that the bodily appetites do in
point of fact furnish the occasion for and form the raw
material of sinful impulse—that they are what a later age
called the *fomes peccati*, the ' tinder of sin '—though in
themselves they are morally neutral.[5]   If they are allowed
to become hypertrophied, the devil may use them as a
fulcrum for pushing us into sin, though even the devil's
assaults do not impair the freedom of our choice.[6]   The

[1] Rufinus does indeed employ the term ' malitia ' to describe the state
in which the fallen spirits find themselves (ii. 9, 1) ; but his method of
translation is so free and arbitrary that it would be unsafe to build too
much upon this word alone.   In any case, for Origen, as for subsequent
Greek Fathers, evil is a negative concept, the mere privation of good
(' certum namque est malum esse bono carere,' *ibid.*).

[2] For the pre-eminence of the Stoa as the champion of free-will, see
Windelband, *Geschichte der Philosophie* (1892), p. 151, 3.

[3] *de princ.* i. 6, 2, 3 (together with this passage should be studied
Koetschau's footnotes, in which are collected summaries of Origen's speculations on this point from the works of Jerome) ; iii. 1, 21.   But this
belief in an eternal indeterminateness of volition, with its corollary of an
eternal possibility of sin, seems inconsistent with the idea of a *necessary*
restitution of all spirits, which appears in iii. 6, 5, 6 ; a fact which illustrates the fluid and provisional character of Origen's thought on questions
belonging to the ' fringe ' rather than to the central core of the Faith.

[4] Gal. v. 17.

[5] *de princ.* iii. 2, 2.   [6] *ibid.* iii. 2, 3.

question why our bodily appetites ever should become hypertrophied is not discussed. It is difficult not to feel that in the *de principiis* the whole treatment of the problem of the ' moral struggle ' is superficial, and reflects, not the ' twice-born ' fervour of Origen's Coptic heart, but the ' once-born ' serenity of his Hellenic brain.[1] Indeed, the structure of his earliest Fall-theory is, if we may so say, of a different composition and consistency from those versions of the traditional Judaeo-Christian doctrine which we have studied hitherto. They are the spontaneous precipitates, the ' rationalisations,' if you will, of crises of poignant feeling ; but this is an intellectual artefact, a cold philosophical hypothesis, divorced from penitential emotion, and designed rather to solve a cosmological than a religious or ethical difficulty.

It is fair to add, in concluding our survey of Origen's first theories in regard to the origin of evil and the pre-existence of souls, that he is at pains to emphasise the tentative and provisional nature of his speculations, and to disclaim any intention of putting them forward as dog-matically certain or as essential parts of the Faith. ' haec prout potuimus de rationabili anima discutienda magis a legentibus quam statuta ac definita protulimus.'[2]

(ii) THE CAESAREAN PERIOD—INFANT BAPTISM

We now turn to the writings which date from the period of Origen's residence at Caesarea in Palestine (A.D. 231— ? 254). In them we shall find—juxtaposed, but by no means synthesised, with the highly ' once-born ' version of the Fall-theory sketched in our last section—another, more sombre and pessimistic, view, the unmistakeable product of the ' twice-born ' elements in his strangely composite personality. According to a very probable hypothesis, first suggested by Bigg[3] and endorsed by Harnack,[4] the

---

[1] *Cf.* Huet, *Origeniana*, ii. q. 7, §§ 1–11.
[2] ii. 8, 5 *ad fin.* ; *cf.* also i. 8, 4 (Koetschau, p. 105, 11).
[3] *Christian Platonists*, p. 246.
[4] *History of Dogma* (E. tr. 1910), ii. p. 365, n. 5.

emergence in his mind of a more thorough-going Fall-doctrine, adhering more closely to the Adam-story as interpreted by St. Paul, and assuming a graver judgment on the weakness of human nature, was due to the fact that at Caesarea he became acquainted for the first time with a custom which is taken for granted by the Churchman of to-day, but which in the third century was not universally practised, or even universally known, amongst Christians—the custom of Infant Baptism.

Exactly when and how this practice originated it is impossible to say with certainty. There is no recorded saying of Christ which can be quoted as referring to the age of the recipients of baptism ; the Acts of the Apostles contain no clear evidence for the administration of the rite to persons other than those of adult age [1] ; the Epistles assume that the mystery of Christian initiation is normally imparted as the crown and consummation of a process of conscious faith in Jesus as Messiah, of repentance from sin, and of conversion from idols to serve the living God— in other words, that the neophyte is a person of full age and responsibility. On the other hand, none of the sacred writings contain any prohibition of the practice. It must be admitted that the New Testament neither approves nor condemns, but ignores, Infant Baptism [2] ; and that, if

---

[1] It has been suggested that the ' households ' which are mentioned in the New Testament as having been baptised (as those of Lydia, Acts xvi. 15, the jailer at Philippi, *ibid.* 33, and Stephanas, 1 Cor. i. 16) may have included children ; but it is obviously impossible to be certain of this.

[2] It is possible to surmise that St. Paul, even if he knew and approved of a custom of baptising the infant children of pagan or Jewish converts to Christianity, would at one period of his life have considered it unnecessary to baptise infants born to parents who were already Christian, or of whom one was a Christian ; see 1 Cor. vii. 14 : ' For the unbelieving husband is sanctified in the wife, and the unbelieving wife is sanctified in the brother ' (*i.e.* her Christian husband) : ' else were your children unclean, but now they are holy (ἅγια).' This passage may imply a belief that baptism so completely cancelled whatever disastrous entail was inherited from Adam that not only was the baptised person thereby made holy, but his or her subsequent children, even by a heathen spouse, were born in a condition of holiness. Hooker's rejection of this interpretation (*Eccl. Pol.* v. 60, 6) seems to be based on dogmatic rather than critical grounds. It is not an argument against the attribution of such a view to St. Paul that according to it the spread of Christianity would eventually make baptism unnecessary and obsolete ; for at the date of the composition of 1 Cor., the Apostle was convinced that ' the time was shortened ' (vii. 29) and the

nothing is lawful save what can be certainly demonstrated to have been sanctioned by one of the sacred authors, the Anabaptist has won his case. We may observe parenthetically that even those who do not accept such a narrowly literal view of the appeal to Scripture, and rely on the *auctoritas* of the universal Christian society as legitimating a sacramental development which goes beyond what can be shown to have been the practice of the Apostolic Church, must feel that the custom of baptising unconscious infants (in virtue of the exclusive emphasis which it seems to lay upon the *ex opere operato* aspect of the sacred action, and the complete absence from it of the subjective and *ex opere operantis* aspect) is not unattended by theoretical difficulties, such as do not arise in connexion with the normal administration of the other sacraments.[1] These difficulties will, however, be dealt with in the proper place.[2] For the purposes of our historical enquiry, it is sufficient to remark that, even if neither our Lord nor His Apostles directly authorised the administration of baptism to those who could not, in the nature of the case, experience either faith or repentance, the custom is one which, in the absence of any explicit prohibition, might well be expected to grow up at an early date and in many places, doubtless as the

---

Parousia at hand, so that *ex hypothesi* comparatively few children could be born under these favoured conditions. If such a view of the hereditary efficacy of baptism was actually held in the Apostolic Church, it would, from the standpoint of later orthodoxy, have to be classed with the companion beliefs in the validity of vicarious ' baptism for the dead ' (1 Cor. xv. 29) and in the impeccability of the baptised (see Lecture III, p. 135) as one of those mistaken but transient inferences from true principles which the student must expect to find in the initial stages of Christian theology. The probability that Christian baptism was, in some quarters, regarded in this way is increased by the fact that a similar view was taken, with regard to the baptism of proselytes, in the Jewish Church ; cf. *Yebamoth*, 78a : ' If a Gentile woman becomes a proselyte when she is with child, her son has no need for baptism ; for the baptism of his mother counts for him in the place of his own baptism.'

[1] Except in the case of absolution given to a dying person who is unconscious (Schieler-Heuser, *Theory and Practice of the Confessional*, 1906, pp. 646 ff.). It may be added that the same *prima facie* difficulties which attach to the custom of Infant Baptism attach also to the customs of Infant Confirmation and Communion, still retained by the Eastern Church.

[2] See below, Additional Note G ' Infant Baptism,' p. 550.

result of popular sentiment rather than of reasoned logic. It may well have been suggested to Jewish-Christian parents by the practice, vouched for by the Talmud as familiar to first-century Judaism,[1] of baptising the infant children of proselytes, and to Gentiles by the custom which permitted young children to be initiated into some at least of the pagan Mysteries.[2]

It is in any case probable that the beginnings of Paedo-baptism run back into the Apostolic age, despite the fact that it is not mentioned in the New Testament ; Polycarp's reply to the proconsul ' Eighty and six years have I been the slave of Christ '[3] must imply that he had been baptised as an infant c. A.D. 69.   Infant baptism is mentioned, possibly by Justin Martyr, and certainly by Irenaeus,[4] in the latter half of the second century, and it is strongly opposed by Tertullian [5] at the beginning of the third : from the middle of the third the evidence for the recognition of its permissibility is continuous, and by the end of the fifth it has become universal and normal, as it is to-day in Christian countries.   A careful study of the historical data, which we have only been able to summarise briefly here, will make it reasonably clear that in the practice of Infant Baptism we have a popular development of the earliest use of the sacrament, a development not at first deduced from theological principle or imposed from above by Church authority, but arising spontaneously from below, out of the subconscious

---

[1] See the passages quoted to illustrate Matt. iii. 6 by J. Lightfoot, *Horae Hebraicae* (1675), p. 219 f.

[2] G. Anrich, *Das antike Mysterienwesen*, p. 55, gives instances, based mainly upon epigraphic evidence, of children of seven and ten years of age who had undergone initiation into several Mystery-cults : one such child is described as μυηθεὶς ἔτι νήπιος.

[3] *martyrium Polycarpi*, 9.

[4] *adv. haer.* II. xxxiii. 2 : ' omnes enim venit per semetipsum salvare ; omnes inquam, qui per eum renascuntur in Deum, *infantes, et parvulos*, et pueros, et iuvenes, et seniores.' The passage from Justin, however, which is often quoted as a proof of the existence of the custom of baptising infants c. A.D. 150 (πολλοί τινες καὶ πολλαὶ ἑξηκοντοῦται καὶ ἑβδομηκοντοῦται, οἳ ἐκ παίδων ἐμαθητεύθησαν τῷ Χριστῷ, ἄφθοροι διαμένουσι, I *Apol.* xv. 6) is inconclusive : for ἐμαθητεύθησαν does not necessarily imply more than admission to the catechumenate, and ἐκ παίδων does not mean ' from infancy.'

[5] *de baptismo*, 18 ; see below, p. 241.

instincts of the Christian society, eventually forcing its way into official recognition, and generating, at least in Western Christendom, a not inconsiderable body of doctrinal ideas in order to effect its own *ex post facto* justification.

The point last mentioned is of crucial importance for the understanding of that part of the history of the Fall-doctrine upon which we are now entering. In treatises of systematic theology, the necessity of infant baptism is usually stated as an inference from the doctrine of Original Sin, and in the order of thought this may be so ; but in order of time the practice was prior to, and largely stimulated the growth of, the doctrine, and not *vice versa*. It is not the case that men said ' Infants are infected from the womb with a hereditary taint ; they must therefore be baptised as soon after birth as possible ' ; what they did say (after the custom, origi-nating, it would seem, in grounds of popular sentiment, had become thoroughly established) was : ' The Church actually does baptise infants as soon as possible after birth, and we cannot suppose that the Church does anything without good reason ; therefore, infants must be infected from the womb with a hereditary taint.' *Legem credendi statuit lex orandi :* there is no clearer instance of the control exercised by liturgical or devotional practice over the growth of dogma than that provided by the study of the relations between the custom of Infant Baptism and the doctrine of Original Sin.

Thus it was, apparently, that Origen argued. If he had previously been unacquainted with the custom, the discovery that newly born, unconscious infants could be, and were, with the sanction of ' Apostolic tradition,'[1] subjected to the same tremendous purificatory ceremonies as adults who had been stained with the darkest vices of the Graeco-Roman world, must have made a profound impression on his mind. Given the rightfulness of the practice (and this it never occurred to him to dispute) it was clear to him that some sort of positive sinfulness or defilement must be supposed to inhere in human nature as such, from the very moment of birth ; and it would seem that the idea of guilt pre-natally acquired by the soul—the only kind of pollution deducible

---

[1] *comm. in Rom.* V. 9 (Lomm. vi. 397) : ' pro hoc et ecclesia ab apostolis traditionem suscepit, etiam parvulis baptismum dare.'

from his theory of individual pre-natal ' falls '—through an act of which the exact nature, and even the bare commission, had *ex hypothesi* been forgotten, now appeared to him far too shadowy and unsubstantial a ground for the introduction of personally sinless babes to the awful mysteries of Christian initiation. His restless mind, therefore, was fain to search in other directions for the required theoretical justification of paedo-baptism.

He seems for a long time to have experimented with the idea of the quasi-material impurity, or ' bad *mana*,' assumed by the Levitical law to infect the physiological processes of conception and child-birth and to need ' expiation ' through the oblation of a pair of turtle-doves or of pigeons, one for a burnt-offering and one for a sin offering.[1] So, shortly after A.D. 231, he writes, in somewhat hesitating terms :

Let us now investigate the question, why a woman who lends help to those being born into this world (*i.e.* a mother) is said to become unclean, not merely when she has received seed but when she has brought forth. Whence she is commanded to offer two young pigeons or turtle-doves for a sin offering . . . as though she required purification of sin, in that she lent help to the birth of a human being into this world . . . I do not venture to lay down any definite *dictum* in such matters, but I feel that certain occult mysteries are contained in these commands, and that there is some hidden and secret cause, why a woman who has conceived of seed and brought forth should be called ' unclean,' and should be commanded, as though she had been guilty of a sin, to offer a sacrifice for sin and so to be purified.

He goes on to point out that the child itself is unclean, according to Job xiv. 4, 5 (LXX),[2] and Ps. li. 5 (' Behold, I was shapen in wickedness ').

---

[1] Lev. xii.

[2] For a note on the Hebrew version of this text, see Lecture I, p. 17. The LXX give 4 τίς γὰρ καθαρὸς ἔσται ἀπὸ ῥύπου ; ἀλλ' οὐθείς, 5 ἐὰν καὶ μία ἡμέρα ὁ βίος αὐτοῦ ἐπὶ τῆς γῆς—' Who shall be pure from defilement ? not so much as one, even though his life on the earth be but a day ' ; which Origen takes as proving the innate corruption of infants. The Hebrew is translated by Driver and Gray (*ICC.*, p. 127) as follows : ' 4. Oh that a clean thing could come out of an unclean ! not one (can). 5. If his (*i.e.* man's) days are determined, the number of his months is known to thee, and his limit thou hast appointed that he cannot pass ; 6. look away from him, and forbear . . .' etc. If this is original, the LXX represents a mere misunderstanding.

We may add to these considerations the question, Why should baptism be given to infants (*parvulis*) as is the use of the Church ? seeing that *if there were nothing in infants which required remission and pardon, the grace of baptism would seem superfluous.*[1]

He re-inforces this hypothesis of a mysterious sinfulness inherent in birth by the quaint argument that none of the saints was ever known to keep his own birthday as a feast, whereas Jeremiah and Job cursed the days of their entrance into this world.[2] Here the pollution of birth is thought of quasi-juridically, as though it constituted guilt. But, a little further on in the same treatise the emphasis seems to shift, and the birth-stain seems to be treated as a predominantly physical quality, from which the pre-existent human soul of Jesus alone was granted exemption at its incarnation, according to the text Wisdom viii. 20—' being good, I came into a body undefiled.'[3] Some years later, the stain derived from the processes of conception and birth has become in Origen's mind purely physical ; and, with considerable daring, as he himself admits (' temerarie forsitan videor dicere '), he asserts that Jesus Himself was subject to it, and stood in need of purification with His Mother.[4] In the Commentary on Romans, however, (after A.D. 244[5]) he returns to the more refined, if less intelligible, idea of the birth-stain as involving or amounting to sin, and appeals

---

[1] *in Lev. hom.* viii. 3 (Lomm. ix. 318).

[2] *ibid.* He also points out in this passage that the only persons mentioned in Scripture as having kept their own birthdays are the tyrants Pharaoh and Herod Antipas, both of whom polluted their celebrations with bloodshed, the former by hanging the chief baker, and the latter by beheading John the Baptist.

[3] *in Lev. hom.* xii. 4 (Lomm. ix. 389 f.).

[4] *in Luc. hom.* xiv. (Lomm. v. 134). This passage distinguishes carefully between *sordes* and *peccatum*, the former of which is said to be transmitted by birth, the latter not. The paragraph significantly concludes (Lomm. v. 135) : ' parvuli baptizantur in remissionem peccatorum. quorum peccatorum ? vel quo tempore peccaverunt ? aut quomodo potest ulla lavacri in parvulis ratio subsistere, nisi iuxta illum sensum, de quo paulo ante diximus " nullus mundus a sorde, nec si unius diei quidem fuerit vita eius super terram " ? et quia per baptismi sacramentum nativitatis sordes deponuntur, propterea baptizantur et parvuli, " nisi enim quis renatus fuerit ex aqua et spiritu, non poterit intrare in regnum coelorum." '

[5] Westcott, *op. cit.*

once more to the 'Apostolic' practice of infant baptism as bearing this out.[1]

Doubtless this line of thought represents one more re-emergence of that primitive subconscious tendency which we have already observed at work in previous hamartio-logical speculation, namely, the tendency to assume that all sex-activity is intrinsically dangerous and wrong,[2] and that the ground or origin of all actual sins is somehow to be found in it. This tendency, characteristic, as we have seen, of the 'twice-born' man, may be assigned to the Coptic, as distinct from the Hellenic, side of Origen's personality. Two facts are in any case clear : (1) that the idea of the birth-stain never assumes complete fixity of outline : like the barbarous idea of 'bad *mana*,' of which it is indeed merely a form, it wavers between the meanings of physical, ceremonial, and moral uncleanness ; and (2) that in its more developed statements, it approximates to a doctrine both of 'original sin' and of 'original guilt,' such as is entirely absent from the writings of his earlier period.

It is clear that this theory of a pollution of some kind necessarily inherent in and transmitted by the processes of generation and birth, if held apart from any view as to the *origin* of such pollution, lands us in pure and simple dualism, and involves the tacit surrender of the fundamental Christian conception of God to Gnosticism. Origen was therefore compelled to search for the ultimate fount of the sinfulness of sexuality or of generation—a broad universal fact (as he thought) which could hardly have been produced by a number of pre-natal or transcendental acts of individual souls—in some catastrophic happening upon the plane of matter ; in other words, he was forced back upon the

---

[1] *comm. in Rom.* V. (Lomm. vi. 397) : ' pro hoc et ecclesia ab apostolis traditionem suscepit, etiam parvulis baptismum dare ; sciebant enim illi, quibus mysteriorum secreta commissa sunt divinorum, quod essent in omnibus *genuinae sordes peccati*, quae per aquam et spiritum ablui deberent.'

[2] Origen's ultra-ascetic, almost Manichean, views with regard to this matter are clearly shown both by his act of self-mutilation alluded to above (p. 209) and also by two passages, *in Gen. hom.* v. 4 ad fin. (Lomm. viii. 177), and *in Num. hom.* vi. 3 ad fin. (Lomm. x. 51), quoted by R. Seeberg, *Lehrbuch der Dogmengesch.* (1920), I. p. 538, n. 2. To these might be added *de orat.* 31, 4 (Koetschau, p. 398).

conception of a single historic ' Fall ' in time and in this
world, and therewith upon a more or less literal interpretation of the Adam-story. At first, if the language of the
Commentary on the Canticles is to be construed literally, he
took refuge in that form of the Fall-doctrine based on Gen. iii.
which may be called the theory of the *inquinamentum*,[1]
that is, the theory that Eve was seduced by the serpent and
physically infected by him [2] ; the same treatise contains
a vaguer and less repulsive expression of the idea of
' Original Sin ' in the statement that man's free-will has
been ' inclined to ignominy or wantonness ' by occasion of
the ' transgression ' [3] (*praevaricatio*, which presumably
represents an original παράβασις [4]). The close study of the
Epistle to the Romans, however, which was necessitated
by the preparation of his great Commentary [5] on that book,
had the effect of diverting his mind into more characteristically Pauline channels ; and throughout *Comm. in Rom.* V.,
which contains his exposition of the crucial passage Rom.
v. 13–21, he accepts, in a general sense, the more normal
Adamic theory as implied in the Apostle's words.

It is noticeable that in his exegesis of this passage the
word *praevaricatio* occurs frequently, and appears for all
practical purposes to have assumed its technical meaning of
' the Fall.' The story of Gen. iii. seems to be taken quite
literally (though the sex-*motif* reappears in one passing
allusion [6]) ; and the propagation of sin from Adam to his

---

[1] See above, Lecture II, p. 57 ; Lecture III, p. 122.

[2] *comm. in Cant.* III. (Lomm. xv. 54 f.) : ' cervus quoque amicitiarum
quis alius videbitur nisi ille qui peremit serpentem qui seduxerat Evam,
et eloquii sui flatibus peccati venena in eam diffundens omnem posteritatis
sobolem contagio peccati praevaricationis infecerat ? ' Westcott (*op. cit.*) dates
this treatise *c.* A.D. 240.   Dr. Tennant's description of it as ' one of
(Origen's) earliest works ' (*Sources*, p. 303, n. 2) seems to be founded on a
confusion of it with an entirely different work, the much earlier Commentary on Canticles of which a fragment is preserved in *Philocalia*, vii. 1
(ἐκ τοῦ εἰς τὸ ᾆσμα μικροῦ τόμου ὃν ἐν τῇ νεότητι ἔγραψεν).

[3] *comm. in Cant.* IV. (Lomm. xv. 72) : ' . . . ut ostenderet inesse
unicuique animae vim possibilitatis et arbitrii libertatem, qua possit agere
omne quod bonum est. Sed quia hoc naturae bonum praevaricationis
occasione decerptum, vel ad ignominiam vel lasciviam fuerat inflexum. . . .'

[4] See below, p. 302.   [5] Written after A.D. 244 (Westcott).

[6] *comm. in Rom.* V. 9 (Lomm. vi. 397), where it is pointed out that
Adam did not beget children until after the Fall : ' nec Adam scribitur
cognovisse Evam uxorem suam et genuisse Cain nisi post peccatum.'

descendants is explained in terms of ' seminal identity,' which we have already encountered in Irenaeus.[1] Yet Origen the Biblical exegete has not altogether overpowered Origen the Platonist ; in his last-named character, he is reluctant to surrender altogether the half-mythological, half-metaphysical idea of an extra-mundane Paradise, and of the individual ' falls ' of pre-existent spirits. Hence, in commenting on Rom. v. 18 (' So then as through one trespass the judgment came upon all men to condemnation ') he writes :

It is written that when Adam had sinned, the Lord God drove him out of Paradise, and set him in this earth, over against the Paradise of delights ; and this was the condemnation of his sin, a condemnation which without doubt has extended unto all men. For all have been made to dwell in this place of humiliation and in the valley of weeping ; whether because *all who are born from Adam were in his loins* and were simultaneously with him cast out of Paradise, or whether, in some other ineffable way known to God only, *each individual may be deemed to have been thrust out of Paradise* and so to have received condemnation.[2]

Here two alternative methods of conceiving a pre-natal and transcendental Fall are indicated : the first being the hypothesis of a collective pre-natal Fall of the whole race, contained in Adam, from the heavenly place ; the second being the theory which has been already expounded in the *de principiis*, that of a never-ending series of individual falls into this vale of tears, which is the world of matter.

In his last work (the *Treatise against Celsus*) he appears, though it is impossible to be quite sure of his meaning, to revert to his earlier theory, that of an immense number of

[1] See above, p. 197. The parallel of Levi's pre-natal existence in Abraham is used to support this theory (*comm. in Rom.* V. 1, Lomm. vi. 326) : ' si ergo Levi, qui generatione quarta post Abraham nascitur, in lumbis Abrahami fuisse perhibetur, multo magis omnes homines qui in hoc mundo nascuntur et nati sunt, in lumbis erant Adami, cum adhuc esset in paradiso ; et omnes homines cum ipso vel in ipso expulsi sunt de paradiso, cum ipse inde depulsus est.'

[2] *comm. in Rom.* V. 4 (Lomm. vi. 363 f.) : ' . . . cum deliquisset Adam, scriptum est quod eiecit eum Dominus Deus de Paradiso, et constituit eum in terra hac contra Paradisum deliciarum : et haec fuit delicti eius condemnatio, quae in omnes homines sine dubio pervenit. omnes enim in loco hoc humiliationis et in convalle fletus effecti sunt : sive quod in lumbis Adae fuerunt omnes qui ex eo nascuntur, et cum ipso pariter eiecti sunt ; sive alio quolibet inenarrabili modo et soli Deo cognito unusquisque de Paradiso trusus videtur et excepisse condemnationem.'

individual pre-natal falls. This at any rate is a probable inference from the allegorisation of ' Adam ' (אָדָם = *homo*, mankind in general) contained in the following passage :

> Concerning Adam and his sin those who have knowledge of these matters will philosophise to this effect, namely, that ' Adam ' in the Greek language signifies ἄνθρωπος, 'man,' and that in what appears to be said about Adam < as an individual > Moses is really laying down scientific principles concerning human nature. For when the divine scripture tells us that ' in Adam all die,' and that all were condemned in ' the likeness of the transgression of Adam,' it uses these expressions not so much of a single individual as of the whole race. And in the whole series of sayings which apparently apply to the individual Adam, it will be found that the curse of Adam is really common to all ; and there is no woman who is not subject to the sentence pronounced on the woman < Eve >. And the ' man ' who with the woman is cast out of Paradise, having been clothed in the ' coats of skins,' which God made on account of the transgression (or 'fall,' παράβασις) of men for those that had sinned, conveys a certain ineffable and mystic meaning, far transcending Plato's story of the descent of the soul which sheds her wings and drifts down to this world, 'until she find some solid footing.'[1]

This conception appears equally to underlie a later passage of the same work, in which the idea of the birth-stain described above, and here definitely stated to involve *guilt* and to need expiation, is asserted to be part of the revelation made to the prophets, and is connected, though in vague language, with the expulsion of ' Adam, that is to say Man ' from Paradise and his arrival in this terrestrial place of affliction.[2] It would, accordingly, seem that the view in which Origen, towards the end of his life, finally came to repose represents a combination of his Alexandrian ' pre-natal fall ' theory with his Caesarean ' birth-stain ' theory. We may regard him, like Wordsworth, as concluding that

> the soul that rises with us, our life's Star,
>   Hath had elsewhere its setting,
>   And cometh from afar[3] ;

---

[1] *c. Cels.* IV. 40 (Koetschau, pp. 313 f.). The reference in the last sentence to the myth of the *Phaedrus* is unmistakeable. For the history of the allegorical interpretation of the ' coats of skins,' see below, pp. 251, 275, 285, and J. H. Srawley, *The Catechetical Oration of Gregory of Nyssa*, p. 42, note on l. 14.

[2] *c. Cels.* VII. 50.   [3] *Ode on Intimations of Immortality.*

but we must add that the sense of sin which was rooted in the Egyptian side of his temperament compelled him to think of the soul, not as ' trailing clouds of glory,' but rather as falling to the earth like a meteor, glowing with the lurid and disastrous fires of pre-natal and extra-temporal guilt.

It will have been seen that it is no more possible to educe a single thought-out scheme of Fall-doctrine from the writings of Origen than from those of his Greek-Christian predecessors, the Apologists, Irenaeus, Clement.   The main interest, indeed, which his speculations bear for the purposes of our enquiry resides in the fact that in them we find, lying side by side and not yet articulated into coherent systems, the *disiecta membra* of both the chief versions of the Christian doctrine of man and sin, ' once-born ' or minimising and ' twice-born ' or maximising, which henceforward were destined to compete for the allegiance of the Church.   To the former, or Hellenic-Christian, version of the doctrine, belongs the tendency to allegorise the story of Gen. iii., and in particular to place ' Paradise ' in an extra-mundane ' third heaven,' which easily passes into the Platonic τόπος νοητός or world of Ideas; the lenient description of ' Original Sin,' if such it can be called, as a *levis contagio*,[1] a ' slight infection,' which does not seriously impair the self-determining force of man's free-will ; the large recognition of ' social heredity ' as a factor equally important with, or even more important than, physiological heredity, in the transmission of sin from generation to generation.[2]   To the latter or ' twice-born ' version, which we may describe as specifically ' African ' (not merely because it reflects the native Egyptian elements in Origen's

---

[1] *comm. in Rom.* V. (Lomm. vi. 341) : ' peccatum enim pertransiit etiam in iustos, et levi quadam eos contagione perstrinxit.'

[2] *ibid.* (Lomm. vi. 342 f.) : ' . . . ut hoc sermone omnes qui ex Adam praevaricatore nati sunt indicari videantur, et habere in semetipsis similitudinem praevaricationis eius non solum ex semine sed ex institutione susceptam. omnes enim qui in hoc mundo nascuntur non solum nutri-untur a parentibus sed et imbuuntur ; et non solum sunt filii peccatorum sed et discipuli.' *ibid.* (Lomm. vi. 353) : ' diximus quidem iam et in superioribus quod parentes non solum generant filios, sed et imbuunt ; et qui nascuntur, non solum filii parentibus, sed et discipul i fiunt, et non tam natura urgentur in mortem peccati quam disciplina.'

personality, but because those who were, as we shall
presently see, its principal elaborators also dwelt on the
southern shores of the Mediterranean), are to be assigned
the tendency to assume the inherent sinfulness of sex, the
idea that the inbred evil in human nature is in some way to
be connected with physical generation, the belief that infants
are born not merely with a bias towards evil but actually
subject to some kind of pre-natal guilt, their own or Adam's,
which needs absolution through the waters of baptism.

It is true that some of the positions characteristic of the
'African' doctrine had already been worked out by a somewhat earlier author, living nearer to the Pillars of Hercules,
the fiery Tertullian; but nevertheless, if it is permissible
to fix a definite point of time at which the bifurcation
between the 'once-born' and the 'twice-born' presentations of the Fall-doctrine tends to become clearly visible,
that point may well be placed in the year A.D. 231, the date
of Origen's retirement from Alexandria to Caesarea.

Tertullian and 'Traducianism' [1]

From the Palestine of A.D. 250 the thread of our research
now leads us some twelve hundred miles westwards, into
the Roman province of Proconsular Africa, and some forty
years backwards in respect of time, into the first decade of
the third century. Hitherto we have been concerned with
the earliest, predominantly 'once-born' and 'minimising,'
development of the Fall-doctrine in the Eastern countries
and the environment of Hellenic culture which together
may be said to constitute the primitive matrix of Catholic
Christianity; but now our story touches for the first time
the Occidental division of the Christian world, in which a
sterner and gloomier presentation of the ideas of the Fall
and of Original Sin has played so momentous a part. Of
this great geographical and cultural unity within the Catholic

---

[1] The brief account of Tertullian's contribution to the growth of the
Western Fall-doctrine contained in this section may be supplemented
from P. Monceaux, *Histoire littéraire de l'Afrique chrétienne*, tom. i. (1901) ;
G. Esser, *Die Seelenlehre Tertullians* (1893) ; A. d'Alès, *La Théologie de
Tertullien* (1905) ; J. Turmel, *Tertullien* (1905).

unity, Western Christendom, of which Roman and Anglican and Protestant still share in differing measures the spiritual and doctrinal heritage, the ultimate intellectual *metropolis* or parent-city is neither Rome nor Canterbury nor Geneva, but Carthage ; where Latin theology was flourishing whilst the local Roman Church was still almost purely Greek in language and thought, and where the work of hammering out the specifically Western conceptions of the Trinity, the Church, and the ' Doctrine of Grace ' was first begun.

The earliest of the line of eminent teachers produced by North African Christianity was Quintus Septimius Florens Tertullianus, born *c.* A.D. 160, at Carthage, ' the great craftsman who was the first to give its peculiar aspect and *cachet* to Latin theology.' [1] As is well known, Tertullian was before his conversion to Christianity a lawyer and jurist, and it is possible that the Pandects of Justinian still preserve an excerpt from his legal writings.[2] The influence of his juristic training upon the tone and character of his thought is luminously summed up by the writer just quoted, in the following words :

Tertullian was no philosopher ; speculation was always foreign to him, and he never thought of the Christian revelation as a new light which comes to enlarge our intellectual horizon or as a body of truth which invites our investigation. But he possessed the *juridical sense* in the highest degree. He was a lawyer who, before all things, saw in Christianity a Fact and a Law. It was the business of Christians to prove and to comprehend the Fact—to interpret and, above all, to observe the Law. Relatively to us, God is a master and a creditor : we are His subjects and His debtors. The right method, therefore, of determining our relations with Him is to apply the principles of human legislative codes, and to carry into this application the severity which governs the calculation of our debts and of our civil rights—a method which can be employed with the exactitude which characterises the operations of commerce.[3]

Despite the fact that only a comparatively short portion of his Christian life was spent within the communion of the

---

[1] J. Tixeront, *Histoire des Dogmes* (1909) i. p. 329.

[2] *quaestionum libri* viii, *de castrensi peculio*, ascribed to a jurist Tertullian, whom some identify with the African Father. See *Digesta Iustiniani Aug.*, recogn. Th. Mommsen (1870), ii. p. 897.

[3] Tixeront, *op. cit.*, p. 330 (slightly abridged).

' Great Church ' (he was baptised some time before A.D. 196, adopted Montanist opinions *c.* 207, broke finally with the Church in 213,[1] and, according to Jerome,[2] lived to an extreme old age), Tertullian may nevertheless be said to have constructed the mould in which the classical ' twice-born ' or ' African ' presentation of the Fall-theory was destined to be cast. This mould, which was indeed broken and discarded when it had served its purpose,[3] but without which the Augustinian Fall-doctrine, still imagined by many to be the only Fall-doctrine known to traditional Christianity, could never have assumed its completed and logically rounded shape, was his ' traducianist '[4] psychology : which may now be briefly summarised.

Tertullian's views with regard to the nature of the soul are expounded at length in the treatise *de anima,* which internal evidence shows to have been composed after his definite adoption of the Montanist position, but which none the less exercised a considerable influence within the ' Great Church.' He asserts that his psychology is based upon Holy Writ,[5] though claiming at the same time, in a curiously modern spirit, to have given attention to medical science in this connexion [6] ; and he expresses a vigorous contempt for the psychologies of philosophers, especially for the Platonic theories of metempsychosis and reminiscence.[7] Nevertheless, it is clear that he was indebted both for his psychology and for his physiology to the Stoics, from

[1] P. Monceaux, *op. cit.*, p. 201 f.

[2] *de viris illustr.* 53 (' fertur vixisse usque ad decrepitam aetatem ').

[3] *c.f.* below, Lecture VI, p. 413, n, 1.

[4] It is convenient to use this term as a description of Tertullian's views regarding the origin of the soul ; though, strictly speaking, it is anachronistic, inasmuch as, according to Du Cange (*Glossarium mediae et infimae latinitatis*, ed. Henschel, 1887, s.v. *tradux*), the term *traduciani* belongs rather to the controversies of the fifth century, being applied as a term of reproach by the Pelagians to the Augustinians ; the earliest instance of the term which he quotes is in Marius Mercator, *lib. subnot.* ix. 7, 14.

[5] *de an.* 3.   In giving quotations from this work I have used the text of A. Reifferschied and G. Wissowa, published in the Vienna *Corpus Script. Eccles. Lat.*, vol. xx.

[6] *ibid.* 2 : ' sed et medicinam inspexi . . . sibi quoque hoc negotium vindicantem, quippe ad quam magis animae ratio pertinere videatur per corporis curam.'   He frequently cites the opinions of famous physicians, especially Soranus (6, 8, 15, 25, 44) and Hippocrates (15, 25).

[7] *ibid.* 4, 23–24, 31–33.

whom he has borrowed his cardinal principle, that of the
corporeality of the soul. It is permissible to suggest that,
in Tertullian's case, the legal mind, accustomed to deal
with ' real property ' and other tangible objects, discovered
a special affinity with a philosophy which renders abstract
ideas easier to handle by hardening them into ' bodies '
or quasi-material substances. Just as the Stoics had
affirmed the *Logos spermatikos*, or ' seminal reason,' per-
meating organic nature, to be, or to be immanent in, a
material or quasi-material thing, a ' creative flame '[1] or
' fiery breath,'[2] that is, an exceedingly fine, rarefied, and
imponderable gas, so Tertullian applies this conception
to that which for him appears to take the place of
the *Logos spermatikos*, namely, the ' breath ' (*flatus*) of
God, and develops it with narrow logic to a fantastic
conclusion.

In the beginning, we are told, God moulded man's body
out of clay, and breathed the breath of life itself, materialis-
tically conceived, into his nostrils. The miraculous vapour
poured into every nook and cranny of Adam's body, filling it
completely, and then congealing, as it were, into an ethereal
substance occupying the same space as the fleshly body and
fitting its lineaments and shape exactly, so as to bear its
precise impress.[3] This substance is the soul, an astral body
somehow included within the skin of, and possessing the
same volume as, the body of flesh and blood : it possesses
a complete set of astral or ghostly limbs, whereby it really
performs in the dream-world, during sleep, deeds lawful and
unlawful, for which it will be held to strict account by God.[4]
Hence it is that in Hades Dives, though disembodied, has

---

[1] πῦρ τεχνικόν.

[2] πνεῦμα πυροειδές : for the use of these terms by the Stoics, see
the references given in A. Aall, *Geschichte der Logosidee in der griech.
Philosophie* (1896), p. 118, n. 4.

[3] *de an.* 9 : ' recogita enim, cum deus flasset in faciem hominis flatum
vitae, et factus esset homo in animam vivam, totum utique per faciem
statim flatum illum in interiora transmissum et per universa corporis
spatia diffusum, simulque divina a spiratione densatum omni intus linea
expressum esse, quam densatus impleverat, et velut in forma gelasse.'

[4] *ibid.* 45. The opinion that the soul is morally responsible for dream-
actions is rejected by St. Augustine, *de Gen. ad litt.* xii. 15, and St. Thomas
Aq., *Summa theol.* i. q. xciv. a. 4, ii. iiae. q. cliv. a. 5.

still a tongue, Lazarus a finger, and Abraham a bosom [1] ;
and it is by their ghostly features—the exact counterparts
of those that they wore in life—that the souls of the martyrs
are recognised beneath the heavenly altar by the Seer of
Patmos.[2] The soul even has a colour ; a Montanist sister
saw, during one of Tertullian's sermons, a vision of a soul,
which was ' tenera et lucida et aerii coloris '—' tender and
shining and of the colour of air ' [3] (apparently resembling
a great soap-bubble in human form)—a description which
reminds us of the wraiths and ' materialisations ' of modern
spiritism. Nevertheless, though soul and body are two
substances distinct in thought, in fact they interpenetrate
and suffuse each other so subtly and intimately that man
is a single unity,[4] resoluble into its constituent elements
only by death.

It is on the basis of this materialistic theory of the soul
that Tertullian builds his explanation of the *rationale* of
procreation.   This, according to him, is essentially a process
of fission, as well in regard to the psychological as to the
physiological domain ; the paternal germ is not merely a
portion of the progenitor's body, but is (or is charged with)
a definite quantity of his soul-stuff, which through the act
of generation is diminished by so much.[5]   When conception
takes place, this detached fragment of the father's soul
shapes itself into a new soul, bearing all the hereditary
characters inherent in the parental stock.   It seems that
the functions of the mother are regarded as being purely
passive and receptive ; and, though Tertullian himself does
not develop this consequence, the supposed biological law
(now finally exploded by the discoveries of Mendel), that
heredity only operates through the father,[6] will later be
used by incautious apologists to show that a miraculous

---

[1] *de an.* 7, 9.   The same curious idea appears in Irenaeus, *adv. haer.*
ii. 55 ; see Grabe's note, quoted by Harvey.

[2] *ibid.* 8, 9.   [3] *ibid.* 9.

[4] *ibid.* 9 : ' a primordio enim in Adam concreta et configurata corpori
anima, ut totius substantiae, ita et condicionis istius semen effecit ' ; *cf.*
also 36.

[5] *ibid.* 27.

[6] This ancient belief has been given a poetical expression by Aeschylus
in *Eumen.* 658-661, where Apollo explains to the Areopagus that the connexion of son and father is very much more intimate and organic than that

conception was necessary in the case of Christ, in order to ensure the sinlessness of His human nature.   Every human being is, therefore, a ' chip of the old block ' in an almost literal sense, with many, if not all, of his mental and moral qualities hereditarily pre-determined,[1] though a place is still left for free-will, which is here as elsewhere strongly asserted.[2]

The first instance of this alleged reproduction by way of fission is to be found in the creation of Eve, who was made not merely out of a rib of Adam but also out of a portion of his soul-stuff.[3]   Though devoid of sexual accompaniments and carried out in a purely supernatural manner, this event was the type of all subsequent acts of generation, which represent so many subdivisions of the initial *quantum* of soul-stuff or condensed divine breath originally concentrated in Adam alone.   Each individual soul now existing is, metaphorically speaking, a *surculus* or twig, cut from the *matrix* or parent-stem of Adam, and then planted out to

---

of son and mother, in order to support his contention that Orestes was justified in slaying his mother in order to avenge his father :

> οὐκ ἔστι μήτηρ ἡ κεκλημένου τέκνου
> τοκεύς, τροφὸς δὲ κύματος νεοσπόρου·
> τίκτει δ' ὁ θρῴσκων, ἡ δ' ἄπερ ξένῳ ξένη
> ἔσωσεν ἔρνος, οἷσι μὴ βλάψῃ θεός.

It is found in the ' Hippocratic ' treatise περὶ γονῆς, which Dr. Singer dates *c.* 380 B.C. (E. Littré, *Hippocrates*, tom. vii.), in Aristotle, *de gen. animal.* i. 21 (729 a 21), though here it appears as the theory that the male parent contributes the *form* or active principle and the female the *matter*, and in Galen (*d.* A.D. 199) *de facult. natural.* i. 4, *de sanit. tuend.* i. 2 ; Tertullian may have been influenced by the last-named.   It was, however, rejected by the Epicureans ; *cf.* Lucretius, *de rerum nat.* iv. 1229–31

> semper enim partus duplici de semine constat,
> atque utri similest magis id quodcumque creatur
> eius habet plus parte aequa.

[1] *de an* 20 : ' et hic itaque concludimus omnia naturalia animae ut substantiva eius ipsi inesse et cum ipsa procedere atque proficere, ex quo ipsa censetur.   Sicut et Seneca saepe noster : '' insita sunt nobis omnium artium et aetatum semina, magisterque ex occulto deus producit ingenia,'' ex seminibus scilicet insitis et occultis per infantiam, quae sunt et intellectus. ex his enim producuntur ingenia.'

[2] *ibid.* 21, 22 ; *cf. adv. Marcion.* ii. 5, 6.

[3] *ibid.* 36 : ' ceterum et ipsam (sc. Evam) dei afflatus animasset, si non ut carnis, ita et animae ex Adam tradux fuisset in femina.'   Here ' tradux ' must mean a ' slip ' or ' off-shoot ' ; see below, p. 240, n. 2, for a note on this word.

grow by itself into a separate tree.[1] Tertullian's biology here seems to approximate to the theory associated with the name of Weissmann, which exhibits the whole life-process of a species as a progressive sub-division of an original immortal germ-plasm, and heredity as the unfolding of characteristics which have not been acquired, but were always implicit in the primitive plasm. It is clear that this whole line of thought leads directly into the theory of 'seminal identity,' already hinted at by Irenaeus and Origen, according to which Adam was the sum of his own posterity,[2] and conversely, the human race as it now exists is an atomised or comminuted Adam : a position from which the step to an interpretation of the conventional Fall-tradition (as it may by this time be called) in terms of ' Original Guilt ' would appear easy and tempting, at any rate to a thinker of ' twice-born ' temperament. If all human souls are detached portions of the original soul (of Adam) which fell, they must bear with them, not merely the psychological effects of, but the moral responsibility for, the primordial Fall ; they sinned ' in Adam,' and his trans-gression is their transgression, for they were he. So at least reason theologians, whose hypertrophied emotions have hurried them into a fanatically pessimistic estimate of human nature and human instincts. ' Traducianism,' ' seminal identity ' and ' original guilt ' constitute an apparently necessary sequence of ideas which is an effective ' rationali-sation ' of, or conceptual disguise for, the keen feelings of shame and remorse with which the ' twice-born ' Christian contemplates the life which he lived before his conversion.[3]

[1] *ibid.* 19 : ' <homo> cuius anima velut surculus quidam ex matrice Adam in propaginem deducta et genitalibus feminae foveis commendata cum omni sua paratura pullulavit tam intellectu quam et sensu.'

[2] A curious argument for this theory is found in the language of Gen. i. 26, which almost in the same breath refers to ' man ' both in the singular and in the plural number : ' Let us make *man* in our image . . . and let *them* have dominion over the fish of the sea, etc.' ; *ibid.* 27 : ' igitur ex uno homine tota haec animarum redundantia . . . nam et in ipsa prae-fatione operis unius, " faciamus hominem," universa posteritas pluraliter praedicata est—" et praesint piscibus maris." '

[3] It has been maintained (1) that ' traducianism ' is the necessary basis of any doctrine of ' Original Sin,' the opposite hypothesis, that of ' creationism ' (*i.e.* the view that each soul is, not the product of the father's soul or the parents' souls, but an immediate and *ad hoc* creation of

Did Tertullian himself take this momentous step, that of advancing from the idea of a hereditary bias towards evil derived from Adam's fall (' Original Sin ') to that of a hereditary responsibility *for* Adam's fall, which, as we shall see in succeeding lectures, is the chief *differentia* of the Augustinian version of the Fall-doctrine ? Scholars are divided in opinion on this point, and it is not easy to give a decided reply.   It is certain that he held the idea of ' Original Sin,' though his demonology, which was even richer and more luxuriant than that of his contemporaries, often tends to cross and blur the lines of his exposition of the Fall-theory. So, in the treatise which we have been considering, c. 39 tells us that the source of the evil with which pagans are tainted from their mothers' wombs is the idolatrous cere-monial which surrounds childbirth, and conveys demonic infection to the newly born babe. From this kind of pollution the children of Christians are born free.[1]   Yet even they in due time [2] need regeneration by water and the Spirit ; for

every soul is enumerated as being ' in Adam,' until that moment when it is re-enumerated as being ' in Christ ' ; and it is unclean,

---

God), destroying the moral continuity and solidarity of the race ; *cf.* the Jewish ' creationism ' lying behind the doctrine of the *yēçer ha-ra*', Lecture II, p. 69, n. 2 ; and (2) that ' the traducian theory is the only one which modern biological knowledge supports ' (J. F. Bethune-Baker, *Introduction to the Early History of Christian Doctrine*, 1903, p. 304).   I would suggest that both these contentions, in so far as they assume ' creationism ' and ' traducianism ' to be mutually exclusive alternatives, are antiquated by the fact that our modern realisation of the immanence of God in all natural processes, combined with the recognition of what is called ' emergent evolution,' has in principle abolished the distinction between these two views.   When water is experimentally generated in a laboratory by the combination of hydrogen and oxygen, we do not raise the question whether ' this water ' as such is to be regarded as the direct product of the combined gases, or whether we must suppose that mysterious proper-ties of ' aqueosity ' and ' thisness ' have been catastrophically imposed by God *ab extra* upon them ; no more should we raise the disjunctive question whether the soul is the product of the parents or of God. ' Traducianism ' and ' creationism ' are no more than different ways of looking at the same fact.

[1] This, Tertullian thinks, is the real meaning of 1 Cor. vii. 14 discussed above (p. 220, n. 2).

[2] Tertullian deprecates Paedo-baptism; see below, p. 241.

until it is so re-enumerated. But the soul is a sinner, because it is < in itself > unclean, not because it derives its disgrace from its alliance with the flesh.[1]

A little later we read :

The evil, therefore, which exists in the soul, other than that which is built upon it by the visitation of the wicked spirit, is antecedent < to particular evil actions >, being derived from the fault of our origin (*ex originis vitio*), and is in a certain manner natural. For, as we have said, the corruption of nature is a second nature.[2]

We are here very far away from the *levis contagio* of Origen's more Hellenic mood [3] ; an equally severe judgment is pronounced upon fallen humanity in the treatise *de spectaculis* :

. . . that dread might of the envious angel, the arch-corrupter of the universe, has cast down man, the work and likeness of God, the lord of the whole world, from his ancient integrity, and changed into a state of rebellion against his Creator his whole substance, which had together with him been fashioned for integrity. . . .[4]

Yet neither of these passages contains any clear trace of the idea that we are justly *culpable* for having fallen ' in Adam ' or for being fallen creatures. An incidental reference to the Fall, in the work *de carnis resurrectione*, is more suggestive of this idea :

[1] *de an.* 40 : ' ita omnis anima eo usque in Adam censetur, donec in Christo recenseatur, tamdiu immunda, quamdiu (? non) recenseatur ; peccatrix autem, quia immunda, nec recipiens ignominiam ex carnis societate.' The word ' nec ' at the beginning of the last clause has been added by Wissowa : but it seems necessary in order to save Tertullian from Manicheism : and as only one manuscript containing the text of the *de anima* survives (cod. Agobardinus, *saec.* ix.), such a restoration is not unjustifiable. Parity of reasoning suggests the insertion of ' non ' after ' quamdiu.'

[2] *ibid.* 41 : ' malum igitur animae, praeter quod ex obventu spiritus nequam superstruitur, ex originis vitio antecedit, naturale quodammodo. nam, ut diximus, naturae corruptio alia natura est.'

[3] *v. supra*, p. 230.

[4] *de spect.* 2 : ' cum ipsum hominem, opus et imaginem Dei, totius universitatis possessorem, illa vis interpolatoris et aemulatoris angeli ab initio de integritate deiecerit, universam substantiam eius pariter cum ipso integritati institutam pariter cum ipso in perversitatem demutavit adversus institutorem ' (Wissowa's text ; but the repetition of ' pariter cum ipso ' must surely be a mere dittography).

When the Lord says that He is come to save that which was lost, what are we to understand by ' that which was lost ' ? Undoubtedly man.   Is man ' lost ' as a whole, or only in part ? Surely as a whole, seeing that the transgression, which is the cause of man's ruin, was committed both by an impulse of the soul, that is through concupiscence, and also by an action of the flesh, that is through the tasting < of the forbidden fruit >, has branded the whole man with the judicial record of his transgression, and therefore has deservedly filled him with ruin.[1]

Here the ' elogium ' or ' judicial record ' of the sin of Adam seems to be understood as binding his posterity also ; and with this may be compared a passage of the *de testimonio animae* :

Finally, in every expression of annoyance, scorn, and abhorrence thou dost utter the name of Satan, whom we call the angel of malice, the contriver of all error, the corrupter of the whole age ; by whom man was deceived in the beginning, that he should overstep the commandment of God ; wherefore man was given over to death, and has made his whole race, drawing contamination from his seed, a stock or breed (*traducem*) stained with his own condemnation [2] :

[1] *de carnis resurrect.* 34 : ' in primis cum ad hoc venisse se dicit, uti quod periit salvum faciat, quid dicis perisse ? hominem sine dubio. totumne an ex parte ? utique totum, siquidem transgressio, quae perditionis humanae causa est, tam animae instinctu ex concupiscentia quam et carnis actu ex degustatione commissa totum hominem elogio transgressionis inscripsit atque exinde merito perditionis implevit ' (Kroymann's text, in Vienna *Corpus*, vol. xxxvii.).   *cf.* also *adv. Marcion.* i. 22 : ' homo damnatur in mortem ob unius arbusculae delibationem, et exinde proficiunt delicta cum poenis, et pereunt iam omnes qui paradisi nullam cespitem norunt ' (a sentence which, though it occurs in a context devoted to a criticism of Marcion's theology, nevertheless appears to express Tertullian's own point of view) ;   and *de resurrect. carnis* 49 : ' portavimus enim imaginem choici per collegium transgressionis, per consortium mortis, per exilium paradisi.'

[2] *de test. animae,* 3 (Wissowa) : ' Satanan denique in omni vexatione et aspernatione et detestatione pronuntias, quem nos dicimus malitiae angelum, totius erroris artificem, totius saeculi interpolatorem, per quem homo a primordio circumventus, ut praeceptum dei excederet, et propterea in mortem datus exinde totum de suo semine infectum suae etiam damnationis traducem fecit.'   The word ' tradux,' which plays an important part in Latin speculation on this subject during the early patristic period, does not seem to have been satisfactorily dealt with by English commentators or translators, who take it as meaning, in a vague sense, either ' transmitter ' or ' transmission.' According to Lewis and Short's *Latin Dictionary* (1922), its original meaning is a ' vine-layer ' or ' vine-branch ' trained for propagation, for which they quote Varro, Columella, Pliny

in which the last phrase might easily be interpreted as meaning that every member of the race is born subject to the judicial sentence pronounced against Adam.

Nevertheless, it is a striking fact that Tertullian objects to the custom of Infant Baptism, which, whether ultimately justifiable on other grounds or not, is an obvious practical inference from the doctrine of ' Original Guilt ' ; if infants are born subject to ' God's wrath and damnation,' and if baptism releases from this, it is clearly inhuman to delay the administration of the Sacrament to them for a second longer than is necessary. Tertullian, however, knows nothing of this line of reasoning, and thinks rather of the terrible danger of post-baptismal actual sin which haunts those who receive the rite without long and searching preparation, and mature purpose ; hence he vehemently urges the post-ponement of baptism in the cases of children and of un-married adults. ' Why hurries the age of innocence to the remission of sins ? ' [1] The conclusion must be that, though he may have been drifting in the direction of a conception of ' Original Guilt,' he had not consciously arrived at it. It is probably safe to sum up this Father's position in the statements (1) that he taught no explicit doctrine of ' Original Guilt ' ; (2) that, however, he held a much more severe doctrine of ' Original Sin ' than any which we have hitherto come across, regarding the hereditary consequences of Adam's fall as a positive corruption, not a mere weakness, a *depravatio* rather than a *deprivatio* ; and (3) that he shows at least a strong tendency to view this corruption *juridically* or *forensically*, as though it were a crime, rather than *medically*, as would be natural if it were a mere infirmity.

---

and Tacitus. Du Cange (*Glossarium*, 1887 ed., *s.v.*) gives four meanings as current in later Latin, viz. (1) stirps vel propago, (2) origo (3) peccatum originale (4) propagatio. The first of these meanings seems to me most appropriate in this context. There seems to be no authority for the sense ' transmitter.'

[1] *de bapt.* 18 : ' itaque pro cuiusque personae condicione ac disposi-tione, etiam aetate, cunctatio baptismi utilior est, praecipue tamen circa parvulos . . . ait quidem dominus, "nolite illos prohibere ad me venire." veniant ergo, dum adolescunt ; veniant, dum discunt, dum quo veniant docentur ; fiant Christiani, cum Christum nosse potuerint. quid festinat innocens aetas ad remissionem peccatorum ? '

It will be clear that this severe, ' twice-born ' conception of the inherited bias towards sin, and the tendency to envisage it under specifically legal categories, when combined with the theory of the ' seminal identity ' of Adam's descendants with Adam himself, were bound eventually to generate the formal idea of ' Original Guilt,' even if they did not generate it immediately upon their first juxtaposition.

The central and distinctive elements in Tertullian's Fall-doctrine have now, it may be hoped, been sketched with a degree of detail sufficient for our purpose. It will, however, be appropriate to add a few words regarding his views on some of the more peripheral of the ' five issues ' enumerated at the beginning of this lecture as arising out of the Pauline ideas of the Fall and of ' Original Sin.' There can be little doubt that he took the Genesis-story as a record of plain historic fact. There is no trace in his writings of the allegorical interpretation, which would have been peculiarly uncongenial to his juristic habit of mind, or of the characteristically Greek removal of ' Paradise ' into some extra-mundane sphere ; all his allusions to the subject are marked by the most naïve literalism, and he seems to claim it as a privilege of Christians (and presumably also of Jews) that they alone are in possession of exact information about the origin of man. As regards his conception of man's unfallen condition, it is noteworthy that, although holding a gloomy view of the consequences of Adam's sin, Tertullian betrays no trace of the tendency, afterwards manifested by Augustine and his successors, towards heightening the ' original righteousness ' and ' perfection ' of man to the greatest possible degree of exaltation, in order thereby to increase the depth and criminality of the ' Fall.' His beliefs on this point do not differ substantially from the Greek-Christian theory of Adam's ' infantile condition ' or undeveloped innocence. Before the first sin, he tells us, man was ' innocent, a close friend of God, and the husbandman (*colonus*) of Paradise.' [1] Adam's state is elsewhere described as one of ' integrity,'

---

[1] *de patient.* 5 : the whole of this chapter, which is too long to quote here, is devoted to an exposition of the Fall and its consequences as springing from the fundamental sin of impatience.

which does not seem to imply more than the absence of any positive defect.[1]   It included, however, the gift of immortality ; ' if he had never sinned, he would never have died.' [2]

Tertullian's view of the present condition of human nature, which is the object of Redemption, is more difficult to define with precision.   We have already quoted passages in which he affirms that through the Fall man has perished as a whole, or in respect of the whole of his substance, that is, both in soul and body ; and his ' traducianism ' might be construed as involving the consequence that the seat or *nidus* of inherited evil extends over the whole personality, from its highest spiritual faculties down to its physiological instrument or basis—a position which seems to discard, at any rate in words, the Pauline antithesis between the disposition or $\phi\rho\acute{o}\nu\eta\mu\alpha$ of ' the spirit,' assumed to be good, and that of ' the flesh,' which is *ex hypothesi* bad. Such a view might easily be pressed so as to become, in effect, the doctrine of the ' total depravity ' of fallen human nature, as held by Calvin.   Yet Tertullian himself never draws this conclusion, and indeed expresses opinions clearly inconsistent with it.   Even after the Fall, he tells us, much that is good still survives in human nature ; the natural goodness of the soul is overshadowed, not extinguished, by the corruption of nature, and reappears in its former beauty when the ' curtain of sin ' has been swept away by baptism.[3]   There is some good in the worst of men and some evil in the best.[4]   Moreover, free-will remains even in fallen man, so that real repentance and real change of life are possible under the impulsion of divine grace.[5]

Yet all men alike are subject to ' concupiscentia,' a term which is one of Tertullian's most momentous legacies

---

[1] *de spect.* 2, quoted above, p. 239, n. 4.

[2] *de an.* 52 : ' si non deliquisset, nequaquam obisset.'

[3] and [4] *de an.* 41 : ' propterea nulla anima sine crimine, quia nulla sine boni semine.   proinde, cum ad finem pervenit, reformata per secundam nativitatem ex aqua et superna virtute detracto corruptionis pristinae aulaeo totam lucem suam conspicit.'

[5] *ibid.* 21 : ' . . . genimina viperarum fructum paenitentiae facient, si venena malignitatis expuerint.   haec erit vis divinae gratiae, potentior utique natura, habens in nobis subiacentem sibi liberam arbitrii potestatem, quod $\alpha\mathring{v}\tau\epsilon\xi o\acute{v}\sigma\iota o\nu$ dicitur . . . inesse autem nobis $\tau\grave{o}$ $\alpha\mathring{v}\tau\epsilon\xi o\acute{v}\sigma\iota o\nu$ naturaliter iam et Marcioni ostendimus et Hermogeni.'

to the Latin and Western theology of sin. ' Concupiscentia '
is the standing translation, both in the Old Latin versions
(as it would seem) and in the Vulgate, of ἐπιθυμία, ' desire,' as
used by St. Paul[1] : and, as we have already seen, the Apostle's
conception of ' desire ' seems to be ultimately identical with
the old *yēçer*-conception of the Rabbis. *Yēçer*, ἐπιθυμία,
' concupiscence,' *libido*—these terms, representing a train of
human thought which stretches from Ben Sirach through
St. Paul and St. Augustine down to Freud, really denote the
same fundamental psychological fact, though they contain
varying implications of moral approval or disapproval of the
fact. The Rabbinical theology could not make up its mind
whether the *yēçer* was in itself morally colourless, only
becoming sinful *per accidens,* or whether it was essentially
the *yēçer ha-ra',* the ' *evil* impulse ' : St. Paul was impelled
by his ascetic and ' twice-born ' temperament to choose the
latter view, and in his writings ' desire ' (ἐπιθυμία) almost
invariably[2] bears a bad sense. Yet Tertullian, for all his
African fanaticism, seems here to go behind St. Paul, and to
revive the view of the more liberal Rabbis, that appetite
in itself is ethically neutral. Those for whom the word
' concupiscence ' is bound up with Augustinian and scholastic
associations will probably be surprised to find Tertullian
declaring that concupiscence existed in Christ as perfect
Man[3] ; and he asserts that there is a reasonable and laudable
concupiscence which any Christian may have, ingenuously
citing the Pauline dictum, in the Latin version familiar to him :
' si quis episcopatum concupiscit, bonum opus concupiscit.'[4]

[1] The Old Latin MSS. d e translate our Lord's words in Luke xxii. 15,
ἐπιθυμίᾳ ἐπεθύμησα, as ' concupiscentia concupivi ' ; but Vulg., apparently
disliking the ascription of ' concupiscence ' to Christ, prefers ' desiderio
desideravi.'

[2] The one instance of the use of the word in a good sense appears to be
Phil. i. 23 : τὴν ἐπιθυμίαν ἔχων εἰς τὸ ἀναλῦσαι.

[3] *de an.* 16 : ' ecce enim tota haec trinitas et in Domino, et rationale,
quo docet, quo disserit, quo salutis vias sternit, et indignativum, quo
invehitur in scribas et Pharisaeos, et concupiscentivum, quo '' pascha cum
discipulis suis edere concupiscit '' ' (Luke xxii. 15 ; see n. 1, above). In
de cult. fem. ii. 2, however, ' concupiscentia ' is used specifically of sexual
desire, in a bad sense.

[4] 1 Tim. iii. 1 : εἴ τις ἐπισκοπῆς ὀρέγεται, καλοῦ ἔργου ἐπιθυμεῖ. Vulg.,
disliking the term ' concupiscere ' in this connexion, has ' si quis episcopatum desiderat, bonum opus desiderat.'

After pointing out this liberal element in the thought of one who is popularly reputed to be the most fanatical of theologians (though indeed there are many parts of his writings which are humble, gentle, persuasive, and beautiful) it is disappointing to be compelled to add that Tertullian frequently enunciates that somewhat morbid view of sex to which, as we have shown, the ' twice-born ' temperament is inclined in its most exaggerated form. It is well known that (at least after his lapse into Montanism) he proclaimed sins of impurity to be the worst of all sins, beyond the reach of any absolving power on earth,[1] and that his normal view of the married state ranked it as far inferior to virginity, and as an entanglement to be avoided by good Christians so far as was possible [2]—though, as M. Monceaux drily remarks, ' ce grand ennemi du mariage était marié, naturellement.'[3] It would seem that a legal training provides no absolute guarantee for consistency either in theological theory or in practical life.

It may be noted that Tertullian is the first writer to give us a phrase for the hereditary moral handicap, which, though it cannot be described as ' technical,' yet has a technical suggestion and flavour about it—namely, the phrase *originis vitium*.[4] When we read these words, we seem to see the shadow of the tremendous term *peccatum originale* already falling across the theological world ; and we are no less conscious that we are moving in an atmosphere very different from that of primitive Greek-Christian theology, in which the thought of the consequences of Adam's sin, or of his or ' our ' expulsion from Paradise, is far too vague and indefinite to have demanded a single technical or quasi-technical term for its expression.

---

[1] See especially *de pudicitia*.

[2] In *de exhort. cast.* 9 he permits himself to write ' ergo, inquis, iam et primas, id est, unas nuptias destruis. nec immerito, quoniam et ipsae ex eo constant, quo et stuprum.'

[3] *op. cit.* p. 388.

[4] *de an.* 41 : ' malum igitur animae, praeter quod ex obventu spiritus nequam superstruitur, ex *originis vitio* antecedit, naturale quodam modo.'

History of the 'Hellenic' and 'African' Theories to the End of the Fourth Century

Our historical research has now reached the middle of the third century of the Christian era, a point some two hundred years distant from the dates of 1 Cor. and Rom., which mark the first appearance of the Fall-doctrine in Christian literature. And it is now possible to discern, clearly differentiated from each other, the outlines of the two classical-versions, ' once-born ' or Hellenic and ' twice-born ' or African, of the somewhat indeterminate doctrines propounded or reaffirmed by St. Paul. It will conduce to lucidity if we pause for a moment in order to state and contrast these two presentations of the ideas in question ; and the best method of doing this will be to summarise the answers given by the ' once-born ' and ' twice-born ' theories respectively to the ' five crucial questions ' which were pointed out at the beginning of this lecture as implicit in the Pauline teaching. These questions, it will be remembered, were those (1) of the literal or allegorical interpretation of Gen. iii., (2) of the original state of man before the Fall, (3) of the exact nature of the disastrous consequences flowing from the first man's sin, (4) of the manner in which these consequences are perpetuated, whether by physiological or ' social ' heredity, (5) of the present condition of human nature, whether suffering from a grave *depravatio* or from a comparatively slight *deprivatio*.

The ' Hellenic ' doctrine shows a strong tendency to allegorise the Paradise-story, or, at least, some of its details. It is inclined to construe ' Adam ' etymologically, as merely the universal of ' man,' to remove ' Paradise ' into some extra-cosmic sphere which easily transforms itself into a purely metaphysical world of ideas or of *noumena*, and to interpret the eating of the forbidden fruit as a symbolic parable of sensual, sometimes of sexual, indulgence. At the same time, man's Paradisal condition is not invested with fantastically exalted attributes of intellectual and moral perfection [1] : he is conceived as a childish and imperfect creature, and his inexperience is sometimes taken as extenuating his Fall, which indeed is said to have had beneficial results in so far as it increased his knowledge of himself and of the world. The evil consequences of the Fall are conceived as expulsion from Paradise, subjection to the hardships of this world, and a certain moral weakness, due to loss of the assistance of the Logos or the Spirit, and sometimes described as the loss of the ' likeness ' of God ; the idea of ' Original Guilt ' is, on the whole, conspicuous by its absence. These evil consequences are transmitted partly by ' social heredity,' children being influenced by the examples and instruction of their parents and by the fact of being born outside ' Paradise,' partly, it would seem, by physiological heredity, in so far as the human race is vaguely thought of as organically united with Adam, its head and progenitor. It follows from this mild and minimising conception of the Fall-idea that the hereditary moral handicap of human nature is not depicted in very gloomy colours ; it is much more a *deprivatio*, a negation or absence of strength, than a positive *depravatio*, and even so far as it is conceived as a positive miasma, it does not amount to more than a *levis contagio*.[2] The main source of sin lies in man's free, self-determining will, and the main hindrance to a life of virtue consists in the invisible assaults of the demons, who, much more than any abstract ' Original Sin,' are invoked as the explanation of evil desires, thoughts, and suggestions.

The ' African ' doctrine, on the other hand, starts from a prosaically literal acceptance of the Paradise-story. On the question of man's original state, it does not differ materially from the other version : the ' integrity,' that is, ' wholeness ' or ' completeness,' which Tertullian predicates of Adam's nature, is clearly not incompatible with the ' childishness ' ascribed to the first man by Irenaeus. But, as we have seen, it shows a decided tendency to treat the

---

[1] Except, perhaps, in Origen's theory of pre-natal falls ; but this, as we have pointed out, is rather a substitute for the Adam-theory than a version of it.

[2] Origen's phrase ; see above, p. 230.

inherited bias towards sin as a substantive and very grave disease or corruption, and to superadd to this, as part of the dreary legacy of the Fall, the idea of ' Original Guilt ' or hereditary legal responsibility for the first transgression. These conceptions are closely bound up with the idea of the ' seminal identity ' of the race with its first father as the true explanation of heredity. And they naturally lead to a severe and gloomy view of man's fallen state, which, though not as yet accused of ' total depravity ' in the Calvinistic sense, is nevertheless regarded as involving the contamination of both body and soul with the poison of congenital sinfulness. This scheme of ideas does not, indeed, amount to the full Augustinian position, for the beliefs in man's ' Original Righteousness ' or ' Perfection ' and in the practical destruction of free-will by the Fall are still lacking ; but it will have become clear that the earliest thought of Christian Africa, as represented by Tertullian and by Origen (when writing as a Copt rather than as a Greek), contains the unmistakeable presage of what was to come.

The remainder of this lecture will be devoted to a sketch of the development of these two types of Fall-doctrine during the rest of the pre-Augustinian period, that is, down to the end of the fourth century of our era—or rather to a sketch of the development of the ' African ' theory, and to a record of the unprogressive oscillations of the ' Hellenic ' theory. For, as we shall see, it is only in reference to the vigorous and prosaic West, with its predominantly ethical and practical interests, that we can speak of a ' development ' of the doctrines of human nature and of sin in the sense of an expansion of content and an ever-growing precision of form ; the contemplative and metaphysically minded East tended rather to fix its gaze upon the eternal verities of the Being of God, upon the idea of the unchanging, impassible Logos and the mysteries of His relation to God and of His assumption of flesh, and it devoted little energy to the elucidation of the Fall-doctrine, contenting itself for the most part with repeating the unsystematised statements of the early Greek-Christian writers whom we have already noticed. Nevertheless, we must not expect to find the doctrines generally characteristic of East and West divided by a rigid geographical frontier. In a supra-racial body like the Great Church of Catholic antiquity the currents of living thought are bound to intermingle ; the colours of the theological map, though their main masses are distinct, tend to overlap and run into each other like those of a badly executed aquatint. Hence we shall have occasion to note the presence of ' twice-born,' almost Augustinian, traits in the teaching of some fourth-century Greek Fathers, and of a ' once-born ' element in the thought of one or two Latin writers : though these overlappings will not prove sufficiently extensive to invalidate the application of the adjectives ' Hellenic ' and ' African ' to the ' once-born ' and ' twice-born ' theories respectively. It will be natural in the first place to complete our survey of Greek-Christian thought with regard to the origin of sin down to the close of what may be called the primitive and formative period of Fall-speculation, and then to retrace our steps in order to carry the story of the more vital and clear-cut Western theory down to the same point ; concluding this lecture with an attempt to indicate the bearing of the results so far attained upon the fundamental question ' What statements regarding the origin and ground of sin may reasonably claim to have been held in the Christian Church *ubique, semper, et ab omnibus* ? '

(a) THE ' HELLENIC ' THEORY DOWN TO THE END OF THE PRE-AUGUSTINIAN PERIOD

(1) *Methodius of Olympus.* The history of Eastern thought with regard to the questions of the primal sin and its consequences, as with regard to other and even profounder questions, between the middle of the third and the end of the fourth century, is in great measure the history of alternating reactions against and regressions toward the characteristic positions of Origen. Both of these tendencies manifest themselves in the writings of Methodius, bishop of Olympus in Lycia (or according to some authorities,

of Patara[1]), who is said to have suffered martyrdom *c.* A.D. 311, in the persecution of Maximinus Daza. Despite this author's relative obscurity, a study of his Fall-doctrine forms the necessary introduction to the Greek-Christian anthropology and hamartiology of this period, not only because his life roughly covers the interval between the generation of Origen and that of Athanasius, but also because his relation to later Eastern orthodoxy is not unlike that of Tertullian to the thought of Ambrose and Augustine in Western Christendom ; for, in both cases, the main ideas afterwards set forth by the great classical writers of the fourth and fifth centuries—the golden age of creative theological thought—already appear, in germinal and confused form, amidst the less mature speculations of their third-century predecessor.

The principal tenet of the Origenistic system to which Methodius objects most strongly is its conception of the relations of soul and body : this is attacked in an intolerably diffuse dialogue, laboriously imitating the Platonic model, though without any tincture of the Attic master's wit and charm—the dialogue *de resurrectione*. In the course of this work he takes occasion to denounce the allegorical interpretation of Gen. iii., the idea of a supra-mundane Paradise, the hypothesis of a number of pre-natal falls, and the contention that evil in the human soul is due to its immersion in the world of matter [2]—that is, the whole ' Transcendental Fall-theory ' which we have seen to be characteristic of Origen's Alexandrine period. He asserts emphatically that Paradise is a definite area of this world's surface, ingeniously pointing out that if it had been located above the firmament

---

[1] See Bardenhewer, *Patrology*, pp. 175 ff., and the articles ' Methodius ' in *DCB* (Salmon) and *PRE* (Bonwetsch). The standard editions of this Father's works are (*a*) G. N. Bonwetsch, *Methodius von Olympus* (1891), i. *Schriften* ; [this does not appear ever to have been completed, and has now been largely superseded by] (*b*) Methodius (1917), edited by the same scholar, in *Die griech. christl. Schriftsteller der erst. drei Jahrhund*. For the purposes of this section I have used the text as given in the latter work, which is cited as ' Bonwetsch (b).' A brief but excellent summary of his general doctrinal position will be found in F. Loofs, *Leitfaden zum Studium der Dogmengesch.* (1906), pp. 224 ff.

[2] *de resurr.* i. *passim*. For the sources from which the text of this work has been reconstructed, see Bonwetsch (b), *Einleitung*, pp. xxxiv-xxxvii.

the four sacred rivers, which according to Gen. ii. 10 ff. take their rise in it, must necessarily have poured down from the skies in a single mighty cataract, which would have washed the earth away altogether.[1] The earlier Greek exegesis [2] of 2 Cor. xii. 2–4 ('I know a man in Christ . . . such a one caught up even to the third heaven. And I know such a man . . . how that he was caught up into Paradise,' etc.) is repudiated, and the passage is explained as referring to *two* separate raptures, which translated the Apostle in spirit to two distinct places, the 'third heaven' above this sublunary world, and 'Paradise' within it.[3] And he devotes interminable pages to confuting Origen's allegorical interpretation of the 'coats of skins,' wherewith God clothed Adam and Eve after the Fall, as fleshly bodies— an interpretation which for some reason he seems to find peculiarly exasperating.[4] So far as the first of the 'five cardinal issues' implicit in the Fall-doctrine is concerned, Methodius, though an Eastern of Easterns, stands for the characteristically 'African' view, and affords a good example of that theological overlapping of East and West which the reader has already been warned to expect.

With regard, however, to three of the other issues (the primal condition of man, the *rationale* of the process whereby the consequences of the first sin are transmitted, the resultant state of human nature) the opinions of Methodius are specifically 'Hellenic' and in line with the teaching of the early Apologists and of Irenaeus. He tells us that Adam was overcome by evil whilst still imperfect, and expresses this idea by the fanciful assertion that, whilst the protoplast was still a clay image, moist and soft from the Creator's hands, the streams of sin overflowed and dissolved

---

[1] *de resurr.* i. 55 [Bonwetsch (b), p. 313] : πρῶτον γὰρ ὁ παράδεισος, ὅθεν καὶ ἐξεβλήθημεν ἐν τῷ πρωτοπλάστῳ, ἐκ ταύτης ἐστὶ τῆς γῆς προδήλως τόπος ἐξαίρετος . . . ⟨ὡς⟩ δῆλον ἀπὸ τοῦ καὶ τὸν Τίγριν καὶ τὸν Εὐφράτην καὶ τοὺς λοιποὺς ποταμοὺς τοὺς ἐκεῖθεν προχεομένους ἐνταῦθα φαίνεσθαι τῶν ῥευμάτων τὰς διεκβολὰς εἰς τὴν καθ᾽ ἡμᾶς ἤπειρον ἐπικλύζοντας. οὐ γὰρ ἀπὸ τῶν οὐρανῶν ἄνωθεν καταράσσονται χεόμενοι· ἐπεὶ οὐδὲ ὑπέστη ἂν ἡ γῆ ὄγκον τοσοῦτον ἀθρόως ἐξ ὕψους καταφερόμενον ὑποδέξασθαι ὕδατος.

[2] *v. supra*, p. 192, n. 2.

[3] *ibid.* [Bonwetsch (b), p. 313 f.]

[4] These 'coats of skins' seem to have exercised a curious fascination over early Christian writers ; see above, p. 229, n. 1, and below, p. 275, n. 4.

him.[1] It would be rash to extract any minutely detailed
meaning from this highly imaginative metaphor : but it
at least suggests that the conception of unfallen man as
a ' babe ' (νήπιος) which we have seen to be characteristic
of the earliest Greek-Christian thought on this subject still
dominates his mind, and that the belief in the ' Original
Perfection ' and ' Righteousness ' of man is still below the
intellectual horizon of Eastern Christianity.

This conclusion may appear at first sight to be somewhat
discounted by the fact that Methodius revives the ' recapitulation ' theory of Irenaeus in a form so extreme that it
asserts the Logos to have been personally united with the
first Adam as with the second, thus hardening the Pauline
parallelism of Adam and Christ into an all but absolute
identity [2] ; and in one passage at least he affirms that man
was originally immortal, and not merely capable of immortality, physical death being introduced in order that
man might not live for ever in a state of sin.[3] We notice
also what appears to be the first instance, in any Christian
writing which can be regarded as a systematic discussion
of the subject,[4] of the application of the significant term

---

[1] *symposium* iii. 5 [Bonwetsch (b), p. 31] : ἔτι γὰρ πηλουργούμενον τὸν
Ἀδάμ, ὡς ἔστιν εἰπεῖν, καὶ τηκτὸν ὄντα καὶ ὑδαρῆ, καὶ μηδέπω φθάσαντα
δίκην ὀστράκου τῇ ἀφθαρσίᾳ κραταιωθῆναι καὶ ἀποπετρωθῆναι, ὕδωρ ὥσπερ
καταλειβομένη καὶ καταστάζουσα διέλυσεν αὐτὸν ἡ ἁμαρτία.

[2] *symposium* iii. 4 [Bonwetsch (b), p. 30 f.] : φέρε γὰρ ἡμεῖς ἐπισκεψώμεθα,
πῶς ὀρθοδόξως ἀνήγαγε ⟨Παῦλος⟩ τὸν Ἀδὰμ εἰς τὸν Χριστόν, οὐ μόνον αὐτὸν
τύπον ἡγούμενος εἶναι καὶ εἰκόνα, ἀλλὰ καὶ αὐτὸ τοῦτο Χριστὸν καὶ αὐτὸν γεγονέναι
διὰ τὸ τὸν πρὸ αἰώνων εἰς αὐτὸν ἐγκατασκῆψαι λόγον. According to Victorinus
Afer, on Gal. i. 19 (*PL* VIII. 1155 B), this idea was held in an even cruder
form by certain Judaising Christians, ' qui ad dominum nostrum Iesum
Christum adiungunt iudaismi observantiam : quamquam etiam Iesum
Christum fatentur : dicunt enim eum ipsum Adam esse, et esse animam
generalem, et alia huiusmodi blasphema.'

[3] *ibid.* ix. 2 [Bonwetsch (b), p. 116] : ἦν γὰρ ἡμῶν καὶ πρόσθεν ἄπτωτος
ἡ σκηνή· ἀλλὰ διὰ τὴν παράβασιν ἐσαλεύθη καὶ ἐκλίθη, τοῦ θεοῦ τὸ ἁμάρτημα
λύσαντος θανάτῳ, ἵνα μὴ ἀθανάτως ἁμαρτωλὸς ὁ ἄνθρωπος ὢν, ζώσης ἐν αὐτῷ
τῆς ἁμαρτίας, αἰωνίως κατάκριτος γενήθη. For the development of this idea
by Gregory of Nyssa, see below, p. 280.

[4] It is true that the word *casus* is used to describe Adam's transgression
in the Latin version of 4 Esdras (Bensly, vii. 118, ' non est factum solius
tuus casus sed et nostrum,' quoted above, in an English translation,
Lecture II, p. 80) ; and that in Hilgenfeld's conjectural restoration of the
lost Greek text from which the Latin version was made (*Messias Iudaeorum*,
Leipzig, 1869, p. 67) this word is represented by πτῶμα. If this restora-

'Fall' (πτῶμα) to the sin of Adam.[1]   This term is entirely
non-scriptural in this connexion, the word used by St. Paul
being παράβασις, a 'stepping aside' from the path marked
out for man by God; and it was destined later to have
momentous consequences in the way of fostering a belief
in 'original righteousness,' inasmuch as the conception of
a 'Fall' implies an exalted condition previously enjoyed by
the being who 'fell,' an implication from which the Biblical
and early Patristic word παράβασις is entirely free.[2]   It is
fair, however, to observe that the term has not yet assumed
the technical sense of 'the Fall,' but is employed rather in
the general sense of a 'calamity' or 'disaster.'   We may
accurately sum up the ideas of Methodius with regard to
man's original state by saying that he adheres in the main
to the position of Irenaeus, though there are not wanting
in his works faint premonitions of the coming invasion of
Christian thought by the Rabbinical figment of Adam's
supernatural perfection.

---

tion were certain, we should have to conclude that the use of πτῶμα in
this connexion runs back at least into the second century A.D.   (The Greek
version of 4 Esdras must be prior to Clement of Alexandria, as it is quoted
by him, *Strom.* iii. 16 ; see G. H. Box, *The Ezra-Apocalypse,* p. xi.)   But
there is no proof that *casus* is a translation of πτῶμα, 'fall'; it may
equally well have been used to translate a vaguer term like συμφορά,
'disaster.'   Violet and Gressmann (*Die Apok. des Esra und des Baruch,*
Griech. Christl. Schriftst. XXXII. p. 99, note *in loc.*) think that *casus* must
represent πτῶμα, and that πτῶμα must have represented an original
מַפָּלָה ; but, even so, this latter word need mean no more than 'ruin'
in a general sense (see Brown, Driver, and Briggs, *Hebrew and English
Lexicon of the O.T.,* *s.v.* נפל, p. 658).

Note that Wisdom x. 3 has παράπτωμα for Adam's sin ; but this
word cannot be pressed to mean much more than παράβασις.   In the New
Testament πτῶμα invariably means 'corpse'; see Moulton and Geden,
Concordance, s.v.   It is, however, curious that Hippolytus, *de antichristo*
64 (*Griech. Christl. Schriftst.,* ed. H. Achelis, p. 44), after quoting
Matt. xxiv. 28, 'wheresoever the πτῶμα is, there will the eagles be gathered
together,' observes πτῶμα δὲ γεγένηται ἐν παραδείσῳ· ἐκεῖ γὰρ Ἀδὰμ
ἀπατηθεὶς πέπτωκεν : a use of the word which at least points the way
towards its later technical use.

[1] *symposium* iii. 6 [Bonwetsch (b), p. 32] : . . . συνέβη ⟨τὸν ἄνθρωπον⟩
παρεληλυθότα τὴν ἐντολὴν ὀλέθριον πτῶμα καὶ δεινὸν πεσεῖν, εἰς θάνατον
ἀναστοιχειωθέντα.

[2] For observations on the use and significance of the parallel Latin
words, *praevaricatio* (= παράβασις) and *lapsus* (= πτῶμα), see below,
p. 302.

The question of the exact nature of the sinister legacy
of the Fall, which had hardly been faced by Eastern theology
up to this point, receives for the first time, in the treatise
known as the *Banquet of the Ten Virgins*,[1] what is in effect
a philosophical answer, albeit expressed in a somewhat
confused form—an answer which was destined to be further
elaborated by the great Greek Fathers of the fourth century.
This answer describes the evil principle introduced into
human nature by the Fall as φθορά, a word which was
doubtless suggested in the first instance by its use in
Rom. viii. 21 to describe the effects of Adam's transgression
upon sub-human nature. This word is usually translated
' corruption ' ; but in the writings of Methodius and his
successors, saturated as they were with the influence of
Greek philosophy, a better rendering would be ' disintegration '[2] ; for ' corruption ' conveys an inevitable suggestion of a change which is offensive to the senses or
(metaphorically) to the conscience, whereas φθορά used in
philosophical context is an aesthetically colourless term, a
connoting, at least in Aristotle, no more than the modern
term ' katabolism,' that is, the break-down of a highly
organised structure into its components or into simpler
combinations of them.[3] No doubt as used by Plato the
term possesses associations of a severer kind, which may
well have been in the mind of this Father (*Methodius
platonizans*[4]) : for, in Platonic thought, γένεσις and
φθορά, ' coming-to-be ' and ' passing-away,' are characteristic of the world of matter, which is erroneous, manifold, self-contradictory, and evil.[5] But, whether the term

---

[1] *symposium* iii. 7 [Bonwetsch (b), pp. 33 ff].

[2] This rendering is confirmed by the fact that the inbred infirmity of
man's nature is also described as ἀναρμοστία ' disharmony ' (*symp*. ii. 7),
and (by implication) as τὸ ἀναστοιχειωθῆναι—' being resolved into its
component elements,' *ibid*. iii. 6 [Bonwetsch (b), p. 32].

[3] It is true that St. Basil once alludes to δυσωδία as arising from φθορά
(*hom*. Quod Deus non est auctor malorum, 5) ; but the highly metaphorical
context makes it clear that φθορά is not used in its philosophical sense.

[4] Loofs, *Leitfaden*, p. 225. (Professor Loofs has been good enough to
inform me that this phrase was suggested to him by the title of A. Jahn's
work, *S. Methodii opera et S. Methodius platonizans*, Halle, 1865.)

[5] For φθορά in Aristotle, see the treatise περὶ γενέσεως καὶ φθορᾶς,
314ᵃ–338ᵇ (edited by H. H. Joachim, under the title ' On Coming-to-be
and Passing-away,' 1922). It is clear that for Aristotle the term φθορά

is employed with the Platonic or the Aristotelian *nuance*, it does not suggest, as the word ' corruption ' does, a quality or a process which naturally awakens horror or disgust in the mind of the beholder : and it is therefore reasonable to assume that the state of φθορά produced in man by the Fall would have been deemed by Methodius to be regrettable indeed both in itself and in its effects, but not *per se* morally censurable or involving those who suffer from it in personal guilt, any more than hereditary phthisis or colour-blindness can be imputed to those who suffer from them as morally censurable offences. It is, in other words, probable that he would have been very far from agreeing with the Augustinian position that the mere possession of ' concupiscence ' is in itself a sin.[1]

Though Methodius himself does not give any clear explanation as to what he means by the ' disintegration ' to which man has been subjected by the Fall, it has seemed worth while to reconstruct its probable significance at this point : for, as stated above, this author is the herald of the fourth-century Greek Fathers, some of whom employ the conception as the basis of that presentation of Christ's redeeming work which unsympathetic critics have labelled ' ethico-physical ' or ' physical-materialistic '—that, namely, which concentrates the believer's attention on the idea of the union of the ' disintegrated ' soul with the Logos, Who through the sacraments—especially that of the Eucharist—floods it with His own essence, which is true Being, thereby arresting its tendency to relapse into non-being and restoring it to full and concrete existence. Formally, this conception is Platonic rather than Aristotelian, in so far as it assumes that evil is *non-ens* ; but we may surmise that what

---

covers what may be roughly called *clean* kinds of disintegration, such as the melting of ice. And, even in Plato, γένεσις and φθορά are correlative and equally necessary characteristics of the material world, the latter not being *more* essentially evil than the former. In later Greek-Christian usage, the original, purely physical meaning of φθορά and its secondary, ethical meaning became hopelessly confused ; this confusion is specially evident in the ' Aphthartodocetic ' controversy at the beginning of the sixth century (see R. Draguet, *Julien d'Halicarnasse et sa controverse avec Sévère d'Antioch*, Louvain, 1924, pp. 100 ff.).

[1] For this, see below, Lecture V, p. 373, n. 2.

Methodius and his greater successors were really trying to express by the term φθορά is ' weakness of will-power,' the defect which the modern psychologist describes by the bastard neologisms ' aboulia ' and ' psychasthenia.' In any case, however, our author is a convinced adherent of the continuous ' Hellenic ' tradition that the inherited infirmity does not seriously prejudice the essential freedom of the will, which in the treatise de autexusio is said to be possessed by all members of the human race in the same measure as by Adam at his creation [1]—a dictum which, if it had been uttered a century later, might have been described as explicitly Pelagian.

The foregoing exposition of Methodius' Fall-doctrine will, it may be hoped, have placed in the reader's hand the main guiding threads which run through the hamartiological teaching of his great fourth-century successors— Athanasius, and the Cappadocian triad, Basil the Great, his brother Gregory of Nyssa, and their friend Gregory of Nazianzus. Their writings deserve a specially careful examination, inasmuch as in them the primitive ' once-born ' version of the Fall-doctrine attained as much fixity of outline and definiteness of articulation as it was destined to attain before Augustinianism descended on the Western Church like a flood, and Eastern thought had been drawn off into the sterile intricacies of the Monophysite, Monothelite, and Iconoclastic controversies. Though these illustrious doctors were by no means unconscious of the pervasive influences of Manicheism (the third great wave of Oriental dualism which was now beginning to assail the faith of Israel), the focus of their attention was occupied by the great Trinitarian and Christological problem, and they were not able to spare more than a place in the penumbra of their thoughts for the question of the origin of sin. Much of our

---

[1] de autexus. xvi. [Bonwetsch (b), p. 186] : αὐτεξούσιον δὲ τὸν πρῶτον ἄνθρωπον γεγονέναι λέγω, τουτέστιν ἐλεύθερον, ἀφ' οὗ καὶ οἱ διάδοχοι τοῦ γένους τὴν ὁμοίαν ἐλευθερίαν ἐκληρώσαντο. It may be noted that this treatise is penetrated by the master-motive which, as we have seen, lies at the root of all Fall-speculation, viz. the desire to safeguard the infinite goodness and power of God both against monism and against dualism ; but, in this work at least, Methodius seems to forget the Fall-doctrine altogether, and to seek the way of escape between the Scylla of the Indian and the Charybdis of the Persian doctrine in unlimited indeterminism.

reconstruction, therefore, in the following section will have, as before, to be pieced together out of incidental allusions and *obiter dicta* ; we shall not expect to find perfect precision of language or coherence of thought ; and we shall be prepared for the occasional emergence of an idea or an expression which seems more akin to the ' African ' or ' twice-born ' mode of feeling than to the sunny genius of Christian Hellenism. It is doubtless unnecessary to repeat the warning that the ' African ' and the ' Hellenic ' versions of the Fall-doctrine, as systematically set out above, though generally representative of the two main tendencies of hamartiological thought in the pre-Augustinian Church, are yet in the nature of composite photographs, which arrive at the expression of an ideal type by the elimination of individual and irrelevant detail.

(2) *St. Athanasius* (b. A.D. 297, d. 373). Though St. Athanasius does not deal with the question directly, it would seem probable that he held a partially allegorising interpretation of Gen. iii. ; for his writings contain few allusions to the details of the story, and one well-known passage describes the Fall of man as consisting, not so much in the physical manducation of a particular fruit as in the aversion of his mind, through slothfulness, from that beatific contemplation of divine things for which he had been created.[1] This idea is presumably inherited from Origen, but with a difference ; for it does not appear to have been coupled by Athanasius with the idea of pre-natal existence or of a purely metaphysical or ' intelligible ' Paradise. He once, indeed, asserts that ' Paradise ' was ' tropically,' or metaphorically, so called by Moses ; but in the same breath he alludes to it as a ' place '[2] ; and, as Adam is

---

[1] *c. gentes* 3 : οὕτω μὲν οὖν ὁ δημιουργὸς, ὥσπερ εἴρηται, τὸ τῶν ἀνθρώπων γένος κατεσκεύασε, καὶ μένειν ἠθέλησεν· οἱ δὲ ἄνθρωποι κατολιγωρήσαντες τῶν κρειττόνων, καὶ ὀκνήσαντες περὶ τῶν τούτων κατάληψιν, τὰ ἐγγυτέρω μᾶλλον ἑαυτῶν ἐζήτησαν. ἐγγύτερα δὲ τούτοις ἦν τὸ σῶμα καὶ αἱ τούτου αἰσθήσεις· ὅθεν τῶν μὲν νοητῶν ἀπέστησαν ἑαυτῶν τὸν νοῦν, ἑαυτοὺς δὲ κατανοεῖν ἤρξαντο. εἰς ἑαυτῶν ἐπιθυμίαν ἔπεσαν, τὰ ἴδια προτιμήσαντες τῆς πρὸς τὰ θεῖα θεωρίας : see also the preceding chapter. (For the text of St. Athanasius I have used the Benedictine edition, Patavii, 1777.)

[2] *ibid.* 2, ad fin. : . . . συνδιαιτᾶσθαι τοῖς ἁγίοις ἐν τῇ τῶν νοητῶν θεωρίᾳ, ἣν εἶχεν ἐν ἐκείνῳ τῷ τόπῳ, ὃν καὶ ὁ ἅγιος Μωϋσῆς τροπικῶς παράδεισον ὠνόμασεν.

conceived as being endowed with a body,[1] even in his paradisal state, it is natural to conclude that the ' place ' is conceived as located somewhere within this concrete universe, whether above the earth, as Irenaeus thought, or upon it, as Methodius maintained.   It is probably safe to assume that, like the former of the authors just mentioned, he accepted the idea of a first man and woman quite literally, but would have been prepared to rationalise some of the more naïve features of the story.

Unlike Irenaeus, however, he holds that the protoplast was anything but a ' babe,' inasmuch as Adam is credited with intellectual, moral, and spiritual powers of the highest order.   His purity of heart endowed him with the vision of God, a vision so far-reaching that he could contemplate the eternity of God's essence and the cosmic operations of His Word.[2]   His mental sight was turned away from ' bodies,' and directed upwards.   Harnack has collected the expressions ' imagination concerning God,' ' knowledge,' ' perception,' ' comprehension,' ' contemplation' of ' divine things' or of ' the intelligible world,' 'contemplation concerning God,' an ' inward grasp of knowledge as to the Father,' [3] which are used by Athanasius to describe the eagle-like, unwavering intensity of the first man's gaze upon the splendour of God.   Besides all this, he was endued with immortality and safeguarded from disintegration into his native nothingness by his intimate union with the Logos [4]—an idea which we have already encountered in the writings of Methodius, though Athanasius does not follow his predecessor in the strange fancy of making the first Adam apparently as much an incarnation of the Divine Word as the second.   The anthropology of this great Father thus marks a definite breach with the primitive Hellenic tradition which conceived the protoplast as frail, unformed, and innocent or morally neutral, 'capable of both' good and evil,[5] and the definite

---

[1] c. gentes 3, quoted above.   [2] ibid. 2.

[3] φαντασία περὶ θεοῦ, γνῶσις, κατανόησις, κατάληψις, θεωρία τῶν θείων, θεωρία τῶν νοητῶν, θεωρία περὶ τοῦ θεοῦ, ἔννοια τῆς εἰς πατέρα γνώσεως (History of Dogma, E. tr., 1897, iii. p. 273).

[4] de incarn. 4, 5 ; cf. especially 5 : διὰ γὰρ τὸν συνόντα τούτοις Λόγον καὶ ἡ κατὰ φύσιν φθορὰ τούτων οὐκ ἤγγιζε.

[5] v. supra, pp. 175, 176, 193.

beginning of that naturalisation of the ideas of Adam's
' original righteousness' and ' perfection' within the sphere
of Christian thought, both Eastern and Western, which was
the outstanding event in the history of the Fall-doctrine
during the fourth century of our era.

It is in the highest degree noteworthy that Athanasius,
in exalting the primitive state of man, draws in effect that
very distinction between (a) the qualities belonging to the
first man merely in virtue of his human nature as such, and
(b) the resplendent *supernatural* qualities bestowed on him
by a special act of Divine grace, which was destined to play
a great part in the later development of the ' African'
Fall-doctrine, and to be expressed by the mediaeval Schoolmen as the distinction between Adam's *pura naturalia* and
the *donum superadditum* of ' original righteousness.' [1] Man,
like all other members of the created universe, was made
out of nothing : hence human nature can never continue
in one stay, always tending to slip back into nothing.[2] To
counteract this inherent instability of man's being, God
bestowed upon him ' a further gift ' [3] (a phrase which is
roughly equivalent to *donum superadditum*), namely His
own ' image,' which is none other than the indwelling of
the Logos, the ' image of the invisible God,' [4] and a special
' grace ' [5] (another word which calls up Augustinian associations in the mind of the modern reader). It is carefully
explained that this supernatural grace was bestowed on man
from without, catastrophically, and was by no means bound
up with or involved in his physical constitution as man.[6]

---

[1] See Lecture V, p. 363 ; Lecture VI, p. 401.

[2] *de incarn.* 4 : ἔστι μὲν γὰρ κατὰ φύσιν ἄνθρωπος θνητός, ἅτε δὴ ἐξ οὐκ
ὄντων γεγονώς.

[3] *ibid.* 3 : πλέον τι χαριζόμενος αὐτοῖς.

[4] Col. i. 15. The idea that the ' image of God ' in man *is* the indwelling
Logos is clearly expressed in the following passage : περὶ δὲ αὐτοῦ (SC. τοῦ
Χριστοῦ) ⟨εἴρηται⟩ ὅτι μόνος εἰκὼν ἀληθινὴ καὶ φύσει τοῦ πατρός ἐστιν. εἰ γὰρ
καὶ κατ' εἰκόνα γεγόναμεν καὶ εἰκὼν καὶ δόξα θεοῦ ἐχρηματίσαμεν, ἀλλ' οὐ δι'
ἑαυτοὺς πάλιν, ἀλλὰ διὰ τὴν ἐνοικήσασαν ἐν ἡμῖν εἰκόνα καὶ ἀληθῆ δόξαν τοῦ θεοῦ,
ἥτις ἐστιν ὁ Λόγος αὐτοῦ, ὁ δι' ἡμᾶς ὕστερον γενόμενος σάρξ, ταύτην τῆς
κλήσεως ἔχομεν τὴν χάριν (*or.* iii. c. *Arian.* 10 ad fin.).

[5] *de incarn.* 3 : προλαβὼν ἠσφαλίσατο νόμῳ καὶ τόπῳ τὴν δοθεῖσαν αὐτοῖς χάριν.

[6] *or.* ii. c. *Arianos*, 68 : ὁ μέντοι ἄνθρωπος τοιοῦτος ἐγίνετο οἷος ἦν καὶ ὁ
Ἀδὰμ πρὸ τῆς παραβάσεως, ἔξωθεν λαβὼν τὴν χάριν καὶ μὴ συνηρμοσμένην ἔχων
αὐτὴν τῷ σώματι.

According to Harnack,[1] this bodily and sensuous constitution of man is all that Athanasius means by mere human nature ; our higher faculties, intellectual and spiritual, belong to the *donum superadditum*, which is the ' image of God.' Hence the first sin was a Fall, not from a natural to an unnatural state, but rather from a state which was supernatural to one which was merely natural—another conception which we shall meet again in the thought of some Western Schoolmen.[2]

It may thus be said that Athanasius, despite the touches of anticipated Augustinianism which we have noted, regards the direct consequences of the Fall as being in the nature of a *deprivatio* rather than of a *depravatio*. The ' deprivation ' however involves a ' depravation,' in so far as the loss of the ' image of God ' (that is, of the indwelling of the Logos) releases the connatural tendency of man's being to lapse into non-entity, in other words, renders him liable to ' disintegration ' or φθορά.[3] This word, at least in the fourth-century Greek Fathers, includes the ideas of physical mortality and of that obscuration of man's intellectual powers which rendered him an easy prey to idolatry and the worship of daemons [4] ; but its primary meaning seems to be metaphysical. Round the conception of ' disintegration ' coheres the whole scheme of ideas, the emergence of which was predicted in our discussion of Methodius, and which needs no further explanation at this point—the idea of evil as non-being (by which, verbally at least, God is saved from the charge of originating evil, as He cannot have originated the non-existent : this device was subsequently employed in the theodicies of Gregory of Nyssa,[5] Augustine,[6]

---

[1] *op. cit.* iii. p. 272.

[2] See Lecture VI, p. 401 f.

[3] For the ideas expressed in this and the preceding sentences, compare *de incarn.* 4 : ἡ γὰρ παράβασις τῆς ἐντολῆς εἰς τὸ κατὰ φύσιν αὐτοὺς ἐπέστρεφεν, ἵνα ὥσπερ οὐκ ὄντες γεγόνασιν οὕτως καὶ τὴν εἰς τὸ μὴ εἶναι φθορὰν ὑπομείνωσι τῷ χρόνῳ εἰκότως.

[4] It would seem that the idea of a progressive intellectual decadence in man resulting in idolatry was derived by Athanasius and his successors from Rom. i. 18–end. We cannot, however, go at length into the interesting question of the influence exercised by this passage on later thought, as exigencies of space compel us to limit the scope of our survey very strictly to the history of the Adam-theory.

[5] *v. infra*, p. 278.   [6] Lecture V, p. 371.

and Thomas Aquinas [1])—and the idea of redemption as consisting chiefly in the reunion of the perishing soul with the Logos, Who infuses into it the streams of His own strong and stainless being, thereby arresting the process of ' disintegration,' and eventually exalting the soul to what is daringly described as actual ' deification.' [2] This latter conception is summed up in the famous paradox ' He (the Logos) became Man in order that we might be made God ' [3] ; a sentence which points backwards to the words ascribed to St. Peter ' that through these (the promises) ye may become partakers of the Divine nature, having escaped from the " disintegration " which is in the world through sinful appetite ' [4]—and forwards to the glowing lines of Newman :

> And that a higher gift than grace
> Should flesh and blood refine,
> God's presence and His very Self
> And essence all-divine.[5]

In all three cases, though the Eucharist is not expressly mentioned, it is permissible to surmise that the sacramental idea is in the background of the writer's mind.[6]

There does not appear to be any trace of the idea of ' original guilt ' in the thought of Athanasius. His occasional statements that ' we ' sinned, or perished, in contexts bearing on the Fall of man, might seem *prima facie* to imply a belief in some kind of participation by Adam's posterity in the responsibility for his sin ; but it is, I think,

---

[1] Lecture VI, p. 405.

[2] Complete ' deification ' will, apparently, not be accomplished until the resurrection : see the passage *or*. iii. *c. Arian.* 33, quoted below (p. 262, n. 2).

[3] *de incarn.* 54 : αὐτὸς γὰρ ἐνηνθρώπησεν, ἵνα ἡμεῖς θεοποιηθῶμεν. Compare *or.* ii. *c. Arian.* 70 : οὐκ ἂν δὲ πάλιν ἐθεοποιήθη κτίσματι συναφθεὶς ὁ ἄνθρωπος, εἰ μὴ θεὸς ἦν ἀληθινὸς ὁ υἱός ; *or.* iii. *c. Arian.* 25 : ὥσπερ υἱοὶ καὶ θεοὶ διὰ τὸν ἐν ἡμῖν Λόγον : and many other passages. See A. Robertson, *St. Athanasius On the Incarnation* (E. tr.), p. 93, n. 2.

[4] 2 Peter i. 4.

[5] *Dream of Gerontius.*

[6] The Eucharistic setting in which the idea of ' deification ' was held by the mind of Athanasius is clearly shown in the following sentence : οὐκ ἀνθρώπου τέ τινος μετέχοντες σώματος ἀλλὰ αὐτοῦ τοῦ Λόγου σῶμα λαμβάνοντες θεοποιούμεθα (*ad Maximum philosophum epistola*, 2 ad fin.). *Cf.* St. Ignatius' conception of the Eucharist as the φάρμακον ἀθανασίας, *Eph.* 20.

more natural to interpret such expressions merely as desultory symptoms of the subconscious influence of the ' Recapitulation '-theory in its vaguest and least rigorous form. No explicit statement is made as to the manner in which the consequences of the Fall are transmitted from generation to generation : but the emphatically realistic idea of ' disintegration ' which Athanasius holds in common with Methodius must surely presuppose physiological, and not merely ' social,' heredity as the means of its propagation.

The opinions of Athanasius with regard to the last of the ' five cardinal issues,' the present condition of ' fallen ' man, though severe, are yet, on the whole, of the ' Hellenic ' and ' once-born ' type. We are told that the *débâcle* of human nature, that is, its collapse into nothingness, which was brought about by the Fall and the withdrawal of the sustaining power of the Logos, was a gradual and long-drawn-out process, which is not even yet complete ; for it is implied that man still retains the ' image of God ' (that is, the indwelling of the Logos) in so far as he still possesses faculties of knowing and reasoning, and free-will.[1] It is even asserted that sinlessness is both theoretically and actually possible, some of the saints, such as Jeremiah and John the Baptist, having been pure from every kind of sin.[2]

---

[1] Cf. *de incarn.* 12, in which it is contended that even before the Incarnation men might have improved their state by receiving instruction from the law, the prophets, and other holy men. The vivid simile at the beginning of c. 14, in the same treatise, of the picture overlaid by dirt, implies that the ' image of God ' still existed in human nature, only overlaid by sin to such a degree that it had been ' made invisible ' (παραφανισθεῖσα).

[2] The passage in which this statement occurs is worth quoting at length, as it contains Athanasius' leading ideas relative to the Fall, Sin, and Redemption assembled together.

εἰ γὰρ τὰ τῆς θεότητος τοῦ Λόγου ἔργα μὴ διὰ τοῦ σώματος ἐγίνετο, οὐκ ἂν ἐθεοποιήθη ὁ ἄνθρωπος. καὶ πάλιν, εἰ τὰ ἴδια τῆς σαρκὸς οὐκ ἐλέγετο τοῦ Λόγου, οὐκ ἂν ἠλευθερώθη παντελῶς ἀπὸ τούτων ὁ ἄνθρωπος· ἀλλ' εἰ ἄρα πρὸς ὀλίγον μὲν ἀνεπαύετο, ὡς προεῖπον, πάλιν δὲ ἔμενεν ἡ ἁμαρτία ἐν αὐτῷ καὶ ἡ φθορά, ὥσπερ ἐπὶ τῶν ἔμπροσθεν ἀνθρώπων γέγονε, καὶ τοῦτο δείκνυται. πολλοὶ γοῦν ἅγιοι γεγόνασι καὶ καθαροὶ πάσης ἁμαρτίας· Ἰερεμίας δὲ καὶ ἐκ κοιλίας ἡγιάσθη· καὶ Ἰωάννης ἔτι κυοφορούμενος ἐσκίρτησεν ἐν ἀγαλλιάσει ἐπὶ τῇ φωνῇ τῆς θεοτόκου Μαρίας· καὶ ὅμως ' ἐβασίλευσεν ὁ θάνατος ἀπὸ Ἀδὰμ μέχρι Μωσέως, καὶ ἐπὶ τοὺς μὴ ἁμαρτήσαντας ἐπὶ τῷ ὁμοιώματι τῆς παραβάσεως Ἀδάμ.' καὶ οὕτως ἔμενον οὐδὲν ἧττον οἱ ἄνθρωποι θνητοὶ καὶ φθαρτοὶ, δεκτικοὶ τῶν ἰδίων τῆς φύσεως παθῶν. νῦν δὲ τοῦ Λόγου γενομένου ἀνθρώπου, καὶ ἰδιοποιουμένου τὰ τῆς σαρκὸς, οὐκέτι ταῦτα τοῦ σώματος ἅπτεται, διὰ τὸν ἐν αὐτῷ γενόμενον Λόγον· ἀλλ' ὑπ' αὐτοῦ μὲν ἀνήλωται, λοιπὸν δὲ οἱ ἄνθρωποι

It is natural to append to our account of Athanasius' Fall-doctrine some words with regard to his younger contemporary, (3) *Cyril of Jerusalem* (A.D. 315–386). This Father's writings contain exceedingly few allusions to the ideas of a primitive catastrophe and of an inherited taint. He tells us, in one place, that Adam's sin was the cause of physical death [1] ; he is prepared to use the idiom which makes the first person plural the subject of verbs referring to the Fall,[2] and he admits that our nature is ' wounded,' [3] that is, affected by a hereditary bias towards sin. But he is no less emphatic in asserting that we are personally sinless at birth,[4] and that man possesses the fullest possible freedom of choice, which is not really hampered by the suggestions of the devil or the storms of appetite [5] ; and his references to the ' remission of sins ' imparted in baptism make it clear that he is thinking only of actual personal sins and of adult baptism, and that the idea of ' original guilt ' is completely absent from his mind.[6] As in the case of so many other Greek-Christian writers, it is evident both that the Fall-tradition is for him too much of an authoritative reality

---

οὐκέτι κατὰ τὰ ἴδια πάθη μένουσιν ἁμαρτωλοὶ καὶ νεκροί, ἀλλὰ κατὰ τὴν τοῦ Λόγου δύναμιν ἀναστάντες, ἀθάνατοι καὶ ἄφθαρτοι ἀεὶ διαμένουσιν (*or.* iii. *c. Arian.* 33). Together with this should be considered a passage in *or.* ii. *c. Arian.* 61, which is of interest (*a*) because it affirms the universality of the destruction involved by Adam's sin, thus appearing to contradict the statement just cited as to the sinlessness of many of the saints, (*b*) because it contains an emphatic assertion of the idea of redemption by way of quasi-physical (*i.e.*, presumably, sacramental) incorporation with the human nature of the incarnate Logos : ἐπειδὴ πάντων τῶν ἀνθρώπων ἀπολλυμένων κατὰ τὴν παράβασιν τοῦ ᾿Αδάμ, πρώτη τῶν ἄλλων ἐσώθη καὶ ἠλευθερώθη ἡ ἐκείνου σάρξ, ὡς αὐτοῦ τοῦ Λόγου σῶμα γενομένη, καὶ λοιπὸν ἡμεῖς ὡς σύσσωμοι τυγχάνοντες κατ᾿ ἐκεῖνο σωζόμεθα.

[1] *cat.* xiii. 2.

[2] *ibid.* ii. 5 : ἀπολώλαμεν ἀπατηθέντες . . . πεπτώκαμεν . . . ἐτυφλώθημεν κ. τ. λ.

[3] *ibid.* xii. 7 : μέγιστον ἦν τὸ τραῦμα τῆς ἀνθρωπότητος, ἀπὸ ποδῶν ἕως κεφαλῆς οὐκ ἦν ἐν αὐτῷ ὁλοκληρία.

[4] *ibid.* iv. 19 : πρὶν παραγένηται εἰς τόνδε τὸν κόσμον ἡ ψυχή, οὐδὲν ἥμαρτεν (probably a repudiation of Origen's view)· ἀλλ᾿ ἐλθόντες ἀναμάρτητοι, νῦν ἐκ προαιρέσεως ἁμαρτάνομεν.

[5] *ibid.* iv. 21 : αὐτεξούσιός ἐστιν ἡ ψυχή· καὶ ὁ διάβολος τὸ μὲν ὑποβάλλειν δύναται, τὸ δὲ καὶ ἀναγκάσαι παρὰ προαίρεσιν οὐκ ἔχει τὴν ἐξουσίαν. ὑπογράφει σοι πορνείας λογισμόν· ἐὰν θέλῃς, ἐδέξω· ἐὰν μὴ θέλῃς, οὐκ ἐδέξω.

[6] *e.g. ibid.* iii. 12, 15, xvii. 37.

to be completely discarded, and also that it has never been assimilated into the texture of his thought, which remains strongly indeterministic throughout.

(4) *St. Basil of Caesarea* (b. A.D. 330, d. 379). The writings of the greatest of the Cappadocian Fathers contain some clear and unmistakable affirmations of, or allusions to, the Adamic Fall-doctrine in its most general sense,[1] side by side with assertions of human free-will so vehement and unqualified as to seem logically incompatible with that doctrine. His position with regard to the question of the origins and ground of sin is thus typically ' Hellenic,' both in its inconsistency and in its libertarianism ; and, but for the testimony which it bears to the rapid growth of the idea of ' original perfection,' might have been described as entirely free from any traits of the kind which we have designated as ' African ' or ' twice-born.' The most extended discussion of the subject which St. Basil has

---

[1] The following are the passages alluded to (all quotations are taken from the Benedictine text, *S.P.N. Basilii Caesar. Capp. archiep. opera omnia*, ed. D. Julianus Garnier, Parisiis, 1722—hereinafter cited as ' Garnier ' or ' G ') : (a) *hom. in ps.* xxix. 5 (G. i. 129 A) : καλὸς μὲν γὰρ ἤμην κατὰ τὴν φύσιν· (notice that Basil does not, apparently, accept Athanasius' distinction between human nature as such and the *donum superadditum*) ἀσθενὴς δὲ διὰ τὸ ἐξ ἐπιβουλῆς τοῦ ὄφεως νεκρωθῆναι τῷ παραπτώματι ;

(b) *hom. in ps.* cxiv. 3 (G. i. 202 A) : ἡμεῖς ἡμέν ποτε ἔνδοξοι ἐπὶ τῆς τοῦ παραδείσου διαγωγῆς, ἐγενόμεθα δὲ ἄδοξοι καὶ ταπεινοὶ διὰ τὴν ἔκπτωσιν :

(c) *hom. in fam. et sicc.* 7 (G. ii. 70 D) : ὡς γὰρ 'Αδὰμ κακῶς φαγὼν τὴν ἁμαρτίαν παρέπεμψεν (presumably by physical heredity) ;

(d) *hom. de humilit.* (G. ii. 156 D, E)—a strong assertion of man's original glory and perfection, from which he was cast down by the devil by the hope of a feigned glory ;

(e) *hom. de renunt. saec.* 6, 7 (G. ii. 207 D, 208 C)—these passages, however, are allusions to the story of Gen. iii. rather than affirmations of the Fall-doctrine ;

(f) *de spir. sancto*, 15 (G. iii. 28 C) : ἡ τοῦ θεοῦ καὶ σωτῆρος ἡμῶν περὶ τὸν ἄνθρωπον οἰκονομία ἀνάκλησίς ἐστιν ἀπὸ τῆς ἐκπτώσεως.

(g) *ep.* 261 (ad Sozopolitanos) (G. iii. 402 A, B)—a general but quite definite assertion of the doctrine of the Fall in order to vindicate the reality of the Incarnation against those who attributed a ' celestial body ' to our Lord. There is an interesting touch of ' anticipated Augustinianism ' in the use of the word φύραμα, ' lump,' to describe mankind considered as included in Adam (v. *infra*, p. 310, n. 2, p. 328, n. 2) : τίς δὲ χρεία τῆς ἁγίας παρθένου, εἰ μὴ ἐκ τοῦ φυράματος τοῦ 'Αδὰμ ἔμελλεν ἡ θεοφόρος σὰρξ προσλαμβάνεσθαι ;

bequeathed to posterity—though, as we shall see, even
this does not amount to very much—is to be found in the
Homily *quod Deus non est auctor malorum*,[1] a title which
bears witness to the fact, often emphasised in these Lectures,
that the Fall-doctrine is fundamentally an exercise in
theodicy-making. A brief summary of this discussion will
sufficiently indicate the general tenor of his thought upon
a matter to which he has evidently devoted but little
sustained attention.

After some introductory remarks upon the evils which
God permits to afflict mankind, and the difficulties which
these raise against the belief in the divine governance of the
world and of human history, the preacher begins his treatment of the subject by distinguishing sharply, much as a
modern philosopher might, between physical evil (that is, in
the last resort, pain) and moral evil or sin. We are not here
concerned, nor does space permit us, to examine his vindication of the justice of God in regard to the terrible chastise-
ments, such as storms, floods and earthquakes, with which
from time to time He visits offending communities or sections
of the human race. These things, according to St. Basil,
are relatively evil ; sin alone is absolutely evil ; and the
root of sin is emphatically asserted to be free-will,[2] ' seeing
that it is in our power either to abstain from evil or to be
wicked.' [3] If this unqualified autonomy can really be
attributed to the human will, one half and that the most
important half of a complete theodicy has already been
constructed, and nothing more remains to be said on the
moral side of the problem of evil.[4] But Basil appears to be
uneasily conscious that the facts of human nature are not
quite so simple as unlimited indeterminism supposes them
to be ; at any rate, he adds two arguments which, on the
extreme libertarian hypothesis, are logically superfluous,

[1] Garnier, ii. 72–83.

[2] *op. cit.* 3 (Garnier, ii. p. 74 A) : ἀρχὴ γὰρ καὶ ῥίζα τῆς ἁμαρτίας τὸ
ἐφ᾽ ἡμῖν καὶ τὸ αὐτεξούσιον.

[3] *ibid.* 5 (p. 76 E).

[4] Later on in this Homily (7, Garnier, p. 79 D, E) Basil gives the
correct reply to those who impugn the righteousness of God on the ground
that He might have made us moral automata and did not—the reply,
namely, that the possibility of moral action involves freedom of choice
and therefore freedom to go wrong.

namely, (1) the contention already adduced by Athanasius, that evil is a *privatio*, supervening upon ' mutilations of the soul,' [1] and therefore a negation or non-entity—and that the Creator cannot be supposed to have created that which does not exist ; (2) that a good Creator cannot in any case be the author of anything save that which is good, a contention which is confirmed by the Scriptural record. ' And God saw all that He had made, and, behold, it was very good.' [2]   Nevertheless, he is forced to admit that evil does exist empirically, even though it may be ' non-existent ' metaphysically [3] ; and he poses once more the question—already answered, if extreme indeterminism be allowed—'If God is not the first cause of evil, who or what is ? '

The reply is again ' Human free-will,' but this time with a difference. For the freedom which is now in question seems to be, not the freedom which we possess or think ourselves to possess at the present moment, but rather the complete capacity for self-determination with which the soul in its unfallen condition was once endowed.[4]   There follows an exceedingly vague and elusive statement of what appears to be in essence Origen's first or ' Alexandrine ' Fall-theory, that which postulates a great number of pre-natal falls.   We are told that ' the soul '—by which is apparently meant each individual soul—was created for the contemplation of God and of eternal beauty ; that it allowed itself to be overcome by satiety [5] and a kind of drowsiness,

---

[1] *op. cit.* 5 (p. 78 A) : στέρησις γὰρ ἀγαθοῦ ἐστὶ τὸ κακόν: *ibid.* (p. 78 B) : οὕτω καὶ τὸ κακὸν οὐκ ἐν ἰδίᾳ ὑπάρξει ἐστίν, ἀλλὰ τοῖς τῆς ψυχῆς πηρώμασιν ἐπιγίνεται.

As was suggested above, in our discussion of Methodius (p. 255), the idea of the anhypostatic character of evil naturally leads to an interpretation of ' inherited sinfulness ' as weakness, or a defect of will-power, issuing in failure to control the natural impulses in accordance with the dictates of reason, rather than as a positive propension towards wrong-doing as such ; and this conception of ' weakness ' as the result of the Fall is actually expressed by St. Basil in quotation (*a*), *supra*, p. 264, n. 1.

[2] Gen. i. 31.

[3] *op. cit.* 5 (p. 78 C) : ἀλλὰ μήν ἐστι τὸ κακὸν, καὶ ἡ ἐνέργεια δείκνυσι πολὺ κατὰ τοῦ βίου παντὸς κεχυμένον.   πόθεν οὖν αὐτῷ τὸ εἶναι, εἰ μήτε ἄναρχόν ἐστι, φησὶ, μήτε πεποίηται ;

[4] *op. cit.* 6 (p. 78 E).

[5] κόρος (*ibid.* 6, p. 79 A) : the word is used by Origen (*v. supra*, p. 213).

so conceiving the desire of carnal pleasures, which caused it
to slide down from the heavenly sphere and to be mingled
with flesh.[1]

Hardly, however, has St. Basil formulated this position
before he seems to be attacked by misgivings with regard to
the wisdom or justifiability of identifying himself so explicitly
with the teaching of one so suspect by many members of
the Church, albeit so beloved by himself,[2] as Origen : and
he consequently decides to redress the balance of his
discourse by subjoining a statement of what had by this
time almost become the ' orthodox ' theory, in the following
words :

There was a time when Adam lived on high, not locally, but
in respect of the direction of his will [this is evidently meant to
repudiate both a supra-mundane, but yet concrete, Paradise,
and also the idea of human pre-existence on the plane of the
intelligible world] when, only just endowed with life, he raised
his eyes to heaven ; and, rejoicing exceedingly in those things
which he saw, he was filled to overflowing with love for his
Benefactor, who had freely given him the enjoyment of eternal
life, had made him to repose amidst the delights of Paradise,
had granted him a princedom like unto that of the angels and
a share in the food of archangels, and had made him a listener
to the Divine Voice. And besides all this, he was shielded by
God<from evil> and enjoyed all His good things. Nevertheless, being soon sated with all these things, and being as it
were impelled to insolence by his satiety, he preferred that
which appeared pleasant to the eyes of flesh above the intelligible
beauty, and counted the satisfying of his belly more precious
than the spiritual joys. So then, being forthwith outside Paradise, and outside that blessed manner of life, he became evil,
not through necessity, but as the result of folly.[3]

---

[1] For Origen's own statement of this theory, v. supra, pp. 212 ff.

[2] It will be remembered that we owe the *Philocalia* to the collaboration
of Basil and Gregory of Nazianzus.

[3] *op. cit.* 7 (Garnier, p. 79 B, C) : ἦν ποτὲ ὁ Ἀδὰμ ἄνω, οὐ τόπῳ ἀλλὰ
τῇ προαιρέσει, ὅτε ἄρτι ψυχωθεὶς καὶ ἀναβλέψας πρὸς οὐρανὸν, περιχαρὴς τοῖς
ὁρωμένοις γενόμενος, ὑπεραγαπῶν τὸν εὐεργέτην ζωῆς μὲν αἰωνίου ἀπόλαυσιν
χαρισάμενον, τρυφαῖς δὲ παραδείσου ἐναναπαύσαντα, ἀρχὴν δὲ δόντα κατὰ τὴν τῶν
ἀγγέλων, καὶ ἀρχαγγέλοις αὐτὸν ποιήσαντα ὁμοδίαιτον, καὶ φωνῆς θείας ἀκροατήν·
ἐπὶ πᾶσι τούτοις ὑπερασπιζόμενος παρὰ θεοῦ, καὶ ἀπολαύων τῶν αὐτοῦ ἀγαθῶν,
ταχὺ πάντων ἀναπληθεὶς καὶ οἷον ἐξυβρίσας τῷ κόρῳ, τὸ τοῖς σαρκίνοις ὀφθαλμοῖς
φανὲν τερπνὸν τοῦ νοητοῦ προετίμησε κάλλους, καὶ τὴν πλησμονὴν τῆς γαστρὸς
τῶν πνευματικῶν ἀπολαύσεων τιμιωτέραν ἔθετο. ἔξω μὲν εὐθὺς ἦν τοῦ
παραδείσου, ἔξω δὲ τῆς μακαρίας ἐκείνης διαγωγῆς· οὐκ ἐξ ἀνάγκης κακὸς
ἀλλ' ἐξ ἀβουλίας γενόμενος.

This passage clearly asserts a high view of ' original righteousness ' and ' perfection,' [1] and it is consequently not surprising to find elsewhere [2] in the writings of St. Basil instances of the use of the word ' Fall ' (ἐκπτῶσις, πτῶμα) in this connexion. We naturally expect, after such an exordium, some explanation of the consequences flowing from the ' folly ' of the first man. But the Adam-theory, as here set forth, remains a torso, running down into vagueness ; the only statements suggestive of a connexion between the acquired sinfulness of the protoplast and the sinfulness of his descendants are to be found in the employment from time to time of an idiom which we have already noted in Greek writers on this subject, namely, the use of the first personal pronoun plural in expressions referring to the Fall.[3] ' We ' are said to have drawn death upon ourselves as the result of an evil disposition [4]; the Tree of the Knowledge of Good and Evil was fair to look upon in order that ' our ' obedience might be tested [5] ; the devil has become our adversary on account of the Fall (πτῶμα) which happened to ' us ' of old as the result of our insult (to God).[6] Such expressions may naturally be construed, both in Athanasius and in Basil, as symptomatic of the subconscious influence of the Recapitulation-theory. But it is clear that the conviction which our author really holds with his whole heart and which springs out of the depths of his own vital experience is the virile ethical belief in the fullness of man's free-will. The Fall-doctrine comes to him from without, on the authority of Scripture and ecclesiastical tradition, and it is accepted by him in a minimising form, we need not doubt sincerely, but yet superficially ; it has not gripped his emotions or even the whole of his intellect, and he has made little effort to harmonise the uncompromising libertarianism natural to his own Hellenic temperament with the measure of determinism which even a minimal statement of the Fall-doctrine must logically involve.

It may be noted that this Father adds a curious

---

[1] Cf. quotations (a), (b) and (d), supra, p. 264, n. 1.

[2] e.g. de spir. sancto 15 ; hom. in ps. cxiv. 3.

[3] v. supra, pp. 196, 261.

[4] hom. quod Deus non est auct. mal. 7 (Garnier, p. 79 C).

[5] ibid. 9 (Garnier, p. 81 A). [6] ibid. 9 (Garnier, p. 81 D).

hypothetical decoration to the idea of Adam's ' original perfection,' when he tells us that, although unfallen man had no need of clothing, nevertheless, if he had persevered in virtue, a lucid aureole would have formed itself about him, more beauteous than the daedal hues of the flowers and more brilliant than the light of the stars, which would have been an angelic garment bestowed on him as the reward of his perseverance by the hand of the Creator himself.[1]

From the writings of St. Basil we pass by a natural transition to those of (5) his younger brother, *St. Gregory of Nyssa* (b. *c.* A.D. 335, d. *c.* 395).[2] Though it cannot be said that this acute psychologist and brilliant rhetorician did much to fix the changeful and elusive lineaments of the ' Hellenic ' Fall-doctrine, he nevertheless deserves the credit of having devoted much more attention and interest to the subject than any of the Greek-Christian writers whom we have reviewed so far, with the exceptions of Irenaeus and Origen ; and his works contain a wealth of material for the reconstruction of the opinions and speculations regarding the origin of sin which were current in Eastern Christendom during the age immediately prior to that of St. Augustine. It will conduce to clearness if in summarising the ideas held by this Father we employ once more the five-fold scheme of 'cardinal issues ' defined at the beginning of this Lecture as arising directly out of the Pauline doctrine of the Fall and of its consequences for man. (1) It is clear that, following his master Origen, Gregory was a partisan of the allegorical, as opposed to the prosaically literal, interpretation of Gen. iii. We need only refer to the phrases used by him in the *oratio catechetica*— ' . . . all the matters whereof Moses treats in more or less historical form, placing before us

---

[1] *hom.* quod Deus non est auct. mal. 9 (Garnier, p. 81 D).

[2] For more extended discussions of St. Gregory's doctrines of Man and of Sin, see the following : *Gregorii Nyss. doctrinam de hominis natura et illustravit et cum Origeniana comparavit* E. W. Möller, Halle, 1854 ; A. Krampf, *Der Urzustand des Menschen nach der Lehre des hl. Gregor von Nyssa,* 1889 ; Fr. Hilt, *Des hl. Gregors von Nyssa Lehre vom Menschen,* 1890 ; J. Rivière, *Le dogme de la rédemption,* 1905, pp. 151–159, 384–386, 420, 422. Quotations from the *oratio catechetica* are given in accordance with Dr. J. H. Srawley's text (*The Catechetical Oration of Gregory of Nyssa,* Cambr. Patristic Texts, 1903) ; for quotations from other works, I have used Migne (*PG* XLIV–XLVI).

doctrines in the guise of a narrative ' [1] . . . ' now it is such a
doctrine which Moses sets forth unto you in more or less
historical form and by means of riddles ; yet the teaching
which these riddles contain is plain and manifest.' [2] Thorough-
going allegorism is for him, as for Origen, a means of escape
from servitude to the letter of the Paradise-story into the
free atmosphere of philosophical speculation, in which the
Fall-theory can be developed in accordance with what we
have seen to be its true nature, as a hypothesis framed by
reason to account for the actual existence of evil whilst
safeguarding the infinite power and goodness of God.

(2) The question, what was Gregory's view of the original
state of man, is much more obscure and complicated. It
can, however, be considerably simplified if we abandon the
attempt to harmonise all his allusions to the subject, and
recognise that two somewhat different theories of ' original
perfection,' involving correspondingly diverse theories of the
nature and effects of the Fall, appear in his writings. The
earliest of these attempts to articulate the Fall-theory is
to be found in the treatise *de hominis opificio* (' on the making
of man ') which may be dated *c.* A.D. 380 ; the later is
contained in the *oratio catechetica*, written *c.* A.D. 385.
A brief survey and comparison of these two views will both
help to complete our picture of the various tendencies which
the ' Hellenic ' Fall-speculation of this period was elastic
enough to include, and also suggest ideas which may prove
to be of use in our final evaluation and re-formulation of the
basic Christian doctrines of human nature and of sin.

(a) ' *Original perfection* ' *and the Fall in the treatise* ' *On the making of man.*' [3]

The first of these trains of thought finds its nominal
starting-point in the words of Gen. i. 26, 27. (26) ' And
God said, Let us make man in our image, after our likeness :
and let them have dominion over the fish of the sea . . . ,'

---

[1] *or. cat.* 5 : ὅσα περὶ τούτων ἱστορικώτερον ὁ Μωσῆς διεξέρχεται, ἐν
διηγήσεως εἴδει δόγματα ἡμῖν παρατιθέμενος.

[2] *ibid.* 8 : τὸ δὲ τοιοῦτον δόγμα ἱστορικώτερον μὲν καὶ δι' αἰνιγμάτων ὁ
Μωσῆς ὑμῖν ἐκτίθεται. πλὴν ἔκδηλον καὶ τὰ αἰνίγματα τὴν διδασκαλίαν ἔχει.

[3] *de hom. opif.* 16–18.

etc. (27) ' And God created man in his own image, in the image of God created he him ; male and female created he them.' This text is made, by a somewhat forced exegesis, to yield the theory of a double creation of man, or (in other words) of the creation of the human race as involving two distinct and separate Divine acts. The first of these acts brought into existence ' man ' as such, that is, the idea or universal concept of humanity. This archetypal or ideal ' man ' was made ' in the image of God,' and was consequently endowed with all possible moral and intellectual excellences, including the completest freedom of self-determination ; and, though at the beginning numerically one, and contained in one body,[1] he included in himself the potentiality of all subsequent individual men. His nature was entirely free from irrational passions and appetites, more particularly from the sexual appetite ; and if he had never fallen, he would have propagated himself in the same manner as the angels, presumably (though Gregory does not say this, and disclaims exact knowledge of the angelic mode of procreation) by some kind of fission.[2]

Nevertheless, though made in the image of God, he was distinguished from God by his creaturely status, which involved instability and mutability ; for God alone is uncreate and immutable. This mutability inherent in man carried with it the possibility of sin : and, though God did not predestine man to sin, He foresaw that in point of fact he *would* sin,[3] and would consequently forfeit the power of

---

[1] *de hom. opif.* 16 (*PG* XLIV. 185 C) : οὕτως οἶμαι καθάπερ ἐν ἑνὶ σώματι ὅλον τὸ τῆς ἀνθρωπότητος πλήρωμα . . . περισχεθῆναι.

[2] The view set out in this paragraph must be carefully distinguished from Origen's theory of the pre-natal existence of individual human spirits, which is emphatically repudiated by Gregory of Nyssa. (*de an. et resurr.* [*PG* XLVI, 112 C].) This passage does not mention the name of Origen, doubtless owing to Gregory's *pietas* towards him, and appears to be nominally directed against the idea of a pre-natal fall as expounded in the myth contained in Plato's *Phaedrus* (*v. supra*, p. 214) ; but to condemn the theory of the *Phaedrus* myth is to condemn the theory of Origen's Alexandrine period. Another repudiation of this view occurs in *de hom. opif.* 28 (*PG* XLIV. 229 B).

[3] *Cf.* Milton, *Paradise Lost*, iii. 116 : ' They themselves decreed
Their own revolt, not I. If I foreknew,
Foreknowledge had no influence on their fault,
Which had no less proved certain, unforeknown.'

reproducing himself after the manner of the angels. In view, therefore, of the foreseen, though not fore-ordained, catastrophe of the Fall, and to preserve the possibility of the numerical increase of mankind, God subdivided the one archetypal man into ' male ' and ' female ' : that is, He added to man's original intellectual nature those sexual organs and appetites which are the instruments of genera- tion in the sub-human brutes. ' Hence also ' (he adds) ' the great David, pitying the misery of man, mourns over his nature with such words as these, that " man being in honour knew it not " (meaning by " honour " the equality of the angels) ; therefore, he says, " he is compared to the beasts that have no understanding, and made like unto them." [1] For he truly was made like the beasts, who received in his nature the present mode of transient generation, on account of his inclination to material things.' [2] This partial degradation of man, through his subdivision and ' sexualization ' (if this coinage may be pardoned) in view of a *foreseen* Fall, is the second act of creation, described in Gen. i. 27 ' male and female created he them.'

The assumption of an animal nature and of sexual feelings by man necessarily carried with it (according to this author) the assumption of other appetites and passions, such as pride, ferocity, greed, and timidity. All these evil impulses came into human nature concomitantly with sex and because of sex, so that man became a Janus-like creature, with two faces, one bearing the ' image of God,' the other the image of the brutes. Nevertheless, free-will can bridle these passions and harness them to good ends, thus trans- forming the dispositions from which they arise into heroic virtues ; this had actually been done by Moses and other saints of the elder Covenant.[3] On the other hand, free- will may accept and endorse the animal passions, and set the intellect to work at the excogitation of lawless and fantastic means of satisfying them, so that monstrous crimes, unknown to the brute creation, result. Yet Gregory seems to recognise, in a startlingly modern spirit, that all

[1] Ps. xlix. 13 (LXX).
[2] *de hom. opif.* 17, 5 (*PG* XLIV. 189 D).
[3] *ibid.* 18, 8 (*PG* XLIV. 193 D).

so-called 'evil passions' in man are exaggerations, or perversions, of instincts which in themselves are necessary for the continuance of animal life upon the earth ; anger, for instance, is the perversion of the self-assertive instinct, timidity of the self-preserving instinct, and so on. The affinities of this conception with the Rabbinical idea of the *yēçer ha-ra'*, and with the doctrines of more recent psychology of the psycho-analytic school, do not need to be emphasised.

Gregory's earliest version of the Fall-doctrine, then, does not regard the connatural disorder of the human soul as a direct consequence of the Fall : it is, rather, a direct consequence of man's endowment by God with a bodily, and more particularly with a sexual, nature, in view of his divinely foreseen Fall. This position represents an exceedingly subtle and original revision of the traditional doctrine, and cannot now be considered on its merits : it must suffice to note its key-conceptions, some of which, as we shall see, were discarded by our author in his later presentation of the doctrine, that which appears in the *oratio catechetica*. These key-conceptions are :

(i) The attribution of 'original perfection,' not to the first sexually differentiated pair of human beings, but to the archetypal Man, the universal of humanity ; this idea may well be derived from the hypothesis of a single pre-existent Adam tentatively suggested in Origen's Commentary on the Epistle to the Romans [1] :

(ii) The conviction that sex is an intrinsically evil, or at least undesirable and regrettable, phenomenon—an instance of the appearance of a specifically ' twice-born ' or ' African ' trait in an otherwise thoroughly ' Hellenic ' scheme of thought. The emergence of this familiar piece of morbidity will cause no surprise to anyone who remembers the ascetic tendencies common to the three Cappadocians, or who has read the terrible indictment of marriage contained in Gregory's treatise *de virginitate*.[2]

---

[1] *v. supra*, p. 228.

[2] c. iii. (*PG* XLVI. 325 ff.). Like Tertullian, Gregory of Nyssa was a married disparager of marriage : his wife was named Theosebia (see S. Greg. Naz. *ep*. cxcvii, ed. Paris. ii. p. 162, written to console Gregory of Nyssa on

(iii) The ultra-'Hellenic,' almost Pelagian, belief that free-will is capable—apparently by itself—of taming the passions, and that sinlessness was actually achieved by a few men even before the coming of Christ.[1]

(b) 'Original perfection' in the Catechetical Oration.

The chief *prima facie* objection to the scheme of ideas just described is that, in so far as it regards sin as a natural consequence of our animal constitution, and attributes our animal constitution to a specific creative act of God, it appears to make God the ultimate first cause of sin—the very conclusion which the Fall-doctrine was originally designed to destroy, but into which it tends, when carelessly handled, to convert itself. Five years later, however, Gregory had been driven by the silent but persistent pressure of Manichean dualism to realise the true issues at stake. 'All through the *oratio catechetica*' (says Dr. Srawley) 'Gregory has the Manicheans in view.'[2] What we have called the theodicy-making motive dominates his later presentation of the Fall-doctrine. 'Seeing that man is the work of God, who out of His goodness brought this living creature into existence, no one can rationally suppose that he, whose constitution has its source in goodness, was created by his Maker in a state of evil.'[3]

In the light of this principle, the whole theory of a double creation and of a distinction between the one archetypal man and the two sexually differentiated beings, Adam and Eve, is tacitly dropped, and there is substituted for it what was now becoming, in both East and West, the normal view—that, namely, of a single glorious protoplast, belonging both to the intelligible and to the sensible world,

---

her death ; Nicephorus, *H.E.* xi. 19, ed. Fronto Ducaeus, 1630, ii. p. 137 ; Tillemont, *Mémoires*, ix. p. 252, thinks that she was a deaconess, as well as a priest's wife).

[1] *Cf.* the opinions of St. Athanasius on this point, *supra*, p. 262.

[2] *op. cit.* p. 27, n. 5.

[3] *or. cat.* 5 (Sr. p. 25, 15) : ἐπειδὴ γὰρ θεοῦ ἔργον ὁ ἄνθρωπος, τοῦ δι' ἀγαθότητα τὸ ζῷον τοῦτο παραγαγόντος εἰς γένεσιν, οὐκ ἄν τις εὐλόγως, οὗ ἡ αἰτία τῆς συστάσεως ἀγαθότης ἐστί, τοῦτον ἐν κακοῖς γεγενῆσθαι παρὰ τοῦ πεποιηκότος καθυποπτεύσειεν.

the meeting-point of spirit and matter, the ruler of the earth, immortal and impassible, ' revelling in the manifestation of Deity even face to face.' [1] Inflamed with envy by man's splendid prerogatives, the archangel who governs the earth and its surrounding sphere resolved to bring him to naught [2]; and, being unable to work man's ruin by force, he persuaded him by guile to renounce his communion with God, and so to infect his whole being with a fatal weakness. Gregory illustrates this conception by a quaint yet significant simile, comparing the malevolent Spirit to one who, not having sufficient strength of lung to blow a lamp out, mixes water with the oil and so reduces the flame to a feeble flicker [3]; a simile which implies that the image of God in man is obscured but by no means destroyed. From the error of the protoplast flow all human ills, including physical mortality (the ' coats of skins ' of Gen. iii. 21 are explained as symbolising the sensuous and irrational nature with which mortality is necessarily bound up, but not bodies as such [4]); and the God of Christianity is thus vindicated against the indictment of the Manicheans. We may note that in Gregory, as in other fourth-century writers, an exalted conception of man's primal state finds its logical consequence in an occasional use of the word ' Fall ' to denote the first transgression. [5]

---

[1] *or. cat.* 6 (Sr. p. 36, 8) : αὐτῆς κατὰ πρόσωπον τῆς θείας ἐμφανείας κατατρυφῶν.

[2] Note that in the Catechetical Oration the real and ultimate ' Fall ' is that of the angel of the earth, who became the devil.

[3] *ibid.* 6 (Sr. p. 36, 15).

[4] *ibid.* 8 (Sr. p. 43, 2 ff.), where Gregory draws attention, in an eminently critical spirit, to the difficulty of supposing that animals were literally killed and flayed for the purpose of providing these garments. The explanation which he gives seems to represent, like so much else of greater importance in fourth-century Eastern thought, the resultant of the forces of attraction towards and revolt against Origen (*v. supra,* p. 249). *Cf. de an. et resurr.* (*PG* XLVI. 148 D), where the ' skin ' is expounded as typifying ' the form of the irrational nature, wherewith we were clothed, when we had been made familiar with passion,' and *de virg.* 12, where it is identified with the ' mind of the flesh ' (φρόνημα τῆς σαρκός). For earlier discussions of this point, *v. supra,* pp. 229, 251, 275.

[5] *Cf. or. cat.* 8 (Sr. p. 51, 22) : ἡ τοῦ πεπτωκότος ἀνόρθωσις : *ibid.* 15 (Sr. p. 63, 11) : ὁ ἐν τῷ πτώματι ἄνθρωπος ; *de vita Moysis* (*PG* XLIV. 337 D) : λόγος τίς ἐστιν ἐκ πατρικῆς παραδόσεως τὸ πιστὸν ἔχων, ὅς φησι, πεσούσης ἡμῶν εἰς ἁμαρτίαν τῆς φύσεως, μὴ παριδεῖν τὸν θεὸν τὴν πτῶσιν

(3) What, in Gregory's view, was the exact nature of the disastrous legacy of the primal catastrophe ? According to the treatise *On the making of man*, it was nothing other than our irrational, sensuous, appetitive, and emotional nature itself. But, as we have already pointed out, to brand appetite, instinct, and emotion as evil, as things which had better not have been, is to leave the door ajar for the entrance of Manicheism. We may suppose that it was the realisation of this fact which impelled Gregory in the *Catechetical Oration* to affirm emphatically that the seat of evil lies in the power of choice [1]—though even in this work there are not wanting traces of his earlier view.[2] To modern readers it may seem that it would not have been very difficult to clear up the confusion which enwrapped the question of the precise nature of the flaw or disharmony in man's psychic structure by saying boldly : ' appetite is in itself good, or at least neutral ; but appetite permitted to indulge itself without limit or government becomes *per accidens* bad ; it is the business of the will to keep appetite in order ; but, owing to the Fall, the will is weak, so that it is not always capable of opposing a firm inhibition to the clamorous demands of the appetites for satisfaction, with the result that they often break out into action contrary to the dictates of reason and conscience. Hence, the radical flaw of human nature may be defined as " weakness of will ".' He comes near to this position, when he tells us that ' human nature is *weak* relatively to the doing of good, in that it was once for all

---

ἀπαρανόητον. *or. cat.*, however, also employs the words παρατροπή, ' turning aside ' (8, Sr. p. 49, 16), and παρολισθάνειν, ' to slip aside ' (8, Sr. p. 51, 10), which seem to express the older idea of the first sin as a παράβασις, a divergence from the line of progress which God had meant man to pursue.

[1] *op. cit.* 7 (Sr. p. 40, 4) : κακὸν γὰρ οὐδὲν ἔξω προαιρέσεως ἐφ' ἑαυτοῦ κεῖται (in other words, *moral* evil is alone κακόν) ; *cf.* also *c. Eunom.* ii. 13 (*PG* XLV. 545 B) : ἡ γὰρ παρακοὴ προαιρέσεως οὐ σώματος ἁμαρτία ἐστίν· ἴδιον γὰρ ψυχῆς ἡ προαίρεσις, ἀφ' ἧς πᾶσα τῆς φύσεως συμφορὰ τὴν ἀρχὴν ἔσχεν (' for disobedience is a sin of will, not of body ; for will is a property of soul, from which all the disaster of our nature had its beginning '). For this line of thought, see St. Basil, *hom.* quod Deus non est auctor malorum (discussed *supra*, p. 265).

[2] *ibid.* 8 (Sr. p. 45, 7) : τῷ αἰσθητικῷ μέρει, τῷ κατὰ τὸ σῶμά φημι, τῆς κακίας καταμιχθείσης (' wickedness being intermingled with the sensuous part ‹of our nature›, that part I mean which is connected with the body ').

hamstrung by wickedness.'[1]   But he never succeeds in reaching a clear distinction between appetite and the illicit indulgence of appetite ; he sticks fast at precisely the same point at which the Rabbinical artificers of the *yēçer*-doctrine had stuck.[2]   Doubtless in both cases the failure to advance may be attributed to defective terminology, inasmuch as neither the Hebrew nor the Greek language contains a word which exactly expresses the idea of Will as the power, not merely to choose, but to enforce the choice in the teeth of rebellious inclinations by the exertion of effort.[3]

In view of this imperfection of his psychological terminology, it might have been expected that Gregory would fall back upon the metaphysical or quasi-metaphysical conception of ' disintegration,' which we have already noted in Methodius and Athanasius.   This, however, he leaves on one side.   Two fragments, indeed, of the scheme of ideas

---

[1] *de orat. domin.* 4 (*PG* XLIV. 1164 C) : ἀσθενὴς ἡ ἀνθρωπίνη φύσις πρὸς τὸ ἀγαθόν ἐστιν, ἅπαξ διὰ κακίας ἐκνευρισθεῖσα.   (The context consists of a series of eloquent variations on this theme.)   *Cf.* also *or. cat.* 15 (Sr. p. 63, 10) : ἐδεῖτο γὰρ τοῦ ἰατρεύοντος ἡ φύσις ἡμῶν ἀσθενήσασα; *ibid.* 16 (Sr. p. 69, 9), where the ' impulse towards wickedness ' is called an ἀρρώστημα or ' ailment ' of our nature.

[2] *v. supra*, Lecture II, p. 69.

[3] Biblical Hebrew does not contain a word for ' Will,' in the sense defined above : רָצוֹן seems to mean rather ' goodwill,' ' favour,' ' desire,' or ' pleasure ' (see Brown, Driver, and Briggs, *Hebrew and English Lexicon of the O.T.*, *s.v.*, p. 953).   And Dr. A. Büchler, than whom no one can speak with more authority, informs me that the equivalent of ' will ' in this sense is not to be found, so far as he knows, in Rabbinical Hebrew.   He suggests, indeed, (in a letter to me) that the term *yēçer hattōbh* (' the good impulse,' which in later Rabbinical literature is said to contend with the *yēçer ha-ra*ʻ within the soul of man) comes to very much the same thing ; but the ' good impulse,' or ' disposition,' being *ex hypothesi* directed towards good ends, cannot be taken as simply identical with the bare power of exerting effort to overcome inclination, for this latter power may be exerted to overcome conscientious scruples or good inclinations, as in the case of Shakespere's Hubert (*King John*, Act IV, Scene 1) :

> ' If I talk to him, with his innocent prate
> He will awake my mercy which lies dead :
> Therefore I will be sudden, and dispatch.'

The Greek language is no better off in this regard.   προαίρεσις is defined by Aristotle as βουλευτικὴ ὄρεξις τῶν ἐφ' ἡμῖν (*Eth. Nic.* iii. 3, 19)— a definition which implies that in προαίρεσις ' appetite ' and ' deliberation ' are harmoniously united ; and θέλημα is defined by St. John of Damascus (*orth. fid.* ii. 22, quoted by Suicer, *Thesaurus*, *s.v.*), in substantially identical terms, as ὄρεξις λογική τε καὶ ζωτικὴ μόνων ἠρτημένη τῶν φυσικῶν.

which coheres round this term appear in the *Catechetical Oration*. He several times takes occasion to point out that evil is a ' privation,' absence, or negation of good, not a thing-in-itself existing in its own right ; and bases on this the conventional anti-Manichean contention that God is not the author of evil, as it would be absurd to describe Him as the author of that which does not exist.[1] And the idea of the ' deification ' of human nature through sacramental incorporation into the Incarnate Logos is expressed with almost startling realism and definiteness, in a chapter [2] which sets forth a doctrine of Eucharistic ' transelementation ' [3] which is hardly, if at all, distinguishable from the later ' transubstantiation.' But the disease which is to be healed by this ' deification ' is here described, not as a mere negative tendency to relapse into nothingness, but as a substantive ' poison ' [4] which can only find its antidote in the reception of the Body of Christ. We seem, in short, to be here confronted with a momentary emergence of the characteristically ' African ' tendency to conceive the results of the Fall as involving a positive *depravatio*, and not a mere *deprivatio*. The only comment that can usefully be made upon this will be a repetition of the familiar reminder that too much consistency must not be expected from the pioneers of scientific theology.

It is of great importance to note that Gregory, in harmony with the strongly marked tendency of the ' once-born ' and ' Hellenic ' line of thought, repudiates the idea of ' Original Guilt.' Ample proof of this statement is supplied by the whole tenor of the treatise *On the untimely deaths of infants* [5] ; in which the question of the future destiny of babes who die

---

[1] *op. cit.* 7. [2] *ibid.* 37.

[3] *ibid.* 37 (Sr. p. 152, 6) : ταῦτα δὲ δίδωσι τῇ τῆς εὐλογίας δυνάμει πρὸς ἐκεῖνο μεταστοιχειώσας τῶν φαινομένων τὴν φύσιν. See Srawley's note *in loc.*, and D. Stone, *History of the Doctrine of the Holy Eucharist*, i. pp. 71 ff., 103 f.

[4] δηλητήριον (Sr. p. 142, 4).

[5] *de infantibus qui praemature abripiuntur* (PG XLVI. 161–192). That the infants contemplated in this treatise are *unbaptised* infants is not indeed expressly stated, but follows (1) from the presumption that no doubt could have arisen in the mind of any primitive Christian about the salvation of *baptised* infants, and (2) from the fact that Gregory seems to be almost unconscious of the existence of the custom of infant baptism ; *v. infra*, p. 279.

without baptism is handled with the completest apparent
unconsciousness of any idea that a newly born babe is as
such subject to God's wrath or stained with any kind of
' sin.' [1] Gregory's humane and reasonable suggestion of
some state analogous to what was later called the *limbus
puerorum*, as the solution of this problem,[2] stands in the
most vivid contrast to the heartless fanaticism with which
Augustine condemns unbaptised little ones to eternal fire,[3]
and is the surest warrant that he was completely out of
sympathy with the theory which impelled the Doctor of
Hippo to this gruesome conclusion.[4] It is, indeed, remarkable that (for all his devotion to Origen) Gregory seems to
ignore the custom of infant baptism with the theories which
had grown out of it, and to maintain the primitive point of
view according to which the normal recipients of baptism
are adults, and the sins which are forgiven through the
sacrament are the actual sins committed by the neophytes
in their past lives. The only work dealing at any length
with the theology of baptism which Gregory has bequeathed
to us declares that the new-made Christian ascending from
the baptismal font is *as free from accusations and penalties
as the new-born babe* [5]—a statement which is a formal

[1] Note the first appearance of a *sixth* ' crucial issue,' which will in our
subsequent discussions have to be considered together with the five defined
at the beginning of Lecture IV—namely, the *eschatological* issue, ' What is
the future fate of those who die subject to the consequences of the Fall,
without having in this life consciously obtained redemption through
Christ and in His Church ? '

[2] This view is developed in a rhetorical and elusive passage too long
to quote (*op. cit.*, PG XLVI. 177 A–180 D), the gist of which is that the
soul of an infant who has died before attaining the age of reason will enjoy
a beatitude proportionate to its capacities, very much less than that to
which the adult saint may look forward, but nevertheless true beatitude ;
it is suggested that such child-spirits may progressively grow in the knowledge of God until they eventually attain to full mental and spiritual
maturity.

[3] For references *v. infra*, Lecture V, p. 377, n. 1.

[4] Gregory does not condemn even hardened adult sinners (much less
innocent babes) to never-ending hell ; for his usual teaching makes ' hell '
merely a temporary purgatory, which will end in the universal ἀποκατάστασις
or restoration in which he had learned from Origen to believe ; see Bardenhewer, *Patrology*, p. 303 f.

[5] *in baptism. Christi* (PG XLVI. 579 D) : ὡς γὰρ τὸ εὐθύτοκον παιδίον
ἐλεύθερόν ἐστιν ἐγκλημάτων καὶ τιμωριῶν, οὕτως καὶ ὁ τῆς ἀναγεννήσεως παῖς
οὐκ ἔχει περὶ τίνος ἀπολογήσεται, βασιλικῇ δωρεᾷ τῶν εὐθυνῶν ἀφεθείς.

contradiction of the doctrine of ' Original Guilt,' and
may even be thought to undermine the necessity of infant
baptism itself.

(4) Although Gregory nowhere attempts an explicit
definition of the manner in which the ' weakness ' or ' ailment ' of human nature is transmitted from generation to
generation, we may conclude with reasonable certainty that
Gregory regarded the transmission as taking place by way
of biological, and not merely of ' social,' heredity. This
conclusion would seem to be an inevitable inference from
the use of the first person plural in verbs referring to the
Fall (an idiom which, as in previous writers, betrays the
subconscious influence of the idea of ' recapitulation '), from
Gregory's ' traducianist ' conception of the origin of the soul, [1]
and from the phrases which declare sin, or the impulse to
sin, to be knit up with man's constitution, especially with
his bodily constitution.[2] It is indirectly confirmed by the
statement, apparently based upon a suggestion of Methodius,[3]
that man was made subject to physical death in order that
his spiritual nature might be freed from inherent sinfulness
and become capable of receiving the resurrection body, just
as an earthenware vessel into which some malicious person
has poured molten lead must be broken up before the alien
matter can be removed and the fragments recompounded
into a new vessel.[4] We may glance in passing at the curious
fancy that the multiplicity of mankind is itself an evil, and
that it would have been better if the archetypal man had
continued to subsist in his pure intellectual unity and
uniqueness [5]; this, however, is an irrelevant piece of un-

---

[1] de hom. opif. 29 (PG XLIV. 233 D ff.).

[2] e.g. or. cat. 35 (Sr. p. 134, 15) : δι' ὧν ἐκλύεταί πως ὁ ἄνθρωπος τῆς
πρὸς τὸ κακὸν συμφυίας: de vita Moysis (PG XLIV. 336) : ‹τὸν
κύριον› τὸν τὴν ἁμαρτητικὴν ἡμῶν φύσιν περιβαλλόμενον: ibid. (756) : ὁ κοινωνῶν
τῆς φύσεως τοῦ Ἀδὰμ, κοινωνῶν δὲ καὶ τῆς ἐκπτώσεως: in ps. (PG XLIV.
609) : ἡ ἁμαρτία ἡ συναποτικτομένη τῇ φύσει. For the connexion of congenital wickedness with the body, v. supra, p. 276, n. 2.

[3] v. supra, p. 252, n. 3.

[4] or. cat. 8 (Sr. p. 44, 17).

[5] Such is the apparent implication of a sentence in de an. et resurr.
(PG XLVI. 157 A) : ὁ γὰρ πρῶτος στάχυς ὁ πρῶτος ἄνθρωπος ἦν Ἀδάμ·
(Gregory is fancifully embroidering upon St. Paul's comparison of the
resurrection of the body to the growth of corn from the seed, in 1 Cor. xv).
ἀλλ' ἐπειδὴ τῇ τῆς κακίας εἰσόδῳ εἰς πλῆθος ἡ φύσις κατεμερίσθη

digested neo-Platonism, which bears no organic relation to Gregory's other speculations upon evil in man.

(5) The resulting state of human nature, infected as it is by ' weakness ' and the ' impulse to sin,' is one of dis-integration and destruction. Yet, though the objective and *ex opere operato* aspects of Redemption, and, by impli-cation, the presupposed need and helplessness of man, are brought into strong relief by the vividly realistic conception of ' deification ' through the Eucharist, in which Gregory's soteriology culminates, no diminution is admitted in the fullness of man's endowment of free-will. Whatever the strength of our innate propension towards evil, it is not so strong that we cannot overcome it if we choose ; whatever the power of sacramental grace, it does not dispense us from the necessity of spiritual effort in order to its fruitful appropriation.

We may conclude this review of Gregory's speculations about human nature and congenital sinfulness by drawing attention to the tentative and provisional character which he expressly attributes to them. ' Some such explanation as the following have we received from the Fathers ' [1]—' we, imagining the truth as far as we can by means of conjectures and similitudes, do not set forth that which occurs to our mind authoritatively, but will place it in the form of a theoretical exercise before our kindly hearers ' [2]—' here, again, the true answer, whatever it may be, can be clear to those only who, like Paul, have been initiated into the mysteries of Paradise ; but *our* answer is as follows ' [3]

κ. τ. λ. The idea that multiplicity as such is evil appears in Plotinus, *Enn.* vi. 6, 1 : ἆρ' ἐστι τὸ πλῆθος ἀπόστασις τοῦ ἑνός, καὶ ἡ ἀπειρία ἀπόστασις παντελὴς τῷ πλῆθος ἀνάριθμον εἶναι, καὶ διὰ τοῦτο κακὸν ἡ ἀπειρία καὶ ἡμεῖς κακοί, ὅταν πλῆθος ;

[1] *or. cat.* 6 (Sr. p. 28, 15) : τοιοῦτόν τινα λόγον παρὰ τῶν πατέρων διεδεξάμεθα : this formula reminds us of the phrase with which Plato's Critias introduces the Myth of Atlantis—ἐγὼ φράσω παλαιὸν ἀκηκοὼς λόγον οὐ νέου ἀνδρός (*Timaeus*, 21 A).

[2] *de hom. opif.* 16 (PG XLIV. 185 A) : ἡμεῖς δὲ, καθώς ἐστι δυνατὸν, διὰ στοχασμῶν τινων καὶ εἰκόνων φαντασθέντες τὴν ἀλήθειαν, τὸ ἐπὶ νοῦν ἐλθὸν οὐκ ἀποφαντικῶς ἐκτιθέμεθα, ἀλλ' ὡς ἐν γυμνασίας εἴδει τοῖς εὐγνώμοσι τῶν ἀκροωμένων προσθήσομεν.

[3] *ibid.* 17 (PG XLIV. 188 B) : ἀλλ' ἐν τούτοις πάλιν ὁ μὴν ἀληθὴς λόγος, ὅστίς ποτε ὢν τυγχάνει, μόνοις ἂν εἴη δῆλος τοῖς κατὰ Παῦλον τὰ τοῦ παραδείσου μυηθεῖσιν ἀπόρρητα· ὁ δὲ ἡμέτερος τοιοῦτός ἐστιν.

—these are the formulae with which he introduces the subtle though unsystematised ideas which have been summarised above. The Adam-tradition exists, and he admits its general claim upon his allegiance ; but the philosopher's stone of allegorism enables him to transmute its pictorial details into metaphysical or psychological concepts, and he uses this power with great freedom. It is clear that there is as yet no question of a stereotyped ecclesiastical dogma.

(6) *St. Gregory of Nazianzus* (b. A.D. 329, d. *c.* 390). Before we finally leave the field of unsystematised and incoherent speculations presented by the writings of the Greek Fathers, and turn to the swift, consistent, and logical development of the ' African ' or Western version of the Fall-doctrine, the third remaining doctor of the Cappadocian group claims our attention—Gregory of Nazianzus, ' the Theologian ' *par excellence* as Eastern Christendom has loved to style him, and the intimate friend of the brothers Basil and Gregory of Nyssa, whose thoughts with regard to the origin and ground of sin have just been reviewed. Like his predecessors, this Father has bequeathed to us no single treatise dealing with the subject of our enquiry, and his ideas about the Fall and its consequences have to be gathered from incidental allusions scattered through works dealing with other doctrinal questions. It cannot be claimed that his doctrine exhibits any advance upon that of his two friends, in respect either of definition or of synthesisation ; its interest lies partly in the testimony which it bears to the existence and solidity of a ' once-born ' and non-Western type of Fall-theory, or Fall-speculation, during the last pre-Augustinian century, and partly in its employment as a spear-head, not so much against theological dualism (its traditional foe) as, in the more restricted area of Christology, against the Apollinarian tenet of the imperfection or incompleteness of the Lord's human nature. This peculiar Christological bearing imposed by Gregory upon the Fall-doctrine will be explained in the course of our survey of his allusions to the doctrine—a survey which may follow the familiar

land-marks of the ' five crucial issues,' or such of them as emerge in his writings.[1]

A convenient starting-point for our study of this Father's opinions on the subject of our enquiry is provided by a passage occurring in the last of his sermons, preached, after his retirement from the see of Constantinople, at the village of Arianzus, one Easter Day not long before his death.[2] The purpose of this discourse is to glorify the Resurrection of Christ by exhibiting it in its context, as a supreme moment in the whole process of God's dealings with His universe and with man. The first portion of it, therefore, is devoted to the topics of Creation and the Fall. The preacher distinguishes sharply between the creation of the ' intelligible world,' the world, that is, of Platonic Ideas or eternal values, and that of the ' sensible ' or phenomenal world. He continues :

Mind, then, and sense, thus distinguished from each other, had remained within their own boundaries, and bore in them-selves the magnificence of the Creator-Word, silent praisers and thrilling heralds of His mighty work. Not yet was there any mingling of both, nor any mixture of these opposites, tokens of a greater wisdom and generosity in the creation of natures ; nor as yet were the whole riches of goodness made known. Now the Creator-Word, determining to exhibit this, and to produce a single living being out of both (the invisible and visible natures, I mean), fashions Man ; and taking the body from already existing matter, and placing in it a Breath taken from Himself (which the Word knew to be an intelligent soul, and the image of God), He placed him on the earth as a sort of second world, a microcosm,[3] a new Angel, a mingled worshipper, fully initiated into the mysteries of the visible creation, but only partially into those of the intelligible creation [4]—king of all upon earth, but subject to the King above ; earthly and heavenly ; temporal and yet immortal ; visible and yet intelligible ; midway between greatness and lowliness ; in one person combining spirit and

---

[1] Quotations are taken from the Paris edition of 1840, ' post operam et studium monachorum O.S.B. e congreg. S. Mauri ' ; references to the volume and page of this are given in brackets.

[2] *or.* xlv. (i. 845) *in sanctum Pascha.* The Benedictine editor dates this Oration *c.* A.D. 385.

[3] οἷόν τινα κόσμον ἕτερον, ἐν μικρῷ μέγαν. The idea may have been suggested by the account of the creation of man in Plato's *Timaeus.*

[4] ἐπόπτην τῆς ὁρατῆς κτίσεως, μύστην τῆς νοουμένης.

flesh, spirit because of God's favour, flesh because of his exaltation . . . a living creature, governed by God's providence here,
but in process of translation to another sphere, and—to crown
the mystery—in process of being deified through its natural
inclination towards God [1] . . .

Him [that is, Man] God placed in Paradise—*whatever that
Paradise may have been* [2]—having honoured him with the gift
of free-will, in order that good might belong to him as the result
of his choice, no less than to Him Who had provided the seeds
thereof, *as a husbandman of immortal plants, that is, perhaps, of
Divine concepts, both the simpler and the more perfect* [3]—naked in
his simplicity and in his inartificial way of life, and devoid of any
covering or defence ; for such it was fitting that the original
man should be . . . *Now the Tree* [of Knowledge] *was Contemplation* [4] (as I see the matter), which can be safely climbed
only by those who are of a more perfect and settled character ;
but it is not good for those who are simple-minded and of a
somewhat greedy appetite, just as perfect (*i.e.* solid) nourishment
is not profitable for those who are yet tender and stand in need
of milk. But when by the envy of the devil and the caprice
of the woman (that caprice which she both suffered, as being
the more tender, and inspired<into the man>, as being the
more persuasive)—*alas for my weakness ! for that of my first
father is mine* [5]—he forgot the commandment which had been
given to him, and was worsted by the baneful taste ; and for
his wickedness was banished at once from the Tree of Life, from
Paradise, and from God, and was clothed with *the coats of skins*,

---

[1] ζῷον ἐνταῦθα οἰκονομούμενον, καὶ ἀλλαχοῦ μεθιστάμενον, καὶ, πέρας τοῦ
μυστηρίου, τῇ πρὸς θεὸν νεύσει θεούμενον.

[2] ὅστίς ποτε ἦν ὁ παράδεισος οὗτος.

[3] φυτῶν ἀθανάτων γεωργόν, θείων ἐννοιῶν ἴσως, τῶν τε ἁπλουστέρων καὶ τῶν
τελεωτέρων.

The comparison between ideas and growing plants is one which seems
naturally to suggest itself to the mystical genius; *cf.* Keats, *Ode to
Psyche* :

    ' Yes, I will be thy priest, and build a fane
      In some untrodden region of my mind,
    Where branchèd thoughts, new-grown with pleasant pain,
      Instead of pines shall murmur in the wind ' ;

and Francis Thompson, *The Hound of Heaven* :

    ' And now my heart is as a broken fount,
      Wherein tear-drippings stagnate, spilt down ever
      From the dank thoughts that shiver
    Upon the sighful branches of my mind.'

[4] θεωρία γὰρ ἦν τὸ φυτόν.

[5] φεῦ τῆς ἐμῆς ἀσθενείας· ἐμὴ γὰρ ἡ τοῦ προπάτορος (a phrase which
contains a suggestion of ' Original Guilt ' ; *v. infra*, p. 289, n. 2).

that is, perhaps, the coarser kind of flesh,[1] which is both mortal and impatient of control.[2]

A cursory survey of this passage will show that in it our author raises the first of the ' cardinal issues,' that of the allegorical as opposed to the literal interpretation of the Scriptural narrative.   Closer investigation, however, reveals the fact that this first issue is not presented to the reader in clear-cut isolation, but is intertwined with the second—namely, the question of the original state of man.   At first sight, a single consistent scheme of ideas, based upon an allegorical exegesis, and displaying clearly marked affinities with Origen's later or ' Caesarean ' presentation of the Fall-doctrine, seems to run through the passage.   The expression ' whatever that Paradise may have been ' suggests that the ' garden ' is not to be interpreted as a literal plot of ground, but as an exalted state [3] ; and, in view of the sublimation of the flowers of Eden into ' Divine concepts,' this state can hardly be other than a transcendental state of existence on the plane of the intelligible world.   With such an interpretation of the Paradise-story coheres the ascription of super-human and angelic prerogatives to the primal man, and the allegorisation of the Tree of Knowledge as ' contemplation ' ; though it is to be noticed that Gregory seems here to have introduced an ingenious variant into the Origenian scheme (doubtless in order to make type and antitype correspond more exactly), representing the first sin as consisting, not in man's turning away through ' satiety ' from privileges of contemplation which he already possessed, but in his premature grasping at privileges which he did not possess and for which he was, even in his primitive glory, not sufficiently prepared.   The explanation of the ' coats of skins ' given here is in a general sense cognate with the

---

[1] τοὺς δερματίνους ἀμφιέννυται χιτῶνας, ἴσως τὴν παχυτέραν σάρκα : cf. *carmen de anima* 115 (ii. p. 248) :

δερματίνους δὲ χιτῶνας ἐφέσσατο σάρκα βαρεῖαν
νεκροφόρος.

[2] *op. cit.* 7, 8 (slightly abbreviated).   The translation given above is largely based on that of C. G. Browne and J. E. Swallow (*Select Library of Nicene and Post-Nicene Fathers*, 1894).   I have italicised phrases of special doctrinal interest.

[3] *Cf. carmen de anima*, 105 (ii. p. 246) :

ζωὴ δ' οὐρανίη πέλεται παράδεισος ἔμοιγε.

explanations given by Origen and Gregory of Nyssa ; though the Nazianzene's statement that these garments may symbolise ' a coarser flesh ' implies that unfallen man possessed flesh of some kind, presumably of a more subtle, tenuous, or ethereal consistency.

Nevertheless, the three notable allegorisations to which we have drawn attention (of the plants of Paradise, the Tree of Knowledge, and the ' coats of skins ') are introduced with expressions of hesitancy (' perhaps ' and ' as I see the matter ') ; and there are other statements which seem to presuppose a more literal view of the Scriptural narrative. We are told that man was placed ' on the earth,' though ' in process of translation to another sphere ' ; that he was only ' partially initiated ' into the mysteries of the ideal world ; that he was naked of covering and defence, and led a simple and artless life. Mention is, moreover, made of the detail of his temptation by the woman. All this is strongly reminiscent of the earliest Greek presentation of the Fall-theory, as we found it in Tatian, Theophilus, and Irenaeus, according to which man as originally created was a ' babe,' ' capable of either good or evil,' but possessed of a ' starting-point for progress.' The conclusion to which we seem to be driven is that Gregory's thoughts on this subject represent a purely mechanical and inconsistent juxtaposition of the earlier pre-Origenian, and of the later or post-Origenian tendencies of Hellenic Fall-speculation— of the primitive theory which views the first sin as the failure of an infantile being to pursue the upward course of development which God had marked out for him, and of the later conception, which vaguely emerges during the fourth century, of an archetypal man or collective race-spirit who falls from an exalted, possibly a metaphysical, Paradise.[1] It should be noted, however, that Gregory Nazianzen, like all the great Greek Fathers of the fourth and succeeding centuries, unequivocally condemns Origen's first or ' Alexandrine ' view, that of the pre-natal life and sin of the *individual* soul [2] ; and few candid students will fail to be

---

[1] *Cf.* p. 271 ff. (Gregory of Nyssa).

[2] *or.* xxxvii. 15 (i. p. 655). The name of Origen is not mentioned, but the theory is condemned as λίαν ἄτοπον καὶ οὐκ ἐκκλησιαστικόν.

impressed by the instinctive repulsion with which the underlying mind of the Christian society rejected a theory which
was felt to be an infiltration from alien sources, despite the
extreme fluidity and indeterminateness of its own Adamic
tradition.

Gregory's language with regard to the third issue, that
of the precise nature of the sorrowful legacy of the Fall,
is tantalisingly vague. We are told that as the result of
Adam's transgression mankind has become subject to a
' newly sown curse,' [1] to death, to sin, to a ' heavy yoke ' of
toil and trouble [2] ; but, for the most part, no effort is made
to define the undesirable thing, quality, or status, of which
trouble, death, and sin are the symptoms. There seems to
be only one passage which gives us even a momentary
glimpse into his real mind with regard to this point ; it
occurs in the poem entitled *A sorrowful song on the calamities
of his own soul*, and forms the conclusion of a lamentation
over the internal conflict between reason and appetite which
torments the author—a lamentation which may be described
as the substance of Rom. vii. 7–24 hammered out into
somewhat pedestrian elegiac couplets. We will venture
upon the following metrical rendering :

Often our earth owns the sway of the Mind : yet, captive
    unwilling,
  Often the Mind in its turn follows the might of the Flesh.
Yea, though it yearn for the good, it accomplisheth that which
    it hateth,
  Mourning its direful fate, held in calamitous thrall,
Mourning our ancient father's offence, and the sin of our mother,
  Word that she spake in guile, mother of frenzy distraught :
Mourning the impious lie of the crooked bloodthirsty serpent,
  Who in the crimes of men taketh his fiendish delight ;
Mourning the fatal Tree, and the fruit bringing ruin to mortals,
  Taste whereof setteth man e'en fore the gates of the grave,

---

[1] *carmina*, i. (*poemata theologica*), sect. i. 8 (*de anima*), line 128 f.
(ii. p. 248) :

> τοίη πρωτογόνοιο νεόσπορος ἤλυθεν ἄτη
> δειλοῖσιν μερόπεσσιν, ὅθεν στάχυς ἐβλάστησε.

[2] *ibid.* ii. (*poemata historica*), sect. ii. 1 (*ad Hellenium*), line 345 f.
(ii. p. 1014) :

> οὐχ ἅλις, ὅττι βροτοῖσι βαρὺν ζυγὸν ἤγαγε πρώτη
> ἀρχεγόνου κακίη, καὶ φυτὸν ἀνδροφόνον ;

Nakedness shameful of limbs, and banishment dreary from
Eden,
Far from the Tree of Life, heaping dishonour on loss.[1]

It is clear that our author here conceives the Fall to be
the historical cause of the moral struggle within himself ;
in other words, that the legacy of the Fall is to be identified
with inordinate or hypertrophied appetite, as indeed St. Paul
had already taught by implication in the chapter which is
the basis of these lines.   But the term ' hypertrophied,' as
applied to appetite, must necessarily be relative to some
norm or standard, and the ' normal ' amount of appetite
must, presumably, be that which is capable of being controlled by the will.   ' Hypertrophy of appetite ' is thus
merely a synonym for ' atrophy of will ' ;   the phrases
represent different aspects of the same psychic fact, as
' convex ' and ' concave ' represent different aspects of the
same geometric fact.   We may therefore claim that the
underlying conception revealed in these lines is that of the
inherent infirmity of human nature as consisting in ' congenital weakness of will '—the same conception which
Methodius and Athanasius had endeavoured to express
under the figure of metaphysical ' disintegration.'

Did Gregory hold the theory of ' Original Guilt ' ?
Certain phrases occurring in his works seem at first sight to
imply that he did.   These phrases include some very definite
and forcible assertions of our unity and solidarity with the
Adam who fell : typical of them is the following :

---

[1] *carmina*, ii. (*poemata historica*), sect. i. 45, lines 95–107 (ii. p. 922) :

ἄλλοτε μέν τε νόῳ χοὸς δάμναται· ἄλλοτε δ' αὖτε
σαρκὶ νόος κρατερῇ ἕσπεται οὐκ ἐθέλων.
ἀλλὰ τὸ μὲν ποθέει, τό γε βέλτερον· ὃ στυγέει δὲ
ἔρδων, δουλοσύνην μύρεται ἀργαλέην,
πατρός τ' ἀρχεγόνοιο πλάνην, καὶ μητρὸς ἀλιτρὴν
πάρφασιν, ἡμετέρης μητέρα μαργοσύης,
καὶ σκολιοῖο δράκοντος ἀτάσθαλον αἱμοβόροιο
ψεῦδος, ὃς ἀνθρώπων τέρπεται ἀμπλακίαις,
καὶ ξύλον, ἠδὲ φυτοῖο βροτῶν δηλήμονα καρπὸν
γεῦσίν τ' οὐλομένην, καὶ θανάτοιο πύλας,
γύμνωσιν μελέων τε παναίσχεα, καὶ παραδείσου
ἠδὲ φυτοῦ ζωῆς ῥίψιν ἀτιμοτάτην.

It may perhaps be claimed for the versions of Gregory's lines given in the
text that they are not more prosaic than the originals.

<Through the sufferings of Christ> we were re-created, not an individual here and there, but all of us who *partook of the same Adam*, who were deceived by the serpent, were slain by sin, were saved once more by the heavenly Adam, and by the Tree of shame were brought back to the Tree of Life, from whence we have fallen.[1]

Together with this may be grouped many other instances of the use of the first person plural (' we ') and even of the first person singular (' I ') [2]—in verbs expressing the idea of the primal sin. The impression created by these turns of phraseology, that Gregory was at least inclined to play with the idea of ' Original Guilt,' is to a certain extent reinforced by passages which speak of the human race as ' condemned' for Adam's fault.[3] But against these references we must set his treatment of infant baptism, any consideration of which must always force the question of the reality of ' Original Guilt' to the front : the crucial passage is, again, to be found in one of his poetical compositions. He tells us that God has provided many helps for our fickle and wayward nature :

Whereof the Laver is one, fount of grace ; for, e'en as the Hebrew
Children escaped the destroyer, by virtue of blood's dread
  anointing
Cleansing the posts of the doors, what time all the first-born of
  Egypt
Fell in the self-same night of alarm, so also meseemeth

---

[1] *or.* xxxiii. 9 (i. p. 609) : αὐτὰ τὰ χριστοῦ πάθη, δι' ὧν ἀνεπλάσθημεν, οὐχ ὁ μὲν, ὁ δ' οὔ, πάντες δὲ οἱ τοῦ αὐτοῦ Ἀδὰμ μετασχόντες, καὶ ὑπὸ τοῦ ὄφεως παραλογισθέντες, καὶ τῇ ἁμαρτίᾳ θανατωθέντες, καὶ διὰ τοῦ ἐπουρανίου Ἀδὰμ ἀνασωθέντες, καὶ πρὸς τὸ ξύλον τῆς ζωῆς ἐπαναχθέντες, διὰ τοῦ ξύλου τῆς ἀτιμίας, ὅθεν ἀποπεπτώκαμεν.

[2] e.g. *or.* xix. 14 (i. p. 372), a paragraph in which every sentence contains this idiom ; *or.* xxii. 13 (i. p. 422) : ἐχρῆν γὰρ, ἐπειδὴ θεότης ἥνωται, διαιρεῖσθαι τὴν ἀνθρωπότητα, καὶ περὶ τὸν νοῦν ἀνοηταίνειν τοὺς τἆλλα σοφούς, καὶ μὴ ὅλον με σώζεσθαι, ὅλον πταίσαντα καὶ κατακριθέντα ἐκ τῆς τοῦ πρωτοπλάστου παρακοῆς (a piece of anti-Apollinarian sarcasm; *v. infra*, p. 291 f) ; *or.* xlv. 8 (i. p. 851) : φεῦ τῆς ἐμῆς ἀσθενείας· ἐμὴ γὰρ ἡ τοῦ προπάτορος (quoted above, p. 284, n. 5) ; *ibid.* 9 (i. p. 852) : μετέλαβον τῆς εἰκόνος (*sc.* τοῦ θεοῦ) καὶ οὐκ ἐφύλαξα : *ibid.* 12 (i. p. 854) : πεσόντας ἡμᾶς ἐκ τῆς ἁμαρτίας τὸ ἀπ' ἀρχῆς.

[3] e.g. *or.* xxxvii. 4 (i. p. 665) : καὶ εἰ ἡ γεῦσις κατέκρινε, πόσῳ μᾶλλον τὸ χριστὸν παθεῖν ἐδικαίωσεν : and *or.* xxxix. 13 (i. p. 685) : <ἵνα> οὕτως ὁ νέος Ἀδὰμ τὸν παλαιὸν ἀνασώσηται, καὶ λυθῇ τὸ κατάκριμα τῆς σαρκός. Notice also the word κατακριθέντα in *or.* xxii. 13 (quoted above).

Here is the Seal of God our defender, *for innocent infants
Only a Seal*, but for grown men a Seal *and a Remedy
potent*.[1]

The significance of the last two lines will be translucently
clear, and doubtless, to those who have been accustomed
to assume that Augustinianism is Catholicism, somewhat
startling : for the poet draws a sharp distinction between
the effects of Adult and those of Infant Baptism, affirming
the former to include both dedication to God and remission
of sin, but the latter to consist in dedication only—which is
precisely the position maintained by the Pelagians in the
next century.[2]   Evidently our author knows nothing of the
idea that newly born babes are, simply in virtue of their
human nature, born guilty of the sin of Adam.   This conclusion is reinforced by the fact that, like his friend and
namesake of Nyssa,[3] he decides the ' eschatological issue '
(which, as we have seen, was now beginning to emerge) by
means of the hypothesis of *Limbo* [4]—another idea which was
advocated by the Pelagians, and as strenuously denounced
by the Africans.[5]   It will therefore be safest to assume
(as in the case of Athanasius, Basil, and Gregory of Nyssa)
that the phrases mentioned above, which identify ' us '

---

[1] *carmina*, i. (*poemata theologica*), sect. i. 9 (*de testamentis et adventu
Christi*), lines 87–92 (ii. p. 252) :

> ὧν ἐν καὶ λοετροῖο βροτοῖς χάρις· ὡς γὰρ ὄλεθρον
> Ἑβραίων ποτὲ παῖδες ὑπέκφυγον αἵματι χριστῷ,
> τὸ φλιὰς ἐκάθηρεν, ὅτ' ὤλετο πρωτογένεθλος
> Αἰγύπτου γενεὴ νυκτὶ μιῇ, ὡς καὶ ἔμοιγε
> σφρηγὶς ἀλεξικάκοιο θεοῦ τόδε, νηπιάχοις μὲν
> σφρηγὶς, ἀεξομένοισι δ' ἄκος καὶ σφρηγὶς ἀρίστη.

(I do not understand the lengthening of the last syllable of νυκτί in
line 90, but give the line as it stands in the Paris edition.)

[2] *v. infra*, Lecture V, p. 345.

[3] *v. supra*, p. 279.

[4] *or*. xl. 23 (i. p. 708) : τοὺς δὲ (that is, those who have not been able
to receive baptism διὰ νηπιότητα—this implies that there were still
some parts of the Church where paedobaptism was unknown—or through
some other involuntary cause) μήτε δοξασθήσεσθαι μήτε κολασθήσεσθαι παρὰ
τοῦ δικαίου κριτοῦ, ὡς ἀσφραγίστους μὲν ἀπονήρους δὲ, ἀλλὰ παθόντας μᾶλλον
τὴν ζημίαν (*i.e.* the lack of baptism) ἢ δράσαντας.   οὐ γὰρ ὅστις οὐ κολάσεως
ἄξιος, ἤδη καὶ τιμῆς· ὥσπερ οὐδὲ ὅστις οὐ τιμῆς, ἤδη καὶ κολάσεως.   I use
the term *Limbo* in the text as a convenient anachronism for expressing the
idea of a future state which is one neither of punishment nor of glory.

[5] *v. infra*, Lecture V, p. 348, n. 2.

with Adam, are no more than highly rhetorical assertions
of the theory of ' Recapitulation.' It will have become clear
in the course of our review that the idea of ' Original
Guilt '—if considered in abstraction from its *psychological*
grounds in the self-condemnation of the ' twice-born ' saint
or converted rake—may be said to have two main *logical*
antecedents, namely, the conception of ' Recapitulation '
(which, if pressed, easily converts itself into ' seminal
identity '), and the belief that baptism is always ' for the
remission of sins,' even when administered to unconscious
infants. But we have seen that Gregory did not hold the
latter view : and, if allowance be made for the vivid modes
of expression natural to an Asian orator, there will be no
reason for supposing that he had in his own mind pressed
the former to its logical conclusion.

Gregory, then, though not a believer in ' Original Guilt,'
is an enthusiastic ' recapitulationist.' In the light of this
fact his opinions with regard to the *fourth* and *fifth* of
the cardinal issues become easily intelligible. The means
whereby ' weakness of will ' is transmitted cannot, for a
believer in ' Recapitulation,' be anything other than physiological heredity.[1] And his characteristic opinion with
regard to the present state of human nature is this—that
man's intellect (νοῦς), as well as his will, emotions, and
physical constitution, has suffered deterioration through the
Fall. It is here that he brings the Fall-doctrine to bear
upon the Apollinarian controversy. Adam sinned with his
mind first of all, in that he mentally denied the supreme
claim of God's command upon his loyalty and obedience.
Hence, in virtue of Adam's ' recapitulation ' of humanity
within himself, the human mind as such became in some
undefined manner subject to the consequences of the Fall.
Gregory never faces the question, What precisely are the
consequences of the Fall in the purely mental sphere ?
but we may suppose that he means in a general sense error
and delusion. In order, therefore, that man as a whole
might be redeemed, it was necessary that the Saviour should
assume human intellectual faculties together with the rest

[1] *cf.* p. 198.

of man's nature [1] ; ' for that which was not assumed could not have been healed.' [2]

We need only point out, without commenting upon, the fact that the conception of redemption here pre-supposed appears, as in the writings of Athanasius and Gregory of Nyssa, to be that of union with the Incarnate Logos, and ultimate ' deification,' through sacramental reception of Him in the Eucharist. This is not, indeed, expressly stated : but it is difficult, if not impossible, to see how the assumption by the Logos of a human νοῦς could have the effect of Redeeming the νοῦς of mankind in general, unless the final ' recapitulation ' of our race in Christ is conceived as consummated through the sacramental incorporation of its wayward and sinful individuals into Him. It may, indeed, be said that healing and sanctification through sacraments constitute the goal to which the *medical* way of conceiving ' innate sinfulness ' favoured by Greek thought naturally leads, just as juridical absolution and ' justification ' are the end which the *forensic* conception more congenial to the Latin mind presupposes.

' THE DEVIL'S RIGHTS '

If Gregory of Nazianzus died in A.D. 390, as seems most probable, the end of his life may be regarded as roughly synchronising with the beginning of Augustine's Christian career [3] ; so that the consideration of his writings forms the natural *terminus ad quem* for the present section of our enquiry. We may appropriately pause at this point, before taking up the thread of the ' African ' or ' twice-born ' development of the Fall-tradition, to explain our deliberate

[1] The classical passages for this anti-Apollinarian use of the Fall-doctrine are to be found in the two Epistles to Cledonius, *epp*. ci., cii. (ii. p. 83 ff) ; *cf.* also *or*. xxii. 13 (i. p. 422), a part of which is quoted above (p. 289, n. 2), and *carmen de se ipso*, line 167 ff. (ii. p. 874) : τέμνουσι δ', ὡς θεόν μου, καὶ θεοῦ μέγαν βροτὸν (*i.e.* ' exalted humanity ') ἄνουν τιθέντες, ὡς ἄνου 'Αδὰμ πεπτωκότος.

[2] *ep*. ci. (ii. p. 87) : τὸ γὰρ ἀπρόσληπτον, ἀθεράπευτον· ὃ δὲ ἥνωται τῷ θεῷ, τοῦτο καὶ σώζεται : a celebrated epigram which Tixeront (*op. cit.* ii. p. 115) justly describes as a ' sentence lapidaire.'

[3] Augustine was baptised in A.D. 387.

omission of any mention of a theory which may well appear at first sight to form an integral part of the subject-matter of our research, and which exercised a powerful influence over Christian soteriology for a thousand years—the theory, namely, that by virtue of Adam's sin the Devil acquired legal or quasi-legal rights of property over mankind, rights which the justice of God forbade Him to disregard and which consequently had to be bought out in some way or other.[1] On this was founded the popular view of the Atonement, which saw in the death of Christ the payment of His life as a ' ransom ' to the Devil, designed to induce the latter to surrender his commercially conceived interest in the posses- sion of human souls. The soteriological scheme so consti- tuted can claim the support of many illustrious teachers, belonging both to Eastern and to Western Christendom, amongst whom may be enumerated Irenaeus (its apparent originator[2]), Origen (though he may not have regarded it as much more than an elaborate metaphor[3]), Basil, Gregory of Nyssa, Tertullian, Augustine ; though sturdy protests were raised against it by the otherwise unknown author Adei- mantius, Gregory of Nazianzus, and John of Damascus.[4]

We have left this once popular theory on one side—not so much because of its bizarre and mythological nature, or of the childishly immoral idea to which it gave birth, that of a trick played by God upon the Devil in offering him Christ's Humanity as his prey without telling him that it veiled the Godhead—nor yet because of the fact that

[1] Detailed histories of the growth of this theory may be found in H. Rashdall, *The Idea of Atonement in Christian Theology* (1919), pp. 243 ff., 259, 303 ff., 311, 313, 332 ; J. Rivière, *Le dogme de la rédemption*, I. (*Essai d'étude historique*) (1905), cc. xxi–xxiv. See also A. Ritschl, *Rechtfertigung und Versöhnung* (1882), i. pp. 16–19, and A. Sabatier, *La doctrine de l'expiation et son évolution historique* (1903), p. 47 ff.

[2] Rashdall (*op. cit.* p. 245) suggests that this theory may have been derived by Irenaeus from the doctrine of Marcion. According to the latter ' it was because, by bringing about the death of Jesus, the God of the Jews —the generally just but not benevolent Demiurge—had violated his own laws, that it became just for the true and benevolent God to set man free from the Demiurge.' Rashdall adds ' Irenaeus simply substituted the devil for the Demiurge.' The dualistic affinities of the conception are in any case obvious.

[3] So Rashdall (p. 259, n. 1).

[4] For references, see the works of Rashdall and Rivière, mentioned above.

Anselm's *Cur Deus homo* eventually drove it from the field
of Christian thought, so that, whether or not it was ever
believed *ubique*, it cannot even assert a claim to fulfil the
test of *semper* ; but rather because it is completely unknown
to the New Testament. Though our Lord speaks of men
as subject to the domination of evil spirits,[1] He gives no
countenance to the monstrous notion of the Devil's ' rights ' ;
the power of Satan is always regarded by Him as a lawless
usurpation. Nor does He anywhere connect the beginnings
of such usurpation with the sin of Adam ; if the simile of
the ' house swept and garnished ' may be pressed, He
affirms them rather to be due to the folly or weakness of
the individual. The theory is merely a mistaken inference
from the use of the word ' ransom ' in Mark x. 45, and forms
an apt illustration of the dangers involved in riding a
metaphor to death. It is a parasite on, and not an organic
branch of, the genuine and Pauline Fall-tradition, only
deserving of notice in so far as its tenacious vigour is an
index of the vitality inherent in the trunk to which it clings ;
and we need not, therefore, complicate our history by taking
further account of it.

(b) The ' African ' Theory down to the End of the pre-Augustinian Period

In accordance with the plan outlined above, our story
now returns to the West and to the third century A.D.,
with the object of tracing the development of the more
severe or ' twice-born ' version of the Fall-doctrine, from
the ' point of bifurcation ' between the two presentations
of this doctrine marked by the writings of Tertullian and
Origen, down to the end of the pre-Augustinian period.
The writers whose opinions will claim attention in this
section of our narrative are Cyprian, Lactantius, Hilary of
Poitiers, Ambrose, and the anonymous commentator on the
Pauline Epistles known by the sobriquet of ' Ambrosiaster.'
The evidence provided by the first three of these writers
may be summed up in a few sentences, whilst the last two
will require a somewhat more detailed treatment, in view

---

[1] *v. supra*, Lecture III, p. 110 f.

of their position in time as the immediate precursors of Augustine, and of the peculiar influence which they (in particular Ambrose, as the bishop who instructed and baptised Augustine) appear to have exercised upon his thought.

(1) *St. Cyprian* (beheaded A.D. 258). The extant writings of this illustrious prelate and martyr, the third [1] great African lawyer to embrace Christianity, contain half a dozen or so of references to Adam's sin and its melancholy consequences, which, whilst generally in accord with the views of Tertullian, Cyprian's 'master,' [2] add no fresh developments to them. There is, however, one passage of great significance, which represents the first explicit emergence of the idea of 'Original *Guilt*' as the theoretical justification of infant baptism. We have spoken above of the stimulating influence exerted by this custom on the growth of a doctrine of birth-sin or birth-pollution [3] ; and we have noted the fact that Tertullian's elaboration of the doctrine of 'seminal identity,' on the basis of his 'traducianist' psychology, naturally pointed in the direction of a theory of all Adam's descendants as hereditarily invested with the legal responsibility for his Fall, a responsibility which to the mind of a juristic theologian might seem to constitute the 'pollution' apparently presupposed by infant baptism. But Tertullian, because of his dread of increasing the possibility of *post*-baptismal sin, strongly objects to paedobaptism, and hence never explicitly develops the idea of Original Guilt. Cyprian, disregarding on this point the authority of 'the Master,' took a step which has proved momentous for Western thought concerning birth-sin and baptism when he wrote his fifty-sixth Epistle, in the name of himself and of a Council of sixty-six bishops, to a certain bishop Fidus, who had thought that the baptism of an infant should be delayed until the eighth day after its birth, on the analogy of the Jewish rule regarding circumcision. Cyprian urges that, on the contrary, baptism

---

[1] The first two were Minucius Felix and Tertullian.

[2] Jerome tells us (*de viris ill.* 53) that Cyprian used to spend some time every day in reading the works of Tertullian, demanding the volume from his secretary with the words ' da magistrum.'

[3] *v. supra*, p. 220 ff.

should be administered as soon as possible after birth ; the passage of immediate interest for our purpose runs as follows :

Assuredly, if the remission of sins is given even to the worst offenders and to those who have previously sinned much against God, when afterwards they have believed, and if no one is forbidden the reception of baptism and of grace, how much more ought an infant not to be forbidden, who being newly born has committed no sin, *save that being carnally born according to Adam he has by his first birth contracted the infection of the ancient death ?* and, indeed, an infant approaches to receive the remission of sins more easily through this very fact, that *the sins which are remitted unto him* <in baptism> are *not his own but another's*.[1]

Here it is clearly taught (a) that to be carnally born as a descendant of Adam involves participating in a hereditary infection by sin, (b) that the sin in question, which is remitted in baptism, is not the newly born's own, but the sin of ' another '—that is, presumably, of Adam. The thought of the passage is obviously confused, and oscillates illogically between what we have called the medical and the forensic ways of regarding sin [2] ; but such a confusion, as we shall see, is inherent in the idea of Original Guilt. It is certainly curious that the transgression of Adam, the guilt whereof is said to be forgiven to infants in baptism, should be described in the plural number as *peccata* ; but the phrase is no doubt chosen in order to avoid admitting an essential difference between the spiritual effects of infant baptism and of adult baptism, both alike conveying the *remissa peccatorum* ; and if challenged on the point, Cyprian would doubtless have contended, like Augustine later,[3] that Adam's primal sin

[1] *ep.* lxiv. (Hartel's text, in Vienna *Corpus Script. Eccl. Lat.* III. 2) : ' porro autem si etiam gravissimis delictoribus et in Deum multum ante peccantibus, cum postea crediderint, remissa peccatorum datur et a baptismo adque (= atque) gratia nemo prohibetur, quanto magis prohiberi non debet infans qui recens natus nihil peccavit, nisi quod secundum Adam carnaliter natus contagium mortis antiquae prima nativitate contraxit, qui ad remissam peccatorum accipiendam hoc ipso facilius accedit quod illi remittuntur non propria sed aliena peccata.' This passage was read out, with great rhetorical effect, by St. Augustine, in the anti-Pelagian sermon preached by him on June 25, 413, in the ' basilica Maiorum ' at Carthage (*serm.* ccxciv. ; *cf. de gestis Pel.* 25).

[2] *Cf.* pp. 133, 241. The passage quoted above almost, but not quite, falls into the absurdity of alluding to the ' remission ' of an ' infection.'

[3] See Lecture V, p. 364.

included within itself several distinct sins, such as pride, greediness, disobedience, and others.

(2) *Lactantius*. Curiously enough, the fourth great member of the African succession of jurists turned theologians, Lucius Caecilius Firmianus Lactantius (b. *c.* A.D. 250, d. 325), represents, in regard to the development of Fall-speculation, an abrupt reversion to an ultra-' Hellenic ' and ' minimising ' position comparable to that of the Alexandrine Clement. This is, perhaps, the more surprising because Lactantius appears to possess a good share of the fanaticism characteristic of the African Church, the general tone of his treatise *de mortibus persecutorum*, in which he narrates with evident gusto the miserable ends of the Emperors who had oppressed the Church, being strongly reminiscent of the conclusion of Tertullian's *de spectaculis*, the famous passage in which the father of African theology anticipates with glee the sight, which he expects to enjoy at the Last Day, of pagan kings and philosophers writhing in eternal flames.[1] Nevertheless, though in his systematic defence and exposition of Christianity, *divinarum institutionum libri vii*, he duly narrates the substance of the Scriptural Fall-Story, he noticeably refrains from attaching any theory of ' Original Sin ' to it, and attributes only external and mechanical consequences to the Fall, such as man's loss of physical immortality and of Paradise.[2]   His own view of the ground of human sin is that man is naturally prone to evil because of the earthly or physical elements in his nature ; and though he uses the actual phrase *depravatio naturae <humanae>*, the *depravatio* is illogically regarded as inherent in the necessary conditions of man's being.[3]   He does not appear to face the

---

[1] Gibbon's comments on this passage (*Decline and Fall of the Roman Empire*, ed. J. B. Bury, ii. p. 27) are well known, and not unjustifiable.

[2] *op. cit.* ii. 13 ; see also *epitom. div. inst.* 27.   *div. inst.* ii. 15 contains an original version of the ' angel-story ' of Gen. vi. which asserts that the ' sons of God ' were sent to earth by the Lord Himself, in order to be guardians of the human race, but that through their sin they became daemons themselves and begat daemons.

[3] *de ira dei*, c. xv. (ed. Brandt, *Corpus Script. Eccl. Lat.* XXVII) : ' sic et nos ex duobus aeque repugnantibus conpacti sumus, anima et corpore : quorum alterum caelo adscribitur, quia tenue est et intractabile, alterum terrae, quia conprehensibile est : alterum solidum est et aeternum, alterum fragile atque mortale.   ergo alteri bonum adhaeret, alteri malum,

fact that this position makes the Creator ultimately responsible for man's sin.[1]   The theology of Lactantius is in general somewhat eccentric and defective—he was better at attacking Paganism than at expounding Christianity—and it would therefore be unjustifiable to cite his words as evidence for a supposed reaction against the Fall-theory at the end of the third or the beginning of the fourth century.   As in the earlier case of Clement of Alexandria, it is probably truer to suggest that even a scanty and (so to speak) grudging mention of the Adam-story, by an author whose characteristic positions demand the uncompromising maintenance of free-will, is an unconscious testimony to the amount of general acceptance which the Fall-theory had obtained ; though this doctrine is alien to his whole way of thinking, it is now too firmly rooted in Christian tradition for him to be able to ignore it altogether.

(3) *St. Hilary of Poitiers* (d. A.D. 368).   However this may be, it is at least certain that we have no evidence for any further development of the specifically ' African ' Fall-doctrine until we come to the writings of Hilary of Poitiers, in the fourth century.   At this point our narrative leaves Africa, the original home of the ' twice-born ' doctrine, for Western Europe, not to return until we come to consider the final formulation of this doctrine by the last and greatest of the African doctors, St. Augustine himself.   The passing allusions made by Hilary to Adam's sin and its consequences are, on the whole, in line with Tertullian's doctrine, with the

---

alteri lux vita iustitia, alteri tenebrae mors iniustitia.   *hinc extitit in hominibus naturae suae depravatio,* ut esset necesse constitui legem qua possent et vitia prohiberi et virtutis officia imperari.'   (This position is described as ' illogical ' in the text, because a ' depravation ' implies a previous good state of that which has suffered the depravation.)   c. xviii. contains an expression of the same idea—' sed ideo <homo> procedit in vitium, quia *de terrena fragilitate permixtus* non potest id quod a deo sumpsit incorruptum purumque servare.'   Lactantius, in fact, shares the view which we have already found in the Book of Job (see Lecture I, p. 17) and shall find again in the writings of Dr. F. R. Tennant (see Additional Note E), the view, namely, that man's moral weakness is simply due to his creaturely nature, and that there is no more to be said on the subject.

[1] See Additional Note E (' Dr. F. R. Tennant's Alternative Theory of the Origin of Sin '), p. 530.

important exception that ' traducianism ' is emphatically repudiated.[1] The *vitium originis*[2] (we notice that this phrase, taken over from Tertullian, has now become all but technical) is not transmitted directly from the soul of the progenitor to the soul of the offspring, but is acquired by the newly created soul through its union with the flesh[3] ; hence the flesh is the seat of ' Original Sin,' a theory which represents a return to the strictly Pauline view. But, though the mould in which the idea of ' seminal identity ' had been shaped into consistency and toughness is thus discarded, the idea itself stands fast ; and there are two or three passages which seem to imply that the human race was in Adam, or was Adam, when he fell—such as the following ' in unius Adae errore omne hominum genus aberravit.'[4] It is, however, clear that this Father took no very great interest in the theology of the Fall and its conse-quences, and the aggregate amount of space occupied by his few incidental allusions to the subject is almost infini-tesimal in comparison with the length of his great treatise on the Holy Trinity and of his polemical writings against the Arians. Not as an elaborator of the Fall-doctrine, but as the ally of Athanasius and the champion of the Nicene Christology in the West, did Hilary earn the titles conceded him by both East and West of Doctor and Confessor of the Church.

(4) *St. Ambrose* (bishop of Milan, A.D. 374–397). This great man is popularly conceived as illustrious through practical rather than through intellectual gifts—as a powerful administrator, a zealous pastor, a princely prelate, a friend and on occasion a severe monitor of emperors, an organiser

---

[1] *tract. in* cxviii. *ps., litt.* iv. : ' anima, quae alterius originis est, terrae corporis adhaesisse creditur'; *de trin.* x. 20 : ' cum anima omnis opus Dei sit, carnis vero generatio semper ex carne sit ' ; *ibid.* 22 : ' <anima> nunquam ab homine gignentium originibus praebetur.'

[2] *tract. in* cxviii. *ps., litt.* xiv. 20 : ' natura quidem et origo carnis suae cum detinebat : sed voluntas et religio cor eius ex eo in quo manebat *originis vitio* ad iustificationum opera declinat.'

[3] So I understand the difficult passage *comm. in Matthaeum*, x. 23, 24.

[4] *ibid.* xviii. 6 ; the context contains what appears to be the first instance of the application of the Parable of the Lost Sheep to the Fall of man. *Cf.* also *tract. in* cxxxvi. *ps.* 5 : ' quisquis ergo *in crimine primi parentis Adae* exsulem se factum illius Sion recordabitur . . .' ; *ibid.* 7 : 'qui *in Adam* extorres se factos esse caelestis Ierusalem meminerunt.'

of liturgical worship, rather than as a learned doctor or subtle theologian. It is doubtless true that no one original enrichment of Christian thought can be placed to his credit : but the part which he played in the elaboration of the ' maximising ' version of the Fall-doctrine was of no little importance, inasmuch as in his mind the cardinal elements of this version were for the first time assembled and held side by side, though not yet wrought into a single coherent unity. Though his writings do not contain a systematic treatise on the doctrine of the Fall (the book *de paradiso* is rather a mystical commentary on the whole narrative of Gen. ii. and iii. than an exposition of the ' Fall ' in particular), yet his numerous allusions to the subject when collected together give us an ultra-' African ' type of Fall-theory, which may not unreasonably be described as Augustinianism before Augustine. If we remember that it was in great part the attraction of Ambrose's majestic personality which drew Augustine through his great spiritual crisis to Catholic Christianity, and the hand of Ambrose which baptised and anointed him,[1] we shall find it difficult not to believe that the brilliant young neophyte must have drunk in Ambrose's teaching on the Fall together with the rest of his dogmatic exposition of the Faith, through private catechetical instruction or through the homilies which the great bishop was accustomed to deliver in the basilica of Milan and to which the not-yet-converted Augustine listened entranced. If this is so, the place occupied by Ambrose in the history of the ' maximising ' Fall-doctrine may be defined as that of the workman who collected the materials out of which the more gifted master-builder Augustine constructed the finished edifice.

Ambrose is the first of the Latin Fathers to teach in unequivocal terms the doctrine of the ' Original Righteousness ' or ' Perfection ' of man, an idea which seems to be the necessary starting-point of the ' maximising ' Fall-theory, considered as a logical scheme ; for only if the original state of man be made one of unqualified perfection and bliss is it possible to represent the primal transgression

---

[1] *Cf.* S. Aug. *Conf.* v. 13, 14 ; vi. 4 ; ix. 5 ; *c. Iulian.* i. 4, 10 ; *op. imp. c. Iulian.* i. 2.

as a sin against the fullest possible light, as an act of wanton, unmotived, inexcusable malice, and therefore as invested with an infinite degree of guilt. He tells us that Adam in Paradise was a ' heavenly being,' [1] ' breathing ethereal air,' [2] like unto an angel,[3] exempt from the cares and weariness of this life,[2] resplendent with celestial grace and accustomed to speak face to face with God,[4] endowed from the moment of his creation with that perfect balance of reason, will, and appetite [5] which fallen man can only recover by painful effort and the continuous assistance of the Holy Spirit.[6] It is a remarkable fact that this Rabbinical figment was, as we have already pointed out, being propagated by Gregory of Nyssa in the East just about the same time that Ambrose appeared as its champion in the West [7] : and it would seem probable that the same ultimate cause lay behind both of these happenings, namely, the invisible pressure of the second great wave of Oriental dualism which was then silently flooding Europe, Manicheism. We have already, in speaking of Gnosticism, called attention to the reaction which the impact of dualistic theories tends to stimulate within the Church : the affirmation of the co-eternity of good and evil inevitably drives the mind of the Christian society back upon the principle implied in its fundamental

[1] *in ps.* cxviii. *expos. serm.* xv. 36 : ' Adam cum in paradiso esset coelestis erat.'

[2] *ibid.* iv. 5 : ' beatissimus auram carpebat aetheream, curas vitae huius et taedia nesciebat.'

[3] *de parad.* ix. 42.

[4] *in ps.* xliii. *enarr.* 75 : ' in conspectu Dei erat Adam, in paradiso vigebat, coelesti gratia refulgebat, loquebatur cum Deo.'

[5] *expos. ev. sec. Luc.* vii. 142 : ' quod utique tunc facit, cum caro in naturam regressa vigoris sui agnoscit altricem, atque ausu deposito contumaciae moderantis animae coniugatur arbitrio : qualis fuit cum inhabitanda paradisi secreta suscepit, antequam veneno pestiferi serpentis infecta sacrilegam famem sciret.'

[6] Note that Ambrose follows the exegetical tradition (for which *v. supra*, pp. 192, 251) which identifies the ' Paradise ' of Gen. iii. with that of 2 Cor. xii. 2 : *in ps.* cxviii. *expos. serm.* iv. 2 : ' denique eiectus de paradiso, hoc est, ex illo sublimi et caelesti loco ad quem raptus est Paulus sive in corpore sive extra corpus nesciens.'

[7] It may be noted that Ambrose, unlike Augustine, had an excellent knowledge of the Greek language, and was much influenced by Origen and Basil : it is possible that he may have derived the idea of ' original perfection ' directly from the Cappadocians.

monotheism, that of the absoluteness and necessity of good
and of the *contingency* of evil, a principle which since the
Maccabean age has been embodied in the Fall-theory.
And doubtless it was the peculiar vigour and compactness
of the doctrines of Mani,[1] as contrasted with the vagueness
and variety of the systems collectively known as Gnosticism,
which impelled Gregory of Nyssa in the East, and Ambrose
in the West, all unconsciously to accentuate the idea of the
Fall by prefixing to it the idea, borrowed from Jewish
legend, of a state of paradisal ' perfection,' which goes far
beyond the conception of that ' infancy ' which was
attributed by the earliest Greek-Christian writers to the
ancestors of the race.   It is interesting, however, to note
that (if a passage in one of Ambrose's letters is to be taken
as containing his permanent thought on the subject) man's
' Original Righteousness ' was not, in this Father's view,
destroyed at one blow by the first transgression, as Augustine
and Calvin were later to maintain ; it became progressively
diminished in each succeeding generation of Adam's
descendants and eventually died out altogether, in much
the same way that the attractive force of a magnet holding
a series of iron rings becomes weaker in each ring that is
added to the series.[2]

The influence of this significant addition of ' Original
Righteousness ' to the growing fabric of the ' African '
theory is reflected in a terminological tendency exactly
analogous to that which we have noted in the writings of
the Cappadocian Fathers—the tendency, namely, to speak
of Adam's sin not merely as a ' transgression ' (*praevaricatio*,
which literally means ' walking crookedly,' and is an almost
exact rendering of the Scriptural and primitive term
παράβασις) but as a ' Fall,' or *lapsus*.[3] We have already

---

[1] For an authoritative summary of Manicheism, based upon the latest
researches, see F. C. Burkitt, *The Religion of the Manichees* (Donnellan
Lectures for 1924).

[2] *ep*. xlv. 14 : *cf*. St. Athanasius, *de incarn*. 12 (commented on above,
p. 262).

[3] *Cf. hexaemeron* vi. 42 : ' secundum hunc imaginem (*sc*. Dei) Adam
ante peccatum : sed ubi *lapsus* est, deposuit imaginem caelestis, sumpsit
terrestris effigiem ' ; *de excessu fratr. sui Satyri*, ii. 6 : ' *lapsus* sum in
Adam ' (see below, p. 305, n. 4, for the rest of the passage) ; *in ps.* cxviii.
expos. xxii. 30 : ' suscipe me in carne, quae in Adam *lapsa* est ' ; *apol.*

pointed out that the idea of a *failure* on the part of man to pursue an upward line of moral progress marked out for him by his Maker is very different from the idea of a *fall* from a pre-existing condition of moral and spiritual perfection ; and it is hardly necessary to add that the former conception of the primal catastrophe is not contradicted by the information given us by science with regard to the origin and primitive condition of our race, whereas the latter would seem in the light of modern knowledge to be purely mythological. It is fair to observe that the use of the term ' fall ' (that is, of the verb *labi* and its cognate substantive *lapsus*) in this connexion is not predominant in Ambrose ; and it is not until the close of the patristic period that *lapsus* takes the place of *praevaricatio* as the technical designation in Latin of the primordial sin.

The allusions in St. Ambrose's writings to ' Original Sin,' in the sense of the inherited bias towards evil, are so numerous that it is impossible to do more than summarise their general import.[1] The phrase ' all we men are born under sin '[2] gives the key-note of his thought on this matter ; and the ' sin,' or ' danger of sinning,'[3] which dogs man's path from his birth is described as ' the iniquity of our heels, which compasseth us about . . . of that heel which was bitten by the serpent, and causes us to go limping '[4] —as the net in which Adam enveloped his whole posterity,[5] or the chain with which he bound the human race [6]—as the inheritance of a *vitium* [7] (Tertullian's and Hilary's word)— as the entailed curse, which makes our flesh to be sin.[8] But the question, what is the precise psychological account to be given of this *vitium*, or curse, is left in judicious vagueness.

David, xi. : ' nec conceptus iniquitatis exsors est, quoniam et parentes non carent *lapsu* ' ; *apol. David altera*, iii. 19 : ' post primi hominis *lapsum* ' ; *de paradis*. xiii. 62 : ' <Adam> vitio uxoris *lapsus* est ' ; *de Cain et Abel*, i. : ' Adam et Evae *lapsus*.'

[1] Some of these passages were collected by St. Augustine, *de pecc. orig.* xli.

[2] *de poenitent*. I. iii. 13 : ' omnes homines sub peccato nascimur.'

[3] *in ps*. xlviii. *enarr*. 9.

[4] *ibid*. 8, 9.

[5] *in ps*. cxviii. *expos*. 47 ; *ep*. lxxiii. 9.

[6] *ep*. lxxiii. 10.

[7] *in ps*. xliii. *enarr*. 75.

[8] *in ps*. cxviii. *expos*. 21.

When he does raise it, he shows the influence of that curious vein of subconscious feeling which we have noted as running all through the history of the Fall-doctrine, a feeling which may be described as a horror or phobia of sex. It is not surprising to discover traces of this feeling in the writings of so prominent a champion of virginity and asceticism ; and the reader will doubtless remember what has been said above concerning the tendencies of the ' twice-born ' temperament in regard to the matter.[1] Hence in one passage [2] he toys with the repulsive notion, already suggested by Origen,[3] of a ' bad *mana* ' inherent in the physiological processes of conception and birth ; and in the same passage he implies that sexual intercourse is itself sinful, so that we are ' born in ' the ' sin ' of our parents. This leads on to the lamentable suggestion that the miraculous birth of Christ was necessary in order to the avoidance of the physical or quasi-physical pollutions inherent in normal birth. Full use is made of the familiar proof-texts, Ps. li. 5, ' Behold, I was shapen in wickedness,' and the Septuagintal mistranslation of Job, ' There is no one free from defilement, not even if his life has been but a day upon the earth.' [4] Nevertheless, the wound of man's nature, whatever its kind and seat, does not abolish free-will or reponsibility ; and it is impossible not to appreciate the manliness and common-sense of Ambrose's declaration, ' Let him not fear the danger of heredity, who desires to hold the standing-ground of virtue.' [5]

In view of the general character and tone of Ambrose's Fall-doctrine as indicated by these preliminary observations, we shall naturally expect to come across some strong affirmations of ' Original Guilt.' It is true that the context of the passage last cited contains a declaration that ' the iniquity of our heels,' which is identified with the sin of Adam or its inherited results, will not be laid to our charge at the Day of Judgment—a declaration which is clearly tantamount to a denial of our personal responsibility for the first sin.[6] But we may set against this isolated utterance

---

[1] See Lecture III, p. 155.   [2] *apol. David*, xi.
[3] *v. supra*, p. 224.   [4] *v. supra*, p. 224, n. 2.
[5] *in ps.* xlviii. *enarr.* 9.   [6] *ibid.*

other passages which with equal clearness affirm this idea, together with its logical foundation of ' seminal identity.' In the writings of the great bishop of Milan the theory that we all were in Adam and were Adam, and therefore fell in his Fall, or ' sinned in ' him, attains to conscious and explicit formulation.   There is no mistaking the significance of such passages as this : ' Assuredly we all sinned in the first man, and by the inheritance of his nature there has been transfused from that one man into all an inheritance of *guilt*. . . . So then Adam is in each one of us ; for in him *human nature itself sinned.*' [1] (We notice in this last clause the first appearance of a refined form of the theory of ' seminal identity,' which sublimates the concrete individual Adam into the abstract universal of ' humanity,' and regards this universal as having somehow ' sinned ' ; this is a thought which runs through the whole subsequent history of the Western theology of sin and redemption, finding its latest expression in Dr. R. C. Moberly's great work on the Atonement.[2])   Equally striking utterances of the same view are the following : ' Adam existed, and in him we all existed. Adam perished, and in him all perished ' [3] ; and ' In Adam I fell, in Adam I was cast out of Paradise, in Adam I died ; how may God recall me, unless He find me in <the second> Adam, justified in Christ, even as I was rendered subject to guilt, and the destined prey of death, in the first Adam ? ' [4]   Here the full implications of Irenaeus' ' recapitulation '-theory are drawn out with a plainness from which its original author would, perhaps, have shrunk.[5]   It is one of the many paradoxes

[1] *apol. David altera*, 71 : ' nempe omnes in primo homine peccavimus, et per naturae successionem *culpae* quoque ab uno in omnes transfusa successio est . . . Adam ergo in singulis nobis est. in illo enim *conditio humana deliquit*, quia per unum in omnes pertransivit peccatum ' ; *cf.* also *ibid.* 69 : ' cui se fateatur noster David non solum in se ipso, sed etiam *in primo homine peccasse*, dum praecepta divina temerantur.'

[2] R. C. Moberly, *Atonement and Personality* (1904), p. 88 f.

[3] *expos. ev. sec. Luc.* vii. 234 : ' fuit Adam, et in illo fuimus omnes ; periit Adam, et in illo omnes perierunt.'

[4] *de excess. fratris sui Satyri*, ii. 6 : ' lapsus sum in Adam, de paradiso eiectus in Adam, mortuus in Adam ; quomodo revocet, nisi me in Adam invenerit, ut in illo culpae obnoxium, morti debitum, ita in Christo iustificatum ? '

[5] *v. supra*, p. 197.

revealed by a close study of the history of dogma, and one of
the many facts which warn us against an over-rigid classification of primitive Christian thinkers, that the idea of
' Original Guilt,' which became the most characteristic
constituent of the African and Latin presentation of the
Fall-doctrine should have been suggested in the first
instance by a theologian so typically Hellenic in thought
and feeling as the great second-century bishop of Lyons.

Like Hilary, Ambrose finds himself able to hold the
theory of the identity of the race with its first father, whilst
discarding the ' traducianism ' which in Tertullian's thought
had supported and reinforced this theory. So far as
Ambrose is concerned, we may safely attribute this
phenomenon to the fact that (as we have just suggested) the
identity of mankind with Adam is ceasing, in his mind, to
be a merely material or ' seminal ' identity, and is becoming
a logical or metaphysical identity ; following, we may
suppose, the lead of those Fathers who had recognised that
the Hebrew $'\bar{A}dh\bar{a}m$ merely means ' man,' [1] he seems to
think of Adam as (so to speak) the Platonic Idea of man, as
hypostatised ' human nature,' *conditio humana*. It would
not be germane to this historical portion of our enquiry to
raise the question whether the statement that a hypostatised
class-concept ' sinned,' and so infected the particulars subsumed under it with sin, is ultimately intelligible or not.

It is hardly necessary to add that in the thought of
Ambrose the divinely appointed remedy for the hereditary
disease of human nature is baptismal regeneration. We
may note that in the treatise *de mysteriis* [2] he seems to ad-
vocate the curious view that ' original guilt ' is remitted by
the liturgical washing of the neophyte's feet after baptism,
or at least that this was effected in the case of the Apostles
through the washing of their feet by our Lord, as narrated
in St. John xiii. 1–11.

Though they have no bearing on the logical structure

---

[1] *v. supra*, pp. 192, n. 2, 203, 229.

[2] *de myst.* vi. 32 : ' mundus erat Petrus, sed plantam lavare debebat ;
habebat enim primi hominis de successione peccatum, quando eum sup-
plantavit serpens, et persuasit errorem. ideo planta eius abluitur, *ut
haereditaria peccata tollantur* ; nostra enim propria per baptismum
relaxantur.'

of Ambrose's Fall-doctrine, we may notice here two mythological decorations of the Adam-story which occur in his
works, and which illustrate the fact that even after two
centuries of gradual crystallisation the tradition was still
plastic enough to admit of *haggadic* additions at the will of
each of its exponents. The first is the curious idea that
Adam, after his expulsion from Paradise, was banished to
a ' castellum,' to do penance for his sin [1] ; he is also said to
have been clothed with skins and not with silk, for the same
reason, the skins being apparently conceived as a kind of
hair-shirt.[2] The second is a belief which still survives as an
artistic convention ; this is the idea that Adam was buried
on the hill which was afterwards to be consecrated by the
Passion of the Son of God, immediately under the spot upon
which the Cross was destined to be reared, an idea from
which has sprung the familiar custom of portraying a skull
as lying at the base of the Cross, in painted or sculptured
representations of the Crucifixion.[3] It is fair to add that
this is only mentioned as a possible opinion. This drapery
of folk-lore which clings about the developed Fall-doctrine,
even in the last half of the fourth century A.D., shows that
the pseudepigraphic and Rabbinical Jewish writings still
exercised a certain influence upon Christian thought, and
that the sentimental ties which had bound the Catholic
Church to its Jewish mother were even at this date not
completely severed.

(5) '*Ambrosiaster.*' This writer [4] clearly indicates by
his comments on Rom. v. vi. vii. that he accepts the idea
of ' Original Sin ' ; but he has only one sentence which
(apparently) implies the idea of ' Original Guilt.' The
sentence to which we refer is, nevertheless, of the most

---

[1] *in ps.* cxviii. *expos.* 23 ; *in ps.* xxxvi. *enarr.* 20.

[2] *de poenitent.* II. xi. 99.

[3] *ep.* lxxi. 10 ; *in Luc.* x. 114. Maldonatus, commenting on Matt.
xxvii. 33, gives a list of other Fathers who held the same opinion. Louis
Ginzberg (*Monatsschrift für Gesch. u. Wissensch. Judentums*, xliii. 69 ff.)
has shown that this story is a Christianised version of the Jewish legend
that the body of Adam was compounded from dust gathered on the future
site of the altar of burnt-sacrifice.

[4] For a discussion of the question of his identity see A. Souter, *A Study
of Ambrosiaster* (Cambridge Texts and Studies), 1905, which contains a
full bibliography.

crucial importance in the development of the ' twice-born '
Fall-theory, because Ambrosiaster thereby provided, perhaps unwittingly, the doctrine of ' Original Guilt ' with
what it had hitherto lacked, namely, a Scriptural proof-text
to be its formal basis : the ignorance of Greek now prevalent
in the West, and the consequent inability of many Latin
theologians to read the actual words of the New Testament,
effectually screened the fact that the supposed proof-text
rested upon a blunder in translation.   Its relevant portions
run as follows :

In whom, that is, in Adam, *all sinned*.   The Apostle said
' in whom ' in the masculine gender (*in quo*) although he is speaking about the woman, for this reason, that his reference is to the
whole race of man, not to the particular sex <which as a matter
of fact sinned first>.   So then it is plain that all have sinned
in Adam as in a lump (*quasi in massa*) ; for all the children whom
Adam begat, having been himself corrupted by the woman
(*ipsa*) through sin, have been born under sin.   From him therefore all are sinners, because from him are we all ; for Adam
lost the gift of God when he transgressed, having become unworthy to eat of the tree of life, so that he died.[1]

The cardinal error in this sentence lies in the mistranslation of St. Paul's phrase ἐφ' ᾧ πάντες ἥμαρτον, ' for
that all sinned ' (R.V.), as though it were ἐν ᾧ πάντες ἥμαρτον,
' in whom, *sc.* the " one man " just mentioned, all sinned.'
Ambrosiaster is, of course, relying on a Latin version which
renders ἐφ' ᾧ as *in quo*, a translation which has been perpetuated in the Vulgate.   This rendering is inexact and
ambiguous enough in all conscience, but it does not compel
us to assume that *quo* is masculine ; a reader who possessed
only the Latin version, without any knowledge of the original
Greek, and read it without any preconceived ideas as to
' Original Guilt,' would probably understand *in quo* as
equivalent to *quod* or *quantum*, ' in so far as all sinned.'   In
any case the words *unum hominem* are too far distant from

---

[1] *comm. in Rom.* v. 12 : ' *in quo*, id est, in Adam, *omnes peccaverunt.*
ideo dixit *in quo*, cum de muliere loquatur, quia non ad speciem rettulit,
sed ad genus. manifestum itaque est in Adam omnes peccasse quasi in
massa ; ipsa enim per peccatum corruptus, quos genuit, omnes nati sunt
sub peccato.   ex eo igitur cuncti peccatores, quia ex eo ipso sumus omnes ;
hic enim beneficium Dei perdidit, dum praevaricavit, indignus factus edere
de arbore vitae, ut moreretur.'

the relative *quo* to be its grammatical antecedent. Ambrosiaster has therefore bequeathed to Western Christendom as the supposed Scriptural foundation of its characteristic doctrine of ' Original Guilt ' a gratuitous misunderstanding of a faulty rendering of what St. Paul actually wrote.

The fatal legacy was received only too gladly : Augustine quotes this passage, mistranslation and all, as from the writings of ' sanctus Hilarius,' [1] who is undoubtedly ' Ambrosiaster.' Nor has its malign influence even yet come to an end : I have in my possession a Roman Catholic pamphlet [2] in which the words of Rom. v. 12 are quoted in defence of the idea of ' Original Guilt,' in the form ' . . . in whom all have sinned,' without the slightest apparent consciousness that St. Paul wrote nothing of the kind.

It is, indeed, doubtful whether Ambrosiaster himself really intended to place on this clause (*in quo omnes peccaverunt*) the sense which Augustine took him to intend, and which has been adopted without question, on Augustine's authority, by so many later writers in Western Christendom. For, in commenting on *v.* 14 of the same fifth chapter of the Epistle to the Romans, he lays down a principle which logically seems to exclude ' Original Guilt ' altogether. His text of this verse runs ' sed regnavit mors ab Adam usque ad Moysen, in eos qui peccaverunt in similitudinem praevaricationis Adam ' ; which, it will be noticed, like Origen's text, pre-supposes a Greek original not containing the word μή before ἁμαρτήσαντας.[3] This reading, right or wrong, clearly connects the incidence of death with the commission of *actual sin ;* and Ambrosiaster expounds it to mean that only actual sin deserves the ' second death,' or Gehenna.

---

[1] *c. ii. epp. Pelag.*, IV, iv. 7. By ' sanctus Hilarius ' Augustine apparently means Hilary of Poitiers : but this is almost certainly mistaken. Souter (*op. cit.*, pp. 161 ff.), following Dom Germain Morin, concludes tentatively that the ' Hilarius ' who is to be identified with ' Ambrosiaster ' is Decimius Hilarianus Hilarius, a distinguished Christian layman who was proconsul of Africa in 377, *praefectus urbi* in 383, *praefectus praetorio Italiae* in 396, and *praefectus urbi* for the second time in 408.

[2] *Original Sin*, by the Rev. C. C. O'Connor (Catholic Truth Society), p. 22. F. X. Schouppe, S.J. (*Elementa Theologiae Dogmaticae*, tom. i. tract. 7, c. 3, 2, § 195) appears to rely on this traditional mistranslation ; but Pohle-Preuss (*God, the Author of Nature*, 1912, p. 249) have grave doubts about it.

[3] For a note on this reading, *v. supra*, p. 125, n. 2.

Moreover, like most Latin writers after Tertullian, he
repudiates ' traducianism.' [1]   It is, therefore, possible that
by the assertion that all men ' sinned in Adam, as in a
lump ' he may merely mean that they ' became sinners ' or
' acquired a sinful tendency ' ;   in other words, he may
intend to affirm merely ' Original Sin,' and not ' Original
Guilt.'   But the idea of ' Original Guilt ' had by this time
become so popular, and the apparent discovery of a Scriptural basis for it was so welcome, amongst thinkers who
knew no Greek, that critical considerations of this kind do
not seem to have occurred to any of Ambrosiaster's readers ;
and his mistranslation of ἐφ' ᾧ πάντες ἥμαρτον took its place in
the armoury of controversial arguments for the ' twice-born '
version of the Fall-doctrine.   This momentous error, and the
emergence of the conception of fallen humanity as a sinful
massa,[2] or ' lump,' bring us up to the very threshold of
Augustinianism ; where it will be appropriate to pause, and
survey the ground which has been covered in this lecture.

CONCLUSION

It must be confessed that the section of our journey
which has just been completed very considerably exceeds in
length those which have preceded it ; but it may be hoped
that the cardinal importance for our enquiry of the Church's
pre-Augustinian infancy will have justified a somewhat
detailed examination of this period.   We are now in a
position to attempt answers to the two main questions
formulated at the beginning of this lecture as necessarily
arising out of our historical method of determining what is
' the ecclesiastical doctrine ' of Man and of Sin—namely :
(1) Can it be said that the ideas of the Fall and of Original
Sin were held universally within the Christian Church—that

---

[1] *comm. in Rom.* vii. 22 : ' si enim anima de traduce esset et ipsa, et in
ipsa habitaret peccatum, quia anima Adae magis peccavit quam corpus :
sed peccatum animae corrupit corpus . . . in anima autem si habitaret
<peccatum>, numquam se cognosceret homo : nunc autem cognoscit se,
et condelectatur legi Dei.'

[2] This term may have been suggested by the use of φύραμα (Vulg.
' massa ') in Rom. ix. 21.

they were believed *ubique, semper, et ab omnibus*—during this period ? and (2) if they were, can any given set of solutions of the ' five crucial problems ' implicit in the Adamic Fall-theory claim a similar degree of oecumenical acceptance ?

(1) To answer this question with exactness, we must distinguish between the doctrine of the ' Fall,' that is, the belief that there has been some great prehistoric moral catastrophe which has separated man from God, and the doctrine of ' Original Sin,' that is, the affirmation that the ground of this separation lies in man's consequent infection by a hereditary weakness or taint which is interior or psychological in nature. It may reasonably be concluded from the evidence which we have adduced from the greatest teachers of the pre-Augustinian Church (to which, if space allowed, might be added more cursory references to the subject by writers of lesser importance [1]) that the doctrine of the Fall was accepted, in a vague and general way, by most Christians of this period, at least from the canonisation of St. Paul's Epistles onwards : and we have shown reason for dismissing the contention that the uncertainty which appears to have reigned in the Church with regard to this matter destroys the claim of the Fall-doctrine to fulfil the second of the Vincentian qualifications, that of acceptance *semper*. Though in all probability the rank and file of the Christian society took little interest in the matter,[2] and though the thought of the consequences of Adam's sin would seem to have possessed little vividness or reality for their imagina-

---

[1] See Additional Note H, p. 554, ' Passages bearing on the Fall-doctrine from pre-Augustinian writers not mentioned in Lecture IV.'

[2] This popular lack of interest in the subject seems to be reflected in the Apocryphal Gospels, which are the products of vulgar and non-theological Christianity, both Catholic and heretical. In the whole of Dr. M. R. James' convenient collection of these documents (*The Apocryphal New Testament*, 1924) there appear to be only three references to the Fall of Adam, one of which occurs in the ' Book of John the Evangelist ' (*op. cit*. p. 189 f.), a Bogomil work which in its present form is not earlier than the twelfth century, and is therefore of no value as evidence for primitive Christian opinion ; the other two occur in the ' Questions of Bartholomew ' (pp. 173, 178), which *may* represent the ' Gospel of Bartholomew ' mentioned by Jerome (*praef. in comm. super Matt.*, Vallarsi, vii. 2), and, if so, is a version of a pre-Augustinian writing—but this is highly doubtful see James, p. 166).

tions in comparison with the idea of invisible daemons swarming around them and instilling subtle suggestions of evil into their minds—an idea which came to them with the direct authority of our Lord's own words—they would at least not have denied the teaching of Rom. v. 12–21 ; it is not conceivable that, after the recognition of St. Paul's letters as Scripture, any member of the Church would have asserted that the Apostle was mistaken when he connected the universal prevalence of death and sin with the transgression of the first man.

The question whether the idea of ' original sin,' in the sense defined above, enjoyed an equal measure of explicit acceptance is *prima facie* more disputable.   It was shown in Lecture III that the language of Rom. v. vi. vii. is most naturally and easily comprehensible on the supposition that St. Paul meant to weld together the Fall-theory of the apocalyptists and the *yēçer*-theory of the Rabbis, and to exhibit the ' evil impulse ' as the legacy of the primordial sin. If this is so, the Pauline teaching is that the disastrous entail of the Fall involves, not merely physical mortality, but evil consequences of an interior, psychological, and spiritual nature.   But the Apostle's obscure and complicated sentences, in which he is struggling to express ideas which are not completely articulated or defined even in his own mind, though they would seem to be penetrated by this assumption of the psychological character of the main legacy of the Fall, do not contain any express affirmation of it ; and hence it was possible for a tendency to manifest itself in some quarters towards construing the consequences of the first sin as of an external or mechanical kind, as consisting in the circumstance that since the Fall men have been born outside Paradise, or subject to some commercially conceived obligation or servitude to the Devil.   Nevertheless, a reasonable interpretation of the Vincentian Canon will allow for temporary misunderstandings and local failures to grasp the full inwardness of these vast and mysterious ideas ; and the conceptions of ' banishment from Paradise ' and ' legal servitude to the devil ' may well be regarded as superficial and mythological rationalisations of that profound and poignant experience of self-condemnation, which is the heart of true penitence and the foundation of the whole Fall-doctrine.

(2) The ideas of the Fall and of ' Original Sin,' in a broad general sense, may thus be taken on the whole to satisfy the Vincentian test (interpreted in that elastic sense which does not exclude doctrinal development) so far as the first four centuries of Christian history are concerned. But it will have become clear in the course of our exposition that neither of the two classical versions of the Fall-doctrine— neither the Hellenic, ' once-born,' and ' minimising,' nor the African, ' twice-born,' or ' maximising ' version (which includes as a characteristic constituent the formidable conception of ' Original Guilt ')—enjoyed oecumenical acceptance during this period. Neither the one nor the other can claim to have been believed *ubique, semper, et ab omnibus* down to the point which our narrative has reached. This fact would seem by itself to dispose of the common assumption that the African theory is ' the ecclesiastical ' or ' the Catholic ' doctrine, in an exclusive sense. Given the Vincentian criteria of Catholicity, it is clear that the title of the ' Catholic ' doctrine can only be claimed by the common substratum, or the highest common factor, of the Hellenic and the African views. And this highest common factor is nothing more or less than the teaching of St. Paul—that ' Adam ' sinned (however ' Adam ' is to be construed, whether as archetypal idea, race-spirit, or historic individual) and that in consequence all men inherit a congenital inordination of appetite or debility of will (whichever mode of expression be preferred), with liability to physical disease and death. It may be predicted, without improper anticipation, that at the end of the historical portion of our enquiry we shall not see reason to revise the provisional judgment to which our study of the first four centuries of Christianity has led us, that the genuinely ' Catholic ' doctrine of the Fall and of Original Sin is simply and strictly identical with the New Testament doctrine.

It should be added, in order to complete our picture of the mind of the Church with regard to this subject during the pre-Augustinian epoch, that none of the writers who have been reviewed so far asserts that the Fall-doctrine belongs to

the essence of the Christian message, that is, to ' the Gospel '
or ' the Deposit of Faith.'   The ideas of Adam's sin and of
its gloomy consequences would seem rather to have been
placed in the not very precisely limited category of indispensable prolegomena to Christianity, contained in the
Jewish sacred books.   It is a significant fact that no mention
of these doctrines occurs either in the local baptismal creeds
of the period or in the great oecumenical symbol of Nicaea.[1]
It was reserved for Augustine to declare that they belonged
to ' the very foundations of the Faith.' [2]

[1] By this is meant, of course, the Creed as promulgated by the Council
(' N '), though the statement is equally true of ' C,' the so-called Niceno-
Constantinopolitan symbol.   The phrase ' who for us men and for our
salvation came down from heaven ' does not, so far as its verbal form is
concerned, necessarily mean more than that the object of the Incarnation
was to redeem us from *actual* sin.

[2] *c. Iulian.* i. 6, 22 : ' hoc autem unde nunc agimus ad ipsa fidei
pertinet fundamenta.'

V.

THE 'TWICE-BORN' VERSION OF THE FALL-DOCTRINE FULLY DEVELOPED— AUGUSTINIANISM

ἀλλ' εἰ ἄνθρωποι ἄκοντές εἰσι κακοὶ καὶ τοιοῦτοι οὐχ ἑκόντες, οὔτ' ἄν τις τοὺς
ἀδικοῦντας αἰτιάσαιτο, οὔτε τοὺς πάσχοντας ὡς δι' αὐτοὺς ταῦτα πάσχοντας. εἰ δὲ
δὴ καὶ ἀνάγκη οὕτω κακοὺς γίνεσθαι εἴτε ὑπὸ τῆς φορᾶς εἴτε τῆς ἀρχῆς διδούσης τὸ
ἀκόλουθον ἐντεῦθεν, φυσικῶς οὕτως. εἰ δὲ δὴ ὁ λόγος αὐτός ἐστιν ὁ ποιῶν, πῶς
οὐκ ἄδικα οὕτως; ἀλλὰ τὸ μὲν ἄκοντες, ὅτι ἁμαρτία ἀκούσιον· τοῦτο δὲ οὐκ
ἀναιρεῖ τὸ αὐτοὺς τοὺς πράττοντας παρ' αὐτῶν εἶναι, ἀλλ' ὅτι αὐτοὶ ποιοῦσι, διὰ
τοῦτο καὶ αὐτοὶ ἁμαρτάνουσιν· ἢ οὐδ' ἂν ὅλως ἥμαρτον μὴ αὐτοὶ οἱ ποιοῦντες ὄντες.

PLOTINUS : Enn. iii. 2, 10.

'Tis the faith that launched point-blank her dart
    At the head of a lie—taught Original Sin,
The Corruption of man's heart.

BROWNING : Gold Hair; a story of Pornic.

LECTURE V

THE 'TWICE-BORN' VERSION OF THE FALL-DOCTRINE FULLY DEVELOPED— AUGUSTINIANISM

Rom. vii. 22, 23 : 'For I delight in the law of God after the inward man: but I see a different law in my members, warring against the law of my mind, and bringing me into captivity under the law of sin which is in my members.'

In our last lecture it was shown that the primitive pre-Augustinian Church, whilst holding the doctrines of the Fall and of an inherited taint or weakness in a vague and undefined shape, did not regard these ideas as constituting parts of the 'Gospel,' that is, of the revelation of Himself made by God through Christ. They are nowhere described as essential elements of the Canon, Rule, or Deposit of Faith. For the Church of the first four centuries, 'the Faith' was that which was contained in the baptismal Creeds, consisting mainly in the doctrines of God and of Christ. But this central nucleus of the Faith, though invested with a unique majesty and authoritativeness, was never regarded as standing alone : it was set in a frame or context of presuppositions and corollaries, less definite and clean-cut, but not less generally accepted. To the category of *presuppositions* or prolegomena belonged the ideas which Christianity had inherited from Judaism, the belief in the unity of God, in the inspiration of the Old Testament scriptures, and that which forms the subject of our present enquiry, the belief in the first sin and its disastrous legacy ; to the latter, the category of *corollaries* or consequences, belonged the as yet undeveloped doctrines of the Church, the Ministry and the Sacraments, things which for the most part [1] were taken for granted as facts, and used rather than theoretically analysed. In other words, the central body of Trinitarian and Christological ideas which constituted ' the Faith ' was surrounded by a fringe or penumbra of less defined ideas, which had not yet formed the subject-matter of authoritative definition, and in regard to which individual speculation was as yet un-trammelled, or limited only by the words of Scripture. This rudimentary organisation of Christian thought con-trasts vividly with those later systems of theology which are most familiar to ourselves, which contain, as integral parts of a defined and coherent whole, not merely the two great original sections dealing with the doctrines of God and of the Incarnation or of ' the Person of Christ,' but three further sections, to all appearance equally authori-tative, devoted to the doctrines of Grace or of ' the Work of Christ,' of the Church, and of the Sacraments—additions which represent the gradual expansion of the sphere of dogma proper by the progressive embodiment into the central nucleus of large tracts of the penumbra. Hence the doctrines of the Fall and of Original Sin now appear to the student of Christian thought as permanently em-bedded in the main fabric, forming as they do the founda-tion of that segment of it which is known as ' the doctrine of Grace ' ; they are now very generally regarded as dogmas of the Christian Church, constituting parts of its essential message just as truly as the ideas of the Incarnation, or the Second Coming. It would be premature to express any opinion now with regard to the validity and desirability of this development ; our immediate task is to reconstruct the way in which it came to pass. The development of the third section of Christian doctrine, the doctrine of. Grace, carrying within it the doctrines of the Fall and of Original Sin, is associated with the name of Augustine, whom we have already observed as it were from a distance, standing on the frontier which separates classical antiquity from the

---

[1] It is true that the ' holy Church ' is mentioned in the Old Roman Creed, ' remission of sins through the holy Church ' in the African Creed of the third century, and baptism in the Jerusalem Creed of c. A.D. 348 : but no specific doctrine about these things is defined.

Middle Ages, and of whom it has been strikingly said that the miserable existence of the Roman Empire in the West would seem to have been providentially prolonged into the fifth century solely in order that Augustine might arise within the shelter of its domain, in order to discharge his predestined task of infusing, through his writings, the thought and culture of the old world into the rude and barbarous vitality of the new.

The history of Christian thought, like that universal history of which it forms a part, is in great measure the history of its creative spirits ; and though the plan of our enquiry, seeking to determine that which has been believed *ubique, semper, et ab omnibus,* necessarily involves the laying of a special emphasis upon the continuous life of the Church and the unbroken self-identity of that diffused corporate consciousness of the Christian society which is the real bearer of its traditional ideas, this conception needs to be perpetually balanced by the recognition of the part played in dogmatic development by the fresh bursts of spontaneous energy which spring from great individual personalities. One such creative personality we have noted in St. Paul, who laid down the lines on which Christian anthropology was to develop. Another has been marked in Origen, the Platonist of Alexandria, some of whose speculations may provide useful material when we come to the constructive part of our task. But the end of the ancient world and the beginning of the Middle Ages was marked by the figure of an even greater Platonist, greater, that is, in the immediate effect which his life and writings produced upon the thought of Christendom. Origen's influence during his life affected only part of the East and did not extend into the West ; and, three centuries after his death, his most daring speculations were repudiated, and he himself was branded as a heretic, by Justinian's ecclesiastical henchmen.[1] But Augustine from his obscure seaport on the North African coast swayed the whole Western Church as its intellectual dictator, a position from

---

[1] See Fr. Diekamp, *Die origenistischen Streitigkeiten im sechsten Jahrhundert und das fünfte allgemeine Concil,* Münster, 1899 ; L. Duchesne, *L'Église au vième siècle* (1925), p. 171 f.

which he has not even yet been deposed, and the mighty energies of his mind and spirit initiated reverberations which affected every sphere of thought. According to Eucken, he was the greatest of purely Christian philosophers,[1] whose fame not even Thomas Aquinas can rival. Like his great master Plato,[2] he was gifted with the resplendent imagination and the flow of gorgeous imagery which spring from the union of poetic and philosophic genius, and he wielded a passionate yet lucid style, which at times could rise, as in the *Confessions*, to heights of almost dithyrambic power ; the derisive nickname of ' Punic Aristotle ' [3] bestowed upon him by his opponent Julian of Eclanum falls harmlessly to the ground in so far as it may be thought to have implied a disparagement of his literary skill, whilst it admirably describes the encyclopaedic range of his intellectual interests. He fused Neo-Platonism and Christian theism into a far more intimate and organic synthesis than had been effected by the Alexandrine Fathers, educing therefrom a vast cosmic picture of the *ordo naturarum* stretching continuously, in hierarchical gradation, from that Divine nature, which is the supreme and unchangeable Good, down to the lowest level of irrational and inanimate natures, a picture of Being not less magnificent than the Plotinian, but unlike it, portraying God as personal and Matter as real.[4] He expounded the argument, *cogito, ergo sum*, before Descartes,[5] and the relativity of Time before Kant.[6] His *Confessions* represent the most penetrating achievement of Christian

---

[1] R. Eucken, *Die Lebensanschauungen der grossen Denker*[2], p. 216.

[2] *Cf.* E. Norden, in *Die Kultur der Gegenwart* (1905) i. 8. p. 394.

[3] ' Aristoteles Poenorum ' (*op. imp. c. Iul.* iii. 199) : ' philosophaster Poenorum ' (*ibid.* v. 11).

[4] A brilliant study of St. Augustine's metaphysic will be found in T. A. Lacey, *Nature, Miracle, and Sin* (1916), Lectures II and III.

[5] *de civit. Dei*, xi. 26 : ' nulla in his veris Academicorum argumenta formido, dicentium, quid, si falleris ? si enim fallor, sum. nam qui non est, utique nec falli potest : ac per hoc sum, si fallor ' ; *cf. de vera relig.* 73 ; *soliloq.* ii. 1 ; *de lib. arbitr.* ii. 3.

[6] *de civit. Dei*, xi. 6 : ' quis non videat quod tempora non fuissent, nisi creatura fieret, quae aliquid aliqua motione mutaret ? ' *ibid.* : ' procul dubio non est mundus factus in tempore, sed cum tempore ' ; *conf.* xi. 26 : ' inde mihi visum est nihil esse aliud tempus quam distentionem—sed cuius rei, nescio, et mirum, si non ipsius animi,' and the whole of 27.

antiquity in the domain of introspective psychology. His treatise ' On the City of God ' created the science of the philosophy of history, and by its workings in the mind of Charlemagne may well have helped to bring that strange romantic phantom, the Holy Roman Empire, to the birth.[1] In Christian theology, he developed the Western conception of the Triune Being of God to a point on which no substantial advance has since been made, and by his influence on Pope Leo the Great helped to determine the final formulation of the Chalcedonian Christology.

But more remarkable than any single one of these mental achievements is the general domination exercised for centuries by his spirit, ideas, and manner of thought over the religious life of Western Europe, a domination which has not even yet entirely passed away. Through the doctrine of the Church and the ministry, as articulated by him to meet the exigencies of the Donatist controversy, and through the doctrine of Grace, as elaborated against the Pelagians, his genius played a foremost part in fixing upon Western Christendom that predominantly institutional and practical bias, which, reinforced by racial antipathies, inevitably tore it loose from the enfeebled Byzantine East (temporarily in the schism of Photius, and finally in the catastrophe of A.D. 1054), and shaped it into a self-contained organism, a mighty theocratic empire of souls, the Latin Catholic Church of the Middle Ages.[2] Yet, all through the mediaeval period, within the bosom of the most imposing ecclesiastical system which the world has ever known, Augustine the predestinarian mystic was silently contending with Augustine the hierarch, and the Reformation of the sixteenth century was in great measure the posthumous rebellion of Augustine against Augustine.

---

[1] Charlemagne ' delighted in the books of St. Augustine, and specially in those that bear the title " Of the City of God " ' (Einhard, *Vita Caroli*, 24, quoted by B. B. Warfield, *ERE* ii. p. 222).

[2] *Cf.* H. Reuter, *Augustinische Studien* (1887), vii. (' Zur Würdigung der Stellung Augustins in der Geschichte der Kirche '), p. 499 : ' (Er hat) durch sein geniales litterarisches Schaffen, durch die Wucht der Persönlichkeit, in so epochemachender Weise auf das theologische Denken in Occidente *ein*gewirkt, in demselbe *nach*gewirkt, dass man sagen darf, *die spätere Trennung desselben von dem Oriente sei wider seine Absicht dennoch von ihm vorbereitet.*'

From Augustine the leaders of the Protestant revolt inherited the overwhelming sense of God's universal causality, of the impotence of human nature and the emptiness of human merit, which in logic makes all sacramental and institutional religion otiose : and in Augustine, too, is to be found that lofty conviction of the divine mission of the institutional, visible Church, which nerved Loyola, Borromeo, and Peter Canisius to roll back the flood of rebellion against the Papacy beyond the Alps and the Rhine. The two main camps into which the Reformation sundered the mediaeval Western Church continued to take the authority of Augustine for granted, as second only to that of the inspired writers. The Preface ' Of Ceremonies ' in our own Prayer Book enquires, with rhetorical passion, ' What would St. Augustine have said . . . ? ' as though a dictum from him would constitute a final solution of any ecclesiastical dispute. The doctrines of Grace set forth in the Canons of the Council of Trent, in the Thirty Nine Articles, in the *Institutio* of Calvin, in the Augsburg Confession, are so many modified and competing versions of Augustinianism.[1] As in St. Paul's interpretation of the Old Testament Abraham was the spiritual father of circumcised and uncircumcised Christians alike,[2] so in the genealogy of Western religious thinkers Augustine is the ancestor both of the Ultramontane and of the Evangelical[3] ; and it is no wonder that his version of the Fall-doctrine has stamped itself so deeply upon the imagination of his descendants that it is still very generally believed to be the only Fall-doctrine.

There could hardly be a greater contrast than that which is presented by the fortunes of Origen, exiled, largely repudiated during his lifetime and anathematised after his death, and those of Augustine, for centuries the unchallenged master of Western theology. Yet it may now be said, without undue anticipation, that one of the conclusions

[1] See Lecture VI.　　　　　　　[2] Rom. iv. 11, 12.

[3] See Reuter, *op. cit.* vii. pp. 497–513. This author, however, finds more of the Catholic than of the Evangelical in Augustine ; *cf.* the following two judgments : (*a*) ' Augustin gilt auch mir als Begründer des römischen Katholizismus im Occidente ' (p. 497) ; (*b*) ' fragmentarisch, aber wirklich Evangelisches ist in Augustin ' (p. 513).

which will emerge from our historical review will be that
in regard to the particular subject-matter of our enquiry,
the 'once-born' or 'Hellenic' scheme, as worked out
(however imperfectly and confusedly) by the Greek Fathers
of the fourth century on the basis of Origen's speculations,
represents not merely the maximum of doctrine to which
historical Christianity as such can be said to be committed,
but also the only type of Fall-doctrine which is capable
of reconciliation with modern knowledge : and that the
characteristic elements in the 'twice-born' or 'African'
theory, as completely elaborated by Augustine, possess
neither oecumenical authority nor intrinsic reasonableness.
The greater part of this judgment has been already established in the preceding lecture ; its remainder must now be
vindicated by what, in view of the vast field to be covered,
will necessarily be a relatively brief and summary sketch
of Augustine's teaching with regard to human nature and
the origins of sin.[1]

Augustine's Early Life and Teaching

As was observed in the case of Origen, any attempt to
estimate the value of a great thinker's work must begin
with some indication of the most important facts of his life.
Augustine was born in A.D. 354 at Tagaste,[2] a small town in
Proconsular Numidia, as the son of Patricius, a citizen of
curial rank, at that date still a pagan, and his Christian wife
Monnica, who has been canonised by the piety of subsequent
generations as a pattern of Christian motherhood. He was

---

[1] The incomparable wealth of documents at our disposal makes it
impossible to give anything like an exhaustive list of references and
quotations in the course of this highly compressed review, and we shall,
therefore, confine ourselves to printing a few of the more important or
interesting. The reader desirous of more detailed information must be
referred to the monumental works of G. J. Vossius (*Historiae de contro-
versiis quas Pelagius eiusque reliquiae moverunt*, lib. vii, 1655) and Petavius
(*De Pelagiana et semi-Pelagiana haeresibus*, 1644) ; *cf.* also J. Turmel,
Le dogme du péché originel dans St. A. (*Revue d'histoire et de littérature
religieuse*, vii. p. 128).

[2] Now Souk-Aras, 'à vingt-cinq lieues de Bone' (Portalié, in *DTC*,
col. 2268).

made a catechumen in his youth, but, owing to Monnica's dread of the responsibilities which full membership of the Church would impose upon his passionate nature, was not baptised. At the age of sixteen he became a student at Carthage, where his sensuous temperament hurried him into the immoral connexion described in the second book of the *Confessions*[1]; and, three years later, his restless intellect, which had already begun to busy itself with the problem of evil, became enmeshed in the toils of that superficially attractive solution which, as we have seen, always has been and must be the deadly foe of Christian monotheism, namely, dualism; which manifested itself at that time and place in the form of Manicheism. For nine years[2] he remained in a prison of his own creation, morally shackled by the *liaison* to which we have alluded, and intellectually fettered by the terrible theory of an eternal and indestructible principle of evil, of equal power with God Himself. It would seem that though during this period he accepted dualism as the starting-point for his enquiries into the origin of evil, he never arrived at any completely satisfying conclusions; and that his *status* in regard to the Manichean sect was that of a 'hearer,' or catechumen, attached to it in the hope of eventually obtaining full enlightenment concerning the questions which tormented him, and not that of the 'elect' or fully initiated members.[3]

The double stress to which Augustine was subjected during this period—the moral agony involved in fighting a losing battle with his own animal passions, and the mental strain of a seemingly futile search for the truth as to the

[1] It was then that the celebrated prayer was uttered—'da mihi castitatem, sed noli modo' (*Conf.* viii. 7, 17)—the cry of a divided personality. Loofs' suggestion (*PRE*, ii. p. 261, art. 'Augustinus') that concubinage was then tolerated by the Church, and that Augustine's conduct was therefore not as reprehensible, from the point of view of *de facto* Christianity, as he himself believed it to be, appears to rest on a misunderstanding of the 17th canon of the Council of Toledo, held in A.D. 400 (Hardouin, i. 992); see Portalié, *op. cit., DTC*, col. 2269.

[2] That is, from 373 to 382, the date of his departure from Africa—'novem totos annos' (*de moribus manich.* 19).

[3] On the two grades of membership in the Manichean Church, see F. C. Burkitt, *Religion of the Manichees*, pp. 44 ff. Augustine was later accused of having been a priest of the sect (*c. litt. Petil.* iii. 20).

origin of evil—constituted the psychological conflict which
eventually gave birth to his characteristic doctrines of
Grace. At the age of twenty-eight he abandoned the formal
profession of the Manichean creed, on discovering that
Faustus of Milevis, the archpundit of the cult, who had
been held up to him as an inspired teacher capable of solving
all his difficulties, was nothing but a pretentious quack.[1]
There followed his sojourn in Italy and his contact with
Ambrose,[2] whose life and teaching induced in him the conviction that the Catholic Christianity of his boyhood was
in possession of the key to the intellectual problem, without,
however, communicating to him the means of solving the
moral problem, that is, of regaining control over his sensual
appetites. We need not recount again the world-famous
story of the spiritual crisis which gripped him in the garden
at Milan,[3] of the childish voice chanting the sentence *tolle
lege, tolle lege*, of the solemn words which met his eye as he
opened the New Testament—' Not in rioting and drunken-
ness, not in chambering and wantonness, not in strife and
envying ; but put ye on the Lord Jesus Christ, and make not
provision for the flesh, to fulfil the lusts thereof.'[4] With the
perusal of these words the long-repressed complex in his
subconscious mind was broken up, the powerful stream of
sexual feeling which had for so long stormed and fretted
against, and every now and then by sheer force broken
through, the repressing activities of the moral censorship,
was diverted into a new channel, and henceforward fertilised
his whole life with a passion for God—' the beauty so ancient
yet so new,'[5]—expressed under the form of ascetic monasticism. His new-found Christianity[6] was deepened and

---

[1] *Conf.* v. 3–6. Other reasons contributed to bring about his secession,
notably the scandalous lives of the Manichean ' elect ' (*de moribus manich.*
ii. 18–20).

[2] *v. supra*, Lecture IV, p. 300. This period covers the years 383–386.

[3] *Conf.* viii. 12.   [4] Rom. xiii. 13, 14.

[5] *Conf.* x. 27 : ' sero te amavi, pulchritudo tam antiqua et tam nova,
sero te amavi.'

[6] I assume that the narrative of the *Confessions* may be taken ' at its
face value,' and that the theory advocated by M. Gourdon (*Essai sur la
conversion de St. Augustin*, 1900), according to which the experience in the
Milanese garden was a conversion to philosophy, not to Christianity, need
not be seriously considered ; see Portalié, *op. cit.*, col. 2273, 4.

philosophically formulated in dialectical converse with his friends at the sylvan retreat of Cassiciacum, where doubtless his private leisure was devoted to the further exploration of those ' books of the Platonists '[1] (probably the *Enneads* of Plotinus, in Victorinus' Latin translation) with which he had already become acquainted at Milan. The year 387 witnessed his baptism by Ambrose, the death of Monnica, and his return to Africa, where he began that monastic life[2] for which the newly transfigured instincts of his nature craved, and which later caused many of the religious orders of the mediaeval Church, friars, eremites, and canons regular, to claim him as their spiritual father and legislator.[3] Four years before the close of the century he became bishop of Hippo Regius, the modern Bona, a small seaport on the Mediterranean coast which his name has immortalised for ever.

It is not necessary for our present purposes to carry this sketch of his biography any further, inasmuch as his theology of grace, with its core of anthropology, was already complete in essentials by the time of his consecration to the episcopate, long before he had heard the name of his great opponent Pelagius. We note here a fact which must be borne in mind when we approach our final evaluation of the Augustinian ideas—the fact that they represent that version of the Christian theory of the origin of evil into which his powerful and ardent spirit was naturally drawn in its recoil from the Iranian theory of an eternal dualism. Augustine's conception of the Fall and its consequences was the product of a reaction, not against Pelagianism but against Manicheism, thus constituting the most impressive and celebrated instance of the law which seems to determine the movements of Christian opinion with regard to the subject of our enquiry—the law, namely, that contact with dualism stimulates the mind of the Church towards a fresh accentua-

---

[1] *Conf.* vii. 9 ; viii. 2.

[2] At first in the home which he had inherited from Patricius at Tagaste, then at Hippo in a house attached to the church, and finally in the episcopal residence itself.

[3] The so-called ' Rule of St. Augustine ' is an adaptation of a letter (*ep.* ccxxi.) of general direction and guidance, which he wrote in A.D. 423 to a community of women at Hippo.

tion of the Fall-doctrine ; and it would seem to have been worked out in comparative peace, not under the stress of controversy, during the first ten years which immediately succeeded Augustine's conversion.

We find it, mildly phrased but already complete in essential outline, in the first book of the treatise *de diversis quaestionibus ad Simplicianum*, a work written in A.D. 397 to explain certain difficult passages of Scripture for the benefit of Simplician, Ambrose's successor in the see of Milan.[1] Augustine here asserts that ' sin,' which for the moment seems to be synonymous with ' concupiscence ' (the passage under discussion is Rom. vii. 7–25, in which, as we have already seen,[2] ἁμαρτία and ἐπιθυμία appear to be more or less convertible terms) originated in the transgression of Adam.[3] This ' sin ' has become ingrained into human nature and is transmitted by physical heredity.[4] Here for the first time in the history of Christian thought we meet the epoch-making phrase *originale peccatum*, meaning a sinful quality which is born with us and is inherent in our constitution. But this sinful quality, it is clear, is conceived by Augustine to be ' sin ' in the fullest sense of the term, albeit involuntarily acquired, for it deserves ' punishment,'[5] and therefore involves guilt ; and a little later we find the actual term *originalis reatus*, ' original ' or ' connatural ' ' guilt.'[6] The guilt in question, however, appears at this early stage of Augustine's thought to be, not so much the supposed

---

[1] In later years Augustine was accustomed to appeal to this work as evidence for the continuity and consistency of his teaching with regard to Grace throughout his episcopate ; see *de don. persev.* xxi. 55 ; *de praedest. sanct.* iv. 8.

[2] Lecture III, p. 142 f.

[3] *ad Simplic.* i. q. 1, 4 : ' sane quod ait, *peccatum revixit adveniente mandato*, satis significavit hoc modo aliquando vixisse peccatum, id est notum fuisse, sicut arbitror, in praevaricatione primi hominis, quia et ipse mandatum acceperat.'

[4] *ibid.* 10 : ' quod si quaerit aliquis unde hoc scit, quod dicit habitare in carne sua non utique bonum, id est peccatum : unde nisi ex traduce mortalitatis et assiduitate voluptatis ? illud est ex poena *originalis peccati*, hoc est ex poena frequentati peccati. cum illo in hanc vitam nascimur, hoc vivendo addimus.'

[5] *ibid.* 10 : ' ex poena originalis peccati.'

[6] *ibid.* 20 (quoted below, p. 328, n. 3).

hereditary responsibility for Adam's transgression,[1] as the guilt of having ' concupiscence ' in us at all.   It is in any case certain that *originale peccatum* in Augustine always includes the idea of ' original guilt ' ; and we shall, therefore, for the purposes of this lecture suspend the popular use of the English term ' original sin ' as meaning merely the bias or tendency towards sin (which Augustine denotes by *con- cupiscentia*), and employ the phrase as the strict equivalent of *originale peccatum*.   By virtue of its intimate saturation with ' concupiscence ' and ' original guilt,' the human stock constitutes a single *massa peccati* or ' lump of sin ' (this terrible phrase was presumably suggested by Ambrosiaster's words ' all have sinned in Adam as in a lump '[2]) which as such is justly doomed to everlasting death.[3]   The freedom of the individual will is indeed nominally preserved [4] ; but inasmuch as in unregenerate man the will is invariably determined by ' sin,' that is, by an inborn aversion from the Creator and propension towards creatures, this freedom appears to be little more than a phrase.

---

[1] So far as we have found traces of the idea of ' original guilt ' in pre-Augustinian writers, this is the form which it seems to have taken.

[2] *comm. in Rom.* v. 12, quoted above, Lecture IV, p. 308, n. 1.

[3] *ad Simplic.* i. q. 2, 16 : ' sunt igitur omnes homines (quandoquidem, ut apostolus ait, *in Adam omnes moriuntur*, a quo in universum genus huma- num origo ducitur offensionis Dei) una quaedam *massa peccati*, supplicium debens divinae summaeque iustitiae, quod sive exigatur sive donatur nulla est iniquitas ' ; 20 : ' tunc facta est una *massa* omnium, veniens de traduce peccati et de poena mortalitatis . . . concupiscentia carnalis de peccati poena iam regnans, universum genus humanum tamquam totam et unam conspersionem, *originali reatu in omnia permanante*, confuderat ' (' con- spersio ' here means ' dough ' or ' paste,' as in 1 Cor. v. 7 *Vulg.*, where it represents φύραμα, Tert., *adv. Marcion.* iv. 24, *et al.*, and carries on the metaphor of *massa*).   The following variants of the phrase *massa peccati*, as applied to fallen mankind, have been collected by the learned Benedictine, Dom O. Rottmanner (*Der Augustinismus*, p. 8) : *massa peccatorum, luti, iniquitatis, irae, mortis, damnationis, offensionis, massa tota vitiata, damnabilis, damnata.*

[4] *ibid.* i. q. 1, 11 : ' *velle enim*, inquit, *adiacet mihi, perficere autem bonum non invenio.* his verbis videtur non recte intelligentibus velut auferre liberum arbitrium. sed quomodo aufert, cum dicat, *velle adiacet mihi* ? certe enim ipsum velle in potestate est, quoniam adiacet nobis ; sed quod perficere bonum non est in potestate, ad meritum pertinet originalis peccati . . . quod non vult malum, hoc agit, superante concupiscentia, non solum vinculo mortalitatis, sed mole consuetudinis roborata.'   21 : ' liberum voluntatis arbitrium plurimum valet, immo vero, est quidem ; sed in venumdatis sub peccato quid valet ? '

In God's resultant dealings with the human race His mercy and justice are equally exhibited. Out of the *massa peccati* His mercy selects a fixed number of souls, who through no merits of their own are brought to baptism, ' justified ' (which in Augustine's terminology means ' sanctified '), and saved. The rest of mankind is left by His justice in the ' lump of sin,' rolling on its way unhindered to the bottomless pit. The equity of this procedure, which glorifies a small body of arbitrarily chosen favourites, and abandons all other human beings (who are *ex hypothesi* not more deserving of damnation than the fortunate objects of predestination) to their fate, is defended partly by the consideration that the lost have in any case no right to complain, inasmuch as they only get what they have deserved (by ' original guilt '), and that the predestined have every reason to be satisfied with the arrangement, so far as it affects themselves [1] : partly by an appeal to mystery and to the transcendental nature of the workings of the Divine Mind.[2] ' How unsearchable are his judgments, and his ways past finding out ! '

It will be recognised at once that we have now reached the fully rounded, logically coherent expression of that ' African ' or ' twice-born ' type of Fall-doctrine which in our last lecture was seen, slowly assuming definite shape and consistency, in a succession of Latin writers reaching from Tertullian to Ambrosiaster. Considered as a formal dogmatic scheme, it purports to be based upon the well-known Scriptural texts which we have already met with in previous

---

[1] *ad Simplic.* i. q. 2, 22 : ' debitum si non reddis, habes quod gratuleris : si reddis, non habes quod quereris '—an epigram in which, we may surmise, the reprobate would find but cold comfort, if Augustinianism represented objective fact. *Cf.* also *de praedest. sanct.* viii. 16 : ' cur autem fides non omnibus detur, fidelem movere non debet, qui credit ex uno omnes isse in condemnationem sine dubitatione iustissimam : ita ut nulla Dei esset iusta reprehensio, etiam si nullus inde liberaretur.'

[2] *ibid.* i. q. 2, 16 : ' atque ita tenacissime firmissimeque credatur, idipsum quod Deus cuius vult miseretur et quem vult obdurat, hoc est, cuius vult miseretur et cuius vult non miseretur, esse *alicuius occultae atque ab humano modulo investigabilis aequitatis.*' *ibid.* : ' eorum autem non miseretur, quibus misericordiam non esse praebendam *aequitate occultissima et ab humanis sensibus remotissima* iudicat. " inscrutabilia enim sunt iudicia eius, et investigabiles viae ipsius." ' For comments on this conception of an ' occult justice ' as an attribute of God, see below, p. 381 f.

writers, reinforced by the predestinarian passages in the Epistle to the Romans : but, considered as a psychological document, it proclaims itself to be the product of Augustine's own personality and of the unique circumstances of his life. It was doubtless natural that an African Christian, meditating on the problems of human nature and sin, should have taken the teaching of Tertullian and Cyprian for granted, and that one of Ambrose's catechumens should have reproduced and developed the Fall-doctrine of his princely master.[1] And Augustine's imperfect acquaintance with Greek would inevitably shut him off from contact with that ' minimising,' more humane and reasonable type of Fall-doctrine which we have seen to be characteristic of primitive and Hellenic Christianity. But the ultimate factors, psychological and environmental, which underlay Augustine's Fall-doctrine, are susceptible of a deeper analysis. Augustinianism embodied some of the more unlovely features of North African Christianity in a peculiarly concentrated form. The crude lights and hard shadows which the burning sun of Africa casts upon its desert sands seem to have sunk into the minds of Tertullian and Cyprian and to have been there transmuted, as by some refracting medium, into the legalistic precision and the pitiless logic of Latin-Punic theology. The narrow, clean-cut idea of the Church and the indifference to the fate of those outside it, the predominantly forensic mode of conceiving sin, and the quasi-commercial treatment of merit which had become traditional in the Christian thought of his native country, left unmistakeable marks upon Augustine's fully elaborated notions of ' seminal identity,' ' original guilt,' and the *massa peccati*. Equally patent is the influence exerted upon his convictions by the less admirable traits of his own character. The downright brutality which led him to discard his mistress of fifteen years' standing, the mother of Adeodatus, without, apparently, so much as a thought of making reparation for his fault by marrying her, appears in his theology as the heartlessness which leaves the great bulk of mankind, even

---

[1] But see E. Buonaiuti, *Agostino e la colpa ereditaria* (*Ricerche religiose*, Sept. 1926, pp. 401 ff.), who minimises the influence of Ambrose on Augustine's Fall-doctrine, and emphasises that of Ambrosiaster.

helpless infants, in the *massa perditionis*, doomed to ever-lasting flames for a sin which is not their own. The terrible strength of the sexual passions which devastated his youth and early manhood accounts for the prominence which the idea of ' concupiscence ' assumes in his writings ; and the apparently instantaneous sublimation of these emotions through his conversion explains the feeling of irresistible grace upon which his theology of predestination and election was founded, as well as the ultra-puritan fanaticism which, as we shall see, coloured his opinions with regard to wedlock and procreation. Augustine's personality, in short, was that of the typical ' introvert,' or ' twice-born ' religious genius. We have in a previous lecture shown how such ' sick souls,' distracted by the conflict between their stormy passions and the no less insistent longing for immediate communion with and possession of God, attain to peace and unification only through a mental and emotional explosion which diverts the greater part of the obscure energies of sex into the channel of mystical religion, through an interior *bouleversement* which appears in consciousness as the hand of God reaching down from the clouds to pluck the brand from the burning, the favoured sinner from the ' lump of perdition.' The theology which is based upon experience of this kind will always appeal to Augustine's psychological kinsfolk, those who not merely believe but intuitively know the Eternal God to be the supreme fact of life, the one immediately apprehended and luminously self-evident presupposition of thought, emotion, and action. Paul, Augustine, Luther, Newman— the great succession of the ' twice-born ' giants of religion stretches across the centuries, transcending denominational and credal barriers, and doubtless will stretch through ages yet unborn.

The Catholic or Universal Church, however, if it is to be true to its name, must provide spiritual shelter and nourish-ment, not merely for the minority of introverts or mystics, but also for the more normal, prosaic, and healthy-minded type of man, to whom the ideal of ethical goodness makes a direct and intelligible appeal, but whose strictly religious feelings are naturally weak and need nursing throughout the whole of his life. If the Christian society is to be more

than a select coterie of mystics, it must reckon with the fact
that the majority of its members will be—and, given the
facts of human nature, ought to be—of the extravert,
practical, and 'hard-headed' type.   In a favourable environment, there is no reason why the normal unimaginative man
should not develop a Christianity as sincere and as intense,
in its own way, as the more passionate and introspective
strain of devotion which commends itself to the small band
of those who are ' born religious.'   It is a singular coincidence—a believer in the Divine governance of history will
call it providence—that whilst the fiery African monk,
Augustine, was working out what seemed to be the implications of repentance, as experienced by the ' twice-born '
temperament, and systematising the severer version of the
Fall-doctrine, which naturally arises from it, another monk,
born in these islands, was simultaneously and independently
constructing a doctrine of human nature and of sin, which is
the classical product, within the sphere of Christian anthropology, of the ' once-born,' healthy-minded, strongly ethical
but feebly religious type of personality.

PELAGIANISM

Pelagius, according to Jerome, was ' natione Scottus,'
that is, an Irishman.   His name is presumably the Hellenic
equivalent of some such Gaelic appellation as *Muirchu,*
' hound of the sea.' [1]   He was not in Holy Orders, and does
not seem, at the date of his appearance on the stage of
history, to have been attached to any particular monastic
community.   In his youth he may have been a coenobite
and so sheltered by the cloister from those temptations
which had left ineffaceable scars upon Augustine's soul.
He is admitted even by his adversaries to have been a man
of great piety and virtue,[2] except in regard to the single

---

[1] J. B. Bury, *Life of St. Patrick,* p. 43.
[2] *Cf.* Aug. *de pecc. merit.* iii. 1 : ' Pelagii quaedam scripta, viri ut
audio sancti et non parvo provectu Christiani ' ; 5 : ' bonum et praedicandum virum.'   I do not know on what ground Dr. W. Bright accuses
Pelagius of a ' defect of humility ' (*Select Anti-Pelagian Treatises,* Introd.

point of truthfulness ; and even here it is probable that the
assertions of vehement controversialists require to be considerably discounted. He is first heard of in Rome, at the
beginning of the fifth century, engaged in what appears to
have been a kind of ' mission ' to the capital city. The
moral standard of Roman Christianity was low enough as
the result of a century's influx into the Church of half-
converted heathens ; and the figure of Pelagius presents
itself to us, if we may so say, as a combination of Savonarola
and Charles Kingsley, denouncing the sins of society and
inculcating a highly ethical and puritan type of religion,
which represented the external and disciplinary element in
monasticism as contrasted with the interior and mystical
element which so largely inspired the thought of Augustine.
This fifth-century exponent of ' muscular Christianity '
found his most fervent disciple and colleague in a man
of very different type from himself, the anaemic lawyer
Caelestius, who carried his monastic enthusiasm so far as
to insist upon literal and absolute poverty as an indispensable condition of true Christian life. The strongly
ethical and non-mystical type of religion inculcated by the
two missioners necessarily presupposed an intense insistence
upon the absolute, uncontrolled, undetermined freedom of
the will. Pelagius had no patience with moral weaklings
or invalids ; he could not understand the idea of the ' moral
struggle.' The contention, that the frailty of human
nature made conformity with the highest ideals a matter
of striving and effort, seemed to him merely a dishonest
excuse, put forward by hypocrites who intended to go on
sinning, and a disparagement of the justice and benevolence
of God, in that He is thereby accused by implication of
having given commandments which are difficult of fulfilment
by man. This naturally led to a revival of the position
maintained by Lactantius in the previous century, in which
the emphasis is laid on the rational nature and autonomous
free-will of man, as efficient causes of his salvation, rather

---

p. viii) and even of ' unchristian pride ' (*The Age of the Fathers*, ii. p. 164)—
unless it be on the ground that disbelief in original sin is *per se* an infallible
symptom of these qualities.

than on the grace of God. Human nature is asserted to be absolutely unimpaired, in a condition of perfect poise and equilibrium ; and all sin, instead of being the rebellion of the lower part of man's nature against the higher, is regarded as the deliberate, conscious self-expression of the whole personality.   There are no such things as ' sins of weakness ' ; men sin according to Pelagius because they choose to sin, because they have calmly and deliberately faced the question of sin, and decided that sin represents for them the most desirable course of conduct. We may postpone for the moment any comments upon this amazing psychology, and content ourselves with pointing out that such a position went far beyond the libertarianism of the Greek Fathers, qualified as this was by the admission of a ' weakness ' or tendency to ' disintegration ' inherent in man ; and necessarily led to the repudiation of the whole of that floating tradition as to an innate flaw or disease of human nature, which, though not part of the Faith, was very generally accepted throughout the Church as part of the necessary presuppositions of the Faith. Pelagianism was not an extreme development of the ' once-born ' form of the Fall-doctrine, but a round denial of that doctrine in all forms.

Whilst the Celtic monk was thus developing a puritan and semi-monastic type of religion at Rome, the African monk Augustine was absorbed in the duties of his episcopal office, and in the controversy with the Donatists.   We have already drawn attention to the fact that the systems of the two great antagonists Augustine and Pelagius were developed in entire independence of each other. The characteristic ideas of Augustine, as we have seen from the treatise *ad Simplicianum*, had assumed their essential shape as early as 397, long before he had ever heard of Pelagius. The views of Pelagius, on the other hand, appear in his commentary on the Epistles of St. Paul,[1] and particularly in his

---

[1] This commentary seems in the first instance to have been issued anonymously, though the secret of its origin leaked out here and there : hence it survived the downfall of its author, and continued to be quoted and copied throughout the Middle Ages, eventually coming, by some inexplicable chance, to be included in a codex of the works of St. Jerome used by Erasmus for his edition of the works of that Father, and so passing into all the standard editions of Jerome, down to Migne's *PL*. Its true

exposition of the crucial passage Romans v. 12 ff.[1]; this commentary, according to Dr. Souter, was written between A.D. 406 and 410.[2] We must conceive of Augustinianism and Pelagianism as two great cycles of teaching which during the first ten years of the fifth century were slowly spreading from two centres, Carthage and Rome. Sooner or later they were bound to collide ; and the only question was, which would be the first to secure the allegiance of the greater part of the West. The Augustinian system had

---

provenance has now been established, and its text critically re-constructed, by Dr. A. Souter, *Pelagius's Expositions of Thirteen Epistles of St. Paul* (Cambridge Texts and Studies, IX.) Vol. I, Introduction (1922), Vol. II, Text (1926).

[1] The specifically ' Pelagian ' character of his exegesis may be illustrated by the following comments : Rom. v. 12 : ' *propterea sicut per unum hominem in hunc mundum peccatum introiit et per peccatum mors.* exemplo vel forma . . . *et ita in omnes homines (mors) pertransiit, in quo omnes moriuntur* dum ita peccant, et similiter moriuntur : non enim in Abraham et Isaac (et Jacob) pertransiit, de quibus dicit Dominus : " omnes enim illi vivunt " . . . Sive : in eos pertransiit qui humano (et) non caelesti ritu vivebant.' Rom. v. 15 : ' *si enim unius delicto multi mortui sunt* etc. plus praevaluit iustitia in vivificando quam peccatum in occidendo, quia Adam tantum se et suos posteros interfecit, Christus autem et qui tunc erant in corpore et posterosl iberavit .hi autem qui contra traducem peccati sunt, ita illam impugnare nituntur : " si Adae " inquiunt " peccatum etiam non peccantibus nocuit, ergo et Christi iustitia etiam non credentibus prodest ; quia similiter, immo et magis dicit per unum salvari quam per unum ante perierant." deinde aiunt " si baptismum mundat antiquum illud delictum, qui de duobus baptizatis nati fuerint debent hoc carere peccato : non enim potuerunt ad filios transmittere quod ipsi minime habuerunt." ' (See below, p. 367, nn. 3, 4, for Augustine's reply to this objection.) ' . . . iniustum esse dicentes ut hodie nata anima, non ex massa Adae, tam antiquum peccatum portet alienum, dicunt etiam nulla ratione concedi ut Deus, qui propria homini peccata remittet, imputet aliena.' (Augustine, who quotes part of this extract, from ' deinde aiunt ' onwards, in *de pecc. merit.* iii. c. 3, suggests that Pelagius' use of the third person to introduce his own opinions betrays a consciousness that those opinions were contrary to the received faith of the Church. This does not seem a justifiable inference : the form of speech in question need not imply more than the dominance of the theory, which Pelagius wishes to controvert, at Rome and in the West.) Rom. vii. 8 : ' *occasione ergo accepta peccatum per mandatum* '—the innate ' sin ' which appears in this chapter is explained to be the personal Devil. 18–24 : the agonising moral struggle depicted by the Apostle is represented as a struggle against voluntarily acquired habit, not against congenital weakness or sinfulness. *Cf.* also 1 Cor. xv. 22 : ' *sicut in Adam omnes moriuntur* etc. sicut per Adam mors intravit, quia primus ipse mortuus est.'

[2] *op. cit.* i. p. 4.

the advantage of being embodied, not in express words but as a pervading inspiration, in one of the greatest literary and devotional classics of all time, namely, the *Confessions*, which, it would seem, were as much a household book in serious Western Christian families of the fifth century as was *The Christian Year* in those of the Victorian epoch, and doubtless did as much to spread the Augustinian point of view as did Keble's volume to disseminate the principles of Tractarianism. The first shot in the great battle was fired when an unnamed bishop [1] quoted in the presence of Pelagius the famous prayer *da quod iubes, et iube quod vis* [2]—' give what Thou dost command,' that is, ' give me the power to fulfil Thy commands,' and then ' command whatever Thou dost will.' This seemed to Pelagius to contain teaching of the most pernicious kind, as implying the utter helplessness of man to raise himself out of the morass of sin, and as therefore likely to weaken that tone of healthy self-reliance which he wished to encourage in his disciples. Dr. W. Bright imaginatively reconstructs the thoughts of Pelagius on *da quod iubes* as follows :

Give what Thou commandest ! . . . Is God to be expected to save us ' without our stir ' ? Are we to sit with folded hands, instead of striving, wrestling, taking the kingdom by force, labouring and energizing in the work of our salvation ? Surely Christians are too ready, as it is, to excuse their own idleness under the pretence of depending on God's working ; to deceive themselves by talking of their weakness ; to forget that they can serve Him if they will ; to fancy that they honour Him by a listlessness which wears the mask of pious humility, but is in fact no better than undutiful and ungrateful sloth.[3]

From this moment onwards, Pelagianism and Augustinianism, the final expressions of the extravert and introvert types of religious and ethical experience, stood before the Christian world as two opposed theories of man, sin, and

[1] *de dono persev.* 53 : ' quae mea verba Pelagius Romae, cum a quodam fratre et coepiscopo meo fuissent eo praesente commemorata, ferre non potuit.'

[2] *Conf.* x. 29 : ' O amor, qui semper ardes et numquam extingueris, caritas, Deus meus, accende me ! continentiam iubes : da quod iubes, et iube quod vis.' ' da quod iubes ' also occurs in *de pecc. merit.* ii. 5 ; *de spir. et litt.* 22.

[3] *The Age of the Fathers* (1903), ii. p. 163.

grace, destined for the next generation to be locked in deadly conflict, and pushing each other, by virtue of their mutual repulsion, into more and more undesirable extremes.

It will be appropriate here to sketch the completed form of Pelagianism, as the issues raised in the fifth century are fundamentally identical with those which confront the Christian speculator on the problem of the origin of evil to-day : and by Pelaganism I do not mean so much the personal views of Pelagius as the whole coherent and rounded system which grew out of his controversy with Augustine, and for the elaboration of which his two chief disciples, Caelestius and Julian, bishop of Eclanum, were as responsible as Pelagius himself. This sketch must be prefaced by the warning that it will be necessary, for the sake of lucidity, to keep our attention strictly concentrated upon the anthropological sector of the battlefield fought over by the two great champions, that is, upon the ideas of the Fall and Original Sin only, and to neglect the vast and mysterious questions which lie on either side of these ideas, the question of Divine predestination, on the one hand, and of the nature, operation, and efficacy of Divine grace, on the other. Such an artificial abstraction of the anthropological development from its soteriological context will, indeed, involve a certain relative mutilation of history ; which, nevertheless, will not be censured by those who accept the Bergsonian position, that every particular science must necessarily mutilate Reality, by isolating a given aspect of it, in order to render it intelligible. What follows, therefore, does not purport to be a conspectus of the whole of Pelagianism or of the Pelagian controversy, but merely of such elements in them as are relevant to the scope of our present enquiry.

The practical and evangelistic interests which lay at the roots of Pelagius' thought have been already explained. We have now to lay bare the theoretical assumptions on which it was formally based. Pelagius meant to be, and believed himself to be, an orthodox Catholic Christian ; and both he and his disciple Caelestius professed a special reverence for the *auctoritas* of the Apostolic see.[1] Those who are familiar

---

[1] Pelagius (*libellus fidei ad Innocent. papam, ap.* S. Aug. opera, 1700, tom. x., appendix ii, pp. 64–65) says : ' haec est fides, papa beatissime,

with the history of the primitive Church will find nothing
paradoxical in the statement that in his veneration for
ecclesiastical tradition Pelagius resembled all the great
heresiarchs of antiquity.   Apart from the Gnostic leaders
alluded to in our last lecture, most of whom were heathens
endeavouring to borrow some of the clothes of Christianity
rather than erring or eccentric Christians,[1] those thinkers
whose speculations were destined to ultimate rejection by
the common mind of the ' Great Church ' wrote and taught
under the influence of one or other of two beliefs—either
that they were explaining, not impugning, some hitherto
unformulated portion of the deposit of Faith, or that the
questions with which their characteristic opinions had to do
were such as had been left open by the Apostolic tradition.
Pelagius was dominated by the latter conviction.   He was,
of course, perfectly familiar with the Pauline texts which
assert a causal connexion between the sin of Adam and the
sinfulness and mortality of his descendants : and he was
well aware, as his commentary on the Pauline Epistles
shows,[2] of the existence of the widely diffused theory which
interpreted that connexion in terms of psycho-physiological
heredity.   But he believed that the consensus of opinion
in support of the *tradux peccati* was not so great as to constitute this theory a doctrine of the Church or to make it a part
of the essential Gospel.   Hence, at the synod of Diospolis,
when reproached with certain indiscreet passages in his
letter to the pious widow Livania, he replied ' I anathema-
tise these words as foolish, but not as heretical, seeing that
there is no question of a matter of dogma ' [3] ; and Caelestius
at Carthage affirmed that, whilst well aware that the Fall-
doctrine was widely held *in* the Church, he had always
understood that it was not held *by* the Church, having known
various orthodox presbyters who had denied it without cen-

---

quam in ecclesia catholica didicimus . . . in qua si minus perite aut
parum caute aliquid forte positum est, emendari cupimus a te, qui Petri et
fidem et sedem tenes.'   For the attitude of Caelestius, *cf. de pecc. orig.*
7 : ' immo se omnia quae sedes illa damnaret damnaturum esse promisit.'

[1] *v. supra*, Lecture IV, p. 182.

[2] For quotations see above, p. 335.

[3] *de gest. Pelag.* 6 : ' anathematizo quasi stultos, non quasi haereticos,
siquidem non est dogma.'

sure.[1] As an instance of such a person, he quoted ' Rufinus,
who stayed at Rome with the holy Pammachius ' [2]; he
might with greater effect have cited Clement of Alexandria.[3]
If the state of Church opinion on this subject down to the
conversion of Augustine has been correctly summarised in
our preceding lecture, it must be allowed that the Pelagians
were, at the moment, well within their rights in taking up
this attitude.   From the standpoint of the modern historian,
as he looks back upon the Pelagian controversy over an
interval of sixteen centuries, it may be (and we shall, at the
right time, argue that it is) fair to regard the wide diffusion
of a basic though ill-defined essence of Fall-doctrine in the
pre-Augustinian Church as sufficient, when taken in combination with the persistence of this belief until now, to
vindicate its claim to satisfy the Vincentian test of *semper*,
interpreted with reasonable elasticity : but it would be
manifestly unjust to censure a thinker of the fifth century
for not anticipating this standpoint.   Given the assumptions of his day, Pelagius was perfectly justified in challenging
the Fall-doctrine, in that ' twice-born ' shape which it then
wore in the West ; it may be added, that a dispassionate
student of dogmatic development will feel no regret that the
experiment of producing an entirely indeterministic version
of Christianity should have been made.   Theology, like
other sciences, progresses very largely by means of false
starts and experiments which come to nothing.   The
gradual comprehension of Christian truth is a dialectical
process zig-zagging from side to side—an extreme and
exaggerated thesis provoking an equally over-emphasised
antithesis, until, in the course of ages, the final synthesis
which commends itself to the diffused consciousness of the
Christian society is ultimately attained.

[1] *de pecc. orig.* 3 : ' dixi de traduce peccati dubium me esse, ita tamen
ut cui donavit Deus gratiam peritiae consentiam ;   quia diversa ab eis
audivi, qui utique in ecclesia catholica constituti sunt presbyteri ' ; *ibid.*
4 : ' iam de traduce peccati dixi, quia intra catholicam constitutos plures
audivi destruere, nec non et alios adstruere : licet quaestionis res sit ista,
non haeresis.'

[2] *ibid.* 3 : ' sanctus presbyter Rufinus Romae qui mansit cum sancto
Pammachio ; ego audivi illum dicentem, quia tradux peccati non sit.'

[3] *v. supra*, Lecture IV, p. 207, n. 4, for a passage in which Clement at
least verbally seems to deny ' original sin ' in any sense.

As an intellectual system, Pelagianism claimed to base itself upon the essential goodness of God. God is good, and therefore everything that He has made is immutably good. Here at the outset we come across a *non sequitur* ; Pelagius does not allow for the possibility that the specific goodness or excellence of a particular form of created being may presuppose freedom, and a consequent capacity for temporary or even permanent self-injury. It is explained that Adam was endowed at his creation with a special ' grace,' a statement which at first sight seems to echo the Augustinian language ; but the content of this ' grace ' is defined as consisting solely in the powers of reason and of free-will which distinguish humanity from the beasts. According to Julian, Adam's intellectual attainments were very low and his moral character very high. He and his descendants would have died whether there had been any transgression or not ; the Divine institution of marriage, indeed, presupposes death, as the begetting of children is designed to fill up the gaps left in the ranks of humanity by physical dissolution. Adam was also liable to pain and disease—a contention against which Augustine directed shafts of ponderous and tasteless sarcasm, dilating upon the ' Pelagian Paradise,' [1] full of aches, pains, cramps, diseases, and other ills, in much the same style as that unhappily employed upon a well-known occasion by Bishop Wilberforce in commenting on Huxley's view of the animal ancestry of man. The primal sin injured Adam himself—and presumably Eve—alone, and that in a purely mechanical and external sense, in so far

---

[1] *op. imperf. c. Iulian.* iii. 154 : ' naturam humanam a Deo bono conditam magno inobedientiae peccato ita fuisse vitiatam, ut etiam posteritas inde traheret mortis meritum atque supplicium . . . et contra vos et contra Manichaeos catholica fides dicit. sed vos qui hoc negatis, quaeso, paulisper paradisum cogitate. placetne vobis, ut ponamus ibi castos et castas contra libidinem dimicantes (the psychologist will find it highly significant that this is the first instance of human misery to occur to Augustine's mind) ; gravidas nauseantes, fastidientes, pallentes ; alias in abortu puerperia immatura fundentes, alias in partu gementes et ululantes . . . ? (there is much more in the same style) certe si talis paradisus pingeretur, nullus diceret esse paradisum, nec si supra legisset hoc nomen inscriptum : nec diceret errasse pictorem, sed plane agnosceret irrisorem. verumtamen eorum qui vos noverunt, nemo miraretur, si adderetur nomen vestrum ad titulum, et scriberetur, *paradisus Pelagianorum.*' Cf. *ibid.* iii. 95, 147 ; vi. 25, 27, 28.

as it procured their banishment from the happy Garden.
Hence human nature, as such, is unaffected by Adam's
or any other individual's misdeeds. Whatever the sins of
previous generations may have been, every birth represents
a fresh start in human history—every infant is born in the
same condition as that enjoyed by Adam before the Fall,
with unimpaired free-will and no inherited psychological
handicap of any kind. Free-will is defined as consisting in
a mere capacity or possibility either of good or of evil,[1] that
is, in pure indetermination, in a mathematical point of
uncontrolled and unmotived spontaneity. We may compare this perfect equilibrium of the will, as the Pelagians
conceived it, inclining in itself neither to virtue nor to vice,
with a balance of exquisite poise, of which the beam remains
absolutely horizontal, yet hung with such tremulous
delicacy that the faintest breath may incline it either this
way or that. So immutable is the freedom of the will that
the Pelagians, contradicting the most patent facts of human
experience, appeared to deny the existence of any such thing
as the tyranny of habit. A man may commit a sin one
hundred times, and yet after the hundredth sin he is no more
inclined to commit it, his will is no more biassed or trammelled
than it was before he began the series of sinful acts.[2] It
follows that this mechanically flawless free-will is quite
sufficient in itself to enable man to live without sin; and

---

[1] Pelagius, *libellus fidei*, ad fin. : ' nos vero dicimus, hominem semper
et peccare et non peccare posse, ut semper nos liberi confiteamur esse
arbitrii ' ; Julian, *ap. op. imperf.* i. 78 : ' libertas arbitrii, qua a Deo
emancipatus homo est, in admittendi peccati et abstinendi a peccato
possibilitate consistit ' ; *ibid.* vi. 9 ; ' liberum arbitrium, quod non est
aliud quam possibilitas peccandi et non peccandi.'

[2] *op. imperf. c. Iulian.* i. 91 (Julian) : ' liberum autem arbitrium et
post peccata tam plenum est quam fuit ante peccata ' ; *ibid.* 96 : ' nos
dicimus peccato hominis non naturae statum mutari, sed meriti qualitatem.'
Pelag. *ap.* Aug. *de nat. et grat.* 19 : ' quomodo potuit humanam debilitare
vel mutare naturam quod substantia caret ? ' (Notice that both the great
protagonists accept the traditional Christian-Platonist view of the
anhypostatic nature of evil.) The Pelagians were, however, by no means
invariably consistent, permitting themselves occasionally to invoke the
' tyranny of habit ' as an explanation of the fact of the moral struggle ;
cf. Pelag. *comment. in epp. S. Pauli*, on Rom. vii. 7–24 (Souter, *op. cit.*, ii.
p. 56 ff.) ; *op. imperf. c. Iulian.* iv. 103 (Aug.) : ' nam et ille qui dicit,
" non quod volo ago," certe secundum vos *necessitate consuetudinis*
premitur.'

in point of fact there were sinless individuals even before the Incarnation—Abel, Enoch, and many others amongst Biblical characters,[1] and many philosophers amongst the Pagans.[2] Hence, there never can be any sort of excuse for, or palliative of, sin of any kind.   In his letter to Demetrias Pelagius denounces the idea of human frailty as a delusion.

We contradict the Lord to His face when we say, It is hard ; it is difficult ; we cannot ; we are men ; we are encompassed with fragile flesh. O blind madness ! O unholy audacity ! We charge the God of all knowledge with a two-fold ignorance, that He does not seem to know what He has made nor what He has commanded, as though, forgetting the human weakness of which He is Himself the author, He had imposed laws on man which he cannot endure.[3]

This unbalanced insistence upon the power of the will, which takes no account of the innumerable types of morbid, per- verted, asthenic wills which actually exist, seems to have prevented the Pelagian school as a whole from arriving at a single coherent theory of the relation of appetite, impulse, and feeling to conscious volition, or at a single unanimous judgment as to the moral value to be attributed to the sub- rational elements in human nature.   To denote these latter, they had no other word than the unsatisfactory, already somewhat question-begging, term ' concupiscence.' Though his fundamental axioms forbid him to speak of concupiscence as sinful, Pelagius is monk enough to insist that it must be perpetually repressed by will-power. Julian, however, the jovial and worldly bishop of Eclanum, who may perhaps be described as a fifth-century Talleyrand, was acute enough to see that this view really conceded one of the key-contentions of Augustinianism. For him, all the instincts of human nature are innocent, and require only to be regulated, not

---

[1] de nat. et grat. 42 ; Pelag. ad Demetriad. ep. iii. (ap. S. Aug. opera, 1700, tom. ii., appendix, pp. 4–13).

[2] ad Demetriad. iii.

[3] ibid. xvii. : ' . . . verum e contrario fastidioso ac remisso animo, superborum ac nequam servorum more, in os Domini reclamamus ac dicimus, durum est, arduum est, non possumus; homines sumus, fragili carne circumdamur. o caecam insaniam ! o profanam temeritatem! duplici ignorantia accusamus Deum scientiae, ut videatur nescire quod fecit, nescire quod iussit : quasi oblitus fragilitatis humanae, cuius auctor ipse est, imposuerit homini mandata quae ferre non possit.'

suppressed, by reason using will as its instrument ; they only become evil *per accidens*, when indulged to excess. He does not hesitate to affirm that concupiscence, even in the more restricted sense of the term, existed in Christ.[1] Julian may thus claim the credit of having been the first Christian writer to grasp with absolute clearness the crucial idea of the moral neutrality of bodily appetite—an idea which, as we have seen, the Jewish elaborators of the *yēçer*-doctrine and Gregory of Nyssa were on the verge of attaining, but never actually attained, and which would have saved the later Church from endless confusion of thought, had theological passion not refused it the opportunity of a fair hearing.

From the unqualified libertarianism which has just been sketched it follows that the empirical universality of sin neither requires nor is capable of any explanation other than the bald statement that most men have as a matter of fact chosen to sin. There could, of course, be no question in the minds of Pelagius and his associates of repudiating St. Paul's language as to the causal connexion between the transgression of Adam and the sinfulness of mankind : but this causality is explained as operating solely by way of ' social,' as contrasted with biological, inheritance, and as having no concern with or effect upon the interior constitution of the soul. Evil is transmitted from generation to generation by bad examples, unjust laws, profligate manners and customs ; and the whole idea of a physiological propagation of sin is rejected with indignation, as making God responsible for the perpetual creation of evil natures, and as being, in effect, Manichean.

Pelagius' adversaries were not slow to confront him with a difficulty arising out of the assumed mutual implication of the practice of infant baptism and the theory of

---

[1] *op. imperf. c. Iulian.* iv. 45–64 (note especially Julian's rhetorical question with regard to the incarnate Christ) : ' quae autem gloria castitatis, si virilitas magis aberat quam voluntas, et quod putabatur fieri de vigore animi veniebat de debilitate membrorum ? ' The form of this question can hardly be said to be characterised by the maximum of reverence or good taste ; but the point which it contains, that the denial of any fundamental instinct to our Lord's human nature is Apollinarian, is a perfectly sound one, and Augustine can only meet it by the disastrous argument that concupiscence cannot have existed in Christ, as His birth, being miraculous, was not preceded by concupiscence.

' original sin ' (in the Augustinian signification of the term) :
our study of Origen and Cyprian, it will be remembered,
led us to the conclusion that whether or no there be a
logical connexion between the practice and the doctrine,
there is undoubtedly a historical and psychological connexion, in the sense that the former was very largely
responsible for the growth of the latter. The difficulty
may be expressed as follows : ' If newly born infants, who
in the nature of things cannot have committed actual sin,
are also free from any kind of birth-sin, what is the use
of infant baptism ? ' A modern Pelagian would doubtless
not admit the existence of any difficulty ; we may reasonably imagine him as replying ' Considered *per se*, infant
baptism is of no use at all, at any rate so far as any direct
effects upon the infant are concerned : but considered in
regard to its subjective influence upon parents, sponsors,
and others who may assist at the ceremony, it is often a
source of edification, as vividly symbolising the enrolment
of the newly born in the ranks of the Christian society, and
the love and care with which humanity at its best surrounds
its weakest and most helpless members.' Pelagius, however, as an orthodox Catholic Christian of the fifth century,
was disabled from dealing with the question in so trenchant
a manner. For him, as for all his contemporaries, baptism
was a sacramental mystery which *ex opere operato* imparted salvation to its recipients, and his loyalty to Church
authority forbade him to challenge the now firmly established custom which sanctioned its administration to
infants [1] ; indeed, his followers anathematised all those
who denied the *necessity* of infant baptism.[2] He therefore
drew a distinction between the positive and the negative
effects of baptism. The positive effects, which are received
by infants, are spiritual illumination, the adoption of the
sons of God, citizenship in the heavenly Jerusalem,
sanctification, admission into the number of the members

---

[1] *libellus fidei* (*op. cit.* p. 65) : ' baptisma unum tenemus, quod iisdem
sacramenti verbis in infantibus quibus etiam in maioribus asserimus esse
celebrandum.' *Cf.* also *c. ii. epp. Pelag.* iv. 1, 2.

[2] *op. imperf. c. Iulian.* i. 53 : (Julian) ' nos igitur in tantam gratiam
baptismatis omnibus utilem aetatibus confitemur, ut cunctos qui illam
non necessariam etiam parvulis putant, aeterno feriamus anathemate.'

of Christ, and possession of the kingdom of heaven.[1] The
negative effects of the Sacrament, which consist in the
remission of sins, are not experienced by infants, because
they have no sins to be remitted. Adults, on the other
hand, receive both the positive and the negative effects.[2]
His opponents were not slow to detect a weak spot in his
orthodox armour. The Creed of the one hundred and fifty
Fathers of Constantinople (our ' Nicene ' Creed), which had
already acquired a position of great authority in the Church,
though a generation was still to elapse before it received
the stamp of formal oecumenicity from the Fathers of
Chalcedon, affirmed ' one baptism for the remission of sins ' ;
but, said the Augustinians, Pelagius was setting up two
kinds of baptism—adult baptism for spiritual illumination
and the remission of sins, and infant baptism for spiritual
illumination only. The Pelagians never succeeded in
parrying this dialectical thrust ; the Constantinopolitan
Symbol had gained so strong a hold on the mind and
affections of Christendom that the repudiation of any one
of its phrases, even of those which did not occur in the
original Nicene Creed, had become impossible for those who
claimed to be orthodox Christians ; and various expedients
were invoked for the purpose of finding a way out of the
difficulty. Most of the Pelagians, it would seem, explained
the ' remission of sins ' believed to be imparted to babes,
in a hypothetical and proleptic sense, affirming that infants
are baptised in order that they may become Christians and,
as such, capable of receiving (presumably through Penance)
remission of the sins which they probably will commit
after arriving at years of discretion. We need not comment
now on this phase of the controversy, save by repeating

---

[1] *op. imperf. c. Iulian.* i. 53   (Julian) ' Christus enim qui est sui operis
redemptor auget circa imaginem suam continua largitate beneficia ; et
quos fecerat condendo bonos facit innovando adoptandoque meliores.
hanc igitur gratiam [*sc.* baptismatis] per quam reis venia, inluminatio
spiritalis, adoptio filiorum Dei, municipatus Ierusalem caelestis, sanctificatio, atque in Christi membra translatio, et possessio regni caelorum
mortalibus datur, qui aliquibus negandam putat, omnium bonorum
exsecrationem meretur.'

[2] This was, as a matter of fact, precisely the position held by St.
Gregory of Nazianzus (*carm.* i. [*theol.*] sect. i. 9. 87–92, quoted above,
Lecture IV, p. 289 f.).

the observation that the practice of infant baptism presents a considerable problem to the critical, even though sympathetic, student of Catholic custom, and that there is a stronger *prima facie* case for the Anabaptist position than most English Church-people have hitherto been willing to admit.[1]

With the question of the precise reasons for which infant baptism is to be deemed necessary is inextricably bound up the further question, What is the destiny in the next life of infants who die unbaptised ? It will be remembered that in our last lecture we noted the first emergence of the ' eschatological issue,' necessarily raised by the Fall-doctrine when thought out to its ultimate consequences, in the writings of the two Cappadocian Gregories.[2] Like them, the Pelagians solved the problem by the mild and humane hypothesis of a *limbus puerorum*, of a state of natural beatitude to be enjoyed by those who through no personal fault but solely through lack of the baptismal character are excluded from the immediate presence and vision of God—a conception which we shall meet again in scholastic theology and in the immortal epic of Dante.[3] This conception followed inevitably from the Pelagian belief in the inborn, unimpaired goodness of human nature, and stood in diametrical contradiction to the lurid eschatology arising from the Augustinian idea of mankind as a *massa peccati*, according to which all the unbaptised without exception, and also such of the baptised as had not been predestined to receive the gift of final perseverance, were justly doomed to everlasting flames. The Augustinians pressed Pelagius with a rigidly literal interpretation of the Saviour's words ' except a man be born of water and of the Spirit, he cannot enter into the kingdom of God ' ; he could only counter this argument by drawing a somewhat forced distinction between ' eternal life,' on the one hand—which need not mean more than existence in a *Limbo* of natural beatitude, and to which the innocent unbaptised might accordingly

---

[1] For a discussion of infant baptism on its merits, see Additional Note G, p. 550.

[2] *v. supra*, Lecture IV, pp. 279, 290.

[3] Lecture VI, p. 406 f.

be held entitled—and ' entrance into the kingdom of God,'
that is, into heaven in the fullest sense, on the other, which
since the Incarnation has been exclusively reserved for the
baptised.

THE CONDEMNATION OF PELAGIANISM

Such were the strictly anthropological tenets of Pelagianism, as gradually hardened and systematised through
a generation of controversy. We have been obliged to
anticipate somewhat the course of history in the foregoing
sketch ; but this anticipation may be justified by the consideration that nothing was really added to Pelagianism
from without, and that the effect of the struggle was merely
to draw out ideas and implications which were latent in it
from the first. The actual course of the controversy may
be read at length in the standard histories of the Church
and of dogma,[1] and need only be summarised here in the
briefest possible manner. The condition of suppressed
hostility between the two systems, which may be deemed
to have been initiated by Pelagius' denunciation of *da quod
iubes*, flamed up into a definite state of war when Pelagius
and Caelestius, on the approach of the Goths to Rome
(A.D. 410), left Italy for North Africa, thereby walking
into the lion's den. Pelagius himself went on to Palestine ;
but Caelestius, the *enfant terrible* of the Pelagian movement, remained in Africa ; and his tactless utterances
drew down upon him the condemnation of the African
Church, expressed by a great Synod held at Carthage
(A.D. 411–12).[2] Having declared their opinion of Pelagian-

---

[1] *e.g.* B. J. Kidd, *History of the Church to* A.D. 461, iii. pp. 65–133 ;
L. Duchesne, *Histoire ancienne de l'Église*, iii. c. 6 ; Harnack, *History
of Dogma* (E. tr. 1898), v. pp. 168–188 ; Seeberg, *Lehrbuch der Dogmengeschichte* (1923), ii. pp. 546 ff. ; Loofs, *Leitfaden* (1906) pp. 417 ff.

[2] The Acts of this Council have perished, save for a fragment which is
preserved by St. Augustine, *de pecc. orig.* iii. The positions of Caelestius
which were then condemned are given as follows, in *de gestis Pel.* 23 :
' (1) Adam mortalem factum, qui sive peccaret, sive non peccaret, mori-
turus esset. (2) quoniam peccatum Adae ipsum solum laeserit, et non
genus humanum. (3) quoniam lex sic mittit ad regnum, quemadmodum
evangelium. (4) quoniam ante adventum Christi fuerent homines sine

ism within their own territory, the Africans, with the implacable fanaticism of their race, despatched the narrow and embittered Orosius to stir up trouble against the author of the movement in Palestine. To the great disgust of the Augustinians, the more tolerant Easterns showed a certain disinclination to follow their lead ; Pelagius was acquitted by two Palestinian synods—as the result of verbal prevarication, say Augustine and Jerome—and by the Pope Zosimus, a Greek by birth,[1] and therefore antecedently likely to be deficient in sympathy with the characteristically ' twice-born ' point of view. The African bishops, none the less, stuck to their heresy-hunt with the grim tenacity of hounds in full cry ; the condemnation of Pelagianism and the affirmation of the Augustinian position were renewed in a second plenary council held at Carthage in A.D. 418.[2] Simultaneously, by a remarkable coincidence, the Emperor Honorius intervened in the controversy, decreeing exile against Pelagius, Caelestius, and their followers, and the whole weight of the secular sword was flung into the balance on the side of Augustine. This may have been due to genuine conviction on the part of the Emperor ; but the Pelagians were not slow to suggest that the imperial action had been procured by the Africans through bribes judiciously administered amongst the monarch's *entourage*.

These events exerted a notable influence on the policy of Pope Zosimus. Faced with the open revolt of Africa, on the one hand, and the coercion of the civil Government, on the other, the terrified pontiff changed his tune and issued an encyclical letter known as the *epistula tractoria*,

---

peccato. (5) quoniam infantes nuper nati in illo statu sunt, in quo Adam fuit ante praevaricationem. (6) quoniam neque per mortem vel praevaricationem Adae omne genus hominum moriatur, neque per resurrectionem Christi omne genus hominum resurgat.'

[1] ' natione Grecus ' (*liber pontificalis*, ed. L. Duchesne, i. p. 225).

[2] For the text of those canons of this Council, which directly refer to the Fall-doctrine, see Additional Note B, p. 391.

Canon iii. condemns the belief in Limbo as the destiny of unbaptised children, a belief which subsequently became part of the accepted teaching of Latin Christendom ; Duchesne (*hist. anc.*, iii. p. 236, n. 1) notes that this canon ' manque à plusieurs des collections canoniques d'où nous vient le texte de ce concile,' and adds, significantly, ' c'est là une suppression voulue, car le canon est certainement authentique.'

which affirmed the essentials of the Augustinian position
and condemned the ideas of Pelagius and Caelestius. Subscription to this document was enforced by the Government
throughout the West ; but nineteen Italian bishops, headed
by Julian of Eclanum, refused to submit. This latter
prelate kept up the fight for another five years, alternately
appealing for a new hearing before a General Council and
endeavouring to gain the ear of Honorius. Failing in both
attempts, Julian and the remnants of the Pelagian party
then (A.D. 423) took refuge in the East, which, loyal to its
more vague and liberal conception of the Fall and of transmitted sinfulness, does not seem to have been deeply impressed by the *tractoria*[1] ; they found their natural allies
and protectors amongst those Eastern bishops who belonged
to the Antiochene school of Christological thought. Of
these, the most illustrious was Theodore of Mopsuestia,
a prelate distinguished alike for pastoral zeal and massive
erudition, who welcomed the exiles to his Cilician see-town.

We may digress for a moment in order to draw attention
to the fact that there is both a historical and a logical
connexion between the Pelagian doctrine of man and of
sin and the Antiochene presentation of the doctrine of the
Person of Christ. The historical connexion lies in the fact,
vouched for by Marius Mercator, that the opinions expressed
by Pelagius in his commentary on the Epistle to the Romans
had been suggested to him by one Rufinus, an otherwise
unknown Syrian, who himself had derived them from
Theodore and his immediate circle.[2] If this is so—and
there seems to be no reason for doubting Marius Mercator's
word—it will be a true and complete account of the genesis
of Pelagianism to state that its *matter* arose out of the
' once-born ' piety and moral earnestness of Pelagius and
Caelestius themselves, as explained above, and that its
intellectual *form* was borrowed by them from the thought

---

[1] *v. infra*, pp. 386, 388.

[2] *lib. subnot.*, 2, 3 (*PL* XLVIII. 111). As is well known, Theodore was
the author of a work against the doctrine of original sin ; the surviving
fragments of it are printed by H. B. Swete, *Theodore of Mopsuestia on the
Minor Epistles of St. Paul*, ii. pp. 332–7. Photius (*Bibliotheca*, cod. 177)
gives the title of this work as Θεοδώρου ᾿Αντιοχέως πρὸς τοὺς λέγοντας φύσει
καὶ οὐ γνώμῃ πταίειν τοὺς ἀνθρώπους.

of Christian Syria. The logical connexion has been
luminously summed up by Dr. Gore in an epigram which
has now become famous, ' The Nestorian Christ is the
fitting Saviour of the Pelagian man ' [1] ; as the Christology
of Nestorius did not differ in essence from the teaching of
Theodore, he might well have made ' the Antiochene Christ '
the subject of the sentence.[2]   A few words will suffice to
draw out the implications of this dictum, which expresses
a far-reaching principle of permanent validity, concerned
with the very essence of the Christian religion, and with
the nature of that redemption which it professes to offer.[3]

Pelagianism, as we have seen, assumed the complete
indetermination of the human will, even in habitual sinners ;
man can save himself, if he chooses, by the exertion of
volitional effort. He does not, therefore, require more
external assistance in order to his salvation than may be
provided by sound moral instruction and the example of a
perfect human life set before him for his imitation. Given
these premises, it is natural to conceive the Redeemer
simply as a man, with his own human individuality and *ego*,
who has himself triumphed in the moral struggle and beaten
down the fiery assaults of desire, and thereby presented all
subsequent generations with an object-lesson of the power
of human will. But, if this example of supreme moral
achievement is to be efficacious, it must be real ; and if it is
to be real, the temptations which the Redeemer overcame
must have been real ; and, if those temptations were real,
poignant, and distracting (it was argued) He cannot have

---

[1] ' Our Lord's Human Example,' in *CQR* xvi. p. 298 (July 1883).

[2] Nestorius' own attitude towards Pelagianism was curiously
ambiguous ; *v. infra*, p. 353.

[3] The logical connexion between the Antiochene and the Pelagian
systems was fully recognised, at least by the Augustinians, in the fifth
century : it is strongly insisted upon by Cassian (*de incarn. Christ.* i.
3–5, *PL* L. 20 sq.) in reference to the case of the monk Leporius, who had
advanced from Pelagian premises to Nestorian conclusions ; for this
personage's subsequent retractation, see *Leporii libellus emendationis,
PL* XXXI. 1221–1230, and Kidd, *op. cit.* iii. p. 137 f. A celebrated utterance on this point is the ironical poem of Prosper of Aquitaine, *epitaphium
Nestorianae et Pelagianae haereseos* (*PL* LI. 153), which begins

' (*Nestoriana haeresis loquitur*)
Nestoriana lues successi Pelagianae
quae fuit in utero praegenerata meo.'

been theoretically impeccable, though He was sinless in fact.
Like Julian, Theodore does not hesitate to affirm that
concupiscence must have existed in Christ, and that He
must have known the agony of wrestling with bodily
appetite [1]; though it is apparently implied that after the
Resurrection and the Ascension He attained to formal
impeccability in the fullest sense.[2]   Hence it is not possible
simply to equate the human Jesus with God the Word, for
God *ex hypothesi* is impeccable.   The relation between the
human and the divine in Christ must be conceived as the
conjunction of two persons, the man Jesus and God the Son
Who indwelt and inspired Him.   Doubtless the union
between them was so intense and intimate that the man may
be described as a ' vesture ' [3] worn by the Divine Son, and
the Antiochenes fiercely repudiated the suggestion that
they were setting up two Sons or two Christs ; yet, though
the unity of Jesus and the Word was such that it justifies
the worship of Jesus, it is nevertheless only a moral unity,
resting on God's ' good pleasure,' which in no way abolishes
the ultimate ontological duality existing behind it.   The
man and the Son of God were blent in a unity of sympathy
and moral harmony far transcending that of the most
devoted friendship or conjugal union ; yet in the last resort
they remain two and not one.

It is not likely that the Antiochene Christology will ever
be revived in this precise form.   But the general conception
of a supremely inspired man, who ' redeems ' free human
beings only in the sense that he helps them towards right
living by his exalted ethical teaching and by the example of
his own interior triumph, is still with us, and forms the

---

[1] *de incarn.* xv (reprinted in H. B. Swete, *op. cit.* ii. p. 311) : πλέον
γὰρ ὠχλεῖτο ὁ κύριος καὶ ἠγωνίζετο πρὸς τὰ ψυχικὰ πάθη ὑπὲρ τὰ τοῦ σώματος,
καὶ τῷ κρείττονι λογισμῷ τὰς ἡδονὰς ἐχειροῦτο, τῆς θεότητος δηλαδὴ μεσιτευούσης
καὶ βοηθούσης αὐτῷ πρὸς τὴν κατόρθωσιν.

[2] *ibid.* vii (Swete, ii. p. 297) : οὕτως δὲ λοιπὸν μετὰ τὴν ἀνάστασιν καὶ τὴν
εἰς οὐρανοὺς ἀνάληψιν ἐπιδείξας ἑαυτὸν καὶ ἐκ τῆς οἰκείας γνώμης τῆς ἑνώσεως
ἄξιον, προσειληφὼς δὲ ταύτην καὶ πρὸ τούτου ἐν αὐτῇ τῇ διαπλάσει τῇ τοῦ
δεσπότου εὐδοκίᾳ, ἀκριβῆ λοιπὸν καὶ τῆς ἑνώσεως παρέχεται τὴν ἀπόδειξιν,
οὐδεμίαν ἔχων κεχωρισμένην καὶ ἀποτετμημένην ἐνέργειαν τοῦ θεοῦ λόγου κ.τ.λ.

[3] The phrase διὰ τὸν φοροῦντα τὸν φορούμενον σέβω is apparently attributed
to Nestorius in Cyril's synodical letter *Cum salvator* (conveniently reprinted in T. H. Bindley, *The Oecumenical Documents of the Faith*, 1906,
pp. 121 ff.).

foundation of the Ritschlian or Liberal Protestant reconstruction of Christianity ; it is as true to-day as it was in the
fifth century that a purely indeterministic anthropology
necessitates a merely ' exemplarist ' soteriology.[1] The traditional scheme, to which this Pelagian-Antiochene sequence
of ideas stands in the sharpest opposition, consists in the
notions of human nature as hamstrung by the Fall, and of
redemption as meaning the restoration of human nature
through sacramental union with a Divine-human Saviour.
In Catholic theology, the inbred malady of mankind and the
sacramental remedy mutually imply each other[2] ; and some
modern thinkers who wish to get rid of the conception of
objectively efficacious sacraments have shown a true instinct
in attacking that idea of the origin and ground of sin which
alone gives sacraments any vital significance.   It must not
be supposed that these logical connexions were consciously
realised by the Pelagians or the Antiochenes : they attached
as much importance to baptism, penance, and the Eucharist
as did the rest of the Great Church.   But it remains true to
say that in so far as they insisted on a merely ' exemplarist '
conception of redemption, they were, all unwittingly, doing
their best to render the sacraments otiose and obsolete.

Nevertheless, the Antiochenes, and the Pelagians in so
far as they consciously adopted the Christology of Antioch,
deserve the credit of having stood for a true and fundamentally Scriptural position—that of the thoroughgoing
reality of our Lord's human experience, of His human
example, of His human triumph over genuine temptations.
How, clothed in a sacred Humanity which knew no disharmony between reason and will, and in which all the
functions and faculties of our nature maintained relatively
to each other that due and lovely proportion which God had
originally willed, He could yet be ' in all points tempted like
as we are,' [3] so that He could express gratitude to His friends

[1] A striking fifth-century instance of the logical necessity of this
inference is provided by the treatise of the Pelagian monk Leporius
(*Leporii libellus emendationis, PL* XXXI. 1221–1230) ; see Kidd, *op. cit.*
iii. p. 137 f.

[2] Of all the writers of antiquity, Gregory of Nyssa seems to recognise
this most clearly ; *v. supra*, Lecture IV, p. 278.

[3] Heb. iv. 15.

for ' continuing with ' Him in His ' temptations,' [1] is a question too grave and mysterious to be investigated here. Yet any explanation of our Lord's sinlessness, which makes His temptations even more unreal than the ' temptation ' which the opportunity of stealing a farthing might present to a millionaire, must inevitably fall under the stigma of Docetism : if it is true to say, with Dr. Bright, ' a peccable Christ could not be a lifegiving Christ,' [2] it is equally true to say the same of an imperfectly human Christ.

We return from this digression to resume the thread of our historical narrative. On the death of Theodore in A.D. 428, Julian, Caelestius, and their adherents (Pelagius himself has now disappeared from sight [3]) took refuge at Constantinople, hoping to be protected by the new archbishop, of tragic fame, Nestorius. This prelate's attitude towards them was curiously vacillating. At first he seems to have favoured them, and wrote to Rome for information concerning the causes for which they had been condemned : then, when the Government of Theodosius II expelled them from the capital of the Eastern Empire, at the instance of Marius Mercator, he preached publicly against Pelagianism, while condoling with Caelestius in private. The controversy about the Fall and original sin now became overshadowed by the gigantic duel between Cyril and Nestorius, which arose out of the attack made by the latter's chaplain, Anastasius, upon the term *Theotokos*. Amidst the din and excitement of this vast conflict it seemed as though the issue raised by Pelagius had been forgotten, especially after the death of Augustine in A.D. 430. It was, however, at least momentarily recalled to men's minds by the Cyrilline Council of Ephesus (A.D. 431), now usually known as the Third Oecumenical Council. This body, in its first and fourth canons,[4] pronounced ecclesiastical censure upon ' those who hold the opinions of Nestorius or of Caeles-

[1] Luke xxii. 28.

[2] *The Age of the Fathers*, ii. p. 262.

[3] The last we hear of him is Marius Mercator's notice of his banishment from Jerusalem in A.D. 424 (*comm.* iii. 5) ; probably he died not long afterwards.

[4] Hardouin, i. 1621, 1623 ; W. Bright, *Canons of the first Four General Councils* (1892), pp. xxvii, xxviii.

tius'[1]; and in a synodical epistle it informed Pope Caelestine that it had renewed the condemnations of Pelagianism enacted by his predecessors[2]—though, as Duchesne points out, the Acts of the Council contain no evidence that this was actually done.[3]

Though the Cyrilline Council, in view of the irregularity both of its constitution and of its proceedings, had at the time of its meeting no genuine claim to oecumenicity, yet the subsequent acceptance of its decrees by the Great Church has been generally regarded as tantamount to the imposition of an oecumenical character upon it. The detailed examination of the two Ephesine canons which touch our subject must be reserved for a later section of this lecture : but it may be said here that the condemnation of the opinions of Caelestius, vaguely expressed though it is, would seem to amount to the elevation of the Fall-doctrine, at least in a minimal form, to the rank of a Catholic dogma. So far as the Church of the Graeco-Roman Empire was concerned, Pelagianism was officially at an end ; and its subsequent recrudescences in Gaul and Britain are of no importance for our present enquiry.

A Critique of Pelagianism

It is probable that the immediate reaction of the average Englishman (one, that is, whose judgments in matters of religion are not controlled either by expert theological knowledge or by stringent denominational loyalties), upon considering the summary of Pelagianism contained in this lecture, would be to approve this system whole-heartedly as the embodiment of the soundest and most healthy common sense. Pelagianism originated in our island, and may,

---

[1] *can.* I : εἴ τις ὁ μητροπολίτης τῆς ἐπαρχίας . . . τὰ Κελεστίου ἐφρόνησεν ἢ φρονήσει . . . *can.* 4 : εἴ δέ τινες ἀποστατήσαιεν τῶν κληρικῶν, καὶ τολμήσαιεν ἢ κατ' ἰδίαν ἢ δημοσίᾳ τὰ Νεστορίου ἢ τὰ Κελεστίου φρονῆσαι. The absence of any mention of Pelagius confirms the supposition that he was by this time dead.

[2] *relatio ad Caelestinum*, ad fin. (Hardouin, i. 1509).

[3] *hist. anc.* iii. p. 357 ; he appends the dry comment ' De ces choses-là on ne parle qu'au pape, avec l'intention évidente de s'en faire bien voir.'

indeed, be said to be endemic in it ; and the dispassionate student will find much that is attractive in the speculations of the first great British theologian. Julian's view, at least, of the moral neutrality of ' concupiscence ' in its broadest sense has now won a practically universal acceptance amongst those who have shaken themselves free from the savage conception of ' bad *mana* ' and the dualistic idea of the inherent evil of matter ; and the Pelagian position as to the other-worldly destiny of unbaptised infants and of the heathen would seem to be far more in accordance with a genuine belief in the infinite love and mercy of God than the opinions of Augustine with regard to the same subject. Most attractive, at first sight, of all the Pelagian tenets is the belief in the unimpaired sovereign freedom of the will. Pelagius would have us declare, in the well-known words of Henley,

> I am the master of my fate :
> I am the captain of my soul [1] ;

and we may be reasonably sure that, in his evangelistic campaign at Rome, the burly British monk must have dealt with his converts in the spirit of a judicious psychotherapist, who, far from insisting on the miserable condition in which his patient finds himself, puts forth every effort to develop the latter's will-power, courage, and self-reliance. It is hardly too much to say that on point after point of detail Pelagianism stood for sanity and reason as against pathological fanaticism.

Yet when all this has been admitted, and when we have expressed the justifiable indignation which the suppression of Pelagianism by the civil sword rather than by reasoned argument naturally evokes, we are constrained to record the judgment that its triumph would have been an unqualified disaster for Christianity. The principal ground for this judgment is the fact that the fundamental assumption of Pelagianism—the assumption of an absolutely undetermined, autonomous, sovereign free-will residing in all human beings without exception—is simply untrue. It ignores the agonising facts of ' incontinence ' and the moral struggle.

[1] *Invictus.*

It represents a purely artificial conception of freedom, deduced from the bare consciousness, which we have at certain moments, of the power of choice. It leaves out of sight the parts played by feeling, instinct, impulse, in the inner life of man ; it recks not of the mighty tides of sensual emotion, of self-assertive impulse, of ideal aspiration, of the love of God, which swirl and mingle together in the seething maelstrom of the human soul. It forgets that the affections are as capable of being harnessed to bear the will up to heights of heroic endeavour as of dragging it down to depths of moral infamy. It reduces the spiritual life to a dull, mechanical process of conformity with an external code ; it is the negation of the profound maxim, of which the truth is daily receiving fresh confirmation from psychological study, ' No virtue is safe which is not enthusiastic.'

Some further consequences of this vicious doctrine of unlimited indeterminism may be briefly summarised. Its complete lack of correspondence with the facts of human nature may be seen in its denial of the terrible power of habit ; on the Pelagian hypothesis, the dipsomaniac, the libertine, the recidivist, the gaol-bird are just as ' free,' just as instantaneously capable of the highest virtue and self-sacrifice as the saint who has grown grey in the service of God and man. Most damning indictment of all—the Pelagian system is fundamentally irreligious, in so far as it tends to destroy in the heart of man the feeling of childlike dependence upon his Maker. By the possession of free-will, Julian did not hesitate to say, man is ' emancipated from God.' [1] God creates a man, and thenceforward ceases to play any part in his life, only re-entering it for the final judgment. Pelagianism is a system of moral Deism, which makes the God of Christianity into an Epicurean divinity throned upon a distant Olympus and exercising no influence upon the lives of His human creatures ; and its adherents did not shrink from the declaration that prayer for spiritual blessings is to be condemned, because man has it in his power to acquire all spiritual blessings by the exercise of his sovereign free-will. Lastly must be mentioned the fact that Pelagianism abolishes the reasonable and humane distinction

[1] *op. imperf. c. Iulian.* i. 78.

formulated by the author of the first Johannine Epistle[1] between a ' sin unto death ' and a ' sin not unto death,' that is, roughly speaking, between what are now called ' mortal ' and ' venial ' sins. As every sinful act proceeds *ex hypothesi* from an entirely free and conscious self-determination of the will, it follows that even the most trivial lapses must be regarded as wilful defiances of the majesty of God, and relatively harmless peccadilloes assume a mountain-like importance. On this showing, the adage which asserts that to steal a pin is as great a sin as to steal any other thing is amply justified. The mild and liberal ethics of Christianity, which allow for the frailty of human nature, are thus invested with a harsh and censorious rigorism,[2] and are made to presuppose an ideal standard of self-control which may be attained in another world, but which the facts of experience show to be inapplicable to our inchoate, raw, and unfinished personalities in this.[3] Pelagianism has often been accused of minimising the ' sense of sin ' ; but the exact opposite is the truth : by insisting on the unlimited freedom of the will, and by sweeping away the excuses which may be found in natural weakness or the power of habit, it exaggerates the sense of sin (of actual sin, that is) to a degree at which it must become a burden to the sensitive conscience no less intolerable than the opposite error, which bids us mourn for the ' original guilt ' of a nature which *ex hypothesi* we cannot help possessing.

These considerations suggest that if Christianity had accepted Pelagius' account of human nature as its presupposition, it would have ceased to be a ' religion ' in any intelligible sense of the term. Religion is a fire, a passion, an elemental pulsation of man's being, an inborn yearning

---

[1] v. 16, 17.

[2] This rigoristic aspect of Pelagianism, which was largely ignored by earlier historians of doctrine, has been brought into prominence by the Pelagian documents edited by C. P. Caspari in *Briefe, Abhandlungen und Predigten* (Christiania, 1890) : a single sentence, from the first of these documents (p. 5), will give their key-note : ' de maioribus criminibus taceo, quia nulli dubium est, maiora exercere delicta non licere, cui nec minora conceduntur.'

[3] An extreme instance of the ascetic tendency in Pelagianism is to be found in Caelestius' declaration that rich Christians could not enter the kingdom of heaven unless they renounced all their riches : *de gest. Pel.* 23.

and aspiration towards the unknown Infinite Good which is God. Pelagianism would have made Christianity into a compound of Judaism and Stoicism, a dull and joyless puritanism, an external code of civic and secular morals. Its interior spirit is aptly summed up in the third of the propositions attributed to Caelestius and condemned at the Carthaginian Synod of A.D. 411–12—' That the (Mosaic) Law is as good a guide to heaven as the Gospel.' [1]

It is therefore both possible and reasonable, without invoking any authoritarian assumptions whatever, to conclude that the Third Oecumenical Council was, as a matter of fact, in the right when it decided that the Pelagian view of human nature, despite the good and noble elements in it, was untrue; inasmuch as this view rests upon an artificial conception formed by the abstraction of one psychical phenomenon—the consciousness of choice—from its context in the rest of our interior experience. But the assertion that the root-idea of Pelagianism represents such an exaggeration of one side of our moral experience as to be untrue, and that its failure was on the whole a blessing for the Church and for humanity, is not by any means to admit that its mighty victorious rival, Augustinianism, was necessarily in the right. Before we can formulate a final judgment with regard to St. Augustine's view of human nature and the origin of sin, we must pick up again the thread of our historical survey, and supplement the provisional sketch of Augustinianism as it stood in its embryonic form before the clash with Pelagianism, which we drew just now, by a picture of St. Augustine's system as it stood at the close of his life, embodied in such a work as the *opus imperfectum contra Iulianum*, and fully developed, with every nerve and lineament drawn out into high relief, through twenty years of controversy. It will be convenient to group the data yielded by the fifteen works which are generally styled ' the anti-Pelagian treatises,' and by occasional passages in other works, under heads corresponding to the five fundamental issues which were defined at the beginning of Lecture IV as necessarily arising

---

[1] ' quoniam lex sic mittit ad regnum, quemadmodum evangelium ' (quoted above, p. 347, n. 2).

out of the Pauline Fall-doctrine, and the two further issues
which emerged during the course of the pre-Augustinian
patristic development ; for the sake of clearness, these
seven problems shall be here reformulated.   They are :

(i) Is the Paradise-narrative of Gen. iii. to be interpreted literally or allegorically ?

(ii) What was the condition of man before the Fall—
one of ' non-moral innocence,' or one of ' original
righteousness ' and ' perfection ' ?

(iii) What is the undesirable thing, state, or quality
asserted to have been acquired by the first man
in consequence of the Fall, and to have
been thereafter transmitted by him to all his
descendants ?   Is it the lack of the supernatural endowments originally possessed by
him, weakness of will, inordinate ' concupiscence,'
legal responsibility for the initial act of sin, or
any or all of these taken together ?

(iv) What is the mode of transmission whereby Adam
transmits this *damnosa haereditas* to his posterity
—biological or merely ' social ' heredity, mystical
or ' seminal ' identity ?

(v) What is the resulting state of human nature, with
which Redemption now has to deal ? is free-
will intact and complete, gravely hampered,
or for all practical purposes annihilated ?

(vi) What is the *rationale* of infant baptism ? can any
theoretical basis be found for this custom other
than the supposition that ' original guilt ' is
thereby remitted to beings who, in the nature
of the case, cannot be subject to the guilt of
actual sin ?

(vii) What is the destiny in the next life of persons—
such as unbaptised infants and virtuous pagans
of adult age—who, without having committed
actual sins, die subject to the consequences of
Adam's Fall, not having obtained redemption
through Christ and His Church ?

The number and the complexity of these issues show vividly the greatness of the tree into which the seed sown by the Jewish apocalyptists had grown.

DEVELOPED AUGUSTINIANISM

(i) During the greater part of his life as a Christian thinker St. Augustine's exegesis of the Biblical Paradise-story is strictly literalistic. He had, indeed, at one time played with the allegorical interpretation, tentatively suggesting, in the treatise *de Genesi ad Manichaeos*, which was written between A.D. 388 and 391, that Adam's body was transparent, celestial, and in no need of physical nourishment, and that the union of our first parents was of a purely spiritual nature, designed solely ' ut copulatione spirituali spirituales fetus ederent, id est bona opera divinae laudis.' [1]   Only a few years later, however, uncompromising literalism makes its appearance in the treatise *de Genesi ad litteram*,[2] and thenceforward its domination of Augustine's anthropology is unquestioned.

(ii) Augustine's beliefs as to the Paradisal state of unfallen man represent the culminating point of that tendency to exalt it to the highest pitch of ' original righteousness ' and ' perfection,' which we have already noted as beginning to emerge in some great writers of the fourth century, both Western and Eastern : which doubtless represents a subtle infiltration of Rabbinical ideas into the mind of the Great Church, though why such an infiltration should have taken place at this precise epoch we cannot tell : and which has always exercised a powerful influence on Fall-speculation of the ' twice-born ' type, inasmuch as, the more glorious man's original state and endowments are made, the deeper, by contrast, become the criminality and the guilt of the Fall.[3]   So we find, according to Augustine, that Adam in

[1] ii. 15 ; cf. *de catech. rud.* 29.

[2] vi. 30–36, 39 ; viii. 7 ; etc.   It is noteworthy, however, that even in this treatise he still retains what may be described as a symbolical interpretation of the ' days ' of creation : *cf.* iv. 51–53.

[3] For the development of this Augustinian tendency by Baius and the Reformers, see Lecture VI, pp. 422, 427.

Paradise was exempted from all physical evils, and endowed ✓
with immortal youth and health which could not be touched
by the taint of sickness or the creeping debility of old age.[1]
The gift of immortality lay within his reach [2] ; the taste
of the Tree of Life would have enabled him to transcend
physical limitations, to refine and transubstantiate his
earthly nature into pure spirit, so that it would have
passed painlessly from this life to the fuller life of Heaven,
without the gloomy passage through the grave and gate
of death.[3] His intellect was endowed with an ' infused
knowledge ' which, we are told, made his mental powers
as far superior to those of the most brilliant modern
philosophers as the flight of birds surpasses in swiftness
the sluggish movements of the tortoise.[4] This speculation
is supported by the curious contention that Adam's intellectual abilities are proved to have been of this transcendent order by the feat which he performed in thinking
of appropriate names for the various species of animals
which were brought to him by the Creator [5]—an idea
developed by Bishop Bull some thirteen centuries later in
a famous passage which I cannot refrain from quoting :

I might here insist upon that admirable philosophy lecture
which Adam (appointed by God Himself to that office) read on
all the other animals, for although his theme here was a part of
natural philosophy yet his performance herein, if we look to its
circumstances, cannot but be judged by every considering man
to be the effect of a more than human sagacity : that, in the
infinite variety of creatures never before seen by Adam, he
should be able, on a sudden, without study or premeditation, to
give names to each of them, so adapted and fitted to their
natures as that God Himself should approve the nomenclature.

---

[1] *de Gen. c. manich.* ii. 8. (References are given only to one or two
typical passages on each point ; for others, see the Benedictine indices.)

[2] *de Gen. ad litt.* vi. 36 ; *op. imperf. c. Iulian.* vi. 39.

[3] *de Gen. ad litt.* ix. 6 : ' . . . si iuste omnes obedienterque viverent,
tunc fieret illa commutatio, ut sine ulla morte animalia corpora conversa in
aliam qualitatem, eo quod ad omnem nutum regenti se spiritui deservirent,
et solo spiritu vivificante sine ullis alimentorum corporalium sustentaculis
viverent, spiritalia vocarentur. potuit hoc fieri, si non praecepti transgressio mortis supplicium mereretur ' ; *cf.* also 10.

[4] *op. imperf. c. Iulian.* v. 1.

[5] Gen. ii. 19, 20 ; for the modern critical interpretation of this passage
see Lecture II, p. 41, n. 2.

How astonishing a thing is it : what single man among all the philosophers since the Fall, what Plato, what Aristotle amongst the ancients, what Descartes or Gassendi among the moderns, nay, what Royal Society durst have undertaken this ? [1]

These exalted intellectual attainments were combined with a moral character equally lofty. Man as originally created had freedom in the proper sense, that is, undetermined autonomy, the faculty of being able not to sin, *posse non peccare*.[2] This autonomous free-will was the absolute sovereign of his microcosm, exercising a most calm and perfect control over all the movements of appetite and feeling. A tendency towards evil did indeed exist in Adam, but only in a faint degree ; there was just enough of it in him to constitute his Paradisal condition a state of trial or testing, but no more.[3] The sexual appetite in particular was entirely subject to the control of the will. If Adam had remained in Paradise he would indeed have begotten children, but in accordance with the dictates of reason, and without any excess of concomitant emotion.[4] His will, moreover, was confirmed in goodness by an implanted rectitude, an interior spirituality, a settled bias and determination towards virtue, which was the equivalent of that steadfast character which the greatest saints have acquired through a lifetime of struggle.[5] Yet Adam in Paradise knew no struggle : his character of perfect holiness was presented to him as it were ready-made by his Creator. He had no temptations with which to contend ; all he had to do was to keep out of the way of temptation, and to preserve the ' original justice ' with which God had endowed him.

The question has been raised, whether Augustine in his

---

[1] *Works* (Oxford, 1846), ii. Discourse V, p. 125 f.

[2] *de corrept. et grat.* 33 ; the *posse non peccare* in the moral sphere was parallel to the *posse non mori* in the physical. But Adam's *posse non peccare* was a state inferior to the *non posse peccare* now enjoyed by the blessed.

[3] So J. B. Mozley, *Augustinian Doctrine of Predestination* (1855), p. 91, drawing out the implications of *op. imperf. c. Iulian.* v. 61.

[4] *de nupt. et concup.* i. 1, 6, 7, 8.

[5] *op. imperf. c. Iulian.* v. 61 : ' illa itaque perfectio naturae quam non dabant anni sed sola manus Dei non potuit nisi habere voluntatem eamque non malam.'

own mind separated sharply between the glorious supernatural qualities which he believed to have been enjoyed
by Adam before the Fall, and the qualities of reason and
voluntary action which distinguished him from the beasts
and which he continued to possess even after the Fall :
in other words, whether he consciously recognised a contrast
between what the Schoolmen were later to describe as the
donum supernaturale of ' original righteousness ' and ' perfection,' and the *pura naturalia*, or properties belonging
simply to human nature as such. According to some
scholars, notably M. Turmel,[1] Augustine drew no such
distinction. For him, it is contended, the primitive state
of Adam was merely the state which is natural to man as
such. Human nature as it now exists is in a wounded and
abnormal condition : the paradisal perfection of the protoplast is the norm from which it has declined.[2] On the
other hand, it is the case that some at least of Adam's more
splendid endowments are expressly attributed by Augustine
to a special grace, a superabundant generosity on the part
of God : such are his holiness, his freedom from concupiscence, his immortality—possibly also his immunity
from disease and his colossal intellectual powers.[3] It
appears safest to say that Augustine never made his mind
decisively up with regard to this point, and that the germs
of both opinions—both that of the Schoolmen, who distinguished the *donum superadditum* from the *pura naturalia*,
and that of the Reformers and Baius, who identified them—
are to be found in his writings.

It follows from this exalted view of man's paradisal
condition that the malice of the first sin was infinite in its
demerit, precisely because it was the *first*. (It is probably

---

[1] *Revue d'hist. et de littér. relig.* vii. p. 224 f.
[2] This is apparently implied by *retract.* i. 15, 6 : ' itemque in eo quod
dixi, *natura esse malae animae nullo modo queunt* ; si quaeritur quomodo
accipiamus quod ait Apostolus, *fuimus et nos natura filii irae sicut
et ceteri* ; respondemus, naturam in his verbis meis me intelligi voluisse
illam, quae proprie natura vocatur, in qua sine vitio creati sumus. nam
ista propter originem natura appellatur ; quae origo utique habet vitium,
quod est contra naturam.'
[3] See numerous references given by J. Tixeront, *Histoire des dogmes*,
ii. p. 465.

unnecessary to utter the warning that we are for the moment engaged in stating Augustine's ideas, not in criticising or evaluating them.)   All subsequent sins, indeed, (according to Augustine) have been due to the inordinate power of concupiscence and the corruption of man's nature engendered by the Fall.   But the Fall itself was not due to concupiscence, because that *ex hypothesi* barely existed in unfallen man.   It was therefore due to pure senseless perversity ; it was a sin solely of the will and not of the appetite, and it was committed, not as a result of weakness or frailty, but against a settled habit of virtue.[1]   It was not a mere floating with the stream of human tendencies, but a deliberate attempt to swim against the stream. Hence, apart from the question of its consequences, it was an unique and dreadful tragedy, because it was the moral *débâcle* of a saint.   Trivial as the act of tasting the forbidden fruit may appear to us, it was none the less a direct transgression of the divine command, and as such included in itself all possible forms of sin.   It involved the sin of pride, which claims to be independent of God ; of infidelity, which refuses to believe in His word ; of homicide, in that it rendered both Adam and his descendants liable to death ; of spiritual fornication, inasmuch as it corrupted his moral integrity ; of avarice, which claimed more than was man's just due.   The passage of the *Enchiridion* which discovers all these forms of vice in the first sin concludes with an anticlimax, of which Augustine is not often guilty : the first sin included the sin of theft, inasmuch as the forbidden fruit was not Adam's property.[2]

In retribution for this infinitely malicious self-determination of his free-will in hostility to and contempt of his Maker, Adam was justly pronounced by the dread judicial sentence to lie under the doom of everlasting death, both of body and of soul.

(iii) The universal sinfulness, which, in the words of the Apostle, ' has passed unto all men,'[3] is original or

---

[1] *op. imperf. c. Iulian.* i. 71 : ' praecessit mala voluntas, qua serpenti subdolo crederetur ; et secuta est mala concupiscentia, qua cibo inhiaretur inlicito.'

[2] *enchirid.* xlv.   [3] Rom. v. 12.

transmitted sin—*peccatum originale* or *peccatum ex traduce*. But what precisely is the nature of this communicated taint? The direct question is one which somewhat embarrassed St. Augustine, for the anti-Pelagian treatises do not yield any explicit definition of original sin, and he himself excuses his failure to supply a logically perfect conception of transmitted sin by the abstruseness and difficulty of the subject; ' nihil est ad praedicandum notius, nihil ad intelligendum secretius.' [1] Subsequent thought, however, is indebted to him for clearing up the confusion which had hitherto reigned in regard to the two metaphors, medical and legal, under which men had found it natural to describe the spiritual effects of Adam's Fall upon his posterity. By distinguishing between the *vitium* and the *reatus* of original sin he showed, in effect, that the Western version of the Fall-doctrine (which, of course, he himself believed to be the primitive and Catholic doctrine) contained two independent propositions, either of which could theoretically be held without the other, namely, (*a*) ' Man suffers from a hereditary moral disease, first acquired by Adam and since transmitted from generation to generation of his posterity,' and (*b*) ' Man is born subject to the inherited legal liability—to judicial punishment for Adam's sin.' It will be convenient to consider these two propositions, which together constitute the specifically Augustinian doctrine of original sin, separately.

(*a*) First of all what, according to Augustine, is the *vitium* of original sin, the flaw in human nature which is inherited from Adam? When the question is narrowed down to this point it is not difficult to discern the answer. The *vitium* consists precisely in the unbridled and inordinate tyranny of concupiscence over the rest of man's interior microcosm. In Augustinian thought, concupiscence may be generally defined as the tendency which impels man to turn from the supreme and immutable good, which is God, in order to find his satisfaction and comfort in that which is mutable and less than God, that is, in creatures. Even in the best of men its involuntary, undesired ebullitions are symptomatic of the flaw inherent in human nature as such.

[1] *de mor. eccl. cath.* i. 40.

It is a languor or malady of the soul, consisting in the hypertrophy of those bodily instincts which in themselves are necessary for the preservation of the individual or the race—so far Augustine does not appear to go beyond the Pauline teaching as to the ' innate infirmity ' [1]—and (a more disputable position) it is both sin and the penalty of our first father's sin : ' sic est hoc peccatum, ut sit poena peccati.' [2]

Of man's disordered instincts, however, the most violent and the least amenable to the commands of reason and of God is the reproductive instinct : and hence in Augustine's thought ' concupiscence ' tends to be predominantly used in its most restricted sense.   We thus arrive at an equation [3] : ' original sin ' (considered as *vitium*) = ' concupiscence ' = sexual passion : an equation which determines his view as to (iv) the mode of transmission of the malady of the soul.   Inasmuch as sex-feeling of the kind now experienced by fallen man is for Augustine intrinsically sinful, it follows that the very act of begetting a child inevitably stains it with ' original sin,' so that we are in a quite literal sense ' born in sin,' that is, in the ' sin ' of our parents.[4]   It is for this reason, he thinks, that it was necessary for the Saviour to be born miraculously, in order that His human nature might be free from the entail of sin.[5]   The Pelagians were not slow to challenge this apparent condemnation of one of the primary instincts of human nature as essentially Manichean ;   and they enquired, with considerable cogency, ' How is it, then, if baptism entirely abolishes " original sin," that baptised persons are still tormented by " con-

---

[1] Lecture III, p. 156.

[2] *de pecc. mer. et rem.* ii. 36.

[3] I find that Buonaiuti (*op. cit.* p. 401, n. 1) has independently arrived at the same phrase : ' l'equazione matematica posta fra il peccato originale e l'istinto sessuale.'   In this Augustinian position we reach the high-water-mark of a tendency which we have noticed running all through the history of Fall-speculation, both Jewish and Christian.

[4] *de pecc. mer. et rem.* i. 57 : ' quod igitur in membris corporis mortis huius inobedienter movetur, totumque animum in se deiectum conatur adtrahere, et neque cum mens voluerit exsurgit, neque cum mens voluerit conquiescit, hoc est malum peccati, in quo nascitur omnis homo.'

[5] *c. Iulian. Pel.* v. 52 : ' quia Mariae corpus quamvis inde (*sc.* ex concupiscentia) venerit, tamen eam non traiecit in corpus quod non inde concepit.'

cupiscence," apparently to as great an extent as the
unbaptised ? and why are the children of Christian parents
not born free from original sin ? ' To the former argument
Augustine replied that what he condemned was not the institution of marriage in itself, for that existed in Paradise,
but rather the excessive and irrational exaltation of feeling
due to the dislocation of human nature consequent on the
Fall, which now almost invariably [1] attends even its lawful
use.[2] (Why ' excessive ' feeling merely as such should be
stigmatised as ' sinful,' rather than as pathological, he does
not explain : like many Fall-speculators of the ' twice-born '
school, he easily passes, without knowing it, from the medical to the forensic way of regarding psychic disharmony.)
The latter was parried by means of the distinction between
the *actus* of concupiscence, that is, the psychological fact of
its existence, and its *reatus*, the guilt which attaches to its
possession : baptism cancels the *reatus*, but leaves the *actus*
still in existence.[3] Hence it follows that, even though the
parents may have been freed by baptism from the *reatus*,
their offspring is none the less born with both the *actus* and
the *reatus* of concupiscence inherent in it : for the *actus*
infects the child in the first moment of its conception, and
an unbaptised person who possesses the *actus* is necessarily
also subject in the sight of God to the *reatus*.[4]

This theory, that the *vitium* of original sin is directly

[1] Augustine allows for the possibility of strictly sinless marriages in
de nupt. et conc. i. 9.

[2] This appears to be the general sense of such passages as *de pecc. orig.*
39–43 ; *de nupt. et conc.* i. 8, ii. 25.

[3] *de nupt. et conc.* i. 29 : ' in eis ergo qui regenerantur in Christo cum
remissionem accipiunt prorsus omnium peccatorum, utique necesse est,
ut reatus etiam huius licet adhuc manentis concupiscentiae remittatur,
ut in peccatum, sicut dixi, non imputetur . . . manent ergo <peccata>,
nisi remittantur. sed quomodo manent, si praeterita sunt, nisi quia
praeterierunt *actu*, manent *reatu* ? sic itaque fieri e contrario potest, ut
etiam illud ' (*sc.* malum concupiscentiae) ' maneat *actu*, praetereat *reatu*.'

[4] *de nupt. et conc.* i. 20, 21 : ' propter hanc ' [*sc.* concupiscentiam]
' ergo fit ut etiam de iustis et legitimis nuptiis filiorum Dei, non filii Dei sed
filii saeculi generentur : qua et ii qui genuerant, si iam regenerati sunt,
non ex hoc generant ex quo filii Dei sed ex quo adhuc filii saeculi . . . ex
hac igitur concupiscentia carnis quod nascitur, utique mundo non Deo
nascitur : Deo autem nascitur cum ex aqua et Spiritu renascitur. huius
concupiscentiae reatum regeneratio sola dimittit, ac per hoc generatio
trahit.'

propagated from parent to child in and through the act of generation, would seem to have relieved Augustine of the necessity of deciding between the ' creationist ' and the ' traducianist ' views of the origin of the soul ; for it is equally compatible with either. His personal inclinations pointed in the direction of ' creationism ' ; but he found it difficult to explain why God should have created so many millions of souls in a state of innocence, only to be infused into bodies which He knew were bound to pollute them with concupiscence.[1] Moreover, the Pelagians, it would seem, were ' creationists ' to a man : hence, when charged by them with holding ' traducianism,' Augustine shows a distinct reluctance to repudiate the accusation.[2] His final position with regard to this point seems to have consisted in an affirmation of its indifference, provided that the reality of the innate disease and of its hereditary transmission were firmly maintained.[3]

(v) So oppressive and overwhelming is the tyranny of fleshly appetite over fallen man, that he cannot even begin to raise himself out of the mire of sinfulness without the help of God's prevenient grace. This position would seem logically to involve the negation of human free-will ; and from time to time Augustine uses phrases which can only be construed in this sense.[4] The condition of man after the Fall is described as subject to a *peccatum habendi dura necessitas*.[5] Yet Augustine strenuously refuses to admit that our fallen race does not still possess free-will, and in order to preserve a nominal freedom in man he is driven to make use of shifts and expedients which, with all due respect for his mighty intellect, it is difficult to regard as more than mere verbal jugglery. In reply to Julian he admits that the *libertas* which Adam possessed in Paradise has perished ; this *libertas* is defined as freedom to remain in Paradise and

---

[1] *de anima et eius orig.* i. 6, 13.

[2] Cf. *de pecc. merit. et rem.* iii. 5 ; *c. ii. epp. Pel.* iii. 26 ; *op. imperf. c. Iulian.* ii. 178 ; iv. 104.

[3] *c. Iulian. Pel.* v. 17 : ' ista fides non negetur, et hoc quod de anima latet aut ex otio discitur, aut sicut alia multa in hac vita sine salutis labe nescitur.'

[4] e.g. *enchir.* 30 : ' amissum est liberum arbitrium ' ; *de perfect. iust. hom.* 9 : ' poenalis vitiositas subsecuta ex libertate fecit necessitatem.'

[5] *de perfect. iust. hom.* 9.

acquire the gift of immortality. But although freedom (*libertas*) has perished free-will (*liberum arbitrium*) still exists; and this elusive and all but incomprehensible distinction between ' freedom ' and ' free-will ' is defended, not by metaphysical arguments, but by an exposition of the metaphorical language employed by St. Paul in Rom. vi. 20 with regard to the condition of unregenerate man : ' When ye were enslaved to sin, ye were free in regard to righteousness.' [1] The confusion introduced into Augustine's conception of free-will by his determination to use St. Paul's image, borrowed from the Roman law of slavery, as though it were a metaphysical or psychological definition, is complete. The will of fallen man is free, but in point of fact it always freely chooses evil under the overwhelming influence of concupiscence, or of the devil's power.[2] We are free to do what we like, but we are not free to like what we ought to like. This interpretation of ' freedom ' is justified by the consideration that if freedom means the power to choose either good or evil God Himself is not free, nor will the blessed in Heaven be free, because they will be subject to the *beata necessitas non peccandi*.[3]

It is not necessary to go into this very abstruse and difficult conception of freedom any further, inasmuch as it is clear that Augustine, whether consciously or not, is

[1] *c. ii. epp. Pel.* i. 5.   [2] *Cf. ibid.* ii. 9.

[3] *Cf. op. imperf. c. Iulian.* i. 100, 102 ; *de civ. Dei*, xxii. 30 : ' Deus ipse numquid quoniam peccare non potest, ideo liberum arbitrium habere negandus est ? ' and the whole context. The answer to this argument surely is that God is not free, in the sense in which freedom is predicable of human beings still *in via*, in the state of probation ; if He were, it would be an imperfection in Him, and He would in fact not be God. The same consideration would also apply to the blessed, who are *comprehensores in patria* : their blessedness is based upon the fact that they cannot now fall, in other words, upon the fact that they are not ' free.' The discussion of the whole matter, both by Augustine and by some of his successors, is vitiated by a failure to distinguish between three senses of the word ' freedom,' *viz.* (*a*) *physical*, in which it connotes absence of external constraint : in this sense, God undoubtedly is free, and man may or may not be, according to circumstances ; (*b*) *metaphysical*, in the sense of interior indetermination ; in this sense, God and the saints are not free, but man in the state of probation is ; (*c*) *metaphorical*, in the sense of ' freedom from sin ' or from concupiscence ; this actually means a fixed interior determination towards good, in other words, it implies the exact opposite of freedom in sense (*b*).

really trying to run with the hare and hunt with the hounds. He wants to keep freedom in order to preserve man's responsibility for actual sin, and yet he wishes to throw it overboard in order to provide scope for irresistible grace. If we disregard verbal subtleties and concentrate our attention on realities, we shall find that the Augustinian system implies the negation of free-will in any except a highly recondite and unnatural sense of the term. Mozley's words can hardly be bettered :

(Augustine) explained the corruption of human nature to mean the loss of free-will ; and this statement was the fundamental barrier which divided the later from the earlier scheme and *rationale* of original sin. The will, according to the earlier school, was not substantially affected by the Fall. Its circumstances, its means and appliances, were altered, not itself ; and endowed with spiritual aids in Paradise, deprived of them at the Fall ; re-endowed with them under the Gospel, it retained throughout these alterations one and the same essential power, in that power of choice whereby it was, in every successive state of higher or lower means, able to use and avail itself of whatever means it had. But in Augustine's scheme the will itself was disabled at the Fall, and not only certain impulses to it withdrawn, its power of choice was gone, and man was unable not only to rise above a defective goodness, but to avoid positive sin. He was thenceforth, prior to the operation of grace, in a state of necessity on the side of evil, a slave to the devil and to his own inordinate lusts.[1]

As a result of the Fall, therefore, according to Augustine, the nerve of the human will is severed, and concupiscence rages unchecked.[2] Yet Augustine is not prepared to draw from these facts—or supposed facts—their logical conclusion, which would seem to be the Calvinistic doctrine of the ' total depravity ' of human nature. We may surmise that it was

[1] *Augustinian Doctrine of Predestination*, p. 125 f.

[2] A well-known passage, *de nat. et grat.* 42, appears at first sight to exempt the Blessed Virgin Mary from this law, and has been quoted as an anticipation of the doctrine of her Immaculate Conception : ' excepta igitur sancta virgine Maria, de qua propter honorem Domini nullam prorsus, cum de peccatis agitur, haberi volo quaestionem : unde enim scimus, quid ei plus gratiae collatum fuerit ad vincendum omni ex parte peccatum, quae concipere et parere meruit, quem constat nullum habuisse peccatum ? ' Yet, at their highest interpretation, these words do not appear to do more than suggest that Mary may have been safeguarded, by a special grace, from actual sin.

his Platonic monism which, perhaps subconsciously, restrained him from formulating this final corollary of the 'twice-born' version of the Fall-doctrine. For the Platonist all being, in so far as it is true being, is good; and everything that exists is either God or derived from God. Even the nature of the devil, *qua* created nature, is good; he is only evil as it were *per accidens*, because of the perversion of his will.[1] Hence evil—even the evil of original sin—is nothing positive : it is a defect of goodness, the absence of virtue, just as darkness is not a substantive thing-in-itself but merely the absence of light.[2] These are ideas which we have already encountered in the great Greek Fathers of the fourth century,[3] and which need not be commented on now, save by the observation that their logical effect would necessarily be to blunt the edge of the antithesis between 'nature' and 'grace,' which arose out of Augustine's own specifically 'twice-born' experience. If this suggestion does actually represent the interior workings of Augustine's mind, it would not be the first time that the harsh judgment of human nature generated by the fervid emotions of an African Fall-speculator had been mollified by the genial influences of his Hellenic philosophical background : Origen is an instance of the same phenomenon.[4] At any rate, it is noteworthy that Augustine, in the opening chapters of the treatise *On nature and grace*, explicitly admits that ' all the good qualities which human nature, even as fallen, still possesses in its constitution, its life, its senses, its intellect, it has from the most high God, its creator and artificer ' [5] :

---

[1] *de civ. Dei*, xix. 13 : ' proinde nec ipsius diaboli natura, in quantum natura est, malum est ; sed perversitas eam malam facit.'

[2] Cf. *de nat. boni* 17 : ' non ergo mala est, in quantum natura est, ulla natura ; sed cuique naturae non est malum nisi minui bono ' ; *enarr. in ps.* vii. 19 : ' non quod aliqua sit natura tenebrarum. omnis enim natura, in quantum natura est, esse cogitur. esse autem ad lucem pertinet : non esse ad tenebras. qui ergo deserit eum a quo factus est et inclinat in id unde factus est, id est in nihilum, in hoc peccato tenebratur.'

[3] Lecture IV, pp. 255, 260, 266, 278.

[4] *ibid.* p. 209.

[5] *de nat. et grat.* 3. As against Julian, he repudiates the idea that human nature is essentially, not merely accidentally, evil : ' non dixeram naturam humanam malam non esse sed malum non esse : hoc est, ut planius loquar, non dixeram vitiatam non esse, sed vitium non esse ' (*op. imperf.* iii. 190).

and, in the section of the *Retractations* dealing with this book, he claims to have upheld grace ' not indeed in disparagement of nature, but as that which liberates and controls nature.' [1]

(*b*) We now pass to the question of the results of the Fall as viewed under the legal or forensic category, that is, to the question of ' original guilt,' of the inherited taint considered as *reatus* rather than as *vitium*, together with the allied question of the mode of transmission or communication of such guilt. It is curious and noteworthy that, whereas the transmission of original sin, considered as *vitium*, is said to take place by way of biological heredity (the act of generation being the *nexus* which conveys the fatal legacy of concupiscence from parent to child), the communication of original sin, considered as *reatus*, from Adam to his posterity is explained in accordance with the theory of ' seminal identity.' No doubt it is possible to harmonise these two conceptions of the mode of transmission, but Augustine makes no effort to do so. When ' original guilt ' is in question, the latter theory is affirmed in the stiffest and most uncompromising fashion. Adam, by his wilful transgression, incurred infinite guilt and was therefore justly doomed to eternal damnation. But, at the moment when he committed his sin, he included within himself, in a strictly physiological sense, the whole of the human race, all the countless myriads who were to proceed from his loins ; or, if the more metaphysical way of phrasing the matter be preferred, Adam was the universal of human nature, and as such subsumed in himself all the particular men who have since been born. Consequently, all men sinned ' in Adam,' in the sense that at the moment of the Fall they were all infinitesimally minute portions of the Adam who sinned, or particulars included in the universal nature which sinned : their personalities and wills were all implicit in Adam's personality and will. The possibility of such pre-natal participation in an ancestor's act is demonstrated by the instance of Levi, who was yet in the loins of Abraham when the latter paid tithes to Melchisedek, and who must therefore, in the mind of the author of the Epistle

---

[1] *retract.* ii. 42.

to the Hebrews, be deemed to have 'seminally' shared in the payment of those tithes.[1] It follows, according to Augustine's logic, that all human beings are born subject to the penalty of eternal hell for a sin which they are alleged to have pre-natally committed in Adam's loins : and this appalling sentence is duly executed upon all except those whom the inscrutable decree of God's predestination singles out from the 'mass of perdition,' brings to the absolving waters of baptism, and endows with the grace of final perseverance. The Doctor of Hippo repeatedly and vehemently insists upon the 'justice' of this arrangement whereby millions of the human race are condemned to an eternity of torture as the punishment of a crime for which they have *ex hypothesi* no personal responsibility whatsoever.[2]

This *macabre* doctrine runs through the warp and weft of Augustinianism like an endless black thread. Though the passages in Augustine's works which embody it are innumerable, it may nevertheless be worth while to quote two of the most gloomy and powerful. The first contains its foundation, the theory of 'seminal' or 'metaphysical identity' :

God indeed created man upright, being Himself the author of natures, not of vices. But man, having of his own free-will become depraved, and having been justly condemned, begat a posterity in the same state of depravation and condemnation. For we all were in that one man <Adam>, seeing that we all *were* that one man (*omnes enim fuimus in illo uno, quando omnes fuimus ille unus*[3]) who fell into sin through the woman, who was made of him before the sin. Not yet had we received those individually created and distinct shapes, in which we were as separate individuals to live ; but there was a seminal nature, from which we were to be propagated ; and, this having been vitiated by sin, tied with the chain of death, and justly condemned, it follows that man would be born from man in no other condition <than that in which Adam was after the Fall>.[4]

---

[1] Heb. vii. 9, 10 ; quoted in *op. imperf. c. Iulian.* i. 48.

[2] It should be noted that original sin, according to the Augustinian conception, really contains two distinct kinds of original guilt, *viz.* (1) the guilt of having 'sinned in Adam,' and (2) the guilt of possessing concupiscence, which is both *peccatum* and *poena peccati*.

[3] *Cf.* Ambrose's phrase 'fuit Adam, et in illo fuimus omnes' (*expos. ev. sec. Luc.* vii. 234, quoted above, p. 305, n. 3).

[4] *de civ. Dei*, xiii. 14.

The second illustrates the superstructure, that is, the theory of original guilt :

Banished <from Paradise> after his sin, Adam bound his offspring also with the penalty of death and damnation, that offspring which by sinning he had corrupted in himself, as in a root ; so that whatever progeny was born (through carnal concupiscence, by which a fitting retribution for his disobedience was bestowed upon him) from himself and his spouse—who was the cause of his sin and the companion of his damnation—would drag through the ages the burden of original sin, by which it would itself be dragged, through manifold errors and sorrows, down to that final and never-ending torment with the rebel angels. . . . So the matter stood ; the damned lump of humanity (*totius humani generis massa damnata*) was lying prostrate, nay, was wallowing, in evil, it was ever falling headlong from one wickedness to another ; and, joined to the faction of the angels who had sinned, it was paying the most righteous penalty of its impious treason.[1]

It is, perhaps, better not to speculate with regard to the amount of unhappiness which these ideas must have brought to sensitive souls between the time of their first promulgation and that of the final eclipse of Augustinianism by Darwinism in the nineteenth century.

Two corollaries of the Augustinian doctrine of original sin remain to be noticed. The first of these is the theory which denies the possibility of virtue, good works, or merit in the unbaptised, a theory which appears to survive in the thirteenth of our Thirty-Nine Articles, in the intensified form of the assertion that works before justification [2] ' have the nature of sin.' Inasmuch as human nature, apart from grace, is so deeply depraved, it is impossible for the heathen to possess genuine virtue, though they may perform actions which in Christians would be the symptoms of genuine virtue.[3] ' <Augustine> regards heathen morality as bad

---

[1] *enchirid.* 26, 27.

[2] This phrase is taken from the title of the Article : it is, however, fair to mention the fact that the text of the Article only condemns ' works done before the grace of Christ and the inspiration of his Spirit,' which might, verbally at any rate, be taken to mean works other than good works : though in that case the body of the Article becomes a sonorous platitude.

[3] In the beautiful treatise *de spiritu et littera*, which reveals only the noblest and most humane side of Augustine, he admits that the good deeds of the heathen may be praised ' merito recteque ' : but he adds, as though

at the foundation, and therefore as hollow, false, and only seeming morality itself.' [1]

God forbid [he exclaims against Julian] that we should admit the existence of true virtue in anyone except he be righteous. And God forbid that we should admit anyone to be truly righteous, unless he lives by faith : ' for the righteous lives by faith.' Who then of those who wish to be thought Christians (except the Pelagians alone, or perhaps you alone even amongst Pelagians) will apply the epithet of ' righteous ' to an infidel, to an impious man, to one sold into the power of the devil ?— even though such a one should be a Fabricius, a Fabius, a Scipio, a Regulus, names by which you thought that I could be brow-beaten, as though we were debating in the old Senate-house at Rome ! [2]

Hence even continence and chastity are no virtues when displayed by the ' impious,' that is, non-Christians.[3] The Scriptural basis of this position appears to consist solely in a scrap of the Epistle to the Romans, torn from its context and expanded into a general principle which the Apostle would never have recognised as his own : ' What-soever is not of faith ' (that is, according to Augustine, specifically Christian faith) ' is sin.' [4] Though he did not himself declare the virtues of pagans to be *splendida vitia*, this phrase, coined by his disciples of a later day, is

---

fearing that he has conceded too much, ' quamquam si discutiantur quo fine fiunt, vix inveniuntur quae iustitiae debitam laudem defensionemve mereantur ' (§ 48). In the following passages Augustine appears (some-what inconsistently with his general position) to recognise the possibility of real virtue outside the Church, though such virtue is solely the gift of God : *ep.* cxliv. 2 (Polemo, a pagan, said to have renounced drunken-ness) ; *de patient.* 23 (schismatic martyrs will, in view of their martyrdom, be treated more leniently in the final judgment) ; *de grat. Christi* 25 (Ahasuerus changed by God's interior operation from fury to gentleness).

[1] J. B. Mozley, *Augustinian Doctrine of Predestination*, p. 127.

[2] *c. Iulian. Pel.* iv. 17.

[3] *ibid.* ad fin.

[4] Rom. xiv. 23, cited in *de gestis Pel.* 34 ; *c. Iulian. Pel.* iv. 24. The true meaning of the phrase, in relation to the vegetarian controversy which the Apostle is discussing, has been well summed up by Sanday and Headlam (*ICC.*, p. 393, note *in loc.*) in the sentence ' Weakly to comply with other persons' customs without being convinced of their indifference is itself sin ' ; it has no reference to the ordinary conduct of non-Christians.

not very far from expressing his real thought on the point.[1]

The second corollary which deserves mention is the doctrine of the necessary damnation of all persons dying unbaptised, including personally guiltless infants. This follows inevitably from the conception of the *massa damnata*, which (with the exception of the company of predestined souls arbitrarily picked out of it for exaltation to eternal life) steadily gravitates, under the inexorable pressure of the divine justice, towards the bottomless pit. At one period of his life, indeed, Augustine appears to have shrunk from the full rigour of this pitiless dogma. In A.D. 415 we find him writing to Jerome for help.

> Teach me [he begs] what I am to teach, teach me what I am to hold, and tell me, if souls are individually created for all the individuals who are this day being born, when (? where) do such souls sin in the little ones, that they should need the remission of sin imparted by the sacrament of Christ . . . ? or, if they sin not, by what justice of the Creator are they so bound to another's sin, so soon as they are infused into their new-begotten members, that damnation seizes upon them, unless help is brought to them through the Church ? especially in view of the fact that it is not in their power to secure being helped by the grace of baptism. So many thousands of souls which at the deaths of infants depart from their bodies without the pardon bestowed by the Christian sacrament—with what equity can they be damned, if, newly created, by no previous sin of their own but solely by the will of the Creator, all these individual souls were infused into the individual bodies for the animation of which He created and gave them ? [2]

Jerome excused himself, on the ground of want of leisure, from giving an answer to these questions, which are indeed unanswerable. The fact that Augustine nevertheless maintained this inhuman theory down to the last days of his life is a melancholy illustration of the way in which the best of men may allow the kindly instincts of

---

[1] The phrase is probably an inference from *de civ. Dei* xix. 25 : 'proinde virtutes, quas sibi habere videtur [*sc.* mens veri Dei nescia], per quas imperat corpori et vitiis ad quodlibet adipiscendum vel tenendum, nisi ad Deum retulerit, etiam ipsae vitia sunt potius quam virtutes.'

[2] *ep.* clxvi. 10. It will be noticed that in this passage Augustine assumes ' creationism ' : but the difficulty is equally pressing on the ' traducianist ' hypothesis.

human nature to be overridden by the demands of a fanatical logic.

The Augustinian doctrine on this point is vividly expressed in a woodcut which is prefixed to tom. x. of the Benedictine edition of 1700, the volume containing the anti-Pelagian treatises. This woodcut is meant to illustrate the passage *op. imperf. c. Iul.* i. 39. It depicts the interior of a church in baroque style. On the right of the picture is the baptistery, where a bishop is plunging a naked infant into the font ; this infant is evidently one of the elect, for the Holy Spirit is represented as a dove descending upon him in a stream of supernatural glory. Parents, sponsors, acolytes stand around in various attitudes of edification. On the left is the nave of the church ; here another christening party is seen, suddenly halted with expressions and gestures of horror and dismay, just before the entrance to the baptistery : in their midst, a nurse holds the corpse of an infant, who was being brought to baptism, but has that very moment unexpectedly died (of convulsions, or what not) on the very verge of receiving the Sacrament of regeneration, and whose soul must therefore be presumed to have gone straight to hell, in virtue of original sin. The picture is surmounted by a scroll, bearing the inscription ' Unus assumitur et alter relinquitur ; Quia magna est gratia Dei, et verax iustitia Dei ' (taken from the passage in question : the context adds ' sed quare ille potius quam ille ?—inscrutabilia sunt iudicia Dei '). When the whole theory is so horrible, it is perhaps a small matter that it appears to assume a purely mechanical view of the efficacy of infant baptism.

Augustine must, indeed, be allowed whatever credit may attach to the fact that at various times during the main period of his theological activity he expresses the opinion that the punishment of unbaptised babes, albeit eternal, will be of the mildest kind.[1] No hint of this qualification, however, is shown by his last utterance on the subject, in the unfinished work against Julian. Here he speaks of the

---

[1] *de pecc. merit. et rem.* i. 21 : *enchirid.* 23 (xciii), with reference in general to those who die in original sin only, without having committed actual sin ; *c. Iulian. Pel.* v. 44 (' damnatio omnium levissima ').

ceremony of *insufflation*, or breathing on the face of the
catechumen, which still survives in the modern Roman
ritual of baptism ; and he tells us that this ceremony is
performed in order that the devil, in whose power the little
one is born (as being ' guilty ' through the contagion of
original sin), may be cast forth, and the child transferred to
the power of Christ. But, he adds, if the little one is not
so delivered from the power of darkness, he remains under
it. Why (he naïvely enquires) should it be a matter of
wonder that the little one is doomed to eternal fire with
the devil, seeing that he is not permitted to enter the
kingdom of God ? [1]

Before proceeding to the task of disentangling what
appear to be the permanently valuable elements in the
Augustinian doctrine of man and of sin from those which
are morbid or irrational, it will be well to indicate the
arguments upon which the doctrine was formally based.
(It is doubtless unnecessary to re-emphasise the distinction
between the psychological *ground* of Augustinianism, consisting in its author's ' twice-born ' temperament, and the
logical *premises* from which it was nominally deduced : and
it will be understood that to recognise Augustine's theological
case for his doctrine as being ultimately an *ex post facto*
' rationalisation ' of a peculiarly vehement type of emotional
experience in no way reflects upon his personal sincerity
and good faith in putting it forward.) These arguments,
which recur again and again throughout the vast mass of
Augustine's anti-Pelagian writings, do not when collected
amount to very much. The ' appeal to Scripture ' consists
in ringing the changes on the four or five proof-texts with
which we are already familiar—the Psalmist's cry ' Behold,
I was shapen in wickedness ' [2]; the Septuagintal mistranslation of Job xiv. 4, 5 ' Who shall be free from defilement ?
not one, even though his life be but a day upon the earth ' [3];
the Johannine Christ's affirmation of the necessity of a new
birth through water and the Spirit as a condition of entrance

---

[1] *op. imperf. c. Iulian.* iii. 199.

[2] Ps. li. 5.

[3] For the true text see Driver and Buchanan Gray, *Job* (*ICC.*), 1921,
p. 127.

into the kingdom of God [1] ; the phrase ' children of wrath '
from Eph. ii. 3 ; and the text which Augustine believed to
be his trump card, the clause from Rom. v. 12 (lat.)—' in
quo omnes peccarunt,' misinterpreted in accordance with
Ambrosiaster's fatal blunder as ' in whom (sc. Adam) all
have sinned.' [2] The slenderness of the Biblical foundation
upon which Augustine's terrific dogma is reared will be
realised when it is pointed out that of his five proof-texts
three are mistranslations. The ' appeal to tradition,' in so
far as it is not a mere assertion, bases itself upon an alleged
consensus of the Fathers : but it is impossible not to observe
that the Fathers whom Augustine cites are for the most
part Western, and that the list of authorities which may be
compiled from his various references is a fairly exhaustive
catalogue of upholders of the specifically ' twice-born ' view,
no account being taken of the Apologists or of the Alexand-
rines.[3] This, however, does not prevent him from triumph-
antly exclaiming to Julian ' You are refuted on every side !
so great testimonies of the Saints are clearer than daylight.' [4]
Thirdly, we have the argument which has played so great a
part in this discussion from the time of Origen downwards,
drawn from the actual practice of the Church in administering baptism to infants, with exsufflations, exorcisms, and
renunciations of Satan ; all of which, it is contended, would
be futile if the newly born infant were not in some sense
guilty of Adam's sin. Lastly, and more reasonably,
Augustine bases his theory upon the actual state of man,

---

[1] St. John iii. 5.

[2] For remarks upon Ambrosiaster's misunderstanding of *in quo*, itself
a faulty rendering of ἐφ' ᾧ, see Lecture IV, p. 308f. Typical instances of
Augustine's use of this mistake to support the idea of our ' seminal identity '
with Adam are *serm.* ccxciv. 15 ; *c. ii. epp. Pel.* iv. 7 (here he quotes
Ambrosiaster's comment, ' manifestum in Adam omnes peccasse quasi
in massa,' as from ' sanctus Hilarius ') ; *de pecc. merit. et rem.* i. 11. The
correct translation which the Pelagians gave of ἐφ' ᾧ, viz., *propter quod*,
was denounced by Augustine, despite his imperfect acquaintance with
Greek, as importing ' sensum alium novum atque distortum et a vero
abhorrentem ' (*c. Iulian. Pel.* vi. 75).

[3] Augustine cites in favour of his general scheme of Fall-doctrine
Irenaeus, Cyprian, Hilary, Ambrose, Ambrosiaster, Reticius of Autun,
Jerome : amongst Eastern writers, Gregory of Nazianzus, Basil, John
Chrysostom.

[4] *c. Iulian. Pel.* i. 30 : ' convinceris undique : luce clariora sunt
testimonia tanta sanctorum.'

the immensity of misery, mental and physical, in which he is overwhelmed. There are inexplicable catastrophes of nature, earthquakes and eruptions, bringing pain and death to thousands of innocent people, there are the sufferings of little children ; which even include, so he tells us, the horrors of demoniacal possession. All this mass of apparently meaningless and inexplicable woe points, according to our author, to the presence of a profound hereditary guilt, derived from the beginning of the race and prior to the responsibility of any individual.

An Evaluation of the Augustinian Doctrine

In view of the more shocking and repulsive aspects of Augustine's doctrine of original guilt, as set out above, many will doubtless think it superfluous to subject his system to any reasoned or detailed criticism at all. It is nevertheless possible, within the compass of a few words, to distinguish between the permanently valuable and the worthless elements in his thought on this subject. The doctrine which we have just sketched may be summed up in three great conceptions, those of ' original righteousness,' ' original sin ' considered as *vitium*, and ' original sin ' considered as *reatus* (that is, ' original guilt '). I venture to submit the judgment that the first and third of these conceptions, in their strict Augustinian form, are worthless from the point of view of modern thought, but that the second contains large elements of permanent truth. We need not spend much time upon Augustine's conception of ' original righteousness.' Even if it were possible to treat Gen. iii. as being a literal record of historical facts, Augustine's idealised picture of the superhuman qualities of the first man goes far beyond the language of the Scriptural text, and beyond that conception of man's first condition as one of ' infancy ' which appears in the earliest Greek Fathers ; and it will hardly be disputed in the light of what we now know about the primitive history of man, that his picture of a ' Golden Age ' and of an earthly Paradise tenanted by a saintly couple belongs to the realm of mythology. Nor is it

necessary to do more than point out the absurdity of the
theory of ' original guilt,' which asserts that human beings
are held responsible by an all-just Judge for an act which
they did not commit and for physiological and psychological
facts which they cannot help. At this time of day it is
hardly necessary to bestow the compliment of a serious
refutation upon the theory of ' seminal identity.' Nor can
any verbal manipulation of the ' universal ' of human nature
make it just to punish a man for a sin alleged to have been
committed several millenniums previously by another man.
Those (if there are any such) who demand a formal disproof
of the belief that what is *ex hypothesi* an inherited psychological malady is regarded by God in the light of a voluntarily committed crime may be referred to the scathing
satire of Samuel Butler's ' Erewhon.' [1]

Augustine feels the force of such objections as these,
with which the Pelagians were not slow to press him : and
hence he is fain to shelter himself behind the mystery which
shrouds all the operations of the Divine Being, availing
himself to the full of two convenient texts from the Epistle
to the Romans [2] : ' Nay but, O man, who art thou that
repliest against God ? ' and ' How unsearchable are his
judgments, and his ways past tracing out ! ' and appealing
to the conception of an ' occult justice ' in God, which may
vindicate the apparent arbitrariness of His predestination,
and may differ as far from ordinary human justice as God
Himself differs from man. A typical expression of this
conception is to be found in the following passage :

By how much divine justice is loftier than human justice,
by so much is it more inscrutable, and by so much it differs from
human justice. . . . Think on these things, and forbear to set
God the Judge in comparison with human judges, that God
whom we must not doubt to be just even when He does what
seems to men unjust, or *what, if it were done by a man, would
actually be unjust.*[3]

---

[1] I do not know whether Butler had ever read the treatise *de correptione
et gratia,* in which Augustine maintains that it is reasonable to rebuke men
for defects for the possession of which they are not responsible : but
Erewhon might have been written as a reply to it.

[2] ix. 20 and xi. 33.

[3] *op. imperf. c. Iulian.* iii. 24.

Such a position lies open to the unanswerable retort made by John Stuart Mill to a similar 'appeal to mystery' advanced in this pulpit, in the Bampton Lectures of sixty-six years ago : ' I will call no being good [or just] who is not what I mean when I apply that epithet to my fellow-creatures ; and if such a being can sentence me to hell for not so calling him, to hell I will go.' [1] On the other hand, Augustine's analysis of original sin, in the sense of the *vitium* or inbred disease of human nature, would seem to be marked by psychological acuteness and truth. We need not go all the way with him in his practical denial of free-will to recognise the subtlety of his analysis of the moral struggle, and the aptness of his division of the rebellious forces within the citadel of man's soul into ' pride,' the hypertrophied instinct of self-assertion, and ' concupiscence,' representing mainly, though not exclusively, the ungovern-able instinct of the race to perpetuate itself even at the expense of a particular individual's suffering.[2] We have seen that Augustine's conception of the inherited infirmity, merely as such, does not appear to go beyond the Pauline conception, save in so far as his perverse view of sex is concerned : and his borrowing from Platonism of the anhypostatic notion of evil points ultimately to the idea of original sin as a *deprivatio* rather than a *depravatio*, a defect or absence of good rather than a positive evil substance,[3] a weakness of will rather than a corruption of appetite.

No Christian thinker in his senses will maintain that Augustinianism is a heresy.[4] Yet a theological opinion may be profoundly erroneous without being either formally or materially heretical ; and, if the contention of these lectures has been sound, at least two-thirds of the classical version of the ' twice-born ' doctrine of man and of sin deserve the former note. If Augustine's doctrines of the Fall and of

[1] J. S. Mill, *An Examination of Sir William Hamilton's Philosophy*, 1865, p. 103, replying to H. L. Mansel's Bampton Lectures, ' The Limits of Religious Thought,' 1858.

[2] See Harnack, *History of Dogma*, E. tr. 1898, v. p. 211 : and *cf. infra*, Lecture VII, p. 481.

[3] Augustine, very justly, claims this point as decisively differentiating his conception of evil from the Manichean : *op. imperf. c. Iulian.* iii. 175.

[4] *Cf.* Lecture VII, p. 483.

original sin—with their mythological conception of the
physical, moral, and mental stature of the first man, with
their logically incoherent notion of original guilt, their
fanatical denial of the possibility of virtue outside the
Church, and their horrible corollary of the necessary damnation of unbaptised infants—were really ' the ecclesiastical
doctrine,' that is, the doctrine of the Church, as both friends
and opponents have, at least in Western Europe, hitherto
assumed it to be ; if the whole fabric of orthodox dogma
were really based upon this one-sided theory of human
nature, seamed as it is with so large a vein of mythology
and split by a colossal self-contradiction ; we should be
obliged to conclude that the prospects of defending historical
Christianity in the coming generation were of a singularly
unpromising kind. Pelagius was right when he affirmed
that these questions were not, strictly speaking, parts of
the Faith [1] ; but Augustine was also right when he said
that they belonged to the foundations of the Faith [2] ; and
no structure can stand if the rock on which it is built is
reduced, by a process of attrition or molecular disintegration,
to a heap of dust. If Catholic Christianity presupposes
statements about human nature and about the origin of sin
which are intellectually indefensible and morally revolting,
then all is over with it. If its axioms have been refuted,
it is waste of time to investigate the conclusions which
follow from them. If the key position of the Christian
trenches has already been stormed, the endeavour to hold
the rest of the line is but useless effort. These considerations
have been our justification for the extended review to which
we have subjected the genetic history of these doctrines—
a review which has been designed for no other purpose
than to furnish us with the materials for returning an
answer to the question ' Is " the ecclesiastical doctrine "
identical with the Augustinian doctrine ? ' or, in other
words, ' Is the Christian Church, as such, committed to
Augustinianism ? '

In view of the gradual development of this doctrine,
side by side with the vaguer and less severe ' Hellenic ' view

[1] v. supra, p. 338, n. 3.
[2] v. supra, Lecture IV, p. 314, n. 2.

(which, as we have seen, is the more primitive, as being traceable well back into the second century), it may appear unnecessary even to raise this question : and, indeed, it may now be claimed that whatever pretensions to satisfy the central test of the Vincentian triad, that of acceptance *semper*, were asserted by Augustinianism have now been decisively dispelled.[1] Yet it is theoretically possible—and it has sometimes been the case—that an idea which cannot be discovered in the earliest epochs of Christian history has nevertheless at a later date diffused itself so intimately through the mind of the Great Church as to acquire at least a plausible title to the honour of acceptance *ubique et ab omnibus*. Such an idea could not, indeed, be affirmed to be an integral part of the Faith : but, if its universal acceptance were extended over many centuries, it might be deemed to have acquired a certain prerogative or *auctoritas*, which, if the idea in question were reasonable, might well serve to commend it to Christian thinkers, and, if it were absurd or unreasonable, would correspondingly discredit the corporate judgment of the Christian society. It will therefore be pertinent to conclude this lecture by enquiring ' Did Augustine, either during his lifetime or after his death, succeed in making his characteristic opinions an integral part of orthodoxy, as orthodoxy was understood during the remainder of the period of " undivided " Christendom, down to the schism of A.D. 1054 ? Did he rivet the theories of " original righteousness " " seminal identity " and " original guilt " into the fabric of orthodoxy as firmly as Athanasius had riveted the *Homoousion* ? ' These questions may be answered in a few words.

[1] A typical instance of such pretensions is to be found in *c. Iulian. Pel.* vi. 39 : ' nihil de hac re iam tunc sentiens . . . nisi quod antiquitus discit et docet omnis ecclesia.' Curiously enough, the original author of the ' Vincentian Canon ' (which, on our shewing, deprives the specifically Augustinian doctrine of any claim to oecumenicity) thinks that it confirms the idea of ' original guilt ' ; he enquires rhetorically ' quis ante prodigiosum discipulum eius (*sc.* Pelagii) Caelestium reatu praevaricationis Adae omne humanum genus denegavit obstrictum ? ' (S. Vinc. Lir. *commonit.* 62). The obvious retort is ' quis ante Ambrosium et Augustinum affirmavit ? '

The Extent to which the Augustinian Doctrine was Accepted by the World-Church

The assent of the Universal Church to a doctrinal proposition may be manifested either by some formal and official act or by tacit acquiescence and general though informal adoption. The only official acts which could conceivably be construed as committing the Great Church to the specifically Augustinian points of 'original righteousness' and 'original guilt' are (a) the (alleged) world-wide subscription, enforced by the sword of the Emperors, of the Catholic episcopate to the *tractoria* of Zosimus, and (b) the condemnation of 'the partisans of Caelestius' by the Council of Ephesus.[1]

(a) The few surviving fragments [2] of the *tractoria* contain little of doctrinal import : it may, however, be assumed that it was drafted in such a way as to enforce at least the main points of the Augustinian position, including 'original righteousness' and 'original guilt.' [3] Ecclesiastical historians have hitherto taken for granted the assertion that Julian of Eclanum and his eighteen associates stood alone in refusing subscription to it.[4] This statement appears, however, to be open to question. The sole testimony for a literally universal acceptance of the *tractoria* is found in the writings of Marius Mercator,[5] an ecclesiastically minded

---

[1] The confirmation of an unspecified synod of Carthage, which may or may not be that of A.D. 418, by *can.* 2 of the Council *in Trullo* (Hardouin iii. 1660 C) can hardly be interpreted as signifying an official adoption of Augustinianism by the Eastern Church.

[2] These were collected by P. Coustant, *epistolae Romanorum pontificum*, 1721, tom. i, col. 994–998, and are reprinted in *PL* XX. 693 f.

[3] It is possible that, as Coustant (*op. cit.* col. 996, reprinted in *PL* col. 694 B) suggests, Augustine may be referring to the *tractoria* in the passage *de an. et eius orig.* xii. 17 : 'novellos haereticos Pelagianos iustissime conciliorum catholicorum et sedis apostolicae damnavit auctoritas, eo quod ausi fuerint non baptizatis parvulis dare quietis et salutis locum etiam praeter regnum coelorum.' If this is so, the Pope followed the Africans in their condemnation of *limbo*.

[4] Duchesne, however (*Hist. ancienne de l'Église*, iii. p. 264, n. 1), seems to feel some doubt on the subject.

[5] *common.* iii. 1 : 'illa beatae memoriae episcopi Zosimi epistola, quae *tractoria* dicitur . . . quae et Constantinopolim et per totum orbem missa subscriptionibus sanctorum patrum est roborata ; cui Iulianus et reliqui complices subscribere detrectantes . . . depositi . . . sunt.'

layman who made opposition to Pelagianism and Nestorianism the main business of his life. It is *a priori* not at all inconceivable that Marius, in accordance with the usual Western tendency to forget the existence of Eastern Christendom, and the usual tendency of enthusiasts to assume that the absence of any active protest against their opinions is the equivalent of a positive approval of them, may well have supposed that the *tractoria* had been accepted throughout the East merely because no Eastern had taken the trouble to denounce it publicly. Zosimus, it would seem, addressed his letter to the chief Patriarchal sees, expecting their occupants to secure the signatures of their subordinates : but we have no evidence (other than the general assertion of Marius Mercator just mentioned) to show how far this was actually done. Doubtless the *tractoria* was duly signed wherever the imperial government was in a position to bring civil coercion into play : but the Syriac-speaking Churches at least, which cherished a theological tradition favourable to Pelagianism,[1] and which, moreover, were rooted amidst a population seething with suppressed nationalistic and anti-imperialist feeling, would hardly be likely to welcome a document emanating from the Roman Pope and enforced by the sword of the Roman Emperor. It is difficult to believe that Theodore of Mopsuestia could have signed the *tractoria*, in view of the fact that only a few years after its publication we find him taking the Pelagian exiles under his personal protection. Nor is it likely that the Churches of Asia Minor and Syria, which looked to Theodore as their intellectual guide and teacher, would have subscribed to a formulary which was destructive of their own point of view. It is at least possible that Marius Mercator's assertion as to the universal acceptance of the *tractoria* is an enthusiastic over-statement of the fact that it was universally received in the West and in Egypt, and not overtly denounced in Asia Minor, Syria, and the far Eastern Churches.

(*b*) The encyclical of Zosimus, however, though it cannot be proved to have secured strictly oecumenical acceptance, represents the apogee and high-water-mark of the power

---

[1] *v. supra*, p. 349 f.

and influence of the Augustinian ideas. But the studiously
vague and cautious condemnation of Caelestius pronounced
by the Council of Ephesus shows that thirteen years later
the Easterns, even those of Cyril's party, were not by any
means willing to give their whole-hearted allegiance to the
theories which had triumphed in the West; nor can the
language of the letter addressed by the Council to Pope
Celestine, informing him that it had renewed the condemnation pronounced by his predecessors against Pelagianism,
be taken as more than a very general and complimentary
approval of the anti-Pelagian attitude of Rome; it would
not be reasonable to extract from it an explicit commendation of every detail of Zosimus' letter, even if we knew what
this contained. The first and fourth Canons of this Council,[1]
which censure those who 'hold the opinions of' or 'side
with' Caelestius, cannot be construed as an approval of the
characteristic positions of Augustine: they can hardly be
made to affirm more in the positive direction than that
there *was* a Fall, and that it had hereditary consequences
in the shape of a transmitted bias towards sin.

How far can the Augustinian Fall-doctrine be deemed
to have secured the tacit acquiescence, as distinct from the
credal or conciliar endorsement, of the undivided Church?
In view of the overwhelming triumph of Augustinianism
in the West, this question is, in effect, an enquiry how far
Augustinianism succeeded in penetrating the East, and in
superseding or suppressing the vaguer, more liberal 'once-
born' tendency which we have seen to be associated with
the Hellenic-Christian thought of the first four centuries.
It is difficult to give any very precise answer to this question,
for the reason that after the Council of Ephesus, and the
secession of the Syrian and Persian Churches which sym-
pathised with Nestorius and by consequence with Pelagius,
the remainder of Eastern Christendom seems to have lost
all interest in the matter. During the last five centuries
of the 'undivided' period, the dominant doctrinal issues in
the East were the Christological question, the questions of
the two natures and the two wills, and that of the veneration

---

[1] The text is given in Additional Note F, p. 537, 'Formularies,
I. Oecumenical'; and see above, p. 354.

of icons, not the Western disputes about Adam, sin, and grace. In the scanty references made to the subject by the Greek-Christian writers of this epoch, we note the appearance of the term ' ancestral sin ' (ἁμαρτία προπατορική[1]) which is now used in the dogmatic theology and formularies of the Eastern Orthodox Church as the equivalent of ' original sin '[2] ; but whether in the sixth and seventh centuries it included the idea of ' original guilt ' or not it is impossible to say. There is no doubt that the Monophysite Christology tended to be associated with an Augustinian type of Fall-doctrine,[3] just as Nestorianism had been logically linked with Pelagianism [4] ; but it would be unsafe to dogmatise with regard to the proportion borne by this tendency to the other factors which went to make up the kaleidoscopic picture of Byzantine theology. It is instructive in this connexion to read through the treatise *On the Orthodox Faith* written by the last of the great figures of Eastern theology, St. John of Damascus (?680–?760). This work contains much detailed exposition of the doctrines of the Trinity and the Incarnation, and, indeed, of various cosmological and physiographical theories which we should regard as having nothing to do with the Faith at all ; but the Damascene's language on the subject of the Fall and of its consequences is rhetorical and vague to the last degree.[5] There is some use of the traditional phrases regarding man's ' servitude to the devil,' and the ' disintegration ' (φθορά) of his being ; but it is impossible to extract from the Damascene's pages any doctrine more precise than that of St. Paul, and the specifically Augustinian conceptions are nowhere to be found.

[1] *Cf.* Olympiodorus (*saec.* vi), *fragmenta in Ieremiam, in c.* xxxi. 30 (*PG* XCIII. 689 D) : ἡ τοῦ Ἀδὰμ ἁμαρτία διελθοῦσα εἰς τὸ ἔθνος καὶ ἐπὶ τοὺς μὴ ἁμαρτήσαντας ἦλθεν ὡς εἶπεν ὁ ἀπόστολος· χριστοῦ οὖν συγχωρήσαντος ταύτην διὰ τοῦ λουτροῦ τῆς ἀφέσεως, ἐκαθαρίσθη μὲν ἡ προπατορικὴ ἁμαρτία, ἕκαστος δὲ τῶν οἰκείων ἁμαρτημάτων ὑπέχει λόγον: Maximus Confessor (*saec.* vii), *ep. ad Marinum* (*PG* XCI. 136A) : δίχα τὸν κύριον εἶναι τῆς προπατορικῆς ἁμαρτίας ὡς ἄνθρωπον.

[2] See Additional Note ' Formularies, III Eastern Orthodox ' (p. 542).

[3] See A. Draguet, *Julien d'Halicarnasse*, mentioned above, p. 254, n. 5.

[4] *v. supra*, p. 349.

[5] The chief references to the subject are contained in lib. ii. cc. 10, 11, 12 (a reproduction of St. Greg. Naz., *or.* xlv, quoted above, Lecture IV, p. 283), 30 : lib. iii. 1 : lib. iv. 13 (in Michael Lequien's edition, Paris, 1712, tom. ii. p. 267 E).

So far as this writer is concerned, Augustine, Pelagius, Caelestius, and Julian might never have existed at all.

In view of such facts as these, we shall be safe in formulating the statement that from the Council of Ephesus down to the Great Schism of A.D. 1054 a modified Augustinianism [1] was dominant in the West, and a state of complete vagueness and confusion with regard to the Fall-doctrine prevailed in the East. Augustinianism, though the most widely spread version of the doctrine, never enjoyed an exclusive dominance : it cannot be said to have ever attained to acceptance in a literal sense *ubique et ab omnibus*. Not even in a modified and secondary sense of the term, therefore, can it claim to be ' the ecclesiastical doctrine ' *par excellence*. Nevertheless, it cannot be denied that the original perfection and righteousness of Adam were taken for granted by practically all Christians between the fifth and the nineteenth century : though Gregory of Nyssa's re-interpretation of the subject of ' original righteousness ' as the ideal or archetypal man, not the concrete individuals Adam and Eve, stood on record as indicating a possible solution of the coming clash between the monotheistic religious consciousness, which demands that the works of an infinitely good God must themselves have been good as originally created by Him, and the scientific understanding, which can find no crevice in the smooth continuity of man's evolution from the brute into which an epoch of Paradisal perfection could be interpolated.[2]

CONCLUSION

Meanwhile, the fact that we must needs reject the ideas of ' original righteousness ' and ' original guilt ' as Augustine formulated them involves no disparagement of the spiritual greatness of this heroic saint and doctor, nor does it imply

---

[1] From A.D. 529 onwards, the canons of the second Council of Orange, with the statement which concludes them (Hardouin, ii. 1098 A *sqq.* ; Denzinger-Bannwart, *Enchiridion*, §§ 174–200) may be taken as representing the norm of this ' modified Augustinianism ' ; see Lecture VI, p. 397, and Additional Note ' Formularies, II. Western and Roman,' p. 537.

[2] *v. supra*, Lecture IV, p. 271 ; and *infra*, Lecture VIII, p. 526, n. 1.

any contempt for the highly specialised type of experience in which these ideas were rooted. In the history of Christian thought we have at every turn to distinguish between the kernel and the husk, between the permanent facts of the life of the soul and the intellectual form which in a given epoch is used to body them forth. Augustine's belief in the Golden Age, in the unalloyed bliss of Paradise, in the supernatural glories of unfallen human nature, has been banished by modern knowledge from the domain of historic possibility. But it is still a splendid symbol of the ideal of human nature as God meant it to be and as it exists in the treasure-house of the divine ideas, a symbol cast in a gorgeous pictorial form and projected upon the misty background of the primeval past. The idea of original guilt, of the inheritance of responsibility for the first sin, is one which is inconsistent with our notion of justice; and the affirmation that there is a mysterious kind of divine justice, which has little in common with what we understand by the term 'justice,' has now ceased to have any meaning for us. Yet as the husk of 'inherited racial guilt' splits asunder, it reveals the infinitely true and precious—though humbling and not easily comprehensible—idea of that voluntary and sympathetic self-identification with the sins of the community which was attributed by the Jewish scriptures to Nehemiah [1] and Daniel,[2] and was achieved in fullest measure by our Lord Himself upon the Cross. These are ideas which cannot be neglected in future speculations on this mysterious subject. The mighty structure of Augustinianism has in great part collapsed; but it contains precious materials which may well be used for the new fabric which is to replace it. As the marble columns which had served to rear the pediments of the ancient temples were utilised by the men of Augustine's day to adorn the glittering naves of the new Christian basilicas: so the characteristic doctrines of Man and of Sin evolved through storms of controversy by the 'twice-born' type of religious genius, though rejected as theological truths, may none the less survive as devotional values, enriching and fertilising the common life of the

---

[1] Nehem. i. 6, 7.
[2] Daniel ix. 20.

Church, which must in the main reflect the experience of the ordinary and ' once-born ' man, with the tears and the penitence of the Saints.

ADDITIONAL NOTE B

Canons of the Carthaginian Council of A.D. 418, dealing with the Fall and Original Sin (Hardouin, i. 926, 927 ; Denzinger-Bannwart, *Enchiridion Symbolorum* etc., 1913, p. 47, §§ 101, 102).

can. 1. placuit omnibus episcopis . . . in sancta synodo Carthaginiensi constitutis : ut quicunque dixerit, Adam primum hominem mortalem factum, ita ut sive peccaret sive non peccaret moreretur in corpore, hoc est de corpore exiret non peccati merito, sed necessitate naturae, anathema sit.

can. 2. item placuit, ut quicunque parvulos recentes ab uteris matrum baptizandos negat, aut dicit in remissionem quidem peccatorum eos baptizari, sed nihil ex Adam trahere originalis peccati, quod lavacro regenerationis expietur, unde sit consequens, ut in eis forma baptismatis in remissionem peccatorum non vera sed falsa intelligatur, anathema sit. quoniam non aliter intelligendum est quod ait apostolus : *per unum hominem peccatum intravit in mundum, et per peccatum mors, et ita in omnes homines pertransiit, in quo omnes peccaverunt,* nisi quemadmodum ecclesia catholica ubique diffusa semper intellexit. propter hanc enim regulam fidei etiam parvuli, qui nihil peccatorum in se ipsis adhuc committere potuerunt, ideo in peccatorum remissionem veraciter baptizantur, ut in eis regeneratione mundetur, quod generatione traxerunt.

can. 3. [This is the canon, which, as Duchesne notes (*v. supra,* p. 348, n. 2), has been suppressed in most collections of canons, presumably because it condemns the idea of *limbo.*] item placuit, ut si quis dicit, ideo dixisse Dominum, *in domo patris mei mansiones multae sunt,* ut intelligatur, quia in regno coelorum erit aliquis medius aut ullus alicubi locus, ubi beati vivant parvuli, qui sine baptismo ex hac vita migrarunt, sine quo in regnum coelorum, quod est vita aeterna, intrare non possunt, anathema sit. nam cum Dominus dicat, *nisi quis renatus fuerit ex aqua et spiritu Sancto, non intrabit in regnum coelorum,* quis catholicus dubitet participem fore diaboli eum, qui coheres esse non meruit Christi ? qui enim dextra caret, sinistram procul dubio partem incurret. [On the authorities for this canon, see Hardouin's note, i. 927 B.]

VI.

THE TRIUMPH AND DECLINE OF THE AUGUSTINIAN DOCTRINE

God made this whole world in such an uniformity, such a correspondency, such a concinnity of parts, as that it was an Instrument, perfectly in tune : we may say, the trebles, the highest strings were disordered first ; the best understandings, Angels and Men, put this instrument out of tune.   God rectified all again, by putting in a new string, *semen mulieris*, the seed of the woman, the Messias : And onely by sounding that string in your ears, become we *musicum carmen*, true musick, true harmony, true peace to you.   If we shall say, that Gods first string in this instrument, was Reprobation, that Gods first intention was for his glory to damn man ; and that then he put in another string, of creating Man, that so he might have some body to damn ; and then another of enforcing him to sin, that so he might have a just cause to damne him ; and then another, of disabling him to lay hold upon any means of recovery : there's no musick in all this, no harmony, no peace in such preaching.

JOHN DONNE.

LECTURE VI.

THE TRIUMPH AND DECLINE OF THE AUGUSTINIAN DOCTRINE

Rom. ix. 18. 'So then he hath mercy on whom he will, and whom he
will be hardeneth.'

IT was shown in our last lecture that the sombre and
pessimistic version of the Fall-theory, which springs from
the characteristic experience of the 'sick soul' or the
'twice-born' type of religious man, which received its chief
development in the stern and fanatical atmosphere of the
North African Church, and which was wrought into a
rounded, coherent, and classical doctrine by the genius of
St. Augustine, though victorious all along the line in the
field of Western Christendom, yet exercised only a superficial influence on the mind of the Christian East; which,
on the whole, remained faithful (at least until the seventeenth century) to that milder view of the presuppositions
of Redemption which we found in the writings of the earlier
Greek Fathers, more particularly in those of Irenaeus,
Origen, and the Cappadocians. It follows that, for those
who recognise a palmary and normative authority as residing
in the mind of the primitive undivided Church, the question
'What is "the ecclesiastical doctrine"'—the doctrine accepted
by the Christian Church as such—in regard to the origin
and nature of the inherited tendency to sin?' has been
conclusively answered. The doctrine of the Undivided
Church as a whole can only be taken to be the highest
common factor of the maximising and minimising versions
of the Fall-doctrine held by its Western and Eastern areas
respectively; and this highest common factor is evidently
identical with the lesser of these quantities, that is, with

the minimising theory. If, then, we were at liberty to assume without question the validity of that appeal to the witness of Christian antiquity as a whole which is implied in a literal interpretation of the word *semper*, as it occurs in the Vincentian formula, and which is in many quarters assumed to be the corner-stone of the specifically Anglican position, the purely historical part of our enquiry might well end at this point. But it will be remembered that, in our first lecture, at the very outset of our review of the development of the Fall-doctrine, we deliberately renounced this liberty, and undertook to employ the Vincentian Canon solely as a scientific, and not as an authoritarian test, in order that our conclusions as to the amount, or the kind, of Fall-doctrine which is necessarily pre-supposed by the Christian religion as such might be invested with as much objectivity and breadth of appeal as possible. Given this method of employing the formula *ubique, semper, et ab omnibus,* it might very plausibly be urged that the term *omnes* should not be interpreted in a grossly literal, mechanical and numerical sense, so as to include all Christians without exception, no matter how ignorant and unprogressive many of them may be : but that it should rather be restricted to designating the intellectually vital and fruitful areas of Christendom, which until recently were confined to Western Christendom, Catholic and Reformed. It would follow from such a contention that the non-acceptance of the Augustinian teaching by the primitive and mediaeval East did not necessarily invalidate the claim of this teaching to be ' the Christian doctrine,' inasmuch as the intellectual life of the Eastern Church was (not exclusively through its own fault) comparatively stationary from the time of the Great Schism down to the seventeenth century ; and that it would be unfair to dismiss a theory which has so deeply affected the religious life of the Western nations, including our own, without having considered the forms which it assumed in the thought of some of the greatest Christian teachers who have flourished since the Patristic age, both Schoolmen and Reformers. It would be irrelevant to our purpose, and would confuse the development of our argument, if we allowed ourselves to be drawn into a discussion of the true meaning of *ubique* and *omnes*; and an enquiry which aspires to scientific impartiality cannot afford to expose itself to the suspicion of having neglected fields of thought which are of the highest interest in themselves, and might conceivably yield considerations of such a nature as to induce us to revise or modify the adverse verdict which in our last lecture was passed upon the classical expression of the ' twice-born ' theory.   The present lecture will, therefore, be devoted to an examination of the post-Augustinian history of the Fall-doctrine in Western Europe, designed with the object of deciding whether or not, within this restricted sphere, the ' twice-born ' theory can reasonably claim acceptance ' by all,' in the sense of all, or nearly all, intellectually alert and progressive Christians.

Our historical review need not pause to consider the Semi-Pelagian controversy, which, though the direct sequel of the great duel between Augustine and Pelagius noticed in our last lecture, was concerned rather with the operations of ' grace ' than with the nature and results of the Fall: we may note, however, that the Second Council of Orange, which brought this controversy to an end, contents itself with affirming a modified Augustinianism, which only predicates ' integrity ' of unfallen man, abstains from affirming ' Original Guilt,' and makes the important assertion that whilst free-will was weakened by the Fall it was not destroyed.[1] Little of interest is to be gleaned from the so-called ' Dark Ages '; of the four great writers whom the Western Church produced during this period, Gregory the Great, Bede, Alcuin, and Scotus Erigena,[2] the first three were largely absorbed in pastoral, historical, juristic, and liturgical interests, and made few original contributions to the progress of thought, whilst the last named did little more than emphasise that Platonic aspect of patristic thought for which evil is mere non-entity. The Doctor of Hippo continued to dominate the West down to the beginning of the thirteenth century, though Anselm in discussing original sin lays all the stress upon our lack of Adam's

<hr />

[1] For the relevant Canons of Orange, see Additional Note F, ' Formularies, (II) Western and Roman,' p. 537 f.

[2] See H. Bett, *Johannes Scotus Erigena*, 1925, pp. 65–70.

original righteousness,[1] and Abaelard repudiates 'original guilt.' [2] It is not until the rise of Scholasticism that signs of an onward movement can be detected in the somewhat stagnant waters of Western-Catholic anthropological thought.[3]

The development of Scholasticism is intimately bound up with the history of the great mendicant Orders of the thirteenth century, notably with that of the Friars Preachers, founded by Dominic Guzman, and that of the Friars Minor, which owes its origin to the life and personality of Francis of Assisi. In regard to the doctrines of man and of sin, the theologies characteristic of these two illustrious Orders exhibit differences which may without undue fancifulness be traced to the differing circumstances of their origins. In the previous lectures of this course, we have had more than once occasion to emphasise the fact that the doctrines of the Fall and of original sin were evolved in the first instance by that ethical monotheism which is the heart both of Judaism and of Christianity, as an intellectual self-defence against the attacks of Oriental dualism ; and this character, that of being in essence a protest against dualism, has clung to them all through their history. They were first shaped in the minds of the Maccabean Jews by the desire to save the unique sovereignty and holiness of Jehovah as against the evil God of Mazdeism. St. Paul and St. Irenaeus reaffirmed them as against the second historic wave of Westward-surging dualism, that which we know as Gnosticism. Augustine perfected his scheme as a bulwark against the third invasion of dualism in the form of Manicheism. And it may be suggested that the strongly Augustinian tone of Dominican thought on these subjects is due to the fact

---

[1] de conceptu virginali, 22, 27 (see also Thomasius, DG. ii, pp. 152, 153, 163–5).

[2] in ep. ad Rom. (Opera, ed. Victor Cousin, 1859, ii. pp. 238 ff.).

[3] An excellent summary account of the evolution of the Fall-doctrine during the scholastic period may be found in Gustav Ljunggren, Det Kristna Syndmedvetandet intill Luther, Uppsala, 1924, pp. 236–265. This book is written in Swedish, and there appears to be no English, French, or German translation : I have only been able to use it through the kindness of the Rev. G. C. Richards, D.D., Fellow of Oriel College, Oxford, and Vicar of the University Church, who has been good enough to supply me with a translation of the pages referred to.

that the Order of Preachers was founded by a saint of stern if heroic character, in Languedoc, in the very midst of a life-and-death struggle between Catholic Christianity, as it then existed, and a fourth invasion of Eastern dualism, that which is known as the ' Albigensian ' or ' Catharist' movement, which was in great part based upon a recrude-scence of the doctrines of Mani.[1] But the Order of Friars Minor was born, not from the crisis of a fierce battle with semi-heathen heresy, but rather from the pure impulses of love towards God and man which flowed forth from the humble and gentle nature of the *poverello* himself, the ' minstrel of the Lord,' and spouse of the Lady Poverty, ' Sweet Saint Francis of Assisi,' as Tennyson calls him :

> He that in his Catholic wholeness used to call the very flowers Sisters, brothers—and the beasts—whose pains are hardly less than ours.[2]

Given a founder whose character was marked by an almost feminine tenderness towards the sufferings of mankind and by that intuitive sympathy with sub-human nature which hitherto we have noted in St. Paul alone of Christian saints, it is not a matter of surprise that the theologians of this Order should have championed a comparatively anti-Augustinian and all but Semi-Pelagian anthropology, in which the sharpness of the distinction between ' nature ' and ' grace ' tends at least to be blunted, and the human will is restored to its dignity as essentially free, though weakened by the Fall.   It will conduce to clearness if we first of all survey briefly the modifications introduced by St. Thomas Aquinas, the ' Angel of the Schools ' and the typical repre-sentative of the Dominican theology, into the hitherto dominant Augustinian scheme, and then set side by side with the Thomist doctrine a brief sketch of the Franciscan point of view, as depicted in the works of one of the most famous sons both of St. Francis and of Oxford, the ' subtle Doctor ' Duns Scotus.

[1] H. J. Warner, however (*The Albigensian Heresy*, 1922), denies the historical derivation of Catharism from Manicheism.
[2] *Locksley Hall Sixty Years After.*

THE THOMIST POSITION

The results of an analysis of the specifically Augustinian Fall-doctrine may be summarised by the statement that it can be reduced to seven fundamental ideas. These are (1) an exalted conception of Adam's original righteousness and perfection ; and the ideas (2) of the infinite malice of the first sin, as being the ethical suicide of a saint ; (3) of ' original sin ' as a *vitium*, consisting in the tyranny of concupiscence ; (4) of ' original sin ' as guilt (*reatus*), inhering in each and every member of the human race in virtue of the race's seminal identity with Adam ; (5) of the transmission of original sin, considered as a disease, in and through the act of generation, which is itself intrinsically sinful, owing to the concupiscence which accompanies it, though it is condoned by God in the case of the baptised ; (6) of the practical abolition of free-will which thus results, though, as we have pointed out, Augustine strenuously maintains freedom—at least in name ; and (7) of the necessary and rightful damnation of the whole of Adam's posterity, including infants, with the exception of those who are arbitrarily predestined to be recipients of baptism, justification, and the ' gift of final perseverance.' We will take these points one by one, and note the modifications introduced by the Angelic Doctor.

(1) In essence the Augustinian conception of man's original state is left unchanged. It is, however, to be noted that the category which Augustine had employed to define this conception is subjected to a certain measure of reconstruction. This leading category of Augustinianism is the antithesis between ' nature ' and ' grace,' which, in the thought of St. Thomas, is made necessary instead of contingent, becomes logical rather than ethical, and instead of being restricted to the domain of human nature is made to apply to the whole realm of created being. It thus appears as the celebrated scholastic distinction between the natural and the supernatural orders or planes of being, or, in modern phrase, between ' nature ' and ' supernature.' This distinction has the effect of sharpening the difference between the qualities of human nature considered in itself—the qualities

known in scholastic terminology as Adam's *pura naturalia*, which God, so to speak, was under the necessity of conferring upon him if He was going to make a ' man ' at all—and the supernatural splendours of ' original perfection,' with its perfect sanctity and its mighty intellectual powers,[1] which God was under no necessity, logical or otherwise, to bestow upon man, but which represents a *donum indebitum*—a purely gratuitous piece of munificence on the part of the Almighty. Even if man had remained endowed solely with the *pura naturalia*, and had never received the splendid present of ' original justice,' he might, St. Thomas tells us, have attained to a certain natural knowledge of God by speculating upon His works. With infinite generosity, however, the Creator destined His creature to a much more wonderful destiny. He raised him at the first moment of his creation to the supernatural plane, and designed to lead him upward, along an ever-ascending pathway, to the supernatural knowledge and possession of Himself in the Beatific Vision. If Adam had stood firm under the tests imposed upon him, his spiritual and physical evolution would have progressed so rapidly that he would have been enabled to transcend death and to ascend to his eternal abode without the necessity of physical dissolution. We need not now discuss the ingenious refinements with which this revised Augustinianism was decorated, or follow out the chain of syllogisms by which Aquinas determines, to his own satisfaction, what would have been the moral, social, physical and economic condition of mankind if Adam had never fallen.[2] It is enough to note that St. Thomas takes an essentially optimistic view of human nature in itself, even apart from the added splendours of the supernatural endowments enjoyed by Adam. Man in himself is not a mere animal, but a citizen of the divine kingdom, who, by the special favour of his Almighty Sovereign, was created a prince at his birth.

(2) The infinite malice of the first sin is assumed, without much argument, on the authority of St. Augustine ; and its prime effect is conceived of as being the instantaneous fall of man, *from* the supernatural plane to which he had been

---

[1] *Summ. theol.* i. qq. xciv, xcv. [2] *ibid.* i. qq. xcvii–ci.

raised, *to* the natural plane on which he would have lived but for the gratuitous exaltation involved in the bestowal of the *donum supernaturale*. To continue the metaphor indicated above, the prince who has offended his sovereign is punished indeed, but not by outlawry or execution ; he merely forfeits his princely rank and privileges and reverts to the status of a *bourgeois*. This has an important bearing upon (3) the nature of original sin considered as a psychological flaw, or disease of the soul. It means that ' original sin,' viewed under the ' medical ' or ' therapeutic ' category, is to be formally defined as the ' lack of original righteousness ' (*defectus originalis iustitiae*), but not of any of the *pura naturalia*, a definition which makes it a mere negation, and as such not, apparently, a very tragic matter ; the inheritor of modest means, who, having been presented with a colossal fortune by a munificent benefactor, then loses the fortune by misconduct, without forfeiting his original patrimony, would appear *prima facie* to be at least no worse off than he would have been if he had never received the fortune. At this point, however, the influence of Augustine makes itself felt, and St. Thomas feels compelled to affirm that although original righteousness is no part of the endowment of man as man, yet the loss of it, when it has once been possessed, introduces a certain disorder into the faculties of human nature. The *pura naturalia* are not destroyed ; but their due harmony and proportion are disturbed and disarranged. This thought leads St. Thomas back into the Augustinian conception of original sin, psychologically considered, as consisting in ' inordinate concupiscence ' ; and he produces what does not appear to be more than a verbal reconciliation of his own position with that of his master by asserting that the material element in original sin is concupiscence, but that its formal element is the defect of original justice [1]—

---

[1] St. Thom. Aq. *de malo*, q. iv. a. 2 : ' et ideo cum carentia originalis iustitiae se habeat ex parte voluntatis, ex parte autem inferiorum virium a voluntate motarum sit pronitas ad inordinate appetendum, quae concupiscentia dici potest, sequitur quod peccatum originale in hoc homine vel in illo, nihil est aliud quam concupiscentia cum carentia originalis iustitiae, ita tamen quod carentia originalis iustitiae est quasi formale in peccato originali, concupiscentia autem quasi materiale ' ; *cf.* also *in I Sent., dist.* xxx. q. i. a. i.

they never avail themselves, whilst the predestined receive
' efficacious ' grace, which they never resist. Yet, despite
its imprisonment in the iron framework of an all-pervasive
divine causality, the will remains ' free ' ; in other words
St. Thomas asserts that psychological freedom can subsist
simultaneously with metaphysical necessity. If he is asked
how this can be, he takes refuge in mystery. He tells us
' As it behoves divine Providence to preserve, not to pervert,
the natures of things, God will move everything according
to the requirements of its nature . . . So God moves the
human will in such a manner that its motion remains contingent and not necessary,' [1] and with this *prima facie*
contradiction in terms he leaves the question. When pressed
by the objection that this universal divine causality inevitably makes God the author of sin, he escapes by means of
the time-honoured verbal device of asserting that sin is a
defectus, a mere vacuity or privation which as such cannot
be due to the operation of the first and supreme Being.[2]

(7) The last point which demands consideration in treating of the Thomist republication of Augustinianism is the
eschatological issue. What is the destiny reserved in the
next world for those who die in original sin only, without
having committed actual sin ? For St. Thomas this means,
What will be the fate of unbaptised children ? because, as
already pointed out, he cannot conceive of a non-baptised
adult who is free from actual mortal sin. The humanity of
Aquinas shrank from the ruthless severity of Augustine, who
condemned unbaptised infants to eternal punishment (even
though of the ' mildest kind ') [3] : hence he takes refuge in
the Pelagian conception of a *limbus puerorum*. For the
purpose of justifying this conception, original sin is regarded
solely on its negative side as being the lack of original
righteousness. This lack of man's Paradisal sanctity has as
its corollary in the next life lack of the Beatific Vision. But
this is not in the strict sense of the term punishment. The
inhabitants of *Limbo*, which for other mediaeval thinkers
includes both the *limbus puerorum*, the eternal home of

[1] *Summa theol.* i. iiae. q. x. a. 4.
[2] *ibid.* i. iiae. q. lxxix. a. 2.
[3] *v. supra*, Lecture V, p. 327.

unbaptised infants, and the *limbus patrum*, in which the
saints of the Old Testament dwelt before the descent of
Christ into Hades, and in which the souls of virtuous pagans
still are confined, never having received through Baptism the
capacity for the Beatific Vision, do not feel the lack of it as
in any way painful ; and consequently their state may well
be one of natural happiness.　They may even know God
through His works as intimately as Adam might have done
if he had never received the endowment of original righteousness.　They would no more complain, or consider it a
grievance that they do not possess the Beatific Vision, than a
horse or a dog complains that it is not a highly educated or
cultured man.　In fact, they may very well remain in blissful
ignorance that there is such a thing as the Beatific Vision at
all.　It is true that a more sombre conception of this state
has received a poetic consecration in the immortal verse
of Dante, who identifies *Limbo* with the first circle that
surrounds the abyss of Hell, but paints it as a realm of
pensive melancholy rather than of agonising pain :

> Here, as mine ear could note, no plaint was heard
> Except of sighs, that made the eternal air
> Tremble, not caused by tortures, but from grief
> Felt by those multitudes, many and vast,
> Of men, women, and infants.　Then to me
> The gentle guide : ' Inquirest thou not what spirits
> Are these which thou beholdest ?　Ere thou pass
> Farther, I would thou know, that these of sin
> Were blameless ; and if aught they merited,
> It profits not, since baptism was not theirs,
> The portal to thy faith.　If they before
> The Gospel lived, they served not God aright ;
> And among such am I.　For these defects,
> And for no other evil, we are lost ;
> Only so far afflicted, that we live
> Desiring without hope.' [1]

---

[1] *Inferno*, iv. 25–42 :

> ' Quivi, secondo che per ascoltare,
> 　　non avea pianto, ma'che di sospiri,
> 　　che l'aura eterna facevan tremare :
> e ciò avvenia di duol senza martiri,
> 　　ch'avean le turbe, ch'eran molte e grandi,
> 　　d'infanti e di femmine e di viri.

Yet even this dun region contains an enclave of passionless tranquillity, approximating to happiness, which is tenanted by the poets, sages, and heroes of pagan antiquity. Dante and Vergil are led through the dreary wood, by the spirits of Homer, Horace, Ovid, and Lucan, to a place depicted as :

> . . . a mead with lively verdure fresh.
> There dwelt a race, who slow their eyes around
> Majestically moved, and in their port
> Bore eminent authority : they spake
> Seldom, but all their words were tuneful sweet . . .
> There on the green enamel of the plain
> Were shown me the great spirits, by whose sight
> I am exalted in my own esteem . . .
> . . . The master of the sapient throng,
> Seated amid the philosophic train.
> Him all admire, all pay him reverence due.
> There Socrates and Plato both I mark'd
> Nearest to him in rank, Democritus,
> Who sets the world at chance, Diogenes,
> With Heraclitus and Empedocles,
> And Anaxagoras, and Thales sage,
> Zeno, and Dioscorides well read
> In nature's secret lore.[1]

> Lo buon maestro a me : " Tu non dimandi
> che spiriti son questi, che tu vedi ?
> Or vo' che sappi, innanzi che più andi,
> Ch'ei non peccaro ; e s'egli hanno mercedi,
> non basta, perchè non ebber battesmo,
> ch'è porte della fede che tu credi ;
> e se furon dinanzi al Cristianesmo,
> non adorar debitamente Dio ;
> e di questi cotai son io medesmo.
> Per tai difetti, non per altro rio,
> semo perduti, e sol di tanto offesi,
> che senza speme vivemo in disio." '

(The translations given in the text are taken from Cary's version, first published in 1814.)

[1] *Inferno*, iv. 111 :

> ' . . . prato di fresca verdura.
> Genti v'eran con occhi tardi e gravi,
> di grande autorità ne' lor sembianti ;
> parlavan rado, con voci soavi . . .
> Colà diritto, sopra il verde smalto,
> mi fur mostrati gli spiriti magni,
> che del vederli in me stesso n'esalto . . .
> Vidi il maestro di color che sanno
> seder tra filosofica famiglia.

We shall have occasion again to treat of the conception of *Limbo* as the eschatological corollary of Original Sin apart from Actual Sin, and need not devote more time to the examination of its specifically Thomist form : it will suffice for our present purpose to point out that its adoption by St. Thomas, after its stern rejection by St. Augustine, is the most striking instance of the fact that, even in the minds of the African Doctor's most loyal disciples, the rigidly ' twice-born ' anthropology had to be perceptibly softened in order to be preserved at all.[1]

THE SCOTIST POSITION

The Franciscan version of the Fall-doctrine represents a more definite and decided revolt against Augustinanism and shows distinct affinities with what we have designated as the primitive, ' once-born,' and ' Hellenic ' view. In accordance with the method previously explained, we take the opinions of John Duns Scotus as typical of his school.[2]

> Tutti lo miran, tutti onor gli fanno ;
>   quivi vid' io Socrate e Platone,
>   che innanzi agli altri più presso gli stanno ;
> Democrito, che il mondo a caso pone,
>   Diogenes, Anassagora e Tale,
>   Empedocles, Eraclito e Zenone ;
> e vidi il buono accoglitor del quale,
>   Dioscoride dico.'

[1] The full Augustinian doctrine was, however, embodied in the great text-book of mediaeval canon law, the *Decretum* of Gratian : Pars iii, dist. 4, c. 3 : ' firmissime tene, et nullatenus dubites, omnem hominem qui per concubitum viri et mulieris concipitur cum originali peccato nasci, inpietati subditum mortique subiectum . . . firmissime tene, non solum homines ratione utentes, verum etiam parvulos, qui sive in uteris matrum vivere incipiunt et ibi moriuntur, sive iam de matribus nati sine baptismatis sacramento . . . de hoc seculo transeunt, *sempiterno igne puniendos* ; quia etsi peccatum propriae actionis nullum habent, originalis tamen peccati dampnationem carnali conceptione ex nativitate traxerunt.'

[2] Scotus' interpretation of the doctrines of the Fall and of Original Sin is expounded at length in *quaestiones in ii. lib. sentent., distinct.* xvii.-xxxiii. (Paris edition, 1893, tom. xiii. pp. 61–332). It will be understood that the sketch given in the text only endeavours to pick out some of his more characteristic points, and does not attempt to review the whole discussion. Except where otherwise indicated, the reference ' *dist.*' denotes one of these *distinctiones*.

So far as words go, the exalted Augustinian conception
of ' original righteousness ' is preserved in this scheme ; the
idea of the Paradisal perfection of man was at this date too
deeply rooted in Christian thought to be frankly discarded.
It is, nevertheless, modified to a certain extent. ' Original
justice ' is asserted to have been a *donum supernaturale*,
which had the effect of producing a perfect harmony and
balance between the various faculties and functions of the
human soul, a harmony involving the due subordination
of appetite to reason.[1] This harmony, however, was not
absolutely stable, even in Paradise ; for the experience of
successful resistance to temptation was needed in order that
human nature might be confirmed in grace. Until he had
been tempted once, Adam's blissful condition bore a provisional character. If he had triumphed on the first occasion
when he was tested, he would have acquired a more solid and
permanent habit of virtue [2] ; and the same rule would have
applied, if he had not fallen, to each of his descendants.
Each member of the human race subsequently born would
have been tested once, and, if triumphant, would have been
confirmed in grace.[3] It may be suggested that Scotus shows
signs of a desire to return, so far as was possible within the
bounds of mediaeval Western orthodoxy, to the primitive,
second-century conception of man's unfallen state as being
one of ' infancy ' ($\nu\eta\pi\iota\acute{o}\tau\eta\varsigma$), though including a ' starting-
point for progress ' ($\acute{\alpha}\phi o\rho\mu\grave{\eta}$ $\pi\rho o\kappa o\pi\hat{\eta}\varsigma$). Congruous with
this is the affirmation that the ' immortality ' enjoyed by

---

[1] *dist*. xxix. (Paris edn. tom. xiii. p. 272) : ' potest dici ergo quod si
originalis iustitia habuit illum effectum, facere scilicet perfectam tran-
quillitatem in anima, quantum ad omnes potentias, ita quod natura
inferior non inclinaretur contra iudicium superioris, aut si inclinaretur
quantum est ex se, posset tamen a superiori regulari et ordinari sine diffi-
cultate superioris et sine tristitia inferioris, cum hoc non habuerit potentia
facta in puris naturalibus, necesse est ipsam ponere donum supernaturale,
quo sit ista tranquillitas perfecta in anima.'

[2] *dist*. xx. q. 1 (*op. cit.* p. 116) : ' . . . pater primus fuisset con-
firmatus, si primae tentationi restitisset, in ista iustitia,' etc.

[3] *dist*. xx. q. 1 (pp. 115 ff.). This ' confirmation in grace ' would,
however, not have conferred the state known as *non posse peccare*, which is
only possible for *comprehensores* (*i.e.* the blessed who possess the Beatific
Vision), but only the privilege *quod non peccat vel peccabit*, which alone is
appropriate to *viatores* (*i.e.* those still living on this earth in a state of
probation).

unfallen Adam consisted, not in the impossibility of dying,
but in the possibility of not dying.[1]

Corresponding to this somewhat modified conception
of original righteousness we have a milder estimate of the
degree of wickedness involved in the Fall. The root of
Adam's sin, according to Scotus, was not (as in Augustine's
view) an incomprehensible, unmotived impulse to defy his
Creator, but the very natural, and, as it were, pardonable
defect of ' immoderate desire for the affection of his wife '
(*immoderatus amor amicitiae uxoris*), and the wish not to be
separated from her even after her sin, a wish that under
the circumstances almost inevitably transformed itself into
the will to do that which was not lawful (*voluntas explendi
illud quod non licuit*).[2] As the primal sin sprang from so
human and genial a source, it is a gross exaggeration to
describe its ' malice ' as ' infinite '[3]; and the foundation
has been removed, on which the Augustinian conception of
fallen mankind as corporately constituting a *massa damnationis* is built. The same tendency to soften the harsh
outlines of the Augustinian system appears most noticeably
in the discussion of original sin in its character of *vitium*,
that is, of a psychological disease. For Scotus, the essence
of original sin consists only in the ' lack of original justice '
(*carentia originalis iustitiae*), and does not consist in con-

---

[1] *dist.* xxix. 5 (p. 274) ; *cf. dist.* xix. 2 (p. 103). This, however, is
precisely St. Augustine's position : *v. supra*, Lecture V, p. 361, n. 2.

[2] *dist.* xxi. q. 2 (p. 139) : ' primum autem peccatum Adae non fuit ex
immoderato amore sui, sicut fuit primum peccatum Angeli . . . primum
ergo peccatum hominis non potuit esse immoderatus amor sui, sed . . .
immoderatus amor amicitiae uxoris. nam dicit Augustinus quod *noluit
contristare eam, quam credebat sine suo solatio contabescere, et a se alienatam
omnino interire*, ut habetur in littera. *c. illo* : *ex quo manifeste.* patet ergo
quod non fuit amor concupiscentiae vel libidinis, quia ille nondum fuerat ;
ex isto autem amore inordinato peccatum gravius sequebatur, scilicet
voluntas explendi illud quod non licuit, puta praeceptum de esu pomi
violare.'

[3] *ibid.* (p. 141) : Adam's sin arose from an excess of love for his neighbour (*i.e.* Eve) ; ' ergo sequitur quod peccatum hominis primi non fuit
quantum ad hoc gravissimum, imo dico quod multa peccata fiunt modo a
multis quae sunt graviora, ita quod si Adam debuisset fuisse damnatus
pro illo, multo minorem poenam sustinuisset.' On p. 143 will be found an
apportionment of the guilt of the Fall, such as it was, between Adam and
Eve : ' Adae peccatum *accidentaliter* fuit gravius peccato Evae : *formaliter*
tamen, *per se mere*, et *praecise in se*, peccatum Evae fuit gravius.'

cupiscence at all[1]; this is one of his capital divergences from St. Thomas. Concupiscence, indeed, is said to be 'natural,' as being merely the necessary reaction of the sensitive part of the soul to intrinsically desirable objects.[2] It would seem probable that the Subtle Doctor is here using the word in its etymological sense, as signifying merely 'desire as such,' not 'inordinate desire'[2]; and we may fairly set the name of Duns Scotus by the side of Julian of Eclanum, as the name of one of the few Christian thinkers who have firmly grasped the idea of the moral neutrality of physical appetite.

It might have seemed that the affirmation of the innocence of concupiscence would naturally bring in its train the further consequence of a denial of original guilt or *reatus*, at any rate of the guilt which on Augustinian principles attaches to a nature infected with concupiscence. Here, however, the courage of the Franciscans would seem to have failed them. Frankly to throw over the conception of original guilt would have seemed to the thought of the Middle Ages to involve the condemnation of the practice of

[1] *dist.* xxx. q. 2 (p. 293) : ' peccatum originale non potest esse aliud quam ista privatio (*sc.* originalis iustitiae) ; non enim est concupiscentia, tum quia illa est naturalis *ex dist.* 29, tum quia ipsa est in parte sensitiva, ubi non est peccatum secundum Anselmum,' etc.

[2] He draws this very distinction between these two senses of the word in *dist.* xxxii. 7 (p. 311), and admits that in the latter sense ' concupiscentia est materiale peccati originalis,' thus coming verbally into accord with St. Thomas. It is, however, not unreasonable to regard this admission as a mere passing act of lip-homage to Augustinianism, and to hold that Scotus' real mind is expressed by a significant silence in *dist.* xxxi. q. unica. Here he is commenting on *Sent.* ii., in which the Lombard quotes and endorses a passage from St. Augustine, expressing in its crudest form the theory that original sin is transmitted from parent to child through the concupiscence accompanying the act of generation. This passage deserves to be quoted in full : it runs : ' quia, dum sibi invicem vir mulierque miscentur, sine libidine non est parentum concubitus ; ob hoc filiorum ex eorum carne nascentium non potest sine peccato esse conceptus, ubi peccatum in parvulos non transmittit propagatio, sed libido ; nec foecunditas humanae naturae facit, homines cum peccato nasci, sed foeditas libidinis, quam homines habent ex illius primi iustissima condemnatione peccati. ideo beatus David, propter originale peccatum quo naturaliter obstricti sunt filii irae, dicit " in iniquitatibus conceptus sum, et in peccatis concepit me mater mea " ' (*de fide ad Petrum*, 2). Scotus passes this unpleasant citation over without a word, evidently dissenting from it, though the combined authority of St. Augustine and of the Master of the Sentences is too great to be explicitly repudiated.

infant baptism. Once more the actual practice of the
Church, as in the fifth century, exercised an irresistible
influence over the development of thought. The Church
actually does baptise newly born infants, and we cannot
suppose that the Church has acted wrongly or without good
reason ; therefore infants, even of a day old, stand in urgent
need of baptism. But, in the ' Nicene ' Creed, we profess
our belief in ' *one* baptism,' which is ' for the remission of
sins.' There are not two different kinds of baptism, one of
adults conveying remission of sins, and the other of infants
conveying no remission of sins ; *therefore*, infants are baptised
' for the remission of sins,' and must accordingly be supposed
to have some real sin, in the sense of guilt, which can be
remitted. Adequate historical knowledge regarding the
growth of the custom of paedo-baptism, and regarding the
relation of the Constantinopolitan (the so-called ' Nicene ')
Creed to the original ' Nicaenum ' might have made this
chain of reasoning seem very much less than cogent.[1] Such
knowledge, however, was not at Scotus' disposal : and hence
he endeavours to explain original guilt under the somewhat unsatisfactory category of ' debt.' God entrusted man
in Paradise with the gift of original righteousness, and
man has lost it ; hence man, collectively considered, is in
a condition of ' indebtedness ' to God, because he has lost
the treasure with which his Father had endowed him. It
is this condition of indebtedness which descends from generation to generation, and is forensically regarded as involving
' guilt ' in the sight of God.[2] The possibility of such
inheritance appears to be based upon a theory of ' seminal

---

[1] See Additional Note G ' Infant Baptism ' (p. 550).

[2] *dist.* xxxii. 7 (p. 311) : ' peccatum originale est . . . formaliter
carentia iustitiae originalis *debitae*, et non qualitercumque debitae, quia
acceptae in primo parente et in ipso amissae, cui correspondet poena
damni dumtaxat ex praemissa criminis transgressione proveniens ' ;
9 (p. 312) : ' ex illa collatione (*sc.* originalis iustitiae) facta patri, filius est
debitor iustitiae sic datae ' ; but see the whole *distinctio*. The ' debt ' of
original justice is remitted (or, in other words, the inherited guilt of having
lost the supernatural endowments of unfallen human nature is pardoned)
by God through baptism, and for it is substituted the obligation to possess
the ordinary Christian virtues : *ibid.* 13 : ' ideo in baptismo cum redditur
gratia, simpliciter dimittitur illud peccatum (*sc.* originale) . . . solvitur
enim debitum habendi istud donum (*sc.* originalem iustitiam), et
commutatur in debitum habendi aliud donum.'

identity,' which, however, only has reference to man's body ; for Scotus' ' creationism ' forbids him to assume that Adam's soul included all subsequent human souls at the moment when he fell. [1]

It has been suggested before that the theory of a material identity of the human race with Adam can hardly be held by a philosophically trained mind except in the form of the theory of logical or metaphysical identity ; and, as Scotus himself was a logical Realist, the idea that we, or at any rate our bodies, were ' in Adam ' is not difficult for him. But the Nominalism which was characteristic of other Franciscan thinkers, by denying the real objective existence of universals, implicitly denied that Adam was the universal of humanity, and thereby cut at the root of the idea of original guilt, in so far as this implies the pre-natal acquisition of responsibility for Adam's sin. The antinomies in which later Franciscan schoolmen found themselves involved by the attempt to justify some sort of defecated Augustinianism on a purely Nominalist basis were such as could only be solved by the application of the sceptical principle, which, by a singular irony, was the final intellectual product of the Ages of Faith—that propositions may be true in theology which are false in philosophy, and *vice versa*.[2]

---

[1] *dist.* xxxi. 2 (p. 299) : ' contraximus istud peccatum in quantum fuimus in Adam secundum rationem seminalem . . . hoc autem fuit secundum corpus, non secundum animam ; anima enim non est ex traduce.'

[2] *Cf.* the following observations on Occam's Fall-doctrine : ' As a church-theologian, Occam was obliged to maintain this conception [that of original sin], and likewise also the traditional definition of it as the defect of original righteousness. But from the standpoint of the possible . . . it in no way appears, according to Occam, that man is under obligation to possess a supernatural gift in addition to his natural equipment. Original sin is no real loss in man's nature : it is the ideal imputation of Adam's sin with regard to all his descendants. It simply means that the race of man, by virtue of God's *potentia ordinata* and by reason of another's trespass, has been included in a sentence of condemnation. There is no question here of a man's own sin. *It is axiomatic with the Nominalists that there is no real connexion between Adam and the rest of humanity.* These theses show with the greatest plainness what a tremendous gulf separates this doctrine of original sin from the motives which led to its first formulation by Augustine. In effect we have only the empty formulae left, now that that which formerly gave them life is gone. The doctrine is a *locus theologicus*, which is without any other *raison d'être* than that which is imposed upon it by ecclesiastical tradition. How little understanding

We pass to the consideration of the present state of fallen man according to the Scotist conception. The Franciscan doctrine is naturally determined by the fundamental position that the essence of original sin consists in no positive corruption of human nature, but merely in the lack of certain splendid endowments which human nature once possessed. Hence the Franciscans are able to maintain a real and not merely nominal freedom of the will. For Scotus the will is free, both in the psychological sense of freedom from exclusive determination by habit and character, and also in the metaphysical sense of freedom from exclusive determination by an all-embracing divine causality. Both these positions have interesting consequences, which may be pointed out without straying too far from the main path of our enquiry. The concession of psychological freedom to fallen man necessitates the admission that he can perform morally good works of a natural order, even prior to the reception of grace. These works of merely natural virtue must, it is explained, be sharply distinguished from supernatural actions, for which grace is necessary; but they are nevertheless truly moral, and so far are pleasing to God. They may even merit the bestowal of grace *de congruo* or *de condigno*, that is, as a congruous or as a deserved reward —a position which is naturally distasteful to the severe Augustinianism of the compilers of our Thirty-Nine Articles [1]; and Scotus emphatically repudiates the idea that the virtues of the heathen are no more than ' splendid vices.' The metaphysical freedom which Scotus attributes to the human soul is reconciled with the universality of divine causation by the supposition of a pre-established harmony

---

Occam has of the original import of the doctrine is shown in his mode of treating *concupiscence* . . . Concupiscence or *fomes* is to him entirely of sensual nature, a merely bodily defect. It is simply to be compared with bodily diseases, and like them must be supposed to rest on an unequal distribution of the " humours " in man. To *fomes* he assigns also the whole circle of the vegetative life ; hunger, thirst, sleep, etc., are results of the same, inasmuch as it is not possible to control them. In this last sense neither Christ nor the Virgin Mary was free from concupiscence. [Thus Occam returns to the position of Julian, which once roused Augustine's vehement indignation].' G. Ljunggren, *op. cit.* p. 248 f. (tr. G. C. Richards).

[1] It is strongly condemned in Art. xiii.

between the eternal decrees of God and the results of human choice. I have, here and now, perfect freedom to choose between two alternatives, A and B. If I decide for B, I am perfectly free in so doing, and bear the full responsibility for my choice : nevertheless, in eternity God foresaw that I should choose B, and ratified my decision by anticipation in His divine counsels, designing the rest of human history on the assumption that B would actually be my choice ; hence the Franciscans are able to approximate very closely to semi-Pelagianism in regard to the function of prevenient grace.

This modified version of the traditional Western presentation of Christian anthropology naturally culminates in an exceptionally mild view of its eschatological corollaries, that is, in a view of *Limbo* even gentler than that of St. Thomas. Scotus is compelled by tradition to describe those in *Limbo* as ' damned ' [1]; but their damnation is, it would seem, of an exceedingly pleasurable and soothing kind. Those who are lost merely because of the original sin of their nature, and are free from actual or personal sin, have no pain or sadness of any kind ; they are exempt both from the *poena sensus*, the torments of unending flames, and from the *poena damni*, the penalty of the loss of God.[2] Though they will not have the Beatific Vision of God in His intimate essence, it is probable that they will know God through His works, perhaps as perfectly as He can be so known ; and this knowledge will give them a certain positive pleasure.[3] Scotus quotes Bonaventura as saying that Augustine spoke *excessive*—' with exaggeration '—in denying the intermediate state postulated by the Pelagians in the case of the virtuous or sinless non-baptised.[4] So far as the conception of *Limbo* is concerned the Franciscan theory won all along the line in the Middle Ages. The few rigid Augustinians, like Gregory of Rimini (d. 1358), who clung

---

[1] *dist.* xxxiii. 2 (p. 328) : ' damnati pro solo peccato originali.'
[2] *ibid.* 2 (p. 329).
[3] *ibid.* 3 (p. 330) : ' videtur probabile concedere quod omnium naturaliter cognoscibilium possunt naturaliter cognitionem habere excellentius quam aliqui habuerunt pro statu isto, et ita aliqualem beatitudinem naturalem de Deo cognito in universali poterunt attingere.'
[4] *dist.* xxxiii. 4 (p. 331).

to the idea of positive torments to be inflicted on unbaptised infants, were scoffingly nicknamed *tortores infantium*. It was reserved for Calvin to revive this part of the Augustinian teaching in its full horror.

Two further consequences of the Scotist doctrine should be mentioned for the sake of completeness—one which has reference to the person of the Redeemer, and the other to that of His Mother. It is naturally difficult for those who minimise the seriousness of the Fall to suppose that such a tremendous event as the Incarnation was contingent upon it. Franciscan thought on this subject is fundamentally out of sympathy with the idea expressed in the famous phrase of the *Exultet* : ' O certe necessarium Adae peccatum ! O felix culpa, quae talem et tantum meruit habere redemptorem ! ' Hence comes the characteristically Scotist view that the Incarnation would in any case have taken place, even if there had been no Fall, and that it was purposed by God from all eternity as the crowning moment of human history.[1] And the purely negative or deprivational notion of original sin, as consisting solely in the absence of certain supernatural graces, made it easier to believe that those graces were as a special privilege conferred upon the Mother of Christ in order to make her body and soul a fitting habitation for the Divine Word.[2] Harnack's dictum, however, that it is easy for Roman Catholics to affirm the immunity of Mary from original sin, because original sin means nothing to them, is an obvious exaggeration,[3] which ignores the fact that the post-Tridentine

---

[1] A classical presentation of the theory of the *absolute* purpose of the Incarnation is found in Westcott's essay ' The Gospel of Creation ' (*Epistles of St. John*, 1883, pp. 273-315).

[2] J. Turmel (*ERE* vii. p. 166, art. ' Immaculate Conception ') reverses the relation of cause and effect suggested in the text, and thinks that popular enthusiasm for the feast and the idea of the Immaculate Conception compelled official theology to mitigate its conception of original sin, and in particular to drop the belief in the inherent sinfulness of concupiscence. On strict Augustinian principles, the Immaculate Conception is ruled out, as the soul of Mary would have been automatically infected with original sin by the concupiscence which *ex hypothesi* must have attended her generation by Joachim and Anne. St. Bernard, as is well known, had strenuously opposed the introduction of the feast (*ep.* clxxiv, *PL* CLXXXII. 332).

[3] *History of Dogma* (E. tr., 1899), vii. p. 100, n. 1.

Latin doctrine of the inherited wound of human nature is more stringent than the Scotist, though not so severe as the Thomist or the Augustinian teaching.[1] And it is also fair to point out that the difference between St. Thomas and Duns Scotus in regard to the privilege of Mary turned, not upon the question whether Mary after her birth was exempt from original sin—for both admitted this—but upon the question whether this exemption was conferred on her at some unknown moment during her intra-uterine life, as the Angelic Doctor affirmed,[2] or in the very first instant of her existence, that is, at the moment of her conception, as the Subtle Doctor maintained.

The foregoing summaries of the anthropological thought

---

[1] It will be appropriate to append here a few words with regard to the bearing of our discussion upon the Roman doctrine of the Immaculate Conception of the Blessed Virgin Mary. The Bull *Ineffabilis Deus*, dated Dec. 8, 1854, affirms that ' the doctrine which holds, that the most blessed Virgin Mary was in the first instant of her conception, by a singular grace and privilege of Almighty God, in view of the merits of Christ Jesus, the Saviour of the human race, preserved immune from all stain of original sin (*ab omni originalis culpae labe praeservatam immunem*) has been revealed by God and is therefore by all the faithful to be firmly and constantly believed ' (Denzinger-Bannwart, *Enchiridion*, § 1641). As the definition is promulgated by Roman authority, it presumably presupposes the present Roman conception of original sin, which (as pointed out in the text) is somewhat severer than the Scotist doctrine, inasmuch as it includes not merely the guilt of being devoid of original righteousness, but also the guilt of having sinned ' in Adam.' Immunity ' from all stain of original sin ' must therefore mean, *inter alia*, immunity from original guilt. From the standpoint of the thesis developed in these lectures, it follows that the main objection to the doctrine of the Immaculate Conception is—not so much the fact that no trace of any such belief can be found in the New Testament or in the Christian writers of the first four centuries, but rather—the fact that (if our contentions have been sound) the idea of responsibility for pre-natal participation in Adam's sin is both mythological and irrational. If, as we have argued, ' original guilt ' is merely an Augustinian nightmare, it is meaningless to assert that Mary was ' immune ' from it.

[2] The doctrine of St. Thomas on this subject is contained in *summa theol.* iii. q. xxvii, ' de beatae Mariae virginis sanctificatione.' This doctrine is (*a*) ' rationabiliter creditur quod beata Virgo sanctificata fuerit antequam ex utero nasceretur' (a. 1); (*b*) 'sanctificatio beatae Virginis <fuit> post eius animationem' (a. 2); (*c*) ' per sanctificationem in utero non <fuit> sublatus beatae Virgini fomes secundum essentiam, sed <remansit> ligatus' (the ' fomes' is, of course, concupiscence) 'postmodum vero in ipsa conceptione carnis Christi, in quo primo debuit refulgere peccati immunitas, credendum est quod ex prole redundaverit <? gratia> in matrem, totaliter fomite subtracto ' (a. 3).

of the two leading doctors of the Middle Ages will, it may be hoped, have made it clear that the history of our subject during the scholastic period is the history of the gradual decline of rigid Augustinianism. In the eleventh century the first blows were struck at its supremacy by Anselm, who introduced the conception of the 'lack of original righteousness' as a prime constituent of original sin, thereby paving the way for the substitution of the idea of hereditary weakness for that of hereditary wickedness, and by Abaelard, who was the first to challenge the idea of original guilt. St. Thomas and the Dominicans stood for a modified type of Augustinianism, in which the lack of original righteousness is described as the 'form,' and concupiscence as the 'matter' of original sin. Scotus and the Franciscans developed a still further modified version of Augustinianism (if such it can be called) in which original sin for all practical purposes comes to consist *solely* in the lack of original righteousness, and concupiscence ceases to be in any real sense sinful. Naturally such a highly artificial and abstract notion as that of the mere non-possession of certain splendid endowments, which were believed to have for a brief space belonged to the remote ancestor of human kind, had little power to weigh upon men's consciences or even to excite their intellectual interest : and if the Franciscan and Nominalist tendency to whittle the Fall-doctrine down to nothing had continued, the whole of Augustine's work in regard to these ideas might have been undone, even within the sphere and period of mediaeval Catholicism. It is a striking fact that the comprehensive commentary on the 'Sentences' written by Pierre d'Ailly [1] ignores the whole subject of original sin. The short-lived Augustinian reaction associated with the names of Bradwardine and Wycliffe had comparatively little effect on the general thought of Europe. *What really gave Augustinianism a new lease of life was the Reformation.* It will, however, conduce to clearness if for

---

[1] Pierre d'Ailly (1350–1420) was successively chancellor of Notre Dame de Paris, bishop of Cambrai, bishop of Orange, and cardinal. He played a leading part in the 'Conciliar' movement at the beginning of the fifteenth century. For a study of his life and writings, see P. Tschackert, *Peter von Ailli*, Gotha, 1877. The statement in the text is made on the authority of Ljunggren, *op. cit.*, p. 249.

the moment we ignore this cataclysmic event, and continue the story of the gradual decadence of Augustinianism within Latin Christianity down to modern times.

THE COUNCIL OF TRENT

The discussion of these doctrines between the theologians of the two great mendicant Orders was largely an affair of the study and the schools. The questions involved did not affect practical life in any way,[1] nor were they of interest to the laity or to such of the clergy as were not theological experts. They belonged to the same world of discourse as the interminable controversies with regard to angels, whether they occupy space or not, whether one angel can occupy the same space as another, whether the thought of angels is discursive or intuitive. But the Reformation, challenging as it did the whole fabric of mediaeval Church life and thought, had the remarkable effect of dragging the doctrines of the Fall and of original sin out from the cloister and the lecture-room into the market-place, and of making them issues of the greatest interest and importance for the religious life of hundreds of thousands of ordinary people.[2] Hence, when the Latin Church, after the defection of the Northern nations, took stock of itself, and proceeded to reorganise itself on a military basis, like a besieged city, with

---

[1] G. G. Coulton, however (*Five Centuries of Religion*, vol. 1, 1923, p. 145), thinks that the gloom of the severe Augustinian doctrine helped to stimulate the growth of the cultus of the Blessed Virgin, the thought of whose intercessory powers provided men with some mental relief from the prospect of probable damnation.

[2] This popularisation of the Fall-doctrine is illustrated by the liturgical confessions of sin embodied in many Protestant Church Orders, which require the congregation to accuse itself of original as well as of actual sin : for a collection of such confessions, see Additional Note C, ' Congregational Confessions of Original Sin in the Churches of the Reformation' (p. 443). The enormous growth of interest in original sin which these formulae manifest can be gauged if they are compared with their mediaeval predecessor, the Catholic ' confiteor Deo omnipotenti, beatae Mariae semper virgini, omnibus sanctis . . . quia peccavi nimis cogitatione, verbo, et opere, mea culpa ' which is a confession of actual sin only. It may be noted that the Confessions contained in the daily Offices and Communion Service of the Church of England, though showing literary relationship with the Continental confessions, abstain from mentioning original sin.

a stern discipline designed to safeguard its life against the attacks of its enemies, it was necessary that these doctrines also should be reduced to a stiff, defined form, in order to keep the reforming influence at a safe distance. Consequently what is still the official doctrine of the Roman Church on these subjects was formulated at the Council of Trent, despite the nervousness of the Emperor Charles V, who would much have preferred that the Council should have left such thorny topics alone. The Dominicans were represented at the Council by Catterino and de Soto, two of the most learned theologians of their order ; but it is remarkable that we hear very little of the Franciscans. The Order of Friars Minor had fallen upon evil days, having produced no great theologian since William Occam. It was at this period distracted by the schisms between the Capuchins and the Conventuals ; and the mantle of Duns Scotus, as the upholder of the anti-Augustinian position, had fallen upon the newly founded Society of Jesus. The decisions of the Souncil were contained in the *Decree concerning original sin*, Cession 5, affirmed on June 17, 1546, and the *Decree concerning Justification*, Session 6, affirmed on January 13, 1547.[1]   The former consists of five canons verbally repeating the first two canons of the second Council of Orange, and containing also a long passage taken from the second canon of the second Council of Carthage, which had condemned Pelagius and Caelestius in A.D. 418. These facts sound as though the Tridentine decision ought to have been a triumph for Augustinianism. Actually, the result was a compromise which cannot have satisfied either party completely, as a brief analysis of it will show. We will take the cardinal points at issue *seriatim*. (1) ' Original righteousness.' Adam is said to have been ' constituted ' in holiness and righteousness. The Council is silent on the subject of his supposed intellectual attainments. (The word ' constituted ' is obviously meant to avoid raising the question whether Adam was created in original righteousness, as the Dominicans asserted, or created in a state of pure nature and subsequently endowed with supernatural holiness, as

---

[1] For the text of the relevant portions of these documents, see Additional Note F, ' Formularies (II), Western and Roman,' p. 538.

the Franciscans maintained.) (2) Original sin considered as *vitium*. Here the Council is studiously vague, contenting itself with repeating the indefinite affirmation of the second Council of Orange, to the effect that by the Fall Adam was changed for the worse, in both body and soul, and that he injured his posterity and not merely himself. (3) Original sin considered as *reatus*, that is, ' original guilt.' This is emphatically affirmed. Canon 3 (of the Decree concerning original sin) seems to imply the theory of ' seminal identity,' though its language is very vague. Canon 4 asserts that infants have sin, which must be expiated in the laver of regeneration. Canon 5 uses the actual phrase *reatus peccati originalis*, and asserts that something undefined, which has the true and proper nature of sin, is abolished by baptism. (4) With regard to the state of human nature which has resulted from the Fall, the Council affirms that concupiscence is not sin but merely the *fomes* or tinder of sin and that it is left in the regenerate *ad agonem*, for them to struggle against. It is declared also that man's free-will was by no means extinguished, but rather attenuated and warped so that apart from grace men cannot rise and free themselves from the chains of sinful desire. It will be seen at once that these positions represent a compromise between the Dominican and the Jesuit points of view, in which, on the whole, the Jesuits get very much the best of the bargain. The Dominicans secure the affirmation of original guilt in terms which go a long way beyond the debt theory of Scotus. The anti-Augustinian party, on the other hand, secures a strong affirmation of the reality of human free-will, the denial of concupiscence as in any real sense sin, the exemption of the Blessed Virgin Mary from the scope of the decree affirming the universality of original sin, and the denial of the Augustinian position that the good works of non-Christians are sins. It may therefore be said that Tridentine orthodoxy on this subject is, on the whole, Scotist, with one unassimilated fragment of pure Augustinianism, namely, the conception of original guilt, adhering awkwardly to it.

The subsequent history of these doctrines in the Latin Church may be passed over in a few words. The main controversy between the Dominicans and the Jesuits tended to veer away from anthropology and to become more and more entangled in the question of ' grace,' with which, as was pointed out in Lecture V,[1] we are not immediately concerned. Mention must be made, however, of one attempt to revive the full Augustinian scheme within the Roman communion—an attempt which by its failure and suppression had the indirect effect of accentuating the Scotist and anti-Augustinian character of Latin orthodoxy on these points. This is associated with the name of Michael de Bay, or Baius.[2]   Baius, a professor at the University of Louvain, who had attended the Council of Trent as a theological expert, denied the scholastic distinction between the *donum supernaturale* of original righteousness and the *pura naturalia* (thereby asserting that Adam's splendid gifts of mind and soul belonged to the essence of human nature, and so increasing the guilt of his fall), and also reaffirmed the Augustinian position that the mere presence of potential concupiscence in a newly born infant is in itself a deadly sin.[3]   The condemnation of these two propositions,[4] amongst many others gathered from the works of Baius, exerted, so to speak, a reflex influence on the current teaching of Roman theologians. The distinction between mere human nature and the ' supernatural gifts ' was sharpened and stereotyped ; and in practice the idea of original sin came to be interpreted in the Scotist manner, as a mere deprivation of these supernatural gifts, with only some slight deordination of the proper relations of reason and appetite as its result. The idea of original guilt is still retained in words, but it is explained in such a way as to evacuate the term ' guilt,' and the forensic terminology which naturally coheres with this conception, of all real meaning.   To illustrate this, we need

---

[1] p. 337.

[2] Born 1513, died 1589 : the forerunner of the more celebrated Cornelius Jansen.

[3] These two positions, as will be explained below, constituted the *differentia* of the version of the Fall-doctrine characteristic of the Reformation. Baius was, in effect, endeavouring to naturalise the Protestant anthropology within the sphere of post-Tridentine Latin Catholicism. See Vacant-Mangénot, *DTC.*, art. ' Baius.'

[4] By the Bull of Pius V, *Ex omnibus afflictionibus* (1567). For the principal propositions condemned, see Denzinger-Bannwart, *Enchiridion*, §§ 1001 ff. ; notice especially 1021, 1023, 1025–27, 1047, 1051.

only quote a recent authoritative statement of the Roman Catholic point of view, contained in the volume of essays called ' God and the Supernatural.' [1]   Speaking of the term ' uncleanness ' as applied to original sin, the writer on ' The Problem of Evil ' says :

> No physical defilement nor uncleanness of nature as such does the Church intend by such language, but simply and solely birth into a nature-self deprived of the supernature which should have completed it.   Thus is the personal innocence of the new-born babe, its innocence in the natural order, compatible with a guilt of its nature in relation to the supernatural order.   Thus also is it dear to God because substantially united to Him as its natural ground and end, yet ' a child of wrath ' in its separation from Him and aversion from Him as its supernatural end. [2]

He adds in a footnote : ' Yet surely such language as " child of wrath " or " hateful to God " should not be used of naturally and personally innocent children without careful explanation of its highly technical and non-natural sense.' In this part of our enquiry we are concerned rather to record the movement of ideas than to criticise them.   It is impossible, however, to refrain from observing that if the term ' guilt ' can only be applied to original sin in a non-natural sense it would seem much better that it should not be so applied at all.

AUGUSTINIANISM AND THE REFORMATION

It will thus be seen that within Latin Catholicism, which still constitutes the greater part of Western Christendom, the influence of St. Augustine's characteristic Fall-doctrine has steadily declined during that whole period of its history which may be regarded as beginning with the rise of Scholasticism and as ending with the definition of the doctrine of the Immaculate Conception by Pius IX.   If the fluctuations in the degree of power exercised at different epochs by a given doctrine over the minds of men could be represented

---

[1] Ed. Fr. Cuthbert, O.S.F.C. (1920).
[2] p. 150.

under the form of a mathematical graph, we should see the index-point of Augustinian dominance rising to its zenith shortly after the death of St. Augustine himself, continuing at this exalted level across an area denoting some six centuries, beginning to fall at the point corresponding to the teaching activity of St. Anselm, and descending in a gradual and elongated curve down to the period of the Reformation. Here our chart would have to be doubled, in order to conform to the religious partition of Europe effected by that event ; and we should notice the remarkable fact that, whereas in the Latin section of the chart the line of Augustinian influence continues to sink, until it reaches its nadir at the canonisation of Alfonso Liguori, in the Reformed section it rushes steeply and suddenly upwards, like the edge of the Matterhorn's silhouette, and for more than two centuries preserves an elevation equal to that which it maintained within those divisions of the single chart which we suppose to symbolise the period known as the ' Dark Ages.'   In other words, we are at this stage of our enquiry brought face to face with a colossal recrudescence of the rigidly ' twice-born ' anthropology, combined with a remorseless accentuation of all its sternest lineaments—a process which has given birth to that puritan doctrine of original sin still so largely believed to be the primitive, Christian, and Biblical doctrine.   The details of this process, and the merits of its results, now demand examination.

It is natural in the first instance to raise the question, why the Reformers should have felt it necessary to draw up an elaborate system of doctrines with regard to these abstruse and mysterious subjects at all ? The Reformation proclaimed itself to be a return to Gospel simplicity, a revolt against the subtleties and quiddities of the Schoolmen, a rediscovery and republication of the pure and undefiled Christianity of the New Testament : why, then, could its leaders not have been content with the very general, loose, and undefined teaching of St. Paul ? Why did they feel it necessary to bequeath to posterity the interminable definitions with regard to predestination, the Fall, original sin, grace, and free-will, which crowd the pages of the innumerable formularies produced in the sixteenth and seventeenth centuries ? What constrained them to impose upon their followers anthropological schemes, no less complicated and far more gloomy than anything that appears in the pages of St. Thomas or St. Bonaventura ? The answer to these questions is partly historical, partly psychological. The Fall-doctrine of the Reformation grew from a double root, of which one fibre was embedded in (a) the hitherto dominant Augustinian dogma, whilst the other sprang from (b) the personal idiosyncrasy of the revolting leaders, Luther and Calvin themselves.

(a) In our last lecture it was pointed out that the thought of St. Augustine, considered as a whole, is permeated by two dominant elements which have never been finally fused or synthesised, the predestinarian element, which regards salvation as the direct work of God upon the individual soul, a work to which the saved man contributes little or nothing, and the institutional or hierarchical element, according to which the Christian works out his own salvation through the devout use of the Sacraments, within the warmth and shelter provided by a great and august society.[1] During the Middle Ages it was the ecclesiastical and sacramental element in Augustine's teaching which, as embodied in the mighty theocratic fabric of the Western Catholic Church, exercised the most powerful influence over the lives of ordinary men, and his predestinarianism was little heard of outside the lecture-room and the cloister. But the mystical craving for immediate, personal, unhampered access to the Divine— the longing which impels the solitary soul to overleap all external, ecclesiastical, and liturgical forms, and to wing her way in a flash to the arms of her solitary God—was still working underground, in the dim subconsciousness of the Teutonic nations : and in the Reformation it found a volcanic and earth-shattering expression. Hence it was, humanly speaking, inevitable that the Reformers, nourished as they had been on the thought of St. Augustine, and representing as they did that individualistic method of envisaging the Godward impulse which had determined his predestinarian teaching, should, in their revolt against his institutionalism, have revived, with unbalanced enthusiasm, his

[1] *v. supra*, p. 321 f.

' twice-born ' anthropology ; that their declaration of war upon the Mass, penance, the cultus of the saints, pilgrimages, monasticism, and other external works and forms, should have been accompanied by the promulgation of a theory of man and of sin which was designed to rule out human merit, and to make salvation exclusively God's work, and which therefore was obliged to presuppose the lowest possible view of unredeemed human nature.

(b) To these considerations we must add the fact that both Luther and Calvin appear to have possessed that ' twice-born ' religious temperament indicated by the experience of instantaneous conversion, whether complete or incomplete, or by experiences analogous thereto. There seems no reason for discrediting the story of the voice which sounded in Luther's ears, pronouncing the words ' The just shall live by faith,' when as a young Austin Friar he had ascended half of the Scala Sancta at Rome on his knees [1] ; and, though this phenomenon took years to work its full effect in Luther's mind, it would seem not unjustifiable, from the standpoint of human psychology, to class it with the ' Saul, Saul ' of the Damascus road or the ' Tolle, lege ' of the Milanese garden. Calvin, too, was visited by a similar experience in his youth, though of this no details are known.[2] It is not too much to claim that temperament alone would have guided the great Reformers into the paths of a severe and gloomy anthropology, even had they not been intellectual heirs of mediaeval theology, with its overwhelming tradition of the African Doctor's immemorial authority.

[1] This incident occurred during Luther's stay in Rome, Dec. 1510– Jan. 1511. The version of the story assumed in the text is that given by Luther's son Paul, who says that he had it from his father. The Reformer himself, however, in a sermon of Sept. 15, 1545, alludes to the incident, merely describing his experience as a sudden feeling of doubt whether the system of indulgences was true. Dr. J. Mackinnon (*Luther and the Reformation*, 1925, i. p. 144, n. 78) thinks that the two versions of the story are incompatible, and that Luther's own account must be accepted in preference to his son's ; it appears to me, however, that there is no real incompatibility, and that the Reformer may well have preferred in the pulpit to employ an indefinite mode of allusion to his experience, whilst feeling free to narrate it in detail in the privacy of his family.

[2] Calvin, *in librum psalm. comment.*, praefatio (ed. A. Tholuck, Berlin, 1836, i. p. ix).

The differences between Lutheranism and Calvinism in regard to the doctrines of man and of sin are inconsiderable, so that it is possible to state the Fall-theory characteristic of the Reformation as a single dogmatic scheme. This scheme was based upon a position which seems curiously dry, abstract, and unreal to us to-day, but which was in the sixteenth century defended by the Reforming leaders with the most passionate fervour : it consists in the denial of the scholastic distinction between the *donum supernaturale* of Original Righteousness assumed to have been received from his Creator by unfallen man and his *pura naturalia*, that is, the qualities belonging to him merely in right of his human nature.[1] It will be remembered that this distinction made possible a comparatively mild view of the Fall, at any rate for the Franciscan Schoolmen : a citizen who is elevated to princely rank and then deposed from it is not necessarily worse off than he was before his elevation. But, for the reasons just mentioned, the Reformers were determined to paint the present condition of fallen human nature in colours as gloomy as possible. Hence the magnificent endowments supposed to have been possessed by the first man are affirmed to have been, not superadded adornments, but essential constituents of human nature as God originally created it ; and their loss means, not merely that human nature has been stripped of some adventitious splendours, but that it has been wrecked and confounded in its inmost being. The Fall was not

---

[1] *Cf*. the position of Baius, mentioned above, p. 422. Though this dispute between Latin Catholic and Protestant theologians (whether the splendours of ' original righteousness ' were a *donum indebitum*, *i.e.* a separable accident of the protoplast's nature, as the Catholics maintained, or an essential quality thereof, as the Protestants contended) may seem to us now purely academic, yet (as Ritschl, *Rechtfertigung u. Versöhnung*[2], iii. p. 308, acutely points out) it was vividly symptomatic of the divergence between the mediaeval Catholic and the Protestant *Weltanschauungen*. For the Protestant view implies that the idea of Christian perfection was included in the idea of human nature itself as conceived in the Divine mind : from which it follows that man should seek his perfection along strictly human lines (as a citizen, husband, father, etc.). Whereas the Latin Catholic opinion, that ' original righteousness ' was a *donum supernaturale*, catastrophically imposed upon man's *pura naturalia*, involves a supernaturalism according to which human perfection can ultimately be found only in the *vita angelica* of monasticism.

a fall from supernature to mere nature, as the Schoolmen had taught, but from mere nature to sub-nature. Man is not a citizen, who, after receiving a princedom from the generosity of his sovereign and forfeiting it by his own fault, has reverted to his former *bourgeois* condition ; he is a citizen who has degraded himself by his own act to the status of an outlaw or a felon.

This view of the nature of original righteousness, with its corollary as to the infinite ruin wrought by the Fall, gives rise, by a logic which we might regard as inexorable if we did not know that the conclusion has really determined the premises, to the doctrine of human nature generally known as that of ' total depravity.' Though the essence of this doctrine is common to both the great schools of Reformation thought, certain differences manifest themselves in the expositions which Luther and Calvin give of it. It may be said at once that the Lutheran doctrine on this point is by far the more pessimistic and severe. According to the strict Lutheran conception, human nature by the Fall was deprived of one of its essential faculties—the faculty of knowing, loving, and serving God. The God-apprehending powers of the human soul were totally extirpated. The so-called ' Synergist ' Lutherans, under the leadership of Victorinus Strigel, endeavoured to mitigate the harshness of this doctrine by maintaining that the moral and religious faculties were not so much permanently destroyed as temporarily paralysed.[1] This view was, however, hailed by the majority of Luther's followers with shouts of vituperation, as being grossly Pelagian, and was condemned by the ' Formulary of Concord,' one of the official documents of the Lutheran Church, which says ' They also are likewise repudiated and rejected, who teach that our nature has indeed been greatly weakened and corrupted because of the Fall of the human race, but nevertheless has not altogether lost all goodness relating to divine and spiritual things. . . . For they say that from his natural birth man still has remaining somewhat of good, however little, minute, scanty and attenuated this may be.'[2] It is true that the

---

[1] J. A. Möhler, *Symbolism* (E. tr., 1847), pp. 79, 80.
[2] *solid. declar.* i. *de pecc. orig.* § 23.

Confession of Augsburg leaves man some little power of fulfilling what it calls ' civil justice,' that is, duties enjoined by purely political or secular morality [1] ; but this power has no reference to spiritual or supernatural virtue, of which fallen man is totally and absolutely bereft. To quote once more the emphatic language of the Formulary of Concord, fallen man as such possesses no more power of loving God or turning towards Him than a stone, a tree-trunk, or a piece of mud.[2] From this position, in the thought of Luther himself an even more startling consequence follows. It seemed self-evident to him that original justice and original sin must be exactly equal and parallel. He seems, by a curious piece of confused thinking, to infer from this premise the consequence that the annihilation of the moral and religious faculties of the soul must have been followed by the substitution in their place of similar, but contrarily orientated powers—what might be called immoral and irreligious faculties.[3] Hence we are led to the idea of original sin as a substantive thing or hypostasis—an idea which the Reformer expresses in crude phrases, such as these : ' It is the essence of man to sin,' ' original sin is that very thing which is born of a father and a mother,' ' Man, as he is born of father and mother, is with his whole nature and essence not merely a sinner but sin itself.' [4] It is difficult to avoid the conclusion that Luther has plunged headlong into the abyss of Manicheism, on the verge of which Augustinianism had always trembled but into which it had never, up to this moment, actually fallen.[5] His followers did not indeed go so far ; but the conception of original sin as a positive malignant power, and not a mere deprivation,

---

[1] conf. August., art. xviii. : ' de libero arbitrio docent quod humana voluntas habeat aliquam libertatem ad efficiendam civilem iustitiam, et diligendas res rationi subiectas.'

[2] solid. declar. ii. de lib. arb. § 24 : ' antequam homo per Spiritum Sanctum illuminatur . . . ex sese et propriis naturalibus suis viribus, in rebus spiritualibus nihil inchoare, operari, aut cooperari potest, non plus quam lapis truncus aut limus.'

[3] Möhler, op. cit., i. p. 85.

[4] These expressions were collected by J. A. Quenstedt (Theologia didactico-polemica, Wittenberg, 1691, ii. pp. 134 f.).

[5] The Formulary of Concord, however, expressly condemns the Manichean theory that evil is a substance (solid. declar. i. § 27).

is unequivocally expressed by the Formulary of Concord
in words which may be quoted here :

> Moreover, it is affirmed that original sin in human nature is
> not merely that total lack or defect of virtuous powers in spiritual
> things which pertain unto God ; but also that into the place of
> the image of God which has been lost there has succeeded an
> intimate, grievous, most profound and abyss-like, inscrutable
> and indescribable corruption of the whole nature and of all the
> powers of man, most chiefly of the superior and principal
> faculties of the soul, a corruption which infects the mind, intellect,
> heart, and will. Wherefore after the Fall man receives from his
> parents by heredity a congenitally depraved impulse, filthiness
> of heart, depraved concupiscences and depraved inclinations.[1]

This sweeping condemnation of human nature as it
stands previously to the operations of divine grace raised
once more the old enigma of the apparent virtues and
good works of non-Christians. Generally speaking, the
theology of the Reformation, in regard to this point as to
others, obediently follows the lines laid down by its master,
Augustine. The supposed ' good deeds ' of Jews or pagans
are really sins : for, given the doctrine of ' total depravity,'
all that issues from unregenerate human nature is necessarily
sinful.[2] So the *Apology for the Confession of Augsburg*
asserts : ' it is both false and an insult to Christ, to assert
that men do not sin when they fulfil the commandments
of God, apart from grace '[3] (and grace *ex hypothesi* is only
bestowed upon members of the Christian Church). This
position is developed, and based upon the familiar proof-
text discovered in the Epistle to the Romans by the

---

[1] *solid. declar.* i. 11 : ' praeterea, quod peccatum originale in humana
natura non tantummodo sit eiusmodi totalis carentia seu defectus omnium
bonorum in rebus spiritualibus ad Deum pertinentibus, sed quod sit
etiam, loco imaginis Dei amissae in homine, intima, pessima, profundissima
instar cuiusdam abyssi, inscrutabilis et ineffabilis corruptio totius naturae
et omnium virium, inprimis vero superiorum et principalium animae
facultatum in mente, intellectu, corde, et voluntate. itaque iam post
lapsum homo haereditario a parentibus accipit congenitam pravam
vim, internam immunditiam cordis, pravas concupiscentias et pravas
inclinationes.'

[2] *Cf.* Calvin, *instit. christ. rel.* ii. 3, title : ' ex corrupta hominis natura
nihil nisi damnabile prodire.'

[3] *apol. conf. Aug.* ii. § 29 : ' falsum est et hoc et contumeliosum in
Christum, quod non peccent homines facientes praecepta Dei sine gratia.'

ingenuity of Augustine,[1] in the following sentence of the same formulary : ' Seeing that contempt of God and doubt concerning His word, His threats, and His promises are rooted in the nature of man, men truly sin even when they perform good works apart from the Holy Spirit : for they perform such works with an impious heart, as it is written, *whatsoever is not of faith is sin.*' [2] Thus the whole of human nature and the sum of man's moral aspirations and efforts, apart from Christianity, are stigmatised as corrupt and worthless in the sight of Almighty God.

Compared with this crude and violent version of the dogma of ' total depravity,' Calvin's doctrine on the same subject assumes from time to time a comparatively humane and reasonable form. There is one sentence of the *Institutio* which in words denies the idea of total depravity, in connexion with this vexed question of the virtues of pagans, which, he tells us, have been ordained by God *ne hominis naturam in totum vitiosam putemus*, lest we should think that the nature of man is altogether depraved.[3] And the psychological analysis of the various faculties of human nature which occurs in the second book of the Institutes contains a singularly generous tribute to triumphs won by the human intellect, even apart from the grace of Christianity, in the spheres of secular ethics, of philosophy, of political and social science, of the liberal and mechanical arts.[4] He exclaims, with patent sincerity, ' How many good things the Lord hath left to human nature, even after it had been despoiled of the one true good ! ' [5] Yet against this liberal and enlightened view we have to set many passages which merely repeat the gloomy doctrine of Luther. Even in

[1] Rom. xiv. 23 ; see Lecture V, p. 374 f.

[2] *apol. conf. Aug.* ii. § 38 : ' cum igitur haereant in natura hominis contemptus Dei, dubitatio de verbo Dei, de minis et promissionibus, vere peccant homines etiam cum honesta opera faciunt sine Spiritu Sancto, quia faciunt ea impio corde, iuxta illud, *quicquid non est ex fide peccatum est.*'

[3] *instit.* ii. 3, 3.

[4] *ibid.* ii. 2, 13–16.

[5] *ibid.* ii. 2, 15 : ' ergo cum homines istos, quos scriptura ψυχικοὺς vocat, usque eo fuisse pateat in rerum inferiorum investigatione acutos et perspicaces, talibus exemplis discamus quot naturae humanae bona Dominus reliquerit, postquam vero bono spoliata est.'

the case of the virtuous pagans, such as Camillus, who appears to have been a stock example of non-Christian virtue, he suggests that their apparently good deeds must have been due to one of two causes—either to hypocrisy, or merely to the sovereign will of God, mechanically impinging upon them *ab extra* and restraining them from acts of external vice without healing the interior corruption of their souls.[1]   Many passages can be quoted which in fact affirm the idea of total depravity, despite the verbal denial of it which we observed just now.   The whole of human nature is saturated with ' concupiscence,' which is in itself mortally sinful, even before and apart from the consent of the will.[2] Man is covered from head to foot with sin as with a flood.[3] Infants bring their own damnation with them from their mothers' wombs ; the moment they are born their natures are odious and abominable to God.[4]

It is not necessary to devote many words to the question of original guilt, because, as will have been seen, this idea is implicit in the Augustinian theory, whole-heartedly accepted by both of the great Reformers, of the intrinsic sinfulness of concupiscence, that is, of any kind of appetitive movement or impulse towards action forbidden by the law of God, even though such movement be not endorsed and even though it may be resisted by the conscious will.   This is fortified by its connexion with the theory of ' seminal identity ' or of the physical solidarity of the race with Adam, which appears explicitly at any rate in Calvin,[5] and seems

---

[1] *instit.* ii. 3, 3 : 'ita sua providentia Deus naturae perversitatem refraenat, ne in actum erumpat : sed non purgat intus.'

[2] *ibid.* ii. 1, 8 : ' qui dixerunt esse concupiscentiam, non nimis alieno verbo usi sunt, si modo adderetur . . . quicquid in homine est, ab intellectu ad voluntatem, ab anima ad carnem usque, hac concupiscentia inquinatum refertumque esse, aut, ut brevius absolvatur, totum hominem non aliud ex se ipso esse quam concupiscentiam.'

[3] *ibid.* ii. 1, 9 : ' totum hominem quasi diluvio a capite ad pedes sic fuisse obrutum, ut nulla pars a peccato sit immunis.'

[4] *ibid.* ii. 1, 8 : ' atque ideo infantes quoque ipsi, dum suam secum damnationem a matris utero afferunt, non alieno, sed suo ipsorum vitio sunt obstricti. nam tametsi suae iniquitatis fructus nondum protulerint, habent tamen in se inclusum semen : imo tota eorum natura quoddam est peccati semen : ideo non odiosa et abominabilis Deo esse non potest.'

[5] *ibid.* ii. 1, 6 : ' certe habendum est, fuisse Adamum humanae naturae non progenitorem modo, sed quasi radicem, atque ideo in illius corruptione

to underlie a position which is common to both the great schools of Reformation divines, namely, that in the last analysis original sin—the sin of universal human nature as such, apart from the actual sins of individuals—is the only real sin that exists. Actual sin is regarded as being merely an *epiphenomenon*—a loathsome efflorescence of which the foul root is the inherent sinfulness of humanity. The sin of Adam, which is the sin of mankind, is regarded as a perennial fountain of filth and uncleanness which is perpetually bubbling up in black streams of perverted and degraded impulse, manifesting itself not merely in those acts which the moral law stigmatises as sinful but in all the daily, hourly, momentary acts, even though in appearance innocent or virtuous, performed by the unconverted man—a doctrine which, if seriously accepted, would make this life indeed a prison-house, a penitentiary, and a vale of tears. On this showing, it would seem to be criminal in the sight of Heaven to be a human being at all. The prolegomena to the Gospel would appear to have been well summed up in the gloomy aphorism of the Spanish dramatist Calderon : ' The greatest crime of man is that ever he was born.'

The last department of the Reformation doctrine which claims consideration, a department which is closely connected with the belief in the ' total depravity ' of man, is that concerned with the freedom of the will. It may be briefly stated that both great schools of Reformers carried the speculations of Augustine to their logical conclusion in the shape of a relentless and iron determinism. In regard to this matter, again, the Lutherans are more emphatic and more violent even than Calvin and his followers. The title of Luther's treatise against Erasmus, *de servo arbitrio*, leaves room for no mistake as to his conclusions. Two quotations from this work will be sufficient : ' Accordingly this doctrine is most chiefly needed and

---

merito vitiatum fuisse hominum genus ' : ' ipse (*sc*. Adam) peccando non sibi tantum cladem ac ruinam ascivit, sed naturam quoque nostram in simile praecipitavit exitium. neque id suo unius vitio, quod nihil ad nos pertineat : sed quoniam *universum suum semen* ea in quam lapsus erat vitiositate infecit.'

2 F

salutary for the Christian to know that God foresees nothing contingently, but that He both foresees, determines, and actually does all things, by His unchangeable, eternal and infallible will. By this thunderbolt the whole idea of free-will is smitten down and ground to powder' (*hoc fulmine sternitur et conteritur penitus liberum arbitrum*).[1] 'All things which we do, even though they may seem to us to be done mutably and contingently . . . in reality are done under the stress of immutable necessity (*necessario et immutabiliter*) if regard be had to the will of God.' [2] It is to be noted that the Formulary of Concord gives express sanction to this treatise.[3] Calvin's doctrine is identical with this, though he attributes real freedom of the psychological order to Adam before the Fall. Yet even this psychological freedom conceded to unfallen Adam is not metaphysical freedom—a conception which is strictly impossible for Calvin, as it had been for St. Thomas and St. Augustine, in virtue of the irresistible, all-embracing, ineluctable omnipresence of the divine causality. For him, as for his great predecessors, the will of God is the direct and immediate cause of suffering or unhappiness in the world ; there is no room for secondary or contingent causes. Though it is not our purpose to enter into the deeper and vaster problems of predestination, it will be seen how inevitable was the consequence which made the arbitrary, inscrutable will of God the ground of an absolute double predestination—of the elect to eternal life and of the reprobate to eternal loss—a grim conclusion from which the Lutherans always shrank. This overwhelming, almost suffocating doctrine of the absoluteness of God, which can find room for not the faintest motion of spontaneity on the part of His creatures, has been summed up by one who will not be suspected of any prejudice against Calvinism, the late Dr. Fairbairn, in the sentence : ' Calvin was as pure, though not as conscientious or consistent, a Pantheist as Spinoza.' [4]

---

[1] *op. cit.*, pars i, § 10 (*opera lat. D.M. Luth.*, ed. Ien., 1567, i. fol. 165).
[2] *ibid.* (*op. lat.* ed. Ien. i. fol. 165 verso).
[3] *solid. declar.* ii. § 44.
[4] A. M. Fairbairn, *The Place of Christ in Modern Theology*, 1893, p. 164.

The denial of human freedom and the reference of all effective causality to the will of God naturally raised for the Reformers, as it had raised for the Schoolmen, the question of the *extra*-human origin of evil. It will be seen at once that any system of rigid determinism possessing a theistic basis can only escape from making God the direct author of evil by the unsatisfactory device of asserting that God cannot have originated that which does not exist.[1] Hampered, doubtless, by the tendency already noted in Luther, to conceive evil as a positive hypostatic substance, the Reformers were slow to avail themselves of this way out, and hence, strange though it may seem, one or two of them do not hesitate to attribute evil to the direct causality of God.   Melancthon, in the edition of his commentary on the Epistle to the Romans published in the year 1525,[2] makes the following assertion : ' Not merely does God permit His creatures to act, but He Himself is the proper agent in all things that happen ; so that as men confess that the conversion of Paul was God's proper work, so they ought to confess both that morally indifferent actions, such as when men eat, are God's works, and also actions which are bad, like David's adultery ' ; he goes on in the same strain to assert that the treachery of Judas was just as much an act of God as the conversion of St. Paul. These conclusions were, however, so revolting to the general mass of Lutherans that they found no support, and the responsibility for the origin of evil was transferred to Satan, with whom it was left—no attempt

---

[1] *Cf. supra*, Lecture IV, p. 260.

[2] The passage has disappeared from later editions, and is known to us only through its preservation by Melancthon's pupil, Martin Chemnitz (*loc. theol.*, ed. Leyser, 1610, pars i, p. 173) : the original is ' nos dicimus, non solum permittere creaturis ut operentur, sed ipsum omnia proprie agere, ut sicut fatentur proprium Dei opus fuisse Pauli vocationem, ita fateantur opera Dei propria esse, sive quae media vocantur, ut comedere, sive quae mala sunt, ut Davidis adulterium : constat enim Deum omnia facere, non permissive, sed potenter, id est, ut sit eius proprium opus Iudae proditio, sicut Pauli vocatio.'   Chemnitz excuses this audacious dictum on the ground that the extreme libertarianism which then prevailed (doubtless under Franciscan influence) in the Schools was calculated to provoke equally extreme utterances on the other side.   *Can.* 6 of the Tridentine *decretum de iustificatione* is directed against this utterance of Melancthon : see Additional Note F, ' Formularies,' p. 540.

being made to investigate the question how Satan became evil. The Calvinists, however, were dominated by a more rigorous logic, and possessed to a greater extent the courage of their convictions.[1] If the origin of evil, as it exists at present, be traced to the Fall, the question arises ' What was the cause of the Fall ? ' and for Calvin there could be only one answer—the will of God. Calvin's pre-destinarianism is, therefore, of what is called the ' supra-lapsarian ' kind ; that is, it assumes that the decree which arbitrarily destined certain elect souls to salvation and con-demned the rest of mankind to perdition, was made by God in eternity, before the Fall, and that the Fall itself was preordained as the means of procuring the infection with sin of those destined to be damned. Calvin leaves us in no doubt as to his tremendous meaning. Such a dictum as the following speaks for itself : ' Man falls, the providence of God so ordaining '[2] ; and, alluding to the sovereign, pre-temporal decree of God which he regards as the direct cause of the Fall of man, with all its consequent misery and horror, ending in the eternal ruin of the greater portion of the human race, he observes : ' It was in truth a horrible decree, I confess : but none can deny that God foreknew the final fate of man before He created him, and that He foreknew it precisely because it was appointed by His own ordinance.'[3] How this terrible doctrine can be reconciled with the love of God Calvin nowhere explains ; it is harmonised with His justice by the familiar Augustinian expedient of postulating a peculiar, mysterious and ' occult ' kind of Divine ' justice ' which has little or nothing in common with what we know as human justice.[4] Critics

---

[1] For quotations from Zwingli appearing to make God the author of sin, see Möhler, *op. cit.* i. p. 54 ff. ; for the opinions of Beza, *ibid.* i. p. 60 ff.

[2] *instit.* iii. 23, 8 : ' cadit igitur homo, Dei providentia sic ordinante, sed suo vitio cadit.'

[3] *ibid.* iii. 23, 7 : ' decretum quidem horribile, fateor : infitiari tamen nemo poterit quin praesciverit Deus quem exitum esset habiturus homo antequam ipsum conderet, et ideo praesciverit quia decreto suo sic ordinarat.'

[4] *Cf. ibid.* iii. 23, 8 : ' si enim praedestinatio nihil aliud est quam divinae iustitiae, *occultae quidem*, sed inculpatae, dispensatio . . . iustis-simum quoque esse interitum quem ex praedestinatione subeunt aeque certum est.'

who are not satisfied with this arbitrary device are silenced
by a convenient quotation from St. Paul—'Nay, but,
O man, who art thou that repliest against God? Shall
the thing formed say to him that formed it, Why hast thou
made me thus? Hath not the potter power over the clay,
of the same lump to make one vessel unto honour, and
another unto dishonour?'[1] It is conceivable that the
Apostle might have expressed himself in less absolute terms
had he foreseen the use to which his words were destined to
be put; but that is a question which cannot be discussed
now. Meanwhile, it is not unfair to conclude this summary
of the Augustinian anthropology, as republished and
developed by the leaders of the Reformation, with the
remark that in the hands of Melancthon and Calvin, at least,
who make God the ultimate author of evil, it would seem
to have transformed itself into precisely that unmoral
Hindu monism—that belief in a God, or an Absolute, who
transcends the distinction between good and evil—which,
as we saw at the beginning of this enquiry, is one of the
Fall-doctrine's two traditional foes: a curious revolution
of the wheel of thought.[2]

The Anglican Doctrine

We have now reviewed the history of the Augustinian
Fall-doctrine between the fifth and the sixteenth centuries,
and have failed to discover any considerations calculated to
induce us to revise the unfavourable judgment which was
passed upon it in our last lecture. Neither the Schoolmen nor
the Reformers seem to have succeeded in placing the ideas
of Original Righteousness, ' seminal identity,' Original Guilt,
and the intrinsic sinfulness of ' concupiscence ' in a more

Rom. ix. 20, 21.

[2] It should be added, however, that the chief Protestant Confessions
explicitly and strongly condemn the view that God is in any sense the
author of sin : the more extreme *obiter dicta* of individual Reformers
quoted in the text are meant to illustrate the subconscious tendencies and
the logical implications of their thought, and are not cited as representing
the official mind of the Lutheran and Calvinistic Churches, for which see
Additional Note F, ' Formularies ' IV and V, pp. 543–548.

favourable light ; on the contrary, the former proved able
to defend these conceptions only by modifying them or by
taking refuge in mystery, whilst the latter appear to have
achieved nothing beyond bringing out into fuller relief all
their more irrational and horrifying features. As for the
suggestion in which this Lecture's argument found its
starting-point, that the ' twice-born ' doctrine has a *prima
facie* claim to be considered as having fulfilled the Vincentian
test, inasmuch as it has been accepted by all the intellectual
vital and progressive areas of Western Christendom, that
has been sufficiently refuted by the gradual decline of
Augustinianism within the Latin communion, and by its
almost complete disappearance, consummated within the last
hundred years, from the thought of Continental Protestantism.   In a rapid and summary review such as the present
(which is all that the vastness of the period to be covered and
the necessity of compressing our discussion within the limits
of a single lecture permit), it is impossible to do more than
allude to the great break-up of traditional evangelical
orthodoxy in the Continental homes of the Reformation, due
to the collapse of the belief in the literal inerrancy of the
Bible—a break-up in which the ultra-Augustinian Fall-
doctrine of the Reformers, based as it was believed to be upon
the historicity of Gen. iii, was swept away with the rest of
the Protestant scholastic system. The philosophic attempts
of Kant and Hegel to restate what they considered to be the
permanent essence of the doctrine must be reserved for consideration in our final lecture.[1]   Only the barest mention can
be made of Schleiermacher's attempt to save the form of the
idea of original sin whilst abandoning its content, by explaining ' hereditary sin ' (*Erbsünde*) in terms of ' social,' as
opposed to biological, heredity [2] : or of the explicit substitution of a communal sinfulness (*gemeinsame Sünde,
Gesammtsünde*) handed on by example and tradition for the
idea of a weakness innate in the individual, by Albrecht
Ritschl,[3] whose recasting of the whole dogmatic system of
Christianity presents the latest and the clearest illustration

---

[1] pp. 497–506.

[2] *Der christliche Glaube*[4], §§ 66–67 (Berlin, 1842, pp. 361–436).

[3] *Rechtfertigung und Versöhnung*[2], iii. 5 (Bonn, 1883, pp. 304–357).

of the mutual co-inherence and interdependence of the Pelagian doctrine of man, the Adoptionist or Antiochene doctrines of Christ, and the merely ' exemplarist ' doctrine of redemption.[1]

The circumstances, however, under which we are gathered together demand that a few concluding words should be devoted to a particular version of the Western Fall-doctrine which has hardly been mentioned hitherto, namely, the doctrine of the Church of England. This is contained in the IXth Article of Religion ' Of Original, or Birth-Sin,' in the Xth ' Of Free will,' and in the XIIIth, ' Of works before justification.' These were all included in the original 42 Articles drawn up in 1553 by Cranmer at the instigation of the Council of Edward VI, at a period when the influence of the Swiss Reformers was at its height. The Tridentine doctrines of Sin and Justification which have been considered in this lecture were promulgated in the year 1546. It follows that Cranmer and his collaborators must have been well acquainted with them, and that the ultra-Augustinian affirmations contained in the Articles were meant to be direct contradictions of the doctrine put forward at the Council of Trent. It is, therefore, not surprising that a superficial perusal of these formularies should seem to justify the celebrated dictum of William Pitt, that the Church of England possessed a Popish liturgy and Calvinistic Articles. A closer study, however, will disclose the fact that whilst these Articles would seem to have been drafted in such a way as to be patient of a Calvinistic interpretation, they cannot be said of necessity to contain more than a fairly strong affirmation of those Augustinian conceptions with which our historical survey has made us familiar. So much is indeed certain. In Article IX we find at least one side of the characteristically Augustinian conception of original guilt, namely, the idea that we are in some inexplicable way responsible for being born with disordered natures ; and it is asserted that this hereditary corruption and fault of human nature, which *ex hypothesi* we cannot help, as found in every person born into this world deserves God's ' wrath and

---

[1] *Cf.* Lecture V, p. 349 f.

damnation.' [1] There can be little doubt that in the original intention of the compilers these tremendous words carried with them the terrible consequences of the necessary damnation of the heathen and of unbaptised infants [2] ; and the gloss with which Dean Church attempts to soften their formidable import—a gloss which in effect amounts to this, that original sin itself may be said in the abstract to deserve God's wrath and damnation, but that its individual possessors do not necessarily deserve anything but His compassion [3] —whilst no doubt practically convenient, as making it easier for men of the twentieth century to consent to a formulary drawn up in the sixteenth, seems to be rather an evacuation than an explanation of the ' literal and grammatical ' sense of the Article.   The same Article contains the statement (attributed to ' the Apostle ') that concupiscence and lust hath of itself the nature of sin ; which, if it means anything at all, would seem to be a re-affirmation of the Augustinian doctrine of the intrinsical sinfulness of one of the elementary

---

[1] *Cf.* the formula prescribed in the Book of Common Prayer for the reception of a privately baptised child into the congregation (' The Ministration of Private Baptism of Children in Houses '), in which the infant is described as ' born in original sin, and in the wrath of God.'

[2] It may be noted, however, that Hooker (*Eccl. Pol.* V. lx. 6) is inclined to think that the unbaptised children of Christian parents may possibly be saved.

[3] The reference is to a letter, in *Life and Letters*, p. 248 : ' The *fact* of what is meant by original sin is as mysterious and inexplicable as the origin of evil, but it is obviously just as much a fact.   There is a fault and vice in the *race*, which, given time, as surely develops into actual sin as our physical constitution, given at birth, does into sickness and physical death. It is of this inherited sin in our nature, looked upon in the abstract and without reference to concrete cases, that I suppose the Article speaks. How can we suppose that such a nature looks in God's eyes according to the standard of perfect righteousness which we also suppose to be God's standard and law ?   Does it satisfy that standard ?   Can He look with neutrality on its divergence from His perfect standard ?   What is His moral judgment of it as a subject for moral judgment ?   What He may do to cure it, to pardon it, to make allowances for it in known or unknown ways, is another matter, about which His known attributes of mercy alone may reassure us ; but the question is, How does He look on this fact of our nature *in itself*, that without exception it has this strong efficacious germ of evil within it, of which He sees all the possibilities and all the consequences ?   Can He look on it, even in germ, with complacency or indifference ?   Must He not judge it and condemn it, as *in itself*, because evil, deserving condemnation ?   I cannot see what other answer can be given but one, and this is what the Article says.'

instincts of mankind, though a loophole is left for those who cannot accept this Manichean opinion in its full rigour by the use of the ambiguous phrase ' the nature of sin,' *ratio peccati*.[1] Article XIII contains another, somewhat hesitating, re-affirmation of a position common to both St. Augustine and the Reformers, namely, that works done before justification, which ' spring not of faith in Jesus Christ,' are not pleasing to God and, in fact, ' have the nature of sin.' There can be no doubt that this Article was meant to traverse the teaching of the Council of Trent that the virtuous actions of pagans are not sins ; but on this point, at any rate, there are very few modern Christians who in their heart of hearts do not agree with Trent. We have already pointed out the intellectual and moral antinomies which these propositions, taken at their face value, necessarily involve. In an age, however, of passionate feeling and of unquestioning acceptance of St. Augustine's authority these difficulties were not likely to occur to anyone ; and circumstances with which we are all familiar have brought it about that these obsolete positions are still embedded in the doctrinal standards of the English Church. Nevertheless, even before the publication of Tract 90, with its exposition of a *benignior interpretatio*, which may be employed as a kind of intellectual shoe-horn for accommodating the stiff formularies of the past to the living religious experience of the present, protests had been raised both in the seventeenth and in the eighteenth centuries against the severity of these doctrines. The idea of original guilt, which, as we have suggested, is both the most characteristic and the least defensible element in the whole Augustinian scheme, involving as it does the assertion that a newly born infant *deserves* eternal damnation on the mere ground of the fact that it is a human being, was manfully combated by the illustrious Jeremy Taylor ; a single quotation will make his position clear :

And truly, My Lord, to say that for Adam's sin it is just in God to condemn infants to the eternal flames of Hell, and to say that concupiscence or natural inclinations before they pass into

[1] The Augustinian view of sex finds a striking expression in the opening exhortation of the Marriage Service, as contained in the Prayer Book of 1662.

any act would bring eternal damnation from God's presence into the eternal portion of devils, are two such horrid propositions that if any Church in the world should expressly affirm them, I, for my part, should think it unlawful to communicate with her in the defence or provision of either, and to think it would be the greatest temptation in the world to make men not to love God, of Whom men so easily speak such horrid things.[1]

Considerations of this nature prompted the application addressed by Dr. Porteus, subsequently Bishop of London, together with several other distinguished divines, in the year 1772 to Archbishop Cornwallis, asking him to consult with the episcopate whether a revision of the Articles could not be carried out, with the object of eliminating what appeared *prima facie* to be their more Calvinistic features. The Archbishop replied that he and his brethren, having considered the matter, were unanimously of the opinion that nothing could be done—a conclusion which was dictated in all probability rather by practical caution than by theological conviction. The relaxation, however, of the terms of clerical subscription to the Articles, which was effected by the combined authority of Convocation and Parliament in the year 1865, has had what is in practice the same effect as a revision of their text, and it is safe to say that no minister of the national Church at the present day conceives himself as being committed to the statements that newly born infants deserve damnation, that those impulses which subserve the perpetuation of the race are inherently sinful, and that the virtuous acts of non-Christians are all crimes. Nevertheless, although practical difficulties in connexion with subscription have solved themselves, it is not a good thing that any branch of the Universal Church should continue to be cumbered with obsolete formularies inherited from the past which are in practice repudiated by the thought and conscience of the present ; and it may, therefore, not be presumptuous to suggest that it would be well if the

---

[1] *Works* (London, 1822), ix. p. 373. From ' An Answer to a letter written by the Rt. Rev. the Lord Bishop of Rochester, concerning the chapter of Original Sin in the " Unum Necessarium." ' Taylor's own views about original sin, which approximate to the Scotist position, are developed in the *Unum Necessarium, or The Doctrine and Practice of Repentance*, cc. vi. vii. (*Works*, ix.).

Doctrinal Commission, which has been entrusted by the two Primates of England with the task of endeavouring to secure a greater unity of fundamental belief amongst members of the Church of England, would turn its attention to this particular area of Christian doctrine, and endeavour to arrive at formulations which might ultimately be substituted for the crude assertions which have come down to us out of the passions and conflicts of the sixteenth century. Revision of the Liturgy, as Porteus saw a century and a half ago, must involve as its logical corollary revision of the Articles, and in some ways the latter is the more important task of the two. If and when it is undertaken by ecclesiastical authority, it must surely include the task of presenting Christendom with a carefully balanced statement of Christian anthropology which does not go beyond the positive contents of Revelation and is free from all contradiction with the teachings of modern science and the deliveries of a tolerant and enlightened conscience. By her unique position in Christendom, seated as she is in the West, and heiress to the treasures of both Latin and Teutonic thought, yet united by ever-growing bonds of sympathy and mutual knowledge with the Christian and Hellenic East, by her splendid intellectual tradition, which combines unswerving loyalty to the historic revelation of God in Christ with the most tremulous sensitiveness to new light, through whatever windows it may pour in—the English Church possesses both the power and the opportunity to wrestle with this ancient problem anew, and to win one of those triumphs in the world of thought which are only less glorious than her invisible achievements in the sphere of grace.

ADDITIONAL NOTE C

CONGREGATIONAL CONFESSIONS OF ORIGINAL SIN IN THE CHURCHES OF THE REFORMATION

I. *Origins.*

Strassburg, 1537 (F. Hubert, *Die Strassburger liturgischen Ordnungen, im Zeitalter der Reformation*, Göttingen, 1900, p. 92) : Almechtiger, ewiger got vnd vatter, wir bekennen

vnd veriehen, das wir leyder inn sünden empfangen vnd
geporen seind vnd daher geneygt zu allem argen vnd treg
zu allem guten. . . .

Calvin, *La manière de faire prières*, 1542 (Alfred Erichson,
Die Calvinische und die altstrassburgische Gottesdienstordnung,
Strassburg, 1894, p. 16) : Seigneur dieu pere eternel et
toutpuissant nous confessons sans feintise deuent ta saincte
majesté, que nous sommes pouures pecheurs, conceuz et nez
en iniquitez et corruption, enclins à mal faire, inutiles à tout
bien. . . .

II. *Development.*

(1) Calvin, *Precum ecclesiasticarum formula* (B. J. Kidd,
Documents of Cont. Reform, p. 615) : Domine Deus Pater
aeterne et omnipotens, agnoscimus et ingenue profitemur
apud sanctam majestatem tuam, nos miseros peccatores
esse, conceptos, et natos in iniquitate et pravitate, ad
nequitiam proclives, ad omne autem bonum opus inutiles . . .

, (2) Valerand Pullain, *Liturgia sacra seu Ritus Ministerii
in ecclesia peregrinorum Francofordiae ad Moenum* (A. L.
Richter, *Die evangelische Kirchenordnungen des* 16. *Jahrhun-
derts*, ii. p. 150) : Domine Deus Pater aeterne et omnipotens
agnoscimus et fatemur ingenue apud sanctam majestatem
tuam peccatores esse nos miseros, adeoque a prima origine,
qua concepti et nati sumus, tam ad omne malum esse pronos
quam ab omni bono alienos. . . .

(3) Laski (Jo. a Lasco) *Forma ac ratio tota Ecclesiastici
Ministerii, in peregrinorum, potissimum uero Germanorum,
Ecclesia instituta Londoni in Anglia*, 1551, p. 66 : Omnipotens aeterne Deus misericors Pater . . . Etenim praeter-
quam quod in peccato concepti ac nati, omnis boni prorsus
expertes, pleni omni iniquitate sumus. . . .

III. *In English Puritanism.*

(1) English exiles at Geneva (Calvin's *Common-Prayer
Book, or the Service, Discipline and Form of the Common
Prayers, & Administration of the Sacraments us'd in the
English Church of Geneva*, in *The Phenix*, Vol. ii. p. 214),
and J. Knox, *Book of Common Order*, 1564 (*The Liturgy of
the Ch. of Scotland, or John Knox's Book of Common Order*,
London, 1840, p. 1) : O Eternal God and most merciful
Father, we confess and acknowledge here before thy divine
Majesty, that we are miserable Sinners, conceiv'd and born
in Sin & Iniquity, so that in us there is no Goodness ; for
the Flesh evermore rebelleth against the Spirit, whereby we
continually transgress thine holy Precepts and Commandments, and so purchase to ourselves, through thy just
Judgment, Death and Damnation.

And *Book of Common Order*, p. 6. If thou shouldst begin to reckon with us even from our first conception in our mother's womb, thou canst find nothing at all in us but occasion of death and eternal condemnation ; for truth it is that first we were conceived in sin, and in iniquity was every one of us born of our mother. . . .

(2) *A booke of the forme of common prayer*, 1584 (' The Puritan Liturgy ' ; in P. Hall, *Fragmenta liturgica*, i. p. 25) : O eternal God, and most merciful Father, we confess and acknowledge here before thy divine majesty, that we are miserable sinners, conceived and born in sin and iniquity, so that in us there is no goodness.

(3) *Disciplina Ecclesiae sacra, c.* 1588 (in F. Paget, *Introd. to the Fifth Book of Hooker's Eccl. Pol.*, p. 301): sequatur precatio continens confessionem generalem reatus peccati originalis et actualis : et poenae ob utrumque ex lege debitae.

(4) *A Directory for the Publike VVorship of God Throughout the Three Kingdoms*, London, 1644 (P. Hall, *Reliquiae liturgicae*, iii. p. 25) : the minister . . . is to endeavour to get his own and his hearers' hearts to be rightly affected with their sins, that they may all mourn . . . by proceeding to a more full confession of sin . . . to this effect :—To acknowledge our great sinfulness : First, by reason of original sin ; which (beside the guilt that makes us liable to everlasting damnation) is the seed of all other sins, hath depraved and poisoned all the faculties of soul and body, doth defile our best actions, and (were it not restrained, or our hearts renewed by grace) would break forth into innumerable transgressions, and greatest rebellions against the Lord, that ever were committed by the vilest sons of men.

(5) *Exceptions of the Ministers*, 1661 (Cardwell, *Conferences*, 309) : The Confession is very defective, not clearly expressing original sin.

(6) *The Reformation of the Liturgy*, 1661 (' The Savoy Liturgy,' by Baxter ; in P. Hall, *Reliquiae liturgicae*, iv. p. 15) : . . . we confess that we are vile and miserable sinners, being conceived in sin ; by nature children of wrath, and transgressors from the womb.

(7) Ευχολογιον : *a Book of Common Order* (Scottish Church Service Soc.), 1877, p. 48 : O Lord our God, eternal and almighty Father, we acknowledge and confess before thy holy majesty, that we are miserable sinners ; born in iniquity, prone to evil ; unable by ourselves to do that which is good. . . .

IV. *At Cologne.*

Hermann von Wied of Cologne, *pia ac simplex deliberatio*, 1545 (the italicised words are added in the Latin to the

German of 1543), p. xciv : Omnipotens aeterne Deus, Pater *Domini nostri Iesu Christi, Creator rerum omnium, iudex cunctorum hominum,* agnoscimus et deploramus nos in peccatis conceptos et natos ideoque ad quaevis mala pronos et abhorrentes a *ueris* bonis. . . .

V. *In Sweden.*

E. Yelverton, *The Mass in Sweden* (Henry Bradshaw Soc., 1920).

1531 : Mass of Olarus Petri, p. 33 : I, poor sinful man, who am both conceived and born in sin, and ever afterwards. . . .

1576 : Mass of John III, p. 85 : Confiteor tibi Deo Patri omnipotenti, me miserum peccatorem in peccatis conceptum et natum nimis peccasse in vita mea . . .

1602 : Communion Office of Charles IX, p. 131, as 1531 above.

1917 : Modern Mass, p. 157 : I, poor sinful man, who was born in sin, and ever afterwards &c.

VII.

'ORIGINAL SIN' RE-INTERPRETED

To consider the world in its length and breadth, its various history, the many races of men, their starts, their fortunes, their mutual alienation, their conflicts; their ways, habits, governments, forms of worship; their enterprises, their aimless courses, their random achievements and acquirements . . . the greatness and littleness of man, his far-reaching aims, his short duration, the curtain hung over his futurity, the disappointments of life, the defeat of good, the success of evil, physical pain, mental anguish, the prevalence and intensity of sin, the pervading idolatries, the corruptions, the dreary hopeless irreligion, that condition of the whole race, so fearfully yet exactly described in the Apostle's words, ' having no hope and without God in the world '—all this is a vision to dizzy and appal; and inflicts upon the mind the sense of a profound mystery, which is absolutely beyond human solution.

What shall be said to this heart-piercing, reason-bewildering fact ? I can only answer, that either there is no Creator, or this living society of men is in a true sense discarded from His presence . . . I argue about the world; *if* there be a God, *since* there is a God, the human race is implicated in some terrible aboriginal calamity. It is out of joint with the purposes of its Creator. This is a fact, a fact as true as the fact of its existence ; and thus the doctrine of what is technically called original sin becomes to me almost as certain as that the world exists, and as the existence of God.

JOHN HENRY NEWMAN : *Apologia pro Vita Sua,* c. V.

LECTURE VII.

'ORIGINAL SIN' RE-INTERPRETED

Matt. xiii. 52 : ' Therefore every scribe who hath been made a disciple
to the kingdom of heaven is like unto a man that is a
householder, which bringeth forth out of his treasure
things new and old.'

It is natural for the traveller who has slowly climbed a
long and precipitous ascent, to pause on reaching the
mountain crest, and look back upon the road by which he
has come ; and it is no less appropriate that, at the end of
our historical survey, which has led us through twenty-five
centuries of Jewish and Christian history, we should sum
up in retrospect the results which our enquiry has yielded,
before pushing on into the almost untrodden region of
abstract speculation and construction. We have seen that
the doctrines of the Fall and of Original Sin were born in
the minds of the Maccabean saints as the fruit of the experience of penitence, and that they were designed to safeguard
this experience against interpretations which were ultimately
destructive of ethical monotheism, especially against the
Iranian explanation of evil as the work of a second and
malevolent God, and the Hindu theory of evil as a necessary
moment in the finite self-expression of an impersonal and
non-moral Absolute. Thus a vague and wavering conception of a primitive moral catastrophe and of a train of
disastrous hereditary consequences flowing from it slowly
arose in later Judaism, clothed itself with the Paradise-
story of Gen. iii. as its supposedly historical integument,
passed on into Christianity with, it would seem, the tacit
permission of the Master Himself, and was stereotyped by
St. Paul as the official Christian explanation of the origin
of evil in Nature and in man. The impact of successive
waves of Oriental dualism stimulated the Christian Church

2 G

to clarify and articulate the ideas which it had adopted as the presuppositions of its redemptive scheme. But, as this development advanced, two distinct versions of the Fall-doctrine began to define themselves, corresponding to the two differing emotional forms which penitence assumes in the experience of the ' once-born ' and ' twice-born ' types of religious man. The former of these versions wears a milder character, appropriate to the sunny genius of Christian Hellenism, recognising as it does the good that survives even in fallen man ; the latter, elaborated into rigid severity by the fanaticism of Northern Africa, and condemning human nature as largely or entirely depraved, was riveted on Western Christendom by the genius of St. Augustine, exaggerated into fantastic and repulsive forms by Luther and Calvin, and until recently was generally believed by Englishmen to be the only traditional Fall-theory. But the Augustinian theory never took captive the mind of the Christian East, and even in the West its millennial domination has now passed away. The right of the highly specialised ' twice-born ' *dévot* to force his despairing estimate of human nature upon the sober majority of ' once-born ' Christians is now universally denied ; and the primitive, Hellenic, ' once-born ' version of the Fall-doctrine now stands clearly revealed as the basic or residual Christian belief, the only scheme of ideas regarding human nature and sin which commits its adherents to nothing that cannot truly claim to be Scriptural, Oecumenical, and accepted ' everywhere, always, and by all.'

We now turn, in conformity with the plan set forth at the beginning of this enquiry, to the constructive task of verifying and elucidating these ideas, and of correlating them, so far as is in our power, with the modern universe of philosophic thought. It has been frequently pointed out during the course of this discussion that the belief in the Fall as a historical event, though for long believed to rest upon the testimony of an inspired and inerrant record, is in reality an inference, a logical construction based upon the observed fact, or what was believed to be such, of ' original sin,' together with the revealed fact of the infinite power and goodness of the Creator ; in the order of thought, therefore, as distinct from the order of time, original sin comes first, and the Fall last.   It will conduce to lucidity if we follow the order of thought, devoting the present discourse to a consideration of the validity of the idea of original sin as a psychological hypothesis, reserving the idea of the Fall, with its deeper theological and metaphysical implications, for our final lecture.

There is, however, one task which must necessarily be dealt with at the outset, if the argument of our two concluding lectures is to be presented with the highest degree of perspicuity ; and that is the task of formulating, with greater precision than has been possible hitherto, the traditional theory which is now to be put to the test.

Before we can verify in the facts of human psychology that which on the basis of the Vincentian Canon we have found to be the most truly 'catholic' or universal doctrine of human nature, it will be necessary first of all to state it *in extenso*, as a single coherent theory, collecting together into an ordered whole various fragments and aspects of it which have from time to time emerged in the course of our historical review. As this minimising, 'once-born' Fall-doctrine has never been officially formulated, but merely exists, as it were, in solution, or like radium, diffused as a common element through a heterogeneous series of chemical compounds, but nowhere discoverable in isolation, it will be understood that this formulation does not lay claim to more than approximate accuracy. We must, therefore, occasionally assume the liberty to supply a few minor links or logical connexions which the structure of the theory seems to demand, but for which no specific patristic or conciliar texts can be quoted. In the light of what has been already said with regard to the real basis of the Fall-doctrine in spiritual experience, and its relatively accidental connexion with the Paradise story of Gen. iii., we shall confine ourselves to a formulation of the intellectual essence of these ideas, carefully avoiding the use of pictorial terminology drawn from the Adam-story, so as to avoid exposing ourselves to the suspicion of substituting legend for logic. It will be convenient to include in this summary a statement of the doctrine of the Fall, that is of the origin of human evil, which, as already explained, is reserved for exhaustive consideration in our final lecture, as well as the statement of that with which we are immediately concerned in this lecture, namely, the doctrine of original sin, so that we may have before our minds a synoptic view of the whole intellectual fabric constituted by these ideas. The full significance borne by the substitution of the milder for the more gloomy version of Christian anthropology will be brought out with greater clearness, if in the course of this formulation we indicate once more the chief Augustinian or ' twice-born ' positions which, if our argument so far has been well founded, must now be decisively repudiated, both on the ground of their lack of genuinely universal acceptance, and also on that of their incompatibility with the facts of modern historical knowledge and with a real belief in the infinite goodness and justice of God.

This basic essence of Fall-doctrine, which may be regarded as the highest common factor of the various competing versions of that doctrine which have from time to time been current within the orthodox Christian world, can be conveniently summarised in the form of seven distinct propositions, of which the first five taken together constitute the doctrine of the ' Fall,' in the strict sense, and the remaining two that of ' original sin,' so called. These propositions are the following :

(1) *God is infinite, not merely in power but in love and goodness, and therefore the world of created being as He made it must have been purely good, including no element of evil at all.* (We note in passing, though it is impossible now to go into the subject at length, that the idea of the Fall necessarily presupposes the idea of Creation, and would be quite incapable of harmonisation with any theory implying that the universe of finite being is an eternal or necessary mode of God's self-expression.)

(2) *The origin of evil is therefore to be sought in the voluntary rebellion of created and finite wills, such rebellion*—and here we touch upon a point of considerable importance—*having taken place prior to the appearance of the human species on this planet.* In other words, the ultimate Fall, which is postulated in order to avoid an infinite regress, is conceived

as being extra-terrestrial; and this extra-terrestrial character of the primal catastrophe may be imagined either
in accordance with the view, hinted at by Origen,[1] of an
extra-temporal Fall of the race-soul from a transcendental
Paradise, or in accordance with the more popular theory
of a 'fall of the angels,'—not that which has hitherto
claimed our attention, the descent of the lustful 'Watchers'
to earth, as narrated in Gen. vi., but a much more ancient,
pre-human revolt of spiritual beings against their Almighty
Lord, such as was imagined at the beginning of our era
by the author of the Slavonic Enoch,[2] was read by Christian
imagination into the Apocalyptic vision of the celestial
conflict between Michael and the dragon,[3] and is familiar
to English readers in the magnificent Homeric vesture
which the genius of Milton has imposed upon it.[4]

(3) *Man, at his first appearance on this planet, was in
moral and intellectual stature a babe, created frail, imperfect,
ignorant and non-moral, but endowed with self-consciousness
and the power of self-determination, which constituted, in the
penetrating and memorable words of Theophilus, an ἀφορμὴ
προκοπῆς, a starting-point for progress and upward evolution.*

Here, for the first time, the theory decisively joins issue
with Augustinianism. It involves the complete abandonment of the belief in the view technically known as the
'original righteousness' or 'perfection' of the first men.
The Talmudic theory of the 'protoplast,' as endowed with
Olympian strength and beauty, with all the gifts of philosophical subtlety and scientific and theological erudition, and
with a character of settled virtue and sanctity—a theory
which does not possess the slightest foundation in Scripture
—is frankly relegated to the limbo of discarded fables.
We cannot stay to enlarge upon this point; but it is
permissible to point out how enormously the repudiation
of 'original righteousness' as an alleged phase of human
history [5] eases the strain of the *prima facie* discordance

---

[1] *v. supra*, Lecture IV, p. 228. [2] *v. supra*, Lecture III, p. 161.
[3] Rev. xii. 7, 8. [4] *Paradise Lost*, v., vi.
[5] For a discussion of the question whether the conception of 'original
righteousness' might not be re-used in an extra- or pre-human connexion,
see the next Lecture, p. 526.

between traditional theology and modern science as to the origins and primal condition of man. With an avowed return on the part of theology to such a picture of primitive man as was sketched by Irenaeus,[1] the conflict between the Fall-doctrine and the evolutionary view of human history would largely disappear, and the atheist lecturer of Hyde Park would find one of his favourite dialectical weapons smitten from his hand.

(4) *The growth of man's moral ideas brought in its train some action, or system of actions, whereby man aligned himself with the rebellious power, showed that he had partially thrown in his lot with the forces of evil which were already at work in the universe, and entered on a path largely divergent from that upward career of spiritual evolution which God had meant him to follow.*

Here again we note a significant divergence from the Augustinian and traditional Western view. Augustinianism, positing the doctrine of ' original righteousness,' assumes that man was placed at his creation on the summit of the mountain of perfection, and that the first sin was tantamount to an instantaneous, headlong ' Fall,' over a sheer precipice, into the abyss of sin and damnation. The view, however, which we are now endeavouring to articulate, represents primitive man as born at the bottom of the mountain, as refusing to follow that path which led most directly to its summit, and as preferring to follow a tortuous route of his own devising, which, whilst leading generally upwards, has plunged him into many bogs and crevasses, and involved him in many unnecessary hardships and miseries. A fully developed systematic theology might continue the metaphor by pointing out that the road of man's own choice has, so far, not led him much higher than the foothills or lower slopes of the peak which he would fain ascend, that a Guide has come to meet him and restore his footsteps to the right track, but that the only short cut from the lower to the higher path must of necessity now lead through ' the grave, and gate of death,' on the further side of which alone complete perfection is to be attained.

Such a theory does not deny that the record of human

[1] *v. supra*, Lecture IV, p. 193 f.

history has, on the whole, been that of a slow millennial ascent from low and brutish beginnings to our present state ; its upholders are only committed to the proposition that the direction of this progress has not been so direct and unswerving as it might have been, and was meant by God to be—that the graph of man's moral and intellectual development, slowly climbing through half a million years at an almost imperceptible angle to the horizontal, with sierra-like undulations of advance and set-back, like those which mark the temperature chart of a feverish patient, stands in the strongest possible contrast to the steep, upward-rushing line of intellectual, spiritual, and moral growth which represented God's original design for His creature. Given this point of view, it would seem very desirable that the word ' Fall,' which occurs nowhere in the Bible, which does not appear to be older than Hippolytus or Methodius,[1] and which is almost inextricably bound up in the popular mind with the idea of ' original perfection,' should be used as little as possible in connexion with the sin of man. (In our next lecture [2] we shall consider the question whether it is possible to believe in anything corresponding to the supposed pre-human rebellion of the angels, an event to which the term ' Fall ' would be more appropriately applied.) When man alone is in question it would seem more appropriate to employ the term which we have seen to be both historically and logically associated with the primitive or ' once-born ' theory, that is, ' transgression ' ($\pi\alpha\rho\acute{\alpha}\beta\alpha\sigma\iota\varsigma$, *praevaricatio*), in the sense of a ' stepping-aside ' from the straight or proper path. The hypothetical ' first human sin,' or the first human action which we should have been justified in classing as ' sin,' had we been able to observe the history of our remotest ancestors,[3] should thus be regarded not so much as a ' Fall,' but rather as *a failure to climb*—to be exact, a failure to climb as directly and perpendicularly as God had desired.

In any case, however, and whatever may be thought with

---

[1] *v. supra*, Lecture IV, p. 252, n. 4.

[2] p. 527.

[3] On the question whether it is possible to assume a historical event which could be absolutely described as ' the first human sin,' *v. infra*, p. 514 f.

regard to the question of terminology, it is clear that this
mode of conceiving the first human sin entirely rules out
Augustine's contention that it was characterised by infinite
malice and a correspondingly infinite guilt. We shall agree
with Irenaeus that the primal sin of man was in a sense
pardonable [1] ; and it is a possible speculation that, as being
the sin of a frail, imperfect, and ignorant creature, so far
from being the greatest, it was really the least of the crimes
which have stained the history of human kind.

(5) *Ever since this first human transgression, our nature
has displayed an inherent moral weakness or bias towards sin.*

This proposition is modelled on a phrase in which
Justin Martyr formulates his primitive and undeveloped
conception of the Fall-theory.[2] It will be noted that it
abstains from asserting that the first human transgression
was the direct cause of the innate bias towards evil which
has revealed itself since, and leaves open the possibility
that the Jewish Rabbis may have been right when they
said that Adam sinned because the ' evil inclination ' was
already rooted in him.[3] It is true that this modified and
cautious assertion does not solve the question how the
evil which was already at work in the universe managed to
find, or to retain, a foothold in human nature : but it does
not raise a difficulty which is inherent in the Augustinian
theory and even in the language of St. Paul, if rigidly
interpreted—the difficulty, namely, of understanding how
a single wrong act could have such illimitably ruinous
results, especially if, as we have just suggested, it was of
a comparatively venial nature. It is true that under the
complicated conditions of our modern world a single false
step may wreck a whole life ; but that is largely due to the
clumsiness and inhumanity of our present social conventions ;
and even they do not involve the penalisation of the sinner's
unoffending posterity until the end of time. We shall find
in our concluding lecture that we are relieved of many other
difficulties by the liberty, which the primitive doctrine

---

[1] *v. supra*, Lecture IV, p. 195.

[2] *dial. c. Tryph.* 88 . . . τοῦ γένους τοῦ τῶν ἀνθρώπων, ὃ ἀπὸ τοῦ
Ἀδὰμ ὑπὸ θάνατον καὶ πλάνην τὴν τοῦ ὄφεως ἐπεπτώκει : the whole passage is
quoted above, Lecture IV, p. 174, n. 1.

[3] Lecture II, p. 70.

allows us, to regard the sin of the protoplast as being not a Fall but a failure—not a wanton plunge into crime but rather a wilful neglect to emancipate himself from tendencies already existing in him, which he both could and should have overcome.

For the sake of clearness it may again be observed that the five propositions just formulated are concerned with the idea of the Fall or ultimate origin of evil, and have therefore received only cursory comment. We now approach the last two of our seven theses, which, taken together, embody the primitive, Hellenic, or ' once-born ' version of the idea of ' Original Sin,' and therefore claim a more detailed and exhaustive examination.

The sixth proposition may be formulated as follows : *This innate bias or tendency towards evil is the effect and symptom of ' weakness of will,' or defective control of the lower emotional and instinctive nature by the higher self.*

The question of the exact nature of the inherited infirmity is one in regard to which the area of agreement between the thought of Eastern and Western Christendom is exiguous and ill-defined. Of one thing we can be certain : historical Christianity as such is not committed to the assertion that ' original sin,' so called, is sin in the strict sense of the term. The word sin either means a conscious act carried out with full purpose and deliberation in defiance of a known law of God, or it means nothing at all. It is therefore, strictly speaking, a solecism to apply this term to a pre-determined state, independent of conscious volition, which is alleged to belong to unconscious infants. We must, accordingly, admit that the term ' original sin,' *peccatum originale*, which (like the term ' Fall ') has no Scriptural authority, which we have seen to be the legacy of Augustine's semi-Manichean view of human nature, and which is inextricably bound up in the popular mind—as, indeed, it was meant to be—with the idea of ' original guilt,' is a singularly unfortunate and misleading expression. It should be beneath the dignity of theology to use a term of which the *prima facie* meaning has to be elaborately explained away on every occasion of its use ; if our religion is to regain its ancient power in an age which demands remorseless clarity of thought and fearless sincerity of expression, it cannot afford to disregard a maxim dictated by common sense, namely, that if a term cannot be used in a given connexion without a non-natural interpretation, it had better not be used in that connexion at all.   I propose, therefore, during the remainder of these lectures, to substitute for the word ' sin,' in speaking of the hypothetical flaw in human nature, the word ' infirmity,' which avoids the implication irresistibly conveyed, and meant to be conveyed, by the Augustinian phrase, namely, that we are morally culpable in the sight of God for possessing natures which we had no share in choosing and which we cannot help possessing.   It is hardly necessary to point out that, with the term ' original sin,' we discard all those Augustinian and Western theories which have historically been bound up with it—the idea that physical appetites, especially the sexual appetite, are inherently sinful, that we are morally guilty because we were born without the imaginary splendid endowments enjoyed by the first man in Paradise, that we were physically parts of Adam at the moment when he ate the forbidden fruit and are therefore justly deemed to have eaten it ourselves.   To this list of obsolete words and conceptions may be added the time-honoured but ambiguous term ' concupiscence,' which for seventeen centuries has wavered, with more than Protean elusiveness, between the meanings of ' physical appetite in general,' ' inordinate physical appetite,' and ' lust,' and through the interminable confusion thereby engendered, has amply earned the sentence of perpetual banishment from the realms of exact theology.

If our argument so far is well founded, we may claim that this particular area of the ground—the question of the exact nature and seat of the inbred tendency to sin—has thus been cleared of a great quantity of obsolete intellectual structures, and now presents a fair open site for the erection of a more solid and permanent fabric, composed of the materials supplied by the universal Christian tradition and cemented together by the best modern thought.   But the question has not yet been answered, What are those materials ? in other words, What is the psychological account given of the ' inherent flaw ' by the basic and truly

'Catholic' tradition, as distinct from, though doubtless underlying, the specifically Latin and Western view of 'hereditary sin'? If we examine those Greek theologians of the early centuries, in whose writings, as we have already seen, the essential Christian doctrine of human nature and sin appears in its purest and most unadulterated form, we find no unanimous, clear-cut answer to this question. Tatian[1] and Theophilus[2] regard the inborn defect as consisting in the loss of the special assistance of the Holy Spirit, assumed to have been enjoyed in full measure by unfallen man; Origen, in his Caesarean period, reverts for a time to the barbarous conception of bad *mana*, supposed to be inherent in the processes of generation and child-birth[3]; Athanasius takes refuge in the Platonic identification of Being and the Good, and explains the bias towards evil as a tendency inherent in the soul to disintegrate and relapse into non-being[4]; Gregory of Nyssa, in a well-known passage of the Catechetical Oration, describes the condition of unregenerate man as 'weakness,' 'a state of prostration,' 'failure to attain to life,' 'lack of participation in the Good,' 'imprisonment in darkness.'[5] But no single psychological conception can be extracted from these heterogeneous statements; and in general it must be observed that the Greek Fathers prefer to employ, in describing that unregenerate condition of human nature which is the necessary presupposition of any theory of Redemption, the somewhat different, if not alternative, idea of servitude to a personal devil, which both afforded greater scope for glowing rhetoric and also cohered with the then popular view of the Atonement as the temporary payment of Christ's life to Satan in ransom for captive humanity.[6] To ascertain, therefore, what is the common underlying element which is the basis of all views of the 'inherent infirmity '—to fix that highest common factor of all the competing theories as to the nature of the moral flaw, which alone can claim acceptance *ubique, semper, et ab omnibus*—we must recur to the teaching of the great Apostle who laid the foundations of Christian

---

[1] Lecture IV, p. 175.
[2] *ibid.* p. 176.
[3] *ibid.* p. 224.
[4] *ibid.* p. 260.
[5] *or. cat.* 15 (Sr. p. 63).
[6] Lecture IV, p. 292 f.

view *tout savoir, c'est tout pardonner*, but it does carry with it the implication that *tout savoir, c'est beaucoup pardonner*. It steers a middle course between the extreme positions of Augustine and Pelagius, asserting against the former that the occurrence of sin is not inevitable, and against the latter that it is in every age, and under every combination of circumstances, highly probable.

It will be well to complete this sketch of the universal basic essence of the Christian Fall doctrine, as extracted by our historical method from the materials provided by Scripture and tradition, by indicating two consequences which seem to follow irresistibly from it.

The first is this : that with the disuse of the phrase ' original sin ' as describing the inherited infirmity of man's nature it is desirable also to discard all phrases which imply that this involuntary weakness, which is *ex hypothesi* simply given in the conditions of human birth and existence and for the possession of which the individual cannot reasonably be held responsible, is in itself, and quite apart from any actual sins to which it may lead, the object of the Divine ' wrath.' The conception of God as regarding the newly born but still unbaptised infant with ' wrath,' that is, presumably, with anger and hostility, is indissolubly bound up with those Augustinian conceptions of seminal identity and original guilt which we have already seen reason to reject ; and it is well known that the phrase of Eph. ii. 3, ' children of wrath,' merely means persons guilty of actual sin.[1] It is doubtless true that all attributions by theologians of human emotions to the Divine Being represent the language of conscious anthropomorphic metaphor ; and that they are nothing but symbols, imperfectly describing the permanent attitude of God, which is implied in His character, towards the various actions or states of His creatures ; and it cannot be doubted that the present condition of human nature, contrary as it is to His holy will, must, if we are to use this human and almost materialistic language at all, provoke in the Divine nature a reaction which can only be described as one of abstract disapproval. But such an attitude falls far short of anything that could be appropriately described by the

[1] Lecture III, p. 113, n. 1.

metaphor of 'wrath.' It would seem truer to say that God regards the nature of the newly born infant, containing, as on this hypothesis it does contain, the seeds of moral failure and possibly of tragedy, with sorrow and compassion, not with resentment or vengeful indignation : these are terms which should be kept to express His attitude towards wilful transgression, towards 'sinning with a high hand,' towards the conscious adoption of the maxim of Milton's Satan, 'Evil, be thou my good.'[1] In this matter we shall be content, if we decide that the whole theory is well founded, to follow the customary language of the Greek Fathers, and speak not so much of the 'wrath' of God as provoked by human nature, prior to human actions, but rather of His *philanthropia*, the loving-kindness which impelled Him to send His Son to seek the sheep that was lost and by 'a higher gift than grace' to restore the disordered faculties of human nature to that harmony, health, and peace which in the beginning He meant them to possess.

The second of the corollaries to the Fall-doctrine, as just restated, is concerned with the eschatological problem first raised by the two Cappadocian Gregories,[2] and forced into prominence by the Pelagians,[3] namely, the question 'What becomes in the next world of those who die in original sin' —or, as we prefer to phrase it, 'subject to the inherited infirmity'—'without having committed actual sin ?' It is unnecessary to say that the view which we have sketched provides no justification whatever for Augustine's condemnation of all such persons to eternal flames. If I may in passing express a personal view on a mysterious and terrible subject, which it is impossible here to examine at length, I would suggest that the total elimination of the idea of hell from our religion must eviscerate and emasculate it, and annul much of its power to chain the tornadoes of human passion. But the only conception of hell which is morally or intellectually tolerable is one which regards it as the sinner's own free choice, as the freely willed culmination of a deliberate course of self-degradation and of conscious rejec-

---

[1] *Paradise Lost*, iv. 110.
[2] *v. supra*, Lecture IV, pp. 279, 290.
[3] Lecture V, p. 346.

tion of God and goodness.[1] As for the destiny of those, whether infants or adults of infantile mind, who pass into the next world, never having rejected God because they have never known Him, nothing has been revealed, and we must be careful not to be wise above that which is written. But, if it is permissible to give the rein to speculation at all, there is, I would suggest, much to be said for the conception of *Limbo*, which, according to the merciful Scotist interpretation, is a state of natural beatitude, representing the utmost perfection of which its tenants are capable; these tenants, unbaptised infants, virtuous pagans, and the like, are conceived as feeling no regret for their lack of the Beatific Vision of God, either because they know themselves to be incompetent to enjoy it, or because they are ignorant that it is possible.[2] Some such hypothesis as this, enlarged in a manner consonant with the generous tendencies of modern Christian thought in regard to the future destiny of non-Christians, might form a theoretical justification for the Church's practical insistence upon the all-importance of the evangelisation of the heathen, and upon the urgency of bringing infants to baptism as soon as possible after their birth.[3] If there are many mansions in the house of God, it would seem not improbable that the forms of life and consciousness which inhabit them may display a variety as

[1] For an eloquent exposition of the idea of hell on these lines, see F. von Hügel, *Essays and Addresses on the Philosophy of Religion* (1921), 7, ' What do we mean by heaven ? and what do we mean by hell ?'

[2] *v. supra*, Lecture VI, p. 415. The conception of *Limbo* has inspired a modern French lyric, Casimir Delavigne's *Les Limbes*, in which, however, the negative aspect of this state—that is, deprivation of the Beatific Vision —is emphasised at the expense of its positive aspect, that of ' natural beatitude ' : *cf.* this stanza :

> ' Loin de Dieu, là, sont renfermés
> Les milliers d'êtres tant aimés,
> Qu'en ces bosquets inanimés
> La tombe envoie.
> Le calme d'un vague loisir,
> Sans regret comme sans désir,
> Sans peine comme sans plaisir,
> C'est là leur joie.'

Milton utilises *Limbo* as a convenient receptacle for ' embryos' and ' idiots,' friars, scapulars, rosaries, and papal bulls (*Paradise Lost*, iii. 445 ff.).

[3] See Additional Notes D, ' Original sin, eschatology, and foreign missions,' p. 486, and G, ' Infant Baptism,' p. 550.

inexhaustible and multitudinous as is provided by the
spectacle of animate nature on this planet ; and the problem
presented by the dwarf, the crétin, the imbecile, and other
stunted or helpless types of human flotsam and jetsam, may
be lightened if we allow ourselves to imagine that such beings
are capable of a perfection of their own, and may grow into
a mode of existence like that of the ethereal choir of child-
spirits, the cloud of *selige Knaben*, whom Goethe has painted
in the final scene of the second part of *Faust*, and on whose
lips he has placed the blissful song :

> Sag' uns, Vater, wo wir wallen,
>   Sag' uns, Guter, wer wir sind ;
> Glücklich sind wir, allen, allen,
>   Ist das Dasein so gelind ! [1]

Time, however, does not permit us to pursue these
fascinating speculations further, and we must return to the
idea of ' original infirmity,' which is the main subject of this
lecture.   Though the whole drift of our argument has been
towards a denial of the authority and validity of the specifically Western versions of the Fall-doctrine, we have already
admitted that one passage in one particular Western formulary appears very accurately to embody the fundamental
and truly Catholic essence of this idea, namely, the first
chapter of the Tridentine decree ' concerning Justification '
which, borrowing a phrase from the Second Council of Orange,
affirms that in unregenerate human nature ' free-will is by
no means extinguished, although weakened in its strength
and warped ' (*liberum arbitrium minime exstinctum, viribus
licet attenuatum et inclinatum*).[2]   The kernel of the whole
idea, which comes to light when the wrappers of Augustinian
and scholastic accretion are stripped away, consists solely in
the conception of an inherent ' weakness of will,' which
to a certain degree diminishes,[3] but does not by any means

---

[1] ' Tell us, father, whither float we : tell us, good father, who we are.
Happy are we, to all of us existence is so delicious ! '

[2] *Conc. Trident.* Sess. VI, *decret. de iustificat.*, cap. 1 (Denzinger-
Bannwart, *Enchiridion*, 1913, p. 266) : cf. *conc. Arausic.* II, *can.* 25
(Denzinger-Bannwart, p. 84).

[3] *Cf.* F. H. Bradley, *Ethical Studies* (1876), p. 42 : ' violent emotion
may make it impossible for the person to keep two courses before him and
decide—impossible to separate himself from the strain put on him, so as

abolish, moral responsibility. (It may be observed in parenthesis that the responsibility with which we are dealing here is
strictly individual responsibility ; the question whether there
is any such thing as racial responsibility belongs to that
complex of deeper and more metaphysical problems which
cluster around the idea of the Fall.)   The phrase ' weakness
of will ' which we have employed hitherto belongs to the
vocabulary of the so-called ' plain man,' and is doubtless an
unsatisfactory instrument of exact thought : if analysed,
however, it would seem to disclose two ideas underlying it,
namely that of volition, as involving effort, and that of this
effort as impeded, or opposed, by non-volitional factors.   We
are, therefore, justified, without spending time in a more
minute analysis, in translating this conception of ' weakness
of will ' into philosophical terminology as the conception of
' partial determinism,' or ' partial indeterminism,' which
comes to the same thing, though the former expression is
perhaps preferable as bearing a positive connotation.   Such
a doctrine would clearly stand in an equal opposition to
absolute or rigoristic determinism and to absolute or anarchic
libertarianism.   It would, if intellectually defensible, represent the safe middle channel between a Scylla which devours
morals and a Charybdis which drowns Science.   The result of
our historical survey has, in fact, been to suggest that the
only doctrine of human nature which is necessitated by the
Vincentian canon involves one particular answer to the world-
old enigma of free-will, and it is inevitable, therefore, that
our ensuing discussion should be to a certain extent concerned with this all-too-hackneyed theme.   No one who
possesses any acquaintance with the history of the discussion
of free-will can be under the delusion that he has anything
new to say on the subject—his only justification for touching
upon it must lie in the hope that he may be able to speak

---

either to resist it or to identify himself with it.   In such cases the agents
can not collect themselves so as to will, and though with knowledge, yet
with pain and feeling of guiltiness, as in a dream, they perform some act
which is abhorrent to them, and which they impute to themselves as guilt,
but which (provided always their fault has not led to it) the sober onlooker
may be unable to impute to them, in their character of a moral agent.'
The last clause, in my opinion, is an overstatement of the case.

nove, non nova—to lay before his hearers not fresh considerations but the familiar arguments envisaged from a novel point of view.

It was pointed out just now that the hypothesis of 'partial determinism,' which is presupposed by the irreducible residuum of the doctrine of so-called original sin, finds two competitors in the field: the rival theories of absolute indeterminism or libertarianism, and of absolute determinism. It is not necessary for us to spend any time in refuting the former theory; the question was fought out as long ago as the fifth century, and the criticisms which were formulated against the views of Pelagius in our fifth lecture would appear to have a permanent validity as against his modern successors. If any further argument be needed it may be briefly pointed out that absolute indeterminism, by making all human action unpredictable, entirely destroys the possibility of the moral sciences—psychology, pedagogy, criminology, politics, economics, and ethics. Nor need we pay much attention to that slightly modified form of absolute libertarianism which admits the external determination of the will by the influences of environment but refuses to acknowledge its interior determination by heredity, and, like the Pelagians of old, finds the medium through which evil is transmitted solely in what is called 'social heredity.' Such a theory, even if it had not been sufficiently refuted by the teachings of biology, as summed up in a phrase associated with the name of Galton 'the all-importance of nature in comparison with nurture,' would seem to be untenable on the simple *a priori* ground that Society is made up of human beings and is not a mysterious abstract hypostasis existing apart from or above them. Social heredity is merely the epiphenomenon of biological heredity: bad laws only exist because there have been bad legislators; and to lay the blame of man's moral deformities upon 'Society,' conceived as something other than and apart from its members, is a fallacy analogous to the political delusion which imagines that it is possible to throw the expense of extravagant schemes upon an imaginary entity known as 'the State' without increasing the burden of the individual taxpayer. The most formidable antagonist which confronts our minimising doctrine of the ' inherited infirmity ' is absolute determinism.   In the present condition of thought it is the partial freedom of the will, not its partial determination, which needs defence.   By a paradoxical revolution of thought, the residual doctrine of original sin has become the last citadel and refuge of the idea of the freedom of the will ; whilst, on the hypothesis of absolute determinism, all the fiendish cruelties of the Inquisition, the Jacquerie, or the Soviet, all the nauseous abnormalities which crowd the pages of Krafft-Ebing [1] or Havelock Ellis,[2] with their minor roots and ramifications which extend into the subconscious selves of us all, must be regarded as necessary, inevitable, predetermined manifestations of a principle of moral evil, saturating the whole body of mankind and making the general sum of human nature into a *massa perditionis* which would more than merit Augustine's most lurid and terrifying descriptions.

The classical nineteenth-century discussions of the problem of free-will, such as those of Bain, Mill, and Leslie Stephen, presuppose that now antiquated view of the mind which regarded it as a piece of clockwork set in motion by the insertion into it of hard, metallic objects, known as ' motives.'   With the remarkable development of the study of human personality which has taken place during this century the problem has assumed a new aspect.   Both the leading schools of psychology—the school which studies human nature as revealed in moral behaviour and political conduct, and the more specifically medical school which draws its data from the study of mental pathology—agree in regarding the soul, or *psyche*, as an organism, living and growing and displaying the fundamental characteristic of organic life, that of perpetual self-adaptation to environment ;   and, despite certain inevitable differences of emphasis and proportion which flow from the different interests and objects of the academic and the medical psychologists, there is a very large measure of agreement as to the general picture of the soul, its essential fibre and structure, which results from recent research and discovery.

[1] *Psychopathia sexualis*, New York, n.d.
[2] *Studies in the Psychology of Sex*, Philadelphia, 1923.

It is inevitable that such a picture should be built up of metaphors, which may sometimes assume such a materialistic complexion as to give the impression that we are dealing with mythology and not with science ; and it is no less inevitable that the outlines of the picture should be invested with a vague, fluctuating, and dreamlike quality, so that we seem to be looking not at realities but at some phantasmagoric dance of shadows, such as that which played and leapt upon the walls of Plato's cave. But psychology is not the only science which is under the necessity of employing pictorial thought-forms and categories moulded in the furnace of imagination ; and if metaphor is frankly recognised for what it is, there is no reason why it should lead us astray.

With this caution in mind we may now proceed to outline that composite portrait of the soul which seems to have resulted from the two branches of psychological research just mentioned. The soul is a living organism ; and in material organisms, such as form the subject-matter of the biologists' study, a clear distinction can be drawn between the structure or tissue of the organism and the vital energy, which informs and builds up this structure and is in turn determined by it as regards the modes and channels of its discharge. In the soul we can similarly distinguish between structure and energy ; and it will conduce to clearness if we devote a separate examination to these two factors in psychic life.

The structural plan of the soul is marked out by the frontiers, vague and undefined yet intensely real, between its three areas, which are commonly known as the conscious, the fore- or pre-conscious, and the unconscious. It is usual and convenient to speak of these areas as though they were vertically superimposed one upon another like storeys in a building, a *usus loquendi* which we will here follow ; and, as we are concerned with the present and normal condition of human personality and not with its genetic history, we will briefly describe the contents of these storeys in an order contrary to that of their chronological development, beginning with the latest addition to the fabric, the attic or garret which is tenanted by, or rather which *is*, consciousness, and working gradually downwards to the obscure and unexplored basement of the Unconscious which rests, perhaps, upon the living bed-rock of God.

For our purpose the most important fact to notice about this top storey, which we call the Conscious Self, is that it is furnished with certain wide and spacious windows, which are the senses, and which are never completely closed, even during sleep. Through these windows there beats in a perpetual blizzard of sense-impressions, derived mainly from the outside world, but including also a not inconsiderable number which originate in the body and which, taken together, constitute what is known as the *coenesthesia* or sum of the organic sensations. This flux of sense-impressions, perpetually pouring in through the windows of the Soul, is flung into the broad framework of the subject-object relation, sorted out and built up into percepts by means of the forms of perception and the categories of the understanding, and organised, with a never-ceasing readjustment of content, perspective, and proportion, into a continuously flowing, cinematographic representation of the objective world. The details of this process belong to the subject-matter of epistemology or the theory of knowledge and do not, therefore, interest us now ; the important fact for our purposes consists in the no less perpetual drain of the impressions, images, percepts and concepts, after they have played their part in the diorama of consciousness, through what, if we are to keep to our metaphor, must be imagined as a series of cracks or holes in the floor, into the storey immediately below, the area of the preconscious, which is the domain of Memory. Here these discarded elements are caught, held suspended, and organised into more or less coherent conglomerates by the force of the vital energies, of which more will presently be said, welling up from the obscure depths of the Unconscious. These constellations of ideas and images, which are often charged with strong emotional feeling much as a thundercloud is charged with electricity, which hover, as it were, in the preconscious area just below the threshold of the Conscious, and which exert, as we shall see, the most powerful reflex influence upon the field of consciousness, are called by one school of psychologists ' sentiments ' ; by Dr. Jung, however, they are known as ' complexes ' ; and there is yet a third method of terminology which describes them as ' sentiments ' when occupying their normal position in the preconscious and as ' complexes ' only when repressed or driven down into the deep prison of the Unconscious. This hierarchy of ' complexes ' (we adopt the term in Dr. Jung's sense) which occupies the preconscious area, constitutes what is generally known as ' character ' in its more obvious and perceptible aspects, though in the conception of character we have to include ' sentiments ' or complexes, which have been repudiated by the whole self, conscious and preconscious, as incompatible with external facts or with the conscious organisation of its purposes, and repressed in the manner just explained. The lowest room of all, the region of the Unconscious, is almost entirely unexplored, and only reveals its contents by vague and uncertain glimpses in the dream. All that we know about it can be summed up in this—that its obscure recesses contain the fountain of that mysterious energy or life-force which penetrates and vitalises the whole superincumbent structure, that it houses the uneasy and rebellious prisoners known as ' repressed complexes,' and that the exit from it is guarded against any possibility of their escape by a kind of psychic Cerberus known as the ' censorship,' whose lair is on the landing between the unconscious and the preconscious, and which is a metaphorical personification of the intellectual, social, and moral dispositions and conventions which forbid the emergence into consciousness of ideas and impulses felt to be inconsistent with its dominant organisations.

These divisions, however, only represent part of the structure of the soul ; if we utilise the metaphor of a building, they represent the horizontal elements in it, the floors or storeys, and we have yet to consider certain highly important vertical elements which pierce through the various floors at right angles to them ; or, if we prefer the metaphor of a woven tissue or fabric, what we have considered so far constitutes merely the warp of human personality, consisting of the various grades of consciousness, and we have now to consider the weft, consisting of the cross-threads of Instinct, running up from the selvedge of the Unconscious through the preconscious, the ends of which are gathered, ravelled and matted together, in manifold and bewildering intricacy, in the sentiments or complexes. Perhaps it would be well, for the sake of clearness, to drop metaphor for a moment, and to take as the basis of our exposition the austerely scientific language of Dr. W. McDougall's definition. He describes an instinct as ' an *inherited* or *innate* [1] psychophysical disposition which determines its possessor to perceive, and to pay attention to, objects of a certain class, to experience an emotional excitement of a particular quality upon perceiving such an object, and to act in regard to it in a particular manner, or at least to experience an impulse to such action.' [2]   It will be seen from this that an instinct is not Energy ; it is rather an arrangement of the psychic structure which determines the course which Energy takes upon a given occasion in order to discharge itself. If we may now relapse into what has already been indicated as inevitable, the use of metaphor, we may say that an instinct is a path, a channel, a pipe, or a wire, into which the fundamental energy of the soul is attracted by the impact of a given stimulus.   Strictly speaking, therefore, it is inaccurate to speak of the Instincts as being the efficient causes of action. The efficient cause of action is psychic energy, that which the medical psychologists have named *libido*, which we shall have occasion to discuss presently.   Nor, in the light of this conception of the instincts as paths or channels is it appropriate to speak of them as ' strong ' or ' powerful.'   What we know as an ' imperious ' instinct should rather be described as one ' of high conductivity,' if we think of the fundamental energy of the soul as something analogous to electricity, or as a ' deeply graven channel,' which attracts into itself a great volume of *libido*, if we think of the energy under the metaphor of a fluid. It is not necessary for us to come to any conclusion on the disputed question of the exact number of the fundamental instincts. As is well known, Dr. McDougall enumerates twelve—Flight, Pugnacity, Repulsion, Curiosity, Self-assertion, Self-abasement, Parental instinct, the reproductive instinct, the instinct towards

---

[1] I have italicised these words in order to draw attention to their importance for our enquiry.

[2] *An Introduction to Social Psychology*, 18th edn., p. 29.

feeding or self-maintenance, Gregariousness, Acquisition, and Construction.[1] Medical psychologists, on the other hand, seem to recognise only three fundamental instincts: those directed towards the preservation of the *ego* or self, towards conformity and homogeneity with the herd to which the individual belongs, and that directed towards the reproduction of the species; in other words, what are generally known as the ' *ego-*,' the ' herd-,' and ' sex- ' instincts. We need not go into the question whether Dr. McDougall's twelve fundamental instincts are differentiations of the psychotherapist's three, or whether the psychotherapist's three are compositions built up out of Dr. McDougall's twelve. It is sufficient for our purpose to know that, piercing the psychical structure perpendicularly upwards, there is a web of pipes, channels, or paths, which is innate and given by heredity, which guides and determines the uprush of the fundamental energies of the soul, and which can, at least in thought, be separated out into three divisions or sets directed towards the maintenance and development of the self, the preservation of harmony between the self and the herd, and the perpetuation through the individual of the life of the race.

We have now to consider the way in which the fundamental energy, or force of the soul, flowing along one or other of these fixed, innate paths or channels, appears in consciousness as volition and in the external world as action. It would seem that in the adult individual, in so far as he is adult in personality, the instincts do not discharge the vital energy directly into action. If and when they do, we are accustomed to say that the person in question is acting like a child, or an animal. Purely automatic actions, sometimes described as purely instinctive, whereby a given stimulus instantaneously causes a given external reaction, are *characteristic* only of organisms in which self-consciousness does not exist. The growth of self-conscious personality involves the growth of the sentiments, or complexes, stored in the preconscious area, which are continually being built up and charged with energy by the life-force transmitted to them through the instincts. In the adult individual, therefore, an instinct is not, or ideally should not be, directly

[1] *op. cit.* c. iii.

connected with the mechanism of muscular innervation leading to act ; it is, on the contrary, a pipe or a channel which ends in the complex or sentiment, which must be conceived as a kind of reservoir or accumulator, lying just below the threshold of consciousness, containing the potentiality of action in the shape of psychic energy, or *libido*, which is being perpetually conducted to it by the channel of the appropriate instinct. If we may employ yet another type of metaphor, we may think of the complex as a kind of sponge made up of associated ideas and images, which is kept in a state of perpetual saturation with psychic energy by the pipe of the appropriate instinct ending in it. The account of action and conation which results from this general conception may be formulated as follows. A stimulus enters the conscious area, either from above, through the windows of sense, or from beneath, dragged up from the preconscious by the machinery of association. The appearance of the stimulus in consciousness calls the appropriate complex or sentiment into activity, and one of two things happens : either the stimulated complex discharges the psychical energy stored in it into the usual conative channels, from which it emerges as muscular innervation, and a bodily action follows ; or the stimulus simultaneously or after an infinitesimal interval excites another complex inhibiting the action of the first. When this latter contingency occurs, the particular rivulet of energy which has been dammed up and refused an outlet into action may return upon itself, still further saturating the appropriate complex, and increasing its potential explosiveness ; or it may be drained off and go to reinforce some other sentiment which is not debarred from finding practical satisfaction. In this way combative energy may be side-tracked and find a harmless outlet in competitive games and sport, and reproductive energy may be diverted and utilised as motive power for artistic creation or philanthropic activity. When the individual is able to resolve the conflict between the sentiments by starving the weaker sentiment—that is, by depriving it of the psychic energy which keeps it in being, and by using up this rejected energy in some other form, harmonising with the general organisation of his complexes—

he is said to have achieved 'sublimation.' Too often,
however, a mind, which has no comprehension of itself and
its workings, takes a short and superficially easy cut to
interior peace by thrusting the rebellious complex, still alive
and charged with vital energy, down into the *oubliette* of
the Unconscious, from which it often emerges as a neurosis
or pathological symptom, disguising itself in some fantastic
or irrational form in order to evade the vigilance of the
'censorship.'

Such, then, is the portrayal of conation and action which
is given in the modern picture of human personality. Action
means the release of stored-up energy by a complex in
response to an appropriate stimulus ; abstinence from action
means the inhibition of a weaker complex by a stronger ;
and interior conflict, such as is manifested in the 'moral
struggle,' represents the overlap and collision of two complexes, which must end either in the 'sublimation' or in the
'repression' of the weaker. This simple scheme—perception of stimulus, excitation of complex, discharge of energy
—represents, of course, the simplest type of conscious action ;
but the most elaborate and complicated concatenations of
mental procedures, directed towards the most ideal and
abstract ends—the activities of a general working out a
strategic design, of a statesman planning and executing a
great measure of social reform, of a scientist or philosopher
pursuing a train of abstruse research or speculation—can
ultimately be dissected and resolved into such elementary
reactions of complex to stimulus, though the true character
of these conational units, if the phrase may be allowed, is
often disguised by the high degree of co-ordination and
integration which they have undergone. The conduct of
the most subtly organised and highly moralised personalities
can, in theory, be exhaustively explained on these lines,
given liberty to postulate a sufficiently numerous hierarchy
of 'sentiments,' fed with power, not merely by the primary
instincts but by a multiplicity of secondary and derivative
conduits carved out for itself by the elemental energy of the
soul, like the network of minor watercourses which link up
with labyrinthine intricacy the main channels enclosing and
dividing the delta of a great river.

Having now before our eyes what may be described as a cross-section photograph of the Self, displaying the interior mechanism of conduct to view, we naturally enquire if in this structure, the main outlines of which, as we have seen, are given solely by heredity, we can recognise any lacuna, any misfit or dislocation, corresponding to the 'inherited infirmity' alleged by theology to inhere in human nature. It must be emphasised, for the sake of clearness, that the 'infirmity' of which we are in search is a strictly moral infirmity; it would complicate our task to an impossible extent if we took account, at this stage, of pathological and morbid phenomena which no one would regard as bearing an ethical character. And a moral infirmity must, presumably, mean an infirmity of the moral 'sentiment' or 'complex,' resulting in a tendency for it to be overborne by complexes more highly charged with psychic energy and endowed with a more pleasurable affective tone. We must, therefore, examine with some care the psychologist's account of the moral sentiment, inasmuch as in it, or in the primitive instincts which have contributed to its formation, we shall either find—or not find—the fundamental flaw which Catholic Christianity declares itself to presuppose.

The 'moral sentiment' is capable of pure and lovely efflorescence in ideal loyalties, self-sacrificing heroisms, and self-transcendent yearnings for the Absolute and the Infinite, in Whom the world of eternal values, like the world of ultimate truths, finds its supporting pillar and stay. Yet this interior power, which has been adored by poets and thinkers under the name of 'Conscience' or 'Duty,' 'stern daughter of the voice of God,' is, from the psychologist's unsentimental point of view, an artificial and secondary construction, built upon one of the three primary, or at any rate most massive and dominant complexes, that which consists of ideas and images clustering round the idea of the 'herd.' It is, doubtless, unnecessary to urge a cultured audience not to allow itself to be prejudiced against the information which psychology has to give us in this connexion by the apparent brutality of this technical term, or by the postulation of a lowly basis for our most exalted feelings; 'a rose by any other name would smell as sweet,' and a diamond sparkles none the less brilliantly because it is made of the same carbon as a lump of coal. The ' herd-complex,' then, with its various roots and ramifications, constitutes the field in which the ' inherited infirmity,' if it is a reality, is to be found.

We must, however, delimit this field with some minuteness before proceeding to its investigation. It would clearly be waste of time to analyse the higher developments of the ' moral sentiment,' or to trace the process whereby, in ethically gifted individuals, the partial fusion of the *ego*- and the herd-complexes gives birth to an autonomous moral ideal, independent of external or social sanctions. Nor are we concerned with the weird and monstrous aberrations of the specifically criminal temperament, such as formed the subject-matter of the studies of Nordau and Lombroso— the temperament in which the ' moral sentiment ' is either non-existent or so much atrophied as hardly to be recognisable. It is, indeed, tempting to identify ' original sin,' so called, with criminality ; and such an identification was implied in the half-serious, popular and journalistic *cliché* which attributed the atrocities committed in the late war to a ' double dose of original sin ' in their perpetrators. It would certainly seem that criminal dispositions are transmissible by heredity ; the progress of statistical research may prove that in certain strains of mankind they behave as Mendelian dominants ; and it is probable that a reasonable system of applied eugenics might do much towards their elimination from the human stock.[1] We shall certainly not be able to ignore the question of criminality when we approach our final problem, that of the ultimate origin of evil. But we cannot simply identify it with the ' inherited infirmity ' of which we are in search ; for the innate flaw or wound of human nature, which Christian tradition presupposes, purports to be, not a varietal factor borne by

---

[1] In so far as ' eugenics ' is a genuine science, no Catholic Christian can claim to have a conscientious objection to it : if and in so far as it is an art, it does not seem possible to find limits for its scope other than those dictated by the inalienable rights and dignity of the individual. Such limits would clearly rule out both the system of State-breeding suggested by Plato in *Republic* V, and also the ' sterilisation of the unfit ' enjoined by the law of certain American States.

particular individuals or stocks, but a generic quality, existing in all men (with one, or, as some hold, with two exceptions), inhering deeply in the fundamental plasm of the race, beyond and below the reach of eugenics, psychotherapy, manipulation of the endocrine glands, or of any remedial agency other than the delicate and viewless influences of God's redeeming grace. We must therefore neglect the superficially more interesting qualities of the ethical genius and the ethical degenerate, and dig deep, in quest of the alleged ' inherited infirmity,' into that instinctive structure which is the basis of human personality in saint and criminal alike.

The ' herd-complex,' then, as it exists, not in the ethically highest or lowest types of mankind, but in the generalised average of humanity, is the starting-point of our search. But here, again, a further limitation has to be added. Civilised man belongs to many herds, and his preconscious mind therefore contains many herd-complexes of greater or lesser strength, built up round the ideas of his school, college, regiment, social class, trade, political or religious party, and so on ; these structures tend to generate in the surface mind feelings of *esprit de corps*, party loyalty, ' class-consciousness,' and other quasi-moral emotions familiar to us all. But the particular herd-complex which forms the core and substratum of the moral sentiment clearly cannot be identified with any one of the minor conglomerates just mentioned, though it may on occasion draw upon the energy with which they are charged. It can be found only in that deep-lying psychic structure which coheres round the idea of ' society ' as such, and which, from the standpoint of the morphology of personality, must be regarded as the proximate source of specifically ethical impulses and conations, no matter whether ' society ' be narrowly conceived as the individual's own clan or totem-group, or broadened out so as to include the whole human race or the whole fellowship of conscious beings. In the religious man, indeed, the perfected moral sentiment is largely fused and identified with the mass of ideas, beliefs and emotions which grow out of his conception of God ; but an examination of this loftiest efflorescence of ethical feeling would lead us away from our immediate task, which is to uncover its ultimate roots. And these roots lie in the idea of 'society,' 'the community,' or 'the herd.' Whatever metaphysical explanation of the pure forms or categories of 'right' and 'wrong' may commend itself to the speculative reason, it is a mere statement of historical and psychological fact when we assert that the concrete content of morality, as it exists at any given time, is defined for the individual by the exigencies of the herd, and mediated to his consciousness through the pressure of the herd-tradition upon him.

The 'social complex,' then, created and maintained by 'herd-instinct,' is the basis of the ethical sentiment ; and all interior moral conflicts are due to incompatible conations arising from this on the one hand, and either from the *ego*-complex or the sex-complex on the other. Sometimes, indeed, the moral sentiment may be able to utilise the energy latent in the *ego*-complex—or, in less technical terms, morality and self-interest may combine to inhibit some sensuous impulse ; and a little imagination will show that an alliance between the moral sentiment and the sex-complex, to oppose the dictates of mere selfishness, is not by any means unknown. But—and here we come to the real point of this long excursion into the realm of analytic psychology—experience decisively shows that the 'society' complex, in isolation and devoid of allies, is no match for the powerful systems of thought and feeling cohering round the ideas of the self and of sex—a fact which is indicated in the restrained words of Dr. McDougall: 'We have to recognise that the desire that springs from the completed moral sentiment is usually of a thin and feeble sort in comparison with the fiercer, coarser desires that spring directly from our instincts and from our concrete sentiments.'[1] If we ask why the desire, which issues from the moral sentiment into consciousness, is normally of this 'thin and feeble' character, the answer must be that the moral sentiment emits only a thin and feeble desire, because it itself is only charged with psychic energy of a thin and feeble quality. Just as a powerful electric spark cannot be

---

[1] *op. cit.* c. ix. p. 229.

obtained from a weak battery, so a strong conational effort
cannot issue from a complex endowed with a relatively small
quantum of that *libido* or life-force which is the driving-
power behind actions of every kind, volitional and non-
volitional alike.   And this weak saturation with psychic
energy of the social complex can only be due to the weakness
of the herd-instinct, which feeds it ; which, in the metaphorical and symbolic language necessary for the purposes
of this enquiry, is a narrow and constricted gutter carrying
only a thin trickle of the forces of the soul ; whereas in
comparison with it the two other elemental instincts, those
concerned with the maintenance of the self and the perpetuation of the race, must be imagined as broad and deeply
cut canals, which take fierce swirling volumes of the vital
impulse.   The ultimate psychological fact, therefore, which
gives rise to an interior ' moral struggle ' ending only too
often in the defeat of the social or ethical principle, is the
weakness or shallowness of the ' herd-instinct,' relatively to
the two other primary instincts of human nature.   And this
unsatisfactory proportion which the three cardinal instincts
bear to each other is, it must be remembered, nothing
acquired or artificially constructed ; it is simply given by
heredity, in the total make-up of human personality with
which we are born.   It would seem therefore that we need
search no further, and that at this deep level in the structure of the soul, beneath the area of the preconscious and
lying in the obscure recesses of the Unconscious, we have
unearthed that precise weakness or interior dislocation of
man's being which historical Christianity has steadfastly
affirmed to exist, and which forms the presupposition of its
redemptive and sacramental scheme.

In the light of this identification of the ' inherited
infirmity ' with congenital weakness or shallowness of
' herd-instinct,' it is easy to understand the psychological
rationale of the traditional language employed by Christian
ascetic theology in regard to the forms assumed by ' innate
sin ' as it gradually grows within the growing soul.   In this
traditional language it is often said that all actual sins
spring from one or other of two roots—namely, Pride and
Sensuality ; and that these again run back into Self-love

as their ultimate source.   And 'Self-love' is nothing but a positive manner of describing the same fact which psychology, in agreement with the most primitive Christian modes of thought, conceives as a negation, an ἔλλειψις or *deprivatio*, as deficiency in that 'herd-complex,' that sympathy or love, that corporate or social feeling which all men do possess to some degree (for otherwise they would not be moral beings at all), but which, in normal human nature, as transmitted to us by birth and as it stands prior to moral and religious educative influences, is strong enough only to hamper and not to master the tendency of the life-force to rush impetuously down the channels of the self-asserting and the race-perpetuating instincts.   'Pride' is merely a name for the exaggeration of the *ego*-complex, and 'sensuality' for the hypertrophy of the cluster of ideas and images connected with sex ; and what we have already noted as the somewhat excessive preoccupation of Jewish and Christian anthropology [1] with 'concupiscence' in the more restricted sense of that ambiguous term is doubtless due to the somewhat greater depth and capacity of the latter instinct as compared with the former.   It would not, indeed, be difficult to paraphrase the classical descriptions of the inbred taint and the moral struggle given us by the masters of the spiritual life in terms of the three dominant complexes.   It would be a task of the highest intellectual interest (though considerations of time prevent us from undertaking it now) to work through the great Pauline passage, Rom. vii. 7–25, which we studied in Lecture III, translating it into the terminology of modern mental science, rendering ' the sin that dwelleth in me ' as ' the innate weakness of my herd-instinct,' ' the law of my mind ' as ' my completed moral sentiment,' and the ' law of sin which is in my members ' as the ' powerful complexes perpetually fed with psychic energy by my animal instincts ' ; whilst the cry of despair ' who shall deliver me from the body of this death ? ' would represent the crisis of psychic pain born of the clash of conflicting conations ; and the victorious

[1] See Lecture I, p. 34 ; Lecture II, pp. 58, 66 ; Lecture III, p. 153 ; Lecture IV, pp. 226, 245, 273, 304 ; Lecture V, p. 366 ; Lecture VI, pp. 403 n. 2, 411 n. 2.

reply ' I thank God through Jesus Christ our Lord ' would be the exulting song of a soul which had won its way to interior harmony and peace by the sublimation of the rebellious complexes into the mystic aspirations of a great ideal love.

Yet when, in accordance both with the most primitive Christian thought and the most modern psychological research, we define the inherited wound of human nature in negative terms as a deficiency, a lack, a *privatio*, we must not be supposed thereby to minimise the deadliness and the horror of the results to which it leads in human action. To realise in full the objective evil of what, considered subjectively, is nothing but a defect, a gap, a blank, a *minus* quantity, we need only borrow the method used by Plato for the detection of righteousness, and study that enlarged and generalised portrait of the soul which is presented by the state or the nation in its corporate bearing towards other states or nations. It is instructive to review that world-wide society constituted by the unity of our race, in which peoples are the individuals, and humanity as a whole is the ' herd ' to which the individual owes allegiance. The history of peoples, in their relations one with another, is marked by an almost complete absence of collective ' herd-instinct ' and by the unrestrained dominance of the ' ego-instinct ' in its most brutal and least disguised form. The events of the last decade lend a melancholy confirmation to words recently written, not by any Augustinian or Calvinistic divine, but by a thinker whose theological impartiality will nowhere be disputed, Mr. Bertrand Russell. ' Men's collective passions are mainly evil ; far the strongest of them are hatred and rivalry directed towards other groups. Therefore at present all that gives men power to indulge their collective passions is bad. That is why Science threatens to cause the destruction of our civilisation.' [1] It would be difficult to find a more apposite commentary upon our Lord's own grave and awful saying : ' From within, out of the heart of men, evil thoughts proceed . . . thefts, murders . . . coveting, wickednesses, deceit . . . an evil eye, railing, pride, foolishness : all these evil things proceed from within, and defile the man.' [2]

[1] *Icarus* (1924), p. 63.   [2] Mark vii. 21 f.

It may thus be reasonably claimed that the existence of
a hereditary psychic factor which tends to promote the
indulgence of self-assertive and sensual impulses in despite of
' conscience,' or the ' moral sentiment,' is a hypothesis which
finds ample verification both in ordinary daily life and in
the scientific study of human personality. But, it may be
objected, this line of thought, if followed out consistently,
proves too much for our purposes : for it lands us, not in
' partial determinism,' but in a determinism just as absolute
as that which results from the older mechanistic view of
the mind. In the preceding description of the *rationale* of
conation and action, hardly anything was said about the
conscious *ego*, which occupies—or rather is—the uppermost
storey of the house of personality : and modern psychology,
especially that of the medical type, is largely epipheno-
menalistic, regarding the feeling of effort and struggle as an
illusion, and the ' I ' as the passive mirror of events which
it has had no share in causing. The logical result of such
a view, when combined with a recognition of the fact
which we have described as man's congenital deficiency of
herd-instinct, would be (as we have pointed out above [1])
something very like the ' twice-born ' view of human nature
characteristic of Latin and Western Christendom : some
elements at least of Augustinianism, having been driven
from the field of theology by the Vincentian Canon, would
have returned in triumph under the aegis of Freud.

We have already indicated what seems to us the
inconsistency of Augustinianism with a genuine belief in
the goodness and justice of God, and in the moral accountability of man. But we do not forget that this doctrine has
nevertheless been held by some of the greatest saints and
doctors of the Universal Church, that it is not without roots
in the teaching of St. Paul, and that the type of character
which has been nourished by it is, at its best, virile, austere,
and noble. Whatever may be the case in logic, it is at
least psychologically possible for an orthodox Christian to
be a rigid determinist. It is, therefore, no part of the
contention of these lectures that Augustinianism is a heresy.
We have maintained that the ' once-born ' or 'Hellenic'

[1] p. 468.

doctrine represents the maximum to which historical Christianity is, as such, committed ; but if any individual orthodox Christian believes that he has grounds for going further and adopting the ' twice-born ' view—if he thinks that man can be justly held accountable by God for acts which are completely determined by heredity and environment, and that the potter may justifiably wreak vengeance on the pots for being of the shape into which he has himself moulded them, or allowed them to be moulded—it would seem that, so far as the *auctoritas* of Scripture and tradition is concerned, he is well within his rights in so thinking and believing. It is not, accordingly, necessary for our purposes to embark at this juncture upon an extensive vindication of free-will : and it will suffice to conclude this lecture with the briefest possible summary of the present position of the problem.

The situation in regard to the question whether a true spontaneous causality, acting within limits [1] fixed by heredity and environment, can be ascribed to the *ego* or not, has not essentially altered since its treatment by Kant. Determinism is the necessary methodological postulate of

---

[1] The mere feeling of freedom is not always veridical : sometimes we are most completely determined when we believe ourselves to be most free. The smooth, unimpeded interaction of the psychic organisations sketched in the text is not in itself freedom : freedom is only realised when the conscious *ego*, the transcendental self, deliberately takes control of the situation, with clear knowledge of itself, of its instinctive impulses, and of the effort which it is putting forth in order to guide or restrain them. What appears to be substantially this point has been expressed by Bergson in his own characteristic language, and connected with his peculiar philosophy of time and duration, in the following passage : ' Il y aurait donc enfin deux moi différents, dont l'un serait comme la projection de l'autre, sa représentation spatiale et pour ainsi dire sociale. Nous atteignons le premier par une réflexion approfondie, qui nous fait saisir nos états internes comme des êtres vivants, sans cesse en voie de formation, comme des états réfractaires à la mesure, qui se pénètrent les uns les autres, et dont la succession dans la durée n'a rien de commun avec une juxtaposition dans l'espace homogène. Mais les moments où nous nous ressaisissons ainsi nous-mêmes sont rares, et *c'est pourquoi nous sommes rarement libres* (italics ours). La plupart du temps, nous vivons extérieurement à nous-mêmes . . . nous vivons pour le monde extérieur plutôt que pour nous ; nous parlons plutôt que nous ne pensons ; nous "sommes agis" plutôt que nous n'agissons nous-mêmes. Agir librement, c'est reprendre possession de soi, c'est se replacer dans la pure durée' (*Les données immédiates de la conscience*, 1908, p. 178).

the scientist and the statistician ; but freedom is the no less necessary assumption of the teacher and the judge, an assumption which is largely employed in psycho-therapeutic practice as distinct from theory.[1] We cannot hope with our present faculties to attain a complete logical synthesis of the dictates of the theoretical reason, which repudiates the idea of an uncaused causality, with those of the practical reason, which demands it ; but it remains true to say that determinism is only necessary to a psychology which studies the mind objectively and *ab extra*, whilst the consciousness of ability to exert or not to exert effort is, from the subjective and introspective point of view, a datum of immediate experience.[2] In the light of these considerations, it may reasonably be claimed that the doctrine of ' partial determinism '—which, whilst admitting that conduct is the result of the interplay of stimulus, complex, and instinct, nevertheless affirms that consciousness has, within limits, a real power of guiding the flow of psychic energy into this complex rather than that, and of gradually modifying the contents of the preconscious and unconscious by voluntary ' sublimation '—would seem to be the only one which does justice both to man's moral and to his intellectual experience.

If this be so, we have in the treasure-house of Christian tradition that true conception of human nature, its power and its weakness, which contains the key to the world-old problems of social regeneration and reform.   No readjust-

---

[1] The restrained words of an eminent psychotherapist may be quoted in this connexion : ' . . . one finds such a distinguished neurologist as Dejerine saying in his book on psychotherapy that belief in freedom is essential to the more successful application of the methods of psychotherapy.   He claims, practically at any rate, that we must believe in freedom if we are to hope to influence our patients on the mental side. Without going so far as that, I am inclined to say that a belief in freedom, in self-determination, on the physician's part, strong enough to sustain or originate a similar belief in the patient's mind, is a very important factor in mental cure ' (William Brown, *Mind and Personality*, 1926, p. 47).

[2] *Cf*. O. Tansley, *The New Psychology* (1922), p. 296 : ' The fundamental postulates of the new science of the mind, the doctrines of psychic determination and of the derivation of the springs of all human action from instinctive sources, are essential as working hypotheses.   But this science need not commit itself to the conclusion that the play of instinctive forces exhausts the meaning of the human soul, any more than biology need commit itself to the conclusion that the play of chemical and physical forces exhausts the meaning of life itself.'

ment of governmental or economic machinery, no perfection of scientific or hygienic efficiency, will in itself avail to bring the Kingdom of God upon earth one step nearer, apart from a ' change of heart ' in the individual member of society. The essential condition of such a change, which is the co-operation of human freedom and Divine grace, stands written for all time in the great saying of the Apostle,[1] ' Work out your own salvation with fear and trembling,' recognising and using to the full the God-given endowment of self-consciousness, self-determination, and individual autonomy, yet remembering, in humble acknowledgment of the connatural flaw of human nature, that it is God, Who alone can ' order the unruly wills and affections of sinful men,' ' that worketh in you both to will and to work, for His good pleasure.'

ADDITIONAL NOTE D

ORIGINAL SIN, ESCHATOLOGY, AND FOREIGN MISSIONS

One of the master-motives which spurred on the great missionaries of the last four centuries, both Catholic and Evangelical, to their heroic labours amongst the heathen was a burning desire to snatch as many souls as they could from the eternal perdition assumed to await all non-Christians as such in the next world, in virtue of ' original sin.'   In other words, Augustinianism and its concomitant eschatology lay at the root of the apostolic zeal manifested alike by a Francis Xavier and a Henry Martyn : and these ideas still seem to appear in the missionary intercession printed in the well-known devotional manual *Sursum Corda* (1906, p. 121) : ' O God of all the nations of the earth, remember the multitudes of the heathen, who, though created in Thine image, are *perishing* in darkness and ignorance '—where there is little point or force in the word ' perishing ' unless it means ' perishing eternally.'   If the contention embodied in these lectures is correct, this particular incentive to missionary effort has ceased to exist.   But the conception of *Limbo*, in some form or other, as a possible destiny of the spiritually undeveloped, may still provide a non-Augustinian Christianity with a satisfactory, though not so dramatically appealing, substitute.   The

[1] Phil. ii. 12, 13.

desire to lead the child-like members of the human family up to far higher planes of spiritual vision and power than any to which they could have attained, apart from Christ and His Gospel, either in this life or the next, may well prove to be an evangelistic motive more truly inspiring than that which springs from the crude eschatology of Augustinianism.

It may be added that the missionary cause would not suffer by a reverent unwillingness on the part of Christian thinkers to define too narrowly the category of those who may be incapable of the highest beatitude, or by a refusal to draw too sharp a line between *Limbo* and ' purgatory.' The words of a previous Bampton Lecturer are specially pertinent in this connexion : ' Few among us would desire to bar the gates of heaven against the Unitarian Channing, against the Buddhist ascetic, against even the naked savage who on his sea-swept coral reef, forsaken as he may seem of God and man, is yet just and grateful and kind to wife and child. Yet few would think that for these maimed souls no instruction is needed, that the mere rending of the veil can make tolerable the splendour which it reveals. We believe in the many stripes and the few. We believe that star differeth from star in glory, and in these words lies all that any sober-minded man has ever maintained.' [1]

[1] Bigg, *Christian Platonists of Alexandria* (1886), p. 299.

VIII.

THE ULTIMATE 'FALL'

O martyred Spirit of this helpless Whole,
    Who dost by pain for tyranny atone,
    And in the star, the atom, and the stone,
Purgest the primal guilt, and in the soul ;
Rich but in grief, thou dost thy wealth unroll,
    And givest of thy substance to thine own,
    Mingling the love, the laughter, and the groan
In the large hollow of the heaven's bowl.

GEORGE SANTAYANA.

In my folly often I wondered why by the great foreseeing wisdom of God the beginning of sin was not letted : for then, methought, all should have been well. . . . But Jesus answered by this word and said ' Sin is behovable, but all shall be well and all shall be well and all manner of thing shall be well.'

JULIAN OF NORWICH.

LECTURE VIII.

THE ULTIMATE 'FALL'

Rev. xii. 7, 8 : ' There was war in heaven : Michael and his angels
going forth to war with the dragon ; and the dragon warred,
and his angels ; and they prevailed not, neither was their
place found any more in heaven.'

IN our last lecture we dealt with the question of what has
been called ' Original Sin,' and defined the nature of the
inherited infirmity, declared to exist in human nature,
by the basic doctrine of traditional Christianity as held
' everywhere, always, and by all.' We saw that our moral
consciousness, the interplay of ' thoughts accusing or else
excusing one another ' [1] (to use St. Paul's vivid phrase),
necessitates the assumption that in an ideal human personality the ' herd-complex ' would form an adequate
counterweight to the ' *ego*-complex ' and the ' sex-complex '
and also to the aggregate of them taken together, so that the
soul would enjoy a condition of perfect equilibrium or poise
on which conscious free-will could play, reinforcing now one
and now another of the dominant psychical structures and
controlling, modifying, or inhibiting the flow of vital energy
into them. And we saw further that the congenital weakness or disorder of human nature consists precisely in this,
that such an equilibrium does not, in point of fact, exist ;
that, owing to the weakness of the herd-instinct which feeds
it, the herd-complex, and by consequence the moral sentiment which is built upon it, does not possess anything like
the amount of vital energy necessary to place it on equal
terms with the two other primary complexes, so as to
preserve that equilibrium of the empirical self, or ' me,'

---

[1] Rom. ii. 15 : μεταξὺ ἀλλήλων τῶν λογισμῶν κατηγορούντων ἢ καὶ
ἀπολογουμένων.

which the transcendental self, or ' I,' needs in order to be
able to function with freedom. Hence the conscious *ego*
is in the position of an organist condemned to play upon an
instrument in which certain very powerful stops are liable
to speak of their own accord and at the most inappropriate
moments; or, in less metaphorical language, free-will,
though not destroyed, is weakened and hampered, in
comparison with what it ought to be, by the present conditions of human nature, and the self-regarding and race-
perpetuating instincts tend to have things all their own
way. We now approach the final problem—namely, the
question how this state of affairs came into existence; that
is to say the problem of what is known to traditional
theology as the ' Fall.'

It was observed in our first lecture, at the very beginning
of our historical review, that the hypothesis of a ' Fall ' is
essentially an inference from the facts of human weakness
and sin, considered in the light of the infinite holiness of
God.[1] It is not a premise given by history—a fact which
would have been quite sufficiently proved by the existence
in Judaism and Christianity for three hundred years of two
alternative Fall-stories, even if Biblical criticism and natural
science had never shown that the Paradise-story which
ultimately triumphed is just as devoid of historical character
as the ' Watcher '-story which it superseded. The recognition of this fact must compel a certain readjustment of
what has been, at least in Western Christianity, the
traditional view as to the interior structure, if the term may
be allowed, of the fabric of Christian doctrine. It was
pointed out in our first lecture that mediaeval Christians,
at least, thought of the Faith as borne up by the twin pillars
of a historic Fall and a historic Redemption, both vouched
for by written records of divinely guaranteed accuracy and
authority—as leaning upon the Tree of Death which stood
in the midst of the Garden of Eden, and the Tree of Life
which was planted upon the summit of Calvary. If the
argument developed in this course of lectures has been
sound, the first pillar is to be found not so much in the

---

[1] Lecture I, p. 19; and *cf.* the passage from Cardinal Newman's
Apologia pro Vita Sua printed at the beginning of the last lecture.

idea of the Fall as in the idea of ' original sin,' so called, and the basis of this pillar consists in a certain kind of religious experience—namely, the experience of penitence—and not in history. I do not mean to imply that the idea of the Fall ought to be discarded, or that it does not correspond to any reality—I am only concerned to point out that, in view of its *inferential* character, it must for the future be conceived not as a column which supports the Christian Faith, but rather as a pinnacle which is supported by it. It might thus seem as though there were not very much to be said about the Fall beyond the mere assertion that, if God is infinitely good, He cannot be the author of evil, and that the facts of human nature therefore compel us to assume something corresponding to a Fall ; and indeed, when once the literal historicity of Gen. iii. has been given up, that is all that can be affirmed to be of faith—at any rate for Christians other than those of the Latin communion. But because the idea of the Fall is a pinnacle and not a column, it does not follow that it is of no structural importance. A pinnacle need not be a mere ornamental excrescence ; it may exert a downward thrust which plays an important part in the system of stresses ensuring the stability of the fabric to which it belongs. It has, in fact, been recently ascertained in connexion with St. George's Chapel at Windsor that the gravitational pressure of a row of heavy pinnacles is necessary in order to enable its buttresses and columns to resist the lateral pressure of its flattened and floriated vault, and that the threatened collapse of this venerable fabric is largely due to the incautious removal of these same pinnacles, a century ago, on the ignorant assumption that they were nothing but unnecessary adornments.[1] We will therefore make no apology for endeavouring to dispel the mists which surround this particular pinnacle, that is, for devoting our final lecture to the task of arriving at a conception of the Fall which may be congruous both with the essential contents of traditional Christianity and also with the deliveries of human reason.

It will be remembered that the fundamental Christian doctrine of the Fall, as distinct from that of Original Sin,

[1] This was written in 1924.

was in our last lecture condensed into the form of five propositions, which it will be well, for the sake of clearness, to
repeat at this juncture. They were as follows :

(1) *God is infinite, not merely in power but in love and
goodness, and therefore the world of created being as He made
it must have been purely good, including no element of evil at all.*

(2) *The origin of evil is therefore to be sought in the
voluntary rebellion of created and finite wills, such rebellion
having taken place prior to the appearance of the human species
on this planet.*

(3) *Man, at his first entry into this world, was in moral and
intellectual stature a babe, created frail, imperfect, ignorant and
non-moral, but endowed with self-consciousness and the power
of self-determination which constituted a starting-point for
progress and upward evolution.*

(4) *The growth of man's moral ideas brought in its train
some action, or system of actions, whereby man aligned himself
with the rebellious power, showed that he had partially thrown
in his lot with the forces of evil which were already at work in
the universe, and entered on a path largely divergent from
that upward career of spiritual evolution which God had
meant him to follow.*

(5) *Ever since this first human transgression, our nature
has displayed an inherent moral weakness or bias towards sin.*

These are the propositions which must now be vindicated
if the doctrine of the Fall is to be preserved as a member of
the Christian dogmatic scheme. It will be noticed that they
are all couched in a strictly historical form. As they stand,
they purport to describe real events which occurred in past
time, which would, presumably, be capable, if we only had
the requisite knowledge, of being assigned to specific dates
B.C. We are all familiar with the conventional form which
the sequence of these alleged events has assumed in popular
religious thought and scholastic theology, and which has
been shaped into a vast cosmic drama in the mighty epic
of ' Paradise Lost.' The revolt of Lucifer, setting up the
standard of revolt against the Most High in the regions of
the North, the hurling of the apostate angels from the crystal
battlements of Heaven, the desire to fill up the gaps left in
the ranks of His servants by the defection of the rebellious

spirits as being the motive which prompted the Almighty to create Man in His own image and likeness, and the tempter's assault upon our first parents as prompted by a craving for revenge upon the triumphant Deity—these are but the pictorial and mythological husk in which the kernel of the doctrine of the ' Fall,' as expressed in the five more abstract propositions given above, has been for many centuries concealed. Such beliefs are only worth mentioning now for the sake of helping us to realise the total and utter absence of any sort of serious evidence for them. We have already pointed out that the Paradise story of Gen. iii. was not meant to narrate a ' Fall ' in the theological sense of the term, and it may be added that the Scriptural texts which have been adduced as testifying to the fall of the angels have even less relevance to their supposed subject-matter. The battle between Michael and the Dragon, narrated in the twelfth chapter of the Christian Apocalypse, has too many parallels in pagan mythology to be regarded as a literal revelation of pre-mundane history [1]; the reference to the fall of ' Lucifer,' that is, the Day-Star, made by some prophet of the Exile, whose work has been embodied in the Book of Isaiah, is merely a metaphorical description of the collapse of the Babylonian power [2]; and even our Lord's saying, reported in St. Luke's Gospel, ' I beheld Satan fallen as lightning from Heaven,' [3] clearly refers not to any pre-cosmic expulsion of the revolting spirits from the abode of God, but to the triumph just gained over the demons by His seventy disciples through a successful series of exorcisms. There is therefore as little *a posteriori* evidence for the fall of the angels as there is for the Fall, or rather the failure, of Man ; and if the scheme contained in our five propositions, or any part of it, is to be sustained at all, it can only be upon the basis of purely *a priori* reasoning.

At this point we are faced by the consideration that the use of the *a priori* method for establishing historical conclusions lies under profound, and not undeserved, suspicion.

---

[1] For a list of these parallels, and a searching investigation of the origins of the myth, see R. H. Charles, *The Revelation of St. John (ICC.,* 1920), vol. i. pp. 305 ff.

[2] Isaiah xiv. 12.   [3] Luke x. 18.

The argument ' Such and such a thing ought to have happened, and therefore it did happen,' has been so often refuted by the critic's pen or the archaeologist's spade that our modern intellectual conscience will not allow it so much as a hearing until all other possible alternatives have been decisively disposed of.   Before, therefore, we can even begin to consider the hypotheses of a pre-mundane revolt and a failure of man to avoid complicity in this revolt we must give careful consideration to the previous question, which is this : Is it necessary to find the source of evil in a historical event at all ?   If, for the time being, we use the term ' Fall ' as a convenient label for designating that unknown x in which the origin of evil lies hid, is it necessary to interpolate the Fall into the historical time series, and to describe its relation to empirical evil under the category of ' cause and effect ' ?   May it not be simpler to regard the Fall, in this symbolical sense, as standing towards the actual sins of man in the relation of ' ground ' to ' consequent,' and as constituting a timeless, transcendent and metaphysical fact, rather than a phenomenal and historical event ?   The shortest and most convenient method of answering this question will be to examine the two classical attempts which have been made by two of the most subtle and powerful of philosophical intellects to remove the idea of the Fall from the plane of history into that of metaphysic, in order to ascertain whether they fulfil the essential function of the Fall-doctrine, for the discharge of which it was first devised and in which alone we, as Christians, are interested—namely, that of saving the infinite goodness of God by relieving Him from the direct responsibility for the creation of evil. These two restatements or reinterpretations of the traditional Fall-doctrine form part of the systematic attempts made by Kant and Hegel to salve what seemed to them the permanent essence of religion from the wreck in which a destructive Biblical criticism and the remorseless rationalism of the *Aufklärung* seemed to have involved German evangelical theology. Should we conclude that neither of these giants of thought has succeeded in lifting the idea of the Fall out of the phenomenal plane, we shall be entitled to assume that the task is inherently impossible, and that—for good or for evil—the propositions which were formulated above must be taken *au pied de la lettre*, as purporting to describe historical events lying, infinitely remote from us, in the ' dark backward and abysm of time.'

Kant's discussion of original sin is contained in the first section of his treatise entitled ' Religion within the bounds of Mere Reason.' [1] This treatise is concerned mainly with religion on its soteriological side, that is, in its aspect as a way of salvation, and its main divisions are concerned with the entry of the evil principle into human nature, the struggle between the good and evil principles, and the eventual triumph of the good principle.[2] The argument of the first of these sections is based upon the empirical universality of sin, which Kant proves from the not very considerable store of information at his disposal with regard to the habits of savages.[3] He does not regard badness as constituting part of the essence of human nature, but rather as an inseparable accident. Badness is not given in the concept of man, but it is *de facto* so widely spread that it can be predicated of man generically. Though Kant is distinguished amongst philosophers by his contempt of psychology, he makes some show of analysing human nature in order to throw light upon the seat of the evil principle, and it is noteworthy that in describing what he calls ' the animal nature of man,' which is the substratum and foundation of his strictly human and moral being, he designates as its primary psychical constituents, precisely those three instincts with which our last lecture is so largely concerned, those, namely, which are directed towards the maintenance of the self, the propagation of the race, and the maintenance of harmony between the self and the society to which it belongs—in other words, what we now call the ' herd-instinct.' [4] It would seem at first sight as though this analysis might lead to results

---

[1] *Die Religion innerhalb der Grenzen der blossen Vernunft* (*Kant's sämmtliche Werke*, ed. Rosenkrantz and Schubert, Leipzig, 1838, x. pp. 1–244).

[2] The first of these sections (' Von der Einwohnung des bösen Princips neben dem guten, oder, Über das radikale Böse in der menschlichen Natur') has been translated into English by T. K. Abbott (*Kant's Critique of Practical Reason, and other works on the Theory of Ethics*, 1883, pp. 325–360).

[3] p. 36 f. (paginal references are given to Rosenkrantz and Schubert's edition).

[4] p. 28, § 1.

congruous with, and likely to illuminate, the conclusions which were reached in the last lecture. Unfortunately, however, Kant is obsessed by his conception of the Good as a Law, eternal and supersensible, which, in Troeltsch's phrase,[1] is the ' focus ' of the intelligible world, which, like the axioms of mathematics, carries its own authority within itself, and neither requires nor is capable of genetic explanation or logical proof : and his argument in consequence tends to move in the rarefied atmosphere and amongst the bloodless abstractions of metaphysics rather than upon the solid ground of ascertained psychological fact. This Law is communicated to man by the ' categorical imperative ' of conscience, and Virtue, or moral goodness, consists in the adoption by the individual man of the ' maxims,' or concrete universal commands, in which this law expresses itself, as the motives which determine the voluntary choice of the will. As we have seen, however, moral badness is, according to Kant, universally characteristic of mankind, manifesting itself in three stages or degrees which appear to represent three chronologically successive phases of the individual's growth. The first degree of moral badness is designated as ' frailty ' or ' weakness ' (Gebrechlichkeit), in which man recognises the authority of the good maxims but is unable to follow them, owing to the strength of his sensual nature. This condition seems to correspond exactly to Aristotle's ἀκρασία which, as we saw, is the moral state described by St. Paul in Rom. vii.[2] This is succeeded by the second degree of moral evil, which is ' impurity ' (Unlauterkeit), in which the individual does indeed conform his conduct to the dictates of the good maxims but from motives other than the only moral motive—namely, the pure desire to obey the moral law precisely and solely because it *is* the moral law. The third and final stage of moral badness, which Kant describes as ' depravity ' (Bösartigkeit), ' corruption ' (Verderbtheit), or ' perversity ' (Verkehrtheit), is reached when the individual experiences a conscious inclination to adopt as the motives of his conduct maxims which are positively contrary to the moral law (gesetzwidrige). When this state is reached human nature has displayed, in fully developed form, what he

[1] *ERE* ii. p. 657. [2] Lecture III, p. 145.

describes as the innate 'inclination to evil' (*Hang zum Bösen*) or 'radical evil.' These law-contradicting maxims arise out of the sensual nature of man, that is, out of the three primary instincts, egoistic, reproductive, and social. These are, indeed, not bad in themselves—Kant has no sympathy with the Augustinian idea of the essential wickedness of normal sex-feeling—and only become relatively bad when the desirability or necessity of their indulgence is exalted into a 'maxim,' endowed with such authority that it overrides the maxims arising out of the moral law. This inclination to evil, or tendency to adopt maxims dictated by the sensual nature in preference to those provided by the moral law, is expressly identified by Kant with 'original sin,' as understood by the only theology with which he was acquainted—namely, that of Prussian Lutheranism—though the fact that he uses the curious phrase *peccatum originarium* [1] instead of the more usual *peccatum originale* suggests that his familiarity with the official theology of his country was not much more intimate than his acquaintance with the interior of its churches.

So far this exposition of the problem appears to be not unreasonable, though, in the light of modern psychology, we shall naturally demur to the exceedingly abstract and transcendental account of the moral law which it embodies and to the attempt to represent the 'herd-instinct' not as the basis of the moral sentiment, but as something essentially separate from, and independent of, it. These, however, are not fatal objections and need not prevent us from pursuing the immediate object of our enquiry, which is that of examining Kant's conception of the Fall—that is, the source or ground of the inclination to evil. We must now draw attention to a further element in Kant's doctrine of original sin, which appears to have been simply taken over from Lutheranism without much effort to examine its intrinsic merits, to wit, the idea of 'original guilt.' Never having examined the monuments of Christian antiquity for himself, and taking the Confession of Augsburg for granted as the authoritative formulation of Christian anthropology, in much the same way that Anglican divines have been apt to take the Thirty-nine

[1] p. 34.

Articles for granted, Kant assumes that we are responsible for possessing an evil inclination, and justly deserve censure because of it.   But we can only be censured for that which proceeds from the exercise of our own free-will.   He therefore arrives at the frankly self-contradictory definition of original sin as a radical evil, inborn in human nature, which is none the less acquired by ourselves.[1]

It is doubtless true that the contradiction implicit in this definition is merely the reflection of the antinomy which we discover in our own moral experience, which both presents us with the idea of inborn evil as stronger than our own moral instinct and at the same time afflicts us with the consciousness of responsibility and guilt for every actual sin that we commit.   From a philosopher, however, who purports to explain religion within the bounds of mere reason we naturally demand a resolution of this antinomy, and it is in Kant's attempt to resolve it that we come face to face with his conception of the Fall.   The antinomy, we learn, between (a) the consciousness of an irresistible evil inclination and (b) the practically necessary postulate of freedom and responsibility, rests upon the dualism between the phenomenal and the noümenal self.   The phenomenal self, which is the sum of the actual contents of consciousness, the totality of the feelings, ideas and volitions which occupy the field of conscious experience, is part of the phenomenal world.   It is completely immersed in the time-series, an indisseverable portion of the causal nexus which stretches from eternity to eternity.   As such, it is rigidly and utterly determined, and from the point of view of pure reason, which can only legitimately function within the phenomenal sphere, freedom is an illusion.   But from the point of view of the practical reason, which is the guide of our moral life, freedom is an indispensable regulative principle which must consequently be assumed to belong to the noümenal self.   The contents of consciousness, indeed, are empirical, belonging to the world of sense and change, but consciousness itself, or rather the transcendent *ego* which is conscious of these contents, belongs to the world of things in themselves, which are the unknown causes of

[1] p. 33 f.

phenomena. From this it follows that 'original sin,' or the adoption of sensual maxims as the guiding principles of conduct, is due to a timeless, transcendental act of the noümenal self,[1] and that for Kant is 'the Fall'; or perhaps it would be more accurate to say that these transcendental acts committed by our noümenal selves constitute the Falls of man. For the philosopher of Königsberg, like Origen in his Alexandrine period,[2] abandons the idea of one single collective or representative Fall of all humanity, and finds in each man the Adam of his own soul. We will only observe in passing that this emergence of Origenistic ideas after fourteen centuries of obscuration by Augustinianism is not without significance; though, to avoid the charge of going further than the facts warrant, we must subjoin the qualifying statements that there is no reason for supposing that Kant had ever read Origen, and that the views of the later thinker differ from those of the earlier in this important respect—that Origen's Falls, though pre-natal, are strictly in time, whereas Kant's belong to the intelligible world, in which the form of perception known as time has *ex hypothesi* no validity.

Such is the first classical attempt to remove the Fall out of the sphere of History into the plane of transcendental truth, and to interpret it as the metaphysical ground rather than the temporal cause of the innate sinfulness of man. Daring as the attempt is, the criticisms to which it is open will be obvious. The conception of a 'timeless act' is one which seems to involve a contradiction in terms—at any rate if the word 'act' be used in that sense which it bears in ordinary usage. For it would seem that an act of the will necessarily implies change, if not in the external world, at least in the agent; it at least involves the idea of a transition on the part of the agent from a previous condition, either of inertia or of differently directed activity; and a transition is a change, and change involves time. The scholastic conception of the being of God as *purus actus* can hardly be adduced to support or illustrate the conceivability

---

[1] p. 34 : ' Jene (der Hang zum Bösen) ist intelligibile That, bloss durch Vernunft ohne alle Zeitbedingung erkennbar.'

[2] Lecture IV, pp. 210–219.

of a timeless act on the part of the human noümenal self ; because an act which is both an action and a state, an ἐνέργεια ἀκινησίας in which eternal activity and eternal repose are transcended and synthesised, can only be affirmed (if it can be affirmed at all) of the Absolute and Infinite Being Himself, and is not thinkable of the finite and relative selves of men, even when regarded *sub specie aeternitatis* as members of the intelligible world. If, then, we desire to penetrate deeply into the significance of Kant's language, so as to elicit from it a meaning which we can make real to ourselves, we seem shut up to one or other of two alternatives : either the ' timeless act ' is merely the intelligible aspect of man's concrete acts of evil-doing, the fact of actual sin seen, as it were, from above by God or by some hypothetical supra-temporal observer ; or the term ' act ' must in this connexion be taken to be simply equivalent to the term ' state ' or ' condition.' If we choose the former alternative, we are forced to conclude that Kant has totally failed to perform the feat which he has undertaken, namely, that of exhibiting to us the ground of actual sin ; for a mere ' aspect' cannot be the ground of the substantive reality of which it is an aspect, and it would seem that on this interpretation his alleged ' explanation ' of the ' evil heart ' which is present within man reduces itself to a mere feat of terminological jugglery. If, however, we take the term ' act ' to be simply the equivalent to the word ' state,' we are led to conclusions which are at first sight equally disappointing, though they contain a lesson which will in the long run prove a helpful contribution towards the development of our argument. If actual or ' derivative ' sin (*peccatum derivativum*) is the baneful efflorescence in time of an eternally evil state of the soul, it must not be forgotten that the ' categorical imperative ' of duty also springs from the timeless essence of the noümenal *ego*. It would seem, therefore, that evil and good exist side by side as eternally necessary principles in the intelligible world, to which the human soul in its higher aspect belongs. In other words, a very few logical steps have landed us in a highly refined philosophic Manicheism. Kant's attempt to lift the Fall out of the temporal order either amounts to nothing at all,

beyond mere verbal gymnastics, or it involves us in precisely
that Iranian dualism which is intolerable to the Christian
who starts from the Biblical idea of God as infinite both in
power and in goodness. It is possible that this conclusion
might not have appeared particularly disastrous to Kant,
inasmuch as for him God, like Freedom and Immortality, is
merely a regulative principle, which the necessities of the
moral life compel us to assume as a working hypothesis, but
which cannot merely on that account be certainly known
to correspond to any reality. But, for the Christian, to
whom God is a luminously self-evident fact of immediate
experience, whose yearnings are summed up in the words of
the Psalmist, ' Whom have I in heaven but thee ? and there
is none upon earth that I desire in comparison of thee ' [1]—
and for whom it would be impiety to admit the existence of
an evil power co-ordinate and co-eternal with God, these
speculations will stand condemned as soon as they are
formulated or uttered.

We pass to the consideration of the second great classical
attempt to provide religion with a purely metaphysical,
as opposed to a historical, conception of the Fall. This is
expounded, not systematically but by way of frequent
allusion, in the third part of Hegel's Philosophy of Religion.[2]
The problem of the moral struggle which, as we have seen,
is the fundamental psychological fact which has given birth
to all doctrines of ' original sin,' ' radical evil,' or ' inherited
infirmity,' is expressed by Hegel in his common dialectical
form of a superficially contradictory pair of propositions.
The thesis runs ' Man is good by nature ' ; there is in him at
least the promise and potency of harmony and interior peace.
Corresponding to this we have the antithesis ' Man is by
nature bad ' ; in actual life we see that he follows his passions
and impulses even when he knows that their indulgence is
harmful to himself. The synthesis is obtained by referring
the inherent goodness of man to his notion or essence, and
his badness to the conditions of concrete existence upon this

---

[1] Ps. lxxiii. 24.

[2] *Philosophie der Religion*, 3. Theil (*Die absolute Religion*), § II (*Das Reich des Sohnes*) : G. W. F. Hegel's Werke, Berlin, 1832, Band xii. pp. 204 ff.

planet. In the words of Dr. J. E. McTaggart, ' Hegel's doctrine of Original Sin is that man in his temporal existence on earth has in his nature a contingent and particular element, as well as a rational and universal element, and that while his nature is good in respect of the second it is bad in respect of the first.' [1] Now this necessary evil which belongs to man's concrete nature appears to be inherent in his existence as man at all; for, although the ' notion ' of man is good, it is only good potentially, and in order that this notion may realise itself it must necessarily pass into a condition of separation from, and consequently opposition to, the absolute system in which, as notion, it inheres. Hence the natural or animal condition of man prior to education and moral discipline—a condition usually described as ' innocence '—is evil precisely because it is natural; and, indeed, innocence on this showing is the greatest evil of all. Actual sin is indeed wrong, because it represents a deliberate purpose to remain in the animal stage after the possibility of a higher development has dawned upon the individual man; but it is less evil than innocence, which means ' incapability of moral choice.' To choose wrong, therefore, is, according to Hegel, better than not to choose at all, and the choice of right is, apparently, only possible after and by means of previous choice of wrong. The advance from innocence to virtue can only be through sin, because ascent from innocence can only be obtained by means of knowledge, and knowledge reveals the possibility of sin. A quotation will make this conception as plain as it is capable of being made.

It is knowledge which first brings out the contrast or antithesis in which evil is found; the animal, the stone, the plant, are not evil. Evil is first present within the sphere of knowledge; it is the consciousness of independent Being, or Being-for-self relatively to an Other, but also relatively to an object which is inherently universal in the sense that it is the notion or rational will. It is only by means of this separation that I exist independantly for myself, and it is in this that evil lies. To be evil means, in an abstract sense, to isolate myself.[2]

---

[1] *Studies in Hegelian Cosmology* (1901), p. 232.
[2] *op. cit.* (Berlin edition, xii. p. 216): ' Die Erkenntniss ist erst das Setzen des Gegensatzes, in dem das Böse ist. Das Thier, der Stein, die Pflanze ist nicht böse, das Böse ist erst innerhalb des Kreises der Erkennt-

Despite the elusive phraseology in which it is enshrined, this sequence of thought seems fairly clear. Evil is due to knowledge, and a pre-condition of knowledge is that separation of the individual man from the rest of the universe which is involved in his coming into being at all. But moral evil is nevertheless not so objectionable as mere innocence ; for a man who has committed sin has, in the words of Dr. McTaggart, ' at least started on the only road which can eventually lead him upwards.' [1]

It is not surprising to find that Hegel, whilst considering that the Paradise-story of Gen. iii. embodies a profound truth, regards the so-called Fall there narrated (or supposed to be narrated) as having been in reality a successful climb. When the Tempter promised man knowledge as the result of sin, he told the exact truth. ' The Serpent says that Adam will become like God, and God confirms the truth of this, and adds His testimony that it is this knowledge which constitutes likeness to God. This is the profound idea lodged in the narrative.' [2] For Hegel, then, the creation and the fall of man are identical ; they are simply different ways of describing the same event, and the ' Fall ' is also an ascent, for sin is the only road which ultimately leads to virtue. It is hardly necessary to observe that this treatment of sin is diametrically opposed to the Scriptural and Christian teaching, which regards wilful sin as infinitely hateful and loathsome. For the Christian no truly valuable end ever has been attained, or can be attained, by means of sin, which could not have been better attained without it. The acceptance of Hegel's presentation of the Fall-doctrine would have the effect of transforming Christianity into Gnosticism ; for he presupposes precisely that conception of a non-moral and impersonal Absolute, including both good and evil as moments in its infinite non-entity, which is the

---

niss vorhanden, es ist das Bewusstsein des Fürsichseins gegen anderes, aber auch gegen das Objekt, was in sich allgemein ist in dem Sinn des Begriffs, des vernünftigen Willens. Erst durch diese Trennung bin ich für mich und darin liegt das Böse. Bösesein heisst abstrakt, mich ver-einzeln . . .' etc.

[1] *op. cit.* p. 234.
[2] *op. cit.* p. 217 (freely translated and compressed).

basis of Hindu religious thought : and his conception of Redemption bases it upon knowledge.[1] Whilst then Kant, if interpreted seriously, leads us straight into the arms of one of the ancient foes of Jewish-Christian monotheism—namely, the dualism of Persia—Hegel hands us over to its other secular antagonist, the non-moral monism of India ; and we are therefore entitled to conclude that the feat which both claim to perform—namely, that of lifting the Fall out of the time-series into some timeless metaphysical plane, whilst yet leaving the rest of the Christian religion essentially intact—is one of which the achievement is in the nature of things impossible. In the world of thought, as in that of action, ' Things are what they are, and their consequences will be what they will be.' No amount of dialectical ingenuity can nullify or even soften the inexorable rigour of the issue, as it was perceived by the Jews of old with the clearness which comes not of speculative power but of passionate religious devotion. If God is infinite in power, dualism is intolerable, and if infinite in goodness, monism not less so ; the origin of evil must therefore be sought in the world of created being, and within the sphere of time[2] and contingency.

We conclude, then, that the attempts made by the two giants of German philosophy, Kant and Hegel, to provide us with a ' Fall ' which shall be neither temporal nor contingent are, from the point of view of the believer in the Christian God, the God of the Bible and of Jesus, worthless. But a theory which proves to have no intrinsic value may possess an accidental and adventitious importance as a floating cork or straw, revealing the direction of some deep natural current of thought, which invisibly and impalpably determines the conscious speculative tendencies of a given period. I called attention just now to the fact that Kant's theory of the radical evil in human nature, as grounded upon an incalculable number of wrong decisions made on the

---

[1] *op. cit.* p. 217 : ' Die Erkenntniss ist das Princip der Geistigkeit, die aber, wie gesagt, auch das Princip der Heilung des Schadens der Trennung ist.'

[2] On the question whether the Fall-theory involves belief in the ultimate reality of Time, *v. infra*, p. 523 n. 2.

supersensible plane by our noümenal selves—in other words, on millions of separate and individual ' falls '—was reminiscent of the hypothesis put forward by Origen in his first or Alexandrine period, the hypothesis of a series of individual pre-natal falls.[1] I do not know of any evidence for supposing that Kant had ever read Origen, and it is probable that there is no direct relation of dependence between the earlier and the later thinker. But this reproduction by Kant of one aspect of Origen's thought, fortuitous though it may have been, is symptomatic of much. It means that with the collapse of what had hitherto been the all-powerful Augustinian doctrine, which had for thirteen centuries banked up the stream of Fall-speculation, the main current of thought on this subject tended to find its way once more into the old and long dry channels which had been provisionally cut out for it some sixteen centuries previously by the genius of Origen. It is not too much to say that if a single phrase be required for summing up the really progressive and valuable movements of Christian anthropology and hamartiology which took place during the nineteenth century, that phrase must be ' Away from Augustine, and back to Origen.'

This tendency shows itself with even greater clearness in what is perhaps the most exhaustive and laborious treatment of the Christian doctrine of sin which has ever been published, the monumental treatise written some seventy years ago by the learned Lutheran divine, Dr. Julius Müller.[2] Müller realised that there is no strictly historical evidence for the Fall, and that the belief in such an event can only be based upon a priori reasoning, which starts from the fact of the moral struggle. Like Kant he finds the root of original sin in the fact, or supposed fact, that whereas the tendency towards sin is universal, ' interwoven with human nature and, as it were, rooted therein,' yet we feel ourselves, and really are, responsible and culpable for its existence. (It will be noticed that Müller is prevented by his Lutheran orthodoxy from breaking decisively with that indefensible

---

[1] See Lecture IV, p. 210 ff.
[2] E. tr., *The Christian Doctrine of Sin*, 2 vols., Edinburgh, 1852.

Augustinian conception of original guilt, which has done so much to confuse and discredit the clear, reasonable, and fundamentally Christian idea of the inherited infirmity.) In order to solve this contradiction, which need never have existed but for Augustine, he follows the guidance of Kant, taking over the dualism which the latter had established between the phenomenal and the noümenal selves. He sees, however, the two difficulties which were raised just now in our critical examination of the Kantian theory— namely, the unintelligibility of the idea of a ' timeless act,' and the lack of any logical ground for the universality of the supposed extra-temporal wrong decision. He therefore endeavours to emend the Kantian theory so as to eliminate both of these flaws. He gets rid of the difficulties inherent in the idea of extra-temporal falls by (in effect) putting the Falls back into the time-series. It is true that so far as words are concerned he strenuously denies that he is doing this ; but it is impossible to attach any other significance to his description of the fall of the individual soul as occurring in a mode of existence which *precedes* life on this planet.[1] If words have any meaning at all, the tell-tale prefix '*pre-*' obstinately resists all attempts to strip it of its temporal reference, and we must suppose that the heavenly or noümenal life from which man has descended, though doubtless in every other way of a transcendental and incomprehensible nature, is nevertheless as completely enclosed in the framework of temporal succession as is the life which we now live in this vale of tears. The second difficulty, that of accounting for what appears at first sight to be the remarkable coincidence that all men have in point of fact made a wrong decision in their pre-natal lives, is accounted for on strictly Origenistic lines. Origen's solution of this problem, which was noticed in our fourth lecture, and which cannot be denied the merit of considerable

---

[1] *Cf. op. cit.* ii. p. 400 : ' This were now a manifest contradiction, if there were not (timelessly) *preceding* our earthly temporal existence of our personality, as the sphere of that self-decision, by which our moral condition from the beginning is conditioned ' ; p. 401 : ' the recognition of a primitive fall preceding the individual time-life.' I have not been able to verify these passages in the original, but I assume that the translator has not done Müller an injustice.

ingenuity, is this : all men are fallen, and have the tendency towards evil in them, precisely because only those spirits who fell in the heavenly sphere were banished to earth and became incarnate, as human beings. Perhaps it would be more exact to say that only those spirits who sinned venially in the intelligible world become incarnate as men : for Müller is disposed to believe in the real existence of devils, who must presumably be regarded as spirits who sinned more grievously than those condemned to inhabit human bodies, and who, therefore, have been banished to an even lower plane of existence (a thoroughly Origenistic idea). The spirits who did not make a wrong decision continued, and presumably still continue, to exist in the heavenly sphere as angels. In other words, we are not fallen because we are men ; on the contrary, we are men because we are fallen ; and this accounts for the universality of the fallen condition. Müller's Lutheranism makes him nervously anxious to disclaim all sympathy with Origenism, but the differences which he discovers between his own theory and that of the Alexandrine thinker do not appear to be of any great moment. He also endeavours, quite unnecessarily from the point of view of logic, to find room for something like a historical fall of Adam and Eve; but, as the supposed historical sin of our first parents must, in accordance with his main theory, be attributed to pre-creational transgressions on their part, the story of Gen. iii. is really, though he will not admit it, nothing but an otiose excrescence upon the main fabric of his theory.

The theory we have just sketched will doubtless appear to many as unnecessarily elaborate and fantastic, and as partaking equally with the old-fashioned scheme of a fall of Lucifer, succeeded after an indefinite interval by a fall of Adam, in the nature of mythology. But the theory of a pre-natal Fall of individual souls is not one that can be dismissed at first sight as inherently improbable. It enjoys at the moment a certain measure of popularity as being an element in the fashionable cult of theosophy. A well-known philosophic teacher has declared that, in his opinion, there are no arguments for the immortality of the soul after death which would not equally well establish its pre-existence before birth.[1] The hypothesis of a number of individual pre-natal Falls certainly seems fully capable of performing that essential function of the Fall doctrine which is its only *raison d'être*—namely, that of relieving God from responsibility for the origin of evil. It is true that the weight of such *auctoritas* as may be deemed to belong to the language of Scripture, and the almost unanimous consensus of Christian antiquity, is on the side of a single, collective, and racial Fall rather than an undefined number of individual falls ; and, if we were to conclude that this latter conception represents the most probable account of the origin of evil in man, we should necessarily be obliged to revise the definitions which we gave of ' original sin ' in Lecture VII, and substitute for the word ' inherited,' as a qualification of the substantive ' weakness of will ' or ' infirmity of herd-complex,' the adjective ' innate.' But the theory of individual falls has never been explicitly condemned by any authority which English Churchmen can recognise as having a right to the august title of oecumenical. It will therefore not be waste of time if we devote a few words to the task of examining this theory in regard to its intrinsic merits.

When we are faced by the hypothesis of a pre-natal existence, our first impulse is to ask ' What, precisely, is conceived as pre-existing ? ' It is natural to assume that the advocates of this hypothesis mean to assert that the entire human spirit, endowed at least in potentiality with the whole structure of ' instincts ' and ' sentiments ' which was described in our last lecture, pre-existed. But much of this instinctive structure is connected with the functions of the physical organism, and would be meaningless and purposeless apart from it. And all of it, in the generalised form under which we sketched it, is ordinarily assumed by psychology to be given by heredity ; the old controversy between creationism and traducianism which we noticed in our review of patristic opinion has for all practical purposes ended in the victory of the latter.[2] If this assumption

---

[1] Dr. J. E. McTaggart, *Some Dogmas of Religion* (1906), ch. iv. ' Human pre-existence,' p. 113. For other supporters of or sympathisers with the doctrine in recent times, see W. R. Inge, *The Philosophy of Plotinus* (1918), ii. p. 31.

[2] *v. supra*, Lecture IV, p. 237 n. 3.

of psychology corresponds to fact—and in the absence of direct evidence to the contrary it is reasonable to assume that it does—we can only conclude that nothing of the soul existed before its birth into this world except a pure form, empty of any content, an *ego* which possessed merely the potentiality of self-consciousness without any self of which to be conscious. It is difficult to see how such a naked and vacuous pre-existent *ego*, with no instincts to control, and no sentiments to resist or modify, could ' sin ' at all, or how such an abstract pre-existence differs from that merely ideal existence in the thoughts of God which will be conceded to all souls even by the most convinced supporters of a historic Adam. It would, then, seem that, if we are to make the conception of a pre-natal sin intelligible at all, we must regard the pre-existent soul as a monad or atom of soul-stuff, containing the potentiality of its fully developed adult structure, much as the acorn contains the germ and potency of an oak. This, of course, means that the conception of heredity in every department of life is a pure illusion, and that the apparent transmission of such qualities as (to quote two instances at random) mathematical genius or moral imbecility from parent to child is really due to a ' pre-established harmony ' between the developmental capacities of a pair of successively incarnate monads. This is no doubt a thinkable theory ; it is always possible to substitute a pre-established harmony for direct causation in all spheres of thought, from the most abstract and ideal down to the most brute and mechanical, given sufficient determination and ingenuity ; just as it would probably still be possible to explain the apparent movements of the heavenly bodies in accordance with the Ptolemaic astronomy, given unlimited liberty to employ an indefinite number of cycles and epi-cycles. But, though such a hypothesis is not inherently impossible, it becomes inconceivably cumbrous and complicated the moment any attempt is made to explain human history in accordance with it ; and it is not illegitimate to suggest that William Occam's ' razor,' which cuts at the root of all unnecessary multiplication of entities, will prove to possess an equally trenchant edge when turned against the indefinite multiplication of causalities.

It may be further urged against this theory that it involves a view of human life and conditions of existence on this planet so profoundly pessimistic as to make us doubt whether the hypothesis of pre-natal falls has not already tumbled into that abyss of Manicheism, on the edge of which, as we have already seen, the doctrine of original sin is perpetually trembling. According to the Hebrew Scriptures the world, as God made it, is good, and a pleasant thing it is to behold the sun ; but according to the ' pre-natal ' theory, this life is a purgatory and a tearful prison-house, in which the soul expiates a sin of which she no longer possesses even the bare memory ; and it is difficult to see how Christian parents could rejoice that a man is born into the world if they were under the necessity of regarding their new-born offspring as a small culprit who had just been banished from the intelligible sphere in consequence of some gross defiance of the majesty of God. Whilst, therefore, we are not prepared to pronounce dogmatically that Origen's first theory as revived by Julius Müller is inherently impossible, or directly unorthodox, its melancholy implications and its complicated structure justify us in leaving it on one side, and in searching for some theory which will both be free from these objections and also will be more harmonious with the general tenor of Scripture and tradition, and with our instinctive consciousness of the essential, and not merely accidental, unity and solidarity of the human race.

For the sake of clearness we will briefly resume the substance of our argument up to this point. We saw that the collapse of the rigid Augustinian system naturally brought about a reversion, conscious or unconscious, to the Origenistic method of dealing with the problem of the Fall, and a concentration of interest upon the ultimate transcendent origin of evil rather than upon the first of its manifestations in human history, the so-called Fall of Man. But our examination of the theories propounded by Kant and Hegel showed that for believers in the Biblical and Christian idea of God, which I have assumed, without apology, all through these lectures, even this ultimate fall must still be conceived as a member of the time-series ; for any attempt to lift the ultimate origin of evil out of Time plunges us into the gulfs either of dualism or of unmoral monism. And we have just seen reason for regarding the hypothesis which polarises the Fall into an indefinite multiplicity of pre-natal individual falls as open to grave suspicions of the same nature. Of the conceptions, therefore, which have emerged in the course of our enquiry, that which seems to offer the most attractive field for our exploration is the conception of a collective fall of the race-soul of humanity in an indefinitely remote past.[1] But this tentative adumbration of a conclusion probably represents the most we can extract with safety from the purely *a priori* trains of reasoning of which we have made use so far ; and at this juncture it will be well to change our method of approach to the problem, and see if body and substance can be given to this attractive vision by means of *a posteriori* evidence, derived from an examination of the world as we actually know it to be, in the light of that Darwinian revolution in thought and knowledge which the eyes of the great German philosophers were never destined to see.

If, then, we turn our backs on the fascinating but mysterious realm of metaphysics, and bend our gaze upon that vast evolutionary panorama in which the history of this planet and of our race has been depicted by the genius of modern science, we shall naturally concentrate our attention, first of all, upon the facts which have now been ascertained about the origin of man, in so far as they are relevant to our purpose. In this connexion, it is unnecessary to do more than repeat an observation already made, namely, that Augustinianism, with its theory of a Paradisal condition of original perfection, cannot possibly be dovetailed into the picture of a gradual ascent from gross and brutish beginnings which is given us by geology and biology.[2]

---

[1] Coleridge seems to hint at some such theory when he speaks of a ' Spiritual Fall or Apostasy antecedent to the formation of Man ' (*Aids to Reflection*, London, 1836, Aphorism X, p. 285).

[2] Mr. H. J. T. Johnson (*Anthropology and the Fall*, 1923), writing from the Roman Catholic standpoint, does not attempt to adduce any positive evidence for the hypothesis of ' original righteousness,' and is content to argue that science has not *dis*proved the essential positions of Latin theology with regard to the state of the first men, positions which for him are based upon revelation. But, in the last resort, his only ground for thinking that the alleged ' revelation ' *is* a revelation is the authority of the Roman Church.

Few Christian thinkers will now attempt to identify the protoplast of Augustine's imagination with the original owner of the Piltdown skull, none with *pithecanthropus erectus*. In so far as the traditional Christian doctrine of man involves any affirmation about the historic state of the first men at all, it is clear that the only version of this doctrine which has the faintest chance of surviving in the modern world is that taught by the primitive Greek Fathers, which regards the protoplast as a babe, a frail, undeveloped, ignorant creature, and views the first human sin rather as a *praevaricatio*—a stepping-aside from the true line of upward progress—than as a *lapsus* or fall from a high level of moral and intellectual endowment.[1] But this conception of a ' first sin ' needs somewhat closer examination than we have hitherto been able to devote to it. It is very doubtful whether, if we could travel back into the past, on some Time-machine, like that imagined by Mr. H. G. Wells, and observe the whole history of the origins of our race—from a point in Time at which it was certain no human creature existed upon the earth at all, to the point (let us say) at which the race of Neanderthal finally disappeared before the conquering march of the men of Cromagnon—we should be able to lay our finger upon any one single event which could be described as a ' first sin ' at all. The idea of sin presupposes the existence both of self-consciousness and of a developed moral sentiment, built up upon that primitive ' herd-instinct ' of which the deficiency constitutes the innate infirmity ; and the development of both of these cardinal facts, self-consciousness and the moral sentiment, must have been such a slow, gradual and continuous process, that even if we possessed the fullest knowledge in regard to its actual course it would still appear entirely arbitrary to draw a line across it and label all acts disapproved of by the ' herd ' as non-moral accidents on one side of the line, and as moral offences or ' sins ' on the other. We can only say that there was a time, doubtless to be counted by aeons, during which the moral consciousness had not dawned on this planet, and that there was—and now is—an age of responsibility, and conscious ethical obligation. But in regard to the question

---

[1] *v. supra*, Lecture IV, pp. 253, 302.

how the former age passed into the latter, we can only confess ourselves to be totally ignorant ; and all analogy suggests that the transition was mediated, not by a sudden flash of moral illumination, succeeded by a single act in which man turned his back upon the new light, but rather by a period of twilight during which the lineaments of the animal slowly melted into the human, the faint glow of potential self-consciousness which smouldered in the brains of our simian ancestors grew in brightness, consistency, and firmness, and the gregarious impulse which had kept the ancient hunting-pack together gradually flowered in the idea of a communal law and in a rudimentary sense of ethical and tribal obligation.

It might be urged as a counterbalancing consideration that the continuity of evolution in no way prejudices the real distinctness of the main stages passed through by the evolving organism, a distinctness which is self-evident if a pair of such phases be mentally held together for purposes of comparison. The process whereby the child grows into a boy, the boy into an adolescent, the adolescent into a man, manifests this precise quality of smoothness and unbroken continuity. It is impossible, except for legal purposes and on the basis of arbitrary convention, to point to a single date in the calendar at which a given individual ceases to be a youth and becomes a man. But, nevertheless, common sense affirms that there is a time after which it is reasonable and necessary to treat a given individual as being, in point of fact, an adult man, though it may not be possible to say exactly when he attained to this status or how long he has enjoyed it. So it might be urged, with regard to the human race as a whole, that—however long the crepuscular period of semi-humanity and semi-bestiality may have lasted— there must have been a definite date at which it would have been possible for an extra-terrestrial observer to say ' Now, at least, whatever it may have been before, this race of advanced biped mammals must be regarded as having become fully self-conscious and morally responsible.' It would, therefore, be theoretically possible, if we possessed the requisite knowledge, to lay our finger upon some primitive action, and say ' This, at least, may be certainly desig-

the innate deficiency of herd-instinct on which we have fixed as the root of moral weakness, and which would appear to have been characteristic of man from the moment when he first becomes recognisable as a strictly moral and responsible agent, is to be regarded as having been inherited directly from his pre-human ancestors.   There seems no reason for returning an affirmative answer to this question.   There is no evidence to show that the *hominidae* or anthropoid animals, who were the immediate progenitors of the human race, were any less loyal as individuals to the hunting-packs or hordes in which they were associated than the hyenas or the wolves of the present day.   The fact is that when we speak of ' defective herd-instinct,' we mean ' defective ' relatively to the exacting, penetrating and intimate demands of the modern herd, whether we think of this as Church, or State, or civilised society in general, or the whole world of moral beings summed up in God.   What is wrong with the average man, as distinct from the criminal, on the one side, and the saint who has won his way to settled and permanent virtue, on the other, is that although a member of a complex society, which claims the allegiance of his innermost thoughts and feelings, he yet possesses only so much strength of herd-instinct as was sufficient to enable his sub-human ancestors to fulfil the simple and elementary requirements of the primitive horde.   Hence, in every age of human development the innate weakness of herd-instinct is relative to existing social conditions, and its immediate origin is to be attributed, not to a deprivation of something which man once possessed, but rather to an *arrested develop- ment*.   Whereas self-consciousness and intellectual power have during the ages increased enormously in scope and clearness, thus revealing more and more opportunities of indulging the instincts connected with self and sex, there has been no corresponding development of the social instinct, or of the moral sentiment which should grow out of it. We can therefore enlarge and enrich our definition of the inherited infirmity by describing it as ' arrested develop- ment ' of the herd-instinct.   And this conclusion takes us a step further back in our investigation of the origins of evil in man.   We must postulate some unknown factor or agency which interfered to arrest the development of corporate feeling, just when man was becoming man, some mysterious and maleficent influence which cut into the stream of the genetic evolution of our race at some point during the twilit age which separates pre-human from human history. It would seem, then, that the negative pre-condition of sin in man, the *privatio* or mutilation which we have found to consist in relatively defective or atrophied herd-instinct, points to a positive or substantive power which at the moment we can only describe as an unknown x representing evil, or the potentiality of evil, as it existed in the nature of things before man was. This provisional conclusion may appear disappointingly vague ; but it must be expected that the more deeply we penetrate into the tunnel of the past and the further we leave behind the daylight of recorded history, the more general and indefinite our judgments are bound to become.

The history of man's immediate ancestors is involved in such obscurity that it throws no light upon the nature of this positive evil factor, and it would seem as though our exploration had been brought to a standstill by a blank wall. If, however, we follow the lead given by the prince and master of all Christian Fall-speculators, the Apostle St. Paul, we shall, I think, be able to find a way round the obstacle It was shown in our third lecture that, for St. Paul, evil in man is closely connected with the pain and suffering and waste of life which reigns in sub-human nature.[1] The Apostle, indeed, regards the former as the direct cause of the latter, echoing the Jewish speculations which had sought to explain evil in nature by the naïve supposition that the Almighty deliberately infuriated the previously tame and gentle animal tribes in order to provide an uncomfortable environment for man as part of the punishment for his sin. This conception, in its literal form, is impossible for us because we know that the strong preyed upon the weak, that ' tooth and claw ' were ' red with ravin,' and that the ' dragons of the prime . . . tare each other in their slime,' millions of years before our race was born. But it is perfectly possible, and, indeed, necessary,

[1] p. 157.

word. And, superficially regarded, this consideration may appear to relieve the problem of evil in nature of some of its oppressive weight. There is much evil amongst the brutes, but (with the possible exception of some of those higher animals which, through their domestication by man, seem to have acquired the germ of a moral faculty) they are free from sin. The cat which tortures the mouse by playing with it ; the wasp which deftly stings the living caterpillar in the chief ganglia of its spinal cord, so as to keep it, paralysed, as a store of fresh food for her young ; the microbe which destroys a life that might have been the source of un-numbered blessings to the human race ; and that most uncanny manifestation of the spirit of evil in nature—the insectivorous plant, which with cold and Mephistophelean ferocity disguises its death-dealing petals in the form of more innocent blossoms so as to allure and entrap its unwary victims : all these perform functions which are evil in the sense that they rouse the detestation of the refined moral consciousness in man ; but they are free from guilt, they commit no sin, because they are but blindly following the fundamental law of their being.

Yet the problem is only lightened in appearance, for the guiltlessness of the brutes merely emphasises the apparent guilt of Nature, which has made them what they are. If savagery and cruelty are the expressions of a fundamental law, how evil must be that law, and how deep its discordance with the will of the all-loving Creator revealed by Christ, Who clothes the lilies of the field, and without Whom not one sparrow falls to the ground. If we face the facts candidly, we must admit that no one of us, if he had been in the position of Demiurge, would have created a universe which was compelled by the inner necessity of its being to evolve the cobra, the tarantula, and the bacillus of diphtheria. How, then, shall that God, the infinite ardours and pulsations of Whose love bear the same relation to our weak emotions of sympathy and fellow-feeling as the infinity of His wisdom does to our dim and limited knowledge, have done so ? The answer can only be that He did not do so ; that He did not create such a universe ; that, in the words of the most ancient scriptures of our monotheistic faith, in the beginning

'God saw every thing that he had made, and, behold, it was very good.'[1]   To explain evil in Nature, no less than in man, we are compelled to assume a Fall—a revolt against the will of the Creator, a declension from the beauty and glory which God stamped upon His work at the beginning.   And, to account for the vast and intimate diffusion of evil, selfishness and hate amongst all the multitudinous tribes of living creatures, we must place this ultimate Fall, which the argument contained in the first part of this lecture compels us to regard as an event in Time, at a point before the differentiation of life into its present multiplicity of forms and the emergence of separate species.   We must summon to our aid the great conception first elaborated by the Stoics under the title of the 'Logos Spermatikos' or 'seminal reason,' and more recently reformulated, in the light of modern biological conceptions, by M. Bergson under the name of the *élan vital*, the Life-Force which is the immediate ground of our own being as of that of all the multitudinous creatures of the universe.   If we can assume that there was a pre-cosmic vitiation of the whole Life-Force, when it was still one and simple, at a point of time[2] prior to its bifurcation and ramification into a manifold of distinct individuals or entelechies, we shall be in possession of a conception which should explain, so far as explanation is

---

[1] Gen. i. 31.   Unfortunately we cannot add, with Goethe's archangels (in the Prologue to the first part of *Faust*) :

> 'Und alle deine hohen Werke
> Sind herrlich wie am ersten Tag.'

[2] It may be asked at this point 'Does such a transcendental Fall-doctrine necessitate the assumption of the ultimate reality of Time?' The answer would seem to be in the negative.   The doctrine of the Fall does, indeed, imply that the created universe is in Time ; it may, indeed, be taken to involve the assumption that there is what may be called for human purposes an 'absolute' Time or duration, of which the times relative to different percipients or groups of percipients are imperfect and distorted copies.   But such an 'absolute Time' would only be absolute within the realm of created being ; it could have no reference to the eternal Essence of God, Who is the supreme and timeless Reality.   The version of the doctrine of the Fall suggested above does not, therefore, involve the attribution of a higher degree of reality to Time than to the created world of which Time is a dimension ; it ascribes no more than a phenomenal reality to either ; and it is amply consistent with the Platonic and Augustinian position that the world was created, not in Time, but together with Time.

posed condition of palaeolithic man, the idea of 'original righteousness' may be usefully employed.[1]

The World-Soul, then, was created good ; but, our theory must continue, at the beginning of Time, in some transcendental and incomprehensible manner, it turned away from God and in the direction of Self, thus shattering its own interior being, which depended upon God for its stability and coherence, and thereby forfeiting its unitary self-consciousness, which it has only regained, after aeons of myopic striving, in sporadic fragments which are the separate minds of men and perhaps of superhuman spirits. It is not necessary to assume, with Plotinus and Gregory of Nyssa, that the existence of our limited and imperfect consciousness represents a *pis-aller*, an unsatisfactory substitute for the one first-created world-consciousness ; if speculation may be carried so far, we may surmise that the cosmic consciousness was meant from the beginning to develop within itself smaller individual consciousnesses without in any way prejudicing its own unity, and so that if it had developed in accordance with the plan pre-ordained by its Creator, it would have been the ideal society or community, endowed with a corporate mind which would have transcended, without mutilating or repressing the minds of its

---

[1] It will not have escaped the reader's notice that the speculative reconstruction of the Fall-doctrine suggested in the text bears certain resemblances to that expounded by St. Gregory of Nyssa in *de hom. opif.*, and commented on in Lecture IV, pp. 270 ff. Our 'World-Soul' corresponds to his 'archetypal man,' numerically one and endowed with original perfection ; though of course the World-Soul must be conceived as including the potentiality of all life, supra- and sub-human as well as human. On occasions when the use of pictorial language is pedagogically desirable, there seems no reason why the World-Soul should not be described as 'Adam,' 'the Man,' הָאָדָם : the assertion of the 'original righteousness' of 'Adam' would thus cease to be a mere Rabbinical figment, and would become a mythological way of expressing a necessary inference from ethical monotheism. The Greek fancy of an extra-terrestrial or even metaphysical 'Paradise' (*v. supra*, pp. 193, 216) might also be re-utilised in an allegorical presentation of our theory. And, like Gregory, we regard the break-up of the intellectual unity of the general Soul as due to the Fall, though (as stated above) we are very far from regarding multiplicity as in itself evil, and have no sympathy with his semi-Manichean view of sex. The affinity of our conception with the ideas of Origen will be obvious ; and the last paragraph of this lecture suggests the kind of 'Recapitulation'-theory to which it would naturally lead up.

individual members. On this supposition it would seem natural to suppose that the Fall wrecked the unity of the world-consciousness, reducing the cosmic soul to a stream of blind and internally discordant effort, and delaying for millions of years the appearance of conscious individual personalities. In our own infirm wills and circumscribed intelligences, and in the efforts which our race has made to develop sympathy and fellowship through families, tribes, nations, and the still shadowy and embryonic World-State or League of Nations, we may trace the instinctive strivings of the dissociated World-Soul to recover, in all its noonday brightness, the unitary self-consciousness that it had at the beginning.

However this may be, we can at least feel sure that this interior self-perversion, which we have hypothetically attributed to the collective Life-Force which was God's primal creature—this orientation away from God and in the direction of ruthless self-assertion—would necessarily manifest itself in a development of organic life permeated through and through with the spirit of selfishness, manifested in ferocious competition and in a bloodthirsty struggle for existence. It might *a priori* have been expected to appear in the cruelty which ravages the animal world, in the unknown maleficent factor which hindered the due development of herd-instinct just when the anthropoids were becoming men, and in the mysterious ebullitions of pure fiendishness which, within the sphere of responsible human action, are known as 'criminality.' If, in harmony with later Jewish and primitive Christian thought, and with the consensus of those who are known as 'spiritual experts' in every age of the newer dispensation, we are prepared to admit the existence of evil discarnate intelligences, it would doubtless follow that the malevolent nature of such beings was to be regarded as the outcome of the pre-mundane Fall of that World-Soul, of which they, equally with men and beasts, would be the offspring. A place could thus be found in this provisional scheme for the idea which has been expressed in mythological form as the Fall of Lucifer and the apostate angels; though on this showing the fall of the angels would be parallel to and collateral with the fall, or rather the failure, of Man, and need not be (though we know too little about these matters to deny that it may have been) its direct cause or chronological antecedent.

For such a hypothesis it may be claimed that, if we are prepared to make allowances for the vagueness and the indefiniteness of its outline, and for the many lacunae which the imperfection of our knowledge, and the uncertainty of *a priori* speculation, render inevitable, it explains better than any other existing theory the existence and the wide diffusion of evil in a universe which, as Christians, we believe to have been created by an all-powerful, all-wise, and all-loving God. And for those who recognise that a religion which claims to be ' Catholic ' or universal, in an intensive, as well as in an extensive, sense, is thereby endowed with the right, and subject to the duty, to make use of categories and thought-forms drawn from any source for the elucidation of its fundamental ideas, it will not appear an objection to this view that it has certain affinities with the thought of the great Neo-Platonist and mystic Plotinus, who makes the World-Soul, the divine ψυχή, the third member of his Trinity. But, in the light of the Christian revelation, we are constrained to diverge decisively from him with regard to two points. In the first place, the World-Soul for us is a created being, not an element in, a part of, or a necessary emanation from, the Godhead. This position is so self-evidently involved in those Biblical conceptions of God as Creator and as infinitely good, which have been taken for granted all through this discussion, that I need not dilate upon it further. Secondly, whereas Plotinus seems to find the origin of evil in the wilful self-detachment of the human soul from the World-Soul,[1] we find the Fall in the voluntary deviation of the World-Soul from conformity with the will of the Creator ; and we cannot but feel that if Plotinus and Origen had possessed our modern realisation, induced by the scientific study of nature, of the vast diffusion of evil outside of, and apart from, the realm of specifically human life, they would have been constrained to agree with us in enlarging

---

[1] Cf. *Enn.* i. 8, 4, *ad fin.* For Plotinus' not always consistent views with regard to the descent of the soul, and its relation to the Universal Soul, see W. R. Inge, *The Philosophy of Plotinus*, i. p. 254.

the subject of the Fall, that is, the personal being who fell, beyond the confines of Man, individually or collectively regarded, until it becomes conterminous with the totality of organic life.

Yet though for us the World-Soul is erring and sinful, created and not divine, we are constrained by the historic Christian revelation to recognise a certain profound and intimate connexion between the created Life-Force of the universe and the eternal Logos of God, the express image of His substance, Who upholds all things by the word of His power and in Whom all things consist. This connexion was meant to consist in the continuous penetration, inspiration, and guidance of the created *anima mundi* by the Almighty and uncreated Logos : and the rebellion of the former has not banished the patiently working, healing, and refining influences of the latter. Even in marred and vitiated Nature much goodness still survives ; many of the dumb beasts may well put our arrogant race to shame by their gentleness, their humility, their love of their offspring, their devotion to their human masters. Such facts as these may embolden us to believe that, long ages before man was, the Spirit of Christ was at work in the world, sustaining the blinded Life-Force, which otherwise would have lapsed into nothingness, fostering within it the potentialities of goodness and love, combating those elements which made for selfishness and cruelty, and leading it slowly and gently back towards the recovery of its original harmony, peace, and unified self-consciousness. And when the cosmic Soul had so far progressed along the upward path as to be able to find expression in Man, the eternal Logos was present in his birth, assisting and inspiring the growth of reason, will, and social or gregarious feeling. Nor, when our race had finally failed to extricate itself from the pre-existing stream of selfish tendency, and was seen still to bear within it, deeply stamped upon its fundamental plasm, the lack of love and weakness of social instinct which were the legacy of the primal Fall, did the immanent Word of God withdraw from it His interior inspiration : the long line of pre-Christian prophets, saints, and sages, in whom the fire of man's highest aspirations has shone with clear and steady flame,

testifies to the benign and pervasive influences of that Light
which lighteth every man, as it cometh into the world.   In
the fullness of time, the gracious Power which had guided
man so far deigned to enter into an even closer bond with our
race, and through it with the fallen World-Soul, by uniting
humanity to His divinity :

> And so the Word had breath, and wrought
> With human hands the creed of creeds.

Yet not by mere example, or by ' loveliness of perfect deeds '
alone did He design to heal the inherited weakness of human
nature, but also by forming a sacramental society which
would be the extension of His personal being, within which
the defect of love, of social feeling, of gregariousness, of
' herd-instinct '—it matters not how it be named—might
be remedied through the direct transfusion into our souls
of His own self-sacrificed life.   This is the point to which
our revised formulation of the doctrines of the Fall and
of Original Sin has naturally led us, and at which we may
well be content to leave it.   In the completion of the
eternal Christ Who all in all is being fulfilled—in that
summing up and recapitulation in Him, not only of all
humanity but of all forms of created being, in their countless hierarchical gradations, whether things on earth or
things in heaven—all individual spirits will have grown
to their full stature, the perfection of their fellowship will
express itself in the redintegrated consciousness of the
general Soul, the Redemption which is the predestined
sequel of the Fall will be for ever consummated, and the
regenerated universe, in all its multitudinous members, will
know the full meaning of the mystic paradox—' O felix culpa,
quae talem et tantum meruit habere Redemptorem.'

ADDITIONAL NOTE E

DR. F. R. TENNANT'S ALTERNATIVE THEORY OF THE ORIGIN OF SIN

' To the evolutionist sin is not an innovation, but is the survival
or misuse of habits and tendencies that were incidental to
an earlier stage in development, whether of the individual or the

race, and were not originally sinful, but were actually useful. Their sinfulness lies in their anachronism : in their resistance to the evolutionary and Divine force that makes for moral development and righteousness.' [1]   These words, quoted by Dr. Tennant from an address delivered to the Church Congress of 1896 by Archdeacon J. M. Wilson, contain nothing which we desire to contradict : though the argument of Lecture VII has endeavoured to supplement them by exhibiting ' the evolutionary and Divine force that makes for righteousness ' as manifested in the growth and development of ' herd-instinct,' social feeling, and love. Dr. Tennant, however, (if I have rightly grasped the argument of his third and fourth Hulsean Lectures,) appears to consider these words to be, not a statement, but the solution of the problem of the origin of sin.   In so far as the empirical universality of sin is a fact, he finds the explanation of this fact in the chronological priority of feeling, impulse, and instinct to conscience in the historical order both of the race's and of the individual's evolution.   The moral consciousness experiences difficulty and pain in disciplining appetite and impulse, because the moral consciousness itself is a late arrival in the house of human personality.   This I take to be the gist of his third lecture, expressed in such a sentence as this : ' The foundation from which we start is the fact already asserted of the race and now to be repeated of the individual, that we are natural *before* we are moral beings, and that the impulses of our nature are in full sway *before* the moral consciousness begins to dawn ' [2] (italics ours).   The result of this temporal priority of instinct to the ethical sense is that sin must be regarded as ' something empirically inevitable for every man ' though by no means ' theoretically, or on *a priori* grounds, an absolute necessity.' [3]

The temporal priority of instinct to conscience is, of course, a fact.   But it appears to me that two criticisms may be made upon the contention that this fact constitutes an adequate explanation of a second fact—namely, the empirical universality and practical inevitability of sin.   The first criticism is, that this contention ignores the possibility that the two facts in question may be collaterally related, as effects of the same cause, and need not necessarily stand in a direct causal relation.   If there is an evil principle infecting organic life, including human life, it may both have delayed the development of the moral will,

---

[1] Quoted, *Origin and Propagation of Sin* (Hulsean Lectures) (1902), p. 82.   Except where otherwise specified, paginal references given in this Additional Note are to this work.

[2] *op. cit.* p. 93.

[3] p. 110.   But, if ' empirical inevitability ' is a fact, must it not be the index and *epiphenomenon* of an underlying ' theoretical necessity ' ?   Such at any rate appears to be the assumption of physical science within its own sphere.

and ensured that the moral will should be relatively weak when at length it did develop. In any case, there seems no *a priori* reason why temporal posteriority of development should involve weakness; an omnipotent God presumably might, and could, so have ordered matters that the moral consciousness, when it did appear, should have sprung into existence endowed with the fullest control and power over the animal impulses, like Athene springing fully armed from the head of Zeus.

This latter consideration naturally leads to our second criticism, which is that, even if it could be proved that the late emergence of the moral consciousness necessarily involved its practical weakness, Dr. Tennant's position does not logically exempt the Almighty from the responsibility of *causing* evil, as the Fall-theory (except when combined with 'supra-lapsarian' predestinarianism [1]) does. (No theodicy, indeed, that human ingenuity can elaborate will ever exempt Him from the responsibility of *permitting* evil: because He obviously does permit it.) For, on any other than a Deistic view of God's relation to the world and to human souls, the temporal priority of instinct to conscience, which is alleged to be the source of man's observed proneness to evil, must (if the Fall-theory be excluded) be attributed to the Divine appointment; that is to say, we must conclude that the will of God immanent in organic evolution has brought man into existence with a secret flaw in his soul which sooner or later betrays him into actual sin. If man's nature is a 'chaos not yet reduced to order,' *and if the hypothesis of a 'Fall' of any kind be ruled out*, we can only suppose that man started his career as a 'chaos' because God willed that he should so start; and if this his 'chaotic' condition involves the 'empirical inevitability' of sin, then God must be deemed to have laid the foundations of human nature in such a way that sin inevitably results. One sentence in the fourth Hulsean Lecture seems expressly to accept this consequence. 'What introspection really discovers is an internal conflict between nature and nurture, natural desire and moral end': (so far we entirely agree; but the sentence continues) 'and this is the *inevitable* condition of human life and *the expression of God's purpose*' [2] (italics ours). If an arrangement which involves the 'empirical inevitability' of sin be really 'the expression of God's purpose,' the human race may well say to its Maker, in the words of FitzGerald:

> Oh, Thou, who Man of baser Earth didst make,
> And who with Eden didst devise the Snake,
> For all the Sin wherewith the Face of Man
> Is blackened, Man's Forgiveness give—and take! [3]

---

[1] *v. supra*, Lecture VI, p. 436f. [2] p. 115.
[3] *Rubáiyát of Omar Khayyám*, lviii.

This consideration is of such importance for the comprehension of the Fall-theory, and also (as it appears to me) so decisive against the sufficiency, from a theistic and Christian point of view, of Dr. Tennant's ' alternative hamartigeny,' that I make no apology for insisting upon it at some length.   ' Anachronisms,' or ' chronological misfits,' are not accepted by the mind as self-caused or self-explanatory, in any department of human affairs. If an antiquated law or institution lingers on in the State after its original usefulness has departed, needlessly causing friction between classes or wasting the resources of the community, we do not record the judgment ' This is an anachronism, and there is no more to be said ' ; on the contrary, our comment is ' This is an anachronism, and the Government, or Parliament, is very much to blame for not having abolished or reformed the law or institution in question when the conditions which originally justified it ceased to exist.' The idea of an ' anachronism ' seems logically to involve the idea of some conscious agent's (more or less) culpable neglect of his duty as its cause, though the more harmless the anachronism, the less culpable the neglect which has produced it. Now it is a not uncommon practice to apply the term ' anachronism ' to certain vestigial and now useless structures in man's physical organism : Dr. Tennant himself instances ' the troublesome wisdom tooth and the dangerous caecum.' [1] If the term ' anachronism ' is seriously used in this connexion, it implies a teleological view of the universe as its background, and *prima facie* involves a note of censure, or quasi-censure, on the power or powers responsible for the continued existence of the 'anachronistic' structure— a power which may for the moment be vaguely described as ' Nature ' (*natura naturans*). When disease arising from such a source brings pain or death to some dear one, the most im-passive philosopher may well experience a moment's indignation against the apparent negligence of ' Nature,' whose irresistible pressure compels men to adopt changed modes of life, without simultaneously effecting the necessary modifications of their physiological organism.

The thoughtful believer in Christian theism will naturally de-mand an explanation of the existence of such cruel anachronisms in a world which he has been taught to believe was created and is sustained by an all-loving and merciful God ; he will no more take them for granted, as self-explanatory, than the his-torical student takes political anachronisms for granted. Our own explanation has been generally indicated in Lecture VIII ; to the poet who cries ' Are God and Nature then at strife ? ' we answer ' Yes, to a large extent ; because of the pre-mundane rebellion against God of that which men have called the Logos

[1] *The Concept of Sin* (1912), p. 147.

Spermatikos, the World-Soul, *natura naturans*, the *élan vital*, the Will to live.' Underlying all the evil in physical nature we suppose vitiated streams of the disintegrated Life-Force, particular entelechies or *idées-forces* (to quote Fouillée's pregnant term) which owing to the primal catastrophe have become forces of sloth, of cruelty, or of death. Such a view at least relieves God of the responsibility for the origination of physical evil, though not from that of originating its possibility and tolerating its actuality. But it appears that Dr. Tennant's view does not claim to do so much. Speaking of the relative independence *vis-à-vis* of God and of its fellow-creatures which he attributes to the human self, he observes ' It is compatible with solidarity in sin and penalty, and does not necessitate that the ills of the creature are events wholly external to the life of the Creator, though indeed their sins are—so that " the Creator has fashioned suffering in which He Himself has no share and of which He is independent." ' [1]

The sentence is vaguely expressed ; but, if we are justified in arguing from its verbal form, it would seem to imply that 'the ills of the creature' (physical ills are presumably meant) are at least partly included in ' the life of the Creator,' in a way in which men's sins are not. And, a little further on, it is suggested that physical evils, though not ' direct expressions of the will of God,' are yet 'necessarily incidental' to His 'plan of realising His end,' or 'inevitable bye-products of the . . . course of nature.' [2] But is it possible to relieve God of responsibility for ' necessary,' even though ' incidental,' consequences of His own plan ? Surely it would not have been beyond the resources of Omniscience to devise another plan, which would not have necessarily involved such consequences as cancer or syphilis ? In human justice a man is held to intend the necessary, reasonably foreseeable, and foreseen consequences of his acts, even though he may urge that the idea of such consequences was not the motive which prompted the acts or a ' direct expression ' of his will : and a theodicy can hardly be conducted on laxer principles than those which prevail in earthly courts. I venture to suggest that, so far as physical evil is concerned, Dr. Tennant despite the subtlety and brilliance of his dialectic has not really succeeded in evading the ancient dilemma ' *Either* there has been a " Fall " of some kind, *or* God must be deemed to be the author of evil,' and that though he refuses to admit the fact, he is really impaled upon its latter horn.

But if physiological anachronisms of such a kind that they produce disease or death must be regarded either as the consequences of a ' Fall ' or as the products of the Divine will, there is at least a strong presumption that the same holds good of the

---

[1] p. 128 f.   [2] See pp. 132, 133.

psychological anachronisms which predispose man to sin. They must be due to *some* cause : that cause *ex hypothesi* does not lie in the will of the individual man who suffers from them—the bully in whom the combative instinct is endowed with a degree of strength, which would have been appropriate and useful in a Pleistocene anthropoid but is useless and dangerous in a member of modern civilised society, has clearly not willed this anachronistic quality of his nature. And what cause of such anachronisms can be or ever has been suggested, by believers in monotheism, other than the will of God or a primal rebellion of some created will or wills against the will of God ? Those who reject both of these alternatives are surely under an intellectual obligation to produce a third explanation: and this it appears to me that Dr. Tennant has failed to do.

Dr. Tennant has laid Theology at large under an immense obligation by the courage with which, following in the steps of Julian and Scotus, he has proclaimed the moral neutrality of appetite (the *fomes peccati*) as such, thereby sweeping away at one blow the endless confusions which clustered round the word ' concupiscence ' ; and by insisting that the word ' sin ' means, not a psychological state nor yet a forensic status, but an act committed with full and conscious deliberation in defiance of a known law. To criticise the constructive views of one who can claim the credit of such far-reaching and permanently valuable achievements may well appear to many minds in the light of presumption. Yet I must needs think that the argument of Dr. Tennant's third and fourth Hulsean Lectures, eloquent and persuasive though it is, obscures the real logic of the matter, which, I suggest, is perfectly simple. So far as sin is capable of a genetic explanation at all, there are four possible explanations and four only: namely (1) monism, (2) dualism, (3) Pelagianism, (4) the theory of a ' Fall ' of some kind. Dr. Tennant rejects the fourth, and, even more emphatically, the second of these [1] ; but I venture to think that, when rigorously analysed, his own explanation will be found to amount, not to a fifth theory, but to an inconsistent combination of the first and third (monism and Pelagianism). When he tells us that an ' inevitable condition of human life,' which involves the ' empirical inevitability of sin,' is ' the expression of the Divine purpose,' [2] he is speaking as a thoroughgoing monist; when he removes the Divine control from a great part of the world-process, and describes many events as having no teleological import [3] and as mere ' incidental results ' or ' bye-products ' of the Divine plan, he at least approximates to the Deistic view of God which is

[1] p. 135. [2] p. 115.
[3] p. 130 : ' . . . the incidental nature of much that happens in God's world, and from which teleological import is excluded.'

inseparable from the Pelagian view of man [1]; when he asserts that ' the actuality of sin is derived solely from the individual will influenced by its social environment ' [2] and that ' the contents of man's moral life and the quality of his character are . . . the results of his own determination according to his opportunities,' [3] it is difficult to interpret his words otherwise than as expressing the complete indeterminism and the ethical atomism on which the thought of Pelagius and Julian was based.

Nevertheless, there is one sentence in the fourth Hulsean Lecture which, if allowed its fullest meaning, seems to concede the whole principle for which we have been contending. ' Man's condition denotes, on our theory of sin, a *fall* [italics ours] from the divine intention, a parody of God's purpose in human history, though not a fall from an actual state of original righteousness.' [4] With regard to the last clause, it need only be said that we have already repudiated the idea of the original righteousness of *the first concrete human individuals* as unhistorical. But the statement that man's present condition denotes a ' fall ' from God's intention presumably means that the idea of Man, as conceived in the Divine mind from all eternity, included the idea of a perfect moral character ; that ' original righteousness,' though its attribution to any generation of our remote semi-brutish ancestors is mythological, may yet be ascribed to the Ideal or Archetypal Man as existing in the intelligible world ; and that the human race, as we know it in the world of time and sense, represents a grave declension or ' fall ' from the eternal pattern of manhood laid up in the heavens.   Two logical steps forward (neither of them very difficult) from this position would bring Dr. Tennant into complete accord with the general Fall-conception vaguely adumbrated by Gregory of Nyssa, and set out in our last lecture.   The first of these steps consists in the hypostatisation and personalisation of the archetypal Idea, and in the reference to its conscious self-determining activity of the cause of the declension from perfect righteousness manifested by the human race as we know it ; the second, in expanding the content of the Idea so that it becomes the Idea not of humanity alone but of all organic life, so that its self-perversion accounts not merely for the tendency to evil in man but for the equally oppressive and saddening phenomenon of evil in sub-human nature.   The justification of these steps will be found stated at length in Lecture VIII, and need only be summarised here by pointing out (*a*) that unless the relation between the perfect Idea and the degenerate particulars be conceived, as we have suggested, under *causal, contingent,* and *temporal* forms, it can only be conceived under the timeless category of ' ground and

---

[1] See Lecture V, p. 356.

[2] p. 117.

[3] p. 119.

[4] p. 131.

consequent,' which would involve postulating a principle of evil necessarily inherent in the Idea itself, and thus making God the direct author of evil ; (b) that the evolutional continuity between man and the brute requires that evil in both should be brought under the head of a single explanation. It is, perhaps, not temerarious to suggest that a full recognition of the implications of the phrase ' a *fall* from the divine intention ' would entirely eliminate whatever divergence may be thought to exist between the ' evolutionary view ' and the ' ecclesiastical doctrine ' (understood in the historical and Vincentian sense of the term, and construed as we have suggested) regarding the origin and ground of sin.

ADDITIONAL NOTE F : FORMULARIES

[Only such texts are printed as are strictly relevant to the Fall-doctrine.]

I. OECUMENICAL

Council of Ephesus, A.D. 431. *can.* I. εἴ τις ὁ μητροπολίτης τῆς ἐπαρχίας, ἀποστατήσας τῆς ἁγίας καὶ οἰκουμενικῆς συνόδου, προσέθετο τῷ τῆς ἀποστασίας συνεδρίῳ, ἢ μετὰ τοῦτο προστεθείη, ἢ τὰ Κελεστίου ἐφρόνησεν ἢ φρονήσει, οὗτος κατὰ τῶν τῆς ἐπαρχίας ἐπισκόπων διαπράττεσθαί τι οὐδαμῶς δύναται, πάσης ἐκκλησιαστικῆς κοινωνίας ἐντεῦθεν ἤδη ὑπὸ τῆς συνόδου ἐκβεβλημένος, καὶ ἀνενέργητος ὑπάρχων. . . .

can. 4. εἰ δέ τινες ἀποστατήσαιεν τῶν κληρικῶν, καὶ τολμήσαιεν ἢ κατ' ἰδίαν ἢ δημοσίᾳ τὰ Νεστορίου ἢ τὰ Κελεστίου φρονῆσαι, καὶ τούτους εἶναι καθηρημένους, ὑπὸ τῆς ἁγίας συνόδου δεδικαίωται.

[Hardouin i. 1621 D ; Denzinger-Bannwart, *Enchiridion*, § 126 ; W. Bright, *Canons of the First Four General Councils*, 1892, p. xxvii f.]

II. WESTERN AND ROMAN

1. *Canons of the Second Council of Orange*, A.D. 529

can. I. si quis per offensam praevaricationis Adae non totum, id est secundum corpus et animam, in deterius dicit hominem commutatum, sed animae libertate illaesa durante corpus tantummodo corruptioni credit obnoxium, Pelagii errore deceptus adversatur scripturae dicenti : *anima, quae peccaverit, ipsa morietur* [Ezek. xviii. 20] : et, *nescitis quoniam qui exhibetis vos servos ad oboediendum servi estis eius, cui oboeditis ?* [Rom. vi. 16] : et, *a quo quis superatur, eius et servus addicitur* [2 Pet. ii. 19].

can. 2.   si quis soli Adae praevaricationem suam, non et eius propagini asserit nocuisse, aut certe mortem tantum corporis, quae poena peccati est, non autem et peccatum, quod mors est animae, per unum hominem in omne genus humanum transiisse testatur, iniustitiam Deo dabit, contradicens Apostolo dicenti : *per unum hominem peccatum intravit in mundum, et per peccatum mors, et ita in omnes homines mors pertransiit, in quo omnes peccaverunt* [Rom. v. 12].

can. 8.   si quis alios misericordia, alios vero per liberum arbitrium, quod in omnibus, qui de praevaricatione primi hominis nati sunt, constat esse vitiatum, ad gratiam baptismi posse venire contendit, a recta fide probatur alienus. is enim non omnium liberum arbitrium per peccatum primi hominis asserit infirmatum, aut certe ita laesum putat, ut tamen quidam valeant sine revelatione Dei mysterium salutis aeternae per semetipsos posse conquirere . . .

can. 13.   arbitrium voluntatis in primo homine infirmatum nisi per gratiam baptismi non potest reparari : quod amissum nisi a quo potuit dari non potest reddi . . .

can. 15.   ab eo quod formavit Deus mutatus est Adam, sed in peius per iniquitatem suam. ab eo quod operata est iniquitas mutatur fidelis, sed in melius per gratiam Dei. illa ergo mutatio fuit praevaricatoris primi, haec secundum Psalmistam *mutatio est dextrae excelsi* [ps. lxxvi. 11].

can. 19.   natura humana, etiamsi in illa integritate in qua est condita permaneret, nullo modo se ipsam creatore suo non adiuvante servaret : unde cum sine Dei gratia salutem non possit custodire, quam accepit, quomodo sine Dei gratia poterit reparare quod perdidit ?

From the doctrinal statement appended to can. 25.   ac sic secundum supra scriptas sanctarum scripturarum sententias vel antiquorum patrum definitiones hoc Deo propitiante et praedicare debemus et credere, quod per peccatum primi hominis ita inclinatum et attenuatum fuerit liberum arbitrium, ut nullus postea aut diligere Deum sicut oportuit, aut credere in Deum, aut operari propter Deum quod bonum est, nisi eum gratia misericordiae divinae praevenerit.

2. *Council of Trent*

Sessio V (June 17, 1546).
Decretum de peccato originali.

1. si quis non confitetur, primum hominem Adam, cum mandatum Dei in paradiso fuisset transgressus, statim sanctitatem et iustitiam, in qua constitutus fuerat, amisisse, incurrisseque per offensam praevaricationis huiusmodi iram et indignationem Dei atque ideo mortem, quam antea illi com-

minatus fuerat Deus, et cum morte captivitatem sub eius
potestate, qui mortis deinde habuit imperium, hoc est diaboli,
totumque Adam per illam praevaricationis offensam secundum
corpus et animam in deterius commutatum fuisse : anathema sit.

2. si quis Adae praevaricationem sibi soli, et non eius
propagini asserit nocuisse, et acceptam a Deo sanctitatem et
iustitiam quam perdidit, sibi soli et non nobis etiam eum
perdidisse ; aut inquinatum illum per inoboedientiae peccatum
mortem et poenas corporis tantum in omne genus humanum
transfudisse, non autem et peccatum, quod mors est animae ;
A.S., cum contradicat Apostolo dicenti : *per unum hominem
peccatum intravit in mundum* etc. [Rom. v. 12].

3. si quis hoc Adae peccatum, quod origine unum est, et
propagatione, non imitatione, transfusum omnibus inest unicuique proprium, vel per humanae naturae vires vel per aliud
remedium asserit tolli quam per meritum unius mediatoris
Domini nostri Iesu Christi . . . A.S. . . .

4. si quis parvulos recentes ab uteris matrum baptizandos
negat, etiam si fuerint a baptizatis parentibus orti, aut dicit in
remissionem quidem peccatorum eos baptizari, sed nihil ex Adam
trahere originalis peccati, quod regenerationis lavacro necesse sit
expiari ad vitam aeternam consequendam, unde fit consequens,
ut in eis forma baptismatis in remissionem peccatorum non vera,
sed falsa intelligatur : A.S., quoniam non aliter intelligendum
est id, quod dixit Apostolus : *per unum hominem peccatum
intravit in mundum* etc. [Rom. v. 12], nisi quemadmodum
Ecclesia catholica ubique diffusa semper intellexit. propter hanc
enim regulam fidei ex traditione Apostolorum etiam parvuli,
qui nihil peccatorum in semetipsis adhuc committere potuerunt,
ideo in remissionem peccatorum veraciter baptizantur, ut in eis
regeneratione mundetur, quod generatione contraxerunt.[1] *nisi
enim quis renatus fuerit ex aqua et Spiritu Sancto, non potest
introire in regnum Dei* [John iii. 5].

5. si quis per Iesu Christi Domini nostri gratiam quae in
baptismate confertur reatum originalis peccati remitti negat, aut
etiam asserit, non tolli totum id, quod veram et propriam peccati
rationem habet, sed illud dicit tantum radi aut non imputari :
A.S. . . . manere autem in baptizatis concupiscentiam vel
fomitem haec sancta Synodus fatetur et sentit, quae cum agonem
relicta sit, nocere non consentientibus sed viriliter per Christi
Iesu gratiam repugnantibus non valet ; quin immo *qui legitime
certaverit* coronabitur [2 Tim. ii. 5]. hanc concupiscentiam, quam
aliquando Apostolus *peccatum* [Denzinger refers for this to
Rom. vi. 12 ff.] appellat, sancta Synodus declarat Ecclesiam
catholicam nunquam intellexisse peccatum appellari, quod vere

---

[1] This canon is practically identical with *can.* 2 of the Carthaginian
Synod of A.D. 418 ; see above, p. 391.

et proprie in renatis peccatum sit, sed quia ex peccato est et ad peccatum inclinat. si quis autem contrarium senserit : A.S. declarat tamen haec ipsa sancta Synodus, non esse suae intentionis, comprehendere in hoc decreto, ubi de peccato originali agitur, beatam et immaculatam Virginem Mariam Dei genitricem,[1] sed observandas esse constitutiones fel. rec. Sixti Papae IV sub poenis in eis constitutionibus contentis, quas innovat.

[Hardouin x. 27 C ff. ; Denzinger-Bannwart, § 788 ff.]

Sessio VI (Jan. 13, 1547).
Decretum de iustificatione.
cap. 1.   *de naturae et legis ad iustificandos homines imbecillitate.*

primum declarat sancta Synodus, ad iustificationis doctrinam probe et sincere intelligendam oportere, ut unusquisque agnoscat et fateatur, quod, cum omnes homines in praevaricatione Adae innocentiam perdidissent . . . usque adeo *servi erant peccato* [Rom. vi. 20] et sub potestate diaboli ac mortis, ut non modo gentes per vim naturae sed ne Iudaei quidem per ipsam etiam litteram legis Moysi inde liberari aut surgere possent, tametsi in eis liberum arbitrium minime exstinctum esset, viribus licet attenuatum et inclinatum.[2]

[Hardouin x. 33 C ; Denzinger-Bannwart, § 793.]

Canones de iustificatione.
can. 5.   si quis liberum hominis arbitrium post Adae peccatum amissum et exstinctum esse dixerit, aut rem esse de solo titulo, immo titulum sine re, figmentum denique a satana invectum in ecclesiam : A.S.
can. 6.   si quis dixerit, non esse in potestate hominis vias suas malas facere, sed mala opera ita ut bona Deum operari, non permissive solum sed etiam proprie et per se, adeo ut sit proprium eius opus non minus proditio Iudae quam vocatio Pauli : A.S.   (This canon is directed against the dictum of Melancthon, mentioned above, p. 435.)

[Hardouin x. 40 E ; Denzinger-Bannwart, §§ 815, 816.]

For the relation of the foregoing definitions to the drafts submitted to the Council by the ' private congregations,' see J. Waterworth, *Canons and Decrees of the Council of Trent*, 1848, pp. xciii–c.

---

[1] *Cf.* St. Aug. *de nat. et grat.* 42, quoted above, Lecture V, p. 370, n. 2.
[2] *v. supra* (p. 538), canons of the second Council of Orange, statement appended to *can.* 25.

III. EASTERN ORTHODOX

1. *Confessio Orthodoxa.* (ap. E. J. Kimmel, *Monumenta fidei Eccl. orient.*, 1850, p. 83 ff.)

quaest. xxii. 'But seeing that man, whilst he was yet in the state of innocency, forgat the commandment of God, and plucked and tasted of the forbidden fruit : for this reason was he stripped of the honour which he had from the moment of creation, during the time of his innocency, and driven forth from Paradise. Wherefore he became such an one as the Prophet describes : " Man being in honour had no understanding, but was compared unto beasts void of reason, and was made like unto them " (Ps. xlix. 20) : and he heard the sentence " Earth thou art, and unto earth shalt thou return " (Gen. iii. 10).'

quaest. xxiii. ' Of what kind was the state of man's innocency, or purity and sinlessness ? '

Answer. ' There are two kinds of innocency and integrity : the first is a voluntary departure from sin, as when a man after the daily and habitual exercise of vice by his own choice renounces sin ; the second is a simple ignorance and inexperience of sin . . . due to tender age or to other causes. With this latter kind was the innocency of Adam to be compared before his sin, joined as that innocency was with every perfection and innate righteousness, both on the side of intellect and on the side of will ; in his intellect was included every kind of knowledge, and in his will every kind of goodness and virtue. And seeing that Adam had a most perfect knowledge of God (in accordance with that measure which was granted unto him for that time, and in accordance with that which was seemly), for this very reason that he knew God, he also knew all other things in God.' [This is proved by the incident of his naming the animals, which he was able to do because he possessed a perfect knowledge of the nature and disposition of each, due not to scientific investigation but to meditation on God and His goodness.] ' As for his will, this was always subject to reason ; though he always retained his liberty, and though it was always in the power of man either to sin or not to sin, as the Scripture saith [Ecclus. xv. 11–17, 20, quoted at length]. In this state, therefore, of innocence and sinlessness man was like unto the angels. But so soon as he had fallen through the transgression, forthwith in the same place of Paradise, being endued with the state of sin, he became mortal [Rom. vi. 23]. Then forthwith, the perfection of his reason and intellect having been lost, his will also became more inclined to evil than to good. And in this way the state of integrity and innocency passed into a state of sin, man having already experienced evil ; and man who had once been perfect was so much humbled, that he may now say with David, " I am a worm, and no man " [Ps. xxii. 6].'

quaest. xxiv. ' Are all men subject to the same sin ? (εἶναι τάχα ὅλοι οἱ ἄνθρωποι ὑποκείμενοι εἰς τὴν αὐτὴν ἁμαρτίνα;)

Answer. ' As all men were in Adam during the state of innocency, so also from the moment that he fell all fell in him (ὅλοι ἔσφαλαν εἰς αὐτόν) and remained in the state of sin. Wherefore they are subject not only to sin, but also to punishment because of the sin [Gen. ii. 17 ; Rom. v. 12]. Wherefore also we are conceived in our mothers' wombs and are born with this sin, as the holy Psalmist saith [Ps. li. 7]. And this sin is called Ancestral [προπατορικόν—or ' original ']; firstly, because man was defiled by no other sin before it. Though the devil was already corrupted by his own sin ; and at his instigation this which is called " ancestral sin " began to germinate in man, that sin to which Adam became subject and all we who descend from him. Secondly, because no man is conceived except in sin.'

2. *Dosithei Confessio* (*ap.* Synod. Hierosol., Kimmel, *op. cit.*, pp. 425 ff.)

decretum vi. (Kimmel, p. 432 f.).

' We believe that the first man was created by God and fell in Paradise, when, neglecting the divine command, he obeyed the deceitful counsel of the serpent ; and that thence has flowed in succession the ancestral sin (τὴν προπατορικὴν ἁμαρτίαν) ; so that no one is born according to the flesh who does not bear this burden and perceive the fruits thereof in this present world. And by the " fruits " and the " burden " we mean, not sin, such as impiety, blasphemy, murder . . . etc. : for many of the Patriarchs and Prophets, and myriads of others of those both who lived in the shadow of the Law and in the truth of the Gospel, and the divine Forerunner, and especially the mother of God the Word, the ever-virgin Mary, had no share in these or like sins ; but we mean those things which the divine justice sends upon man as a penalty on account of the transgression, such as the sweat of toil, tribulations, bodily infirmities, the pains of childbirth, a toilsome life during this pilgrimage, and finally bodily death.'

[Note that this formulary appears to restrict the consequences of the Fall to external and physical evils.]

3. *The Longer Catechism of the Russian Church.* (R. W. Blackmore, *The Doctrine of the Russian Church*, 1845, p. 60)

Q. 'Why did not the first man only die, and not all as now?'
A. 'Because all have come of Adam since his infection by sin, and all sin themselves. As from an infected source there

naturally flows an infected stream, so from a father infected with sin, and consequently mortal, there naturally proceeds a posterity infected like him with sin, and like him mortal.'

[The definitely Augustinian tone of the sections quoted from the *Confessio orthodoxa* of Peter Mogila is notable, and contrasts strongly with the vagueness which had previously characterised Eastern thought on this subject. It is doubtless to be attributed to the wave of Latinising influence which swept over Eastern theology in the middle of the seventeenth century, as a reaction from the Protestantising tendencies of the unfortunate Patriarch Cyril Lucaris (†1637). To judge by the sketch of modern Greek theology given by F. Gavin (*Some Aspects of Contemporary Greek Orthodox Thought*, 1923, Lecture III, § 3, ' The Fall,' § 4, ' Original Sin,' pp. 165 ff.), the current hamartiological teaching of Eastern divines, as represented by two such eminent scholars as M. Androutsos and M. Dyobouniotis, is still strongly coloured by Augustinianism; though Gavin (p. 168) quotes Damalas as deeming ' concupiscence' to be morally indifferent, whilst Androutsos rejects the Augustinian disparagement of the good works of the heathen (Gavin, p. 167).]

IV. LUTHERAN

[In this and the following section it has not been possible to print more than a few typical texts, owing to considerations of space.]

1. *Confession of Augsburg*, A.D. 1530

art. ii. *de peccato originis.*

item docent, quod post lapsum Adae omnes homines secundum naturam propagati nascantur cum peccato, hoc est, sine metu Dei, sine fiducia erga Deum, et cum concupiscentia, quodque hic morbus seu vitium originis vere sit peccatum, damnans et afferens nunc quoque aeternam mortem his qui non renascuntur per baptismum et Spiritum Sanctum.

damnant Pelagianos et alios qui vitium originis negant esse peccatum, et ut extenuent gloriam meriti et beneficiorum Christi, disputant hominem propriis viribus rationis coram Deo iustificari posse.

[F. Francke, *libri symbolici eccl. Lutheranae*, i. p. 13 f.; B. J. Kidd, *Documents of the Continental Reformation* (1911), p. 262.]

2. *Schmalkaldic Articles*, A.D. 1537

pars iii, I. *de peccato.*

1. hic confitendum nobis est, ut Paulus Roman. v. affirmat, peccatum ab uno homine Adamo ortum esse et introisse in

mundum, per cuius inobedientiam omnes homines facti sunt peccatores, morti et diabolo obnoxii. hoc nominatur originale, haereditarium, principale, et capitale peccatum.

2. huius peccati fructus postea sunt mala opera, in decalogo prohibita, ut sunt diffidentia, incredulitas, falsa fides sive κακοπιστία, idololatria, sine Dei timore esse, praesumptio seu temeritas, desperatio, caecitas seu excaecatio, et ut summatim dicam, Deum non agnoscere, non curare; deinde mentiri, nomine Dei abuti, peierare, non orare, non invocare, verbum Dei contemnere vel negligere, parentibus immorigerum esse, occidere, lascivire, furari, decipere etc.

3. hoc peccatum haereditarium tam profunda et tetra est corruptio naturae, ut nullius hominis ratione intelligi possit, sed ex scripturae patefactione agnoscenda et credenda sit (Ps. li., Rom. v., Exod. xxxiii., Gen. iii.). quapropter meri sunt errores et caligines contra hunc articulum scholasticorum doctorum dogmata, quibus docetur :

4. post Adae lapsum hominis naturales vires mansisse integras et incorruptas, et hominem naturaliter habere rationem rectam et bonam voluntatem, sicut philosophi docent :

5. et hominem habere liberum arbitrium faciendi bonum et omittendi malum et e contra omittendi bonum et faciendi malum, etc.

[Francke, i. p. 20 f.]

3. *The Formulary of Concord*, A.D. 1577

I. *Epitome*, c. i. *de peccato originali*

B. *Affirmativa*

I

credimus, docemus, et confitemur, quod sit aliquod discrimen inter ipsam hominis naturam, non tantum quemadmodum initio a Deo purus et sanctus et absque peccato homo conditus est, verum etiam qualem iam post lapsum naturam illam habemus, discrimen, inquam, inter ipsam *naturam*, quae etiam post lapsum est permanetque Dei creatura, et inter *peccatum originis*, et quod tanta sit illa naturae et peccati originalis differentia, quanta est inter opus Dei et inter opus diaboli.

II

credimus, docemus, et confitemur quod summo studio hoc discrimen sit conservandum, propterea quod illud dogma, nullum videlicet inter naturam hominis corrupti et inter peccatum originis esse discrimen, cum praecipuis fidei nostrae articulis de creatione, de redemptione, de sanctificatione et resurrectione carnis nostrae pugnet, neque salvis hisce articulis stare possit. . .

III

vicissim autem credimus, docemus atque confitemur, peccatum originis non esse levem, sed tam profundam humanae naturae corruptionem, quae nihil sanum, nihil incorruptum in corpore et anima hominis, atque adeo in interioribus et exterioribus viribus eius reliquit. sicut ecclesia canit ' lapsus Adae vi pessima humana tota massa, natura et ipsa essentia corrupta, luce cassa ' etc.

[Francke, ii. p. 20 f.]

II. *solida declaratio*, c. i. B. I

et primum quidem constat, Christianos non tantum actualia delicta et transgressiones mandatorum Dei peccata esse agnoscere et definire debere, sed etiam horrendum atque abominabilem illum *haereditarium morbum*, per quem tota natura corrupta est, inprimis pro *horribili peccato*, et quidem pro principio et capite omnium peccatorum, e quo reliquae transgressiones tamquam e radice nascantur et quasi e scaturigine promanent, omnino habendum esse. et hoc malum aliquando D. Lutherus *peccatum naturae*, item *peccatum personae* appellare solet, ut significet, etiamsi homo prorsus nihil mali cogitaret loqueretur aut ageret (quod sane post primorum nostrorum parentum lapsum in hac vita humanae naturae est impossibile) tamen nihilominus hominis naturam et personam esse peccatricem, hoc est, peccato originali quasi *lepra* quadam *spirituali* prorsus et totaliter in intimis etiam visceribus et cordis recessibus profundissimis totam esse coram Dei infectam, venenatam et penitus corruptam ; et propter hanc corruptionem atque primorum nostrorum lapsum natura aut persona hominis lege Dei accusatur et condemnatur, ita ut natura filii irae, mortis et damnationis mancipia simus, nisi beneficio meriti Christi ab his malis liberemur et servemur.

[Francke, ii. p. 84 f.]

V. Reformed

1. *Confessio Helvetica prior*, A.D. 1536

7. *Von dem menschen.*

Der mensch, die volkomnest bildnus gottes uff erden, under allen sichtbaren creaturen, die edleste und furnemste, der ist uss lib und seel zusamen gesetzt. Der lib ist todtlich, die seel untodtlich, diser mensch als er von gott recht und wol geschaffen war, ist er durch sin eigne schuld in die sund gefallen und hatt das ganz menschlich geschlecht mit ihm in solichn fall gezogen, und solicher arbeitsalikeit underwurflich gemacht.

8. *Von der eerbsünd.*

Dise eerbsucht aber und urspringenliche sund ist das ganz
menschlich geschlecht dermasen durchgangen, und hetts dermasen verwust und vergifft, dz dem menschen, der ein kind des
zorns und fyend gottes worden war, niemā denn gott durch
Christū helffen oder widerbringen mocht, und was in ihm guts
uberbliben ist, dz wirt durch taglich mangell und prasten fur
und fur geschwacht, das es zū eergeren geratet, dann die krafft
der sund und des prestens in uns trifft fur, das weder die vernunfft
dem, dz sy erkendt nachkomen, noch der hochverstand das
gottlich funckli pflanzen und furbringen mag.

[H. A. Niemeyer, *Collectio confessionum in ecclesiis reformatis
publicatarum*, Lipsiae, 1840, p. 106 f.]

2. *Confessio Belgica*, A.D. 1561

XIV. *De hominis creatione, lapsu et corruptione.*

credimus Deum ex limo terrae hominem ad imaginem suam,
bonum, iustum et sanctum creasse, qui proprio arbitrio suam
voluntatem ad Dei voluntatem componere et conformem reddere
posset. verum cum in honore esset nescivit, et excellentiam
suam non cognovit : sed seipsum sciens et volens peccato et per
consequens morti ac maledictioni subiecit : dum diaboli verbis
et imposturis aurem praebens mandatum vitae transgressus
est, quod a Domino acceperat ; seque a Deo, vera ipsius vita,
penitus subduxit, atque abalienavit, vitiata omnino atque
corrupta per peccatum ipsius natura : quo factum est, ut morti
tum corporeae tum spirituali sese obnoxium reddiderit, improbus
atque perversus effectus fuerit, atque in omnibus viis et studiis
suis corruptus, et praeclara illa dona omnia amiserit, quae a
Deo acceperat : adeo ut non nisi exiguae illorum scintillae et
vestigia exilia illi relicta sunt, quae tamen sufficiant ad in-
excusabiles reddendos homines . . . idcirco quaecunque de
libero hominis arbitrio traduntur ea merito reiicimus, cum homo
sit servus peccati : nihilque ex se possit, nisi datum sit illi de
coelo.

XV. *De peccato originali.*

credimus Adami inobedientia peccatum, quod vocant originis,
in totum genus humanum diffusum esse. est autem peccatum
originis corruptio totius naturae et vitium haereditarium, quo
et ipsi infantes in matris utero polluti sunt : quodque velut
noxia quaedam radix genus omne peccatorum in homine producit, estque tam foedum et execrabile coram Deo, ut ad universi
generis humani condemnationem sufficiat. neque vero per
baptismum penitus aboletur aut radicitus evellitur, quandoquidem ex illo tanquam ex infausta ac corrupta scaturigine

perpetui rivuli assidue exoriuntur et effluunt . . . hinc ergo
Pelagianorum errorem damnamus, qui hoc peccatum originis
nihil aliud esse asserunt quam imitationem.

[Niemeyer, pp. 368–70.]

3. *Confessio fidei Gallicana*, A.D. 1561

Article IX

Nous croyons que l'homme ayant esté créé pur et entier et
conforme à l'image de Dieu, est par sa propre faute descheu de
sa grace qu'il avoit reçue, et ainsi s'est aliéné de Dieu . . . en
sorte que sa nature est du tout corrompue : et estant aveuglé
en son esprit et dépravé en son cœur, a perdu toute integrité
sans en avoir rien de residu. . . .

Article X

Nous croyons que toute la lignée de Adam est infectée de
telle contagion, qui est le péché originel et un vice héréditaire,
et non pas seulement une imitation, comme les Pelagiens ont
voulu dire. . . . Et ainsi que en la personne d'iceluy (*sc*. Adam)
nous avons esté dénués de tous biens, et sommes trébuchés en
toute pauvreté et malédiction.

Article XI

Nous croyons aussi que ce vice est vrayement paché : qui
suffit à condamner tout le genre humain, iusques aux petis
enfants dès le ventre de la mère, et que pour tel il est reputé
devant Dieu, mesmes qu'après le baptesme c'est toujours péché,
quant à la coulpe, combien que la condamnation en soit abolie
aux enfans de Dieu, ne la leur imputant point par sa bonté
gratuite : outre cela, que c'est une perversité produisant tousiours
fruicts de malice et de rebellion, tels que les plus sains, encore
qu'ils y résistent, ne laissent point d'estre entachez d'infirmitez
et de fautes, pendant qu'ils habitent en ce monde.

Article XII

Nous croyons que de cette corruption et condamnation
générale, en laquelle tous hommes sont plongez, Dieu retire ceux
lesquels en son conseil éternel et immuable il a éleus par sa seule
bonté et miséricorde en nostre Seigneur Jesus Christ, sans con-
sidération de leurs œuvres, laissant les autres en icelle mesme
corruption et condamnation, pour démontrer en eux sa iustice,
comme ès premiers il fait luire les richesses de sa miséricorde. . . .

[Niemeyer, pp. 316–318.]

4. *The Westminster Confession*, A.D. 1647

Chapter VI. *Of the Fall of Man, of Sin, and of the Punishment thereof.*

I. Our first parents, being seduced by the subtilty and temptation of Satan, sinned in eating the forbidden fruit. This their sin God was pleased, according to his wise and holy counsel, to permit, having purposed to order it to his own glory.

II. By this sin they fell from their original righteousness and communion with God, and so became dead in sin, and wholly defiled in all the faculties and parts of soul and body.

III. They being the root of all mankind, the guilt of this sin was imputed, and the same death in sin and corrupted nature conveyed to all their posterity descending from them by ordinary generation.

IV. From this original corruption, whereby we are utterly indisposed, disabled, and made opposite to all good, and wholly inclined to all evil, do proceed all actual transgressions.

V. This corruption of nature during this life doth remain in those that are regenerated ; and although it be through Christ pardoned and mortified, yet both itself and all the motions thereof are truly and properly sin.

VI. Every sin, both original and actual, being a transgression of the righteous law of God and contrary thereto, doth in its own nature bring guilt upon the sinner, whereby he is bound over to the wrath of God and curse of the law, and so made subject to death, with all miseries spiritual, temporal, and eternal.

[P. Schaff, *The Creeds of the Evangelical Protestant Churches,* 1877, p. 615 f.]

VI. Anglican.   (A.D. 1553 ;   1562 ;   1571)

ARTICLE IX

De peccato originali	*Of Original or Birth Sin*
peccatum originis non est (ut fabulantur Pelagiani) in imitatione Adami situm, sed est vitium et depravatio naturae cuiuslibet hominis ex Adamo naturaliter propagati, qua fit, ut ab originali iustitia quam longissime distet, ad malum sua natura propendeat, et caro semper adversus spiritum con-	Original Sin standeth not in the following of *Adam* (as the *Pelagians* do vainly talk), but it is the fault and corruption of the Nature of every man, that naturally is ingendered of the offspring of *Adam* ; whereby man is very far gone from original righteousness, and is of his own nature inclined to

cupiscat. unde in unoquoque nascentium iram Dei atque damnationem meretur. manet etiam in renatis haec naturae depravatio ; qua fit ut affectus carnis, Graece φρόνημα σαρκός, (quod alii sapientiam, alii sensum, alii affectum, alii studium carnis interpretantur) legi Dei non subiiciatur. et quanquam renatis et credentibus nulla propter Christum est condemnatio, peccati tamen in sese rationem habere concupiscentiam fatetur Apostolus.

evil, so that the flesh lusteth always contrary to the spirit ; and therefore in every person born into this world it deserveth God's wrath and damnation. And this infection of nature doth remain, yea in them that are regenerated ; whereby the lust of the flesh, called in the Greek, φρόνημα σαρκός, which some do expound the wisdom, some sensuality, some the affection, some the desire of the flesh, is not subject to the Law of God. And although there is no condemnation for them that believe and are baptised, yet the Apostle doth confess, that concupiscence and lust hath of itself the nature of sin.

ARTICLE X

De libero arbitrio

ea est hominis post lapsum Adae conditio, ut sese naturalibus suis viribus et bonis operibus ad fidem et invocationem Dei convertere ac praeparare non possit ; quare absque gratia Dei, quae per Christum est, nos praeveniente, ut velimus, et co-operante, dum volumus, ad pietatis opera facienda, quae Deo grata sint et accepta, nihil valemus.

Of free will

The condition of Man after the fall of *Adam* is such, that he cannot turn and prepare himself, by his own natural strength and good works, to faith, and calling upon God : Wherefore we have no power to do good works pleasant and acceptable to God, without the grace of God by Christ preventing us, that we may have a good will, and working with us, when we have that good will.

ARTICLE XIII

Opera ante iustificationem

opera quae fiunt ante gratiam Christi et Spiritus eius afflatum, cum ex fide Jesu

Of Works before Justification

Works done before the grace of Christ, and the Inspiration of his Spirit, are not pleasant

Christi non prodeant, minime Deo grata sunt ; neque gratiam (ut multi vocant) de congruo merentur ; Imo cum non sint facta ut Deus illa fieri voluit et praecepit, peccati rationem habere non dubitamus.

to God, forasmuch as they spring not of faith in Jesus Christ, neither do they make men meet to receive grace, or (as the School-authors say) deserve grace of congruity ; yea rather, for that they are not done as God hath willed and commanded them to be done, we doubt not but they have the nature of sin.

ADDITIONAL NOTE G

INFANT BAPTISM

THE ceremony of baptism, as known to the Apostolic Church, seems to have formed the central act of a process which may be described as ' Christian Initiation.' This began with ' Repentance ' (presumably manifested by an oral confession of sin), was consummated by the immersion of the catechumen in the living waters of a spring or river, symbolising the washing away of sin, and concluded with the imposition of hands, which imparted the gifts of the Spirit. As we have pointed out in the text and elsewhere,[1] the New Testament references to Initiation assume that its recipients are adults, and that the dispositions required in them are those of conscious and deliberate renunciation of sin and idols, and of personal faith in and allegiance to Christ. Thus conceived, the rite illustrates vividly the true principles of ethical sacramentalism, which demand not merely the due performance of a sacred act by the minister but the right response of heart and will on the part of the worshipper, and which regard the objective *opus operatum* as ineffective unless met and completed by the subjective *opus operantis*.

It will be clear from this account of the original institution of baptism that the custom of baptising unconscious infants, which, as we have suggested, seems to have grown up spontaneously on a basis of popular feeling, and not of any reasoned theory, and which has now for many centuries been the normal means of entrance to the Christian Church, involves two very serious difficulties : (1) the apparent incongruity of administering a sacrament, the purpose of which is declared both by its symbolism and by the language of Scripture to be the ' washing away of sins,' to beings who *ex hypothesi* cannot have committed

---

[1] ' The Origins of the Sacraments,' in *Essays Catholic and Critical*, 1926, pp. 369 ff.

any sins ; (2) the exclusive emphasis which the practice appears to lay upon the *opus operatum*, in view of the presumption that unconscious infants are incapable of repentance or of personal faith in Christ. It might in fact be contended, that if the epithets ' magical ' and ' mechanical ' can be applied to any parts of the traditional sacramental system at all, it is the custom of infant baptism first and foremost to which they ought to be affixed ; and such a contention might be thought to derive some force from the curious stratagems employed by the Jesuit missionaries in North America to enable them to baptise dying infants amongst the heathen surreptitiously (by unobservedly flicking a few drops of water over the infant's face, and simultaneously whispering *ego te baptizo*, etc., whilst apparently engaged in conversation with the parents), for the purpose of adding as many souls as possible to the Kingdom of God.[1]

We have already pointed out that the first of these difficulties stimulated the growth of the idea of ' original guilt,' or guilt of nature, as its own solution. If, however, the history of the Fall-doctrine has been correctly portrayed in Lectures I to VI, this idea is no part of the body of revealed Christian truth, but a mere human figment : and in whatever way it be conceived—whether as the guilt of having sinned ' in Adam,' of being destitute of the splendid endowments alleged to have been originally possessed by Adam, or of being infected by ' concupiscence '—it is equally irrational, as involving the self-contradictory assertion that we are held ' guilty ' by God in respect of facts for which we have *ex hypothesi* no personal responsibility whatsoever. If, then, the insistence of the historic Church upon the permissibility, and indeed necessity, of infant baptism is to be justified, some theoretical basis for this custom other than the idea of ' original guilt ' must now be found.

It is necessary at this point to distinguish between the *fact* (assuming it to be a fact) of, and the *reasons* for, the necessity, or at least high desirability, of the baptism of infants. *That* infants may and should be baptised is a proposition which rests solely upon the actual practice of the Church ; as in the fifth century, the sole argument for the fact is simply this: 'The Church does baptise infants, and we cannot suppose that the Church has acted wrongly or without good cause in so doing.' It is not possible here to enter into such vast questions as the nature of the stewardship which the Church holds in regard to the methods and conditions of administering the sacraments, the amount of liberty which our Lord may have intended to leave to His Church in regard to developments or variations of sacramental usage, or the degree of *auctoritas* which attaches to a custom which has come to be accepted by the whole, or

[1] See F. Parkman, *The Jesuits in North America*, i. pp. 185 f., 206 f.

practically the whole, of the Christian society. It must suffice to state that in the author's view the argument *a praxi ecclesiae* is the only, but also a sufficient, ground for affirming the legitimacy and laudability of Paedo-baptism: and that those who do not trust the instincts of the historic Church to the extent which this argument requires should in logic either abandon the custom altogether or interpret it solely as a picturesque and dramatic method of registering the name of the infant as an honorary member of the Christian society.

Those, however, who are prepared on this ground to accept the proposition *that* infant baptism is permissible and desirable, will still demand some explanation as to *why* it should be desirable. If the theory that ' original guilt ' is thereby remitted be ruled out, and if, nevertheless, the baptism of infants be regarded as strictly sacramental and grace-bestowing, and not as merely symbolical, there appears to be no explanation of its efficacy other than that hinted at by St. Gregory of Nazianzus in the words already quoted :

νηπιάχοις μὲν

σφρηγὶς, ἀεξομένοισι δ᾽ ἄκος καὶ σφρηγὶς ἀρίστη [1]

and developed by Julian of Eclanum in the suggestion that whilst infants, not being *rei*, do not need *venia*, they are nevertheless capable of receiving ' inluminatio spiritualis, adoptio filiorum Dei, municipatus Ierusalem caelestis, sanctificatio, atque in Christi membra translatio, et possessio regni caelorum.' [2] We must frankly regard baptism as having two sets of effects, negative and positive, sin-remitting and strength-bestowing. And we must conceive of the baptism of adults as fraught with both kinds of operation, in that it both remits men's actual sins and imparts to them the germ of the supernatural life ; whilst the baptism of infants involves only the positive operation of making its recipients members of the Church and of Christ, capable of receiving the influx of grace which, when their Initiation has been completed by Confirmation, will assist them gradually to overcome that ' inherited infirmity ' which daily experience shows, so far from being abolished by the *opus operatum* of baptism, to remain ' yea, even in them that are regenerated.' It would follow from such a view of infant baptism that the idea of its efficacy cannot be dissociated from the influences of a Christian upbringing and of life within the shelter of Church membership, and that the indiscriminate baptism of children, with regard to whom no guarantee exists that they will be trained as Christians, is both useless and to be deprecated as a cheapening of the Sacrament.

---

[1] *carmina* i. § i. 9, 22, 91, 92 (quoted above, p. 290, n. 1).
[2] *op. imperf. c. Iulian.* i. 53.

Nevertheless, though part of the efficacy of infant baptism must be conceived as *proleptic*, in that by admitting its recipients to the Christian society it makes it possible for them in future years to imbibe the graces which flow from a supernatural environment, the actual practice of the Church clearly assumes that the administration of the rite has its own *immediate* efficacy ; for otherwise there would be no reason for baptising dying infants, who *ex hypothesi* have no prospect of being brought to Confirmation or of being trained up in Christian virtue within the fold of the Church militant here in earth. We must, then, believe that through the act of the Christian society, represented for the time being by the minister of the Sacrament, the beginnings of the Christ-life are planted in the infant soul, even though there may appear to be no conscious effort to prepare for or to appropriate them. Those who find this a hard saying may be asked to weigh well the words of Fr. C. C. Martindale, S.J. : ' Less and less objection should be taken to the Catholic baptism of children or the weak-witted, in proportion as modern psycho-. therapy proves how very deep and active is the sub-consciousness of those who, like children or seeming "idiots," have their superficial consciousness very undeveloped or ill-controlled,' and ' Even in those whose wits do not seem capable of coping with the natural life of man, the germ of the supernatural may yet take root.' [1]

The question may be raised, as it was raised in the fifth century,[2] ' How can such a view of the *rationale* of infant baptism be reconciled with the clause of the Oecumenical Creed which affirms " one baptism *for the remission of sins* " ? ' If it were an admitted principle that the meaning of the clauses of the Creed must be determined in complete abstraction from their history, this question would possess a certain amount of force as an objection to the explanation of Paedo-baptism indicated above. But no such principle has been formulated by any person or body with any claim upon our intellectual allegiance, and the Council of Chalcedon, which first conferred official authority upon the ' Creed of the 150,' did not append to it any commentary or any canons to govern its exegesis. It is therefore reasonable to assume that the true meaning of this clause is its historical meaning—that is, the meaning which it bore in the minds of those who first drew it up. Now it is well known that this clause does not occur in the original *Nicaenum*, which ended with the words 'and in the Holy Ghost' and the anti-Arian anathemas. According to the generally accepted theory of Hort, it is of Jerusalemitic origin, as indeed is the main body of our ' Nicene Creed'; which represents the baptismal creed of

---

[1] *God and the Supernatural* (1920), p. 285.
[2] See Lecture V, p. 345.

the Mother Church of Christendom, revised (perhaps by Cyril of
Jerusalem in A.D. 362–364) by the insertion into it of phrases
drawn from the real Nicene Creed (*i.e.* that actually approved
by the Council of Nicaea).[1]   The true meaning of this clause
must, then, be the meaning which it would have borne for Cyril
and for the Church of Jerusalem in the middle of the fourth
century.   And there can be no reasonable doubt that the thought
in their minds was that of baptism as administered to adults
according to Apostolic and primitive usage, preceded by
' Repentance ' and immediately followed by ' Confirmation '
and first Communion: a glance at Cyril's *catecheses illuminan-
dorum* and *catecheses mystagogicae* is enough to show that
adult baptism was for him and his flock the normal form of
baptism.   When, therefore, we repeat this clause in the Creed
as a part of the Eucharistic Liturgy, what we affirm is our belief
in baptism as anciently administered to adults, for the washing
away of actual sins, and as still so administered, habitually in
the mission field to converts from heathenism, and rarely in
Christian countries : we neither affirm nor deny the legitimacy
of infant baptism, which is a collateral development from the
original idea and institution of baptism, and which depends for
its authority not upon any credal or conciliar formula, but upon
the actual practice of the Church and the semi-articulate instincts
of the general body of Christendom.

ADDITIONAL NOTE H

Passages bearing on the Fall-doctrine from pre-Augustinian writers not mentioned in Lecture IV

(1) *Latin Writers*

Novatian (*flor. c.* A.D. 250)

de trinitate 1.   [*PL* III. 914 A]

(*physical mortality the result of the Fall*)

post quae hominem quoque mundo praeposuit et quidem ad
imaginem Dei factum : cui mentem et rationem indidit et
prudentiam, ut Deum posset imitari : cuius etsi corporis terrena
primordia, caelestis tamen et divini halitus inspirata substantia :
quem, cum omnia in servitutem illi dedisset, solum liberum esse
voluit. et ne in periculum caderet rursum soluta libertas,
mandatum posuit, quo tamen non inesse malum fructu arboris
doceretur, sed futurum, si forte ex voluntate hominis de con-
temptu datae legis praemoneretur.   nam et liber esse debuerat,

---

[1] See A. E. Burn, *Introduction to the Creeds* (1899), pp. 104 ff.

ne incongruenter Dei imago serviret: et lex addenda, ne usque
ad contemptum dantis libertas effraenata prorumperet: ut et
praemia condigna et merita poenarum consequenter exciperet,
suum iam habens illud, quod motu mentis in alterutram partem
agitare voluisset: ex quo mortalitas, invidia utique, in ipsum
redit ; qui cum illam de obedientia posset evadere, in eamdem
incurrit, dum ex consilio perverso Deus esse festinat: cuius
tamen poenam nihilominus indulgenter temperavit, dum non
tam ipse quam labores eius maledicuntur super terram.

COMMODIAN (? *c.* A.D. 250)

instructiones adversus gentium deos. [*PL* V. 201–262]

XXXV.   *de ligno vitae et mortis*

Adam protolapsus, ut Dei praecepta vitaret,
Belias tentator fuit de invidia palmae ;
contulit et nobis seu boni seu mali quod egit,
dux nati [?] nativitatis, morimur indeque per illum,
ex divino ipse ut recedens exsul a verbo.

XLVI.   *catecuminis*

in baptismo tibi genitale solox lavatur

[' genitale solox ' means ' ancestral filth,' *i.e.*, presumably,
' original guilt.'   For the word 'solox,' *v. PL*, footnote *in loc.*,
or Du Cange, *Glossarium med. et inf. lat.* (Henschel-Favre), *s.v.*
But B. Dombart, *Commodiani carmina*, in *Corp. eccl. script.
Lat.*, 1887, p. 66, emends the line so as to read—

in baptismo tibi genitalia sola donantur.]

PACIAN OF BARCELONA (*flor.* A.D. 360–390)

sermo de baptismo.   [*PL* XIII. 1089 c ff.]

accipite ergo, dulcissimi, homo ante baptismum in qua morte
sit positus. scitis certe illud antiquum quod Adam terrenae
origini praestitutus sit : quae utique damnatio legem illi aeternae
mortis imposuit; et omnibus ab eo posteris quos lex una retinebat
haec mors in genus omne dominata est, *ab Adam usque ad
Moysen* . . . interea nos omnes sub peccato tenebamur, ut
fructus essemus mortis : siliquarum escis et pecorum custodiae
destinati, id est, operibus immundis, per malos angelos, quibus
dominantibus nec facere licuit nec scire iustitiam. . . .

Adam postquam peccavit, ut retuli, dicente tunc Domino,
terra es, et in terram ibis, addictus est morti.   haec addictio in

genus omne defluxit. omnes enim peccaverunt, ipsa iam urgente natura, sicut apostolus dicit : *quia per unum hominem peccatum introivit, et per delictum mors, et sic in omnes homines devenit, in quo omnes peccaverunt.* dominatum est ergo peccatum, cuius vinculis quasi captivi trahebamur ad mortem, mortem scilicet sempiternam.

AURELIUS CLEMENS PRUDENTIUS (A.D. 348–†after 405)
apotheosis, 909–931

(*A strongly ' Western ' or ' twice-born ' view of the Fall and its results is expressed, but ' traducianism ' is repudiated.*)

> haec prima est natura anima, sic condita simplex,
> decidit in vitium per sordida foedera carnis.
> exin tincta malo peccamine principis Adae
> infecit genus omne hominum, quod pullulat inde,
> et tenet ingenitas animarum infantia in ortu
> primi hominis maculas, nec quisquam nascitur insons.
> vitandus tamen error erit, ne traduce carnis
> transfundi in sobolem credatur fons animarum
> sanguinis exemplo, cui texta propagine vena est.
> non animas animae pariunt, sed lege latenti
> fundit opus natura suum, quod parvula anhelent
> vascula vitalisque adsit scintilla coactis.
> quae quamvis infusa novum penetret nova semper
> figmentum, vetus illa tamen de crimine avorum
> ducitur, inluto quoniam concreta veterno est.
> inde secunda redit generatio et inde lavatur
> naturae inluvies, iterumque renascimur intus
> perfusi, ut veterem splendens anima exuat Adam.
> quae quia materiam peccati ex fomite carnis
> consociata trahit, nec non simul ipsa sodali
> est incentivum peccaminis, inplicat ambas
> vindex paena reas peccantes mente sub una
> peccandique cremat socias cruciatibus aequis.

(2) *Greek Writers.*

EPIPHANIUS (*c.* A.D. 315–†403)
haer. i. 4. [*PG* XLI. 177 D]

[*Adam before the Fall was innocent and simple.*]

ἁπλοῦς τε ἦν καὶ ἄκακος, οὐκ ὄνομά τι κεκτημένος ἕτερον, οὐ δόξης, οὐ γνώμης, οὐ βίου διακρίσεως ἐπίκλησιν κεκτημένος, ἢ 'Αδὰμ μόνον κληθείς, τὸ ἑρμηνευόμενον ἄνθρωπος.

haer. lii. 2.   [*PG* XLI. 957 A]

[*Against the Adamian sect, who held their meetings in hypocausts
or subterranean heating-chambers.—Adam and Eve before the Fall
were not tormented by heat or cold.*]

Ἀδὰμ γὰρ καὶ Εὔα οὐκ ἐν ὑποκαύστῳ οἴκῳ τὴν δίαιταν εἶχον, οὔτε ἐν φλογμῷ
τινι ὑπεπιέζοντο, οὔτε κρύος αὐτοὺς ἐφόρτου· ἦν δὲ αὐτοῖς ἀὴρ καθαρώτατος,
καὶ πάσης εὐκρασίας εὐτάκτως ἐκ θεοῦ μεμερημένος, οὔτε ἀπηνότητι ψυχρίας
τετονωμένος, οὔτε ἀηδεστάτῃ ἐκπυρώσει καύσωνος ἐπηρτημένος· δίαιτα δὲ
ἀμβροσία μάλα ἐκ θεοῦ πεποιημένη· ὁ χῶρος ἐτέτακτο, θυμηδίας καὶ εὐζωίας
πεποιημένος. καὶ οὔτε ῥίγει ὑπέπιπτον οὔτε καύσωνι, ὡς ἔφην.

haer. lxix. 52.   [*PG* XLII. 282 D, 284 A]

[*free choice the source of sin, both in Adam and in ourselves.*]
[The Word co-operated with the Father and the Spirit in the
creation of the universe] ἵνα δείξῃ, ὅτι τὸ αἴτιον τῆς τοῦ Ἀδὰμ παραβάσεως
οὐκ ἀπὸ τοῦ πεπλακέναι, οὐδὲ ἀπὸ τοῦ πεποιηκέναι τὸ ἁμαρτὲς ἢ τὸ τῆς παρακοῆς
ἔσχεν, ἀλλ᾽ ἀπὸ ἰδίας προαιρέσεως . . . οὐ γὰρ ὁ γέγονεν ἐν τῷ ἀνθρώπῳ, εἰς
τοῦτο ἐκ τοῦ δημιουργοῦ τοῦ ἀναιτίου τῆς τοῦ Ἀδὰμ ἁμαρτίας τοῦ ἁμαρτεῖν γέγονε,
καὶ διὰ τοῦτο ἥμαρτεν· ἀλλὰ τὸ αὐτεξούσιον αὐτῷ ἐπέδωκε, καὶ αἴτιος ἑαυτῷ
ἕκαστος γίνεται ἁμαρτίας.

haer. xxxvii. 1, 3 (ed. K. Holl, ap. *Gr. Chr. Schr.*, ii. p. 51)

[*A vague connexion between the disobedience of Adam and Eve
and the idolatry of their descendants seems to be implied.*]

καθάπερ γὰρ ἐξ ὑπαρχῆς τοὺς περὶ Εὔαν καὶ τὸν Ἀδὰμ ἠπάτησεν, οὕτω καὶ
νῦν, κρύπτων ἑαυτὸν ἔν τε τῷ παρόντι καὶ ἐν τῷ χρόνῳ τῶν Ἰουδαίων ἄχρι τῆς
τοῦ Χριστοῦ παρουσίας. εἶτα καὶ προβαινόντων τῶν χρόνων λίχνους ὄντας τοὺς
ἀνθρώπους τῇ δι᾽ αὐτοῦ ἐκ τῆς παρακοῆς ληφθείσῃ βρώσει ἔτι ὑπονοθεύων καὶ
ἐρεθίζων εἰς περισσοτέραν ἀπάτην ἀπὸ τοῦ ὄντος θεοῦ ἀφίστησι. . . . ἀπὸ γὰρ
τοῦ ἑνὸς καὶ ἀληθινοῦ θεοῦ ἀποστήσας αὐτοὺς ἐνεκίσσησε πάλαι τὴν τῆς
εἰδωλολατρείας καὶ πολυθείας βλάσφημον κενοφωνίαν. . . . οὐκ ἦν δὲ αἴτιος μόνος
ὁ φαινόμενος τότε ὄφις, ἀλλὰ ὁ ἐν τῷ ὄφει ὄφις λαλήσας (φημὶ δὲ ὁ διάβολος) καὶ
τὴν ἀκοὴν τοῦ ἀνθρώπου ταράξας διὰ τῆς γυναικός. καὶ οὐδὲ τὸ ξύλον ἦν ἁμαρτία
(θεὸς γὰρ οὐδὲν πονηρὸν φυτεύει), γνῶσιν δὲ ἐνεποίησε τὸ ξύλον τοῦ εἰδέναι
ἀγαθόν τε καὶ φαῦλον. καὶ οὐχὶ διὰ τὸ εἰδέναι ὁ θάνατος, ἀλλὰ διὰ τὴν παρακοήν.
καὶ γὰρ ἡ πᾶσα τοῦ ἐχθροῦ τότε συσκευὴ οὐχ ἕνεκεν τοῦ βρώματος γέγονεν, ἀλλὰ
ἕνεκεν τοῦ ἐργάσασθαι αὐτοῖς τὴν παρακοήν. ὅθεν παρακούσαντες τότε τοῦ μὲν
παραδείσου ἔξωθεν γίνονται, ἐπιτιμηθέντες δικαιότατα. . . .

haer. lxx. 3.   [*PG* XLII. 344 A]

[*Adam did not lose the image of God by his Fall.*]

ἄλλοι . . . θέλουσι λέγειν τότε μὲν εἶναι τὸ κατ᾽ εἰκόνα ἐν τῷ Ἀδάμ, ἕως
ὅτε ἐν παρακοῇ γέγονε καὶ βέκρωκεν ἀπὸ τοῦ ξύλου, καὶ ἐξεώσθη· ἀφ᾽ οὗ δὲ
ἐξεώσθη, ἀπώλεσε τὸ κατ᾽ εἰκόνα. καὶ πολλή τις ἐστὶ τῶν ἀνθρώπων μυθοποιία·
οἷς οὐ χρὴ οὐδὲ πρὸς ὥραν εἶξαι, οὔτε τούτοις, οὔτε ἐκείνοις τοῖς οὕτως ἢ οὕτω
λέγουσιν· ἀλλ᾽ εἶναι μὲν πιστεύειν ἐν τῷ ἀνθρώπῳ τὸ κατ᾽ εἰκόνα, ἐν παντὶ δὲ
μάλιστα, καὶ οὐχ ἁπλῶς.

John Chrysostom (A.D. 344–†407)

in c. ii. Genes. hom. xvi. [*PG* LIII. 126 f.]

[*Man's paradisal state was devoid of pain.*]

ἐννόησόν μοι μακαριότητος ὑπερβολὴν, πῶς ἀνώτεροι ἦσαν τῶν σωματικῶν
ἁπάντων, πῶς καθάπερ τὸν οὐρανὸν οὕτω τὴν γῆν ᾤκουν, καὶ ἐν σώματι τυγχάνοντες
τὰ τῶν σωμάτων οὐχ ὑπέμενον· οὔτε γὰρ στέγης, οὔτε ὀρόφου, οὔτε ἱματίου,
οὔτε ἄλλου οὐδενὸς τῶν τοιούτων ἐδέοντο. καὶ οὐχ ἁπλῶς, οὐδὲ εἰκῆ τοῦτο
ἡμῖν ἐπεσημήνατο ἡ θεία γραφή, ἀλλ' ἵνα μαθόντες τὴν ἄλυπον αὐτῶν ταύτην
διαγωγὴν, καὶ τὸν ἀνώδυνον βίον, καὶ τὴν ἀγγελικὴν, ὡς εἰπεῖν, κατάστασιν,
ἐπειδὰν ἴδωμεν μετὰ ταῦτα τούτων ἁπάντων ἐρήμους αὐτοὺς γενομένους, καὶ
καθάπερ ἀπὸ πολλῆς πλούτου περιουσίας εἰς ἐλαχίστην πενίαν κατενεχθέντας,
τῇ ῥαθυμίᾳ αὐτῶν τὸ πᾶν ἐπιγράψωμεν.

ep. ad Olymp. iii, 3. [*PG* LII. 574]

[*The Fall of Adam condemned the whole human race.*]

ὅτε γὰρ ἥμαρτεν ὁ Ἀδὰμ τὴν ἁμαρτίαν ἐκείνην τὴν χαλεπὴν, καὶ τὸ κοινὸν
ἁπάντων ἀνθρώπων κατεδίκασε γένος, μόχθῳ τότε κατεδικάζετο.

in c. i. Genes. hom. ix. [*PG* LIII. 79]

[*As a result of the Fall man lost his empire over the animals.*]

παρὰ γὰρ τὴν ἀρχὴν οὐχ οὕτω τὰ πράγματα διέκειτο, ἀλλ' ἐδεδοίκει καὶ ἔτρεμε
τὰ θηρία, καὶ ὑπέκυπτε τῷ δεσπότῃ. ἐπειδὴ δὲ τῆς παρρησίας ἐξέπεσε διὰ τὴν
παρακοὴν, καὶ τὰ τῆς ἀρχῆς ἠκρωτηριάσθη . . . . ἕως μὲν γὰρ εἶχε τὴν πρὸς τὸν
θεὸν παρρησίαν, φοβερὸς καὶ τοῖς θηρίοις ἦν· ἐπειδὴ δὲ προσέκρουσε, καὶ τοὺς
ἐσχάτους τῶν συνδούλων ἐδεδοίκει λοιπόν.

in Matt. hom. xxviii. 3. [*PG* LVII. 353]

[*The souls of children are not evil, and are in the hand of God.*]

οὐδὲ γὰρ ἔνι ψυχὴν ἀπορραγεῖσαν τοῦ σώματος ἐνταῦθα πλανᾶσθαι λοιπόν.
δικαίων γὰρ ψυχαὶ ἐν χειρὶ θεοῦ· εἰ δὲ αἱ τῶν δικαίων, καὶ αἱ τῶν παίδων·
οὐδὲ γὰρ ἐκεῖναι πονηραί.

in Matt. hom. lviii. [*PG* LVIII. 569]

[*Our Lord's calling a child to Him proves that child-nature, and
therefore human nature as such, is not an evil thing.*]

εἶδες πῶς πάλιν ἡμᾶς πρὸς τὰ φυσικὰ κατορθώματα ἐκκαλεῖται, δεικνὺς ὅτι
ἐκ προαιρέσεως ταῦτα κατορθοῦν δυνατόν, καὶ τὴν πονηρὰν Μανιχαίων ἐπιστομίζει
λύτταν; εἰ γὰρ πονηρὸν ἡ φύσις, τίνος ἕνεκεν ἐκεῖθεν τῆς φιλοσοφίας τὰ
παραδείγματα ἕλκει; παιδίον δέ μοι δοκεῖ σφόδρα παιδίον ἐν τῷ μέσῳ στῆσαι,
τῶν παθῶν ἁπάντων τούτων ἀπηλλαγμένον. τὸ γὰρ τοιοῦτον παιδίον καὶ ἀπονοίας
καὶ δοξομανίας καὶ βασκανίας καὶ φιλονεικίας καὶ πάντων τῶν τοιούτων ἀπήλλακται
παθῶν κ. τ. λ.

in ep. ad Hebr. c. vii. *hom.* xii.   [*PG* LXIII. 99]

[*The human will, though free, is prone to evil.*]

2.   . . . προαίρεσις, πολλὰς δεχομένη μεταβολάς, καὶ νῦν μὲν τοῦτο, νῦν δὲ ἐκεῖνο αἱρουμένη· ὀξυρρεπὴς γὰρ αὕτη πρὸς κακίαν.

[*Grace co-operates with, but does not ' prevent,' our wills.*]

3.   οὐ προφθάνει τὰς ἡμετέρας βουλήσεις, ἵνα μὴ λυμήνηται τὸ αὐτεξούσιον ἡμῶν. ὅταν δὲ ἡμεῖς ἑλώμεθα, τότε πολλὴν εἰσάγει τὴν βοήθειαν ἡμῖν (the position later known as ' semi-Pelagianism' : *cf. de verb. apost.* habentes eundem spiritum, i. 5 [*PG* LI. 276]).   οὔτε γὰρ ὁ θεός, οὔτε ἡ τοῦ πνεύματος χάρις τὴν ἡμετέραν προφθάνει προαίρεσιν· ἀλλὰ καλεῖ μὲν, ἀναμένει δὲ ὥστε ἕκοντας καὶ βουληθέντας οἴκοθεν προσελθεῖν· εἶτα ἐπειδὰν προσέλθωμεν, τότε τὴν παρ' ἑαυτοῦ παρέχει συμμαχίαν ἅπασαν.

in ep. ad Rom. hom. x. 2, 3.   [*PG* LX. 477 f.]

(*A ' minimising' discussion of the classical N.T. Fall-passage. St. Paul says ' As through the one man's disobedience the many were made sinners,' etc. [Rom. v. 19]. But it seems unreasonable that one man should be deemed to have sinned, because another has disobeyed: therefore, by ' sinners' the Apostle must mean ' liable to the penalty of sin,' i.e. death. Even so, however, it is difficult to see why mankind should be liable to death for Adam's sin : the Apostle states the fact, but is silent as to the reason for it.*)

ὥσπερ γὰρ διὰ τῆς παρακοῆς τοῦ ἑνὸς ἀνθρώπου ἁμαρτωλοὶ κατεστάθησαν οἱ πολλοί κ.τ.λ.   καὶ δοκεῖ μὲν ζήτημα οὐ μικρὸν ἔχειν τὸ εἰρημένον· ἂν δέ τις ἀκριβῶς προσέχῃ, καὶ τοῦτο εὐκόλως λυθήσεται.   τί ποτ' οὖν ἐστι τὸ ζήτημα ; τὸ λέγειν διὰ τῆς παρακοῆς τοῦ ἑνὸς ἁμαρτωλοὺς γενέσθαι πολλούς.   τὸ μὲν γὰρ ἁμαρτόντος ἐκείνου καὶ γενομένου θνητοῦ, καὶ τοὺς ἐξ αὐτοῦ τοιούτους εἶναι, οὐδὲν ἀπεικός·   τὸ δὲ ἐκ τῆς παρακοῆς ἐκείνου ἕτερον ἁμαρτωλὸν γενέσθαι, ποίαν ἂν ἀκολουθίαν σχοίη ; εὑρεθήσεται γὰρ οὕτω μηδὲ δίκην ὀφείλων ὁ τοιοῦτος, εἴ γε μὴ οἴκοθεν γέγονεν ἁμαρτωλός.

τί οὖν ἐστιν ἐνταῦθα τὸ Ἁμαρτωλοί ; ἐμοὶ δοκεῖ τὸ ὑπεύθυνοι κολάσει καὶ καταδεδικασμένοι θανάτῳ.   ὅτι μὲν οὖν τοῦ Ἀδὰμ ἀποθανόντος πάντες ἐγενόμεθα θνητοί, σαφῶς καὶ διὰ πολλῶν ἔδειξε·   τὸ δὲ ζητούμενον, τίνος ἕνεκεν τοῦτο γέγονεν. ἀλλ' οὐκέτι τοῦτο προστίθησιν·   οὐδὲ γὰρ αὐτῷ πρὸς τὸ παρὸν συντελεῖ·   πρὸς γὰρ Ἰουδαῖον ἡ μάχη τὸν ἀμφιβάλλοντα καὶ καταγελῶντα τῆς διὰ τοῦ ἑνὸς δικαιοσύνης· . . . . διόπερ ἀφίησιν ἄλυτον.   [In any case, our mortality is not such a very great evil : for the thought of death restrains us from many sins and, if there had been no death, the martyrs could not have won their crowns.]

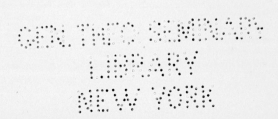

НГЕЛ ЛОМИ
ПЪБУКА
СОЛГ ЦЦС ЕГКОЛЛА

INDICES

I.

SCRIPTURAL, PSEUDEPIGRAPHIC, AND RABBINICAL REFERENCES.

2 O

II.

AUTHORS.

III.

SUBJECTS.

Printed in England at THE BALLANTYNE PRESS
SPOTTISWOODE, BALLANTYNE & CO. LTD.
Colchester, London & Eton